THE SUPPLEMENT TO
THE NINTH MENTAL
MEASUREMENTS YEARBOOK

D1528940

EARLIER PUBLICATIONS IN THIS SERIES

CHIEF EDITORIAL ASSOCIATE

LINDA L. MURPHY

PRODUCTION AND SECRETARIAL

DEBRA S. RUTHSATZ
ROSEMARY G. SIECK

THE SUPPLEMENT TO THE NINTH MENTAL MEASUREMENTS YEARBOOK

Edited by
JANE CLOSE CONOLEY
JACK J. KRAMER
JAMES V. MITCHELL, JR.

The Buros Institute of Mental Measurements
The University of Nebraska-Lincoln
Lincoln, Nebraska

1988
Distributed by The University of Nebraska Press

LC 39-3422
ISBN 910674–30–2

Manufactured in the United States of America.

The paper used in this publication meets the minimum requirements of American National Standard for Information Sciences—Permanence of Paper for Printed Library Materials, ANSI Z39.48–1984.

Note to Users

TABLE OF CONTENTS

INTRODUCTION

The Supplement to the Ninth Mental Measurements Yearbook (9*MMY-S*) represents both a continuation and an innovation of the traditional mission of the Buros Institute of Mental Measurements. The 9*MMY-S* is similar in format and content to the previous 27 publications of the Buros Institute. However, this new publication represents an effort to increase our contribution to the field of testing by providing consumers with a timely tool to assist in decision making regarding assessment products.

With this publication we begin an annual production schedule for the well-known *Mental Measurements Yearbook* (*MMY*) series. In 1989, a hardbound *MMY*, the *Tenth*, will be published containing all the material in this *Supplement*, plus many more reviews and tests, a comprehensive indexing system, and a scholarly paper focused on the current state of measurement and testing. In the years following, *Supplements* and *MMY*s will appear on alternating years. This new schedule will make important evaluative information available to test users in an expedient fashion. Timely access to information was Oscar Buros' objective in founding the Institute more than fifty years ago. Improved computer technology has allowed us to initiate a frequent publication schedule and approach Buros' goal of informing consumers and improving the state-of-the-art in test publishing.

THE SUPPLEMENT TO THE NINTH MENTAL MEASUREMENTS YEARBOOK

The 9*MMY-S* contains reviews of tests that are new or significantly revised since the publication of the *Ninth MMY* in 1985. Unlike previous *MMY*s, however, the 9*MMY-S* is not a comprehensive volume. We have included reviews of tests that were available before our production deadline of December 1, 1987. Reviews of additional new or revised tests since 1985 will appear in the *Tenth MMY*. Reviews, descriptions, and references associated with older tests can be located in other Buros publications such as previous *MMY*s and *Tests in Print III*.

The contents of the 9*MMY-S* include: (*a*) a bibliography of 89 commercially available tests, new or revised, published as separates for use with English-speaking subjects; (*b*) 150 critical test reviews by well-qualified professional people who were selected by the editors on the basis of their expertise in measurement and, often, the content of the test being reviewed; (*c*) bibliographies of references for specific tests related to the construction, validity, or use of the tests in various settings; (*d*) a test title index with appropriate cross-references; (*e*) a classified subject index; (*f*) a publishers directory and index, including addresses and test listings by publisher; (*g*) a name index including the names of all authors of tests, reviews, or references; (h) an index of acronyms for easy reference when a test acronym, not the full title, is known; and (i) a score index to refer readers to tests featuring particular kinds of scores that are of interest to them.

The volume is organized like an encyclopedia, with tests being ordered alphabetically by title. Thus if the title of a test is known, the reader can locate the test immediately without having to consult the Index of Titles.

The page headings reflect the encyclopedic organization. The page heading of the left-hand page cites the number and title of the first test listed on that page, and the page heading of the right-hand page cites the number and title of the last test listed on that page. All numbers presented in the various indexes are test numbers, not page numbers. Page numbers, important only for the Table of Contents, are indicated at the bottom of each page.

INDEXES

As mentioned earlier, *The* 9*MMY-S* includes six indexes invaluable as aids to effective use: (a) Index of Titles, (b) Index of Acronyms, (c) Classified Subject Index, (d) Publishers Directory and Index, (e) Index of Names, and (f) Score Index. Additional comment on these indexes will be presented below.

Index of Titles. Because the organization of the 9*MMY-S* is encyclopedic in nature, with the tests ordered alphabetically by title throughout the two volumes, the test title index does not have to be consulted to find a test for which the title is known. However, the title index has some features that make it useful beyond its function as a complete title listing. First, it includes cross-reference information that is useful for tests with superseded or alternative titles or tests which are commonly (and sometimes inaccurately) known by multiple titles. Second, it provides information on which tests are new or revised. It is important to keep in mind that the numbers in this index, like those for all *MMY* indexes, are test numbers and not page numbers.

Index of Acronyms. Some tests seem to be better known by their acronyms than by their full titles. The Index of Acronyms can provide very useful help in such instances; it refers the reader to the full title of the test and to the relevant descriptive information and reviews.

Classified Subject Index. The Classified Subject Index classifies all tests listed in the 9*MMY-S* into 12 major categories: Achievement, Developmental, English, Fine Arts, Intelligence and Scholastic Aptitude, Mathematics, Miscellaneous, Neuropsychological, Personality, Reading, Speech and Hearing, and Vocations. Each test entry includes test title, population for which the test is intended, and test number. The Classified Subject Index is of great help to readers who seek a listing of tests in given subject areas. The Classified Subject Index represents a very useful starting point for readers who know their area of interest but do not know how to further focus that interest in order to identify the best test(s) for their particular purposes.

Publishers Directory and Index. The Publishers Directory and Index includes the names and addresses of the publishers of all tests included in the 9*MMY-S* plus a listing of test numbers for each individual publisher. This index can be particularly useful in obtaining addresses for specimen sets or catalogs after the test reviews have been read and evaluated. It can also be useful when a reader knows the publisher of a certain test but is uncertain about the test title, or when a reader is interested in the range of tests published by a given publisher.

Index of Names. The Index of Names is an analytical index indicating authorship of a test, test review, or reference.

Score Index. The Score Index is an index to all the scores that can be obtained from all the tests in the 9*MMY-S*. Test titles are sometimes misleading, and even test content is sometimes difficult to define with precision. But test scores represent operational definitions of the variables the test author is trying to measure, and as such they often define test purpose and content more adequately than whatever else is available. When someone is searching for a particular kind of test, the search purpose is usually defined in terms of finding a test that measures a particular variable of interest or perhaps several such variables. Test scores and their associated labels can often be the best operational definitions of the variables of interest. Hence the inclusion of a Score Index represents another effort to help the test user find the test that best fits his or her needs. It is in fact a detailed subject index based on the most critical operational features of any test—the scores and their associated labels.

HOW TO USE THIS SUPPLEMENT

A reference work like *The Supplement to the Ninth Mental Measurements Yearbook* can be of far greater benefit to a reader if a little time is taken to become familiar with what it has to offer and how one might most effectively use it to obtain the information wanted. The first step in this process is to read the Introduction to the *9MMY-S* in its entirety. The second step is to become familiar with the six indexes and particularly with the instructions preceding each index listing. The third step is to make actual use of the book by looking up needed information. This third step is simple if one keeps in mind the following possibilities:

1. If you know the title of the test, use the alphabetical page headings to go directly to the test entry.
2. If you don't know, can't find, or are unsure of the title of a test, consult the Index of Test Titles for possible variants of the title or consult the appropriate subject area of the Classified Subject Index for other possible leads or for similar or related tests in the same area. (Other uses for both of these indexes were described earlier.)
3. If you know the author of a test but not the title or publisher, consult the Index of Names and look up the author's titles until you find the test you want.
4. If you know the test publisher but not the title or author, consult the Publishers Directory and Index and look up the publisher's titles until you find the test you want.
5. If you are looking for a test that yields a particular kind of score, but have no knowledge of which test that might be, look up the score in the Index of Scores and locate the test or tests that include the score variable of interest.
6. Once you have found the test or tests you are looking for, read the descriptive entries for these tests carefully so that you can take advantage of the information provided. A description of the information provided in these test entries will be presented later in this section.

7. Read the test reviews carefully and analytically, as described earlier in this Introduction. There is much to be gained from reading these reviews, and you are well advised to take the time and make the effort to read them thoroughly and with understanding.
8. Once you have read the descriptive information and test reviews, you may want to order a specimen set for a particular test so that you can examine it firsthand. The Publishers Directory and Index has the address information needed to obtain specimen sets or catalogs.
9. The Buros Institute of Mental Measurements also offers an online computer data base service through BRS Information Technologies (BRS). The search label for the Institute data base is MMYD. Coverage begins with *The Eighth Mental Measurements Yearbook* (1978), and the data base provides a vehicle for regularly scheduled updates (typically, monthly updates) to the material. As a means for insuring the most current information possible, the combination of the *Mental Measurements Yearbooks*, *MMY Supplements*, and the online data base service constitutes a remarkable resource for test users.
10. The Buros Institute also sponsors the annual Buros-Nebraska Symposium on Measurement and Testing. The first four symposia have included speakers of national and international reknown in measurement, and each symposium has been very well received. The presentations are later published in book form. Readers of this yearbook are cordially invited to attend the symposia and to examine the symposium books published by Lawrence Erlbaum Associates for their relevance to the purposes of test users.

Making Effective Use of the Test Entries. The test entries include extensive and useful information. For each test, descriptive information is presented in the following order:

a) TITLES. Test titles are printed in boldface type. Secondary or series titles are set off from main titles by a colon.

b) DESCRIPTIONS OF THE GROUPS FOR WHICH THE TEST IS INTENDED. The grade, chronological age, or semester range, or the employment category is usually given. "Grades 1.5–2.5, 2–3, 4–12, 13–17" means that there are four test booklets: a booklet for the middle of the first grade through the middle of the second grade, a booklet for the beginning of the second grade through the end of the third grade, a booklet for grades 4 through 12 inclusive, and a booklet for undergraduate and graduate students in colleges and universities.

c) DATE OF PUBLICATION. The inclusive range of publication dates for the various forms, accessories, and additions of a test is reported.

d) ACRONYM. When a test is often referred to by an acronym, the acronym is given in the test entry immediately following the publication date.

e) SPECIAL COMMENTS. Some entries contain special notations, such as: "for research use only"; "revision of the ABC Test"; "tests administered monthly at centers throughout the United States"; "subtests available as separates"; and "verbal creativity." A statement such as "verbal creativity" is intended to further describe what the test claims to measure. Some of the test entries include factual statements that imply criticism of the test, such as "1980 test identical with test copyrighted 1970" and "no manual."

f) PART SCORES. The number of part scores is presented along with their titles or descriptions of what they are intended to represent.

g) INDIVIDUAL OR GROUP TEST. All tests are group tests unless otherwise indicated.

h) FORMS, PARTS, AND LEVELS. All available forms, parts, and levels are listed.

i) PAGES. The number of pages on which print occurs is reported for test booklets, manuals, technical reports, profiles, and other nonapparatus accessories.

j) MACHINE-SCORABLE ANSWER SHEETS. All types of machine-scorable answer sheets available for use with a specific test are reported.

k) COST. Price information is reported for test packages (usually 20 to 35 tests), answer sheets, all other accessories, and specimen sets. The statement "$17.50 per 35 tests" means that all accessories are included unless otherwise indicated by the reporting of separate prices for accessories. The statement also means 35 tests of one level, one edition, or one part unless stated otherwise. Because test prices can change very quickly, the year that the listed test prices were obtained is also given. Foreign currency is assigned the appropriate symbol. When prices are given in foreign dollars, a qualifying symbol is added (e.g., A$16.50 refers to 16 dollars and 50 cents in Australian currency).

l) SCORING AND REPORTING SERVICES. Scoring and reporting services provided by publishers are reported along with information on costs. In a few cases, special computerized scoring and interpretation services are given in separate entries immediately following the test.

m) TIME. The number of minutes of actual working time allowed examinees and the approximate length of time needed for administering a test are reported whenever obtainable.

n) AUTHOR. For most tests, all authors are reported. In the case of tests which appear in a new form each year, only authors of the most recent forms are listed. Names are reported exactly as printed on test booklets. Names of editors are generally not reported.

o) PUBLISHER. The name of the publisher or distributor is reported for each test. Foreign publishers are identified by listing the country in brackets immediately following the name of the publisher. The Publishers Directory and Index must be consulted for a publisher's address.

p) CLOSING ASTERISK. An asterisk following the publisher's name indicates that an entry was prepared from a firsthand examination of the test materials.

q) FOREIGN ADAPTATIONS. Revisions and adaptations of tests for foreign use are listed in a separate paragraph following the original edition.

r) SUBLISTINGS. Levels, editions, subtests, or parts of a test which are available in separate booklets are sometimes presented as sublistings with titles set in small capitals. Sub-sublistings are indented and titles are set in italic type.

s) CROSS REFERENCES. For tests which have been previously listed in a Buros Institute publication, a test entry includes—if relevant—a final paragraph containing a cross reference to the reviews, excerpts, and references for that test in those volumes. In the cross references, "T3:467" refers to test 467 in *Tests in Print III*, "8:1023" refers to test 1023 in *The Eighth Mental Measurements Yearbook*,

"T2:144" refers to test 144 in *Tests in Print II*, "7:637" refers to test 637 in *The Seventh Mental Measurements Yearbook*, "P:262" refers to test 262 in *Personality Tests and Reviews I*, "2:1427" refers to test 1427 in *The 1940 Yearbook*, and "1:1110" refers to test 1110 in *The 1938 Yearbook*. In the case of batteries and programs, the paragraph also includes cross references—from the battery to the separately listed subtests and vice versa—to entries in this volume and to entries and reviews in earlier yearbooks. Test numbers not preceded by a colon refer to tests in this Supplement; for example, "see 45" refers to test 45 in this Supplement.

If a reader finds something in a test description that is not understood, the descriptive material presented above can be referred to again and can often help to clarify the matter.

ACKNOWLEDGEMENTS

The ongoing efforts to publish the *Mental Measurements Yearbooks* could not be accomplished without the contributions of many individuals. The editors of this volume are well aware and acknowledge gratefully the talent, expertise, and dedication of all those who have assisted in the publication process. Foremost among this group is Linda Murphy, Chief Editorial Associate. Her knowledge of our publication process, willingness to contribute in whatever way necessary, and cheerful attitude made our editorial tasks easier than we could have imagined. Nor would the publication of this volume be possible without the efforts of Debbie Ruthsatz, Secretarial Specialist, and Rosemary Sieck, Word Processing Specialist. Their efforts go far beyond that required as part of normal job responsibilities. The sense of accomplishment and pride we feel with the publication of the 9*MMY-S* have resulted from a team effort and our heartfelt thank you is extended to the three individuals mentioned above.

Our gratitude is also extended to the many reviewers who have prepared test reviews for the Buros Institute. Their willingness to take time from busy professional schedules to share their expertise in the form of thoughtful test reviews is appreciated. The *Mental Measurements Yearbook* would not exist were it not for their efforts.

Many graduate students have contributed to the publication of this volume. Their efforts have included reviewing test catalogs, fact checking reviews, looking for test references, and innumerable other tasks. We thank Stephen Axford, Jerene Bishop, Crystal Grow, Julie Krejci, Christopher Milne, Bunny Pozehl, Debra Sabers, and Mark Shriver for their assistance.

Our appreciation is also extended to our National and Departmental Advisory Committees for their willingness to assist in the implementation and review of the operations of the Buros Institute. The National Advisory Committee consists of Luella Buros, T. Anne Cleary, Ellis Page, Daniel Reschly, Lyle Schoenfeldt, Richard Snow, Julian Stanley, and Frank Womer. The Buros Institute is part of the Department of Educational Psychology and we have benefitted from the many departmental colleagues who have contributed to our efforts including Roger Bruning, David Dixon (now at Ball State University), Terry Gutkin, Ronn Johnson, Kenneth Orton, Wayne Piersel, Barbara Plake, Royce Ronning, Toni Santmire, and Steven Wise.

The very existence of the Buros Institute of Mental Measurements at the University of Nebraska-Lincoln would not be possible without Luella Buros. Her continued involvement with and support of the Institute reflect commitment for which we and the entire measurement community must be eternally grateful.

SUMMARY

Our hope is, of course, that the 9*MMY-S* fills an important need for timely access to critical reviews of testing products. The information contained in this *Supplement* will be superseded in a year by a far more comprehensive *Tenth MMY*. Decisions regarding tests for educational, research, personnel selection, and vocational guidance must often be made rather quickly. The 9*MMY-S* will fulfill its purpose if its effective use creates substantive gains in the selection, use, and interpretation of commercially published tests.

Tests and Reviews

[1]

ACER Primary Reading Survey Tests. Purpose: To provide teachers with assessments of the status of their students in the areas of reading vocabulary and reading comprehension. Grades 3, 4, 5, 6; 1971–84; 2 scores: Word Knowledge, Comprehension; revised teacher's handbook ('84, 32 pages); price information available from publisher; Word Knowledge [20] minutes, Comprehension [30] minutes, (with parallel format); Graham Ward (revised handbook); Australian Council for Educational Research [Australia].*

See T3:42 (4 references).

Review of the ACER Primary Reading Survey Tests by MARILYN FRIEND, Assistant Professor of Learning, Development, and Special Education, Northern Illinois University, DeKalb, IL:

The revised editions of the Australian Council for Educational Research Primary Reading Survey Tests are group administered, timed screening instruments designed to "test the language skills of primary school students" in grades 3, 4, 5, and 6 (Levels A, B, C, and D, respectively). This purpose is accomplished through two subtests: Word Knowledge and Comprehension. For Word Knowledge students select from four alternatives a synonym for a stimulus word presented in boldface type. For Comprehension (for which two forms are available) students read short passages and then respond to several related multiple-choice items. The testing materials include student test booklets, machine-readable answer sheets, answer keys in the form of clear acetate overlays, and a teacher's handbook.

The information contained in the handbook demonstrates that this set of tests is the product of considerable research and development effort. The handbook includes detailed instructions on the proper administration of the test, explanations of the scores obtained (reported in percentile ranks and stanine scores), suggestions on using the test results, cautions about their use, and technical information. It is conveniently organized and well written; its contents should be readily understood by even novice test users, yet the information is precise and detailed.

On the basis of technical quality, the ACER Primary Reading Survey Tests are quite sound. Content validity was established by experts (i.e., teachers, test developers, subject specialists), who rated the correspondence between item content and curricular emphases. Users are urged to carefully assess item suitability for themselves. Further, the developers established the differences in relative difficulty of the tests for the four grade levels for which the test is standardized. For the Reading Comprehension test, variations in the complexity of the topics, vocabulary, overall reading level, and types of questions (factual recall vs. inference) were also evaluated. A final strategy for establishing validity was trial testing followed by revisions and detailed item analyses.

The reliability section of the teacher's handbook begins with a discussion of what reliability is and how it can be established. The KR-20 values reported are acceptable: For the Word Knowledge subtest they range from .79 to .92 for the four test levels, and for the Comprehension subtest the values range from .84 to .93. The handbook mentions test-retest reliability as appropriate for this type of instrument; surprisingly, no data of this sort are presented.

The problems with this set of tests for potential users in the U.S. are primarily the result of its development for Australian students. For example, the norms are based on a rigorous 1983 standardization study in which careful attention was paid to the sampling design in order to accurately represent the school populations in the Australian states. However, it remains unknown how the norms relate to U.S. populations.

The occasional variations in spelling are another drawback for U.S. students. While many students would probably understand "colour" for "color," translating "tonnes" for "tons" might prove more difficult. In a speed test of language skill the potential negative impact of such variations on students' performance is a risk to be considered.

Other cautions concerning these tests should also be noted. First, the Word Knowledge subtest is actually a type of comprehension exercise since students must independently read the stimulus word and then likewise read and select the correct response alternative. Second, in the Comprehension subtest, the short passages limit the types of questions posed, thus tapping only a limited number of comprehension skills. Finally, and hopefully not trivially, the bright pink paper on which the student test booklets are printed seemed to be an unnecessary distractor.

In summary, the ACER Primary Reading Survey Tests are exactly what the developers intended: technically sound assessment instruments for assisting teachers to evaluate students' reading skills. Despite the overall quality, their use cannot be recommended for U.S. students. So many adequate similar assessment instruments have been developed in this country that no reason exists to contend with the vocabulary and norming difficulties presented

by these Australian tests. Such qualifications would not apply to use in Australia.

Review of the ACER Primary Reading Survey Tests by JULIA A. HICKMAN, Assistant Professor of School Psychology, The University of Texas at Austin, Austin, TX:

The ACER Primary Reading Survey Tests are part of a series of Primary Reading Survey tests developed by the Australian Council for Educational Research. The ACER Primary Reading Survey Tests are designed to assess word knowledge and reading comprehension skills of children in grades 3 through 6. The authors group word knowledge and passage comprehension under the rubric of language learning skills.

The Word Knowledge tests consist of one form, Form R, with four levels, one at each grade 3 through 6. Each level of the test is comprised of 40 to 45 multiple-choice items in which the student is required to select among three or four alternatives the one word that has the meaning most similar to the stimulus word. To administer the test, the examiner reads three sample questions to a group of students to insure that they understand the nature of the task. The students then have 20 minutes to complete the remaining items.

A raw score for word knowledge is obtained by summing the number of items the student answers correctly. It may be that the derived score obtained from the raw score is not a valid measure of word knowledge due to the fact that children may choose the correct answer even if they do not recognize the stimulus word. It is impossible to ascertain word knowledge precisely on a paper-and-pencil, multiple-choice test administered in a group format.

There are two forms of the comprehension tests, Forms R and S, each with four levels, one for each grade 3 through 6. The student reads a passage silently and then answers multiple-choice questions (each with four options) concerning the factual meaning or inferred knowledge of the paragraph.

The comprehension tests are also administered in a group format. Prior to administering the actual test, the examiner presents three sample items again to insure the students understand the nature of the tasks. The students are given 30 minutes to complete the remaining items independently. Here again, it is questionable to consider this a complete assessment of reading comprehension as the results may simply reflect a student's word-recognition skills. That is, a student may understand what a paragraph means but may be unable to demonstrate this in the testing situation because of poorly developed word-recognition skills. When only a measure of silent reading is used as an indicator of reading comprehension, the results have little if any diagnostic value. In the test manual, the authors do provide appropriate cautions to test users regarding the limitations of the scores obtained.

Raw scores obtained on the ACER Primary Reading Survey Tests are converted to standard scores. Norm-referenced scores are also presented in the form of percentile ranks and stanine scores. The authors explain the weaknesses of percentile scores and advantages of stanine scores. Although it is preferable to use age-based standard scores when making norm-referenced comparisons, both percentile ranks and stanine scores are superior to age- or grade-equivalent scores often presented in test manuals.

The standardization and technical data reported in the test manual are adequate in some areas but lacking in most. For example, the procedures for construction and standardization of the ACER Primary Reading Survey Tests are described inadequately. The authors state that initial and revised test items were presented to "committees of critics" for review and selection, but no specification of who these critics were or how they chose the final items is forthcoming in the manual. It is implied that item-discrimination and item-difficulty indices were calculated and used to select appropriate test items, but the actual procedures are not described in the test manual.

In addition, although an entire page in the manual is devoted to description of norming procedures, little substantive information is provided. For example, a detailed, albeit confusing, description is presented regarding standardization sampling procedures. Although it is clear that many schools were used as sites from which the standardization sample was drawn, it is not explicit how many subjects were included or how the sample was representative of a normal population according to such relevant variables as sex, socioeconomic status, race, and so forth.

Data regarding the tests' reliability and validity are also incomplete. Kuder-Richardson reliability coefficients are appropriately presented as evidence of the internal consistency of the Primary Reading Survey Tests. The coefficients seem adequate except for the .79 value reported for Level D of the Word Recognition Test. Otherwise, the values range from .84 on Level D of Form S of the Comprehension Test to .92 on several levels of the Word Recognition and Comprehension Test.

It is unfortunate that the authors present no data assessing reliability of the alternate forms of the Comprehension Tests. This is a glaring omission for the Primary Reading Survey Tests.

Standard errors of measurement (*SEMs*) were calculated for the Word Recognition and Comprehension tests using internal-consistency reliability coefficients. The authors give a brief but adequate explanation of *SEMs* and their appropriate use in test interpretation. Cautions concerning interpretation of individual test scores without consideration of this and other sources of errors are adequately described in the manual.

Confirmation of the tests' validity consists of the author's written assurance that the method of item development and selection resulted in satisfactory test content validity. Although content validity is an important and necessary part of the evidence needed to establish the validity of a test, content validity is not sufficient to determine that a test in fact measures what it says it measures. Many more empirical studies supporting the tests' concurrent and construct validity are needed.

In conclusion, although it is not possible to make comparative judgments regarding the Primary Reading Survey Tests and other tests normed in Australia, it is possible to consider its adequacy and usability in relation to other reading tests normed specifically for use in the United States. This reviewer regretfully concludes that the Primary Reading Survey Tests as presented in the test manual do not meet the technical standards described in the *Standards for Educational and Psychological Testing* (AERA, APA, NCME, 1985). The tests also do not realize the purposes stated in the test manual. It is hoped that future manuals will include the data and information necessary to use the Primary Reading Survey Tests in conjunction with other instruments in the never-ending search for good reading diagnostic information.

REVIEWER'S REFERENCE

American Educational Research Association, American Psychological Association, & National Council on Measurement in Education. (1985). *Standards for educational and psychological testing.* Washington, DC: American Psychological Association, Inc.

[2]

Achievement Identification Measure. Purpose: "Determine the degree to which children exhibit the characteristics of underachievers so that preventive or curative efforts may be administered." School-age children; 1985; AIM; parent report inventory; 6 scores: Competition, Responsibility, Control, Achievement Communication, Respect, Total; 1987 price data: $80 per 30 tests, manual for administration (8 pages), manual for interpretation of scores (7 pages), and computer scoring of 30 tests; $10 per specimen set; (20) minutes; Sylvia B. Rimm; Educational Assessment Service, Inc.*

Review of the Achievement Identification Measure by HOWARD M. KNOFF, Associate Professor of School Psychology, Department of Psychological Foundations, University of South Florida, Tampa, FL:

The Achievement Identification Measure (AIM) is a 77-item rating scale completed by parents of school-aged children which, according to its manual, "was developed to provide a measure of the characteristics which distinguish achieving students from underachievers" and to identify underachievers "so that preventive or curative efforts may be administered." The AIM was developed by Dr. Sylvia B. Rimm, who is described as having specialized in the identification and treatment of underachievers, the latter through her work with identified children and their parents and schools. The conceptualization of the AIM and its rating-scale items are based on Dr. Rimm's clinical work. The AIM has six scores (Competition, Responsibility, Control, Achievement Communication, Respect, and a Total Score), which are reported using percentile, normal curve equivalent (Mean = 50, Standard Deviation = 21.06), and stanine scores. Two manuals are provided with the AIM materials, one describing its administration and the other describing the interpretation of its scores.

The six-page Manual for Administration has sections addressing the AIM's purpose and background, administration and scoring, and research base. While the discussion of the AIM's purpose is admirably succinct, it does not define underachievers ("children whose performance in school is below their ability level") in sufficient detail. For example, not specified is whether all exceptional children (e.g., learning disabled, emotionally disturbed, mentally retarded) can be underachievers, nor what effects their exceptionality might have on underachievement in general or their AIM profile in particular. Gifted underachieving children are noted briefly in the manual (this appears to be an area of specialization with Dr. Rimm), but again there is no elaboration that would suggest anything other than one AIM profile or criterion level to identify all under-achieving students. The background section of the manual, meanwhile, simply refers to Dr. Rimm's experience and clinical findings with underachieving students; no other studies or information are referenced to provide a broader foundation towards understanding the AIM.

The background material in the manual would be significantly strengthened by a comprehensive review of the literature on under-achieving students, noting interrelationships with various exceptionalities, and a demonstration that the AIM is related to empirical results that are meaningful and replicable. Unfortunately, the AIM does not appear to be founded on empirical research. The test appears to be based on one individual's perception of under-achievement which, at the very least, may be specific to a limited geographic area and/or a select group of students who have been referred for outside counseling or academic support. This is a serious limitation of the AIM affecting the very roots of its validity. Because of the limited information presented in this manual, these are the only comments possible at this time. Perhaps, with a more extensive background section, different conclusions would be warranted.

The administration and scoring section of the manual is fairly easy to follow. The manual recommends that both parents complete the AIM together unless there are serious disagreements. In such cases separate forms can be completed. The possible effects of single versus joint versus separate parent completion of the AIM are not explored, statistically or conceptually. This section also notes that the AIM evaluates underachievement for all school-aged children, yet the possible use of the AIM with exceptional children, who may be educated in the public schools until age 21, is unspecified. Further, the AIM's standardization sample is not fully described. Thus, it is not clear whether the AIM was standardized with parents who had children who fully represent "all school aged children." The breadth and applicability of the AIM with all school-aged children, therefore, is unclear, is not demonstrated, and cannot be determined. Finally, the acceptability of comparing a completed AIM protocol to the entire standardization sample or the need to compare it to an age-specific subset of the sample, comparable to the target child's specific age, is not addressed.

Unfortunately, the only way the AIM can be scored is to send the completed protocol to the scale's publishers. This is a serious flaw, which is compounded by the lack of reported norms in the manual. Without these norms, this test cannot be fully evaluated, and the accuracy of the publisher's scores and interpretations cannot be determined. This scoring approach may also reduce test users' understandings of the AIM's important details and nuances, while introducing an unnecessary delay between administering the scale and implementing an intervention program based on its results (the manual states that the AIM scoring will be returned within one month, or within one week for special "rush" jobs). The lack of AIM norms also discourages the comparative research that is desperately needed to further validate this test.

The research background section of the manual *appears* to describe the AIM's test construction and psychometric properties; however, the discussion is only cursory at best. The test construction section again alludes to the clinical work of Dr. Rimm, while other parts of the research background section are vague or limited in their scope. There is no description of how the scale items were chosen, whether a group of pilot items were tested and statistically discarded or retained to create the present scale, or whether a factor-analytic procedure was used to identify and/or validate the five AIM scales. A comprehensive discussion of the AIM's reliability is missing, no construct-validity statistics are reported, and criterion-related validity support is based on an author-generated study with an undefined subject pool and methodology. Finally, there is only a vague description of the AIM's standardization and normative sam-

ple (500 school-aged children from rural, suburban, and urban geographic areas in this country), with no statistical or stratification data presented. Overall, the development, integrity, utility, reliability, and validity (construct, concurrent, convergent, and discriminant) of this scale cannot be evaluated or are not present. The manual provides insufficient information in almost all technical areas—even the accomplishment of the AIM's stated goals and purposes cannot be determined. It would surely be unwise to use the AIM for any clinical purpose, or for that matter, any research-oriented purposes.

In five pages, the Manual for Interpretation describes how to evaluate and interpret the percentile scores that are returned with a scored protocol along with the scores for the five AIM dimensions. Again, the validity of these dimensions and interpretations must be seriously questioned—the manuals provide no empirical support for them either through a factor analysis of the present scale or a review of previous research.

The manual reports that total AIM scores above the 80th percentile indicate students who are high achievers. This use of the AIM as a tool which evaluates high *and* low achievers (rather than the latter only) is commendable. However, the manual's statement that those scoring between the 40th and 60th percentiles "probably are having some problems related to school achievement already" is inconsistent with common interpretations of these percentiles as being within average ranges. Finally, the designation of students scoring below the 40th percentile as being at high risk for underachievement is troublesome. First, this cutoff score is not empirically supported, and more importantly, it appears to be unusually high—higher than one might expect from a randomly sampled standardization group. If this is true, the potential for identifying numerous "false-positive" underachievers within a typical population is significant, both in terms of the costs involved in serving them and the possible stigmatization from an inappropriate label.

The remainder of this manual is devoted to describing the five AIM dimensions. Once again, there are no citations to validate the interpretation; they appear to be drawn from the clinical experience of the author. Thus, more questions related to the validity of the AIM's interpretations arise.

To summarize, the AIM manuals do not present sufficient description, standardization data, and/or psychometric support to permit any recommendation for its use—clinically or in research. Indeed, the apparent dependence on the author's clinical experience, devoid of any empirical support for the conceptualization, development, or interpretation of the AIM, is a significant weakness. The validity and utility of the AIM has not been demonstrated, or at least reported, in its manuals. In fact, the notion that parents, who have their own biases and perceptions of schools' academic processes, can reliably identify their children as underachievers, has not been discussed or demonstrated. It is strongly recommended that any revision of the AIM provide the comprehensive information noted above in a *single* manual. While the author has alluded to a forthcoming book and other studies with the AIM, these should be reported in this manual so that users are able to independently evaluate and use the tool for their own purposes.

Review of the Achievement Identification Measure by SHARON B. REYNOLDS, Assistant Professor of Education, Texas Christian University, Fort Worth, TX:

The stated purpose of the Achievement Identification Measure (AIM) is to measure characteristics that distinguish between achieving and underachieving school-age children. The author describes a theoretical framework in which underachievement is viewed as a pattern, learned in early childhood, related to attention "addiction," expressed in either dependent or domineering modes.

ITEMS. The inventory is a Likert-type scale in which the parent checks, for each of the items, one of the following responses: *no, to a small extent, average, more than average, definitely.* The 70 items to which all parents are asked to respond can be categorized as follows: 19 items related to the child's behavior with respect to school, 17 items related to the child's behavior or characteristics in general, 12 items about the child's relationship with either the child's father or mother, 8 items related to the parent's behavior or characteristics, 6 items about the child's behavior toward other children, 3 items about the child's siblings, 2 items

about the behavior or attitudes of the child's father or mother toward school, 1 item about the child's health, 1 item about the child's relationship with grandparents, 1 item about the parents' relationship with each other.

Of these 70 items, some are repeated and some are opposites. An additional 7 questions are to be answered only by two-parent families. These questions all refer to differences between the father and mother.

Some of the items do not use the full range of the scale. These require a yes or no response. Some of the items require factual information or information based on direct observation. Other items require the parent to compare the child to "normal" or "reasonable" behavior. There is no information within the inventory that provides the parent with appropriate norm reference with respect to these items.

No information is given regarding the source of the original set of items, or on the criteria for selecting the final set. The authors stated that item analysis revealed gender differences for some items. These differences resulted in a change in scoring procedures such that some items are now scored for only one gender.

RELIABILITY AND VALIDITY. Reliability coefficients are reported, but the size and characteristics of the reliability sample were not described. In the absence of such information, the reliability coefficients are not useful in assisting the user to determine the suitability of the instrument for the user's purposes.

The information provided on construct validity is just a restatement of the theoretical basis for the inventory, with no empirical data provided. Criterion-related validity is reported as a correlation between AIM scores and parent ratings of their child's achievement on a 5-point scale. The size and characteristics of the validity sample were not described. Thus, in the absence of information about the sample on which the test was validated, the validity coefficients are not useful in assisting the user in determining the suitability of the test for the user's purposes.

MANUALS. The inventory includes two manuals: Manual for Administration and Manual for Interpretation of Scores. The Manual for Administration is divided into three sections: Background Information, Administration and Scoring, and Research Background. The administration and scoring section includes instructions, time suggestions, materials, and age restriction ("school age"). It states that "small problems should be considered more serious when identified in younger children since they are likely to increase with age unless there is intervention." No empirical evidence is cited in support of this assertion.

The Manual for Interpretation of Scores is divided into four sections: Introduction, Scores, Dimension Descriptions, and Further Information.

ADMINISTRATION AND SCORING. The directions for administration of the instrument are clear and simple. Directions for scoring are not included because scoring is provided by Educational Assessment Service, Inc.

The inventory provides scores for overall achiever characteristics as well as "dimension" scores for Competition, Responsibility, Control, Achievement, Communication, and Respect. The Manual for Interpretation of Scores states that scores are reported as percentiles, Normal Curve Equivalent scores, and stanine scores for the five separate dimensions. The instructions for interpreting scores states that the total score is reported as a percentile and Dimension scores are reported as stanines. It does not give any information about the Normal Curve Equivalent Scores. Directions for interpreting both types of scores are given in terms of ranges. A general description of the way in which the theory relates the Dimension score to the overall score is provided. The relationship is not supported by quantitative data. Incomplete information is provided about the reference group on which these norms were established.

SUMMARY. The major flaw in this instrument is its lack of empirical data. It is not possible to determine the appropriateness of the instrument, the relevance of the norms, or even the relationship between the Dimension scores and the overall score. The major advantage of the instrument is its ease of administration. In the absence of empirical data, however, one is left with the opportunity to easily measure something that cannot be interpreted with any level of confidence.

[3]

ACT Proficiency Examination in Statistics.

Purpose: "To give adult learners the opportunity to earn college credit for knowledge gained outside the classroom and to provide institutions with an objective basis for awarding such credit" in statistics. College and adults; 1984–86; test administered 6 times annually (February, March, May, June, October, November) at centers established by the publisher; 1986 examination fee: $40 (includes reporting of score to the candidate and one college); 180(190) minutes; developed by the faculty of The University of the State of New York; American College Testing Program.*

For information on the entire ACT Proficiency Examination Program, see 9:45 (1 reference).

Review of the ACT Proficiency Examination in Statistics by ROBERT P. MARKLEY, Professor of Psychology, Fort Hays State University, Hays, KS:

The ACT Proficiency Examination in Statistics (PEP) test is designed to provide a measure of knowledge or achievement in the topics contained in a traditional elementary statistics course. The purpose of the test (and the PEP program) is to provide a measure of college-equivalent life experiences. Presumably, one could take the test, submit the score to a local educational institution, and (if the score is satisfactory) be given credit for three units of statistics without having formally attended or enrolled in the traditional class. For institutions, there are available a Technical Handbook and User's Guide which provide general information about the total PEP program and some technical information about the Statistics test. A very thorough Study Guide is provided to the enrollee upon registration.

The first version of the test itself has 97 items in multiple-choice format. Items are placed on alternate pages with an interleaved blank page for notes and figuring. According to the Technical Handbook, an attempt was made to have 20% of the items tap rote-memory knowledge, 25% of the items deal with comprehension of the subject, 25% applications and higher order operations, and 25% applications and higher order operations with computations. (Either there is a misprint in the Handbook or 5% of the items are unaccounted for.) Almost all of the topics that are found in the traditional elementary text book appear in test items, including descriptive statistics, graphs, probability, probability distributions, sampling and sampling distributions, estimation and hypothesis testing—including large and small sample tests on single means and pairs of means, Chi Square, regression and correlation, and one-way ANOVA. There are no items dealing with nonparametric statistics. Topics are, for the most part, sequenced in a manner similar to their order of appearance in a standard text. The test taker is provided with a booklet containing a list of standard formulas and excerpts from statistical tables that can be used during the test. Calculators cannot be used during the test.

A group of 1,327 introductory statistics students at 37 U.S. colleges and universities was used to norm the test. The raw score mean for this group was 53.5 items correct (out of 97) with a standard deviation of 12.4. A coefficient alpha of .86 is reported by the ACT. Scores are reported in a standard score form ($M = 50$, $SD = 10$, range $= 80$ to 20). The SE_m is estimated as being 3.7 scaled-score units. The ACT recommends that a scaled score of 45 be considered a passing score. Thirty-one percent of the norm group failed this standard.

As yet there is no information available on performance of actual candidates who are taking this test for course equivalency purposes.

Score reports include a scaled score, percent of items correct, and (apparently) a projected final grade (based upon the norm sample). Apparently there is no provision for a breakdown of topics or areas missed, which the candidate could use for diagnostic or remedial purposes. It would be very helpful for a failed candidate to be informed that further study in a subarea (e.g., probability or correlation) would be beneficial. Such diagnostics would also be helpful to an instructor who might be interested in using this standardized exam to assess students' achievement against a national norm (even though this is not the purpose of the test).

An instructor could quarrel with the relative weighting of topics on the test. There is more coverage of probability on this test than I would want on my final exam and not enough coverage of ANOVA and experimental design. I suppose that a decision-theory-oriented business statistics instructor would like the emphasis upon probability topics. As an instructor, I personally am somewhat put off and frustrated by the traditional textbook reliance upon one and two sample designs to illustrate and introduce inferential hypothesis testing. We just begin to get students to understand what is going on and then tell them that real researchers almost never use the statistical tests they have just learned—that the main action is in

ANOVA and various multivariate procedures which we don't have time to teach in a one-semester course.

Some really minor quibbles: There is at least one item that is pure algebra and not statistics. Throughout the test the lower case x or x_1 is used to refer to individual scores; most social science and psychology texts are now using the upper case X or X_1 to refer to an individual raw score and reserving the lower case x or x_1 to refer to the deviation quantity, $X_1 - M$. Finally, the technical manual consistently commits the error of saying "data is."

Finally, despite some quibbles and reservations, I would, provisionally and until local experience proves otherwise, judge an applicant for a social science graduate program who presents a high score on this test to have satisfied an undergraduate statistics prerequisite and thus allow the student entry to discipline-oriented graduate level methods and statistics courses.

Review of the ACT Proficiency Examination in Statistics by STEVEN L. WISE, Assistant Professor of Educational Psychology, University of Nebraska-Lincoln, Lincoln, NE:

The ACT Proficiency Examination in Statistics (PEP) is intended to be used by postsecondary institutions in decisions regarding the awarding of college credit to individuals who have studied elementary statistical methods. The PEP Statistics examination, currently consisting of 97 multiple-choice items, was developed to test knowledge of material that is normally taught in a one-semester introductory course in statistics.

The test materials include three types of supporting information: a User's Guide, a Study Guide, and a Technical Handbook. The PEP User's Guide provides generic information about the PEP program and examinations. A description of the test development procedures and psychometric properties of the PEP examinations are presented in a general fashion. Because the PEP Statistics examination is administered by ACT, detailed administration instructions are not contained in the User's Guide. Candidates for the PEP Statistics examination are provided a Study Guide containing a general description of the examination, a list of objectives, a description of the content domain covered by the items, the proportion of the items measuring each content area, a list of reference materials for candidate preparation, a list of the tables and formulas used in the examination, and several sample test items. The Technical Handbook contains psychometric and normative information for each of the PEP examinations.

The PEP User's Guide gives a comprehensive description of the PEP program. The test development procedures used in all of the PEP examinations are clearly presented. General descriptions of the methods used to insure reliability and validity of the examinations are also given in the User's Guide. In addition, several methods are presented for choosing an appropriate cutoff score for a PEP examination.

Several aspects of the Study Guide merit discussion. First, the content domain presented in the Study Guide is very broad. I feel that there are few instructors of introductory statistics who cover more than about 90% of these topics within the time constraints of a one-semester course. Several of the topics, such as hypergeometric distributions and Bayes' theorem, are only rarely addressed in an introductory course. Moreover, 25% of the test items deal with probability theory and probability distributions. This is substantially more coverage of probability than is given in many introductory statistics courses. Users should take into account the scope and emphasis of the content domain when choosing cutting scores for the examination.

A second problem with the Study Guide concerns the list of four primary reference textbooks. This list is preceded by the statement "any one of the following general purpose textbooks may be used to study the material listed in the content outline." Inspection of the four textbooks reveals that only one, Freund's *Modern Elementary Statistics*, provides an exhaustive coverage of the content domain. Hence the statement in the Study Guide that any of the textbooks in the list may be used is misleading, because a candidate who studied Freund's textbook would be at a clear advantage over a candidate who studied only one of the other "primary" textbooks. It would be clearer (and more accurate) to state that the content of the PEP Statistics examination is based on Freund's textbook.

The Technical Handbook provides little evidence of the reliability and validity of the PEP Statistics examination. Only one estimate of reliability is given—a coefficient alpha value of .86. No validity evidence is presented. This is somewhat surprising, given the high overall quality of the testing materials. In the beginning of the Technical Handbook, general procedures for obtaining evidence of both content and concurrent validity of the PEP examinations are described. Apparently the user is expected to accept on faith that the validity evidence for a particular examination is adequate. I find this practice to be unacceptable, and hope that ACT will soon provide detailed validity evidence for each of the PEP examinations.

Overall, I feel that the PEP Statistics examination should provide postsecondary institutions with useful information regarding statistics proficiency. In view of the scanty psychometric evidence available for this examination, however, it is difficult to provide a more detailed assessment of the psychometric quality of the PEP Statistics examination.

[4]

The Activity Completion Technique. Purpose: Assessment of personality through sentence completion technique. High school and over; 1984; ACT; developed from the Sacks Sentence Completion Test; 4 areas: Family, Interpersonal, Affect, Self-Concept; 1987 price data: $24.95 per 25 tests, 25 rating sheets, and manual (33 pages); $12 per 50 tests; $8 per 25 rating sheets; $8.50 per manual; (30–40) minutes; Joseph M. Sacks; Psychological Assessment Resources, Inc.*

Review of The Activity Completion Technique by FRED M. GROSSMAN, Assistant Professor of Special Education and Communication Disorders, University of Nebraska-Lincoln, Lincoln, NE:

The Activity Completion Technique (ACT) is a revision of the Sacks Sentence Completion Test (SSCT) (Sacks & Levy, 1959) and, as such, attempts to assess personality characteristics by requesting individuals to complete sentence stems within a standard sentence completion format. According to the author, the test can be administered individually or in groups with an average completion time of 30–40 minutes. Administration procedures are clearly delineated within the ACT manual as are suggestions for the examiner on how to respond to frequently asked questions by examinees. ACT respondents are asked to silently read and subsequently to complete each sentence stem in writing, although the author recommends that for particularly anxious test-takers it may be advantageous for the examiner to read the stimulus items orally and then record the client's oral responses. In addition, examiners are encouraged to conduct an inquiry by asking follow-up questions relating to selected responses that appear to be of clinical significance.

The entire instrument is comprised of 15 categories that are grouped under four major areas. Each category includes 4 stimulus items, resulting in a total of 60 sentence completion items. The four major areas are: (*a*) Family, which has three categories (e.g., relationship with mother, early family relationships, etc.); (*b*) Interpersonal, which is comprised of four categories (e.g., peers, authority figures, etc.); (*c*) Affect, of which anxiety and hostility are the two components; and (*d*) Self-Concept, which has six categories (e.g., competence, needs, fantasy, etc.). The four stimulus items within each category are scored together as a constellation of responses, which is a departure from previous sentence completion methods. In effect, based upon the clinical judgment of the examiner, each category is globally scored on a rating sheet as either (1) no significant disturbance; (2) mildly disturbed; (3) severely disturbed; or (X) unknown, insufficient evidence. Space is provided under each category on the rating sheet for clinicians to write a brief interpretive summary (i.e., usually a phrase or sentence) regarding their impressions of the test-taker's set of responses. After completion of the scoring for all categories, the examiner is expected to complete a clinical summary with respect to outlined areas provided on the rating sheet.

In addition to the previously mentioned scoring procedures, selected ACT items can be scored in accordance with criteria for Self-Actualization personality characteristics. Further scoring criteria are also available for Activity-Passivity personality tendencies and can be assessed for any of the ACT items that the examiner chooses to evaluate in this manner. To the author's credit, several scoring samples are provided in the test manual as are two illustrative cases to aid the clinician in the ratings and narrative interpretations of response constellations.

Although some reliability and validity indices are reported in the manual for the original SSCT, no such data are presented for the ACT. In fact, psychometric data on the ACT are totally lacking, with the exception of minimal summaries of a few correlational studies regarding Self-Actualization and Activity-Passivity constructs. In effect, standardization information, normative data, and reliability and validity indices are conspicuously absent.

In summary, although the ACT differs from some of the previous sentence completion methods in a positive manner (e.g., first-person stimuli, scoring a constellation of responses rather than a single response, etc.), the lack of psychometric data suggests that diagnostic and classification decisions not be made solely on the basis of the results of this instrument. The major problem with the ACT is best represented by the comment of the test author that the validity of ratings is greatly determined by the clinical impressions, experience, and insight of the examiner. This type of interpretive approach poses the potential danger of idiosyncratic and subjective scoring by individual examiners and points to the need for substantially more research on the ACT, particularly with regard to reliability and validity data. In effect, while clinically-oriented psychologists may feel comfortable using the ACT, psychometrically-inclined clinicians are advised to direct their attention toward the use of personality instruments that have more objective scoring systems and psychometrically-derived interpretive systems.

REVIEWER'S REFERENCE

Sacks, J. M., & Levy, S. (1950). The Sentence Completion Test. In L. E. Abt & L. Bellak (Eds.), *Projective psychology* (pp. 357-402). New York: Knopf.

Review of The Activity Completion Technique by MARCIA B. SHAFFER, School Psychologist, Steuben/Allegany BOCES, Bath, NY:

Joseph M. Sacks is known for his development of the Sacks Sentence Completion Test (SSCT), which has been widely used in research and in clinical practice. He is the originator, also, of the Activity Completion Technique, or ACT. The ACT consists of 60 items, each of which is intended to probe a specific characteristic or experience of the subject. In scoring, each item is grouped with three others, e.g., "authority role" is described by items 14, 29, 32, and 47. Finally, these areas are grouped under the four categories listed in the test, e.g., "affect" includes anxiety and hostility. Administration of the ACT is like that of other sentence completion tests, with the addition of an inquiry.

The ACT is described as "a revised form of the Sacks Sentence Completion Test in which the items have been reworded to elicit responses in terms of behavioral, emotional, or cognitive activity." This symbiotic affinity to the SSCT is so strong that there are few statistics in the manual which are based on the actual ACT. There is no reference to factor analysis. The comments on validity and reliability tend to be ambiguous, evasive, or patently derived from SSCT research done several years ago.

The dubious data comprise the major flaw in the construction and interpretation of the ACT. There is one other criticism which might be made, although some potential users may not find it of primary importance. The criticism is of the method of scoring. "The validity of the ACT is dependent . . . upon . . . the clinical acumen of the examiner. . . . [and] highly dependent on the psychologist's experience, insight, and knowledge of the dynamics of behavior." Accuracy in understanding is supposedly enhanced by 20 pages of examples of responses, with interpretation by experts. Whether examples are a safe substitute for the expertise of the examiner is an important question, but is not addressed here. Warning about ethical use of the ACT is contained in a single statement: "For those who have little experience with this method, examples of interpretation and ratings are presented." No additional cautionary advice is given.

Among its assets, the ACT offers the advantage of being in the first person, which has been found to "elicit more valid clinical content than stimuli referring to others." The use of several responses in combination produces information of a richer nature than use of a single response. It is adaptable, it may be given to groups as well as individuals, and it may be read to a subject if necessary. In addition, the ACT places emphasis on strengths, assets, and coping ability rather than simply on pathology.

The ACT is definitely in need of research, and a more carefully written, more explicatory manual. Still, it has a strong visual appeal for possible purchasers; the rating sheet is neatly arranged with the categories defined and a

place for the scorer's interpretive summary. The questions appear relevant and the test can be said to possess a face validity. It would be easy to forget about psychometric data and test interpretation when looking at so tidy a test. In fact, the ACT might be a satisfactory part of an extensive battery in a hospital, an industrial setting, or a college admissions office. Unfortunately, the test's integrity rests chiefly on faith rather than proven performance.

[5]

Adolescent Language Screening Test. Purpose: "Developed to screen for deficits in the dimensions of language use, content, and form" in adolescents. Ages 11–17; 1984; ALST; 7 subtests: Pragmatics, Receptive Vocabulary, Concepts, Expressive Vocabulary, Sentence Formation, Morphology, Phonology; individual; 1988 price data: $69 per complete kit including 50 record booklets, stimulus easel, and administration manual (26 pages); (10–15) minutes; Denise L. Morgan and Arthur M. Guilford; PRO-ED, Inc.*

Review of the Adolescent Language Screening Test by LINDA CROCKER, Professor of Foundations of Education, University of Florida, Gainesville, FL:

The Adolescent Language Screening Test (ALST) is an individually administered test of developmental speech and language, designed for use with examinees from middle school through high school grades. Its seven subtests include Pragmatics (responses to simple instructions and conversational skills), Concepts (answering questions based on information obtained from a sentence spoken by the examiner), Receptive Vocabulary (understanding/identifying words spoken by the examiner), Expressive Vocabulary (picture identification, definitions, and word usage), Sentence Formation (scored for complexity of sentence structure when sentences are generated using specified words), Morphology (sentence completion), and Phonology (pronunciations requiring various consonant blends). Based upon these subtests three separate subscores and a total score are determined. Subtest 1 yields a Language Use score; subtests 2, 3, and 4 yield a Language Content score; and subtests 5, 6, and 7 are combined to obtain a Language Form score.

The ALST is easily administered and easily scored. The notebook format for task presentation is conveniently arranged to facilitate administration. While no special qualifications are needed to administer the test, some practice with the materials is essential for smooth administration. For several subtests the examiner must present stimulus words or sentences and the instructions are explicit that these can be presented only once (without repetition). Consequently there is no margin for examiner error in oral presentation of the stimuli and no alternative items are provided. The manual offers no instructions about the pacing or speed of presentation of verbal stimuli or the length of time that should be allowed between oral presentation of a sentence and questions that follow about the content of that sentence. In giving this test I noted that variations in examiner presentation could result in variations in examinee performance on these items. These matters should be addressed in any future revisions of this scale and manual.

Because of the heavy dependence on oral stimuli and the strictures against repetition of the verbal items, the ALST would not appear to be suitable for administration to hearing-impaired students.

The standardization sample consisted of 775 examinees (approximately 100 at each age level from 11 to 17). The process by which these examinees were selected is not described. The sample included 68 black and 35 Hispanic examinees ranging in numbers from 3–19 across age levels for blacks and 1–13 across age levels for Hispanics. Approximately 26% of the standardization sample were classified as learning disabled or needing speech therapy. Means and standard deviations are reported by age group for examinees receiving special services, those receiving no services, and the two groups combined. The means increase progressively over age-level groups but the standard deviations are noticeably smaller for the 16–17-year-olds, suggesting a possible ceiling effect on the test, at least for normal examinees. The standard deviations, however, remain large for the special services older students.

No data are presented on validity or reliability. Evidence of concurrent criterion-related validity might be inferred from the fact that at every age level the means for examinees qualifying for special services were substantially lower than means for examinees not receiving special services, but the test authors do not mention this. A more serious omission is the

lack of any consideration of construct validity. An important issue in developing or reviewing any language test is whether it measures a construct that is distinct from general verbal aptitude as measured by standardized intelligence measures. Another aspect of construct validity is the internal structure of the scale and its subtests. Collapsing seven separate subtest scores for reporting purposes is a practice that should have some empirical justification. Correlational data or results of a factor-analytic study are sorely needed to support the subscale structure and reporting format of the test. Further evidence of internal consistency of subtest and total scores, test-retest reliability, and reliability of classifications of examinees at the recommended cut-scores (the 25th percentile rank) are also essential before this instrument is used for screening or placement of students.

In summary, the desirable features of the ALST are that it is easy to administer and covers the age range from 11–17, making longitudinal follow-up possible over a wide age span using the same instrument. Norm-group sample sizes at each age level are adequate. These positive features, however, are outweighed by the serious lack of data relating to validity and reliability of the test scores. Until such studies are published or conducted by test users in local settings, use of this test for clinical or educational decision making will remain open to question.

Review of the Adolescent Language Screening Test by ROBERT T. WILLIAMS, Associate Professor of Occupational and Educational Studies, Colorado State University, Fort Collins, CO, and AMY FINCH-WILLIAMS, Assistant Professor of Speech/Language Pathology, University of Wyoming, Laramie, WY:

The authors of the Adolescent Language Screening Test (ALST) maintain there is a need for a screening test of language abilities for adolescents. This test was designed to screen for deficits associated with spoken language in the areas of use, content, and form, as identified by Bloom and Lahey (1978). The authors build a strong rationale for their theoretical position relative to the language tasks included in the screening. The manual includes a review of the language characteristics of language-learning disabled adolescents. The development of this theoretical position and the review of the research establishes the content validity for this instrument.

Although content validity is established, the specific items selected and the scoring procedure for some subtests reduces the value of the screening instrument. This is apparent in both the Language Use and Language Form sections. For example, in the first section of Language Use a good rationale is made for the use of higher-level indirect speech acts with adolescents. However, the stimulus item chosen reflects an earlier developing indirect speech act.

Further, in the second section of Language Use the authors evaluate conversational skills, but the scoring system does not allow differentiation between impaired and normal populations. This problem is reflected in the fact that each subcategory has both early and later developing skills that are weighed equally. A point may be earned for the subcategory by demonstrating only the early developing skill. For example, in the second subcategory the authors are evaluating the functions of language (e.g., imperative, question, and declarative). The students may receive a point for using any function. In screening the language abilities of adolescents, it would be more appropriate to give differentiated credit for use of the question function or higher-level cognitive uses of language (Bereiter & Engelmann, 1966; Simon, 1985).

This same type of problem is found in the Language Form section. The authors state that the Sentence Formulation subtest was modified to evaluate a variety of sentence constructions. Although the scoring criteria for this section differentiate among various constructions, neither the directions nor the stimulus words suggest the expectation of a response more complex than simple, active, declarative sentences. The lack of this expectation could well affect the individual's score on this subtest.

Overall, the Language Content section is appropriate for adolescents. However, at least one of the pictures in the Receptive Vocabulary subtest is confusing. For the stimulus word "destruction" the possible responses include pictures of (1) a building under construction, (2) a car with a dented front bumper and fender behind a car with a dented rear bumper and fender, (3) a building being destroyed, and (4) a building burning. The keyed responses are 3 and 4, but response 2 seems justifiable. In addition the instructions to the examiner and to the student are contradictory. The examiner reads to the examinee, "I will only say each statement one time, so be sure to listen carefully." Then the manual tells the examiner, "At the student's request, one repetition may be given for each item without penalty."

The authors state in their rationale that language-learning disabled adolescents have been noted to have word retrieval difficulties. They maintain that the ALST screens vocabulary knowledge and word-finding skills. The "Naming to Confrontation" section of the Expressive Vocabulary subtest does not adequately screen word-finding skills. It is an expressive vocabulary test (i.e., vocabulary knowledge) because the student is not timed during his/her naming responses.

The manual provides no further evidence of validity or reliability. Caution, therefore, should be used in generalizing the results of this screening instrument.

The authors of the ALST attempt to provide normative data. Additionally, they attempt to account for ethnic diversity by including Black, Hispanic, and other minorities within the 775 students used in the standardization sample. Within the standardization sample they also include information on 208 students who were identified as needing special services. In the tables in which the means and standard deviations are presented, the total sample is divided into two groups: those students identified as needing special services and those identified as not needing special services. However, there is no information indicating in which of these groups the various ethnic groups are to be found. Further, because the group needing special services included a variety of handicapping conditions as well as levels of impairment, the usefulness of these norms is limited. The pass/fail criteria are based on the total sample population ($N = 775$), including students needing special services, 27% of the total population. The reviewers question the inclusion of students needing special services to establish standardizations of screening for normal language functions.

Visual inspection suggests small differences among means and standard deviations across age groups and between various subgroups. The authors do not discuss any significant differences between their populations for any of the subtests or for the total test. Nor do they provide this information for the age groups. The inclusion of this information would enhance the usefulness of the data provided.

In summary, this instrument provides a strong rationale and theoretical position for the need for a screening test of language abilities for adolescents and for the items selected for screening. The review of the research for each subtest is relevant for individuals working with adolescents with language-learning disabilities. However, the overall implementation of this information is affected by the selection of certain items and scoring procedures that reduce the value of the instrument as a screening tool. The normative data provided are affected by the fact that 27% of the standardization sample presents various handicapping conditions with varying levels of impairment. Therefore, the pass/fail criteria are lowered and do not reflect criteria that are based on normal adolescents. Because the authors do not provide any information on validity, reliability, or significant differences among the age groups, the usefulness of this screening instrument is limited.

REVIEWER'S REFERENCES

Bereiter, C., & Engelmann, S. (1966). *Teaching disadvantaged children in the preschool*. Englewood Cliffs, NJ: Prentice-Hall.

Bloom, L., & Lahey, M. (1978). *Language development and language disorders*. New York: John Wiley and Sons, Inc.

Simon, C. (1985). Functional flexibility: Developing communicative competence in speaker and listener roles. In C. Simon (Ed.), *Communication skills and classroom success: Therapy methodologies for language-learning disabled students* (pp. 135-178). San Diego: College-Hill Press.

[6]

Assessment of Career Decision Making. Purpose: "Assesses a student's career decision-making style and progress on three career decision-making tasks." Adolescents and adults; 1985; ACDM; 9 scales: Rational, Intuitive, Dependent, School Adjustment, Satisfaction With School, Involvement With Peers, Interaction With Instructors, Occupation, Major; 1986 price data: $32 per 2 answer sheets including scoring service and manual (84 pages); $17.50 per manual; WPS scoring service, $4.80 or more per answer sheet; (40) minutes; Jacqueline N. Buck and M. Harry Daniels; Western Psychological Services.*

TEST REFERENCES

1. Phillips, S. D., & Strohmer, D. C. (1983). Vocationally mature coping strategies and progress in the decision-making process: A canonical analysis. *Journal of Counseling Psychology, 30*, 395-402.

2. Pinder, F. A., & Fitzgerald, P. W. (1984). The effectiveness of a computerized guidance system in promoting career decision making. *Journal of Vocational Behavior, 24*, 123-131.

3. Phillips, S. D., Pazienza, N. J., & Ferrin, H. H. (1984). Decision-making styles and problem-solving appraisal. *Journal of Counseling Psychology, 31*, 497-502.

4. Phillips, S. D., Pazienza, N. J., & Walsh, D. J. (1984). Decision making styles and progress in occupational decision making. *Journal of Vocational Behavior, 25*, 96-105.

5. Remer, P., O'Neill, C. D., & Gohs, D. E. (1984). Multiple outcome evaluation of a life-career development course. *Journal of Counseling Psychology, 31*, 532-540.

6. Thomas, R. G., & Bruning, C. R. (1984). Cognitive dissonance as a mechanism in vocational decision processes. *Journal of Vocational Behavior, 24*, 264-278.

7. Phillips, S. D., Friedlander, M. L., Pazienza, N. J., & Kost, P. P. (1985). A factor analytic investigation of career decision-making styles. *Journal of Vocational Behavior, 26*, 106-115.

8. Gordon, V. N., Coscarelli, W. C., & Sears, S. J. (1986). Comparative assessments of individual differences in learning and career decision making. *Journal of College Student Personnel, 27*, 233-242.

Review of the Assessment of Career Decision Making by BRUCE J. EBERHARDT, Associate Professor of Management, University of North Dakota, Grand Forks, ND:

The Assessment of Career Decision Making (ACDM) is a 94-item, self-report instrument, the major focus of which is the process of career decision making. The theoretical basis of the ACDM is the Harren Model of Career Decision Making (Harren, 1979), which is "a comprehensive model that takes into account many of the important factors involved in the career decision-making process of students." The instrument assesses aspects of three of the four major components of the model: decision-making process, decision-making styles, and developmental tasks.

Three 10-item scales measure the degree to which students utilize three strategies—Rational, Intuitive, and Dependent—in making career decisions. A 24-item scale, labeled School Adjustment, consists of three 8-item subscales and measures students' satisfaction with school, involvement with peers, and interaction with instructors. These subscales represent the developmental tasks of autonomy, interpersonal maturity, and sense of purpose. Finally, the Occupation and Major scales are both 20-item scales that "measure the degree of commitment and certainty the student feels towards his or her choice of future occupation" or major or field of study, respectively. Both scales represent single, bipolar continua and assess the planning and commitment phases of the career decision-making process.

The ACDM can be administered to students either individually or in groups. The publisher recommends that the purpose of the instrument be explained to students before distribution. The ACDM was intended for use with adolescents and adults. However, particular sections of the test should be deleted when used with certain populations. The entire test can be used for college and university students. For high school students the Major scale should be deleted except for those individuals who have plans for some form of further education. Because of their general wording the Decision-Making Styles scales and the Occupation scale can be used with nonstudents. However, the publisher recommends not using the test with this group because relevant normative data are not available. Although the reading difficulty of the instrument has been estimated at the sixth-grade level, users are cautioned that students with low verbal skills or learning disabilities may have problems completing the test.

The scoring of the ACDM is both a strength and a potential weakness of the instrument. All completed forms must be scored through the publisher's scoring service. The computerized report which is generated from the scored ACDM actually consists of three separate reports: a Group Summary, a Counselor's report, and a Student's report. All of these reports provide extensive, detailed information. Especially impressive in the Counselor's report is a section labeled "Validity Considerations." This section considers two types of validity checks: "(a) invalid responses due to random or systematic response biases, and (b) threats to validity associated with relevant moderator variables such as age or ethnic group membership." The first type of validity concern is assessed using a Random Response Index. This scale was designed to detect random response patterns in the ACDM and was based on the supposition that certain pairs of items are inconsistent, contradictory, or at least statistically unlikely.

The only potentially negative aspect of ACDM scoring is that no hand-scoring option is available. Although the publisher states that for the average user the scoring turn around time is from 2 to 6 working days, it is easy to predict that in some circumstances, depending on the postal service, delays could be longer. For the user wishing to provide immediate feedback to test takers this delay may be prohibitive.

The publishers have done a first-rate job in providing test users with a manual that supplies extensive information concerning the test's theoretical development and standardization and its psychometric properties. The ACDM was standardized on samples of 550 high school and 2,495 college students. For scales where sex and grade-level differences were discovered, separate norms were established for males and females and individuals in the various grades. A shortcoming in the normative data, as noted by the publisher, is that the representation of ethnic minorities in the normative sample is limited. Therefore, caution should be taken when using the norms to interpret the scores of minority group members.

The manual presents the results of several studies investigating both the internal consistency and the test-retest reliabilities of the ACDM. In studies using the present form, alpha coefficients ranged from .49 to .84 for the Decision-Making Styles scales and from .78 to .92 for the Decision-Making Tasks scales. These figures indicate that the ACDM possesses adequate internal consistency for research purposes. However, the .49 for the one Decision-Making Style scale is relatively low and caution should be exercised when using the scale for individual interpretation. The studies examining the temporal stability of ACDM scores all involved only college students; data on test-retest reliability were lacking for high school students. The research investigating the test-retest reliability of the ACDM in its present form yielded correlation coefficients ranging from .66 to .84 with a 2-week time interval.

Numerous studies are cited in the manual that report on the ACDM's validity. Evidence is presented for the content, criterion-related, and construct validity of the test. When considered together, these studies present an impressive argument for the validity of the ACDM. However, more information on the predictive validity of the test would be desirable.

In summary, the ACDM appears to be a useful tool for individuals interested in the career decision-making process. Potential users include teachers, career counselors, and school staff responsible for career orientation programs. Used in combination with instruments assessing vocational interests, it provides students with information to assist in their career decision making. Potential users, however, should be careful when expanding its application to groups for which normative data are not presently available. These groups include nonstudents and members of certain ethnic minorities.

REVIEWER'S REFERENCE

Harren, V. A. (1979). A model of career decision making for college students. *Journal of Vocational Behavior*, 14, 119-133.

Review of the Assessment of Career Decision Making by NICHOLAS A. VACC, Professor and Coordinator of Counselor Education, University of North Carolina, Greensboro, NC:

The Assessment of Career Decision Making (ACDM) is a 94-item measure that assesses, through self-report, an individual's style of career decision making and progress on career decision-making tasks. Originally designed and developed by Vincent A. Harren, the ACDM is based on the Tiedeman and O'Hara theory of career decision. The present form of this instrument is the result of further development and refinement by Jacqueline N. Buck and M. Harry Daniels.

The ACDM is a self-report instrument with a true or false checkoff answer sheet and requires approximately 40 minutes to administer. The price of the answer sheet (i.e., $7.95 per sheet for quantities less than 10 with a slightly reduced cost for quantities greater than 10) includes computer processing, an individualized Counselor's Report, Student's Report, Group Summary if applicable, and postage and handling for returning the reports.

The manual indicates the ACDM, which was designed for high school and college students, can be used individually or with a group. As reported by the authors, the purpose of the instrument is to assist students in making career decisions and "selecting college majors and occupations that are compatible with their interests, skills, and environmental constraints." It is further stated that the test helps determine the "need for career counseling and best type of counseling to use." The latter purpose is particularly ambitious considering that the counseling literature indicates disagreement concerning who needs counseling and the type to use for different groups of clients.

Norms for the instrument are reported based on the performance of 550 high-school-age students and 2,495 college-age students over a 7-year period. As the authors indicate, use with individuals outside schools is limited. Grade-level norms are reported from ninth grade through the senior year in college. The normative sample for the ninth-grade level consists of only 60 subjects. A related concern is the demographic section of the answer sheet, which includes responses for students below the ninth grade; norms are not available for this group. In addition, reporting grade norms for college students is of questionable value because of the wide range of ages among those attending college. For example, differences between 40-year-old college students and stereotypic students who recently graduated from high school would be great. In general, standardization appeared to be nonsystematic, evolving from a series of studies completed over a number of years, with some studies using different forms of the test. The authors, however, have not clearly indicated how many subjects were administered earlier versions of the ACDM.

Several reliability studies were reported. The authors reported alpha coefficients for the ACDM ranging from .49 ($N = 143$) to .84 ($N = 264$) for the Decision-Making Styles scales, and from .78 ($N = 264$) to .92 ($N = 143$) for the Decision-Making Tasks scales. The reliability evidence presented is supportive, but further reliability estimates are needed. A number of validity studies by a variety of authors reported on content validity and estimates of criterion-related and construct validity. Again, earlier versions of the ACDM were used in some of the reported validity studies. Hence, this reviewer believes that the validity data cannot be interpreted with confidence.

Of concern is the interpretation of test results. The authors have reported that the Student Report is "designed to be used as part of a broader effort of giving feedback, including, at a minimum, a face-to-face meeting." However, the 1985–86 Western Psychological Services sales catalog indicates a report that is "jargon-free" and easily understood by the student. In making counselor, student, and group reports readily available, it appears that despite the manual warning, the Student Report is designed to be distributed without an interview with a counselor. This would not be a serious concern except the interpretive language of the Student Report is inappropriately dogmatic. Phrases such as "you are" and "your decision-making style also includes . . . " are prescriptively emphatic and not as tentative as they should be.

In summary, the ACDM has evolved over a period of 20 years. Some of the studies cited in the manual reflect earlier versions of the present instrument, i.e., Vocational Decision Making Q-Sort (1964–65) and Vocational Decision-Making Checklist (1968). Normative information is somewhat fragmented and has been generated from a variety of investigations whose purposes were other than addressing the psychometric properties of the ACDM.

Although recommended for high-school and college students, it seems the ACDM is most appropriately used at the college level. The majority of standardization studies focus on college populations, and the terms used in the instrument (e.g., instructor, course, and major) seem more appropriate to college students than to high school students. Terms more familiar to the latter group would include teacher, class, and program. The authors' recommendation that the ACDM be used with students only is well advised.

The concept of assessing career decision-making components is intriguing. At this time, however, there is a lack of sufficient confidence that the ACDM can provide this information. Until more empirical data using the present instrument are available, the manual and catalog announcement for the ACDM should temper their claims of the instrument's uses and effectiveness.

[7]

Assessment of Fluency in School-Age Children. Purpose: "To determine speech, language, and physiological functioning." Ages 5–18; 1983; AFSC; "criterion-referenced"; assessment includes classroom observation, parent interview, teacher evaluation of child's speech, multi-factored evaluation of child, and post therapy; multi-factored evaluation assesses 5 areas: Automatic Speech, Cued Speech, Spontaneous Speech, Physiological Components, Interview With Student/Assessing Attitudes; individual; 1983 price data: $32.50 per complete set including 32 of each form; $8 per 32 assessment of fluency forms; $2.25 per 32 parent interview, teacher evaluation, or dismissal from therapy program forms; $14.75 per resource guide (220 pages); (45) minutes for student evaluation; (30) minutes for parent interview; (15) minutes for classroom observation; (15) minutes for teacher evaluation;

Julia Thompson; The INTERSTATE Printers & Publishers, Inc.*

Review of the Assessment of Fluency in School-Age Children by LYNN S. FUCHS, Assistant Professor of Special Education, George Peabody College, Vanderbilt University, Nashville, TN:

Assessment of Fluency in School-Age Children is designed to assess fluency for the purposes of screening and making program placement and planning decisions. It incorporates assessment information from different sources, within multiple settings, employing a variety of measurement strategies, on a range of variables including fluency, articulation, voice, semantics, syntax, pragmatics, breath control, and auditory memory. The potential of such an ambitious instrument is great. Unfortunately, the author fails to fulfill this potential because of (*a*) inaccurate and inconsistent representation of the nature of the test, (*b*) confusing and insufficiently standardized directions and procedures as well as a poorly designed protocol, and (*c*) inadequate empirical development and documentation.

With respect to representation of the nature of the assessment, the author makes some questionable and confusing assertions. Examples include inconsistent and vague application of the term *differential evaluation* and the author's definition of stuttering. Perhaps most troublesome is the use of the descriptor *criterion-referenced*, in which the notion of a "threshold" for identifying ineffective communicators is proposed. This concept is promising and suggests a basis for related empirical work. Nevertheless, no relevant empirical development is presented; moreover, no criterion for fluency program placement or for speech and language screening is provided. Rather, the resource guide presents normative guidelines for certain determinations, such as acceptable phonation times and inhalation/exhalation rates, and one set of undocumented guidelines for classifying numbers of performative errors, with no age breakdowns. Most often, however, evaluation decisions are purely subjective. The author states, "There is no formula for making decisions as to whether therapy is indicated. . . . In the final analysis, the decision . . . is . . . individual . . . based on the uniqueness of the assessment." Such unsystematic, subjective decision making not only is unacceptable from a measurement viewpoint, but also is contradicted by some of the author's own recommendations. For example, the author notes that practitioners must determine whether "the child meets . . . eligibility criteria of the . . . district," and should set a fluency training goal representing "normal, human speech, operationally defined as a stuttering rate of 0.5 SW/M."

Directions for administration and protocol design also contribute to the inadequacy of the assessment. The first problem is one of confusion. The protocol has four numeral 2s, each subsumed under a different letter, but the resource guide refers to 2s without clarifying whether A2, B2, C2, or D2 is the relevant item. The top portion of the last page of the protocol has no heading to indicate the summative nature of this section, and this summative section precedes the scoring of the speech sample on the protocol. The level of headings in the outline under "Preliminary Activities" fails to reflect the organization. The "Overview of Activities" misleadingly implies corresponding activities for child and tester. One-to-one correspondence is not maintained between the scoring code and definitions (see pages 32–35). The three-item code for scoring performatives is operationalized dichotomously, with no functional meaning assigned to the "None" code.

Second, directions are incomplete, with (a) no clear instructions on what to score/write for many sections of the test/protocol (in fact, the author contends the only "test" scored is No. 2), and (b) inadequate guidelines and protocol format for integrating data from multiple sources, for summarizing information, and for determining whether performance is adequate (examiners are told to make these decisions using "general impressions"). Because no information is provided concerning appropriate examiner training, the confusing and incomplete nature of directions and protocol and the lack of interpretive guidelines represent serious problems.

Of even more serious consequence, however, is the lack of standardized instructions for administration. Few directions to students are provided; the examiner is required to identify relevant storybooks, four-sequence stories, and reading materials, with no guidelines for determining difficulty; the tester is directed to create another test of spontaneous speech for older students if the material provided seems juvenile; the examiner is required to select syntax

and articulation tests to include in the assessment; the tester is instructed to choose between a stopwatch and second hand of watch when several items seem to require a stopwatch for reliable scoring. This lack of standardization requires validation studies across a variety of testing materials and formats.

Unfortunately, test development and validation are incomplete. Two pilot studies, with a total N of 48 spanning grades K–7, report only minimal descriptive results. Obvious problems are the omission of reliability and validity information, procedures used to develop test items, and norms or empirical guidelines for criterion-referenced decisions. Additionally, it appears that in the studies reported, grades 8–12 were omitted. This is inappropriate because the author claims the assessment is designed for ages 5–18 (although the materials are juvenile and the author repeatedly refers to "young children" in the resource guide). A clinic population of fluency disorders also was excluded, and the percentages of students with high rates of disfluencies are, in fact, low for a sample specifically identified for fluency difficulties. These low percentages are especially problematic because disfluencies included whole word repetitions, which are not usually considered stuttered blocks. Therefore, the samples in these studies are unrepresentative not only of overall demographic variables, but also of the age range and fluency-disordered population the measure was designed to cover.

This test suffers from serious problems including lack of accurate and consistent representation, unclear directions, protocol deficiencies, unstandardized procedures, and insufficient development and validation. Given these problems along with the instrument's time-consuming nature (105 minutes for data collection and 30 minutes for summary and transcription), I can think of no decision-making purpose for which I can recommend its use.

Review of the Assessment of Fluency in School-Age Children by E. CHARLES HEALEY, Associate Professor of Speech-Language Pathology, University of Nebraska-Lincoln, Lincoln, NE:

TEST OVERVIEW. The Assessment of Fluency in School-Age Children (AFSC) by Julia Thompson is one of the few assessment instruments that provides a speech-language pathologist with a comprehensive examination of stuttering in young children. The author has provided a data-based rationale for the assessment approach along with a rather complete set of questions and test items for the professional to use. This assessment instrument includes color-coded forms along with a Resource Guide that provides directions for administration and descriptions of case studies, therapy methods, future research needs, and published materials on fluency disorders.

The major strength of this assessment tool is the multi-factor approach to the evaluation of school-age, nonfluent children. The author recognizes the complex and idiosyncratic nature of this disorder and provides a speech-language pathologist with a number of areas to test that might relate to the detection of problematic stuttering in children. The approach and assessment areas included in this test are sound and organized in a logical fashion.

The Resource Guide that accompanies the AFSC provides the necessary data and information about the test. The procedures used are justified by past research findings and/or commonly accepted opinions by highly regarded professionals in this field. The color-coded forms accompanying the test are easy to understand and provide adequate space for recording information.

The "Directions for Administration" chapter in the Resource Guide gives complete explanations of procedures to be followed in administering this test. The author offers suggestions about the types of questions to be asked to elicit responses from a child as well as specific items to present in order to collect the necessary data for the evaluation. It is also a plus to find definition of terms, normative data on certain test items, and a generous number of examples of responses one could anticipate in each section of the AFSC.

Another strength of the assessment instrument is the inclusion of rather detailed information regarding treatment. Specific treatment techniques and methods are given for those children diagnosed as stutterers. Thus, not only does the author provide an assessment tool, but a fairly complete description of therapeutic methods as well. Justification and rationale for each method is given along with some specific examples of instructions and procedures clinicians might follow. Many professionals will find this information helpful as reference or

review information even if they do not use the assessment materials.

The test has some weaknesses, however. Most of the information provided in the AFSC is taught in graduate level coursework in most training programs. Thus, most professionals do not need to purchase this particular instrument to perform an adequate differential diagnosis of school-age stutterers. None of the forms provided with the kit are unique in their content and most professionals could probably develop better ones than those provided. The assessment tool relies heavily on the evaluation procedures specified in an article by Gregory and Hill (1980), and professionals could easily refer to that article for suggestions regarding the diagnostic procedures supplied in the AFSC.

Another major weakness is the lack of clearly specified reliability and validity data. There is no evidence in the Resource Guide of any test-retest, interjudge, or intrajudge reliability data or standard errors of measurement. Statistical comparisons between data derived from the AFSC and another popular assessment device such as *The Stoker Probe Technique* (Stoker, 1980) are lacking. This lack of validity data is a serious oversight. Moreover, the total sample of young stutterers making up the normative group is also extremely small. All of the assessment data were acquired from children in the east-central Ohio area, a rural, small industrial region of the United States. The author even admits to this weakness in the Preface by stating, "there is a need for data from urban and rural areas in different geographic locations." When the test is used to track the improvement of students (criterion-referenced), this may not be a weakness. However, as a tool used to place children in special programs the small norming group does raise some concern.

SUMMARY. The AFSC is a practical and useful guide to professionals interested in a thorough differential evaluation and assessment of school-age children with a fluency disorder. The Resource Guide that accompanies the test forms provides complete and easy-to-understand materials. In addition to the information provided in the guide about assessment, there are chapters dealing with treatment, criteria for dismissal from therapy, and directions for future research. The major strength of this instrument is the material in the Resource

Guide. It is complete, thorough, and represents sound, objective evaluation of literature in the area of fluency disorders.

Perhaps the biggest concern this reviewer has about the instrument is its relative simplicity and the lack of any really novel assessment procedures for this type of problem. Most, if not all, of the tasks performed in AFSC are those that any professionals could develop on their own. Thus, the basic evaluation tasks included are ones that professionals have been using for several years. Additionally, there is no evidence that the author has conducted any reliability and validity studies. Despite these serious shortcomings, many professionals might find the AFSC helpful in planning assessment and treatment procedures for young stutterers.

REVIEWER'S REFERENCES

Gregory, H., & Hill, D. (1980). Stuttering therapy for children. In W. Perkins (Ed.), *Strategies in stuttering therapy. Seminars in Speech, Language and Hearing.* New York: Thieme-Stratton.
    Stoker, B. (1980). *The Stoker Probe Technique* (2nd ed.). Tulsa: Modern Education Corporation.

[8]

Bader Reading and Language Inventory.
Purpose: "Designed to determine appropriate placement of students in instructional materials." Children and adolescents and adults; 1983; a compilation of graded reading passages, word recognition lists, phonics and word analysis subtests, spelling tests, cloze tests, visual discrimination tests, auditory discrimination tests, unfinished sentences, and evaluations of language abilities; individual; manual including all tests (233 pages); price data available from publisher; administration time not reported; Lois A. Bader; Macmillan Publishing Co., Inc.*

Review of the Bader Reading and Language Inventory by KRISTA J. STEWART, Associate Professor of Psychology and Director of the School Psychology Training Program, Tulane University, New Orleans, LA:

The Bader Reading and Language Inventory is a battery of informal tests developed for use by reading specialists, resource teachers, and classroom teachers. Primary emphasis is on the set of graded reading passages, but the other tests allow examination of specific areas (some more related to reading than others) in which the student might also be having difficulty.

The manual gives little information on the development of the Bader's many tests; less than four pages are dedicated to this discussion. The bulk of this description focuses on the development of the graded passages, but even that information is sketchy at best. Three sets of 12 passages were developed for the graded passages: one set for children; one for children, adolescents, and adults; and one for adults. The passages were either written by the author or, as the author indicates, were selected from materials that appeared to be typical for the grade level designations. After the initial passages were written, they were administered to a total of 70 students. According to the author, passages that were not considered appealing were dropped although no indication is given of how this determination was made.

The author reports that the sets of passages were tested for equivalence, resulting in correlations in the upper .70s and low .80s but does not indicate specifically what scores were correlated (i.e., word recognition, comprehension, or both). To give evidence of the validity of these passages, the author reports a study of 30 students whose performance on the test was compared to teacher report of the child's level of placement in basal reading materials; 60% of these comparisons were identical. The author, however, does not describe the sample used.

Literal comprehension of the passages is assessed by having the child summarize the passage, followed by a series of questions to prompt recall of information not given in the summary. From these responses, total number of "memories" is determined. Interpretative questions are asked but are not counted in the total number of memories. The author gives criteria for instructional reading level, criteria that are less stringent than those used in current practice. The author justifies this difference by stating that traditional cutoffs result in students usually being placed in materials that are too easy for them. No further rationale is given, however, for the precise cutoffs that are used. The author does indicate that if the student's reading is extremely slow, the instructional level may be one level lower than the passage on which comprehension was adequate.

Cutoffs are also given for frustration and independent levels. Comprehension can be determined for oral and silent reading as well as for listening, although the author encourages omitting testing for comprehension after oral reading, which is usually lower than comprehension after silent reading. The author advises that oral reading be tape recorded so that scorer accuracy of the evaluation of reading errors can be checked.

The major purpose for another part of the test, the Graded Word List, is to determine entry level for the graded passages. According to the author, the lists can also serve as a check on the student's word attack skills and provide a comparison with contextual reading. As was the case for the written passages, little specific information is given on how the words were selected for the lists. According to the author, words were chosen from graded sight-word lists and basals that appeared to be appropriate for each level. Validity was evaluated by comparing reading specialists' placement of 64 students and the child's performance on the lists. Besides the Graded Word List, four supplementary functional word lists are included: a list of words frequently used in instructional materials, two lists of words encountered in daily life, and a list of words encountered in completing forms and managing personal affairs.

The remaining parts of the inventory are to be given as desired and are to be interpreted based on the need of the student to perform the skill being evaluated. Virtually no information is given on the development of any of these tests. In some cases the author gives recommended cutoff points and indicates that they are those suggested by research; no specific research is cited, however.

The Phonics and Word Analysis Test contains 14 subtests that, according to the author, may be pertinent to some areas of knowledge and abilities that may underlie word recognition. These subtests are to be given selectively.

Seven Spelling Tests are provided and categorized according to the type of skill being evaluated and the reading level of the child for which the test would be appropriate. Skills being evaluated include words with silent letters, words spelled phonetically, words illustrating common spelling conventions, and commonly misspelled high frequency words.

The four Cloze Tests each contain unrelated sentences rather than a paragraph format. The first test is for beginning readers; the others are a semantic cloze test, a syntactic cloze test, and a grammatical cloze test.

The two Visual Discrimination Tests require matching letters, syllables, words, and phrases. The first test is for children through grade one, and the second is for readers at second grade

level or above. A general guide for evaluating performance is provided although no indication is given of how those guidelines were established.

The first of the Auditory Discrimination Tests requires discrimination of word pairs. Cutoff scores (with no rationale cited) for six-, seven-, and eight-year-olds are given. The second test involves having the student name the initial letter in words that are presented.

The author refers to the Unfinished Sentences task as a "projective technique." The purpose of this test is to evaluate the child's concerns and interests that should be considered during assessment and remediation. The author notes that often students will share problems about which the examiner can do little, a comment that reflects the inappropriateness of untrained personnel administering this test.

The Arithmetic (calculation) Test is included to provide an estimate of the student's ability to perform a skill that is not dependent on reading. Grade equivalents for raw scores are provided, but the method of score derivation is not indicated.

Several methods are described for evaluating expressive language and include describing, retelling, dictating, completing sentences, repeating sentences, and syntax matching. A Sentence Repetition Test and a Syntax Matching Test are included in this section. Also provided are suggestions for evaluating receptive language.

Finally, evaluation of writing is discussed. A checklist for evaluating written language expression is provided.

Also included in the manual are several other forms: a teacher's reading referral form, a form for summarizing the assessment and recommendations, and two checklists for evaluating the student's own learning priorities. In addition, a graphic representation of a model for the test battery is presented. This model, however, is never discussed in the text.

In summary, the Bader is a battery that may be most useful to the expert diagnostician who is particularly interested in evaluating skill development. The test does provide an interesting assortment of materials to be used in assessment; but the user should keep in mind that the tests, because of the lack of psychometric data, must be considered strictly informal.

The cutoffs or grade equivalent scores can be considered only rough estimates at best.

Review of the Bader Reading and Language Inventory by DAN WRIGHT, School Psychologist, Ralston Public Schools, Ralston, NE:

The Bader Reading and Language Inventory was designed as a flexible and largely qualitative inventory of reading and reading-related skills. Constructed for use primarily by reading specialists, resource teachers, and classroom teachers, the actual administration of the inventory could be mastered by anyone with training in individual assessment. The time required for administration will depend not only on student abilities, but on the depth and breadth of inquiry desired by the examiner. Test materials, scoring sheets, and other forms can be detached from the manual, duplicated as needed, and organized and stored to accommodate the examiner's uses.

The central feature of the inventory is a series of graded reading passages, ranging from pre-primer through twelfth grade, and providing alternate passages on three levels of interest at each grade level. The purpose of the graded passages, as succinctly stated in the manual, is "to find the highest instructional level at which the student can comprehend and to analyze oral reading to discover student strengths and problems in reading so that the student can be appropriately placed in materials for instruction." The word recognition lists function primarily to indicate an appropriate entry level to the graded passages, and the other tests generally provide information supplementary to test interpretation.

The manual is somewhat ambiguous regarding test development. The graded word lists and graded word passages rightly appear to have received the most intensive attention, but item selection or construction in these areas seems to have been rather subjective and there is no indication that items were added, deleted, or modified as a result of field testing. Some testing with small, poorly-defined samples was conducted to demonstrate that items were indeed presented in order of increasing difficulty, that alternate passages were roughly equivalent, and that results were in agreement with current reading placements. However, a much stronger case for the adequacy of all the items needs to be built. Reliability is not

addressed, and validity is dismissed with reference to a single, unpublished study.

Shaky as the support may be for the word lists and reading passages, the remaining parts of the inventory fare worse. No information is presented on the development or adequacy of the remaining tests, and there is no coherent articulation on the utility of any results. A student's performance on tests of visual and auditory discrimination, for example, may be of some relevance in interpreting performance on the reading passages, but the examiner is left alone to infer the nature or extent of such relevance.

In summary, it would be better not to consider this inventory as a "test" at all in the sense of providing useful quantitative results. Examiners must make independent and subjective judgements on the appropriateness of the inventory for their populations of students, its relevance to curriculum in use locally, and any inferences to draw regarding instructional programming. What the inventory does offer is a structured series of tasks that provide an opportunity to observe and record much qualitative information regarding students' reading and reading-related abilities. However, there is little reason to recommend this inventory over teacher-constructed, informal reading inventories, and nothing that causes it to stand out positively among other commercially available inventories.

[9]

Behaviordyne Retirement Service. Purpose: "Designed to help you plan for a satisfying retirement." Pre-retirees and people in retirement; 1982–85; BRS; 5 areas: Leisure, Health, Housing, Finances, Legal Issues; 1983 price data: $25 per test including report ('85, 161 pages) and scoring service; (30) minutes; John H. Lewis; Behaviordyne, Inc.*

[This service has been temporarily withdrawn; the Editor has been informed that it will be reintroduced after revision, at a later date.]

Review of the Behaviordyne Retirement Service by CAMERON J. CAMP, Associate Professor of Psychology, University of New Orleans, New Orleans, LA:

The Behaviordyne Retirement Service (BRS) consists of a computer-scored questionnaire, which has 100 statements such as "Most retirement villages are occupied by people with small incomes." Each of these statements is judged to be "true," "false," or "don't know." The items are distributed across five categories of information, ranging from Leisure to Legal. The number of items in each category ranges from 14 to 28. In addition, topics are listed under each category, and respondents can obtain further information on any of these topics by indicating their interests on the questionnaire form. For example, under the category Health the respondent can get additional information about Death and Dying, Heart Disease, Diabetes, Stress, etc. In addition, the questionnaire concludes with a potpourri of "Retirement Specials," which are additional topics of information ranging from Women and Retirement to how to get the President of the United States to send you a birthday card or anniversary greeting.

Upon sending in the questionnaire/booklet, respondents receive a listing of the "actual" answers to the true/false questions, brief (generally 2–3 pages) narratives about the general topics, and information related to the "additional information" choices requested. The additional information usually includes addresses where publications can be obtained from other agencies.

The BRS is not a test, nor is it an interest inventory in the tradition of standardized inventories. The true/false statements "stimulate your thinking about retirement and help us determine if there is retirement information that might be of value to you." The same key of "correct" answers is sent to all respondents, while "additional information packets" are identical and sent to all persons indicating interest in such information. No attempt is made to match patterns of responses with national norms or other profiles. Therefore, issues such as reliability, validity, etc., are superfluous to discussion of this questionnaire.

Basically, the BRS is a marketing tool. It is used as a "hook" to arouse the interest of prospective respondents who then purchase a "product," in this case information. The value or worth of the BRS therefore is best determined by free market forces rather than by criteria of good test design. It is certainly worthwhile for older adults to plan for retirement, and the information that the BRS provides is easily understood and apparently updated on a regular basis. Whether the BRS is "good" can only be judged on the basis of

"getting your money's worth." If $25 seems to be a good buy for obtaining this information, then the BRS is a good questionnaire. If the same or better information can be obtained more easily and/or cheaply (as through the local chapter of the AARP or Administration on Aging), then the BRS is "not good," (i.e., overpriced).

SUMMARY. The Behaviordyne Retirement Service (BRS) contains a questionnaire that has 100 true/false items dealing with respondents' attitudes and knowledge about five aspects of retirement, and also allows respondents to indicate topics dealing with retirement about which they would like to receive more information. After sending in the questionnaire, respondents are sent an answer key for the 100 items, along with narrative information about aspects of retirement and more specific information concerning additional topics of interest. Not a test, the BRS is instead an information dissemination service for individuals interested in planning for retirement.

Review of the Behaviordyne Retirement Service by KEVIN W. MOSSHOLDER, Associate Professor of Management, Auburn University, Auburn, AL:

The Behaviordyne Retirement Service (BRS) is designed to aid in retirement planning. The goal of the BRS is to provide timely retirement information in a nonthreatening manner in order to increase the potential for a satisfactory retirement. Though ideally used prior to retirement, the service could be helpful to many persons who have been retired for some years.

The initial step in using the BRS requires the respondent to answer a series of true-false questionnaire items that tap five areas: Leisure, Health, Housing, Finances, and Legal Issues. The format of the questionnaire booklet allows for individuals to request additional information pertinent to each of the above areas. After responses have been processed, the BRS returns a computer-generated report containing the "correct" responses to the true-false items, extensive narrative concerning topics broached by the items and/or requested by the respondent, and bibliographies indicating sources of further topical, relevant information.

The BRS offers a product that could prove beneficial to an increasing portion of the population. Its ultimate purpose is educational rather than evaluative. Accordingly, the BRS might be more properly judged with respect to this goal rather than more traditional criteria used to assess standardized tests. A positive feature is that its objective format may, in a nonthreatening way, allow the BRS to attract attention to topics that are important but overlooked or taken for granted by the prospective retiree. The BRS questionnaire items are laid out for optical scanning and instructions for completing the questionnaire are adequate. Few if any respondents should have trouble understanding how to use the questionnaire. The instructions emphasize the nonevaluative purpose of the process, which may ease reservations some respondents might have about assessing their beliefs and views on less positive aspects of retirement.

According to the BRS, the computer-generated report should have impact because it contains only information relevant to the respondent. Since the report is not assembled from preprinted material, it can be kept more up-to-date. Apprehensions about others knowing the respondents' feelings on sensitive items are reduced because the resulting report belongs solely to the respondent and can be read in private. Judging from the sample report accompanying the BRS package, the average person should be able to comprehend its contents. Information is presented in a well-organized, straightforward manner. Bibliographies accompanying the narrative portions of the report appear to be current and potentially helpful.

There are some questions that need to be answered about the BRS and some features that could be improved. The BRS emphasizes that reports are individualized, but does not explain further. Individualized could mean the amount of information contained in any of the five areas depends on the correctness of an individual's responses (i.e., how much was known). Individualized could also mean simply that a respondent receives unique information in the reports only because of having specifically requested it. Certainly, the former definition indicates greater sophistication and a higher quality report. The BRS package does not make clear which definition of individualized applies and this information should be made available.

The correctness of a response to the questions in the response booklet may depend on one's perspective. In some cases, presenting answers as being true (or false) when matters of perspective are involved could cause a respondent to discount other information that is actually based on facts. (A BRS advertising flyer indicates that there are no right or wrong answers, but this is not stated in the questionnaire booklet or report.) It is not clear if the respondent's answers are fed back along with the report. It would be desirable if this were done so the respondent could assess areas where more education is needed.

Needless to say, the BRS would not be recommended for research or psychological assessment purposes. However, as a nonthreatening, relatively inexpensive educational tool for retirement, it is acceptable. The BRS could benefit from improved explanations about report generation and information updating. The computer-generated report might also include an expanded introduction section (in addition to its suggestions for use section) to provide better overall integration of the areas of the report. This type of information could strengthen the report overall by promoting the perspective that, while some of the five content areas of the questionnaire may be of greater interest, all are of sufficient importance to satisfactory retirement planning and should receive the respondent's attention.

[10]

The Brief Symptom Inventory. Purpose: "Designed to reflect the psychological symptom patterns of psychiatric and medical patients as well as nonpatient individuals." Psychiatric patients and nonpatients; 1975-82; BSI; essentially the brief form of the SCL-90-R; self-report; 9 primary dimension scores (Somatization, Obsessive-Compulsive, Interpersonal Sensitivity, Depression, Anxiety, Hostility, Phobic Anxiety, Paranoid Ideation, Psychoticism), plus 3 global indices (Global Severity Index, Positive Symptom Distress Index, Positive Symptom Total); 1987 price data: $30 per 100 test forms; $17.50 per manual ('82, 48 pages); (7–10) minutes; Leonard R. Derogatis and Phillip M. Spencer; Clinical Psychometric Research.*

See 9:160 (1 reference).

TEST REFERENCES

1. Cochran, C. D., & Hale, W. D. (1985). College student norms on the Brief Symptom Inventory. *Journal of Clinical Psychology*, 41, 777-779.

2. Cella, D. F., & Tross, S. (1986). Psychological adjustment to survival from Hodgkin's disease. *Journal of Consulting and Clinical Psychology*, 54, 616-622.

3. Verinis, J. S., Wetzel, L., Vanderporten, A., & Lewis, D. (1986). Improvement in men inpatients in an alcoholism

rehabilitation unit: A week-by-week comparison. *Journal of Studies on Alcohol*, 47, 85-88.

4. Noyes, R., Jr., Clarkson, C., Crowe, R. R., Yates, W. R., & McChesney, C. M. (1987). A family study of generalized anxiety disorder. *The American Journal of Psychiatry*, 144, 1019-1024.

Review of The Brief Symptom Inventory by BERT P. CUNDICK, Professor of Psychology, Brigham Young University, Provo, UT:

The Brief Symptom Inventory (BSI) is a 53-item self-report symptom inventory designed to reflect the psychological systems of psychiatric, medical, and normal individuals. It is a brief form of the SCL-90, which was also devised by Derogatis. It is designed to provide a multidimensional symptom measurement in about 10 minutes.

Although only four to seven items are used on each of the symptom scales, the internal consistency reliabilities (Cronbach's alpha) are very acceptable, ranging from a low of .71 on Psychoticism to a high of .83 on Obsessive-Compulsive. The test-retest reliabilities are also good, ranging from a low of .68 on Somatization to a high of .91 on Phobic Anxiety. The three global scores all have test-retest reliabilities above .80. The 53-item total may be somewhat misleading because the response format utilizes a 5-point continuum which greatly increases score points over what would be obtained from a T-F format. A variation of alternate form reliability is also presented where the specific items on the BSI were taken from the answer sheets obtained from a group who had taken the SCL-90 and correlated with the symptom scales they matched. These correlations ranged from .92 on Psychoticism to .99 on Hostility. The effort to represent reliability is thorough and establishes the fact that the scores on the BSI are very acceptable for this kind of measure and that the instrument is an adequate substitute for the SCL-90.

Concurrent validity is reported by showing the correlations on the symptom dimensions of the BSI with the Wiggins content scales and the Tryon cluster scores obtained on the MMPI. The reported correlations range from .30 to .72 with the most relevant average score correlations averaging above .5. A factor analysis on a 1,002-psychiatric-outpatient sample was performed. The results confirmed to a remarkable degree the a priori construction of the symptom dimensions; only the four-item Interpersonal Sensitivity scale was not essentially found as hypothesized.

Predictive and construct validity will take some time to establish. However, the method of deriving the BSI from the SCL-90 suggests that previous studies involving the SCL-90 might reflect on the validity of the BSI.

The norms on the BSI are well described; however, they do not appear to be representative of many areas in the United States and it might be desirable for users to develop local norms. The psychiatric norm groups appear heavily weighted toward lower social classes and also overrepresent blacks. It would have been interesting and more informative to show comparisons with U.S. Bureau of the Census data.

Derogatis has been very careful to look at reading level in developing his items. However, neither the SCL-90 nor the BSI include an attempt at validity scores. Confusion, faking, and illiteracy could all produce individual profiles which might be highly misleading.

In summary, the BSI appears to be technically sound in its test construction procedures. The manual is well written and complete and is convincing on matters of score reliability and initial efforts to establish validity. The BSI would be a good initial screening measure. However, future efforts might be directed at improving the test norms and addressing the issue of validity scores.

Review of The Brief Symptom Inventory by CHARLES A. PETERSON, Staff Clinical Psychologist, VA Minneapolis Medical Center, Minneapolis, MN:

The Brief Symptom Inventory (BSI) is a brief form of the SCL-90-R (9:1082). It is a self-report inventory "designed to reflect the psychological symptom patterns of psychiatric and medical patients as well as non-patient individuals." The authors state the BSI may be used for a "single, point-in-time assessment of an individual's clinical status, or it may be utilized repeatedly either to document trends through time, or in pre-post evaluations." No comparative data are provided, but the authors insist that the BSI can be reliably administered in a narrative mode to patients who cannot read. Brief, clear instructions to the test will enable all but the very deranged to rate each of the 53 items on a 5-point scale of distress (0–4), ranging from *not at all*, (o) to *extremely* (4). Subjects are asked to consider "the past seven days including today" when rendering their self-observing assessment on an easy-to-comprehend answer sheet.

Item content appears to have face validity and is simply stated. A typical example asks, "HOW MUCH WERE YOU DISTRESSED BY:" "Poor appetite?" "Feeling uneasy in crowds?" "Your mind going blank?." Nine symptom dimensions and three global indices can be assessed by the clinician after receiving the answer sheet, quickly scoring the test, and plotting the profile on conveniently normed profile sheets. Interpretation takes place on three different, but interrelated, levels: the global level, the dimensional level, and the level of discrete symptoms. Profile interpretation may be unwarranted, given that no information was provided in the manual on intercorrelations among scales. Scale intercorrelations are "moderate to high, ranging from the mid .40s to the mid .70s" (L. R. Derogatis, personal communication, January 27, 1987). Interpretations should be based on the relevant norms provided in the manual: male and female outpatients, male and female nonpatients, male and female psychiatric inpatients, and male and female adolescents. Additional norms are available for college students (Cochran & Hale, 1985) and for the elderly (Hale, Cochran, & Hedgepeth, 1984).

There is every reason to believe that this test will work as promised. The psychometric underpinnings are impressive and are the result of a careful, sequential research program. Internal consistency ranges from a low of .71 on Psychoticism to a high of .85 on Depression. Test-retest reliability over a 2-week period is excellent, ranging from a low of .68 on Somatization to a high of .91 in Phobic Anxiety. The Global Severity index, touted as "the most sensitive" of the macroscopic measures of psychopathology, has a test-retest reliability of .90. These test-retest reliabilities sound good, but theory-derived predictions of those scales most likely to change over time (states?) and those likely to remain stable over time (traits?) should have been provided. The authors use the parent SCL-90-R as an alternate form and find reliability coefficients ranging from .92 to .99. In line with Loevinger (1957) and Messick (1981), the BSI has been evaluated primarily

in terms of construct validity. When correlated with the MMPI, convergent validity is good but attenuated by less impressive discriminant validity. Factor analytic results demonstrate impressive agreement between the factor precipitates and the a priori dimensional structure. Predictive validity has been underresearched, a sad state of affairs common to most tests in the *Mental Measurements Yearbooks*. Multimodal assessments of BSI constructs could be made by using compatible instruments from the Psychopathology Rating Scale Series; for example, the Hopkins Psychiatric Rating Scale (9:483) allows a clinician to rate the same constructs from interview data.

Surely it is no secret that clinician time has become increasingly expensive and scarce. Less available time and higher costs have prompted many changes in traditional psychological assessment, including less testing, abbreviated testing, and more automated testing. We have witnessed the MMPI shrink from maxi to midi to mini. Tests may become so brief that we must fearfully wonder if psychologists—following Allport (1953)—will simply dispense with tests and just ask the patient, "Are you depressed?" Psychologists must consider carefully the indications for and the implications of this hurried understanding. Compared to the significant interpersonal relationship in traditional psychological testing (cf., Schafer, 1954; especially Chapter 2), a measure such as the BSI may signal a treatment relationship that may seem ephemeral and superficial. Expressed somewhat differently, what patient would be comforted by the sight of a physician reading a book titled *Rapid Interpretation of Grave Conditions*?

The SCL-90-R takes 15–20 minutes to administer, apparently an unacceptable amount of time to today's fevered clinician, causing the BSI's authors to reduce administration time to 7–10 minutes. Is this difference significant? Is the reduction in time sufficient to justify the BSI's existence? In the spirit of brevity, the answer is "Yes," particularly in light of the solid psychometric foundation, the multiple norms which help the clinician remain sensitive to fluctuations in base rates of psychopathology, and the test's ability to survey a fairly broad range of psychopathology. No doubt potential users would be happier if a "Mania" symptom dimension were included, and if the authors more honestly called the test by its true name, The SCL-53.

REVIEWER'S REFERENCES

Allport, G. W. (1953). The trend in motivational theory. *American Journal of Orthopsychiatry*, 23, 107-119.

Schafer, R. (1954). *Psychoanalytic interpretation of Rorschach testing.* New York: Grune & Stratton.

Loevinger, J. (1957). Objective tests as instruments of psychological theory. *Psychological Reports*, 3, 635-694.

Messick, S. (1981). Constructs and their vicissitudes in educational and psychological measurement. *Psychological Bulletin*, 89, 575-588.

Hale, W. D., Cochran, C. D., & Hedgepeth, B. E. (1984). Norms for the elderly on the Brief Symptom Inventory. *Journal of Consulting and Clinical Psychology*, 52, 321-322.

Cochran, C. D., & Hale, W. D. (1985). College student norms on the Brief Symptom Inventory. *Journal of Clinical Psychology*, 41, 777-779.

[11]

Burns/Roe Informal Reading Inventory: Preprimer to Twelfth Grade, Second Edition. Purpose: Allows teacher "to determine students' strengths and weaknesses in reading as well as the levels of reading skills they've attained." Beginning readers–grade 12; 1985; IRI; 2 scores: Word Recognition, Comprehension; 14 levels: Preprimer, Primer, First Reader, Second Grade, Third Grade, Fourth Grade, Fifth Grade, Sixth Grade, Seventh Grade, Eighth Grade, Ninth Grade, Tenth Grade, Eleventh Grade, Twelfth Grade; 1987 price data: $17.50 per manual ('85, 174 pages) containing instructions and graded word lists and graded passages; (30) minutes; Paul C. Burns and Betty D. Roe; Houghton Mifflin.*

Review of the Burns/Roe Informal Reading Inventory: Preprimer to Twelfth Grade, Second Edition by CAROLYN COLVIN MURPHY, Assistant Professor of Teacher Education, San Diego State University, San Diego, CA and ROGER H. BRUNING, Professor of Educational Psychology, University of Nebraska-Lincoln, Lincoln, NE:

The Burns/Roe Informal Reading Inventory is an informal test used to discover the kinds of materials students can and cannot read without assistance. Most often, informal reading inventories (IRIs) are administered by classroom teachers. In the case of the Burns/Roe Informal Reading Inventory, student oral and silent reading of graded word lists and passages is assessed, yielding grade-equivalent scores for independent reading (student can read with understanding alone and with ease), instructional reading (student can read and comprehend with teacher assistance), frustration level (student is unable to function adequately), and capacity (student level of listening comprehension). These scores are seen as suitable for placing students at the correct level in reading programs, for supplying appropriate content-area reading material, and for recommending recreational reading.

Among the many classroom teachers who use it, the Burns/Roe appears to enjoy a generally favorable status. The materials have high interest; there are equivalent forms, which makes the Burns/Roe flexible for use in a variety of situations; it uses the familiar concepts (to reading teachers) of independent, instructional, and frustration levels in reading; and the Burns/Roe is one of the few IRIs that go up to the twelfth grade level. For knowledgeable users, it provides a relatively quick source of information about problems students may be experiencing with reading.

At the same time, the implication of diagnostic capability (e.g., separate scores for different types of comprehension questions) and the fact that the Burns/Roe yields scores used in making individual decisions about students require certain basic psychometric qualities. These are completely lacking. There is no technical manual. There are no data on reliability, standard errors of measurement, comparability of the four forms, or relationship to other measures. No basis for the criteria used to determine levels is given (e.g., in grades 1 and 2, instructional level equals 85 percent or higher in word recognition and 75 percent or higher on comprehension questions). A two-page appendix to the manual contains all the information presented on scale development and validation. Neither the numbers nor characteristics of the students who took part are described.

As a consequence, use of the Burns/Roe Informal Reading Inventory must be an act of faith. While clinical judgments may lead users to the conclusion that the Burns/Roe's assessments may be valid, there are no data to substantiate that claim. The lack of that data severely detracts from what, otherwise, might be considered one of the better informal inventories. Certainly, reading teachers would react with much greater confidence to a measure in which they could make a judgment of probable error in any score, correspondence to other, more formal measures of reading, and expected relationship to classroom performance. In its present form, the Burns/Roe Informal Reading Inventory, Second Edition falls far short of accepted standards for test development and revision.

Review of the Burns/Roe Informal Reading Inventory: Preprimer to Twelfth Grade, Second Edition by EDWARD S. SHAPIRO, Associate Professor and Director, School Psychology Program, Lehigh University, Bethlehem, PA:

The Burns/Roe Informal Reading Inventory (IRI) is a set of informal reading inventories from preprimer through twelfth grade reading levels. The instrument contains both graded word lists and reading passages. The current version is a revision of an earlier edition.

Two sets of word lists, 20 words each, are provided at each level. Words were selected from the Rand McNally and Scott Foresman reading series, although the authors do not provide information regarding which particular series of those publishers were used. Words were assigned to grade levels during field testing; the criteria for classifying a word at a given grade level were that 80% or more of the students at that grade level could successfully pronounce the word, less than 80% of the students could successfully pronounce the word at the grade level below, and more than 80% could pronounce it at the grade level above.

Passages were constructed from the same basal reading series as the word lists and from the reading and literature series of the Houghton-Mifflin company. Again, the authors do not indicate the specific series employed. Passages were evaluated for readability levels using the Spache and Fry formulae. Comprehension questions were constructed to evaluate six areas: Main Idea, Detail, Sequence, Cause and Effect, Inference, and Vocabulary. For each passage, 8 to 10 questions are provided. The questions were evaluated by graduate students in reading education and then revised. Subsequent field testing was conducted, although the authors do not indicate with whom or how many students were tested. Based on the feedback from these students, however, revisions on comprehension questions were made.

Included in the instrument are a number of excellent tables, charts, and clear examples on the administration, scoring, and interpretation of the IRI. The authors discuss their definitions for independent reading level, instructional reading level, frustration reading level, and capacity reading levels. In addition, they offer a suggested system for marking errors and conducting a miscue analysis. Appropriate cautions about the use of error analysis from the limited sample of the IRI are included.

The authors make clear that the intent of their measure is primarily to determine appropriate reading levels. Implied in this use is that a teacher would then be able to accurately place a child within the basal series. Unfortunately, there may be a significant problem with the degree to which IRI results may be generalized beyond the particular basal reading series from which the IRI was developed. Jenkins and Pany (1978), Armbruster and Rosenshine (1977), and Leinhardt, Zigmond, and Cooley (1981) have all provided data that suggest the overlap between the content of assessment instruments and basal reading series is questionable. As such, results on a particular measure may be very different if a different reading series was employed. The IRI measures were all derived from the Rand McNally, Scott Foresman, and Houghton Mifflin series. Although the results may be generalizable to students placed into these series, the authors did not adequately report the exact series employed in developing the inventories.

In addition to the problem of test/curriculum overlap, there are only limited details provided in the manual regarding the field testing. It is difficult to evaluate the degree to which the measures were effectively piloted before publication.

Another concern of this reviewer is the lack of psychometric data reported. Although I would agree the measures are designed as informal inventories, the authors do suggest the use of the measures in a retest format to evaluate student progress. There are no data on test-retest reliability reported. Further, if the measures are to be used to determine placement, validity data should be reported; yet there are no validity data presented. Indeed, the authors have provided very little discussion of potential uses of the measures.

An additional weakness of these measures is their limited usefulness in monitoring student performance across a short period of time. Given that only two equivalent forms of each grade level are provided, any attempt to readminister the IRI frequently would result in biased data due to retesting on the identical information. The authors do not explicitly caution against using the measures to monitor performance. Such cautions should be included in the manual.

Despite these weaknesses, the IRI measure does have a number of significant strengths. The authors have provided all forms, charts, tables, and instructions necessary for conducting IRIs. These items are very clear and easily reproducible. As such, the measure would be particularly valuable as an adjunct assessment measure for reading specialists or classroom teachers.

The measure does offer one of the few available, commercially produced IRIs. Although users should be careful about the potential lack of overlap with the basal reading series employed by their school, the measure may provide an important component to an overall reading assessment.

REVIEWER'S REFERENCES

Armbruster, B. B., Stevens, R. J., & Rosenshine, B. (1977). *Analyzing content coverage and emphasis: A study of three curricula and two tests.* Technical Report No. 26, Center for the Study of Reading, University of Illinois at Urbana-Champaign.
Jenkins, J. R., & Pany, D. (1978). Standardized achievement tests: How useful for special education? *Exceptional Children, 44,* 448-453.
Leinhardt, G., Zigmond, N., & Cooley, W. W. (1981). Reading instruction and its effects. *American Educational Research Journal,* 18, 343-361.

[12]

Career Survey. Purpose: "To provide students, clients, and their counselors with information which may stimulate the counseling process . . . . to encourage students and clients to explore career areas which they may not have previously considered . . . . to provide a means for self-reflection and clarification of long-range plans in order to make short-range educational decisions which are consistent with those plans." Grade 7 through adults; 1984; 12 interest scales: Accommodating/Entertaining, Humanitarian/Caretaking, Plant/Animal Caretaking, Mechanical, Business Detail, Sales, Numerical, Communications/Promotion, Science/Technology, Artistic Expression, Educational/Social, Medical; 2 ability scales: Verbal, Nonverbal; 1987 price data: $26.25 per 35 career survey booklets, 35 orientation booklets, and directions for administration (16 pages); $23.85 per 35 interest survey booklets (includes interests only), 35 orientation booklets, and directions for administration; scoring service and additional packages available from publisher; (60) minutes; American Testronics.*

Review of the Career Survey by CHRISTO-PHER BORMAN, Professor of Educational Psychology, Texas A&M University, College Station, TX:

The Career Survey is a guidance instrument consisting of two parts: an interest survey called the Ohio Career Interest Survey and an ability test called the Career Ability Survey. The interest test has 12 scales with 11 items per scale. The 132 items in the interest test (Part 1) are scored on a 5-point scale going from *dislike very much* to *like very much.* As a part of the Ohio Career Interest Survey, there are seven additional items (Part 2) relating to expressed interests, and these questions ask about best-liked job tasks, best-liked school subjects, and future educational goals. The Career Ability Survey contains two parts: (*a*) Verbal reasoning is measured by 22 verbal analogy items; and (*b*) Nonverbal reasoning is measured by 18 items divided equally between two item types—number series and figural relationships.

A two-dimensional model was used to develop the Ohio Career Interest Survey. Test materials indicate that this survey was developed by staff members from the Ohio Department of Education who worked with Ohio schools in using the Ohio Vocational Interest Survey (OVIS) and used this experience to develop the Ohio Career Interest Survey. Dimensions of the test model are people-things and data-ideas. Twelve interest scales were developed to fit this bipolar model, and these scales can be displayed graphically along the diagonals of a square. Opposite sides of the square are labeled people-things and data-ideas. Originally 600 items were written to relate directly to 1 of the 12 scale definitions, and then the number of items was reduced until there were 11 items per scale. The Counselor's Guide (provided with the test and similar to a test manual) explains how the items were assigned to scales and how the final items were selected, but no data are given to back up this selection process. The items of the interest inventory are stated as job tasks. The Ohio Career Interest Survey results are linked to the Worker Trait Group arrangement of jobs developed by the Department of Labor and to the Military Occupation Specialties used by the Department of Defense.

In developing the Career Ability Survey, approximately 500 ability test items were written and field tested with approximately 8,000 students per grade (7–12). The authors state that from this pool three types of items were selected for inclusion in the test—verbal analogy, number series, and figural relationships. Item selection criteria are described in the Counselor's Guide, but no data are given to support the selection of the 40 items that comprise the ability test.

The Career Survey was designed for students in grades 7 through 12 and for use with adults. The instrument was nationally normed in the fall of 1983 and the spring of 1984. A list of participating schools is included in Part 4 of the Counselor's Guide. The norm sample seems to be similar to a representative sample of students from across the country, but this observation is based only on a visual examination of a table that lists school districts and the number of participants per grade level included in the norm sample. National percentile ranks are provided for both the interest and ability scales. For the 12 interest scales, separate norm tables are provided for males, females, and combined groups (both sexes) for the following grade combinations: 7/8, 9/10, and 11/12. Norm tables for 11–12 are also used for college/young adult. For the two ability subtests (Verbal and Nonverbal), norm tables are provided separately for each grade. It is stated that there are not separate tables for males and females because sex differences on the ability tests were negligible.

Using Cronbach's coefficient alpha, internal consistency of the Ohio Career Interest Survey was tested with Ohio studies of 6,000 to 7,000 students per grade level. The coefficients for the 12 scales range from .86 to .93 indicating very respectable internal consistency for the instrument. Test-retest reliability coefficients, with 10-day intervals, were calculated for samples of students in grades 8, 9, and 10. Test-retest reliability coefficients for the interest survey range from .79 to .92 with the median reliability being .86. Test-retest reliability data indicate that results from the 12 interest scales are stable over time. Reliability of the Career Ability Survey was assessed by the Kuder-Richardson Formula 20 and odd-even approaches with a sample of approximately 1,500 students in grades 7–12. Reliability coefficients for the verbal and nonverbal sections of the test range from .62 to .84 when the coefficients are examined separately for each grade level. Coefficients for all grades combined are .80

(KR-20) and .81 (odd-even) for the verbal test, and .73 (KR-20) and .78 (odd-even) for the nonverbal test. These data indicate satisfactory internal consistency of the ability test, but no data are reported on the test-retest reliability of the ability test.

Construct validity for the interest survey was established by a two-step process: (a) Theoretical relationships were predicted from the two-dimensional model used to develop the instrument, and (b) the "fit" between observed and theoretical relationships was examined. Data presented in the Counselor's Guide tend to support predictions from the test model. Criterion validity of the 12 interest scales was investigated by relating measured interests to satisfaction with the job training experiences in selected vocational training programs. The sample consisted of 996 graduates from nine vocational training programs at 16 vocational schools. Students involved in the validation study completed the interest survey and a questionnaire measuring overall satisfaction with the job tasks that they were trained to perform. The hypotheses that were tested in this study were that a satisfied group of students in a particular training program would show significantly higher interest on certain specified items and scales than a dissatisfied group and that the satisfied group means would be significantly higher than the standardization means for the same scales. The data presented generally support these hypotheses and provide evidence for criterion validity for the 12 scales of the Ohio Career Interest Survey. Additional validation studies with students in other training programs or with actual workers in different occupations would add considerable support to the validity of the instrument.

The Career Ability Survey was written by the four authors who wrote the Developing Cognitive Abilities Test (DCAT), and one of the validity studies described in the Counselor's Guide compares Career Ability measures with DCAT results. Data indicate that the Verbal subtest is moderately to highly correlated with the DCAT Verbal subtest. The Nonverbal subtest of the Career Ability Survey is moderately correlated with the DCAT Quantitative and Spatial subtests. The Career Ability Survey has also been correlated with the General Aptitude Test Battery (GATB), the American College Test (ACT), and the Scholastic Aptitude Test (SAT). Data indicate a substantial relationship between the Verbal scale of the Career Ability Survey and the Verbal scale of the GATB. There is a moderate relationship between the Nonverbal scale of the Career Ability Survey and the Numerical and Spatial scales of the GATB. Finally, the Career Ability Survey subtests have substantial correlations with subtests of the ACT and SAT.

The interest test (Ohio Career Interest Survey) and ability test (Career Ability Survey) are included in one test book and can be taken together. Also, the interest survey is included by itself in a separate booklet if the desire is only to administer the interest test. Directions for administration of the Career Survey are clear and easy to follow. The instrument can be hand scored and scoring directions are given in the Counselor's Guide. Machine scoring is recommended and provided by the test publishers. A career profile is provided where the scores are presented in a visual fashion. Also, the profile reports results in words as a part of a personalized narrative for each student.

The Career Survey is a new instrument among career guidance instruments, but it offers the potential for being a very useful instrument, especially since the Career Survey includes both an interest inventory and an ability test. Reliability data for the interest inventory indicate respectable internal consistency and stability over time. Reliability data for the ability survey indicate satisfactory internal consistency, but no information is reported on test-retest reliability of the test. Evidence is presented supporting the construct validity and criterion validity of the interest survey, but further studies with more diverse populations are needed to add support to the criterion validity of the instrument. Considerable evidence is given in the Counselor's Guide supporting the criterion validity of the ability survey. The Career Survey is well developed in terms of providing support materials for clients or students taking the survey and also providing good reference materials for those administering and interpreting the instrument.

Review of the Career Survey by GEORGE DOMINO, Professor of Psychology, University of Arizona, Tucson, AZ:

The Career Survey is designed to provide measures of a person's interests and abilities through the administration of three separate subtests: (*a*) the Ohio Career Interest Survey (Part 1), made up of 132 items (e.g., pick fruits or vegetables, analyze data from computer printouts) for which the respondent indicates degree of liking on a 5-point scale ranging from "*like this activity very much*" to "*dislike this activity very much*"; (*b*) the Career Planning Survey (designated as Part 2 of the Ohio Career Interest Survey), a set of seven multiple-choice questions that explore the kinds of job tasks respondents like and assesses plans for further education or training (e.g., What school subjects do you like best? In what high school program are you enrolled?); (*c*) the Career Ability Survey, a 40-item timed (24 minutes) test of reasoning ability that consists of 22 verbal analogies, 9 number series, and 9 spatial or concept relationship items.

The use of the words "career" and "survey" for both the overall questionnaire and each of the parts is quite confusing. Adding further to the confusion is the fact that Part 1 was originally called the Ohio Interest Survey, and this in turn was based on the Ohio Vocational Interest Survey.

The Career Survey is designed for students in grades 7 through 12 and for adults, and has three primary purposes: (*a*) to provide students, clients, and counselors with information that will stimulate the counseling process; (*b*) to encourage exploration of career areas not previously considered; and (*c*) to provide a link between long-range career plans and short-range educational decisions. The Career Survey was developed to meet three criteria: (*a*) "efficiency and flexibility in administration and interpretation," (*b*) "high technical quality in materials development and standardization," and (*c*) "links with one or more existing career information systems."

Part 1 of the Ohio Career Interest Survey yields scores on 12 interest scales, each based on 11 items, ranging from Accommodating/Entertaining to Medical. These interest scales are said to cover all 66 job clusters defined by the U.S. Department of Labor. The items that form these scales require a sixth-grade reading level and are free of any racial, gender, or cultural bias. The 12 interest scales appear to intercorrelate substantially, ranging from .88 between Business Detail and Sales (for females), to a low of .14 between Accommodating/Entertaining and Science/Technology (for males). At least $1/2$ of the intercorrelations between the scales are at or above ·35.

The normative sample included almost 3,000 junior high school students, over 7,000 high school students, and 681 freshman and sophomore college students, from diverse geographical areas. Little information is given about these subjects, however, and the impression is that these were samples of convenience rather than selected to be representative.

The reliability of Part 1 was assessed by both internal homogeneity and 10-day test-retest analyses. Results seem quite satisfactory, with median coefficient alphas in the .89/.90 range, and a median test-retest coefficient of .86. Validity information is fairly extensive and centers on (a) the construct validity of the 12 scales as related to a two-dimensional model with "poles" designated as data-ideas and people-things, as well as (b) criterion validity based on comparison of measured interests with satisfaction in training experiences in selected vocational training programs. Much more information is required, but these validity data represent a good beginning.

Part 2, the Career Planning Survey, seems to be disregarded by the test authors, and perhaps that is the way it ought to be. It seems pretentious to call something a "survey" that only asks the respondent which of the 12 career fields is most liked and in which school program the respondent is enrolled. Nonetheless, it would have been nice to know to what degree a person's first and second career choices on this part actually match the results of Part 1.

Part 3 of this battery is the Career Ability Survey and yields two scores, a Verbal Reasoning Ability score based on 22 items, and a Nonverbal Reasoning Ability score based on 18 items. Since each score is based on so few items, the resulting percentile distribution is highly misleading. For example, for seventh graders a raw score of 3 equals the 34th percentile, but a raw score of 5 equals the 50th percentile. Thus on the basis of 2 items, the typical counselor would arrive at quite different conclusions regarding a student's ability.

Reliability seems satisfactory and was estimated by both Kuder-Richardson Formula 20 and odd-even approaches. The reported coefficients for all grades combined are in the .73 to .81

range, but it is not indicated whether the odd-even coefficients were corrected by the Spearman-Brown formula.

The test authors indicate that Part 3, the Career Ability Survey, allows one to predict a student's ACT, SAT, and/or GATB-G scores. This prediction is based on linear regression analyses of two samples of 11th- and 12th-grade students who took the ACT and the SAT ($N = 142$) or the GATB-G ($N = 62$) in addition to the Career Ability Survey. Given the rather large normative samples, one wonders why these analyses are based on smaller samples, the nature of which is not described. In addition, no information is given on how accurate the prediction is, and the typical counselor might well assume a degree of correspondence between tests that is not warranted.

The validity of the Career Ability Survey is explored by relating the Verbal and Nonverbal scores to scores on the Developing Cognitive Abilities Test, the General Aptitude Test Battery, the American College Test, and the Scholastic Aptitude Test. It should be pointed out that the two Career Ability Survey scores (Verbal/Nonverbal) correlate with one another substantially, from .44 to .68 in various samples, and hence one would question whether these two are in fact measuring different aspects of reasoning ability. The two do correlate significantly with the various measures indicated above, and many of the resulting coefficients are in the .50s and .60s.

The Career Survey can be hand scored, although for Part 1 this represents a rather herculean task. Computer scoring services are available from the test publisher, who provides both individual reports for the client and group reports for the counselor. The package of test materials is quite comprehensive and includes very detailed administration guidelines. Most of the materials are clearly written, and a careful reading revealed only one typographical error.

In summary, Part 1 seems quite promising and represents a reliable and well validated questionnaire. Part 2 adds little and one would hope the typical counselor would already have this information. Part 3 is suspect, and much more evidence needs to be presented that in fact the Career Ability Survey measures two types of reasoning abilities, and that these are indeed differentially related to career choice.

Finally, there is no evidence presented that would support what the authors state are the three primary purposes of the Career Survey. There is no empirical evidence that the information generated by the Career Survey (*a*) stimulates the counseling process, (*b*) encourages the exploration of new career areas, and (*c*) provides a link between long range career plans and short range educational decisions. Unless such evidence is forthcoming, career counselors are advised to use other, better validated instruments.

[13]

Children's Version of the Family Environment Scale. Purpose: "Provides a measure of young children's subjective appraisal of their family environment." Ages 5–12; 1984; CVFES; downward extension of the Family Environment Scale (9:408); 10 scores: Cohesion, Expressiveness, Conflict, Independence, Achievement Orientation, Intellectual-Cultural Orientation, Active-Recreational Orientation, Moral-Religious Emphasis, Organization, Control; 1987 price data: $17 per 10 test booklets; $6 per 50 answer sheets; $7 per 50 profiles; $6 per 50 examiner's worksheets; $6 per manual (17 pages); administration time not reported; Christopher J. Pino, Nancy Simons, and Mary Jane Slawinowski; Slosson Educational Publications, Inc.*

Review of the Children's Version of the Family Environment Scale by NANCY A. BUSCH-ROSSNAGEL, Associate Professor of Psychology and Research Associate, Hispanic Research Center, Fordham University, Bronx, NY:

The Children's Version of the Family Environment Scale (CVFES) is a downward extension of the Family Environment Scale (FES) of Moos and Moos (1981). As such, its purpose is to enable children, ages 5 to 12, to provide self-reports of family relationships. Children's perceptions of 10 dimensions in three general areas of family functioning are assessed: Relationship Dimensions (Cohesion, Expressiveness, and Conflict); Personal Growth Dimensions (Independence, Achievement Orientation, Intellectual-Cultural Orientation, Active-Recreational Orientation, and Moral-Religious Emphasis); and System Maintenance Dimensions (Organization and Control).

The CVFES is a 30-item test, with 3 items for each of the 10 scales. These items were taken from the Family Environment Scale (FES) of Moos and Moos (1981). Each item

has 3 pictures; each picture is a cartoon-like drawing of a mother, father, son, and/or daughter. The pictures vary along some dimension, for example, proximity of the family members. The child is asked to pick the picture that "looks like your family." Although the test is described as pictorial, many items require a third-grade reading level. The family's verbalizations are presented in a balloon, comic-strip style. In half of the items, the three pictures are identical except for the written information. The parents' comments differ among the pictures, but the visual cues, such as facial expression and posture, are the same in each of the three pictures in these items. Because of the reliance on reading for many distinctions, the test should be given to younger children (up to fourth grade) only in an individual format. The authors suggest this practice, but do not follow it themselves in their content validity study.

The validity of the CVFES rests on the validity of the FES and the pictures developed to tap its content. While the FES has adequate reliability, the evidence for its validity is weak (Busch-Rossnagel, 1985). In developing the CVFES, the authors grouped the items of the FES so that a smaller number of items would tap the same content as the adult version. They then chose those items which "best" cut across the nine FES scales, but they do not indicate what their criteria were.

The content validity of the pictures is unclear. The authors state that an effort was made to make each item unidimensional, (i.e., to vary only one feature in each of the three pictures comprising the item). However, the variability in facial expression is difficult to see on some items, making the item a test of visual perception rather than family environment. In addition, some items vary two features among the pictures, making the content unclear, (e.g., item 3 varies both proximity and facial expression). The authors attempted to address the issue of content validity of the items in two studies. The first study had a small sample ($N = 16$), but no information was given about the results. The second study raises more questions than it answers (e.g., why include seventh-grade subjects when the standardization sample included only first- through sixth-graders? How many children were unable to understand the items?).

There are problems with scoring as well. Scoring is done by assigning each response a 1, 2, or 3, with 3 representing the highest level in each dimension; the responses for each subscale are then summed. No information is provided as to how the rankings of the pictures were established. The rankings for items 11 and 12 go against common sense: the parents saying "we'll do it for you" is scored as a 2, showing more independence than "if you need help, we'll help you" which is scored as a 1.

The authors report that the 4-week test-retest reliability was .80. No range of reliabilities is given, so one presumes that this is the reliability for the total score, even though no indication is given that a total score should be computed. Because the scoring is done by scales, the reliabilities for each scale should be reported. Information about differences in reliabilities for different ages should also be given.

As noted by the authors, the standardization sample for the CVFES is very restricted: 158 children from grades 1 to 6 of the Buffalo parochial schools. No specific breakdown of the sample is provided, and this seriously limits the usefulness of the norms. For example, family size may affect FES scores, and the authors of the CVFES suggest that children from single-parent families may have difficulty identifying with the four-person family of the picture. Likewise, the authors present the subscale means by grade level and state there are important differences in them, but they do not indicate which differences are significantly different or why they are important. If the grade level differences are important, and if family size may affect responses, the norm sample should be broken down by at least these two factors. Because of the restricted sample and paucity of information, the norms as presented are inadequate. This norm group problem limits the potential for comparison between children's perceptions of the family with the CVFES and parents' and adolescents' perceptions with the FES.

One potential application of the CVFES is for feedback in family therapy, and the authors primarily tie the test to the program for family enrichment they have developed. The authors present a case study using the CVFES and the parents' responses to the FES. Such an application requires comparisons between the CVFES and the FES which, as noted above, should not be done with the current norms. In addition, specifics about this application are not given, (e.g., how is the "line of best fit" determined? What magnitude of differences between parent and child scores should be considered important?).

In summary, the CVFES should be considered as an experimental, downward extension of the FES. The utility of the test rests primarily with the validity of the pictorial format. The content validity studies presented make that validity very questionable. The standardization sample is so restricted the present norms should not be used, thus limiting the potential comparison of the CVFES results with the FES and such applications in therapy. The authors should be encouraged in their efforts to overcome these limitations because a valid evaluation of family environment from children's perspectives would be useful for therapists and researchers alike.

REVIEWER'S REFERENCES

Moos, R. H., & Moos, B. S. (1981). *Family Environment Scale*. Palo Alto, CA: Consulting Psychologists Press, Inc.
Busch-Rossnagel, N. A. (1985). [Review of the Family Environment Scale.] In J. V. Mitchell, Jr. (Ed.), *The ninth mental measurements yearbook*. Lincoln, NE: The Buros Institute of Mental Measurements.

[14]

CLASS—The Cognitive, Linguistic and Social-Communicative Scales. Purpose: "Created to provide the speech-language pathologist, early childhood educator, physician, or other professional concerned with language development in preschool children with an efficient means of assessing cognitive, linguistic and social-communicative systems development in children from birth through five years of age." Ages birth through 72 months; 1984; CLASS; indirect assessment from informant reports; 3 scales: Cognitive, Linguistic, Social-Communicative; individual; 1985 price data: $60 per complete set including manual (91 pages); (45) minutes; Dennis C. Tanner and Wendy M. Lamb; PRO-ED, Inc.*

[The publisher informed us in January 1988 that this test has been discontinued.]

Review of CLASS—The Cognitive, Linguistic and Social-Communicative Scales by DORIS V. ALLEN, Professor of Audiology, Wayne State University, Detroit, MI:

CLASS—The Cognitive, Linguistic and Social-Communicative Scales is intended as an indirect assessment of language behaviors of preschool children. Information concerning language and speech is derived, not from the child, but from the parent. The three systems (Cognitive, Linguistic, and Social-Communicative) are assessed separately. The 157 items comprising this scale have been derived from the research literature. The items span the developmental period from birth through 5 years of age. Within each system, the items are arranged in 11 successive developmental levels. The authors estimate that testing time is about 15 minutes per section, giving a total time of 45 minutes. The directions specify that the child being assessed should not be present during the interview. Each item has two examples that are presented to the parent. The parent indicates whether the child currently exhibits the target behavior or has done so at some time in the past (a positive response), or that the child has never exhibited such behavior (negative response). If the parent expresses uncertainty about whether the child has ever exhibited the target behavior, this is scored as an inadequate response. Directions are given in the manual for identifying the basal and ceiling levels. Performance is summarized ultimately on graphs representing each system and a composite graph, each showing the child's level of performance relative to chronological age.

The manual includes two audiocassette tapes intended for parent training. One tape is an introduction to behavior modification of speech and language and the other covers principles of language development. The manual itself contains no suggestions or directions regarding the use of the tapes. It is not clear how, when, or by whom these tapes should be distributed to parents. The tapes themselves state that they "have been designed to offer constructive advice and general instruction to provide a home program of speech and language therapy to your child" and should be used "under the supervision of a speech-language pathologist." Presumably the tapes should be distributed at the discretion of a speech-language pathologist but this information is not explicitly stated. In addition, the level of the concepts involved and the language used on the tapes suggest that the tapes are best suited for the educated, well-motivated parent.

Using parent report as a source of information regarding speech and language development has both advantages and disadvantages. Studies have found that parents are an accurate source of information about behaviors of their children; however, it is also recognized that parent report is subject to error (e.g., denial, exaggeration). Obviously, the accuracy of a specific parent report is unknown. Thus, the outcomes from administration of this instrument are best viewed as tentative until additional data are obtained from other sources to serve as a referent or basis for comparison. Consistencies across different sources would support the accuracy of the parent report but provide little additional information about the child. Inconsistencies, on the other hand, may be due either to assessment or parent "error"; these would need to be resolved before an accurate evaluation of the child can be made. This weakness precludes the use of this instrument by other than speech-language pathologists. Even these clinicians might elect to use this instrument following language assessment (rather than preceding or replacing such assessment), to gain further information about the child's language behavior in other than the clinical setting.

Another aspect of this instrument that has both advantages and disadvantages is the derivation of the items from the research literature. Research findings and their interpretations form the knowledge base for any discipline, but the status of such information is, at best, tentative until those facts have been confirmed by independent replication. Use of small sample sizes and available samples often produces results that are not replicable. Items in this instrument that are based upon findings reported in several research studies by independent authors may be viewed as valid. However, many of the linguistic and social-communicative scale items are based on single sources. The validity of the placement of the items in terms of developmental level should not be considered as confirmed at this time.

The authors provide no other information concerning either the validity or the reliability of this instrument; normative data are not reported but are promised. A reference entitled "Unpublished Pilot Study Data" by the authors is included in the reference list and serves as a source of some items, but details of the pilot study are not given (e.g., sample size, characteristics, etc.). Analysis suggests that this pilot study was used primarily to obtain linguistic data from infants ranging in age from birth through one year.

In conclusion, while CLASS attempts to provide an alternative approach to assessment of a child's speech and language development, it has serious weaknesses that a potential user should consider. It should not be used by individuals lacking professional training in speech-language pathology. Decisions should not be based solely on CLASS but the test may be used to supplement other assessment procedures. CLASS could provide further insight into the child's behavior as reported by the parent, but, in many instances, the information will be redundant. Without further research, the developmental levels derived from CLASS must be viewed as being of unknown or uncertain validity and reliability.

Review of CLASS—The Cognitive, Linguistic and Social-Communicative Scales by JANICE SANTOGROSSI, Instructor of Special Education and Communication Disorders, University of Nebraska-Lincoln, Lincoln, NE:

CLASS—The Cognitive, Linguistic and Social-Communicative Scales is a standardized instrument for indirect assessment of the language skills of preschool children. The authors' purpose in developing CLASS was to create an assessment tool to supplement direct assessment procedures. The three sections of CLASS assess the child's conceptual development, use and comprehension of English grammar, and communicative effectiveness.

The behaviors assessed by CLASS were selected from "several descriptive studies of child language development, as well as from parental reports and the authors' clinical experience." Items in each section are arranged in 11 levels in developmental sequence. The age ranges assigned to each level are approximate ages at which children typically acquire the behaviors. The sequence was determined from studies of development in young children and from the authors' experience in administering CLASS. The authors present adequate references to support selection and placement of the behaviors at various developmental levels, but no information about their pilot studies with CLASS. The authors do report that they are conducting normative studies, the results of which will be reported when the studies are completed. The authors suggest that "locally developed" norms may be more useful to users of CLASS. While this may be true, it is this reviewer's opinion that conducting such studies is beyond the resources and time constraints of most test users.

The authors report no reliability data for CLASS. In the introduction to the CLASS manual they mention, almost in passing, that "the content validity of the test items is determined by the research on which they are based." There is no mention of attempts to establish other kinds of validity.

CLASS includes a readable manual that contains clear and complete instructions for administering the instrument. For each section of CLASS the manual provides a synopsis of development in preschool children, instructions to be given to the informant, and the test items. The manual also contains information about interpretation and application of the results and one set of response forms. (These forms are apparently to be photocopied for use, though this reviewer could find no mention of this anywhere in the CLASS materials.) A separate Presentation Booklet, which has instructions to the informant and the test items to be used when administering CLASS, is also included. In addition, the CLASS materials include two parent training tapes "Introduction to Behavior Modification of Speech and Language" and "Principles of Language Development." The parent training tapes are an interesting addition, but this reviewer feels such materials are outside the scope of an assessment tool. The authors would have been better advised to have spent their time conducting reliability, validity, and normative studies on CLASS.

CLASS is based on the premise that a knowledgeable informant such as a parent (the authors recommend the child's mother) can provide reliable, accurate, and complete information about the language skills of young children that is equivalent to or, in fact, superior to information that can be obtained from direct testing. The authors offer results of studies reporting high correlations between data from parental report and direct testing to support this premise. The authors provide further justification for using an informant format from their experience that direct testing of young children may "yield inaccurate or incomplete data and result in inappropriate and ineffective intervention programs" due to the difficulty of getting a child's best performance in a formal evaluation situation. The informant format is an advantage and, at the same time, a problem. It is this reviewer's experience that it is indeed difficult at times to obtain from a young child results that are truly representative of the child's skills with direct testing procedures. At the same time, I have found that some parents are reliable informants while others are not. It would require a skilled, experienced interviewer who is familiar with the parent, the child, and the family situation to facilitate and recognize complete and accurate reporting from the informant.

The authors state that CLASS requires 45 minutes to administer (i.e., 15 minutes for each section). The interviewer would need to be thoroughly acquainted with the behaviors and administration/scoring procedures in order to complete CLASS in that time. A procedure for determining basal and ceiling levels for each section precludes the necessity of administering all the items. The scoring procedures for CLASS stress the importance of the interviewer's judgement of the appropriateness of the example of each behavior given by the informant in crediting a child with the behavior. The authors, however, provide no guidelines for making such judgements and, again, report no studies of inter-judge reliability.

The results of CLASS are plotted on bar graphs (one for each section and a cumulative graph). These graphs provide a clear, convenient visual representation of the child's results. The child's ceiling level is his/her "age equivalent" for each section (i.e., the level at which the child is assumed to be functioning). The authors caution that the age range for each level is an approximate age of acquisition of the behaviors and should be used as a general guideline to compare the child's chronological age to his/her developmental age achieved for each of the CLASS sections. The items the child did not achieve below his/her chronological age should be targeted for training in developmental sequence. In this way the results of CLASS may be used to determine objectives for remediation.

SUMMARY. CLASS could serve as a useful adjunct to a direct language assessment battery especially for difficult-to-test children, provided it is administered by an experienced, skilled interviewer to a knowledgeable, reliable informant. The format and content of CLASS promise to fulfill the need for a standardized

measure of a child's communicative functioning in real-life situations. However, in the absence of data to show that CLASS is a reliable, valid instrument with appropriate norms, this reviewer cannot recommend it for use.

[15]

Classroom Reading Inventory, Fourth Edition. Purpose: "Attempts to identify the student's specific word-recognition and comprehension skills." Grades 2–8, high school and adults; 1965–82; CRI; 6 scores: Independent Reading Level, Instructional Reading Level, Frustration Reading Level, Hearing Capacity Level, Word Recognition, Comprehension; individual in part; Forms A, B, C, (for use with grades 2–8), D (for use with high school and adults); manual ('82, 170 pages, includes all forms); price data available from publisher; (24) minutes; Nicholas J. Silvaroli; Wm. C. Brown Co., Publishers.*

For a review of an earlier edition by Marjorie S. Johnson, see 8:749; see also T2:1618 (1 reference); for an excerpted review by Donald L. Cleland, see 7:715.

TEST REFERENCES
1. Paris, S. G., & Jacobs, J. E. (1984). The benefits of informed instruction for children's reading awareness and comprehension skills. *Child Development, 55,* 2083-2093.
2. Connelly, J. B. (1985). Published tests—which ones do special education teachers perceive as useful? *Journal of Special Education, 19,* 150-155.
3. Olson, M. W. (1985). Text type and reader ability: The effects on paraphrase and text-based inference questions. *Journal of Reading Behavior, 17,* 199-214.
4. Gildemeister, J., & Friedman, P. (1986). Sequence memory and organization in recall of black third and fifth graders. *Journal of Negro Education, 55,* 142-154.

Review of the Classroom Reading Inventory, Fourth Edition by IRA E. AARON, Professor Emeritus, and SYLVIA M. CARTER, Associate Professor of Reading Education, University of Georgia, Athens, GA:

The Classroom Reading Inventory, Fourth Edition, consisting of three forms (A, B, and C) for grades 2–8 and a form (D) for high school and adult students, is a useful inventory for assisting teachers to pinpoint strengths and weaknesses in student reading and in estimating student reading level (Independent, Instructional, and Frustration). It also furnishes an estimate of hearing capacity level, and Forms A, B, and C include Spelling Surveys.

The instructions and discussion in the test booklet are sufficient for teachers and prospective teachers to learn how to administer the inventory. However, 16 teachers, asked to review the instructions, concluded that certain sections should be improved. The marking system for recording oral reading errors is practical and easy to master. The two samples of inventory results and accompanying explanations are of considerable help in illustrating inventory administration and interpretation.

Forms A, B, and C contain Graded Word Lists of 20 words each for eight levels, preprimer through sixth grade; Form D contains eight lists, from grade 1 through 8. Though how and why these particular words were selected is not discussed, the difficulty from level to level appears appropriate. Mispronunciations are analyzed for word-recognition errors.

The Graded Oral Paragraphs are interesting and appropriate in difficulty at the various levels from preprimer through grade 8. Approximately three-fourths of the 38 oral reading selections in the four forms of the inventory are informational in content, mainly about science and sports. Several readability formulas were used in checking selections for difficulty levels. No comment was made about equal comprehensibility across levels and forms, but selections appear to be written satisfactorily. Form D selections, designed for use with older readers and not meant to be interchanged with selections in the other three forms, begin at grade 1 rather than at preprimer level as in the other forms.

Each Graded Oral Paragraph in all four inventory forms is followed by five comprehension questions. For the most part the questions are good. However, six Yes/No and True/False questions are included in the total of 190 questions across all four forms. Because of the 50/50 chance of a correct answer just from guessing, such questions are poor. One answer also is given in the title and not in the text, though titles are not included in the word count.

The author states that editing was done to assure that questions were passage dependent. However, a panel of 16 teachers, asked to review the passages and comprehension questions, concluded that many (at least 14 in Form A alone) could be answered by some children from their experiences, independent of the selections. A few examples are these: "At what time of year do we see more spiders?" "Why do you think they called the horse Midnight?" "What does in excess of 90 m.p.h. mean?" The panel of teachers also questioned the effective-

ness of the illustrations accompanying each paragraph; these are in black and white and are of poor quality. The information relative to speed of reading the oral paragraphs is not likely to be of much use since speed of comprehension in silent reading is what teachers are concerned about. Further, rate of oral reading is limited at higher levels by rate of speaking.

Comprehension questions are classified as Fact, Inference, or Vocabulary. According to the labels given the 190 questions on the four forms, 61 percent are classified as Fact, 23 percent as Inference, and 16 percent as Vocabulary. Five questions labeled as Fact appear to be Inference questions, and two Vocabulary questions actually check interpretations of figurative language (i.e., "sensitive nostrils feeling the air") and could have been classified as Inference.

Spelling Surveys, consisting of six 10-word lists, ranging in difficulty from grade 1 to grade 6, are included in each of Forms A, B, and C. This test may be given in a group setting, with responses checked following the administration of each list. As in the case of the Graded Word Lists, the basis for the selection of these particular words is not given, though the spelling words do appear to be suited to the difficulty level assigned them (grades 1–6). On the summary sheet, there is no place to record Spelling Survey results. This test, which is optional, is likely to be far less useful to most teachers than the first two sections of the inventory.

The criteria for determining the hearing capacity and the various reading levels are explained clearly. A good case is made in the instructions for teacher judgment—along with the criteria—for making decisions about levels. As would be expected because of the differing lengths of selections, the error percentages for Independent, Instructional, and Frustration levels are not the same at the different grade levels; (i.e., the error range for the lower limits of the Instructional level varies from 3 to 8 percent [92 to 97 percent correct pronunciation]).

Overall, the Classroom Reading Inventory is a useful tool in the hands of a knowledgeable teacher. This particular inventory compares favorably with the best of other published inventories. To control testing time, this inventory uses brief selections—especially at early levels, and checks comprehension following oral reading, with no assessment of silent reading. Longer selections likely would have increased reliability, and checking comprehension following silent reading would have been more in keeping with school practice. The author does suggest that teachers may use the Graded Oral Paragraphs in Forms B and C to check on comprehension following silent reading for those children who do not react well to the oral reading. Some teachers may prefer to build their own tests to use in place of or in addition to a published inventory such as this— if they have the knowledge and time. Teacher-made tests have the added advantage of instructional and testing passages being comparable because test passages may be taken from student textbooks.

Review of the Classroom Reading Inventory, Fourth Edition by JANET A. NORRIS, Assistant Professor of Communication Disorders, Louisiana State University, Baton Rouge, LA:

The stated purpose of the Classroom Reading Inventory, Fourth Edition (CRI) is to provide a diagnostic tool for teachers that can be used both to identify specific word-recognition and comprehension skills, and to determine the grade levels at which a child reads independently, instructionally, at frustration, and potentially. The test is designed to be administered quickly, within the classroom setting, and individually in order to provide the teacher with some specific insights into a child's reading strengths and weaknesses. The manual provides case examples to illustrate some of the information that can be obtained from the inventory.

The fourth edition of the CRI includes the addition of a fourth form of the test designed to assess the reading ability of more mature students exhibiting low reading achievement levels. Other revisions include the modification of a few of the reading passages, changes or rewording of some of the comprehension questions, the provision of a motivational statement prior to the reading of each graded passage, and revised drawings to accompany the reading passages.

The CRI is designed for use by classroom teachers, and does not purport to be an instrument used to ascertain achievement levels, diagnose reading disorders, or identify handicapping conditions. However, although the test may not have to meet the rigorous test construction or normative procedures of a diagnostic test, the provision of some information in the manual concerning test construction would be useful. For example, the manual states that the passages were evaluated for their readability level and cites several procedures used. No further information is provided about selection criteria, number of measures an individual passage was subjected to, level of agreement of readability between measures for the same passage, or level of agreement of readability between passages among alternate forms graded at the same level by the inventory. The agreement among alternate forms is particularly important because the author states the forms can be used for posttesting, a comparison of oral reading to silent reading, and/or a comparison of oral reading to hearing capacity, therefore implying the forms are equivalent. No studies or evaluations are reported indicating the reliability coefficients across the alternate forms of the test. Variations between passages, such as differences in the complexity of the sentence structures seen between the fourth-grade passages of Forms A and B, may create differences in performance. Similarly, no information is provided on the manner in which the sight words were selected for the word recognition portion of the test.

In this fourth edition of the CRI, modifications were made in the comprehension questions in an attempt to eliminate correct responses derived from general knowledge rather than reading comprehension. The author states that all questions are passage dependent, meaning they can be answered correctly only by reading the corresponding passages. However, several passage-independent questions still remain, such as, "Is there more than one kind of spider?" or "Where do ants live?" Several of the vocabulary questions ask for a generic definition that can be answered if the child knows the word without regard to the reading passage, such as, "What does the word 'grind' mean?" or "What does the word 'submerge' mean?" There are inferential questions such as, "Why do you think they called the horse Midnight?" that not only can be answered independently of the text, but which have very little to do with the theme of the story towards which inferences should be directed. For some questions, such as, "At what time of year do we see more spiders?" the answers are not contained within or implied by the text. The examiner is instructed to accept the answer typical for the area of the country in which the child lives. In general, there are too many factual questions that the child can answer without really understanding the theme, story, or significance of the passage, so that many comprehension problems could go undetected by this inventory. The inferential questions that are asked tend to be relatively low-level inferences, and many of them are only tangentially related to the theme or purpose of the passage. Therefore, the comprehension questions remain the most problematic aspect of the inventory.

The material presented to the child to read is not ideal, and could have an effect on reading performance. The print is small, and is the same size and typeface at all levels. There is only single spacing between lines of the text, even at the preprimer and primer reading levels. Many children reading at that level are accustomed to reading print of larger type and could easily be confused or intimidated by the type size and spacing. Because of the minimal spacing between words and lines, some children may experience a greater number of errors related to skipping across lines of text. The story in Form C, Level 2 is written in paragraph form, while the equivalent passages in Forms A and B are written in the somewhat easier format of one sentence per line. Similarly, on the word recognition lists, there is barely a character of space between the number of the word and the word to be read, making the visual discrimination harder for some children. The numbers themselves on the child's form seem superfluous and may serve as irrelevant distractions.

The pictures accompanying the text in this edition consist of abstract sketches with poorly defined lines, unclear details, and poor use of shading. It is difficult to determine what some of the sketches are supposed to represent. Such ambiguity may mislead a child in predicting what the text is about. Unlike the pictures in previous editions of the CRI, these sketches tend to depict isolated objects hanging within an empty space of dark background rather than a scene representative of the story. Many of the drawings are hard to recognize because much of the object is not visible, such as a sketch of the

back end of a bus, or an airplane with the wing tips and tail end cut off. The penciled lines are so faintly drawn it is hard to distinguish shapes or figures within the pictures. Any child with visual discrimination problems would find it extremely difficult to get any information from these pictures. Rather than supporting the text, the pictures add confusion.

The manual has clear and complete instructions for administration and scoring. Adequate guidelines and explanations are provided to enable an inexperienced examiner to understand the significance of the various obtained reading levels, and to generate some useful interpretations of this information. The examples also help to clarify procedures.

In summary, the CRI is designed to provide the classroom teacher with a quick method of evaluating an individual child's word recognition and comprehension abilities for relative strengths and weaknesses. While there are many problems in the construction of the inventory, the author does not make diagnostic claims that go beyond its use as an informal analysis, and, therefore, the test can be useful in accomplishing its stated purposes. As a quick inventory, it can provide the teacher with information about an individual child that is not available from achievement test scores or group reading activities.

[16]

Clinical Articulation Profile. Purpose: "Designed to assess young children who have severe articulation difficulties." Young children; 1983; CAP; 3 scores: Omissions, Substitutions, Total; individual; 1985 price data: $20 per 100 profiles and information sheet (2 pages); administration time not reported; PRO-ED, Inc.*

[The publisher informed us in January 1988 that this test has been discontinued.]

Review of the Clinical Articulation Profile by JOHN A. COURTRIGHT, Professor and Chair of Communication, University of Delaware, Newark, DE:

The most notable aspect of the Clinical Articulation Profile (CAP) is the complete absence of any information about its reliability, and only the most minimal discussion of its content validity. The CAP has no manual containing this essential information, but rather is accompanied by a single-page instruction sheet. This sheet provides three pieces of information: (*a*) a brief description of "four features of the CAP"; (*b*) an equally brief set of instructions for the administration and scoring of the CAP; and (*c*) an incomplete reference to an article by the authors of the test.

Given the brevity of this instruction sheet, my natural reaction was to locate and read the cited article: Hurvitz, Rilla, and Pickert (1983). Unfortunately, the article is little more than a slightly amplified version of the instruction sheet. At least part of this amplification addresses the issue of content validity, but reliability again receives not the slightest mention.

Hurvitz et al. (1983) present the same four features of the CAP that are outlined in the instruction sheet. In their article, however, they indicate why these features are important and explain how several existing tests are lacking because they do not possess these attributes. There is no doubt as to what the "performance domain" of an articulation test must be: all of the possible sounds in the initial, medial, and final positions of words. How a test assesses the child's ability to produce these combinations of sounds and positions is the issue.

Children with severe articulation disorders— the specified target population for this test— pose a particularly difficult problem for assessment. Hurvitz et al. (1983) make a relatively persuasive case that their approach will provide a more representative assessment of a child's ability to produce combinations of sounds in various positions than do several existing instruments. Without question, these arguments should have appeared in the test materials.

Neither the Hurvitz et al. (1983) article nor the instruction sheet contains information about concurrent validity. What other established tests or diagnostic instruments are related to the CAP? Even though the rationale for the CAP is that it overcomes "difficulties" inherent in several other articulation tests, it surely is not completely unrelated to these tests. The authors have a responsibility to evaluate and discuss where both commonalities and uniquenesses exist between the CAP and other instruments. Their failure to provide this essential information on concurrent validity is a serious shortcoming of the test materials.

Similarly, the authors of the CAP have provided absolutely no information about the reliability of the instrument. For the CAP, test-retest reliability (without intervening therapy,

of course) would have been most useful for estimating the stability of the instrument. The authors maintain that the CAP is a "quantifiable method for documenting change and progress" due to therapy (Hurvitz et al., 1983). Accordingly, it should have been demonstrated empirically that differences between administrations are the result of actual changes in client performance, and not the result of random fluctuations due to measurement error.

In addition, coefficients of interrater reliability should have been obtained by having more than one qualified clinician score the same administration of the test. Given the relatively straightforward method of administering and scoring the CAP, it is likely that interrater reliability would be high. Information on interrater reliabilities is necessary to rule out a potentially significant source of measurement error. Interrater reliability coefficients would also have an important bearing on the interpretation of the test-retest reliability of the instrument. Clearly, the authors are responsible for providing this information and its omission constitutes another serious shortcoming of the test materials.

In summary, the Clinical Articulation Profile has failed to comply with several essential standards for published tests. The CAP offers absolutely no assessment of its reliability or its relationship to other measures of articulation. Moreover, content validity is addressed only indirectly in a separately published article. Because tests of articulation have such a well-defined performance domain, there is no confusion about what should be measured. In contrast, the accuracy and consistency of those measurements, as well as the relationship of the obtained scores to other recognized tests of articulation, are very important to establish in a new test.

Consequently, the authors of the CAP should be strongly encouraged to provide information essential to the evaluation of this test. If the appropriate data were gathered, I suspect the CAP would prove to be highly reliable and acceptably valid. I also believe that clinicians would find this test quite appealing. It presents an efficient way to assess the articulation of a highly problematic population, and it has the potential (assuming reliability and validity) to measure therapeutic progress, even when a child's overall intelligibility is lacking. These are very strong points favoring the utility of the CAP. Nevertheless, until the essential empirical information is provided, it is impossible to recommend its use without several serious reservations.

REVIEWER'S REFERENCE

Hurvitz, J. A., Rilla, D. C., & Pickert, S. M. (1983). Measuring change in children with severe articulation disorders. *Language, Speech, and Hearing Services in Schools*, 14, 195-198.

Review of the Clinical Articulation Profile by LYNN S. FUCHS, Assistant Professor of Special Education, George Peabody College, Vanderbilt University, Nashville, TN:

The Clinical Articulation Profile requires examinees to imitate sounds in isolation as well as at beginning, medial, and ending positions within words and syllables. The authors contend this instrument improves upon other articulation measures for assessing young children with severely impaired speech, because it (a) incorporates sounds in isolation and in syllables to permit assessment of skills prerequisite to successful word production, (b) measures only one sound within each word or syllable to facilitate reliable scoring, (c) uses imitation instead of picture naming to reduce administration time, and to separate effects of word knowledge and retrieval from articulation proficiency, and (d) provides a method for monitoring student growth over time. A measure combining these features is potentially useful. Unfortunately, the two-page supporting document, along with the four-page referenced article and accompanying instructions on the protocol, fail to satisfy primary standards on test and technical manuals as stated in *Standards for Educational and Psychological Testing* (APA, AERA, NCME, 1985). These materials omit most supporting information necessary for meaningful and accurate interpretation of the test results.

Specifically, technical data are inadequate. First, information on test development is limited to the statement in the referenced article that developers were speech-language pathologists at a city hospital, working with preschool speech and language impaired children. Discussions of the development of test stimuli, item order, and other aspects of content and format are omitted. Second, the reliability of the instrument is never addressed. Third, authors' statements on validity are limited to assertions that the instrument provides "a quantifiable

method for documenting change and progress," "documentation of whether therapy objectives were attained," claims of sensitivity to growth, and curricular validity (Yalow & Popham, 1983), respectively. However, only one case study is presented to support these assertions, rather than the necessary empirical documentation for sensitivity to growth, curricular validity, and criterion-related validity. Given (a) that the 50 syllabic and 50 word items, across three positions, contain certain redundancies, (b) the authors' statement that the overall intelligibility of the case-study child's connected speech did not coincide with improvement on the test, and (c) the nature of sample objectives provided, one might question the outcome of such studies. Additionally, the failure to document content validity, along with no clear definition of the universe represented by the test, violates Standard 1.6 of the *Standards for Educational and Psychological Testing* (APA, AERA, NCME, 1985).

Furthermore, directions for administration and scoring are incomplete and at times questionable. No guidelines concerning tester experience and training are provided. This is an omission with potentially serious implications given the lack of information on interrater reliability and the well-known potential for inaccuracy in scoring articulation errors. Specific directions to examinees are not provided, and it is unclear whether the examiner's production of the stimuli should be visible to the child. Without instructions for standardized administration, decisions based on comparisons between students and intra-individual comparisons over time could be affected. A questionable direction is for examiners to code unintelligible responses as substitutions, when the possibility that targeted sounds are omitted seems equally plausible.

Finally, insufficient information is provided on interpretation of scores. There is no clear statement on what decisions can be based on the measure, or the pupils for whom the measure was designed. In terms of decisions, the authors imply a dual purpose in their summary: "provides a . . . tool for assessment of children who have severe articulation disorders . . . also . . . a . . . method for documenting . . . progress." However, the first "assessment" purpose is never specified, and no guidelines for formulating any norm- or criterion-referenced decisions are delineated. With respect to relevant populations, the appropriate age range for the test is omitted, and the supporting document and referenced article provide different information concerning the severity of articulation disorders for which the test was designed. Additional details necessary for adequate test interpretation also are lacking. For example, explanation for the I, M, and F codes on the protocol is omitted, and the articulation categories (e.g., bilabial, tip-alveolar) are neither defined nor addressed for interpretation. Although one might assume that the "profile" aspect of this measure, referenced in the instrument's title, refers to these articulation categories, appropriate profile analysis is never discussed.

The Clinical Articulation Profile has little to recommend it over other measures. It suffers from serious problems of inadequate technical development, unclear purpose, insufficient administration and scoring directions, and inadequate guidelines on test interpretation.

REVIEWER'S REFERENCES

Yalow, E. S., & Popham, W. J. (1983). Content validity at the crossroads. *Educational Researcher*, 12 (8), 10-14, 21.
American Psychological Association, American Educational Research Association, & National Council on Measurement in Education. (1985). *Standards for educational and psychological testing*. Washington, DC: American Psychological Association.

[17]

Coarticulation Assessment in Meaningful Language. Purpose: Designed to assess coarticulatory variability in children using meaningful multisyllabic words and word strings. Ages 2.5–5.5; 1984; CAML; 14 scores: 8 specific phoneme scores, 3 Manner scores (Liquid, Fricative, Stop), 2 Position scores (Arrest, Release), Total; individual; 1987 price data: $20 per 25 scoring forms, test booklet, and manual (36 pages); $7 per 25 scoring forms; (10–20) minutes; Kathryn W. Kenney and Elizabeth M. Prather; Communication Skill Builders.*

TEST REFERENCES

1. Kenney, K. W., & Prather, E. M. (1986). Articulation development in preschool children: Consistency of productions. *Journal of Speech and Hearing Research*, 29, 29-36.

Review of the Coarticulation Assessment in Meaningful Language by JANET A. NORRIS, Assistant Professor of Communication Disorders, Louisiana State University, Baton Rouge, LA:

No purpose is stated in the test manual for the Coarticulation Assessment in Meaningful Language (CAML). This lack of definition leads to methodological problems in the test's design and standardization. The rationale provided for the CAML includes a description of the coarticulation model, as contrasted to phoneme-based models of articulation, and a discussion of the problems inherent in the existing test instruments. However, the CAML never establishes its own purposes, and so it is unknown whether the test is designed as a screening device, a diagnostic instrument, a measure of normal and/or disordered articulation, or as a method for obtaining an in-depth analysis of selected phonemes in various coarticulation contexts. This lack of clear purpose results in many methodological errors in test construction. The errors negate the positive intentions of the test as a standardized instrument.

The CAML reflects 2 decades of research demonstrating that phoneme productions are strongly influenced by the sounds that precede and follow them. The CAML, therefore, systematically tests each of eight targeted phonemes in contexts that both precede and follow bilabial, alveolar, velar-stop, and fricative sounds, to determine effects related to place and manner of production, and to identify contexts of best production. Considerable planning went into the construction of appropriate stimulus items. Efforts were made to control for factors related to stimulus complexity, including the selection of meaningful words and phrases such as "watchdog" or "her shoe," rather than nonsense words or syllables, thereby more closely approximating natural speech productions. Also, stimulus words were selected to be within a preschool child's vocabulary, to maintain simple syllable structure (91% are bisyllabic), and to be composed of the simple canonical forms characteristically used by children in continuous speech samples (89% represent simple CVC, CV, and VC syllabic shapes). Overall, item construction is a strength. Although some of the word combinations are unfamiliar to many preschool children and unlikely to be elicited spontaneously (i.e., pushpin, catbird, steel table, keep right), the protocol specifies that a delayed imitation procedure be used. This reviewer administered the test to a small sample of children ($N = 6$). The delayed imitation procedure was successful in obtaining a response for approximately 80% of the items. For the remaining items, a direct imitation was required to elicit the stimulus words.

The most problematic aspect of the CAML is related to the standardization procedures used and the resulting standard scores. Some major assumptions of a normal curve distribution were violated in both subject selection and in deriving the norms for this test. The 60 children included in the standardization population at each of the six age intervals fall short of the minimum 100 recommended for any normative sample. The problems created by the insufficient numbers are greatly compounded by the lack of representativeness in the normative sample. The 360 subjects in the standardizing population formed a homogeneous and nonrepresentative group across nearly every dimension, including geographic area, socioeconomic status, and most importantly, range of abilities. The children all attended preschool, were all from a single metropolitan area, were all from middle- and upper middle-class homes, were all rated as "normal" across seven developmental areas including intelligence, language, and motor ability, were not members of minority groups, and were all selected voluntarily on the basis of parent permission. Each of these characteristics factors out variability and representativeness as it relates to standardization in general. Several of these variables, such as socioeconomic status, intelligence, motor ability, and language ability, have been shown to strongly influence articulation performance. The resulting population is biased and nonrepresentative of any population other than developmentally normal, white, middle-class children with preschool exposure. Rather than representing a normal distribution of preschool coarticulation abilities, the normative data available for the CAML represent only a narrow range of normal articulation variability. Therefore, the scores ranked as representing extremely poor performances on the CAML (i.e., greater than 2 standard deviations from the mean) in actuality are within the average range of articulation abilities for preschool-aged children. This bias renders the standard scores useless in assessing and making comparisons among children likely to display articulation problems. In their manual, the authors recommend administration of the test to children with delayed and/or disordered articulation development, and provide case histories to illustrate this use. This generalization of use to children not represented in the norm group results in several

statistically and diagnostically unsound interpretations. For example, because only normally developing children were used to establish the norms, when children with relatively mild articulation disorders are assessed, they appear to be in the severely disordered range of performance.

Standard scores are based on the distribution of the normal curve, with less than 1% of all scores falling more than three standard deviations from the mean. The misuse of the norms of the CAML, when applied to children with delayed articulation development, is evident in the manual's reporting of scores up to 12 standard deviations from the mean for children with moderate articulation problems.

Two studies of CAML test-retest reliability yielded adequate results. The authors also established adequate reliability for their scoring procedure. Several studies were conducted to establish validity, including a comparison of performance on the CAML to the McDonald's Screening Deep Test, and a comparison of performance on the CAML to intelligibility of spontaneous speech. A comparison of performance on the CAML with articulation performance within a story-retelling task is erroneously reported as content validity; it is essentially a further confirmation of concurrent validity, and not content validity. Thus, the last three studies cited supported the concurrent validity of the instrument.

Problems were evident in the data the authors used as support for construct validity. The manual reports that the data collected from the normative population support construct validity in that the younger children with normally developing articulation made significantly more errors than older children. However, analysis of their standard score tables reveals that for several of their standard scores across age groups, this relationship did not hold. For example, children between 3.6 and 3.11 years of age received a lower standard score in the category of "stop" productions than children between 3.0 and 3.5 years, indicating that with increasing age the same number of errors would reflect an improved within-age performance according to these norms. These differences were as large as two standard deviations for some scores. This problem was prevalent across all age levels and several production categories, including stops, /r/, /k/, and /t/ at the 3.6–3.11 year age level; fricative, /s/, and /f/ at 4.0–4.5 years; /f/, /l/, and /r/ at 4.6–4.11 years; and arrests, stops, /sh/, and /k/ at the 5.0–5.5 year age levels.

Aside from the problem in supporting construct validity on the basis of the normative data, these discrepancies in the scores across ages also create problems for use of these norms for diagnostic purposes, despite the authors' claims. Without changing any articulation productions, a child's performance can be judged to show improvement as he or she transitions into an older age level, when in fact the results should be the opposite. With increasing age, a continuing error should reflect a greater developmental problem. Furthermore, the interpretation of the scores is confusing by virtue of the manner in which they are reported. When reporting standard scores, the normal distribution is conventionally used in such a way that those respondents displaying the least proficiency in a skill or behavior are distributed below the mean. However, the CAML uses a distribution of errors rather than relative performance. Therefore, the worse a child's articulation performance is, the higher he or she places above the mean. This can add confusion in interpretation, particularly when guidelines for diagnosis of handicapping conditions among preschool-aged children often stipulate a performance below the mean on a standardized measure.

Another problem created by the lack of clarity or purpose in its design concerns the phonemes selected for inclusion on the CAML. The test assesses only eight phonemes, and therefore is not comprehensive enough to constitute a diagnostic test of articulation performance. As a screening device, it does assess high-frequency error phonemes. However, the test is designed to be administered to preschoolers between the ages of 2.5 to 5.5. Of the eight phonemes tested, seven have been normed as relatively late developing sounds, not considered mastered by the majority of children until 4 to 7 years of age (Shames & Wiig, 1986). Therefore, it is questionable whether preschoolers below the age of 4 should be screened on these phonemes. Because the CAML used only average or above preschoolers in its normative population, it is questionable whether these norms can be used as a basis of comparison for many children. Additionally, the manual suggests that an error analysis, reflecting various phonological processes, can be conducted from the phonetic transcription, but neither the stimuli nor the score sheet are systematically set up for this analysis.

The test is easy to administer and score, and does provide some information about production in various phonetic contexts that may be useful in the analysis of a child's articulation. The line drawings used to elicit the target words are sufficiently clear for most children to interpret accurately if they know the concepts depicted. The durability of the stimulus booklet is questionable, consisting of lightweight paper through which pictures and print from other pages can easily be seen, creating a distraction to children during test administration.

In summary, the CAML is a test instrument with well developed test stimuli designed to elicit phonemes in a variety of coarticulatory frames, but with serious problems in its test construction and norms. These problems render the test inappropriate for the assessment of the population to which it is most likely to be administered (i.e., children with articulation delays and/or disorders), at least as a standardized instrument. If used as a criterion-referenced assessment of selected phonemes, it may provide useful information about productions in a variety of phonetic contexts.

REVIEWER'S REFERENCE

Shames, G. H., and Wiig, E. H. (1986). *Human communication disorders* (2nd ed.). Columbus: Charles E. Merrill.

Review of the Coarticulation Assessment in Meaningful Language by RICHARD J. SCHIS-SEL, Associate Professor and Chair, Department of Speech Pathology and Audiology, Ithaca College, Ithaca, NY:

The Coarticulation Assessment in Meaningful Language (CAML) is designed to assess the effects of coarticulation on the articulatory accuracy of preschool children. It was constructed to overcome some of the purported weaknesses of the Screening Deep Test of Articulation (SDTA).

The CAML elicits production of eight of nine sounds examined by the SDTA (/s, f, ch, t, k, sh, l, r/) in meaningful words and word strings.

Each of the eight target phonemes is examined in eight contexts. Each sound is tested as part of an abutting pair: four times each in syllable arresting (bus ride), and syllable releasing (big *s*un) position. The authors attempted to control canonical form (syllable shape), phonetic context, syllable structure, and linguistic structure. For example, 91% of the 57 stimulus items presented are bisyllabic. Eighty-nine percent of the 115 syllables are simple shapes of the type most frequently used by children in continuous speech: CVC, CV, VC. Phonetic context is controlled for place and manner of production. Linguistically the test contains 10 multisyllabic nouns and 47 word strings composed of verbs, adjectives, and possessive pronouns with nouns. Stimulus items are words normally included in a preschool child's vocabulary.

The test was standardized on 360 children between the ages of 2½ and 5½ years of age. All were native English speakers from middle- and upper middle-class homes. Based on the performance of this group, norms are provided for children at 6-month intervals between 2½ and 5½ years of age. Norm tables allow conversion from raw scores (total number of errors) to standard scores for easier interpretation and to allow comparison across children. Norms are provided for the total number of errors on the entire test, errors in releasing position only, arresting position only, liquids, fricatives, stops, and for each of the eight individual phonemes.

The test utilizes a delayed imitation format. Stimulus items consist of black and white line drawings. Each item is identified for the child by the examiner. For example, the examiner would say "This is a pet cat. This is a catbird. What is this?" (points to pet cat). "It's a _____." "What's this?" (points to catbird). "It's a _____."

The manual clearly presents instructions for administering, scoring, and interpreting the results. The rationale for the test is clear. Test materials are unambiguous and the scoring sheet is easy to follow. Most clinicians would find this a useful addition to their test battery. I do not recommend this test, however, and my reservations follow.

First, the content validity of the test is questionable. Content validity was not established on the published version of the test but on "an earlier, but similar version." From material presented in the manual, it appears that the canonical form and phonetic context of 28 of the 64 items were altered. Thus, there is no assurance the data provided in support of content validity are applicable to the version the clinician will be using.

The procedure used to establish this form of validity was flawed. The authors used an analysis of variance to compare total number of errors made by 30 "normally developing children" on the CAML and a story-retell task. The children were between the ages of 4 years 4 months and 4 years 8 months. The authors claim content validity on the basis of finding no significant difference in the total number or type of errors on the two tasks. There are problems with this. First, absence of evidence is not evidence of absence. The fact that the authors found no difference between performance on the two tasks does not mean that no differences existed. The authors did not include a statement regarding the power or ability of their analysis to detect a difference if one existed. Second, their subject group was too limited and homogeneous. They used only 30 "normally developing children," within a 4-month age range. The literature clearly shows that children will make more sound-production errors on spontaneous speech tasks than picture-naming tasks. The use of such a restricted sample decreased the likelihood that these differences would emerge.

The use of the total number of errors in the analysis is misleading. It is possible that subjects made errors on different sounds on the two test conditions, but that the total number of errors did not differ to a statistically significant degree. Such a finding would have suggested that the CAML does not tap the same skills as the story-retell task.

In addition, the authors' treatment of validity issues is incomplete. The approach described in the manual (comparing errors made by normally developing children on a CAML task and a spontaneous story-retell task) is informative but should be supplemented with expert opinions about the content of the test.

An effort to establish predictive validity also should have been made. The relationship between performance on the CAML and a criterion measure must be published, thereby confirming (or disconfirming) the usefulness of the CAML in meaningful treatment decisions.

Of most concern is that an effort was made to establish content validity using children only within a 4-month age range. The test is to be used with, and norms are provided for, children across a 3-year age range. It is incumbent upon test developers to establish validity of the test for all subjects for whom it is intended. Even had the authors successfully established content validity on their sample there is no assurance that the test would have been equally valid for all other children for whom it was designed.

The concurrent validity of the test also is of concern. Concurrent validity is demonstrated when there is evidence that the test correlates highly with external, independent criteria of the variable measured. The authors first compared performance on the CAML with performance on the SDTA and found very close agreement. The SDTA was a poor choice of criterion measure. The SDTA itself has never been validated. To demonstrate that the CAML measures the same behavior as the SDTA is of little usefulness because no evidence exists to show what the SDTA measures.

A further effort to establish concurrent validity was made by comparing performance on the CAML with errors in a spontaneous speech sample of 35 children of unspecified age. This procedure was well done and the results encouraging. The data suggest the test will distinguish between children with and without articulation disorders. However, there remains the problem of a restricted sample. In their comparison with the SDTA the authors used only kindergarten children. In the spontaneous speech comparison the age range of the children was not provided. It is impossible to know whether such concurrent validity as might exist for the test exists across all ages for which the test was developed.

The problems with validity are unfortunate. This test has the potential to be a popular and useful tool. However, I cannot recommend its adoption until such time as its validity has been established.

[18]

Comprehensive Screening Tool for Determining Optimal Communication Mode. Purpose: "To evaluate the clients' performative skills in the areas of vocal production (Oral Skills Battery), gestural and motor production (Manual Skills Battery), and response to symbols and pictorial content (Pictographic Skills Battery)." Low functioning non-speaking clients; 1984; CST; 9 subtests: Manual Training Prerequisites, Movement Patterning, Cognitive Correlates for Manual Communica-

tion, Prerequisites Visual Training, Attending Behaviors and Accuracy Movement, Cognitive Correlates, Pre-Speech and Oral Awareness, Pre-Articulatory and Articulatory Skills, Auditory Awareness; individual; 1986 price data: $53 per 25 scoring summary/profile sheets, 25 record sheets per subtest, and manual (50 pages); (45) minutes; Linda Infante House and Brenda S. Rogerson; United Educational Services, Inc.*

Review of the Comprehensive Screening Tool for Determining Optimal Communication Mode by MARILYN E. DEMOREST, Associate Professor of Psychology, University of Maryland-Baltimore County, Catonsville, MD:

The purpose of the Comprehensive Screening Tool for Determining Optimal Communication Mode (CST) is to promote formal and objective assessment of nonspeaking individuals. Its development was motivated by the authors' awareness of the subjective and unsystematic nature of many clinical assessments. Accordingly, the CST has been designed to be a theoretically and empirically based tool for systematically eliciting, observing, and evaluating communicative behaviors. The primary goal of this behavioral assessment is selection of an appropriate communication mode such as vocal production, an augmentative communication system, or a combination of both. Secondary goals include (a) providing an empirical basis for recommendations to parents, teachers, and administrators; (b) justification of a previously selected communication mode; and (c) planning and evaluation of intervention procedures.

The instrument was designed for clients who are mentally retarded and/or physically limited and suggestions are offered for adapting the testing procedures to the special needs of multiply-handicapped individuals. The target population is not confined to any particular age group, but tasks contained in the CST reflect skills appropriate for a developmental age of at least 6 months.

Steps or stages in the development of the CST, if any, are not described in the manual. The starting point for item construction was the authors' clinical experience and expert judgment, which was corroborated by a review of the literature. Brief reference is made to discussions with other professionals and to field testing of the instrument, but no details are given other than the fact that a variety of ages and handicapping conditions was represented.

Whether the amount and type of feedback from other professionals was sufficient to insure that the CST reflects collective clinical judgment and practice is unknown and remains to be determined.

The CST manual is most comprehensive in its presentation of the rationale for inclusion of each behavioral objective. The behavioral domain is divided into three areas (Manual, Pictographic, and Oral Skills, respectively), and within each there are three subtests, each comprising two or more sections. Theoretical arguments and empirical studies are offered in support of each of the 151 CST items. Although the rationale for individual items is excellent, other aspects of test design are not so well documented. For example, a 5-point rating scale is used for evaluating each task, but there is no discussion of how or why this scheme was adopted. Scoring is accomplished by adding the ratings for items within each battery. Nowhere is it pointed out that these battery scores are each based on 46 items and that the appropriateness of directly comparing battery totals hinges on this fact. Indeed, items in Subtest III of the Oral Skills Battery (Auditory Awareness) are excluded from the battery total because "the authors feel these items are important to oral communication but not necessary for successful use of the oral mode of communication." Had they been included, the battery total would have been based on 59 items; it is tempting to speculate that this fact may also have played some role in the decision to exclude them.

CST materials consist of a recording sheet for each subtest and a scoring summary/profile sheet. The recording sheet states each behavioral objective and gives a brief description of the task to be performed. The manual offers further comments and guidelines on procedures and scoring. Although the manual gives a general guideline for using the 5-point rating scale, its adaptation to individual items is not straightforward. Full credit (4 points) is to be awarded when the client meets the objective without delay and without assistance from the observer. Ratings of 3, 2, 1, and 0 are given for delayed, assisted, partial, and inaccurate responses respectively. It is not clear how this strategy is to be employed when the objective involves *absence* of a response (e.g., absence of startle, self-stimulatory behavior, or rooting reflex). Suggestions are made for awarding partial credit for many items, but they are not sufficiently specific. For example, one objective is to assess the chewing reflex. Up-and-down movement is the target, but 1 point is to be awarded for rotary movement. It is not clear whether or how ratings of 2 or 3 are to be used with this item. Given the raison d'être of the CST is to improve objectivity in assessment, scale values should be more clearly defined for each objective. Clinical judgment should play a role in deciding whether performance satisfies the description for a particular rating; it should not be used to define the scale values themselves.

The authors repeatedly state that the CST is not a standardized test. Although the scope of the assessment and the behavioral objective of each task are given in detail, flexibility in the selection of test materials and in the test procedures are both permitted and encouraged in the interest of eliciting maximum performance from each client. It is also recommended that the test format and the test setting be adapted to the individual. Although these features of test content and administration are justifiable, they do not preclude evaluations of reliability and validity. In fact, given that items are scored and that total scores are calculated, plotted, and interpreted, it is imperative that the psychometric properties of these scores be documented.

Given the ambiguity of the scoring system, it is important that its reliability be established. Both intra- and interscorer agreement should be evaluated using videotaped samples of client performance. In addition, the reliability of the behavioral sample should be evaluated through multiple assessments of the same clients. At present, the only evidence of interobserver reliability for the CST comes from a sample of 10 clients who were independently evaluated by the authors with "consistent scoring on all items." However, there is no indication that other users of the CST will be able to administer and score the items in the same manner. Thus there is little evidence the goal of an objective assessment procedure has been attained.

The most serious omission in the CST manual is the failure to provide evidence supporting the recommended interpretation of battery scores. The authors propose the skill battery or batteries with the highest score "should be considered for training potential." Although this interpretation has strong face validity, it has not been demonstrated that scores on the different batteries are equivalent. That is, there is no evidence that equal scores on different batteries represent equal potential for training or that they would predict equal levels of proficiency after training. Such issues can be addressed only through carefully designed and controlled outcome research. Test users should also beware of claims the CST can be used to support a selected mode of training or to evaluate intervention procedures. The absence of standardization and the potential for observer bias are likely to seriously compromise its validity in such applications.

In summary, the CST represents an important step toward systematic and objective assessment of nonspeaking individuals. The rationale for its scope and for inclusion of individual items is clearly documented, but as a tool for behavioral assessment it suffers from a lack of precision in the definition and application of the rating scale. The manual provides no empirical data on the psychometric characteristics of battery scores and, therefore, it is essential that studies be undertaken to demonstrate (*a*) the interobserver and retest reliability of the assessment, and (*b*) the validity of recommended battery-score interpretations.

Review of the Comprehensive Screening Tool for Determining Optimal Communication Mode by KENNETH L. SHELDON, School Psychologist, Edgecombe County Schools, Tarboro, NC:

The Comprehensive Screening Tool for Determining Optimal Communication Mode (CST) is a nonstandardized assessment instrument used to determine the existence of prerequisite skills necessary for alternative modes of communication in nonspeaking individuals. It was developed by two speech/language professionals for use by speech/language pathologists. The authors reasoned that a tool to assess skills for alternative communication modes was needed, that alternative communication modes are desirable for those unable to use the traditional communication channels, and that many nonspeaking people are not too physically handicapped to be able to use an alternative communication system. Three assumptions derived from an interpretation of current research, discussion with other professionals, and field testing with low-functioning nonspeaking individuals were used to develop the test. The assumptions are that manual communication, communication with a communication board, or oral communication are viable alternatives for communication if the person possesses the appropriate skills.

The goal of the instrument is to determine what alternative communication mode is appropriate and what prerequisite skills may be needed before teaching the new communication mode. Appropriate skills, based on the Piagetian view of the interaction of cognition and language development, are identified for each of the three communication modes. Each of the nine subtests cited above in the test description are further divided into skill areas that follow a developmental sequence of prerequisite skills.

Rationale for the inclusion of the subtests is well documented in the easily read manual. The concise manual lists the objectives, tasks, and guidelines for scoring. Stimuli used to assess each skill are selected by the clinician based on his/her knowledge of the client's likes. This indicates the clinician needs to know the client well before administering the tasks. The authors include a list of materials needed. These are readily available household items.

Administration of the instrument requires a thorough understanding of the task and materials that are organized and ready to use. The entire battery is recommended so that the clinician has information about the client for all three modes of communication. Additional testing is also highly recommended to more fully understand the client. While there is no limit on chronological age, the client must have at least a mental age of 6 months.

Scoring is based on a numerical scale of 0 to 4, with 4 being an accurate, complete, and prompt response without clinician assistance, while 0 is an incorrect or incomplete response. The scores from the items are summed and plotted for each battery. The highest battery score suggests training in that mode. While the guidelines are clear, interpretation is enhanced by the clinician's professional knowledge and observational skills.

Stressed throughout the manual is that the CST is not a standardized instrument. It is behavioral in nature and used only as a tool to give the clinician help in determining the mode of communication for a nonspeaking client.

Validity and reliability are mentioned but no rigorous statistical procedures are described. For content validity, the authors note the instrument is representative of the goals and objectives for which it was developed. Interrater reliability was established by the authors of the instrument and was based on the assessment of 10 clients. Field testing was completed on 50 clients. A description of these clients is not given and would obviously have been extremely helpful. Modifications for use with the mentally retarded, cerebral palsy or neurologically impaired, visually impaired, and/or hearing impaired are included.

Helpful additions to the manual would include: behavior examples with numerical ratings, a case history, interpretation guidelines and examples, and suggestions for training deficient skills. Interrater reliability needs to be established for clinicians other than the authors.

In summary, the CST appears theoretically sound. The authors have developed a useful instrument for assessing a client's potential for different communication modes. The tasks for assessing skills appear complete and well organized along a firm developmental sequence necessary for oral communication, manual communication, and pictographic communication modes. With more field testing, the CST seems promising.

[19]

Data Entry Operator Aptitude Test. Purpose: "Evaluates a candidate's aptitude for success as a Data Entry Operator." Candidates for data entry operators; 1982; DEOAT; 5 scores: Coding, Numerical Skills, Manual Dexterity, Clerical Accuracy/Detail/Editing, Overall; 1987 price data: $20 ($35 if scored by publisher) per test including manual (no date, 7 pages); French edition available; 20(30) minutes; Wolfe Personnel Testing & Training Systems, Inc.*

Review of the Data Entry Operator Aptitude Test by DAVID O. HERMAN, Measurement Research Services, Inc., New York, NY:

The DEOAT is intended primarily for selecting "data entry operators," presumably the computerized successors to keypunch operators. Each of the four sections of the test has a 5-minute time limit and is described as a test of both speed and accuracy. Thus if the test lived up to its claims it would be an attractive and brief instrument to help select workers in an increasingly important occupation. This review will present evidence about how well the DEOAT and its supporting documents meet current test standards.

The first section of the test, Coding, involves substituting one set of letter or number codes for another. The task is similar to that of the familiar Digit Symbol test of the Wechsler scales, but probably calls for more mental processing than does the Wechsler task. Section II, Numerical Skills, requires the examinee to perform one or two arithmetic operations sequentially. The items include no words, but only numbers and the four conventional operations signs. The first 40 items involve only integers, but the remaining 20 items require manipulation of fractions and decimals.

For each item of Section III, Manual Dexterity, the examinee must draw a line along a maze-like pathway without touching the path walls. An unusual feature of the test is that the examinee traces one or more figures with one hand, then draws identical figures with the other hand, and finally traces the figure with both hands simultaneously using pathways printed side by side. The pathways become narrower and the figures smaller as the test progresses, making the task increasingly difficult.

Each item of Section IV, Clerical Accuracy, Detail & Editing, presents four sets of letters, numbers, symbols, or letter-number-symbol combinations. Any number of these sets, from none to all four, may be identical, and the examinee must identify the ones that are the same.

The administration instructions indicate that the DEOAT is essentially self-administering in that examinees read for themselves the directions for each section and work the sample problems. The instructions offer no guidance to the tester should the examinee have trouble understanding the tasks. Although the manual emphasizes that the test must be administered under supervision, it fails to caution users to be alert for applicants who disobey the instructions for Section III and thereby make the task easier. For example, an inattentive examiner may not see an applicant use his preferred hand to mark pathways intended for the nonpreferred hand.

Scoring is usually done by a scoring center in New Jersey, which sends a report of the results to the client company. Under certain restrictions, however, clients may obtain a special Scoring Guide from the publisher and do their own scoring locally. According to instructions in this guide, the raw score on each section of the test is the number of correct answers (weighted in the case of Section III), less some function of the number of errors. Critical portions of the scoring directions are ambiguous, but it appears that the section scores are then weighted and summed to yield an overall total score. In turn the total score is transformed to a "percent score," a needless step and a misleading name for the score that is to be interpreted. (The percent score is not the percentage of items answered correctly, as its name implies.)

The percent score appears to be the only score interpreted. Although the manual notes that the section subscores are converted to stanines, which implies interpretation of performance on the separate parts, the manual and the Scoring Guide are otherwise silent on the issue.

Percentile norms for the percent score are available for a sample of 93 experienced candidates for positions as data entry operators. The sample is in other respects undescribed. The manual presents no reliability data.

An empirical validity study is reported for 40 female data entry operators employed by 12 different companies. The correlation of the DEOAT percent score with supervisory ratings was .41. The relationships between the subscores and the criterion are not reported.

COMMENT. The DEOAT materials include no meaningful discussion of the relevance of its tasks to the job of data entry operator. Measures of an applicant's speed and accuracy in coding and clerical checking tasks have a surface relevance to the work in question. Other abilities tapped by the DEOAT do not share this face validity, however, and should be supported by evidence. An important example relates to the Manual Dexterity section. How does precise line-drawing with a pencil relate to operating a computer or terminal keyboard? This question is most relevant for the portions of Section III that involve drawing with the nonpreferred hand and drawing simultaneously with both hands.

Similarly, the relevance of numerical computation to data entry tasks may be in question, especially because one-third of the items of

Section II require facility with fractions and decimals. It must be added that one of the numbers in this section is printed as "10.001½," reflecting unconventional notation, to say the least; that two of the answers provided in the Scoring Guide are wrong; and that three other answers in the guide have been truncated back to one or two decimal places, so that inexperienced scorers may deny credit to the correct, longer answers.

Three of the four sections of the DEOAT resemble the kinds of tests often used in clerical selection. It is to the author's credit that item formats have novel aspects that should minimize practice effects from exposure to previous employment testing. However, the novelty of the dexterity task appears to offer no advantage, for neither data nor appropriate discussion of construct validity addresses the critical issue of why the dexterity section is included at all. The one empirical validity study summarized in the test materials presents no criterion correlations for the subscores, as noted earlier; these might have provided some of the missing evidence.

Further, it is the reviewer's opinion that the manual indefensibly recommends using the DEOAT for certain secondary purposes. These include determining whether examinees need more training, measuring the effectiveness of training, and reviewing employees' career goals. Such purposes would be met better with measures of job performance than with aptitude measures such as the DEOAT. Unsupported and illogical claims of this kind should have been avoided.

Incompleteness and ambiguity in the directions for obtaining and transforming scores, errors in the scoring key, and lack of reliability information all reflect carelessness in preparing the DEOAT materials. Many of these flaws could be repaired by editing and revision. At present, however, there is little to recommend the DEOAT for its stated purpose on anything but a cautious, experimental basis.

Review of the Data Entry Operator Aptitude Test by RICHARD W. JOHNSON, Associate Director and Adjunct Professor, University Counseling Service, University of Wisconsin-Madison, Madison, WI:

The Data Entry Operator Aptitude Test (DEOAT) was designed to aid in the selection of data entry or terminal operators. It consists of four subtests (Coding Skill, Numerical Facility, Manual Dexterity, and Clerical Accuracy), each of which has a time limit of 5 minutes. Relatively little information is available for evaluating this test.

The brief manual for the DEOAT offers no rationale for the selection of the four subtests. It gives no information concerning the intercorrelations of the subtests or their relative effectiveness in predicting job performance. It provides no data to help determine the influence of speed and guessing on the test results.

Normative data reported in the manual are based on "93 experienced candidates" who are not further described. The degree to which this group is representative of the entire population of data entry operators is unknown.

There is limited information on scoring. According to the Scoring Guide, raw scores for three of the subtests (all but Coding) must first be multiplied by a weighting factor (ranging from 1.5 to 2.0) before they are converted to percentages. No explanation is provided as to why the weighting factors are used. The score for the Manual Dexterity subtest is calculated by subtracting points from a set amount each time a candidate "touches or crosses a boundary line." No data are given regarding the interjudge reliability of this scoring procedure. It is also unclear why so many points are assigned to the Manual Dexterity subtest (210 of 465 total possible points). After the raw scores are converted to percentages, the percentages are interpreted in terms of four categories ranging from "HIRE—candidate is likely to be a superior performer" (84% to 100%) to "DO NOT HIRE" (0% to 44%). No empirical data (e.g., expectancy tables) are provided to justify using these particular cutoff scores.

The test authors provide no information regarding the reliability of candidates' scores. Because of the heavy emphasis on speed, candidates' scores may change considerably upon retesting once they have become familiar with the nature of the test. A test-retest study would be helpful in determining to what extent scores may be expected to change upon retesting.

Only one validity study has been conducted. This study showed a moderate degree of relationship $r = .41$) between the DEOAT total score and supervisor ratings for a sample of 40 workers. It is not clear if the supervisors who evaluated the performance of the data entry operators had knowledge of their test scores or not. If they did, the correlation coefficient could be spuriously high. At any rate, additional validity studies with larger sample sizes are needed before one can place much confidence in the results.

The DEOAT cannot be recommended for commercial use because of the limited amount of information available for evaluating it and because so little research evidence is provided to support its use. According to recent research, the performance of data entry operators and related workers may be predicted with a fair degree of accuracy by special tests of reasoning ability, quantitative ability, or perceptual speed or by general tests of mental ability or clerical aptitude (Pearlman, Schmidt, & Hunter, 1980). Meta-analyses of a large number of studies (Hunter & Hunter, 1984) indicate that ability tests are more successful in predicting performance in clerical jobs or other types of jobs than are nearly all alternative predictors (e.g., biographical inventories, reference checks, interviews, or training and experience ratings). Previous research which indicated that the predictive validity of ability tests varied substantially from job situation to job situation appears to have been unduly influenced by sampling errors and other statistical artifacts (errors of measurement and restriction of range in the criterion variable). When the statistical artifacts are taken into account, the predictive validities of the different types of ability tests are similar for different jobs within broad occupational categories (e.g., computing and account-recording occupations). With this body of research in mind, the test user may wish to select a combination of ability tests from the PSI Basic Skills Tests for Business, Industry, and Government, a general mental ability test such as the Wonderlic Personnel Test, or an established clerical aptitude test such as the Short Employment Tests to help predict the job performance of data entry operators and related workers. Any of these possibilities would be preferable to the DEOAT.

REVIEWER'S REFERENCES

Pearlman, K., Schmidt, F. L., & Hunter, J. E. (1980). Validity generalization results for tests used to predict job proficiency and training success in clerical occupations. *Journal of Applied Psychology*, 65, 373-406.

Hunter, J. E., & Hunter, R. F. (1984). Validity and utility of alternative predictors of job performance. *Psychological Bulletin*, 96, 72-98.

[20]

Decision Making Inventory. Purpose: "To assess an individual's preferred style of decision making." High school and college students; 1983; DMI; 4 scores: 2 Information-Gathering Styles (Systematic, Spontaneous), 2 Information-Analysis Styles (Internal, External); 1984 price data: $6 per 30 inventories; $1 per 2 scoring grids; $10 per manual (72 pages); specimen set included with manual; (10–15) minutes; William Coscarelli, Richard Johnson (test), and JaDean Johnson (test); Marathon Consulting & Press.*

TEST REFERENCES

1. Coscarelli, W. C. (1983). Development of a decision-making inventory to assess Johnson's decision making styles. *Measurement and Evaluation in Guidance*, 16, 149-160.
2. Ferrell, B. G. (1983). A factor analytic comparison of four learning-styles instruments. *Journal of Educational Psychology*, 75, 33-39.
3. Gordon, V. N., Coscarelli, W. C., & Sears, S. J. (1986). Comparative assessments of individual differences in learning and career decision making. *Journal of College Student Personnel*, 27, 233-242.

Review of the Decision Making Inventory by GEORGE DOMINO, Professor of Psychology, University of Arizona, Tucson, AZ:

The DMI is intended to operationalize a theoretical model (Johnson, 1978) that was formulated to assist counselors' understanding of clients' decision-making styles as well as to assist researchers in their investigation of the process of decision making. The theory, based on Johnson's work in a college counseling center, proposes that there are two basic processes of gathering information, the Spontaneous and the Systematic, and two basic processes of analyzing information, Internal and External. The spontaneous and systematic approaches are differentiated along five dimensions: goal orientation, choosing among alternatives, thinking patterns, speed of commitment to new ideas, and reaction to events. The result is a fourfold typology of systematic-internal, systematic-external, spontaneous-internal, and spontaneous-external.

The current DMI is apparently the sixth version, although prior versions seemed to be significantly different from one another; for example, the first version consisted of 29 forced-choice items, while the second version consisted of 66 items of unspecified form. The current version consists of 20 items, but only 12 are scored so that each of the four scales is based on only three items. The items are standard personality-type items, each to be responded to on a 6-point scale where only the end points are

labeled. A representative (but made up) item is: I prefer to think carefully before making a decision (never o o o o o o always). Each item is scored on a 1 to 7 scale, with 4 omitted, so that scores on each scale (e.g., Spontaneous-External) can range from 3 to 21.

The manual presents the results of five administrations of the DMI to: (a) Sample 1—73 undergraduate students enrolled in an introductory interpersonal communication course, in which the DMI was followed by either a 10-, 20-, or 30-minute presentation on the constructs assessed by the DMI, and students were then asked to guess their decision-making style; (b) Sample 2—316 students in freshman orientation courses; (c) Sample 3—113 students also in freshman orientation courses, 58 of whom were retested a week later; (d) Sample 4—313 students enrolled in a second year chemistry course, where information on high school rank, college GPA, chemistry course grade, and ACT scores was obtained (the manual does not indicate whether these were students' reports, registrar's records, etc.); (e) Sample 5—67 students enrolled in a freshman orientation course, who were administered the Kolb Learning Style Inventory, Harren's Decision Making Style subscale of the Assessment of Career Decision Making questionnaire, and the DMI. These five samples are clearly captive samples, with the results of the first three cited in the body of the manual, while the last two are relegated to an appendix.

The first and most striking result from those studies is the low reliability of the DMI. For sample 1, alpha coefficients range from .40 to .68, for sample 2 from .36 to .60, and for sample 3 from .29 to .69; test-retest coefficients for sample 3 range from .41 to .71. Considering the brevity of the scales, these low coefficients are not surprising, and certainly not acceptable. Considering that each scale is actually made up of three different versions of the same item, greater internal consistency might be expected. The results from the various samples are consistent in indicating that the External scale is the most reliable and Spontaneous the least.

The results of each DMI administration were also factor analyzed, and these analyses support the presence of four factors, accounting for approximately 54 to 60 percent of the total score variance. Scale intercorrelations, however, indicate substantial correlations between the

External and Internal scales (-.33 to -.48), the Systematic and the Internal scales (.48 to .66), the External and Spontaneous (.31 to .52), and the Systematic and Spontaneous (-.19 to -.41), calling into question the relative independence of the four scales.

Validity data is scant and the reader has to wade through a variety of tables for which no statistical tests of significance are given. For example, for sample 4, the fourfold typology is analyzed in terms of high-school rank, college GPA, chemistry grade, and ACT scores. The only presumably significant difference is that spontaneous-internal students had a substantially lower high school rank than did the other groups. There is no indication in this table of the relative frequency or sex composition of each type, or whether a statistical analysis such as ANOVA was performed.

Two tables address the question of sex differences, one based on 216 students (part of sample 2), the other on 282 students (part of sample 4). Both tables present the raw frequencies and the percent of the total samples, with no chi-square or other statistical test of significance. It is left up to the reader to do the appropriate analysis, which is made more challenging by the typographical error found in Table A-4, where 112 + 43 is made to equal 185.

Given that Johnson's theoretical observations evolved in a counseling center setting, it would seem natural to test the validity of the DMI in such a setting, but the manual reports no such efforts. Similarly, it would seem basic to assess the validity of the DMI not only against other questionnaires, but against real world criteria. For example, the manual states that spontaneous thinkers excel in divergent thinking, but no evidence to support this claim is presented.

The manual is to a large extent a repetition of the information found in several journal articles, and lacks organized coherence. It contains a discussion of decision making using simple-minded analogies from physics, and a theoretical analysis of task groups, both of which seem out of place in a test manual. Incidentally, the manual gives 16 references, but 7 of these are to convention papers, personal communications, and unpublished manuscripts—all sources unavailable to the typical reader. The manual contains a number of typographical errors and reads like a series of studies rather than a coherent piece of work. Johnson's observations are given the status of a theory, which seems too grandiose a term, and the response options are called a "Likert" scale, simply because they involve something more than a true-false response.

In summary, the DMI has low reliability and there is little evidence of validity. Use of this instrument for any purpose is not recommended.

Review of the Decision Making Inventory by BARBARA A. KERR, *Assistant Professor of Counselor Education, The University of Iowa, Iowa City, IA:*

The Decision Making Inventory is based on a theory developed by one counselor based on his clinical observations. As such, it is probably most useful to adherents who wish to engage in research related to that theory. As an instrument to measure decision-making style for diagnostic or classification purposes, it is severely flawed by its isolation from any empirical work in the areas of information processing and cognition. The test author's (Johnson, 1978) theory states that individuals may be classified as gathering information in either a systematic or spontaneous manner and as analyzing information either internally (that is, silently) or externally (that is, out loud). The Decision Making Inventory is a set of 12 items embedded in a 20-item scale, designed to place individuals on both continua so as to determine a "decision-making style."

The author admits to using a combination of inductive and deductive methodologies in the development of this inventory, and perhaps that is what makes this scale difficult to evaluate. Much work has been put into validation and establishment of reliability by Johnson's colleagues, but the methodologies used in these studies were often inadequate, and the overall results provide weak support for the theory and the instrument. In the three studies reported in the manual, reliability as measured by internal consistency of the scales ranged from moderate (.69 for External) to very low (.29 for Spontaneous). Validity research consisted of weak techniques such as teaching students the theory, asking which style they thought they might be, and comparing their responses to the scores on the instrument. An instrument which required teaching the construct in order to obtain construct validity is not a strong one. Factor analyses of the inventory did not lead to impressive amounts of variance being accounted for by the posited factors, and overlap with other measures of decision-making style was small or nonexistent.

In short, the development of the Decision Making Inventory seems to have been hampered by the original inadequacy of the theory upon which it is based. This instrument would probably not be useful unless completely overhauled, with a comprehensive review of the literature of decision-making as the first step for the developers.

REVIEWER'S REFERENCE

Johnson, R. H. (1978). Individual styles of decision-making: A theoretical model for counseling. *The Personnel and Guidance Journal*, 56, 530-536.

[21]

Detroit Tests of Learning Aptitude (Second Edition). Purpose: "To determine strengths and weaknesses among intellectual abilities, to identify children and youths who are significantly below their peers in aptitude, and to serve as a measurement device in research studies investigating aptitude, intelligence, and cognitive behavior." Ages 6–18; 1935–85; DTLA-2; 20 scores: 11 subtest scores (Word Opposites, Sentence Imitation, Oral Directions, Word Sequences, Story Construction, Design Reproduction, Object Sequences, Symbolic Relations, Conceptual Matching, Word Fragments, Letter Sequences) and 9 composite scores (Verbal Aptitude, Nonverbal Aptitude, Conceptual Aptitude, Structural Aptitude, Attention-Enhanced Aptitude, Attention-Reduced Aptitude, Motor-Enhanced Aptitude, Motor-Reduced Aptitude, Overall Aptitude); individual; 1987 price data: $88 per complete kit including 25 student response forms, 25 examiner record forms, 25 summary and profile sheets, picture book, and manual ('85, 135 pages); $11 per 25 student response forms; $11 per examiner record forms; $8 per 25 summary and profile sheets; $39 per picture book; $24 per manual; $59 per software scoring system; (50–120) minutes; Donald D. Hammill; PRO-ED, Inc.*

See 9:320 (11 references) and T3:691 (20 references); for a review by Arthur B. Silverstein of an earlier edition, see 8:213 (14 references); see also T2:493 (3 references) and 7:406 (10 references); for a review by F. L. Wells, see 3:275 (1 reference); for reviews by Anne Anastasi and Henry Feinburg and an excerpted review by D. A. Worcester (with S. M. Corey), see 1:1058.

TEST REFERENCES

1. DeSoto, J. L., & DeSoto, C. B. (1983). Relationship of reading achievement to verbal processing abilities. *Journal of Educational Psychology*, 75, 116-127.

2. Olson, J., & Midgett, J. (1984). Alternative placements: Does a difference exist in the LD populations? *Journal of Learning Disabilities*, 17, 101-103.

3. Perlmutter, B. F., & Bryan, J. H. (1984). First impressions, ingratiation, and the learning disabled child. *Journal of Learning Disabilities*, 17, 157-161.

4. Simner, M. L. (1984). Predicting school readiness from stroke directions in children's printing. *Journal of Learning Disabilities*, 17, 397-399.

5. Tobey, E. A., & Cullen, J. K., Jr. (1984). Temporal integration of tone glides by children with auditory-memory and reading problems. *Journal of Speech and Hearing Research*, 27, 527-533.

6. Weithorn, C. J., & Kagen, E. (1984). Verbal mediation in high-active and cognitively impulsive second graders. *Journal of Learning Disabilities*, 17, 483-490.

7. Weithorn, C. J., Kagen, E., & Marcus, M. (1984). The relationship of activity level ratings and cognitive inpulsivity to task performance and academic achievement. *Journal of Child Psychology and Psychiatry and Allied Disciplines*, 25, 587-606.

8. Brown, R. T., & Alford, N. (1984). Ameliorating attentional deficits and concommitant academic deficiencies in learning disabled children through cognitive training. *Journal of Learning Disabilities*, 17, 20-26.

9. Webster, R. E. (1985). The criterion-related validity of psychoeducational tests for actual reading ability of learning disabled students. *Psychology in the Schools*, 22, 152-159.

10. Bowers, P. G., Steffy, R. A., & Swanson, L. B. (1986). Naming speed, memory, and visual processing in reading disability. *Canadian Journal of Behavioural Science*, 18, 209-223.

11. Kashani, J. H., Horwitz, E., Ray, J. S., & Reid, J. C. (1986). DSM-III diagnostic classification of 100 preschoolers in a child development unit. *Child Psychiatry and Human Development*, 16, 137-147.

12. Shinn-Strieker, T. (1986). Patterns of cognitive style in normal and handicapped children. *Journal of Learning Disabilities*, 19, 572-576.

13. Silverstein, A. B. (1986). Organization and structure of the Detroit Tests of Learning Aptitude (DTLA-2). *Educational and Psychological Measurement*, 46, 1061-1066.

Review of the Detroit Tests of Learning Aptitude (Second Edition) by ARTHUR B. SILVERSTEIN, Professor of Psychiatry, University of California, Los Angeles, CA:

The original Detroit Tests of Learning Aptitude (DTLA) appeared 50 years ago. When the DTLA was introduced, the second revision of the Stanford-Binet was still 2 years in the future and the Wechsler Intelligence Scale for Children (WISC) was not to appear for another 14 years. The fourth edition of the Stanford-Binet has been recently released and 11 years have passed since the WISC was revised. Thus, to say that the second edition of the DTLA (DTLA-2) is long overdue is quite an understatement. How does the new DTLA compare with its predecessor and competing tests, and has it been worth waiting for?

Instead of the 19 subtests that made up the old DTLA, from which the examiner was to select from 9 to 13 to meet the needs of the individual subject, the DTLA-2 has just 11, all of which are to be administered except in special circumstances. Seven subtests—those preferred by a sample of users of the first edition—have been retained more or less intact, although most of them have been retitled; four subtests are new. The order in which the subtests are to be given is the same as that used in the standardization, and the time required is said to vary from approximately 50 minutes to 2 hours. For comparison, the time required for the Wechsler Intelligence Scale for Children—Revised (WISC-R) is said to be approximately 50 to 75 minutes.

Raw scores on the 11 subtests are first transformed into standard scores with a mean of 10 and a standard deviation of 3, just as with the WISC-R. The standard scores are then summed in various ways. The resulting sums are converted into a series of composite scores, which, in keeping with tradition, are termed quotients. These quotients are actually standard scores with a mean of 100 and a standard deviation of 15, again just as with the WISC-R. Mental ages have been abandoned, which is a change for the better. Provision is made on the examiner record form for presenting both the subtest scores and the composite quotients in profile form.

The standardization was based on a sample of over 1,500 subjects—roughly 100 or more at each age level from 6 through 17 years—living in 30 states, and closely comparable to the population of the United States with respect to sex, place of residence (urban vs. rural), race (white, black, or other), and geographical area. However, much of the psychometric information is based on a stratified random subsample of 300 subjects, 25 at each age level, pooled into six groups of 50 subjects each (ages 6/7, 8/9, . . . 16/17). This information includes a summary of the results of item analyses conducted on each subtest (median discriminating powers and percentages of difficulty), internal consistency data (Cronbach's alpha coefficients and associated standard errors of measurement), and the intercorrelations among the subtests and the composites. The values of alpha, averaged across age groups, are impressively high, ranging from .81 to .95 for the subtests and from .95 to .97 for the composites. For comparison, split-half reliability coefficients for the WISC-R, again averaged across age groups, range from .70 to .86 for the subtests

and from .90 to .96 for the Verbal, Performance, and Full Scale.

Additional psychometric information is based on smaller samples. Stability coefficients over a 2-week interval range from .63 to .91 for the subtests and from .80 to .93 for the composites. Corresponding values for the WISC-R, over a 1-month interval, range from .65 to .88 for the subtests, and from .90 to .95 for the three scales. Validity data of various sorts are also presented. These include correlations between the DTLA-2 and the WISC-R (.83), the Peabody Picture Vocabulary Test (.75), and the SRA Achievement Series (from .58 to .93 for students at different grade levels). However, these coefficients should not be taken at face value—they are too high by some unknown amount—because they were "attenuated [sic] to account for imperfect reliability" (of course, *dis*attenuated is what is meant).

A novel feature of the DTLA-2 is the variety of composite scores that it yields. Besides a General Intelligence Quotient, there are quotients for four pairs of composites: Verbal versus Nonverbal, Conceptual versus Structural, Attention-Enhanced versus Attention-Reduced, and Motor-Enhanced versus Motor-Reduced. All 11 subtests contribute to the General Intelligence Quotient, and every subtest enters into one or the other composite in each pair. The correlations between composites in the same pair range from .61 to .68. For comparison, the correlation between the Verbal and Performance IQs on the WISC-R, averaged across age groups, is .67. Because of overlap in their makeup, the correlations between composites in different pairs are generally higher (range: .63 to .95), as are the correlations with the General Intelligence Quotient (range: .78 to .87). Clinicians are likely to find discrepancies between the composite quotients a fruitful source of hypotheses to account for intraindividual variability in performance. The manual is appropriately cautious in suggesting interpretations of these discrepancies, but if all four are evaluated routinely, the discrepancies required for significance at the .05 level, based on the Bonferroni procedure, are about 12 points rather than the 9 points that the manual suggests.

From a psychometric perspective, the DTLA-2 appears vastly superior to the old DTLA, although users of the first edition will have to make a number of adjustments in administration and scoring if they choose to switch. The toughest competition will almost certainly come from the WISC-R (the new Stanford-Binet is an unknown quantity at this time). Practitioners and researchers are encouraged to try the DTLA-2 . . . they may well like it.

Review of the Detroit Tests of Learning Aptitude (Second Edition) by JOAN SILVERSTEIN, Assistant Professor of Psychology and Director, School Psychology Program, Montclair State College, Upper Montclair, NJ:

The Detroit Tests of Learning Aptitude (Second Edition) (DTLA-2), a revision of the DTLA, is an individual intelligence scale which can be administered to children and adolescents ranging in age from 6 through 17 years. The DTLA-2 consists of 11 subtests, all of which are administered to each subject.

Serious efforts were made to retain and improve the reported strengths of the DTLA, while modifying the weaknesses. Recognized standards for test construction were consulted for decisions related to reliability, validity, normative data, and methods for reporting scores. The representativeness and size of the normative sample have been greatly improved. The scoring criteria for some subtests have been revised in order to make them "objective and easy to apply." Some of the subtests have been shortened through extensive item analysis; others have been lengthened to increase reliability. Standard scores have replaced the mental age equivalents for each subtest and the former ratio IQ has been replaced by a series of composite quotients and the General Intelligence or Aptitude Quotient.

Suggestions have been heeded to improve the level of sophistication and the usability of the test manual; technical data on reliability and validity have been added. Useful sections on testing the limits, sharing the results, and cautions on interpreting test results have been included. The pictures have been improved and updated so that they are generally more readily recognizable by current test takers. (See further discussion of this issue below under discussion of test design.) The straightforward physical layout of the material has been retained, making the test fairly simple to administer.

Based on a survey of test users, seven of the original subtests were retained, generally in modified form and with titles revised in an attempt to reflect more closely the skills tapped (Word Opposites, Sentence Imitation, Oral Directions, Word Sequences, Design Reproduction, Object Sequences, Letter Sequences). Four new subtests have been added (Story Construction, Symbolic Relations, Conceptual Matching, Word Fragments). Subtests have been grouped into eight composite domains, including two for each of four specific aptitude domains (linguistic, cognitive, attentional, and motoric) plus the General Intelligence or Aptitude Quotient. The statistical basis for the selection of the new subtests and for the development of the domains is not reported.

Three principal uses for the DTLA-2 are specified: (*a*) to determine strengths and weaknesses among intellectual abilities, (*b*) to identify children and youth who are significantly below their peers in aptitude, and (*c*) to serve as a measurement device in research studies. Many professionals have used the DTLA and will, presumably, now adopt the DTLA-2 to diagnose individuals "to qualify them for placement in programs for special groups such as the mentally retarded, learning disabled, and other categories of handicap." Therefore, the results of the test can have serious implications for a child's future. Unfortunately, significant areas of concern affect the usefulness of the DTLA-2:

1. *Qualifications for test administrators.* Given the significance of the DTLA-2's uses, it is extremely important that test administrators be adequately trained, particularly for the complex task of interpretation. As discussed below, fairly sophisticated levels of knowledge and skill in areas such as test construction, test administration, diagnosis, and interpretation are necessary if the DTLA-2 is to be used effectively. Otherwise, findings may be misinterpreted. However, the only discussion in the manual about the need for properly trained, qualified examiners is a warning that tests do not diagnose, but that "in the end, practical diagnoses rest on the clinical skills and experience of examiners." No attention is devoted to describing the qualifications, skills, and knowledge required to effectively administer and interpret the DTLA-2.

2. *Issues related to statistical properties of the scale.* While there has been a substantial improvement in the reporting of statistical data concerning reliability and validity, there remain concerns with time sampling and criterion-related validity, as well as the need for more precise statistical data to document some aspects of the author's decision making.

In order to determine stability over time, 33 students from the Hilltop Baptist Academy were tested twice with a 2-week period between tests. A larger, more representative sample and a longer time period is clearly necessary. Criterion-related validity was determined by testing 76 students who were either enrolled in special education classes (mostly for the mentally retarded or learning disabled) or were being screened for possible special education placement. DTLA-2 values were correlated with WISC-R scores. However, this selection of a subset of possible scores has resulted in a truncation of the sample and of the potential correlation.

In addition, as mentioned above, it is important that test users have access to precise factor analytic data, describing the relationship of the specific subtests to *g*, and providing factor loadings to illustrate how the composition of the domains was determined.

3. *Issues related to language bias, design of materials, test procedures, and interpretation.* Because many of the subtests—including those that measure nonverbal abilities—require proficiency in English for understanding of directions and, at times, for responses, the DTLA-2 "has a decided bias regarding the English language." The manual warns that "test results should be viewed with unusual caution when testing persons known to speak English poorly. Of course, the DTLA-2 should not be given at all to non-English speakers." Unfortunately, this very important warning is not prominently displayed in the manual.

As mentioned in the manual, several of the subtests are complex in demands. At one point, for example, the author states in his discussion of the Oral Directions subtest, "At present, we do not know which of these abilities is the most important for doing well on this subtest. All that is known is that the subtest's results are reliable and valid indicators of general learning aptitude (i.e., it seems imbued with lots of Spearman's *g* factor)." In some cases, this complexity may affect a child's ability to succeed on specific subtests. For example, the response sheet for Oral Directions is complex, containing a large number of stimuli on each page. Two other subtests, Object Sequences and Letter Sequences, require a written response on an answer sheet with very tiny spaces. It is possible that such factors as visual perceptual and motor difficulties, developmental delays, or immature motor development common in 6-year-old children may affect a child's ability to perform effectively on these tasks.

Test procedures may also affect performance. For example, the Conceptual Matching subtest measures the ability to see theoretical or practical relationships between objects. Although most of the line drawings are clear, some of the drawings may be confusing to some children either because of the content or the abstractness of the design (e.g., a dome of a capitol building, a tower for power lines, and a schematic of an atom). At no point is the examiner instructed to check to determine whether the child has correctly identified the symbols. Therefore, failure on this subtest may be due to the child's misinterpretation of the symbols, rather than to lack of ability to identify relationships. However, with the current procedures, the examiner may not realize the cause of the error.

Although the manual lists generic suggestions for limit testing, the causes of failure on specific subtests may be subject to misinterpretation. Unfortunately, due to the complex demands of some tasks and the lack of ample guidance in teasing out the factors affecting test performance, the success of interpretation of these complex tasks relies heavily on the sophistication of the test administrator.

It is important that the publishers provide the additional technical information and clarify issues of interpretation. Clarification of the qualifications of test administrators and test takers, including the need for caution when testing persons with limited English skills, should be stated clearly at the beginning of the manual. Specific factors affecting test performance (such as construction of test materials and test procedures) should be discussed in detail, with specific recommendations for testing limits in order to aid accurate interpretation. Without these modifications, there is a significant concern that poor test performance due to linguistic, visual, perceptual, and motor factors may be misinterpreted as due to cognitive difficulties. Unless these issues are resolved, there are major concerns about the use of the DTLA-2 as a test of cognitive ability for purposes of diagnosis, classification, and placement.

[22]

Drumcondra Criterion Referenced Mathematics Test, Level 6. Purpose: "To assess pupil's mastery of the objectives of the primary school mathematics curriculum." Pupils in 6th class or in first-year post primary; 1977–84; DCRMT; formerly Level C; "criterion-referenced"; item scores only for 58 objectives in 10 sections: Operations With Whole Numbers, Whole Number Structure, Fractional Number Structure, Operations With Fractions, Decimals, Sets, Algebra, Geometry, Charts, Problems; 1985 price data: 50p per test booklet ('84, 14 pages); 20p per answer sheet; 35p per scoring stencil; 35p per Pupil Mastery Record; 35p per Class Mastery Record; 50p per manual (no date, 36 pages); £3 per specimen set; price data for machine scoring service available from publisher; (180) minutes total to be administered on 3 or 5 separate days; John S. Close and Peter Airasian; Educational Research Centre [Ireland].*

Review of the Drumcondra Criterion Referenced Mathematics Test, Level 6 by IRVIN J. LEHMANN, Professor of Measurement, Michigan State University, East Lansing, MI:

The Drumcondra Criterion Referenced Mathematics Test (DCRMT) Level 6 is designed to be used with students in Irish schools "to evaluate pupils' mastery of the objectives of the mathematics curriculum for sixth standard in primary school . . . . [or] pupils in first year in post-primary school." This reviewer would interpret this as meaning the DCRMT could be used for American students in middle or junior high school. Because of the possible differences in the mathematics curriculum between American and Irish schools, potential users must exercise extreme care and caution in evaluating the DCRMT.

Fifty-eight instructional objectives are measured by 156 multiple-choice questions. With the exception of one objective that is tested with five items, all others are tested with two to three items. The major emphasis of the test is, according to the test authors, on "mathematical knowledge and comprehension to reflect emphasis of the new curriculum on the development of mathematical understandings." A careful examination of the test blueprint indicates that the authors were somewhat successful in this endeavor as there are items measuring sets, algebra, geometry, and word problems, as well as measurement, charts, and graphs.

As would be expected in any achievement test, and particularly for a criterion-referenced test, content validity was stressed in the test's construction. After a "detailed analysis" of the sixth class mathematics curriculum and textbooks and a consensus of opinion of experienced primary teachers regarding curricular objectives, a list of test objectives was developed. Unfortunately, users are provided with no information concerning some important facts. For example, what textbooks and curricula were surveyed and by whom? How many primary teachers were surveyed? Are these teachers representative of the primary teachers in Ireland? Were any mathematics teachers used in the development of objectives? Was a master list of instructional objectives drawn up by the test developers and given to a panel to obtain a consensus of opinion? Without answers to such questions it is very difficult to draw any valid interpretation regarding the strength of content-validity claims.

Evaluation of the validity of criterion-referenced tests (CRT), like reliability to be discussed later, has been a source of disagreement among psychometricians. However, if and when CRTs are used for instructional decision-making, as most criterion-referenced or mastery tests normally are, should we not have some evidence of empirical validity? This reviewer believes that we should have such evidence; unfortunately, the authors of the DCRMT do not provide these data.

Regretfully, no information is presented regarding the reliability of the test. Granted there .is disagreement among measurement experts as to how to best assess reliability of a criterion-referenced test. Regardless of the point of view of the DCRMT's authors, this reviewer believes they should have presented their position. Instead, they appear to have ignored the significance of this very important psychometric property of tests, be the test criterion- or norm-referenced.

Criterion or cutoff or mastery scores were determined in a somewhat simplistic fashion. For the one instructional objective that had five items, the criterion score was set at 4, that is, the pupil had to answer four items correctly to be classified as having mastered the objective. For the remaining 57 objectives, each of which was measured with two or three items, the criterion score was 2. What justification was there in setting the mastery scores in the DCRMT? If there were some empirical studies conducted in order to set these mastery scores, this information should have been provided. If the test authors simply picked some numbers out of the air (and they are entitled to do so) this should also have been stated. This reviewer feels very strongly that when there are empirical ways to do something, such as setting criterion scores or estimating validity and reliability, they should be used; and data should *not* be reported without an explanation of how it was derived.

Although users may not expect to see a CRT test manual with a description of standardization procedures or normative data, this reviewer strongly believes that data must be presented somewhere in the examiner's/administrator's or technical manual describing in detail the procedure used to select the final items. The test authors allude to the fact that more items than needed were prepared "by an experienced mathematics teacher and 2 or 3 items were selected to represent the objective in the test." Who were these "experienced" teachers and how was it determined that they were "experienced"? How were the two to three items selected, that is, what criteria were used? What p-values are associated with the final selection of items? Are most of them "easy," and if not, should they not be since this is construed to be a mastery test? Again, this type of information would be most desirable and not too difficult to obtain.

The test authors are to be commended for the manner in which the test items are presented. The 11 sections as well as the items within each section are presented in order of increasing difficulty. This reviewer cannot think of anything more frustrating and traumatic than an examinee sitting down to take a test and not being able to answer, for instance, the first four to five items.

The quality of printing and the diagrams used are good. The overall layout of the items is fine. Even though there are many items presented per page, the use of boxes/cells makes for a good separation. The use of bold type helps for those items dealing with fractions.

Although the test is untimed, the authors suggest that it will take about 3 hours to complete and therefore should be administered in three to five testing sessions. The authors also suggest that the test could be administered "section by section as required throughout the school year"; however, this reviewer is somewhat ambivalent regarding this recommendation. Trying to maintain test security in such an endeavor might prove to be an exercise in futility. There is, however, value in such an approach as testing and feedback could immediately follow instruction and provide evidence of whether remedial instruction is needed. Because of the instructional benefit of this approach, we strongly urge the test authors and publisher to give serious consideration to reformatting the sections so that each section appears on a separate page. In this way, section by section testing could take place without compromising test security.

The Temporary Examiner's Manual has sections dealing with the typical phases of test administration—preparing the pupils, planning for effective test administration, test administrator's responsibilities, handscoring, and the like. In addition, instructions are provided on how to prepare the answer sheets for machine scoring, completing the pupil mastery record (PMR), and completing the class mastery record (CMR).

The PMR and CMR provide teachers with information concerning the performance of each individual pupil and the class as a whole on each of the DCRMT's objectives. With this information, the classroom teacher can readily obtain a picture of the strengths and weaknesses of the individual pupils as well as the whole class. Based on this information, appropriate remedial activities may be undertaken. These two charts may also help the teacher evaluate his/her instruction. It would be valuable if the test authors were to provide users with either a list of suggested activities or teaching strategies that could be used for remediation in the areas tested by various sections as is done in some achievement test batteries such as the Stanford or Metropolitan Achievement Tests.

In summary, the DCRMT is a good test if one defines "good" in terms of acceptable principles of item-writing practices. The DCRMT is also a "good" test in the sense that the instructional objectives are specific and behavioral, rather than general. That is, the objectives are written in terms of what the student is expected *to do*. Regarding the validity of the DCRMT for American schools and pupils, only the user's careful study of the instructional objectives, clearly presented in the test manual, will answer this question. It appears to this writer, at least, that there is an overemphasis on fractions, algebra, and geometry. However, for those teachers who emphasize these content areas, the test might be valid.

The major deficiency, in this reviewer's opinion, deals with the determination of mastery of an objective on the basis of a pupil answering two out of two to three items correctly. Surely, a mastery test should have a *limited* number of instructional objectives with *many* items per objective. But this is not so in the DCRMT, or for that matter, in many mastery tests. In addition, if I were a classroom teacher, I would be very hesitant in ascribing strengths or weaknesses based upon the scores on the DCRMT. To obtain a very limited view of middle or junior high school pupils' knowledge in mathematics, the DCRMT may be valid. However, teachers wishing to evaluate the strengths and weaknesses of their pupils might well consider other mathematics tests. This would be especially true for American middle and junior high school mathematics teachers inasmuch as the curriculum between the Irish and American schools may be too dissimilar.

Review of the Drumcondra Criterion Referenced Mathematics Test, Level 6 by LINDA JENSEN SHEFFIELD, Professor of Education and Mathematics, Northern Kentucky University, Highland Heights, KY:

Even though the Drumcondra test was written in 1977 and reprinted in 1984, the Examiner's Manual is labeled as a Temporary Version. It contains no data whatsoever on validity or reliability.

The objectives for the test were decided upon after an analysis of sixth class mathematics curricula and textbooks currently in use, and a survey of experienced primary teachers about their perceptions of the objectives of the curricula. Although the authors state that the Drumcondra Criterion Referenced Mathematics Test (DCRMT) "is weighted in favour of objectives relating to mathematical knowledge and comprehension to reflect the emphasis of the new curriculum on the development of mathematical understandings," there is no evidence that objectives are based upon recommendations from any professional organizations or that there was any input from mathematics educators concerned with primary mathematics. The objectives do include the use of the commutative and distributive properties, interpreting and analyzing charts and graphs and solving one- or two-step word problems, but there is no mention of such topics as actual problem solving, estimation, mental calculations, predicting, or using computers and calculators. The majority of the objectives deal with the structure of whole and rational numbers and operations with whole numbers, fractions, decimals, and percents. Relatively fewer objectives are concerned with sets, algebra, geometry, charts, graphs, and word problems.

The actual test items were written by an experienced mathematics teacher. No mention is made of any testing of the instrument for validity or reliability, or even any analysis by a "panel of experts" for face validity. Most objectives do seem fairly clear, however, and do appear to match the test items. There are two to three test items for each of 57 objectives and the criterion score for mastery is set at 2. For the objective on reading and interpreting charts and graphs there are five questions (all about a histogram) and the criterion for mastery is set at 4.

Some of the questions would cause difficulty if used by students in the U.S. Problems involving money utilize pounds and pence, metric exercises use British spellings such as grammes and metres, and word problems talk about such things as a chip of tomatoes. The presentation of the directed numbers on the number line may also be unfamiliar. Terms are often varied on the exercises that test the same objective. For example, one question asks for the highest common factor and the next for the highest number which will divide evenly into. This may help students who are familiar with one term but not the other, but it may confuse other students who may think two different processes are being asked for.

Both the individual pupil mastery record and the class mastery record would be useful to a classroom teacher for keeping track of students' progress. It is recommended that the tests be used as a pretest to help with lesson planning and again as a posttest to check progress. Tests may be machine scored, but only if all 10 sections of the test are completed at the same time. If teachers wish to pre- or posttest each section separately (the most useful method for diagnostic-prescriptive testing), they must score the tests themselves. A scoring key is included, which can be placed over students' answer sheets for easy scoring, but it is a bit difficult to align.

To summarize, this test might be useful to Irish teachers of pupils in the sixth standard of primary school or the first year of post-primary school, but other teachers should carefully study the objectives to determine if the test is appropriate for their classes. A final version of the Examiner's Manual with reliability and validity data is needed. Objectives should be examined relative to goals for the 1980s and beyond, such as the NCTM Agenda for Action (1980).

REVIEWER'S REFERENCE

National Council of Teachers of Mathematics. (1980). *Agenda for action*. Reston, VA: NCTM.

[23]

The Dyslexia Screening Survey. Purpose: "Screening primary phonetic-auditory, visual, and multisensory processing skills in children who may be dyslexic." Children in primary grades; 1980; checklist of basic developmental skills or criterion tasks divided into 7 steps: Functional Reading Level, Reading Potential, Significant Reading Discrepancy, Specific Processing Skill Deficiencies, Neuropsychological Dysfunctions, Associated Factors, Developmental-Remedial Strategies; individual; no manual; 1988 price data: $7.95 per 10 survey forms; administration time not reported; Robert E. Valett; Fearon Education.*

Review of The Dyslexia Screening Survey by FRED M. GROSSMAN, Assistant Professor of Special Education and Communication Disorders, University of Nebraska-Lincoln, Lincoln, NE:

The Dyslexia Screening Survey is described as a "checklist of basic neuropsychological skills involved in the reading process." In effect, the tasks included in the survey are purported by its author to tap representative neuropsychological and processing functions that are important precursors for reading success. The checklist is intended for use by teachers and others interested in screening children for possible reading disabilities.

The author provides a definition of dyslexia in the scoring booklet and introduces the notion that for preschool children of average cognitive ability, dyslexic disorders may be manifested in immature reading readiness skills and psycholinguistic abilities. Additionally, dyslexia is operationally defined for school-age children of average intelligence as a discrepancy of two or more years between learning potential and functional reading. Checklist users are informed that the Survey is not a standardized instrument that provides normative data and are cautioned against making decisions based solely upon the results derived from the checklist. Users of the survey are urged by the author to supplement checklist findings with other data (e.g., standardized tests of intelligence and language skills, behavioral observations, medical examinations, etc.).

The administration of the Survey is described briefly in the scoring booklet. Survey consumers are encouraged to examine the work of Valett (1980) for a more detailed explanation of administration procedures. The Survey booklet describes the problem solving involved in the diagnosis of dyslexia as taking place in seven steps requiring the determination of: (*a*) functional reading level, as measured by oral and silent reading using the child's classroom basal reader and scores on standardized reading tests; (*b*) reading potential, as measured by aptitude or IQ tests (e.g., WISC-R); (*c*) significant reading discrepancy, which is defined as a difference between a child's functional reading level and reading potential; (*d*) specific processing skill deficiencies, which are primarily assessed by administering tasks encompassing phonetic-auditory, visual, and multisensory skills; (*e*) neurological dysfunctions, as measured by a variety of specific tasks used to evaluate sensory integration (e.g., tandem walk, finger to nose coordination, laterality, etc.); and (*f*) associated factors, such as motivation, physical health, anxiety level, self-esteem, etc. A seventh and final section of the Survey instructs the test user to formulate and prioritize instructional objectives based upon an examination of an individual child's strengths and weaknesses relating to the processing skills assessed by the tasks on the checklist. Users are also urged to recommend at least one remedial-prescriptive strategy for each derived objective.

Scoring procedures for the tasks are generally straightforward. In some instances, however, specific criteria for successful performance or skill mastery (i.e., scoring "yes" or "no") are lacking. In addition, the method of administration of several tasks is not specific (e.g., "copies words and sentences," "follows a sequence of oral directions," etc.), which would most likely result in varied forms of presentation. This lack of specificity may also result in inappropriate content in relation to the chronological age of the child being assessed. Furthermore, scoring for some skill areas requires the subjective judgment of the checklist user, particularly when the performance on a specific task is to be evaluated as "good," "fair," or "questionable."

Significant difficulties arise in the author's discussion of methods by which to calculate a reading discrepancy for children. Several methods of determining a significant reading problem are presented in the scoring booklet as well as by Valett (1980), all of which have psychometric weaknesses. For example, the use of mental age and grade equivalent scores presents major problems when conducting discrepancy analyses, particularly for children at the upper grade levels. Eighth-grade students of average intelligence who are reading 2 years below grade expectancy are defined by the author as potentially reading disabled when, in fact, an examination of the more precise standard scores reported by most reading achievement tests would reveal this level of reading skills to be within the low average-average range when compared to other individuals of the same chronological age and level of cognitive functioning. Similarly, the use of the criterion of functional reading approximately 2 years below mental age is inadequate in terms of the identification of reading problems for children in the lower primary grades.

Although the Survey is described as a screening device and is not a norm-referenced instrument, it is inexcusable that reliability and construct-validity data are not reported either in the scoring booklet or adjunct material (Valett, 1980). The absence of psychometric data, the occasional use of qualitative scoring features, the lack of standardized tasks and administration procedures, and the problems associated with the use of mental age and grade level scores present difficulties in the use of the Survey as a diagnostic instrument for the

screening of dyslexia or reading disabilities. Educational personnel interested in screening for possible reading problems of individual children would be better advised to consider group standardized achievement tests that have a reading component (e.g., Metropolitan Achievement Test, California Achievement Test, etc.) and are routinely administered to children in school settings. In essence, administration time of The Dyslexia Screening Survey appears lengthy and, perhaps, not worth the effort. This is particularly true when less time-consuming and more psychometrically sound screening approaches are readily available.

REVIEWER'S REFERENCE

Valett, R. E. (1980). *Dyslexia: A neuropsychological approach to educating children with severe reading disorders.* Belmont, CA: Fearon Pitman Publishers.

Review of The Dyslexia Screening Survey by DEBORAH KING KUNDERT, Educational Psychology and Statistics, University at Albany, State University of New York, Albany, NY:

The Dyslexia Screening Survey (DSS) is an informal survey of criterion tasks presented in the author's book *Dyslexia: A Neuropsychological Approach to Educating Children with Severe Reading Disorders* (Valett, 1980). Specifically, the DSS provides a checklist of basic developmental skills which, according to the author, are important for success in reading. Results of the survey, when combined with other information (e.g., observation, standardized tests, and medical examinations), may be used to plan educational interventions.

Dyslexia is defined as "a significant disorder in the meaningful integration of perceptual-linguistic symbols due to neuropsychological immaturity or dysfunction." Following this orientation, tasks on the DSS are organized into 7 categories: Functional Reading Level, Reading Potential, Significant Reading Discrepancy, Specific Processing Skill Deficiencies, Neuropsychological Dysfunctions, Associated Factors, and Developmental-Remedial strategies. The author's book, *Dyslexia*, provides some of the details necessary to complete the survey.

To determine a child's functional reading level, standardized reading tests and direct assessment of reading in the classroom are used. At this step, the examiner determines whether the child has mastered critical perceptual-linguistic skills considered necessary in learning to read. Examiners record test scores and also indicate whether the child can perform 20 developmental reading skills (using Yes, No, or ? ratings). Some of these skills are not described in enough detail, which makes accurate rating difficult.

Determination of reading capacity is based on scores on individual intelligence tests and/or "other evaluations of reading potential." Examiners evaluate the child's level of comprehension of grade level materials.

At the discrepancy step, the examiner determines whether the disability is significant or not (a lag of 2 or more years is defined as significant). To calculate this, the child's functional reading grade level is subtracted from the reading grade level expectancy (based on mental age).

At the processing skills deficiencies step, the child is presented with tasks to assess auditory, visual, and multisensory processing skills. Visual stimuli presented in the survey booklet are small, thus impeding the performance of some children. The examiner records the number correct and incorrect on each task for the various skills. In addition, the author indicates that supplemental tasks may be helpful. Examiners are referred to other texts for information on how these processing skills can be used directly in the classroom.

To assess neurological dysfunction, a variety of tasks in walking, coordination, balance, laterality, stereognosis, and school history are used. Examiners rate these skills as Good/Fair/Questionable, Right/Left, or Yes/No depending on the task. In addition, the author indicates that examiners should obtain medical history and information, as well as use supplemental tasks as needed.

The associated factors step involves rating the child's interest and motivation, physical health, self confidence and esteem, and the adequacy of reading instruction as Good, Fair, or Questionable. The associated text offers no concrete guidelines on which examiners may base ratings.

The final step on the DSS is developmental-remedial strategies. At this point the examiner determines the child's strengths and weaknesses and then establishes priority instructional objectives. In addition, the examiner checks one or more of 12 recommended forms of special education for follow-up consideration. Not all of these strategies seem to follow directly from

the survey results, and as such this section would be difficult to complete. The author presents some of the available research on the different interventions in his associated text; however, details are often lacking on how to implement these interventions in the classroom.

The DSS is not a standardized or normative measure. Although informal inventories may serve a purpose, certain, specific information is necessary for examiners to use these instruments appropriately. No manual is included with the survey. The associated text, *Dyslexia*, cannot be considered as a substitute for a manual. Specific information not provided with the DSS includes: indication of the appropriate age range, details on the selection and ordering of items, specific directions for administering and scoring, guidelines for score interpretation, and data on reliability and validity. Other areas of weakness include the vague definition of neuropsychological skills, the limited number of items, and the broad definition of dyslexia.

In summary, the DSS purports to be a screening measure of prerequisite processing skills that are necessary for reading at the upper elementary and secondary school levels. The absence of survey development information, scoring guidelines, and interpretation details, as well as the lack of reliability and validity data, preclude the use of this survey at this time. Additional information from the author and research are needed to determine whether the DSS can contribute useful information in working with children with reading disorders.

REVIEWER'S REFERENCE

Valett, R. E. (1980). *Dyslexia: A neuropsychological approach to educating children with severe reading disorders.* Belmont, CA: Fearon Pitman Publishers.

[24]

The Ennis-Weir Critical Thinking Essay Test. Purpose: "To help evaluate a person's ability to appraise an argument and to formulate in writing an argument in response, thus recognizing a creative dimension in critical thinking ability." High school and college; 1983–85; 1987 price data: $9.95 per complete test including reproducible test, scoring directions, scoring sheet, and manual ('85, 16 pages); (40) minutes; Robert H. Ennis and Eric Weir; Midwest Publications, Inc.*

Review of The Ennis-Weir Critical Thinking Essay Test by JAMES A. POTEET, Professor of Special Education, Ball State University, Muncie, IN:

The Ennis-Weir Critical Thinking Essay Test was designed to be used both as a test and as a teaching instrument. As a test, it is an informal assessment device that requires scoring judgements by examiners who should have had at least a college-level course in informal logic, critical thinking, or the equivalent. The test is most appropriate for high school and college students, although the manual states that it has been used successfully with junior high and sixth-grade students. It takes approximately 40 minutes, which include reading the stimulus and planning and writing the response. The authors grant permission for the purchaser of the manual to reproduce for classroom use the directions to the student, the stimulus letter, and the scoring sheet.

The test stimulus is a letter written to the editor of a fictitious newspaper about the parking problems in a fictitious city. The student must write a response letter to the editor. For each of the eight arguments presented in the stimulus letter, the student is to write a response paragraph judging the quality of those arguments. In addition, a closing paragraph about the stimulus letter's overall quality of argument is to be written by the student. The student is to defend his/her judgments with reasons.

The task described above requires the student to think critically in the context of argumentation in which the student is defending a point. The manual states that "the test is intended to help evaluate a person's ability to appraise an argument and to formulate in writing an argument in response, thus recognizing a creative dimension in critical thinking ability."

For scoring purposes, the examiner is provided with suggested criteria for awarding points for each paragraph written by the student. Thinking ability, not writing ability, is to be judged. The scoring criteria are to be used "flexibly and with judgment." The scoring approach might be described as "loose."

Construct, predictive, and concurrent validity have not been studied, as noted in the manual. Content validity is viewed as acceptable because the stimulus task requires critical thinking. References to earlier works by Ennis are offered to the readers to explore aspects of critical-thinking competence felt to be important by the authors. Interrater reliability for two groups, 27 college students and 28 gifted eighth-grade students, was reported as .86 and .82. The size of these groups, means, and standard deviations are given in the manual. Most of the manual is devoted to offering scoring guidelines and suggestions for each of the paragraphs.

As a teaching instrument, the manual suggests that the instrument can be used by a Socratic teacher by having the students grade either each other's or their own tests followed by a discussion of how to apply the proposed criteria given on the scoring sheet. Also, the students could react to the stimulus letter either orally or in writing and then react to each other's reactions through class discussions. For the didactic teacher, a diagnostic approach might be taken where a teacher evaluates students' responses followed by further instruction based on these responses.

The Ennis-Weir is a cleverly constructed task that is designed to assess a student's skill in critical thinking. Guidelines are given to assist an informed examiner in evaluating student responses. It is not meant to be considered as a norm-referenced test, but more as an informal assessment technique that lends itself well both to informal assessment and to instruction in the area of critical thinking.

Review of The Ennis-Weir Critical Thinking Essay Test by GAIL E. TOMPKINS, *Associate Professor of Language Arts Education, University of Oklahoma, Norman, OK:*

The Ennis-Weir Critical Thinking Essay Test is "a general test of critical thinking ability in the context of argumentation." According to the authors, the following areas of critical-thinking competence are examined in the test: getting the point, seeing reasons and assumptions, stating one's point, offering good reasons, seeing other possibilities, responding appropriately to and/or avoiding equivocation, irrelevance, circularity, reversal of an if-then relationship, straw-person fallacy, overgeneralization, excessive skepticism, credibility problems, and the use of emotive language to persuade. The Ennis-Weir is not a test of formal or deductive argumentation, and examinees are not required to exhibit technical knowledge or use specialized vocabulary in their essays.

In the Ennis-Weir, examinees read a complex argument presented as a letter to the editor of a newspaper about a local parking problem and are asked to formulate another complex argument in response to the letter. In the letter, a proposal is presented and eight arguments in support of the proposal are offered. Each argument appears in a separate numbered paragraph and exemplifies at least one error in reasoning (e.g., irrelevance, circularity, overgeneralization). Examinees read the letter and then write an essay evaluating the argument of each paragraph and the letter as a whole.

Instructions to examinees are straightforward. During the 40-minute testing period, examinees are directed to spend the first 10 minutes reading and thinking about the letter and the remaining 30 minutes writing the nine-paragraph essay evaluating the argument of the letter.

Graders are provided with detailed evaluation criteria and scoring instructions. A scoring sheet is provided in the manual, and graders are instructed to award from -1 to +3 points for each of the first eight paragraphs and from -1 to +5 points for the ninth paragraph, with a total of 29 points possible. Graders are encouraged to use their own judgment in applying the criteria and to add or subtract points for other insights or errors. The manual contains a detailed discussion, paragraph by paragraph, of the arguments in the letter and comments students might make in response to the arguments. This information should help graders make reasonably sophisticated judgements, but no information is provided about how to interpret the scores or about what might be considered "average" performance on the test.

The authors claim content validity for The Ennis-Weir by arguing that examinees demonstrate critical-thinking skills in appraising the arguments presented in the letter and in formulating arguments in their responses. Furthermore, they have called graders' attention to specific relevant aspects of examinee responses in the scoring guide. However, claims for content validity would be much stronger if the authors had compared the results of this test with other tests of critical thinking.

Scanty information on reliability is provided in the manual. Reliability is based on 27 undergraduate students who took the test as part of an introductory course on informal logic and 28 gifted eighth-graders in an English class who had received some critical thinking instruction. The only reliability information reported was interrater reliabilities (.86 and .82) for the

graders who scored the undergraduate and eighth-grade essays, respectively. No other reliability information was reported.

The authors of The Ennis-Weir also suggest that the test can be used as an instructional tool in high school classes. Because of the limited information on validity and the lack of reliability data, this second use may be the more valuable one for this material. The detailed scoring criteria provide useful information for teachers planning a unit on critical thinking, and the test itself can be used as one activity in the unit.

In summary, The Ennis-Weir has the potential to be a valuable test of critical-thinking ability for high school and college students. The authors are to be commended for developing an open-ended and content-specific test that allows students to respond to the arguments presented in the test in a variety of ways. The content of the test minimizes the artificiality of the testing situation, and an interesting and fairly realistic situation is presented in the test. The test manual is another plus. It is easy to read and use, and the detailed scoring criteria simplify grading. Unfortunately, the limited information on validity and the lack of reliability data suggest that The Ennis-Weir may be more appropriately used as a teaching tool than as a testing tool. The essay format of the test prompts another concern. The authors caution that The Ennis-Weir is primarily a test of critical-thinking ability, not of writing ability, and that graders should focus on the quality of thinking in the responses rather than on the quality of writing. But writing ability as well as writing anxiety may influence examinees' performance on the test.

[25]

Evaluating Educational Programs for Intellectually Gifted Students. Purpose: "Designed to guide the evaluation of educational programming relative to the special educational needs of intellectually gifted students, grades K–12, that have been demonstrated to influence socioemotional and cognitive development." Learning environments for grades K–12; 1984; EEPIGS; ratings by educators; Form A: Socioemotional Needs, Form B: Cognitive Development and Intellectual Needs, Form C: Identified Program Strengths, Form D: Identified Program Weaknesses; 1985 price data: $20 per 50 copies of Forms A and B, 25 copies of Forms C and D, and administrative manual (14 pages); $6 per 50 Form A or Form B; $6 per 25

Form C and Form D; Joanne Rand Whitmore; D.O.K. Publishers, Inc.*

Review of Evaluating Educational Programs for Intellectually Gifted Students by LINDA E. BRODY, Assistant Director, Study of Mathematically Precocious Youth (SMPY), The Johns Hopkins University, Baltimore, MD:

The Evaluating Educational Programs for Intellectually Gifted Students (EEPIGS) scales were designed to assist school systems in evaluating how well their programs meet the needs of intellectually gifted students. The author suggests that the scales can be used for making decisions about the needs of an entire school system, one school, or an individual child. It is designed to assess needs prior to the implementation of special programs for the gifted, as well as for evaluative purposes during and after the development of special services.

The scales include four forms. Form A consists of a list of classroom characteristics related to the socioemotional needs of gifted students, and Form B includes classroom characteristics related to the cognitive development of gifted students. The evaluator is asked to assign a rating from o (*not at all*) to 3 (*regularly*) for each item listed based on the frequency with which the characteristic occurs in the program. A total score is computed for each of these scales based on 30 items.

Forms C and D are used to analyze the program strengths and weaknesses identified when Forms A and B are completed. A discussion should follow, and a plan of action for improving the program should be formulated. Then the plan should be reviewed by those affected, and revised if necessary. School systems are encouraged to use these outlined procedures only as a guide and to adapt the instrument to meet their own special needs.

The scales are an outgrowth of the author's extensive experience in designing and evaluating programs for underachieving gifted students. The program characteristics listed reflect the author's philosophical assumptions and beliefs about appropriate programming for gifted students, and these beliefs are listed in the manual. The rationale for the inclusion of each individual item on the scales is not included, however. Users of the instrument need to carefully consider whether the underlying assumptions and the program characteristics are consonant with their own beliefs about educational programming for the gifted and for the particular program being examined before electing to use this instrument.

These scales could be extremely valuable in encouraging schools to do a needs assessment prior to implementing a program for gifted students and also in encouraging schools to include an evaluative component in any program they develop. The inclusion of socioemotional considerations is particularly commendable because they are frequently overlooked in favor of only cognitive results.

I do have some concerns about the scales, however. Although the author encourages schools to adapt the scales for their own purposes, including adding to the list of characteristics, it may be that many schools will use the scales as a checklist and not make any changes. In fact, the computation of total scale scores encourages this. Thus, school systems may be likely to use the scales "as is" without considering whether they agree with the underlying philosophy that the scales reflect or whether the characteristics listed are appropriate for their purposes. Although the manual is well written, my feeling is that the person leading the evaluation may need training in the use of the instrument to ensure its appropriate use in a school's unique situation rather than as a simple checklist.

While traditional measures of validity, reliability, and normative data would not be appropriate for this type of process instrument, some research reporting on the effectiveness of these scales in promoting improvement in a variety of programs would be extremely helpful. The scales may be trying to do too much. It may not be possible to develop one instrument with universally agreed-upon objectives appropriate to evaluate programming for gifted students at all grade levels and in all subject areas. If, on the other hand, the success of the instrument depends upon extensive revision of the scales by school system personnel, a major advantage of the instrument (i.e., ease of administration), is lost.

In conclusion, although instruments are needed to assist schools in evaluating programs, I am not convinced that these scales can be used appropriately for all types of programs without considerable efforts by school personnel to adapt the scales to meet their own needs. If schools fail to make the necessary adaptations, there is danger that inappropriate decisions will be made concerning the programs under consideration. If schools do attempt to modify the instrument, there is reason to be concerned that school personnel may require training in order to do this effectively, and the scales lose their attractiveness as an easily administered instrument. Research is needed to identify the particular kinds of programs for which the scales would be appropriate. Meanwhile, schools are urged to use caution in adopting this instrument without a careful examination of the items.

Review of Evaluating Educational Programs for Intellectually Gifted Students by NICHOLAS COLANGELO, Professor and Chair of Counselor Education, University of Iowa, Iowa City, IA:

Evaluating Educational Programs for Intellectually Gifted Students (EEPIGS) is an instrument designed "to guide the evaluation of educational programming relative to the special educational needs of intellectually gifted students, grades K–12." The EEPIGS has four forms; however, only the first two of these contain items. Form A assesses the socioemotional needs of gifted youngsters, and Form B assesses cognitive development and intellectual needs. Forms C and D will be described later.

The instrument is an outcome of Whitmore's work with gifted underachievers. From this work she found that gifted students become highly motivated to achieve or become underachievers, to various degrees, in response to two sets of characteristics of learning opportunities: (*a*) socioemotional attributes of the learning environment; (*b*) characteristics of the instructional process and curriculum that affect the cognitive development of gifted students. The instrument comprises two scales (Form A and Form B) assessing the attributes of these forces that shape the classroom behavior of gifted students. The author states that both scales are equally important and should not be used separately.

Form A contains 30 items that can be responded to with 0 (*not at all*), 1 (*sometimes, on occasion*), 2 (*often*), 3 (*regularly*). An example of one item from Form A is: "The classroom is well structured for flexibility in learning activities."

Form B contains 30 items with the same 0–3 scale found in Form A. An example of an item from Form B is: "Students are challenged to think critically about what they hear and read and to develop their questioning skills."

It is suggested in the manual that items rated "2" or "3" could be considered a relative strength of the programs whereas ratings of "0" or "1" would signify weaknesses. Scoring for Forms A and B is to be done by adding the "numerical sum of the responses and divide by 30 to obtain the overall rating." It is stated on the forms that a minimally satisfactory score is 60 (or an overall rating of 2.0).

Two other forms are included: Form C is titled, Identified Program Strengths, and Form D is titled, Identified Program Weaknesses. Forms C and D are essentially blank pages divided in half where users of the instrument can list strengths and weaknesses of their program and list what should be done to correct the weakness or sustain the strengths.

The author states that the items for Forms A and B are research-based characteristics of classrooms that foster the full development of the academic potential of intellectually gifted students. However, there is nothing in the manual that gives evidence of the research basis for these items. There is a general reference to three books (Clark, 1983; Purkey, 1978; Whitmore, 1980) but no data on the items themselves. There is no information on how or why some items were selected and others excluded. Also, there is no indication of the relative importance of any single item or cluster of items; I find this a major problem. One can only assume that each item has equal influence. However, an overall score would not provide a sense of what *essential* elements are missing or present in a program.

The EEPIGS is essentially a needs assessment instrument. Instructions are well written and easy to follow. The items do tap a variety of issues in the affective and cognitive development of gifted youngsters.

In summary, EEPIGS is a process tool to help educators make decisions about the educational needs of gifted youngsters. The need for such an instrument is unquestionable. However, EEPIGS does not provide evidence for sound development of items and the scoring system and meaning of scores is ambiguous. The usefulness of the instrument is limited.

[26]

GAP Reading Comprehension Test, Third Edition. Purpose: Assesses reading comprehension and can indicate reading progress. Reading ages 7–12; 1965–85; GAP; cloze technique; 2 equivalent forms; 1985 price data: A$24.95 per 48 copies each of Form B and Form R, and teacher manual ('85, 8 pages); 15(20) minutes; John McLeod; Heineman Publishers Australia Pty Ltd. [Australia].*

See T3:928 (4 references), and T2:1550 (3 references); for reviews by Donald B. Black and Earl F. Rankin of an earlier edition, see 7:688.

TEST REFERENCES

1. Beggs, W. D. A., & Howarth, P. N. (1985). Inner speech as a learned skill. *Journal of Experimental Child Psychology*, 39, 396-411.
2. Bowey, J. A. (1986). Syntactic awareness in relation to reading skill and ongoing reading comprehension monitoring. *Journal of Experimental Child Psychology*, 41, 282-299.
3. Marsh, H. W. (1986). Self-serving effect (bias?) in academic attributions: Its relation to academic achievement and self-concept. *Journal of Educational Psychology*, 78, 190-200.

Review of the GAP Reading Comprehension Test, Third Edition by ALAN S. KAUFMAN, Research Professor of School Psychology, The University of Alabama, Tuscaloosa, AL:

The GAP Reading Comprehension Test is allegedly a "practical by-product from a research study concerned with book readability and the application of information theory to the study of reading"; the test uses a modified cloze procedure to measure reading comprehension. Reliability data are presented for ages 8 to 10 years, but there is nothing else in the eight-page manual of the Third Edition that gives a clue about the suggested age range of the test. Indeed, there is virtually nothing in the test manual: no reference to the study that produced the instrument as a by-product; no explication of the role of information theory in test development; no evidence of a normative sample; and no validity data.

TEST DESCRIPTION AND CONSTRUCTION. The GAP Reading Comprehension Test comprises two supposedly equivalent forms, each with a 15-minute time limit. Although presumably only one form is intended to be given to a child (the manual suggests that there are two forms so that they can be distributed "alternately" to deter cheating), age-equivalent tables are provided for each form separately and for the sum of raw scores on the two forms. Form B3 (which presumably refers to the Third Edition of the blue test) contains seven brief passages (four to six lines), each with four to nine words missing. Form R3 (the red form) contains eight brief passages, each missing four to seven words.

Test-development procedures for the first two editions of the GAP test are discussed sketchily in the current manual, and only a limited description is provided of the construction in 1976 of the Third Edition. Preliminary items for all editions were administered to fluent readers (teachers in training); only items that were answered unequivocally (i.e., by 95 percent or more of the fluent readers) were retained.

Approximately 75 percent of the items selected in this manner for the third revision were from the previous edition of the test; the remaining items were new, written to replace a few of the items that experience had shown to be inappropriate. The revised tests were then administered to 250 children, presumably ages 8 to 10 years, since reliability data are provided for the Third Edition only at ages 8, 9, and 10.

The items on each form are mostly unambiguous, but the passages are not particularly child oriented or interesting, especially on Form B3. The missing words tend to be simple prepositions, auxiliary verbs, articles, and pronouns; very few nonhelping verbs, adjectives (other than articles), adverbs, or nouns are deleted from the passages. The vocabulary in each passage tends to be considerably more difficult than the simple words omitted via the cloze procedure; perhaps reading comprehension would have been assessed with more breadth and depth if a wider variety of words (in terms of part of speech and difficulty level) had been eliminated from the passages.

The format of the test also presents a problem. The print becomes smaller as the items get harder, for no apparent reason. The last two or three items per form are in unnecessarily tiny print.

PSYCHOMETRIC PROPERTIES. The GAP manual is one of the most incomplete I have ever seen. Split-half reliability coefficients are provided for ages 8, 9, and 10, probably for the 250 children tested during the test development phase, but sample sizes for the age groups are not given. The coefficients are good, ranging from .90 to .94 for Form B3 and from .90 to .92 for Form R3. However, the only way that split-half coefficients would be appropriate for the GAP is if all items in a given passage are included on the same "half-test"; otherwise the coefficients would be spuriously high because of experimental interdependence among sets of items. Unfortunately, no mention is made of this important consideration. Of greater concern is the lack of standard errors of measurement to facilitate interpretation of raw scores, and the failure to provide alternate-forms coefficients for the two forms. Test users are asked to accept Forms B3 and R3 as equivalent, but the author of the GAP has provided not one shred of evidence to support the equivalence!

Shockingly, not one validity study is offered in the manual for any edition of the GAP, even though the test was first copyrighted in 1965. There is simply no evidence of any sort that the GAP is a valid measure of reading comprehension.

Normative data are equally lacking. The author states that the sample of 250 children tested during construction of the Third Edition provided data that were used to modify the original norms. How this was done is unclear since 25 percent of the items in the Third Edition are new. No information about the original sample is offered, and the sample of 250 is described in one word: children. Since the test author is from Canada and the test is published in Australia, the likelihood of the "norms" being appropriate for the United States is nil; indeed, the odds of the norms being appropriate for Canada or Australia are only slightly higher.

Norms tables are provided, namely reading-age equivalents of raw scores. Obviously, age equivalents are not adequate as the only type of norm. Conversion of raw scores to standard scores or percentile ranks for separate age groups would have been decidedly superior to age-equivalent conversion tables for Form B3, Form R3, and for both norms combined. Similarly, the presentation of tables to determine retarded readers based on a criterion of Reading Quotients less than 80 (reading age divided by chronological age multiplied by 100) is psychometrically indefensible.

SUMMARY. The GAP Reading Comprehension Test has little to recommend it. The test construction seems flawed, psychometric data are largely missing, and the only converted scores provided by the test author (reading-age equivalents) are of limited usefulness and questionable meaningfulness because of the unknown nature of the normative sample.

Review of the GAP Reading Comprehension Test, Third Edition by GLORIA E. MILLER, Associate Professor of Psychology, University of South Carolina, Columbia, SC:

The GAP Reading Comprehension Test, authored by J. McLeod, is one of the only published instruments to test reading comprehension using a modified cloze procedure. The third edition of this test, published in 1977, is based on the earlier 1965 version. The author reports that about 75 percent of the original test content is retained in the third revision.

As in the past, there are two versions of the test (Form B3 and Form R3). Each test form consists of seven or eight short reading passages. The test is group administered. The exact instructions to be read orally to the children are provided in the manual. Children are given 15 minutes to fill in an average of five words that have been randomly omitted from each passage. The passages are written and presented at a progressively more difficult readability level.

A child's score on each test form is based on the number of correct word replacements produced. Only exact word replacements are accepted; however, incorrectly spelled versions of the keyed responses are scored as correct. Tables are provided so that a child's total raw score on either of the separate test forms or on the combined test forms can be converted into a reading age equivalency level. In a second set of tables, a cutoff score is provided to allow for a diagnosis of reading deficiency based on a child's chronological age.

The author claims that the GAP Test represents a more valid test of comprehension than other tests, in part because it overcomes the problem of content knowledge. However, it is apparent from reading the passages that this claim certainly is overstated. For example, a child who has experience with or knowledge of gardens and the need for constant weeding would be at a distinct advantage in filling in this blank item: "the gardens are overgrown with _____." Clearly, background knowledge is a factor that affects one's speed and efficiency on a timed test. Poorer performance also might be expected from a child who is a slow or meticulous writer since a written response is required.

The GAP Test is recommended as a screening measure to "facilitate the identification of children who are significantly retarded in reading comprehension." However, caution is recommended in employing this measure to identify children for further assessment because of several problems related to the standardization of the third version of the test.

First, the revised GAP Test was standardized on a small sample of children from Australia ($N = 250$). Moreover, the demographic characteristics of this sample are never presented. Although it is assumed that multiple age groups were employed, there is no breakdown of the age, sex, or socioeconomic status of the standardization sample. Thus, the generalizability of the norms from this population to children in the United States remains unknown.

Second, although the reported split-half reliabilities for the revised GAP Test were quite acceptable (i.e., ranges from .90 to .94), it was unclear just how these were calculated. In a one paragraph description of this procedure, the author states that the reliabilities "were calculated . . . on samples of children at three different age groups." Unfortunately, there is no mention either of the characteristics or number of children in these samples. Also, the exact reliability coefficient employed to obtain these estimates is not reported.

Finally, in contrast to past efforts to establish the validity of cloze procedures, no validity studies were conducted on the third revision of the GAP Test. The cutoff scores used to identify children who are "significantly retarded in reading comprehension" are reportedly set at the expected score of an average child whose age is 80 percent of the tested child's actual chronological age. It is unknown whether children identified as "retarded" comprehenders on the GAP Test actually were similarly identified on other measures. Moreover, there is no mention of how scores on the GAP Test correlate with children's scores on other measures of reading comprehension.

In conclusion, the limited documentation and the above mentioned problems associated with the standardization of the third revision of the GAP Reading Comprehension Test limit its usefulness for accurate reading diagnosis. Though there is considerable reason to believe that a standardized cloze test has the potential to be clinically useful for identifying problem readers, the value of the GAP Reading Comprehension Test in meeting this objective has not yet been clearly demonstrated.

[27]

Gifted and Talented Scale. Purpose: "Designed to identify those children who should be admitted into school programs for the Gifted and Talented." Grades 4–6; no date on test materials; 6 scores: Numerical Reasoning, Vocabulary, Synonyms/Antonyms, Similarities, Analogies, Total; 1985 price data: $50 per 25 pupil record forms and manual (17 pages); $45 per 25 pupil record forms; $7.50 per manual; administration time not reported; Dallas Educational Services.*

Review of the Gifted and Talented Scale by LINDA E. BRODY, Assistant Director, Study of Mathematically Precocious Youth (SMPY), The Johns Hopkins University, Baltimore, MD:

The Gifted and Talented Scale is designed to identify students in grades 4, 5, and 6 for placement in programs for gifted and talented students. Untimed and intended to be used for group administration, the scale attempts to measure abstract concepts through five subtests: Numerical Reasoning, Vocabulary, Synonyms and Antonyms, Similarities, and Analogies.

Programs for gifted and talented students have grown in popularity, creating assessment/identification problems for program administrators. The global intelligence test, once very popular for finding gifted students, is now recognized as somewhat limited in terms of assessing specific strengths and weaknesses for placement purposes. Achievement tests provide useful information but often reflect the adequacy of educational programs more than an individual student's potential. The Scholastic Aptitude Test (SAT) has been used successfully to measure verbal and mathematical reasoning ability in students as young as seventh grade, but the SAT would not be appropriate for younger students except in unusual circumstances. Schools, therefore, usually use a variety of measures of achievement and potential to assess a student's unique pattern of abilities in an effort to predict future performance.

This scale attempts to make the identification task easier by combining in one scale a measure of several types of reasoning abilities in an easily administered format. Unfortunately, the scale has been published prematurely. The research that has been done on the scale is inadequate to justify its use to determine the placement of students.

Norming was done in two school systems and involved the comparison of students in the gifted and talented program with students in the regular program. No other descriptive information about the norm group is provided, such as how they were selected for the gifted program, their socioeconomic level, or the racial and gender composition of the group. In school system A, fourth, fifth, and sixth grade gifted students were tested but only fourth grade regular students. No explanation is given as to why older regular students were not included. In addition, the total number of subjects in this sample is omitted, and the only descriptive information provided about the test results are means and standard deviations. More information is provided about the test results in school system B, including histograms, frequency distributions, analysis of variance and *t*-test results, and some descriptive statistics. However, the population is not described; for example, it is not clear which age groups were tested or how the samples were selected. Moreover, only 94 students (47 in each group) were tested, certainly an inadequate number for a normative sample. Furthermore, although the gifted students did score higher on the scale than the regular students, the range of scores for both groups in school system B is quite large, suggesting that this measure would not select all of the same students currently placed in the gifted program. There is inadequate information to determine whether the scale or the current identification system used in the school system is more effective in selecting the appropriate students.

The subtests are quite short; therefore assessment of their reliability as well as of the reliability of the total scale is critical. None is reported.

The validity of this instrument is questionable. It would be desirable to compare students' results on this scale with results on other measures such as intelligence and achievement tests to determine just what this scale is measuring. Predictive validity studies are needed to determine the effectiveness of this scale for predicting later achievement. Moreover, the test should be considered in terms of fourth, fifth, and sixth grade curricula. If students currently enrolled in gifted and talented programs, such as those in the norm group, have been exposed to more of the test content because of an enriched program, the test may actually be measuring achievement rather than

reasoning ability. This issue needs research attention. The manual provides no information concerning how the test was constructed nor any rationale for the selection of particular items.

In conclusion, I would strongly caution against the use of this scale for placement purposes at this time. Extensive research is needed to validate the scale, to provide representative normative samples, and to ensure adequate reliability of the instrument. It would be inappropriate for any school system to use it to make decisions about the placement of students in programs until this is done. The scale should be used only, and quite cautiously, for research purposes by qualified investigators.

Review of the Gifted and Talented Scale by NICHOLAS COLANGELO, *Professor and Chair of Counselor Education, University of Iowa, Iowa City, IA:*

The authors claim that the Gifted and Talented Scale (GTS) is designed to identify gifted and talented children in grades 4, 5, and 6. This claim is incredible given the absence of virtually any conceptual or psychometric supporting data in the manual.

The GTS is a power test designed for group administration. There are five categories in the test; all items in every category are designed to measure abstract concepts. No information is provided on how items were developed or selected. In addition, after reviewing each item, I cannot imagine how it was determined that each item measures an abstract concept.

The five categories are Numerical Reasoning, Vocabulary, Synonyms and Antonyms, Similarities, and Analogies. Each category contains 10 items. The Numerical Reasoning category contains a series of numbers. The student is to determine the next logical number in the series. The Vocabulary category consists of items designed to test a student's ability to define words. Students choose among four options for their answers. Synonyms and Antonyms consists of 10 items (five synonyms and five antonyms) designed to test a student's reasoning ability. Similarities is designed to test a student's knowledge of verbal relationships. Ten pairs are presented and a student is to determine how they are alike, choosing one of the four options provided for each pair. The final category is Analogies. This category is designed to test a student's verbal and abstract reasoning abilities.

There are serious conceptual and psychometric problems with the GTS. A major weakness is that no useful definition of gifted or talented is offered. Gifted is defined as "to be endowed with some power, quality or attribute." What human being would not fit this definition? Talented is defined as "possessing talent, special attribute, mentally gifted, skilled in performing art." Both definitions are taken from Webster's *Third New International Dictionary* and offer no guidance to clarify either concept. A confusing, incoherent array of short statements are made about gifted youngsters. Anyone not familiar with the field would not be able to understand what is being communicated. In essence, this is a scale that does not clearly state exactly what is being measured.

The scale is also weak from a psychometric standpoint. Almost no information is provided on item construction or on reliability or validity. Students in the gifted and talented program in two school districts were given the GTS. In addition, students not identified as gifted and talented were given the test. Not surprisingly, the students identified as gifted or talented scored higher than nonidentified students. It is reported that the mean scores of gifted students were significantly higher than the mean scores of regular students. This kind of comparison suggests that if a student scores "high" (i.e., similar to the scores obtained by gifted students in the sample, an acceptable criterion), then this student would be a candidate for a gifted program. No other validity-related information is presented.

Gifted education is receiving considerable attention in schools today. There is a rush to find straightforward, quantifiable data that will clearly determine who is and who is not gifted. I do not recommend the GTS be used to determine giftedness. There is no evidence for the claims made.

[28]

The Harrington O'Shea Career Decision-Making System. Purpose: "Surveys not only interests, but also values, training plans, and self-ratings of abilities." Grades 7–12 and adults; 1974–85; CDM; 6 scores (Arts, Business, Clerical, Crafts, Scientific, Social) used to identify 3 or more occupational areas, for intensive career exploration, from among 18 clusters (Art Work, Clerical Work,

Customer Services, Data Analysis, Education Work, Entertainment, Legal, Literary Work, Management, Manual Work, Math-Science, Medical-Dental, Music Work, Personal Service, Sales Work, Skilled Crafts, Social Services, Technical) and questions in 5 areas (Abilities, Future Plans, Job Values, Occupational Preferences, School Subject Preferences); 1988 price data: $13 per manual ('82, 102 pages); $9 per audiocassette; $165 per microcomputer edition; $3 per specimen set; (40) minutes; Thomas F. Harrington and Arthur J. O'Shea; American Guidance Service.*

a) SELF-SCORED EDITION. $34 per 25 survey booklets, directions for administration ('82, 6 pages), and interpretive folder ('82, 8 pages); Spanish edition available.

b) MACHINE-SCORED EDITION. 3 scoring reports available: $66 per 25 survey booklets, directions for administration ('82, 2 pages), and profile reports; $70 per 25 survey booklets, directions, and profile reports with group summary report; $8.50 per test with narrative report.

See T3:1059 (3 references); for a review by Carl G. Willis of an earlier edition, see 8:1004.

TEST REFERENCES

1. Galassi, M. D., Jones, L. K., & Britt, M. N. (1985). Nontraditional career options for women: An evaluation of career guidance instruments. *Vocational Guidance Quarterly, 34,* 124-130.

Review of The Harrington O'Shea Career Decision-Making System by CAROLINE MANUELE-ADKINS, *Associate Professor Counseling, Department of Educational Foundations, Hunter College of the City University of New York, New York, NY:*

The Harrington O'Shea Career Decision-Making System (CDM) is a multidimensional interest inventory measuring several variables hypothesized to contribute to effective career decision making. These variables include: occupational preferences, school subject areas, future plans, job values, abilities, and interests. The authors based their systems on Holland's theory of vocational development. The test has alternative scoring systems for counselor and subject use. The available systems are a self-scoring version, a computerized scoring version, a profile and narrative report, a group-reported scoring report (to provide information to curriculum planners and administrators), and most recently, a microcomputer version (Apple II and IIe and TRS 80 models III). There is also a Spanish version, available only in self-scoring format, and an audiocassette version for poor readers.

In brief, the CDM asks respondents to (a) select their first and second occupational preferences from a list of 18 occupational clusters; (b) select two school subjects they liked most from a list of 14 subjects; (c) identify one future educational or training plan from a list of 9 alternatives; (d) select four job values (e.g., security, variety) from 14 values; (e) choose 4 abilities from a list of 14; and (f) indicate on the interest survey how they feel on a scale of 0, 1, 2 about 120 different activities. As respondents proceed through each section they transfer the information to their summary profile, which produces a career code encompassing dichotomous combinations of crafts, scientific, arts, social, business, and clerical codes. Basically, these codes are renamed Holland codes. Similar to Holland's Vocational Preference Inventory (VPI) and Self-Directed Search (SDS), the codes are matched to different occupational areas.

The CDM survey booklet is easy to read and understand. The directions, for the most part, are clear. However, good reading ability and a sufficient level of motivation to follow through with all the scoring steps are required. The items in the booklet have face validity and there is no item overlap in any of the areas. The self-scoring version is accompanied by an interpretive folder to assist respondents in interpreting each area of their summary profile. This is a well designed and important part of the self-scored CDM. The authors developed it for those clients whose time with a counselor was limited. The interpretive folder fills an important need for a system that may be used without professional assistance. In this respect, the CDM is an advancement over the SDS, which is also self-scored but has until recently not provided interpretive information for the person using it alone. The success of the self-scoring systems depends, of course, on the abilities and motivation of the users.

The manual presents evidence for the validity of the CDM. The items and scale correlations analyses done for the interest section of the CDM indicate that the scales are homogeneous and each item is correlated with its own scale .50 or above. The procedures for developing this part of the CDM are thorough and adequate. The manual also presents evidence for construct validity by illustrating how the CDM interest categories exhibit the same correlational pattern as Holland's hexagonal model (from VPI data). Construct validity is also documented by studies which examine the relationship between CDM codes and Holland codes achieved on the Strong-Campbell Interest Inventory (SCII). For four different samples there is an 88, 89, 95, and 61 percent agreement with the first letter code. Concurrent validity data show the similarity between codes received on the CDM and codes of the occupations of a sample of employed people. In most cases they are very similar. The results were similar for college students' codes and choice of major. The authors state in the manual that they are not concerned with the predictive validity of the CDM. They define its purpose as "self-exploration" and not to "predict the job that an individual will finally enter as a permanent career." Some preliminary predictive validity studies are presented, however, that show the CDM has an average 50% predictive rate for high school students' choice of job or college major (4 years later). Comparison with the SCVIB's predictive validity shows strong similarity. Overall there is good evidence for the validity of the CDM.

Alpha coefficients for the internal consistency of the CDM interest scales range from .91 to .94. Thirty day test-retest reliabilities for the interest scales with high school and college students range from .75 to .94 (average mid .80s). They are slightly less stable for college students over a 5-month period of time. While these reliability estimates are good, they are provided only for the interest scales. Reliability data for the other areas are also necessary. Another concern in terms of this measure is the reliability of the scores obtained among the various scoring systems. The manual reports studies that show .96 and .99 correlations between the student-scored and author-scored interest scales. This is very high interrater reliability but the authors still caution that scores should be checked. These same reliability studies should be done for other areas of the CDM.

Data that are similar, but not as extensive, are presented for the reliability and validity of the Spanish version of the CDM. These compare favorably with the English version. The authors describe their efforts to include language that would be understood by diverse Spanish-speaking cultures and to use more widely understood than literal translations of expressions and phrases in the measure.

Extensive male and female norms are provided for each of the CDM areas for junior high, high school, and college freshmen. Only interest scale norms are provided for the Spanish version (grade 7 through adult), for adults, and for adult CETA participants. Normative data are, therefore, needed for the other CDM areas for these groups. The authors have put a lot of effort into making the CDM gender-fair. It uses neither separate scales by sex nor combined sex scales.

In summary, the CDM appears to be a well-developed measure that is particularly useful if one wants a comprehensive self-scored vocational assessment measure. Because of its similarity to the Holland VPI and SDS measures one has to question the advantages of its use over these other measures. The SDS is simpler to use and the VPI is machine scored rather than self scored. The CDM seems more comprehensive in its coverage and offers more interpretive information than the SDS. Its multiple scoring systems may also be advantageous for meeting the needs of diverse client groups.

[29]

Howell Prekindergarten Screening Test.
Purpose: Provides for early identification of children "who may need special assistance to ensure their successful entry into formal education; . . . whose skills seem appropriate for typical kindergarten work; . . . [or those] students with unusually well developed skills which can be most fully enhanced by specially designed educational experiences." Prekindergarten students; 1984; 23 scores: Shapes, Listening Comprehension, Auditory Memory, Colors, Color Words, Vocabulary, Classification, Letter Identification, Rhyming, Letter Writing, Directionality & Spatial Relationships, Consonant Sounds, Visual Motor, Visual Discrimination, Name, Math (Number Identification, Number Writing, Counting Sets, Math Concepts, Addition & Subtraction, Total), Copying, Total; 1986 price data: $17.95 per 10 student test booklets; $12.95 per user's guide and technical manual ('84, 49 pages); $14.95 per specimen set; (60) minutes; Howell Township Public Schools, Joseph P. Ryan (manual) and Ronald J. Mead (manual); Book-Lab.*

Review of the Howell Prekindergarten Screening Test by CARL J. DUNST, Director, Family, Infant and Preschool Program, Western Carolina Center, Morganton, NC:

The Howell Prekindergarten Screening Test is designed to help teachers identify children entering kindergarten who may need supplemental and supportive instructional assistance. The instrument includes 71 items that assess a child's performance in 21 learning areas, including Listening Comprehension, Auditory Memory, Classification, Letter Identification and Writing, Number Identification and Writing, and Addition and Subtraction. The items were selected to tap skills early childhood specialists generally recognize as necessary and important for successful participation in kindergarten classrooms.

The Howell is a group test administered in a paper-and-pencil format. It takes approximately 2 hours to administer. It is recommended that the test be administered in four sittings over a 2-day period. The examiner's manual includes explicit instructions for teachers to follow when administering the test. A filmstrip has been developed in order to facilitate correct administration, scoring, and interpretation of the scale. According to the test developers, the results from the test "can be utilized to develop a diagnostic supplementary educational plan." It must be noted that results are not used for identifying instructional targets for either supplemental or remedial purposes. Rather, the results are used for deciding the next steps to be taken for children whose scores fall below a certain cutoff point, and who, thus, presumably have learning difficulties.

Each of the 71 scale items is scored dichotomously (pass vs. fail). The Howell yields a total scale score, which is simply the sum of the passes on the individual items. (A math subscale score can also be determined.) The total scores are used to classify a child as falling into one of three "score categories": Critical Region (0–30), Regular Performance (31–51), and Very High Performance (52–73). Children in the critical group are thought to need remedial instruction, children in the regular performance category are thought to be prepared for a typical school experience, and children in the very high group are thought to need more challenging educational experiences. The test developers do not provide any rationale, whatsoever, for the parameters of the cutoff points for the score categories, and in no instance is there any discussion of the validity of this categorization scheme.

The method for assigning children to "risk," "nonrisk," and "advanced" categories is especially open to criticism. The selection of cutoff points for assignment of children to the categories appears to have been done either intuitively or based on an approximate tripartite split, and does not appear to have been established empirically. Because no explanation or rationale is provided for the scores demarcating the boundaries of each category, the use of the scale for screening purposes is questionable, especially for children whose scores are close to the cutoff points.

The above criticism is compounded by the fact that no normative or standardization data are presented in the test manual, and no specific information is provided about the subjects (age, sex, parent education, SES, etc.). The Howell was developed in a school district composed of predominantly middle-income families. Consequently, the scale scores may have different meanings depending upon the population being tested. This is not a trivial matter, and caution is warranted in using the Howell even as a screening tool except in cases where scores are either extremely low or high.

The examiner's manual does include numerous bits of data regarding the reliability and validity of the test. The five internal consistency coefficients were all high (Range = .86 to .88) for samples ranging from $Ns = 186$ to 328. Neither short- or long-term test-retest reliability data are reported. Despite the test developers' dismissal of the need for these types of stability indices, such coefficients are needed in order to establish whether the scores allow accurate classification of children administered the scale. This seems especially true because the scale is used primarily with 5-year-olds whose behavior is likely to be affected by taking this type of a paper-and-pencil test. For many children of this age, this test may be their first experience with a paper-and-pencil evaluation.

A number of studies have been conducted with respect to the validity of the Howell. In one study of 229 children, teachers were first asked to classify their students into one of four categories: eligible for compensatory education, possibly needing assistance, prepared for regular program, and eligible for gifted and talented program. Mean Howell scores were then computed for the children assigned to each category. The scores for the four groups were,

respectively, 26.0 (SD = 7.2), 35.5 (SD = 7.8), 43.9 (SD = 10.3), and 53.6 (SD = 6.9), with all adjacent pair-wise comparisons statistically significant. In a second study, Howell scores were used to group 328 students into low-, middle-, and high-score groups. Eight months later, teachers were asked to assign their students to one of three ability levels (low, middle, high). Cross tabulations of the two sets of data showed identical cell assignments for 64% of the cases. Assignment of only 1.2% of the cases differed by two categories. The "hit" rate for assignment to the high and low groups based on Howell scores is generally impressive. However, examination of the data for the middle ability group, which presumably overlaps considerably with the Regular Performance Category (although no scores are given), suggests difficulties in using the test. Of all the students in the study, teachers assigned 117 to the middle ability group. Only 56 students, or 48%, were properly classified by the Howell scores. Thus, for children bordering around the cutoff points, there is about a 50-50 chance of being assigned to the correct category.

The predictive validity of the Howell was examined in two studies in which Howell scores were used to predict California Achievement Test grade levels and percentile rankings with the measurements taken 1 and 2 years apart. The validity coefficients were .71 and .68, respectively, between the total scale scores and the CAT Reading and Mathematics scores for the 1-year measures, and .64 and .72 for the same comparisons for the 2-year measures. These are quite impressive validity coefficients, and indicate that generally (on the average) children who score low on the Howell at entry into kindergarten are the same youngsters who are likely to score low on the California Achievement Test in the first and second grades, whereas the opposite is true for children who initially score high on the Howell.

SUMMARY. The Howell is a screening instrument designed to identify kindergarten children who may potentially require supplemental or remedial instruction. The results are used to classify a child as being "at-risk," "at-no-risk," or "advanced" in performance. Although the reliability and validity data on the Howell are generally acceptable and in some instances even impressive, none of the data are based precisely on the trichotomized categorization scheme for deciding at-risk status. The major task that remains is to ascertain the degree to which the scoring scheme is reliable and valid. Some type of discriminant analysis is clearly warranted. Until this type of validity study is conducted, users should be cautious in using the Howell for screening purposes.

Review of the Howell Prekindergarten Screening Test by CANDICE FEIRING, Associate Professor of Pediatrics, Robert Wood Johnson Medical School, University of Medicine and Dentistry of New Jersey, New Brunswick, NJ:

The Howell Prekindergarten Screening Test is basically a tool that provides a measure for classifying students entering kindergarten into three groups—high, medium, and low—based on skills believed necessary for beginning kindergarten. The low-performance group may need special assistance to facilitate kindergarten entrance; the medium group has sufficient skills; and the high group is considered advanced and in need of special programming. It must be kept in mind that these three groups are based on norms obtained from a series of samples (N = 186–229) from a middle-income community, so that skill levels are based on performance levels necessary to succeed in this type of population. The test is comprised of 73 items easily administered to groups. As a screening tool, the Howell takes a very long time to administer, requiring 2 hours of testing with a recommendation of four sittings over a 2-day period. The items cover 21 skills (see description of test content provided above) believed important by experienced teachers and early childhood experts for kindergarten success. However, these 21 skills cannot be assessed separately as the Howell is a screening tool for general classification of students and is not appropriate for determining children's specific learning profiles.

The psychometric properties of the Howell have been well addressed and the test developers were given technical assistance by the staff at Educational Testing Service. Reliability information on the Howell consists only of information on internal consistency. Split-half reliability, calculated using an odd-even division of items with the Spearman-Brown Prophecy formula to adjust for test length, yielded acceptable levels of internal consistency from .86 to .88 for three independent samples. Test-retest reliability of the Howell was not obtained, the rationales given being the young age of the respondents and the test length. However, it still would have been advisable to obtain an index of the extent to which the Howell reliably classifies children into the same category on two test occasions. An odd-even item split could have been used to create two comparable forms in order to obtain short term test-retest reliability.

Concurrent validity of the Howell was determined by comparing children's test scores to teacher classification of the children into four groups: (1) gifted, (2) regular class, (3) possible assistance, and (4) compensatory program. The teachers who estimated children's skill levels were well experienced with the children's performance and were unaware of the children's test scores. The mean scores on the Howell were shown to be rank ordered as expected (group 1 > 2 > 3 > 4) given the teacher's estimates, and the observed differences were significant overall for the contrasts of adjacent groups (group 1 > 2, 2 > 3, 3 > 4). While these results are quite acceptable, it would also be useful to have information on the comparison of Howell scores to another instrument (e.g., CIRCUS).

Predictive validity of the Howell was determined in two ways using teachers' rankings and California Achievement Test scores (CAT) as outcome criteria. The teachers' rankings of 328 students into Low, Middle, and High groups were obtained 8 months after a 100-item pilot version of the Howell was administered. The Howell scores were used to classify children into High, Medium, and Low groups and these groups were related to the teachers' subsequent ratings. The agreement between test ranks and teacher rank was moderately good for the High (69%) and Low (78%) groups. For the Middle group, agreement was lower (48%) with children who scored in the Middle group on the Howell often ranked in the High (28%) or Low (20%) group by teachers. Test scores on the Howell for two large samples (N = 138 and 194) were correlated with CAT scores in reading and math. All correlations were significant and ranged from .62 to .72, which is very acceptable predictive validity.

In general, the Howell has acceptable internal consistency and good predictive validity. However, as a screening tool the Howell takes an extremely long time to administer in order to obtain three skill-level classifications for children entering kindergarten. The test developers wisely caution against use of the Howell to measure individual skill areas. The guidelines for test administration and interpretation of scores and psychometric information are clear and well presented in the examiner's manual. In using the Howell, caution should be used in regard to misclassification of children in the middle scoring groups, and it must be kept in mind that this test has been normed on a restricted sample of children from middle-income families. Despite these drawbacks, the Howell has been thoughtfully constructed and initial psychometric findings on a large sample are generally good.

[30]

Infant Screening. Purpose: To identify children as possibly "at risk" of educational, social, and emotional difficulties. Ages 5–6; 1981; screening tests, checklists, and diagnostic tests in the areas of Visual Reception, Auditory Reception, Association Skill, Sequential Skill, Expression (Encoding), and Reading Difficulties; 1988 price data: £3.25 per 10 test booklets; £2.75 per 20 checklists; £4.25 per 25 pupil profiles; £9.50 per teacher's book (73 pages) and 8 diagnostic test cards; administration time not reported; Humberside Education Authority; Macmillan Education Ltd. [England].*

Review of Infant Screening by CATHY F. TELZROW, Psychologist and Director, Educational Assessment Project, Cuyahoga Special Education Service Center, Maple Heights, OH:

The Infant Screening System is described as a three-stage procedure for identifying young children who may be at risk for educational failure. The first stage is a brief teacher-completed checklist, of which there are two forms depending upon the age of the child (Checklist 1 for 5-year-old children and Checklist 2 for children aged 5-10 to 6-3). For the older children, Checklist 2 is supplemented by an Initial Screening Test that can be administered in groups of up to approximately 15 children. The third stage of the Infant Screening System is a lengthy diagnostic test to be administered to children who are identified as "at-risk" by the earlier screening procedures. The system was developed in England; hence the use of the term "infant" refers to children of early school age (approximately 5 to 6½ years).

The theoretical model forming the basis of the Infant Screening System is the psycholinguistic model, which represents receptive, expressive, and association types of processing across auditory and visual channels and representational and automatic levels of organization. The Infant Screening procedure incorporates a method of transactional assessment and hypothesis testing, whereby teachers engage in ongoing formal and informal appraisal of pupils' strengths and weaknesses.

Some portions of the Infant Screening System are heuristically interesting. The initial screening checklists, in particular, appear to include broad behaviors of educational relevance that teachers can respond to rather easily. However, the manual (*Infant Screening: A Handbook for Teachers*) does not indicate how the items included on Checklists 1 and 2 were selected, nor whether or not the items listed have demonstrated validity in predicting school failure or "at risk" status. The Handbook includes an extensive chapter entitled "Remediation," where specific intervention strategies matched to various processes in the system's psycholinguistic model (e.g., visual discrimination, auditory figure-ground perception) are described in detail. Although this section may be of interest to teachers, there is no explanation for how the remedial strategies were designed nor whether or not they have demonstrated validity for improving identified weaknesses. A separate chapter ("Management of Maladaptive Behavior") provides a brief introduction to behavioral principles. Although this chapter might serve as background material for more intensive staff development on the topic of behavior management, it is too incomplete for exclusive use by teachers.

With the exception of a few interesting features, the Infant Screening System must be judged inadequate as an assessment tool. The directions for administering, scoring, and interpreting the components of the Infant Screening System are incomplete and frequently confusing. No data are presented on the procedure used for item selection on the Initial Screening Test. Although the Handbook states "there were three pilot runs," the procedure by which items were deleted or modified during pilot testing is not explained. Technical data are not reported separately for the two-teacher checklists (Checklist 1 and Checklist 2), the Initial

Screening Test, and the Diagnostic Test. Instead, the manual states that a group of 594 children, for whom sampling procedures were not specified, "were given the five screening tests and the Carver Word Recognition Test," as well as having their teachers complete "the Bristol Social Adjustment Guide (Children in School) and the checklist for the screening procedure." What is meant by the "five screening tests" is not clear, since the Initial Screening Test has six subtests. From all these tests and screening procedures, a list of 14 variables was generated, and these variables were used in subsequent statistical analyses. Therefore, it is not possible to evaluate the technical qualities of the individual components of the Infant Screening System, nor of the entire system, because all technical data were computed from variables incorporating measures other than those included in the Infant Screening System.

In summary, the Infant Screening System is not recommended as a measure of potential school failure in kindergarten- and first-grade-age children. The absence of any discussion of item selection and validity for certain components of the system (i.e., Checklists 1 and 2 and diagnostic tests) reduces these portions of the system to interesting exercises. Although greater detail is included for the Initial Screening Test, it is not possible to evaluate the technical merits of this component, because all statistical analyses incorporated other measures. Although its restricted sampling complicates its use in some settings, validity data for the Florida Kindergarten Screening Battery (Satz & Fletcher, 1982) suggest this scale is far preferable to the Infant Screening System in identifying children at-risk for school failure.

REVIEWER'S REFERENCE

Satz, P., & Fletcher, J. (1982). *Manual for the Florida Kindergarten Screening Battery*. Odessa, FL: Psychological Assessment Resources.

Review of Infant Screening by STANLEY F. VASA, Professor of Special Education and Communication Disorders, University of Nebraska-Lincoln, Lincoln, NE:

The Infant Screening program is designed to detect children, ages 5 through 6 years of age, who are at risk of having school-related difficulties. The procedures include both teacher observations and judgments and specific screening measures. The program is based on the psycholinguistic model employed in the Illinois Test of Psycholinguistic Abilities (ITPA; Kirk, McCarthy, & Kirk, 1968). Screening tests are provided that measure Visual Reception, Auditory Reception, Association Skill, Sequential Skill, Expression, and Reading Difficulties.

The handbook provides a description of the assessment model, description of the screening tests and materials, remediation guidelines, and guides for dealing with maladaptive behavior. The chapters on remediation and management of maladaptive behavior contribute to the handbook being more of a curriculum guide than a screening test. The remediation section analyzes each of the subtests and provides guides for teacher observations in educational settings. This section overstates the test's power to accurately depict the strengths and weaknesses of a child. In addition, the recommendations provided for the user go beyond the information provided by the tests. The procedures employed are not unique and have a high degree of resemblance to the ITPA subtests.

There is a lack of information about the development of the scale and how items were selected for inclusion. The technical information lacks specificity, and there is not enough information to evaluate the usefulness of the tests in settings other than the ones in which they were developed. No specific information on reliability and validity is provided. The scale is identified as criterion-referenced. The authors report cutoff scores and tables for normal scores, at-risk scores, and moderate to severe difficulties. Unfortunately, no specific description of the standardization population is given beyond the ages of subjects, making the interpretation tables unusable.

The strength of the scale may be in the assessment process utilized. Schools that wish to develop local norms may find the procedures useful. In order to use the screening procedures, it would be necessary to carefully analyze the curriculum of individual programs for agreement with the model utilized by the screening program.

Users should be cautious in making decisions based on the scale. Overall, the content of the scale is a broad-based sampling of abilities and skills of young children. It is fairly ecological in approach and looks at more than basic academic skills.

SUMMARY. The manual accompanying the test appears to be more of a teacher's guide for intervention with young children than a description of the development and psychometric characteristics of this test. The accompanying scale is not well constructed. Concerns regarding this test center on the development of the test items, the standardization sample, and the lack of indicators of concurrent and content validity for the scale. Overall, the Infant Screening program may provide the user with some information, but the lack of standardization data makes interpretations based on the scale suspect.

REVIEWER'S REFERENCE

Kirk, S. A., McCarthy, J. J., & Kirk, W. D. (1968). Illinois Test of Psycholinguistic Abilities. Champaign, IL: University of Illinois Press.

[31]

Instrument Timbre Preference Test. Purpose: "To act as an objective aid to the teacher and the parent in helping a student choose an appropriate woodwind or brass instrument to learn to play in beginning instrumental music and band." Grades 4–12; 1984–85; ITPT; 7 scores: Flute, Clarinet, Saxophone and French Horn, Oboe/English Horn/Bassoon, Trumpet and Cornet, Trombone/Baritone/French Horn, Tuba and Sousaphone; 1986 price data: $39 per complete kit including 100 test sheets, scoring masks, cassette tape, and manual ('84, 53 pages); $13.50 per 100 test sheets; scoring service, $.50 per test available ($10 minimum); (30) minutes; Edwin E. Gordon; G.I.A. Publications, Inc.*

Review of the Instrument Timbre Preference Test by RICHARD COLWELL, Professor of Music and Secondary Education, University of Illinois at Urbana-Champaign, Urbana, IL:

Gordon is the first researcher to suggest that preference for real or an "artificial" timbre is a predictor of success in the study of instrumental music. The claim is that when results of the Instrument Timbre Preference Test are combined with data from his own Musical Aptitude Test and together used to match students with the appropriate musical instrument, this will reduce dropouts and increase achievement in instrumental music. The test is a seven-item forced-choice (which of two timbres do you prefer?) test; seven different timbres are created by the Moog synthesizer, each representing the sound of a specific instrument or a group of related instruments (i.e., Timbre 1 = flute; Timbre 4 = oboe-English horn-bassoon). Gordon pairs each timbre with every other timbre (twice) and asks for a preference between them.

The highest possible score for a timbre is 12; for example, if one chose the flute in all of its pairings the flute score would equal 12.

Gordon's sole concern for criterion-related validity was whether experts could match the Moog sound with an actual instrumental timbre. A more appropriate concern for criterion-related validity would be whether the test aids in predicting success on the accepted objectives of school instrumental music. Material in the test manual consists of a mixture of pedagogical suggestions, accurate technical data, unproven hypotheses, and some folklore. This material raises interesting and unanswered questions about what the test actually does measure.

Gordon's data for his control group are based on the responses of 165 nonparticipants in beginning instrumental music; a sample of 159 comparable subjects constitutes the source of data used by this reviewer. Gordon's experimental group consists of 34 nonvolunteers who studied an instrument selected for them on the basis of test scores. Twenty-two of these students completed a year of study.

Gordon obtains the highest mean score (greatest preference) for Timbre 4 (oboe-English horn-bassoon). This preference by students was confirmed by the reviewer's data. Preference for the pseudo-woodwind timbre over the brass timbre by most students was also confirmed. The reviewer, however, also found ethnic differences in preference for various timbres. In a sample of half blacks and half whites, no blacks scored 12 on clarinet timbre and no blacks gave a score of 11 or 12 to trumpets or trombone-baritone. Sixty-eight percent of the black students disliked the tuba (scores of 0–2) as compared to 35 percent of white students. The standard deviation for tuba timbre (7) was 2.73 with a median score of 1.44 for black students. Sex differences need to be investigated before accepting the independence of timbre differences.

The high mean score for double reeds is meaningless and not an indicator that most students should begin instrumental music by studying these instruments. All mean scores are generally irrelevant; the important data are the timbre preference scores of 0–2 and 10–12. These cutoff scores, apparently arbitrarily established by Gordon, are used in recommending or not recommending a particular instrument to a student. Unfortunately, no indication of the size of the student groups falling into these two groups is given in the manual. Our data indicate that Gordon would recommend between 23–34 percent of the students should begin on a double reed instrument; only 1–3 percent should be discouraged. For clarinet 5–10 percent should be encouraged; 1–7 percent discouraged. The similarity of Gordon's mean scores and our mean scores hints that Gordon's data are comparable.

Gordon's argument that a student will be more successful if he or she studies an instrument that has a personally pleasing timbre makes logical sense. Gordon fails to provide data, however, that present students find the timbre of their own instruments unpleasant and whether those who do are unsuccessful or drop out.

Timbre is a factor in preference, but preference is usually more subtle than that measured by Gordon. The difference between a pleasing and an unpleasant sound on an instrument is a finer discrimination than the comparison between a true French horn sound and that putatively attributed to preference for French horn on the test tape. Gordon also hints at this in suggesting that vibrato or special styles added to a timbre would be an invalidating factor. At that point in the manual, however, the author is making an argument for the synthesized sounds rather than for the genuine sounds.

His loose argument on the reasons for success would be disputed by experienced teachers, (e.g., "as much as 3 percent of the reason or reasons for students' success in instrumental music is associated with their physical and psychological well-being and their home and cultural environments"). Home and cultural environment are thought by most teachers to contribute more than 3 percent.

Gordon uses the test manual as much to promote his other publications as to provide data on this test. "*Jump Right In: The Instrumental Series* will prove to be the most appropriate." Gordon also urges use of the Musical Aptitude Profile or one of his two developmental aptitude tests throughout the manual.

Scoring the test requires the use of seven different templates to obtain the seven scores, a cumbersome and time-consuming procedure. Once the scores are recorded, the teacher is to use a colored marker to highlight high and low scores. Scores greater than 2 but less than 10 are presumably not used. As a preference test has no right or wrong answers, there are no norms; reliability is computed by test-retest and validity should be criterion related.

Gordon's pedagogical statements indicate his concern for unidentified talent and for not discouraging any student from instrumental music study. He states that more than 40 percent of the fourth and fifth grade students who score above the 80th percentile on his music aptitude tests do not volunteer to study a musical instrument. A 60 percent success rate in an elective course in any discipline, however, is commendable, even if 100 percent would be better. These extensive pedagogical arguments contribute little to understanding the value of the timbre preference test.

Gordon's test-retest reliability coefficient after one week is about .70. He reports reliability by grade, school, and test, providing 77 reliability figures that range from .46 to .93. Our reliability figures were only slightly lower and as varied. If the score on a single timbre preference is to be used in making a major decision, a user should expect more consistency than a reliability range such as that for timbre 3 (from .55 to .93). Preference is apparently affected by age. For example, Gordon provides data for students in grades 3–8 in one school. At third grade, students generally do not like the clarinet sound, giving it a mean score of 5.2. The preference score increased to 5.8 at fourth grade, 6.6 in fifth, 7.1 in sixth, and then begins to drop off: 6.7 for seventh grade students and 6.3 for eighth graders. The preference ranking is of greater importance. At third grade the clarinet sound is ranked 7 out of 7 but by fifth grade is ranked second, exceeded only by the saxophone-French horn timbre. Preference for clarinet stays second for 3 years only to fall precipitously among eighth graders. In this school, double-reed preference changed from 5.7 (tied for preference 5 or 6) to 8.2 in grade 6. The highest mean score for any timbre at any grade level in any school is 8.2.

Gordon argues the fact that timbre preference is not related to music aptitude contributes to the construct validity of both his aptitude test and this preference test. The argument is weak and negatively constructed. A manual dexterity test would reveal the same low correlation without providing credence for construct validity of either test. The argument for construct validity, along with the test's recommended use, implies that Gordon believes that instrumental timbre preference is an additional component of musical aptitude. Like the extensive reporting of mean scores that are not pertinent to test interpretation, the reporting of low correlations between timbre scores and IQ scores does not advance the argument for predicting success in instrumental music.

When students did not volunteer to study an instrument but were selected based upon their timbre preference as revealed by this test, they did not join the band. Only 20 percent of these students enrolled as opposed to 92 percent and 83 percent of the students from groups where students had selected their own instrument. Selected students, however, were more successful as judged by performance of three études. A preference test that has little relationship to wanting to play the instrument and produce these pleasing timbres yourself is only one of the questions raised by Gordon's research.

Through the publishing of an instrumental-timbre-preference test, GIA and Edwin Gordon have again raised the issue of the components of success in instrumental music. Gordon's conclusion that aptitude plus timbre preference is a more powerful combination than consideration of motivation, home background, and diligence is not convincingly supported by his data. Had the instrumental timbre data been paired with results from an aptitude test other than the author's, a more convincing argument would have been made. The large dropout rate in the experimental school system, the relatively poor quality of the test tape, and the lack of a rigorous test development schema, despite the innovative aspects of providing free use of an instrument for 2 years for nonvolunteers, add up to the need for considerable additional research before Gordon's Instrumental Timbre Preference Test can attain the credibility of his research in musical aptitude.

Review of the Instrument Timbre Preference Test by PAUL R. LEHMAN, Professor and Associate Dean, School of Music, The University of Michigan, Ann Arbor, MI:
Instrumental teachers have long realized that motivation is enormously important in determining success in instrumental study. They also know that one of the most important aspects of

motivation is the love that some children seem to have for their instruments, and certainly a part of that magical attraction stems directly from the sound of the instrument.

Gordon has sought to document these bits of conventional wisdom and at the same time to provide a test to help identify students' preferences concerning timbre. His test is based on seven synthesized timbres, each of which is "intended to represent the timbre of one or more woodwind or brass instruments." By using carefully controlled synthesized sounds he eliminates the extraneous factors of dynamics, intonation, tempo, phrasing, and expression (although it sounds as though some of the examples are played more legato than others).

The test is simple and straightforward. Each timbre is paired twice with each other timbre. Thus, there are 12 comparisons for each of the seven timbres. In effect, there are seven separate tests.

The student is asked to indicate whether the melody "sounds better" the first time or the second. According to Gordon, a student who chooses a given timbre 10 or more times reveals a distinct preference for that tone quality and should be encouraged to study an instrument represented by that timbre. His assumption is that, other factors being equal, students will do better if they like the sounds of their instruments.

Some students may show more than one preference. Some may show no preference. Because the test is based on preferences, there is no composite score and no norms are provided.

Based on previous studies, Gordon claims that music aptitudes account for approximately 56% of students' success in beginning instrumental music. Another 4% is related to intelligence, he suggests, while 12% represents error of measurement, and 3% has to do with the students' physical and psychological well being and their home and cultural environments. Of the remaining 25%, according to Gordon, at least 10% is associated with timbre preference.

Because of the nature of the test, the only practical way to determine reliability is by the test-retest method. The reported test-retest reliabilities for the seven timbres, based on 11 groups totaling 642 students in grades 3 through 8 in three schools in the Philadelphia area, are more or less evenly dispersed from .46 to .93, with a median of .72. There is a remarkable lack of central tendency in the reliability coefficients from one group to another within each of the timbres, but one should remember that there are only 12 test items for each timbre.

The ultimate question, of course, is what do the test results mean? The answer must be based in part on how closely the timbres "represent" real instruments. To a musician they do not sound much like the instruments at all. They sound like organ stops. One reason is that they lack the distinctive attack and decay characteristics of real wind instruments. Their harmonic content is not stated.

It is not surprising the trombone and baritone are grouped together and represented by one timbre. It is not especially surprising the French horn is grouped with them. But it is surprising the horn appears a second time sharing a timbre with the saxophone. Can one timbre be sufficiently similar to both the French horn and the saxophone that the test results are valid? How can the test identify a student who might prefer the sound of the horn to all other instruments when the horn is represented by two different timbres?

It would have been possible, of course, to reproduce the sounds of the instruments much more closely. Gordon chose not to do so in order to "represent" more instruments. Some teachers might prefer that he had used timbres more like those of the real instruments even if that meant representing fewer instruments. Several of the instruments included are instruments that most teachers do not start beginners on anyway. The less similar the timbres are to those of actual instruments the less useful the test results are.

As evidence of "criterion-related validity" (but actually representing content validity), a study is reported in which 50 music professors and teachers and 136 members of a university band were asked to name the instrument or instruments "represented by" each timbre. Most members of both groups associated each timbre with more than one instrument, but "at least one actual instrument that the test author had previously associated with each of the timbres . . . was associated with the same timbre by a majority of persons in both groups." Given there were two hearings, and that a written list of instruments was provided to work from,

these results scarcely constitute a ringing confirmation that the associations are close.

One way out of this uncertainty is to seek evidence of predictive validity. A longitudinal study is described in which 33 students playing instruments for which they displayed a timbre preference on the Instrument Timbre Preference Test achieved higher scores on three performance measures after 1 academic year of study than did 47 students playing instruments for which they had not displayed a timbre preference. The three measures included an étude prepared in class, an étude prepared independently by the student, and an étude that was sightread. The difference for the combined scores was significant at the .05 level. Still, this is a very small number of cases upon which to base evidence of predictive validity. Additional evidence based on larger samples should be gathered in the future.

This test is the only one of its kind. It is technically excellent. The manual is well written. It bristles with good suggestions and timely caveats. The test is inexpensive and easy to administer in groups. The premise on which it is based is sound. The extent to which instrumental teachers may find it useful will depend entirely on how much confidence they have in the information it yields.

[32]

Kinetic Drawing System for Family and School: A Handbook.. Purpose: "Assessing the pervasiveness of a child's difficulties across both the home and school settings; identifying home/family issues which explain school attitudes or behaviors, or school/classroom issues that affect home behaviors (or both); and isolating setting-specific relationships or interactions which contribute to the child's difficulties or may be available as therapeutic resources." Ages 5–20; 1985; KDS; a combination of the Kinetic Family Drawing and Kinetic School Drawing; 5 diagnostic categories: Actions Of and Between Figures, Figure Characteristics, Position/Distance/Barriers, Style, Symbols; individual; 1986 price data: $21.50 per 25 scoring booklets and handbook ('85, 82 pages including scoring booklet); $7.90 per 25 scoring booklets; $15 per handbook; (20–40) minutes; Howard M. Knoff and H. Thompson Prout (handbook); Western Psychological Services.*

TEST REFERENCES

1. Champion, L., Doughtie, E. B., Johnson, P. J., & McCreary, J. H. (1984). Preliminary investigation into the Rorschach response patterns of children with documented learning disabilities. *Journal of Clinical Psychology*, 40, 329-333.

2. Prout, H. T., & Celmer, D. S. (1984). A validity study of the Kinetic School Drawing technique. *Psychology in the Schools*, 21, 176-180.

3. Knoff, H. M., & Prout, H. T. (1985). The Kinetic Drawing System: A review and integration of the Kinetic Family and School drawing techniques. *Psychology in the Schools*, 22, 50-59.

4. Wood, B. (1985). Proximity and hierarchy: Orthogonal dimensions of family interconnectedness. *Family Process*, 24, 487-507.

Review of the Kinetic Drawing System for Family and School: A Handbook by BERT P. CUNDICK, Professor of Psychology, Brigham Young University, Provo, UT:

The Kinetic Drawing System for Family and School: A Handbook is *not* a technical manual that describes the systematic formulation of a test. There is no guiding rationale for the creation of a task. There are no focused scores with accompanying data concerning reliability. There are no norm groups showing the distribution of scores in various kinds of groups and there is no real evidence of systematic attempts to determine validity. In short, this Handbook is not a report of a test; it is rather a compendium of sources regarding a technique that has been used by many people in many different ways.

The technique described in this Handbook consists of two different administration formats with slightly modified sets of instructions. Instruction 1 is, "Draw a picture of everyone in your family, including you, DOING something. Try to draw whole people, not cartoons or stick people. Remember, make everyone DOING something—some kind of action." Instruction 2 is, "I'd like you to draw a school picture. Put yourself, your teacher, and a friend or two in the picture. Make everyone doing something. Try to draw whole people and make the best drawing you can. Remember, draw yourself, your teacher, and a friend or two, and make everyone doing something." After the tasks are finished separate inquiries are made regarding each drawing. A rather lengthy series of questions are suggested that might be presented to the child completing the tasks regarding each person represented in the drawings.

After the drawings and inquiries are completed, it is suggested that the examiner utilize a "scoring booklet" provided for an analysis of the drawings. The scoring booklet consists of various components of five characteristics of the drawings: Actions Of and Between Figures; Figure Characteristics; Position, Distance, and Barriers; Style; and Symbols. Subcomponents for each characteristic are also given and the examiner is to indicate whether the component is present or absent.

The subcomponent present or absent element is never used additively to arrive at a global score that has a fixed meaning, rather each element present is given a suggested clinical hypothesis that stems from some published source dealing with the technique.

Nine case studies with background and referral information, observations during assessment, drawings, inquiries, and the characteristics and hypotheses are presented. The background information is sketchy, and the inquiry information very brief. The reviewer expected the presentation of an inquiry protocol with questions and responses. Instead only a limited number of responses were presented. In addition, the inquiry is not scored and, apparently, is not a source of hypotheses, except for those responses which might have veracity and, hence, face validity.

There is a section in the Handbook that presents information regarding norms, reliability, and validity. The major difficulty with this section is that it is a potpourri of information on various scores and interpretative schemes that are not systematically related to the protocol developed by the authors. Hence, they may be of interest to those using figure drawings, but they have limited utility at best when attempting to use the present-absent and hypothesis model partially developed in the Handbook.

In fairness to the authors, they do not purport to have a test; rather they indicate that their approach "primarily involves a hypothesis-generating and hypothesis-testing model, rather than a procedure focused on differential diagnosis . . . the clinician chooses hypotheses to entertain and test further based on his or her knowledge and experience with the child."

The Handbook provides a useful summary of literature related to the use of family drawings. In addition, the protocol developed by the authors could indeed lead one to generate hypotheses. These cookbook formulations might be substantiated by cross validation with independent sources; however, there are no traditional group test data to support such a hope. At present the system developed by the authors is in its infancy; in fact it appears only conceived, yet to be developed.

Review of the Kinetic Drawing System for Family and School: A Handbook by RICHARD A. WEINBERG, Professor, Educational Psychology and Co-Director, Center for Early Education and Development, University of Minnesota, Minneapolis, MN:

This Handbook is an attempt to synthesize current research on and interpretation of the Kinetic Family Drawing (KFD) technique and the Kinetic School Drawing (KSD), both of which were developed in the early 1970s. Knoff and Prout contend that drawings such as these can be used in multiple ways for personality assessment—as a sample of behavior in a semistructured situation, as an "ice-breaker," and especially "as a projective technique which assesses a child's perceptions of relationships among the child, peers, family, school, and significant others."

The Kinetic Drawing System argues the advantage of using both the KFD and KSD, "comparing the two differentially." The authors provide a good summary of the history of projective drawings, highlighting the contributions of Goodenough, Harris, Buck, Machover, and Koppitz. The introduction of action into the KFD family drawings by Burns and Kaufman (1970) ("draw your family *doing* something") is seen as having increased the qualitative and quantitative diagnostic information available in drawings. Developed by Prout and Phillips, the KSD directs attention to interactions in school environments.

Accompanying the Handbook is a sample scoring booklet that includes a list of questions to be asked as part of the inquiry phase, after the child has completed the KFD and the KSD. The inquiry process "attempts to clarify the child's drawing and investigate the overt and covert processes which affected its production." The scoring booklet lists five diagnostic categories used for interpretation: Actions Of and Between Figures; Figure Characteristics; Position, Distance, and Barriers; Style; and Symbols. A major portion of the Handbook is a summary of interpretive hypotheses for each characteristic, providing "empirical" data when available as well as indications of clinical evidence. For example, crossing out and redrawing an entire figure may indicate the individual's true or idealized feelings toward the person (Burns & Kaufman, 1970); drawings of a school principal could reflect "signifi-cant concerns or conflicts over issues of power, authority, structure, rules" or "may imply the need for a male identification figure" (Sarbaugh, 1982). Thirteen pages of such hypotheses are presented, drawn from a literature dominated by Burns and Kaufman. This material is followed by nine detailed case studies, representing children between the ages of 5 and 16. The latter will be especially intimidating to "non-believers" of projective methods.

In the final and perhaps most important chapter of the Handbook, Knoff and Prout present the psychometric case for the Kinetic Drawing System and its component drawing techniques. In a nutshell, the case continues to be weak (Gersten, 1978; Harris, 1978). There are a few reported normative studies, primarily done in the early 1970s. No new normative data are provided in this Handbook for either the KFD or the KSD. Two major conclusions about the reliability of the KFD are:

1. High interrater reliability can be achieved when scoring criteria are clearly defined and judges are trained adequately. (Four different "objective" scoring systems are presented with limited data on their objectivity.)

2. Poor test-retest stability is reported, but this is interpreted as "suggesting that certain KFD variables are sensitive to children's transitory personality states."

Although limited data on the KFD's validity are presented, one study evaluated the technique's ability to discriminate among children who were clinically labeled. McGregor (1979) concluded that the KFD is not a valid instrument for discriminating "normal" and "clinical" children. Knoff and Prout counter that "the KFD and other projective techniques may still serve a useful function by identifying state-oriented personality/behavioral issues that may be significant to a child." Unfortunately, even less psychometric data are provided for the KSD technique.

In his foreword to the Handbook, Robert C. Burns articulates well the historical tension between the science of psychometrics and the clinical artistry of projective techniques. Burns argues for clinical validity "as a beginning to ask more sophisticated and wise questions." Unfortunately, patience wears thin, waiting for other kinds of validity data. To date, as reflected in this Handbook, the accumulated psychometric underpinnings for projective drawings, in general, and the Kinetic Drawing System for Family and School, in particular, are lean.

Depending upon one's theoretical biases and penchants, cautious use of projectives as a basis for generating clinical hypotheses may have a place in the professional practice of psychology. But the age of accountability, especially in schools, demands that greater psychometric credibility be demonstrated for kinetic drawings. There are multiple steps in approximating the construct validity of our assessment tools (Anastasi, 1986); more vigorous attempts must be made to take these steps in validating drawing techniques.

In summary, the Kinetic Drawing System for Family and School: A Handbook is an excellent synthesis of up-to-date research on and interpretation of kinetic drawing techniques. Unfortunately, however, clinical validity is the primary support offered for their use. While one could confidently recommend the use of kinetic drawings as an "ice-breaker" and "rapport-builder" in the assessment process, one cannot defend the projective interpretive system presented in this Handbook.

REVIEWER'S REFERENCES

Burns, R. C., & Kaufman, S. H. (1970). *Kinetic Family Drawings (K-F-D): An introduction to understanding children through kinetic drawings.* New York: Brunner/Mazel, Inc.
Gersten, J. C. (1978). [Review of Kinetic Family Drawings.] In O. K. Buros (Ed.), *The eighth mental measurements yearbook* (pp. 882-884). Highland Park, NJ: Gryphon Press.
Harris, D. B. (1978). [Review of Kinetic Family Drawings]. In O. K. Buros (Ed.), *The eighth mental measurements yearbook* (pp. 884-886). Highland Park, NJ: Gryphon Press.
McGregor, J. P. (1979). Kinetic Family Drawing Test: A validity study. *Dissertation Abstracts International,* 40, 927B-928B.
Sarbaugh, M. E. A. (1982). Kinetic Drawing-School (KD-S) Technique. *Illinois School Psychologists' Association Monograph Series,* 1, 1-70.
Anastasi, A. (1986). Evolving concepts of test validation. *Annual Review of Psychology,* 37, 1-15.

[33]

Leadership Skills Inventory. Purpose: "Assess strengths and weaknesses in the area of leadership." Grades 4–12; 1985; LSI; self-administered and self-scored; 9 categories: Fundamentals of Leadership, Written Communication Skills, Speech Communication Skills, Values Clarification, Decision Making Skills, Group Dynamics Skills, Problem Solving Skills, Personal Development Skills, Planning Skills; 1985 price data: $29 per complete kit; $14.95 per 25 inventory booklets; $10.50 per activities manual (52 pages); $14.35 per administration manual (19 pages); $14.95 per computer version; (45) minutes; Frances A. Karnes and Jane C. Chauvin; D.O.K. Publishers.*

Review of the Leadership Skills Inventory by BARBARA A. KERR, Assistant Professor of Counselor Education, The University of Iowa, Iowa City, IA:

The Leadership Skills Inventory (LSI) holds promise as an instrument for self-assessment of leadership skills; more research is needed, however, before it can be used confidently for this purpose. The major difficulty with the inventory lies in the inadequate establishment of its validity.

The LSI comprises nine domains presumed to be related to leadership skills: Fundamentals of Leadership, Written Communication Skills, Speech Communication Skills, Values Clarification, Problem-solving Skills, Personal Skills, and Planning Skills. It is not clear, however, that the construct of "leadership skills" is adequately represented by the instrument. A thorough review of the literature was performed, according to the authors, and the reference list appearing at the end of the manual is a listing of major sources. However, the absence of elements of leadership considered important in much of the social psychology and industrial organizational psychology literature—such as interpersonal influence skills and leadership development skills—is puzzling. A group of adult professionals and a group of youth participants in youth organizations served as panels to review the items developed by the authors, and to make suggestions. The literature review and the use of the panel for item review constituted the only validity research. The use of instruments such as 4-H's Life Skills for Leadership (Miller, 1984) or the Need Dominance Scale of the Edwards Personal Preference Inventory (Edwards, 1953) could have helped to establish concurrent validity. A study comparing the performance of proven young leaders (e.g., successful organization officers) with nonleaders would have lent credibility to claims of construct validity for the LSI. More work is clearly needed before the inventory can be considered to measure what it intends to measure.

The reliability data presented by the authors show the inventory to be internally consistent, with split-half and Kuder-Richardson reliability coefficients mostly in the .80s for the seven regional samples. (A total of 452 students participated in the development of the instrument.) Test-retest reliability was found to be quite low in the one sample featuring this procedure, with six of the subscales having coefficients of .49 and under. Therefore some scales, particularly Fundamentals of Leadership, Personal Skills, and Planning Skills, may lack stability.

The instrument itself is simple, clear, and easily read by most children over 10 years of age. For each category of leadership skills, the respondent is given a set of competency statements followed by Likert 4-point scales anchored by *Almost Always* and *Almost Never*, (e.g., "I know how to get and use written information.") It seems likely that children might learn about the skills of leadership while responding to the inventory.

The authors assume truthful responding to the inventory. In fact, they say that individuals "can obtain a realistic assessment of their current leadership skills. Due to the self-reporting and self-scoring format, individuals can obtain a more objective view of themselves, rather than being rated by others who may be less knowledgeable about the person's individual strengths and weaknesses." This is a novel usage for the word "objective"! Clearly, this instrument is not at all objective, but entirely subjective. Because it is a self-report measure which does not control for socially desirable responding, it would not serve well as a measure of leadership skills for purposes such as identification of potential leaders or selection for leadership positions.

However, the LSI is probably a good self-exploration and learning experience. The authors include a helpful manual of learning activities that form a basis for an experiential learning course in leadership skills. This inventory and activities manual deserve further study.

REVIEWER'S REFERENCES

Edwards, A. L. (1953). *The Edwards Personal Preference Schedule.* New York: The Psychological Corporation.
Miller, R. (1984). *Leader/agents guide/leadership life skills.* Stillwater, OK: Southern Region 4-H Materials.

Review of the Leadership Skills Inventory by STEVEN W. LEE, *Assistant Professor, Department of Educational and School Psychology, Indiana State University, Terre Haute, IN:*

The Leadership Skills Inventory (LSI) was developed to assess leadership skills of a wide range of individuals (age 9 to adults) in school and youth organizations as well as in business and industry. The LSI kit includes an adminis-

tration and an activities manual. The activities manual provides many diverse activities designed to help a group leader foster leadership skills among students. The LSI is an untimed test that can be administered in a group or individually. No special training is required of the examiner, and the LSI may be administered orally. The LSI administration manual states that the LSI is a "self-administered, self-scored inventory," although no scoring directions are provided to the examinee on the test form. The scoring for each of the leadership domains is fairly straightforward: The total raw score for each domain is plotted on a profile sheet that provides *T*-score conversions for each domain raw score. The obtained *T* score(s) can then be compared to the normative group. The instructions for administration properly point out that the LSI is an inventory and not a "test." The instructions are sufficiently clear for an understanding of what is to be done, but no examples or sample questions are provided.

Although the manual states that a "thorough review of the literature pertaining to leadership" was done, no clear method of item development is provided in the manual. Two panels of individuals evaluated the generated items and the "suggestions were incorporated." These panels included one group of professional persons from youth organizations and education, while the other group consisted of youths from the same organizations.

The norms are published in the manual; however, the administrative conditions under which the normative data were obtained are not clearly specified, except to say that the teachers were "forwarded the needed number of inventories and the preliminary manual which stated the purpose of the instrument and guidelines for administration." The normative group is comprised of 452 school children with a mean age of 14.6 years. Of this group, 207 were male and 215 were female, and they ranged in age from 9 to 18. The normative sample was obtained from students in California, Illinois, Kansas, Louisiana, Massachusetts, and Nebraska. The rationale for choosing the sample is not provided. No apparent stratification plan for representativeness of the normative sample was employed. As a result, the representativeness of the normative sample of the LSI can be called into question, particularly for important variables such as age, geographic region, rural vs. urban, income levels, or race.

Although normative data were obtained from various states across the U.S., it was not possible to ascertain the rationale for the geographic sampling procedure, because it is not provided in the manual. The manual states that the LSI is designed to assess leadership skills "at the upper elementary, secondary and post-secondary levels," and norms are provided for children ages 9 to 18. However, only a portion of the Louisiana sample ($N = 107$, mean age of 14.4 years) included students below age 12. Therefore, the age group 9 to 11 is inadequately represented within the normative sample. Since the norms are not reported by age, the LSI consumer cannot ascertain whether age differences were found or have been reported in the leadership literature. Scores by age for each leadership domain should be provided. The norms are reported in raw scores. The mean and standard deviation for each leadership domain is provided; however, no other measures of central tendency or variability are reported. Local norms are provided for the states previously mentioned; however, the samples for these norms are small and they vary in age range and male-female demographics. No other stratification characteristics are reported for the local norms in the manual.

The LSI manual reports estimates of internal consistency (Kuder-Richardson) of .78 or above for each leadership domain for the total sample. Somewhat lower estimates of internal consistency were found for the local norms, but none below .65. The domain entitled Fundamentals of Leadership tended to show the lowest estimate of internal consistency, while Group Dynamics displayed the highest. The temporal stability of the LSI was assessed only for the Louisiana sample ($N = 45$). Test-retest reliability estimates ranged from poor to fair in this sample, with the Fundamentals of Leadership domain exhibiting the lowest test-retest reliability (.30 over 4 weeks), and the domain of Speech Communication exhibiting the highest (.67).

No scorer reliability estimates are provided in the manual. In addition, no estimates of the Standard Error of Measurement (SEM) are reported. The SEM information would help to determine if the scores are sufficiently dependable for the intended use of the LSI.

A paucity of information regarding the validity of the LSI is presented in the manual.

Item content validity is purported to exist due to the expertise and creditability of the members of the panels who made suggestions on item content. However, the panels did not include personnel development specialists in business and industry for which the LSI is purportedly useful. No estimates of concurrent or construct validity are reported in the manual. As a result, we do not know whether the leadership domains of the LSI can empirically be shown to exist, nor do we have any idea of their relationship with other measures of leadership characteristics. Further, no plan for gathering these essential validity data is presented. Given these severe psychometric deficits, cautions should be elucidated by the authors as to the limits of generalizability of the results at the LSI; unfortunately, none are provided.

In summary, the LSI is a test which is purported to measure leadership skills. However, due to a lack of concurrent and construct validity estimates, no empirical confirmation is provided for the trait of leadership the LSI purports to measure. Therefore, it is not possible to ascertain whether the construct of leadership exists separate from other personality characteristics, let alone if separate domains exist within the construct of leadership. The internal consistency reliability of the LSI is high, but the data on temporal stability is weak at best. Fundamental information regarding how the items were developed and the rationale for obtaining the normative sample is not provided. The LSI normative group did not appear to be stratified, and has a very small and unrepresentative sample for certain age groups. The best use of the LSI may be as an informal tool to assess an individual's strengths and weaknesses in leadership-type skills and the use of the ideas in the activities manual for intervention strategies.

[34]

MAC Checklist for Evaluating, Preparing and/or Improving Standardized Tests for Limited English Speaking Students. Purpose: Aids in the review, critique, or preparation of ESL assessment instruments. ESL test developers, reviewers, and users; 1981; 5 criterion categories: Evidence of Validity, Evidence of Examinee Appropriateness, Evidence of Proper Item Construction, Evidence of Technical Merit, Evidence of Administrative Excellence; 1985 price data: $3.95 per checklist ('81, 71 pages); Jean D'Arcy Maculaitis; the Author.*

Review of the MAC Checklist for Evaluating, Preparing and/or Improving Standardized Tests for Limited English Speaking Students by EUGENE E. GARCIA, Professor/Director, Center for Bilingual/Bicultural Education, Arizona State University, Tempe, AZ:

With the continuing increase of students in U.S. schools whose native language is not English, a variety of educational professionals are called upon to make linguistic, intellectual, and academic assessments of these students. As part of these assessments, standardized instruments are likely to be utilized. In recent years the number of instruments available for the assessment of nonnative English speakers and the demand for the use of these instruments has increased. Moreover, the specific demand on educational personnel to judge the adequacy of these instruments provides evidence of the need for a guide to assist in the evaluation, preparation, and improvement of standardized tests for limited-English-speaking students.

The MAC Checklist provides an examination of the issues that should guide test users in determining the adequacy of a standardized test for use with limited-English student populations. It does so by providing: (a) 103 criteria regarding the psychometric and general characteristics of a standardized measure; (b) "rights" and tips for test takers; (c) selected sources of bilingual tests and testing information; and (d) a partial list of selected commercially available English-language measures. The MAC Checklist extracts from the larger testing literature those general aspects of testing that serve to determine a theoretically and methodologically sound measure. In addition, this checklist incorporates specific issues (cultural aspects of items, linguistic diversity, tester bias, etc.) of relevance in the assessment of language minority students. The MAC Checklist professes to be of assistance in test development and modification. Inasmuch as it details the attributes of a "good" test, the MAC Checklist addresses these two issues indirectly. Otherwise, the checklist does not directly deal with test development and modification.

The strength of the MAC Checklist is its direct and satisfactory treatment of standardized test-evaluation criteria. It does provide a useful summary of general test validity, reliability, and administrative criteria. The listing of English-language measures that have become available to educators is useful to professionals unaware of such measures.

Unfortunately for the language-minority professional, the MAC Checklist does not address specific issues of relevance to non-English standardized measures. For determination of educational status and treatment, language-minority students are subjected to assessment of (a) the native language, (b) English, and (c) native language and/or English academic achievement. The MAC Checklist primarily confines itself to issues of relevance to English language measures. In doing so, it is of limited usefulness to the practitioner. Moreover, even in its treatment of English measures, the MAC Checklist does not provide any discussion that will allow a user to determine a yes/no response to a criteria question (e.g., a tester is asked to make a judgement about the test's cultural relevance based on recent research findings; however, a novice test user may have no background to make that judgement).

Most significantly, the MAC Checklist was designed to be of direct assistance to teachers and school administrators. Unfortunately, the vocabulary and terminology used are highly technical and likely to be outside the expertise of a teacher or school administrator. The MAC Checklist is best utilized by the school psychologist or program evaluator. These professionals should already be well versed on test evaluation; however, this summary can be a handy and helpful reference.

As indicated earlier, the MAC Checklist provides one of the few listings of standardized instruments commonly used in language minority education efforts. However, no analysis is provided (i.e., how do these instruments fare when they are evaluated on the criteria identified by the checklist?). Such an analysis would be extremely helpful to the professionals for whom the checklist was developed.

In conclusion, the MAC Checklist can be of assistance in determining the appropriateness of English language measures developed for use with limited-English-proficient students. However, it is not likely to be of significant assistance to individuals who are not already aware of issues related to test theory and application. Moreover, this checklist is restricted to English language measures only.

Review of the MAC Checklist for Evaluating, Preparing and/or Improving Standardized Tests for Limited English Speaking Students by CHARLES W. STANSFIELD, *Director, Division of Foreign Language Education and Testing, Center for Applied Linguistics, Washington, DC:*

The MAC Checklist is a collection of guidelines for evaluating, selecting, and using standardized tests. The name "MAC" is associated with the author, Jean D'Arcy Maculaitis, who has also written a multilevel English-language-proficiency measure known as the MAC Test. The Checklist presents 103 questions about test materials, organized into groups called criterion categories. The user of the Checklist is to mark "yes" or "no" in a space to the left of each question. The Checklist is intended for test developers, reviewers, and users. It is divided into three parts.

Part I is a four-page introduction that describes the author's purpose and approach to developing the Checklist and gives an overview of the text. This information is interspersed with advice about the analysis of standardized tests.

Part II, Criterion Categories, is the main part of the text. The criterion categories are the question groups for evaluating tests. Category A, validity, contains 22 questions dealing with basic issues, including evidence of content validity, criterion-related validity, the availability of norms, subgroup information, and so on. One guideline asks whether the manual contains correlations between each item and the total score as evidence of validity. This question tends to confuse validity with discrimination. An item can be valid without being discriminating. Also, item discrimination values are not ordinarily reported in a test manual.

The second category of questions deals with examinee appropriateness. These 17 questions are intended to allow the reviewer of a test to assess the degree to which the test is suitable for examinees of specific age or grade levels and cultural or ethnic backgrounds. The questions relate to the relevance of items and pictures to the examinees, the adequacy of test directions, whether a sample test is made available to examinees, the quality of the printing and layout of test materials, and whether the time alloted is adequate and the pacing is appropriate.

The third criterion category, proper item construction, deals with the quality of the test items. These guidelines are the most valuable because most books on measurement slight the art of item writing. Maculaitis brings her test development experience to this section of the Checklist. The guidelines ask the test evaluator to assess whether items are written in concise and clear language, whether clues to the correct answer are found in earlier or subsequent items, whether more than one correct answer is possible for any item, whether all distractors are plausible, and whether assignment of keyed items to position (A, B, C, or D) is random. The author also suggests that items be examined in terms of whether content experts, or native English speakers in the case of an English-as-a-second-language test, could answer them correctly. One perplexing guideline is "Are the number of distractors related to the examinees' age/grade level?" This reviewer is not aware of any research suggesting a different number of distractors as optimum for students of different grade levels.

The fourth category, technical merit, pertains to test reliability. The 17 questions ask about the existence of parallel forms, the discrimination power of the test, the appropriateness of the reliability coefficients reported, and the general quality and usability of the technical manual. Again, a couple of guidelines are questionable. For instance, the author states, "Six months is the recommended maximum time interval between administrations of the same or an equivalent form of the test." The basis for this recommendation is unclear. For example, there is no reason why different forms of a test cannot be administered at the beginning and end of a school year to measure progress on a standardized test.

The final category deals with the quality of the instructions for administering the test. There are 20 questions concerning matters such as the qualifications of test administrators, proctors, and test score interpreters, number of proctors required, and so on. A number of questions pertain to the presentation of score interpretation data, such as the existence of norms for subgroups, and the explanation of standard scores. One unusual guideline asks whether the manual gives different norms for the different types of answer sheets that may be used with the test. Although this guideline may pose a legitimate research question, this reviewer is not aware of such a practice nor that it is even recommended by testing professionals.

Part II of the Checklist presents four appendices. These include lists of 50 basic rights of examinees and 50 hints for examinees in preparing for tests. Although these are useful, it is not apparent why they appear in a document that appears to be aimed at test developers, evaluators, and score users rather than examinees. A third appendix presents sources of information on testing and tests, particularly tests for the nonnative English speaker. The reader is urged to join specific professional organizations, including the National Association for Bilingual Education and Teachers of English to Speakers of Other Languages, to write for specific newsletters, and even to contact specific individuals at the New York State Department of Education. These appendices apparently are reprints of handouts that were used by Maculaitis in the testing workshops she offers in New York and New Jersey. The fourth appendix lists some commercially available tests that appear to satisfy her criteria. Few of these are tests designed for limited-English-proficient students.

Following a references section is a glossary of testing terminology used in the text. The glossary is the weakest section of the text. Many of the terms are explained inadequately. For instance, the author defines the Pearson Product-Moment Reliability Coefficient as "one of several methods used to compute reliability coefficients. (It is the preferred method because it more accurately reflects the differences between and among scores.)" The fact that such coefficients are measures of test-retest or parallel-form reliability is not mentioned. The sentence in parentheses contributes little to the definition, particularly since reliability involves only a single group of examinees.

The MAC Checklist seems to be a collection of handouts from a testing workshop. As such, it contains a number of useful questions that practicing teachers could ask when evaluating standardized tests. Its usefulness is limited to that of supplemental material, however. It should not be relied on or used in lieu of a comprehensive text in educational measurement or the *Standards for Educational and Psychological Testing* (APA, AERA, NCME, 1985). Several of the texts on second language

testing listed in the references section of the Checklist would also be more useful than the Checklist. Given its practical format, however, the Checklist may be of some value to a teacher who is in the process of evaluating the suitability of a test for a given purpose and population.

REVIEWER'S REFERENCE

American Psychological Association, American Educational Research Association, & National Council on Measurement in Education. (1985). *Standards for educational and psychological testing.* Washington, DC: American Psychological Association, Inc.

[35]
Macmillan Graded Word Reading Test. Purpose: "To provide a general set of guidelines for the teacher not only on the standard of reading reached by pupils but on what else may need to be required in the reading process." Ages 6–13; 1985; GWRT; individual; 1988 price data: £14.95 per 25 record sheets, teacher's manual (24 pages), and word card; (5–10) minutes; Macmillan Test Unit and Bridie Raban; Macmillan Education Ltd. [England].*

Review of the Macmillan Graded Word Reading Test by BRUCE A. BRACKEN, Associate Professor, Department of Psychology, Memphis State University, Memphis, TN:

The Macmillan Graded Word Reading Test (GWRT) is a sight-word vocabulary scale designed to assess a client's ability to read presented words. The GWRT is packaged in a plastic packet and provides a two-sided stimulus reading chart (two forms), Teacher's Guide, and a tablet of record forms. The test is appropriate for individuals between the ages of 6 years 0 months and 13 years 3 months.

The critique of the GWRT will be divided into three sections: (a) manual, (b) materials, and (c) psychometric adequacy.

MANUAL. The manual (Teacher's Guide) for the GWRT is markedly deficient for a test published in 1985. The user of the GWRT is provided with very little information on such important topics as item construction, item tryouts, item analyses, standardization sample characteristics, interpretation of the test, etc.

In addition to these glaring omissions, the manual is poorly written, with many examples of unclear referents (e.g., they, them), and unsupportable or unusable statements (e.g., "Recording these details is a valuable aid to constructing a suitable teaching programme." In this example, there is no elaboration as to how "these details" will facilitate program development, and in all honesty the solution is less than intuitively obvious.

Rather than providing a sound rationale for the use of sight-word reading tests, the test author provides a defense against common criticisms made toward such tests. It is the opinion of this reviewer that tests should stem from sound theory and rationale rather than in response to one's critics. If the test is theoretically and psychometrically sound, the critics will be hushed.

MATERIALS. The stimulus materials (Word Cards 1 and 2) are eye pleasing in color and layout. Words are nicely spaced and separated. With 50 words per card, the page presents an uncluttered view. Two criticisms of the Word Cards have to do with the size and characteristics of the stimulus words.

First, it is well known that young children read upper case (capital) letters more easily than lower case letters. The easiest words presented on the Word Cards (e.g., the, you, from) should have been printed in an upper case mode to facilitate recognition. These earlier words are larger than the most difficult words by approximately 100 percent in an effort to increase readability. However, this varied letter size leaves one with the feeling they are reading a familiar Snellen Eye Chart, rather than a sight-word list.

Second, more up-to-date reading lists have begun to provide a mix of nonphonetic sight words with those that can be deciphered easily through word-attack strategies (e.g., ache, sword, gnat). Words of this sort truly assess the child's current sight-word reading vocabulary, rather than phonetic deciphering skills.

PSYCHOMETRIC ADEQUACY. The GWRT fails miserably in terms of its demonstration of technical adequacy. The lack of available information on item construction leaves one asking, "Why these words? What kind of item gradient exists? What about content validity?" and so forth. There are no answers to these questions in the Teacher's Guide.

While the Guide provides information on administration and scoring, a minimal number of examples are provided to aid the examiner in those odd cases that eventually surface. The standard scores, converted from obtained raw scores, are also explained minimally. The mean and standard deviation of the standard-score system are not provided, nor are percentile ranks. Thus, the meaning of the converted standard scores is of no greater value than the raw score; neither are easily interpreted in a norm-referenced fashion.

The manual deals with reliability by explaining the test/retest reliability of .85 is an alternate analysis of the KR-21 coefficient of .92. These are not alternate analyses, but both are equally important, depending on which aspect of reliability one is concerned with— stability or internal consistency. This is not explained to the reader and either assumes more psychometric sophistication on the behalf of teachers or the lack of sophistication of the test developer. The samples upon which these coefficients were determined are not described, and the length of the test-retest interval is not identified.

The manual reports nonsignificant sex- or region-related differences. Again, no description of the sample is provided for these studies and the actual obtained scores are not presented in the manual for the reader to inspect.

The standardization sample is not described in detail, and thus its representativeness is unknown. Subject selection according to race, gender, age, socioeconomic, and geographic variables are not described in the Teacher's Guide. However, the manual does reveal that the test was normed in England. Hence, no American norms are available.

The validity of the GWRT rests on a single comparison with the Macmillan Group Reading Test. Not only is this one comparison inadequate in number and description; the comparison of the individual test with its "big brother" group test will surely result in spuriously high correlations.

CONCLUSIONS. This reviewer acknowledges that sight-word reading tests have considerable utility. I have no a priori opposition to them as such. I do believe, however, that tests developed during this current decade should reflect the psychometric advances made during the past century. The publishers of the GWRT seem to have taken a Rip Van Winkle nap and missed out on at least 2 decades of advances in test development. It is recommended that the GWRT not be used, especially in the United States, until it is sufficiently developed to warrant such use. More elaborate development and reporting is needed before this test reaches a minimal standard suitable for public use.

Review of the Macmillan Graded Word Reading Test by DEBORAH B. ERICKSON, Assistant Professor of Psychology, Rochester Institute of Technology and Monroe Community College, Rochester, NY:

The Macmillan Graded Word Reading Test is a 50-word, 5-to-10-minute reading-recognition test developed and standardized in Great Britain. The test is designed to assess reading ability for ages 6 to 14 years. The authors of the test indicate that it is useful, in a qualitative sense, for older students who are below grade level in reading.

The test purports to yield information on grade-level ability and sight vocabulary versus trial and error vocabulary. The test provides for the analysis of errors in word beginnings, word endings, middle of the words, vowels, long vowels, consonant clusters, words inside words, mispronunciations, and reversals. Results are shown through standard scores and reading-age scores.

The test was designed despite recent criticisms toward word-recognition tests. Most reading experts believe reading words in isolation, rather than in context, is of limited use in the interpretation of the total reading process. Also, word-sample sizes are so small in this type of test that any interpretation about reading ability must be made with extreme caution. However, the authors report that 60% of current teachers use word-recognition tests on a regular basis and will probably continue to use such tests due to their simplicity and speed.

The authors believe a thorough explanation of the limitations of word-recognition tests will reduce the abuse of this type of screening instrument. While the authors emphasize the need for a full battery of diagnostic assessment instruments for a diagnostic/prescriptive analysis of reading, the introduction section of the manual describes the test as allowing teachers to monitor standards, investigate the range of reading attainment in a school or class, and examine individual progress in reading if used at appropriate intervals. The authors indicate this test facilitates analysis of errors yielding diagnostic information that teachers can use to plan educational strategies in the teaching of reading.

The section of the manual describing the directions to be given to students is clear and concise. However, basal levels are not specified.

A chart of reasonable starting places is given with directions to credit unread words and to return to an "earlier point" of the test if a mistake is made. While the basal is vague, the ceiling is specific. Failure on five consecutive words ends the test. Directions for scoring are clear and easy to follow. The record sheet is divided into words with columns to allow for the investigation of diagnostic information. The section in the manual discussing the interpretation of the use of this diagnostic information is clear. However, the design to make the word-recognition test more useful by allowing elaborate analysis of errors actually makes the test results more susceptible to abuse. While the use of a word-recognition test may be minimally useful as a screening device, inferring diagnostic information from a sample of 20 to 30 isolated words is not appropriate.

The technical data section of this test does not follow basic test design standards recommended by the joint committee of the American Psychological Association, the American Educational Research Association, and the National Council on Measurement in Education (1985). The sections on item selection, standardization, validity, and reliability are vague and ambiguous.

The item-selection process and the item analysis are not described thoroughly. Standardization of the test was done exclusively in Great Britain. The words and the sequence of difficulty may not be appropriate for use in the United States. While the norming procedure is described in general demographic characteristics, the sample sizes in each area (e.g., sex, residence, geographic area) are not specified. The manual did indicate that updated norms would be made available later due to the small numbers involved in the initial standardization process.

The section on reliability states that "two halves" of the test were correlated, yielding a reliability coefficient of .85. The paragraph then indicates that an alternative method of analysis based on the Kuder-Richardson Formula 21 yielded a reliability of .92. Due to this limited and vague information, the reliability of the test is questionable.

There are other psychometric flaws. Concurrent validity is determined through correlation of the Word Recognition Test with the Macmillan Group Reading Test and with teacher estimates. The validation process is not reported in detail and the one chart demonstrating correlation coefficients is unclear with regard to what comparisons were made. Objective criteria for teacher estimates are also not specified. The lack of information regarding content validity is significant. A systematic examination of item selection and analysis is essential to determine whether the test actually is a representative sample of the behavior domain to be assessed. In addition, reference to construct validity would have been appropriate in light of the controversy over use of word-recognition tests.

SUMMARY. This 50-word, 5-to-10-minute test is designed to yield a reading grade level and a diagnostic evaluation of reading errors. While the directions and interpretation sections of the test manual are generally clear and concise, there are serious concerns with the technical adequacy of the test design. The test manual does not meet the standards recommended by the joint committee of the American Psychological Association, the American Educational Research Association, and the National Council on Measurement in Education (1985). In addition, the exclusive development and standardization in Great Britain limits the use of this test in the United States.

There is a curious paradox in the design of this word-recognition test. The test is a screening instrument with cautions against interpreting a student's total reading ability from 20 to 30 words in isolation. The development of a pattern analysis of these words, however, contradicts the authors' caution against abusing the test in this way.

The test is not recommended for use in the United States. Furthermore, administration and interpretation of any word-recognition test must be done with an awareness of its limitations.

REVIEWER'S REFERENCE

American Educational Research Association, American Psychological Association, & National Council on Measurement in Education. (1985). *Standards for educational and psychological testing*. Washington, DC: American Psychological Association, Inc.

[36]

Macmillan Group Reading Test. Purpose: "A means of monitoring standards of reading and investigating the range of reading attainment in a school or a class." Ages 6-3 to 13-3; 1985; 2 forms; 1988 price data: £4.50 per 25 tests; £4.50 per teacher's manual (23 pages); (30) minutes; The Macmillan Test Unit; Macmillan Education Ltd. [England].*

Review of the Macmillan Group Reading Test by KORESSA KUTSICK, Assistant Professor of Psychology, James Madison University, Harrisonburg, VA:

The Macmillan Group Reading Test is a teacher-administered, multiple-choice test of reading skills. The test was designed for use with children of reading ages 6-3 to 13-3. Two primary reading tasks are included in this test: The first involves picture recognition (students select one of five words that identifies a picture printed in the response booklet); and the second involves sentence completion (one of five words is selected that best fills a blank space in a presented sentence). Two forms of this test (A and B), which are purported to be equivalent forms, are provided. Average administration time is 30 minutes; however, the test has no specific time limit. The Macmillan Group Reading Test provides for transformation of raw scores into standard scores and reading ages.

The overall format of the Macmillan is quite simple. Students complete 48 items that are divided into the two types of tasks discussed above. Due to the limited number of reading tasks presented, the test should be primarily considered a screening tool as opposed to a comprehensive reading test. Publishers of the Macmillan list the utility of this test as: (*a*) a means of obtaining and recording standard reading scores for students; (*b*) a method of comparing student reading skills within a class and within a school; (*c*) an instrument for documenting student progress in reading-skill acquisition; and (*d*) a screening device for identifying students who are poor readers for placement into various kinds of instructional reading groups. Cutoff scores for poor performance are described; however, no diagnostic information regarding specific reading deficiencies can be generated from performances on the Macmillan Group Reading Test.

A Teachers' Guide for the Macmillan is available and discusses administration and scoring procedures in a concise manner. The test is easy to administer and takes little technical skill to score. Clear directions and examples are given regarding the conversion of raw scores to standard scores and reading-age levels.

Psychometric data presented in the Teachers' Guide include information on test construction, reliability, and validity. The Macmillan Group

Reading Test was normed on 7,500 students who attended five of the largest school districts in England. This sample was reported to be representative of various geographical areas of the country; however, no information was given as to socioeconomic stratification. The test publishers noted that items and test scores were analyzed to demonstrate that the instrument did not discriminate on the basis of sex or geographical region; however, no specific data were provided to support this statement.

Reliability of the Macmillan Group Reading Test was reported as correlations between the alternate forms of this scale. Positive correlations (ranging from .85 to .94) between these forms across different age levels were reported. No other reliability data were presented.

The validity of the Macmillan Group Reading Test was demonstrated through a number of procedures. Test items were reviewed by teachers for appropriateness of vocabulary and item difficulty. More formal item analyses were not reported. Additional validity measures were obtained by comparing obtained test scores to teachers' estimates of students' reading skills as well as to test scores obtained on other reading instruments. Moderate to high positive correlations were obtained between the Macmillan Group Reading Test and teachers' estimates of reading skills and student performances on the Schonell Graded Word Reading Test, the Holborn Reading Test, the Young Group Reading Test, the Primary Reading Test, the Kent Reading Test, and the Macmillan Graded Word Reading Test. These instruments are commonly used in English infant, junior, and secondary schools.

The Macmillan Group Reading Test appears to be an adequate reading screening tool. Its use in the United States would be limited, however, by the fact that the test was normed in England. For use in England, the test would provide little additional information than that generated by such instruments as the Primary Reading Test or the Kent Reading Test.

In summary, the Macmillan Group Reading Test is a fairly well constructed, easily administered reading-skills screening tool. Its primary advantage appears to be in its brevity. Adequate reliability and validity information is available; however, additional work in this area would enhance this test. The Macmillan Group Read-

ing Test would be most appropriate for use in English schools.

Review of the Macmillan Group Reading Test by GAIL E. TOMPKINS, Associate Professor of Language Arts Education, University of Oklahoma, Norman, OK:

The Macmillan Group Reading Test (MGRT) is a multiple-choice word-reading test consisting of 48 items. In the first five items, students select a one-word label for a picture, and in the following 43 fill-in-the-blank items, students select a word to complete a sentence. Two color-coded equivalent forms of the test are available.

The MGRT is published in England, and a few Briticisms and British English spellings are used in the test, restricting its usefulness for American students. One form has three items and the other form has five items with British English spellings (e.g., flavour for flavor) or words with British meanings (e.g., chemist for pharmacist).

The authors cite four purposes for the MGRT: (*a*) to monitor standards of reading, (*b*) to investigate the range of reading attainment in a school or class, (*c*) to assess individual progress with reading, and (*d*) to evaluate the effectiveness of various approaches to reading instruction. The authors acknowledge that the MGRT is less useful in assessing reading fluency and comprehension, and they suggest that criterion-referenced tests and informal testing procedures should also be used in evaluating individual students' reading levels and in determining appropriate placement for reading instruction.

A crucial consideration in choosing this test or any word-reading test is whether emphasis at this level can produce an accurate measure of reading ability. The Teacher's Guide does not address this question except to say that this test should be one test in a battery of reading tests at a teacher's disposal. No information is provided about how the words were selected for inclusion in the test, only that a group of teachers evaluated the appropriateness of the words.

The MGRT can be administered to a class of students with reading ages from 6.3 to 13.3 under normal classroom conditions and within a 30-minute period. The test is not timed, but according to the Teacher's Guide, 30 minutes is adequate time for most students to complete the

48-item test. Clear directions for administering the test are provided. The teacher introduces students to the test using two practice items (one picture item and one fill-in-the-blank sentence item) and then students complete the test independently, by circling the correct word for each test item. At the teacher's discretion, older students may skip the five picture items and begin with the fill-in-the-blank sentence items. Students receive credit for the omitted items when the tests are scored.

The MGRT is hand scored using scoring keys for each form that are included in the Teacher's Guide. Standardized scores and reading-age scores may be calculated from raw scores, and some information is provided in the Teacher's Guide about using the test results and interpreting the standard scores and reading-age scores.

Approximately 7,500 students in five of the largest school districts in England were tested to generate normative data. Validity was estimated in two ways. First, validity estimates were calculated by correlating student scores on MGRT with teacher estimates of these students' reading abilities. Correlations, by grade level, ranged from .76 to .89. Second, validity was established by correlating scores on MGRT with scores on other reading tests. For example, student scores on the MGRT were correlated with their scores on the Macmillan Graded Word Reading Test, and correlations ranged from .70 to .86 according to grade level test. Correlations were also reported for five other reading tests at particular grade levels.

Reliability was estimated through the alternate forms procedure, correlating student scores on Forms A and B. Reliability coefficients by grade level ranged from .85 to .94, indicating a high level of agreement between the two forms. No information is provided on the internal consistency of test items.

In summary, the MGRT appears to be a useful instrument in a teacher's battery of reading tests. It can be quickly administered to a class of students and easily scored to produce standardized scores. A high correlation exists among the MGRT, teachers' evaluations of students' reading achievement, and other word-reading tests. However, the philosphical question of whether the MGRT, a word-reading test, can adequately measure reading achievement remains.

The suitability of the MGRT for American students must be carefully considered. The test was standardized using English students and other reading tests published in Great Britain. Also, Briticisms and British English spellings that American students will find unfamiliar were used in several test items.

[37]
Maculaitis Assessment Program, Commercial Edition. Purpose: "Designed for the purposes of: 1) selection, 2) placement, 3) diagnosis, 4) proficiency and 5) achievement" of non-native speakers of English in grades K–12. ESL students in grades K–3, K–1, 2–3, 4–5, 6–8, 9–12; 1982; MAC: K–12; 6 levels; individual; 1985 price data: $195 per MAC: K–12 sampler set including technical manual (296 pages), examiner's manual (142 pages), and 1 each of all other test materials; $19.10–$31.80 per sampler set for any one level; $32.50 per technical manual; $18.45 per examiner's manual; Jean D'Arcy Maculaitis; The Alemany Press.*

a) BASIC CONCEPTS TEST. ESL students in grades K–3; 8 scores: Color Identification, Shape Identification, 2 Number Identification scores (Counting, Spoken), 2 Letter Identification scores (Alphabet, Spoken), Relationship Identification, Total; (15–20) minutes.

b) MAC K–1. ESL Students in grades K–1. 7 scores: 2 Oral Expression scores (Asking Questions, Connected Discourse), 3 Listening Comprehension scores (Commands, Situations, Minimal Pairs), Vocabulary Recognition, Total; (25–30) minutes.

c) MAC 2–3. ESL students in grades 2–3; 16 scores: 2 Oral Expression scores (Answering Questions, Connected Discourse), 2 Vocabulary Knowledge scores (Identification, Noun Definition), 4 Listening Comprehension scores (Identifying Words, Counting Words, Answering Questions, Comprehending Statements), 6 Word Recognition Skills (Alphabetizing, Recognizing Vowels and Consonants, Recognizing Long and Short Vowels, Using Word Families, Determining Singular and Plural Forms, Recognizing Silent Letters), Reading Comprehension, Total; (79–89) minutes.

d) MAC 4–5. ESL students in grades 4–5. 15 scores: 2 Oral Expression scores (Asking Questions, Connected Discourse), Vocabulary Knowledge, 4 Listening Comprehension scores (Positional Auditory Discrimination, Answering Questions, Comprehending Statements, Comprehending Dialogues), 4 Reading Comprehension scores (Recognizing Homonyms, Recognizing Antonyms, Recognizing Abbreviations, Reading Outcomes), 3 Writing Ability scores (Grammatical

Structures, Pictoral, School Information), Total; (119–134) minutes.

e) MAC 6–8. ESL students in grades 6–8; 11 scores: 3 Oral Expression scores (Answering Questions, Asking Questions, Connected Discourse), 3 Listening Comprehension scores (Answering Questions, Comprehending Statements, Comprehending Dialogues), 2 Reading Comprehension scores (Vocabulary, Reading Outcomes), 2 Writing Ability scores (Grammatical Structure, Application Forms), Total; (108–123) minutes.

f) MAC 9–12. ESL students in grades 9–12; 11 scores: same as MAC 6–8; (108–123) minutes.

Review of the Maculaitis Assessment Program by J. MANUEL CASAS, Associate Professor of Counseling Psychology, and DAVID STRAND, PhD Candidate in Counseling Psychology, Department of Education, University of California, Santa Barbara, CA:

Recent increases in the number of immigrants coming into the United States has resulted in a significant increase in the number of students in grades K–12 who are nonnative speakers of English. This increase coupled with consequent legislative action in various states has created a pressing need for instruments that can be used by schools to assess the English proficiency of such students and in turn place them in the most appropriate instructional program. The Maculaitis Assessment Program (MAC) was developed in response to this need.

The test batteries that comprise the MAC were designed to assess the English language competencies of limited-English-proficient (LEP) students in the four basic language skills: listening, speaking, reading, and writing. Relative to each of these skills, the MAC focuses on the functional meaning of language and emphasizes the vocabulary and structures needed by the language learner to respond appropriately in specific situations. Furthermore, the subtests, especially the reading subtest, focus on very important but often overlooked aspects in assessing English proficiency. For instance, "the selection of the correct answer in the reading comprehension subtest must involve interpretation of each passage, not merely matching the words in the choices with the identical words in the passage, thus requiring a careful reading of each passage."

The MAC has both norm-referenced and criterion-referenced applications. Consequently, according to the author, the information it provides can be used by school personnel for a

variety of purposes including selection, placement, diagnosis, proficiency, and achievement. Although providing minimal supportive evidence, the test also purports to provide teachers with the opportunity to spot vision problems and gain insight into the affective aspects of the student.

With respect to the content of the test materials, steps were taken to make the test both age and culture appropriate. A unique aspect of the MAC is the inclusion of sample test materials for levels 2–3 and above. The provision of such materials is extremely important for LEP students, who often lack test sophistication and experience. Separate sets of color-coded materials (i.e., booklets, answer sheets, scoring sheets, etc.) are provided for each of the six levels that comprise the test. Although in the long run this may turn out to be a positive attribute of the test, in the short run it gives the MAC a rather voluminous and complex appearance that could potentially discourage testers from using it. To prevent this from happening, the publishers might consider providing workshops to any school district seriously considering using the MAC. Furthermore, future revisions of the MAC should consider the consolidation of all materials into a shorter and more manageable package.

The MAC contains both examiner and technical manuals. The technical manual provides extensive information on validation and standardization procedures, scoring, reporting, understanding, and using test results. The manual states that experts—including professors of tests and measurements, foreign language, and ESL/BE education, and certified ESL/BE classroom teachers—were used to establish content validity. Very methodical piloting procedures were followed to establish the validity of each subtest and of the testing program as a whole. Great care and detail were given to identifying the discriminatory power of the test items. In general, all the validity and reliability data reported throughout the piloting process are very acceptable. Extensive data are provided to demonstrate test fairness and to insure that the MAC is not ethnically or sexually biased for those for whom it was designed. While the MAC provides data showing the relationship between specific subtests and school grades, it would be helpful if future revisions of the test provided information on its concurrent validity vis-a-vis instruments currently used to assess English proficiency.

At present, national norms for the MAC are lacking. Consequently the MAC norms apply only to those urban public school districts and urban private and parochial schools whose enrollment includes non-English proficient and/or limited-English-proficient kindergarten through 12th-grade students from low- and middle-income families. The author does contend, however, that the lack of national norms neither diminishes the appropriateness nor the usefulness of the MAC for any school district. Additional data from varied school districts across the United States are needed to affirm this contention.

The examiner's manual goes into great detail describing the MAC materials and provides information relative to the administration and scoring of the test. Careful reading and use of the examiner's manual will facilitate standardized administration of the MAC.

There is no doubt that much of the information contained in both manuals is a positive attribute of the MAC. Unfortunately, although the author contends the manuals provide information in a quick and concise manner, the fact of the matter is that both manuals are quite formidable in length. The information they provide is exceedingly detailed and, oftentimes, redundant relative to testing in general and the MAC assessment process in particular. For instance, 67 pages of tables are presented to demonstrate that the MAC is not ethnically or sexually biased for those for whom the testing program was designed. In future revisions of the MAC, a careful editing of the manuals should occur in order to ensure that all needed information is provided quickly and concisely.

In summary, the Maculaitis Assessment Program was developed to assess the English language competencies of LEP students. The information it provides can be used for a variety of purposes including selection, placement, diagnosis, proficiency, and achievement. Extensive efforts were taken to demonstrate both its validity and reliability. National norms are lacking; consequently the generalizability of the instrument is somewhat limited. To insure standardization in its administration, detailed procedural information is contained in the examiner's manual. Although the MAC has many positive aspects, the numerous materials provided to assess kindergarten through 12th-grade students give this instrument a voluminous and complex appearance that could potentially discourage testers from using it.

Review of the Maculaitis Assessment Program, Commercial Edition by EUGENE E. GARCIA, Professor/Director, Center for Bilingual/Bicultural Education, Arizona State University, Tempe, AZ:

The continued growth in the number of language minority students requiring linguistic and educational assessment has challenged present-day test developers. These students come from a variety of native language and cultural backgrounds, necessitating extreme precautions in the administration and interpretation of standardized measures. However, such measures are required by state statutes with the intent of assisting local schools in meeting the needs of these diverse limited-English-proficient students. Few highly reliable, valid comprehensive English language and literacy measures are available for grades K–12. The Maculaitis Assessment Program (MAC) is among these few.

The MAC consists of six assessment packages designed to assist in the selection, placement, and diagnosis of language minority students through the comprehensive evaluation of English language proficiency and English literacy. The theoretical framework of this assessment package considers as important the vocabulary and structural forms needed by a language learner to respond to "real-life" contexts and the diverse communicative needs and functions of the student. At early grade levels the assessment focuses on receptive and expressive proficiency of English vocabulary, phoneme differentiation, interrogatives, connected discourse, letter identification, and other morphological and syntactic abilities. At later grades (grades 2–12), reading and writing assessments are added. Overall, each grade level assessment provides a comprehensive evaluation of a student's English language proficiency by taking into consideration various structural aspects and communicative functions.

Both a highly descriptive examiner's manual and a thorough technical manual serve to inform the potential test administrator. The examiner's manual provides brief but necessary descriptions of the skills tested, theoretical rationale, and the contents of the MAC. A complete description of examiner qualifications and proper testing conditions/preparations is also made available. These descriptions combined with those provided in the actual test booklets assist in assuring appropriate use of this measure. The technical manual provides comprehensive data useful in judging the psychometric adequacy of the instrument including validity, reliability, and score interpretation information. Standardization procedures, populations, and data are available for review. Significantly, data regarding gender and home language background for the norm-referenced populations are available for use in interpreting scores. The authors are to be congratulated for the comprehensiveness and usability of these manuals.

Unfortunately for the language minority professional, the MAC does not address specific issues of relevance to non-English standardized measures. For determination of educational status and treatment, language minority students are subjected to assessment of (*a*) the native language, (*b*) English, and (*c*) native language and/or English academic achievement. The MAC confines itself to measures of relevance to English language and literacy. In doing so, it limits its usefulness to the language minority practitioner.

In summary, the MAC is a comprehensive measure of English language proficiency and English reading and writing. It can be of specific use in the identification of limited English proficiency as well as selected aspects of communicative functions. It is recommended for serious consideration by language minority educational professionals.

[38]

Mastery Test in Consumer Economics.
Purpose: Measures knowledge in consumer economics. Grades 8–12; 1984; performance objectives in 15 areas (Consumer in the Marketplace, Consumer in the Economy, Personal Money Management, Consumer Credit Fundamentals, Wise Use of Credit, Food Buying, Housing, Transportation, Furniture/Appliances/Clothing, Personal and Health Services, Banking Services, Saving and Investments, Insurance, Taxes and Government, Consumer in Society), and total score; 1985 price data: $26.50 per test kit including manual (23 pages), 20 test booklets, and 20 answer sheets; $12 per 20 test booklets; $12.50 per 50 answer sheets; $5.50 per manual; $9 per specimen set; STS scoring

service, $1.10 per student ($20 minimum); 30(35) minutes; Les Dlabay; Scholastic Testing Service, Inc.*

Review of the Mastery Test in Consumer Economics by IRVIN J. LEHMANN, Professor of Measurement, Michigan State University, East Lansing, MI:

When I discuss the distinctions between criterion and norm-referenced tests (hereafter referred to as CRTs and NRTs respectively) in my testing courses, I do so in terms of the following differences between the two: (*a*) CRTs are designed to *describe* the strengths and weaknesses of an individual whereas NRTs are designed to *discriminate* among individuals; and (*b*) CRTs have a limited number of instructional objectives with many test items per objective whereas NRTs have a large number of objectives with just one or two items per objective. Both, however, share certain characteristics. For example, the principles generally espoused in measurement textbooks regarding the construction of test items, regardless of what type of test one is developing, are the same: The language should be unambiguous, there should be only one correct answer, there should be no clues in the item to reward the testwise student, etc. In addition, it is necessary for any achievement test, (but especially for CRTs) to demonstrate at least content validity and to offer some type of reliability evidence. Keeping in mind the purposes, psychometric properties, and item-writing practices of any CRT, let us look at the Mastery Test in Consumer Economics (MTCE) in greater detail.

The MTCE is a criterion-referenced test designed for high school students. The test has 45 items grouped into 15 major sections with each section representing a major consumer economic topic. Examples of these topics are The Consumer in the Marketplace, Housing, The Consumer in Society, and Taxes and Government. For each major topic "an overall objective . . . has been developed," and for each of these overall objectives three specific instructional objectives have been written, and one item has been written for each of these three specific objectives.

For example, the major overall objective for MTCE Saving and Investments is "The student will recognize factors related to savings and investments." The three specific instructional objectives are as follows: The student will be able to "(1) recognize the differences among various investments regarding rate of return, (2) identify factors considered by consumers when selecting an investment, and (3) recognize factors which affect stock [market] prices." The major topical sections and the specific instructional objectives within each section are reasonable for a CRT because they meet the requirements of knowledgeable people that a CRT should have a limited number of instructional objectives. However, a CRT, especially a mastery test, should have many test items per instructional objective. In this respect this reviewer feels the MTCE falls short. How confident can a teacher be that Johnny, for instance, has the knowledge needed "to recognize factors which affect food costs among various items" when only one item is used to measure this instructional objective? If I were the teacher, I would be very hesitant to draw any conclusion regarding my students' knowledge of consumer economics based on such a shallow sampling of the domain.

The test author claims content validity on the basis of the following statement: "Selection of test items was based on desired objectives, competencies, and knowledge as set forth in various state education agency and professional organization curriculum guides." This is fine, but what about test authors also consulting textbooks, curriculum specialists, and teachers? Surely sources such as these should have been used in developing the overall test blueprint, but regretfully they were not. This reviewer agrees that for any type of achievement test, be it CRT or NRT, content validity is the sine qua non. Unfortunately, although the test author may also have felt this way, limited information was presented to substantiate the claim for content validity.

There is dispute among some test developers and psychometricians regarding the application of traditional approaches of computing reliability estimates to criterion-referenced tests. Even among those who disagree with the manner in which a CRT's reliability is estimated, however, there is nearly universal agreement that CRTs should present evidence attesting to their reliability. The author of the MTCE apparently disagrees with most measurement persons. He presents no reliability data. Possibly even more disconcerting, at least to this reviewer, is the

fact that this psychometric property was not even alluded to in the test manual.

Two other psychometric properties—item difficulty and item discrimination—are a "must" for cognitive tests in general and achievement tests in particular. The author did present data on the former but not on the latter. The average ps for the 15 major sections ranged from .33 to .80, with all but two of the average ps being over .50. Seven of the sections were somewhat easier, with average ps of .70 and higher. This reviewer would have expected a CRT test like the MTCE to be easier. It goes without saying that the MTCE is *not* a mastery test despite the inclusion of mastery in the test name. It should also be noted that the item-validity data must be interpreted with the utmost caution because only 334 students in four Illinois high schools were used to compute the item-analysis statistics. This reviewer would be satisfied with a simple test standardization design; however, the sample description, consisting only of limited information such as the number of subjects, their locale, and their class standing, is inadequate. It is reported that 292 students were upper classmen. But how many were in grades 9, 10, 11, and 12? How many males and females? Surely the author could and *should* have provided the user with more information than "About one-half ($N = 173$) had completed a course in consumer education."

The author is to be commended for the quality of the multiple-choice test items. They are clear, the problem is in the stem, no clues to the correct answer are given the examinee, the options are listed logically, etc. However, this reviewer feels that in a few instances the distractors are not always plausible. And in a few instances one might disagree with the answer keyed as correct. For example, the author states that "The most reliable source of consumer information about a product may be obtained from the label." One of the foils provided is "other consumers." Why is that not correct? Is it not true that the only reliable information provided by the label pertains to the chemical composition of the product, its weight or volume, etc.? This reviewer believes that "the label" is correct only if one interprets consumer information in a very restricted sense. Other than these few instances, however, the quality of the items is very good.

The instructions for test administration are simple and clearly presented. Although it appears the test can be scored only by the publisher, there is no reason why the teacher cannot score the answer sheets. The scoring agency furnishes a score report that presents pupils' performance by objective, the percentage of the group answering each item correctly, the percentage of the group mastering each objective, and how each student performed (mastered/nonmastery/partial mastery) on each item/objective. Although we are told that an examinee must answer all three items to show "mastery" for a particular performance objective, no rationale is provided for this cutoff score.

Although the author supplies the user with a supplementary list of resource materials, little if any information is provided to either help the user teach economics or to help teachers diagnose pupil strengths and weaknesses. And if a CRT serves any useful purpose, it is to assist teachers in gaining a better understanding of their students' strengths and weaknesses. No test that has only three items per major objective can hope to do this validly.

In the final analysis, the test makes a good attempt to demonstrate content validity (albeit not too successfully) but is deficient in demonstrating reliability. The quality of the items is good except for a few instances where some improvement could be made. Regretfully, well written items do not a valid test make. The author is to be commended for using simple, yet realistic situations. If I were a consumer economics teacher I would be very careful to examine the test in relation to its validity and lack of reliability data. I would also be cautious in interpreting the item-analysis data, since the analyses were conducted on a very small, unrepresentative sample.

Review of the Mastery Test in Consumer Economics by LINDA JENSEN SHEFFIELD, Professor of Education and Mathematics, Northern Kentucky University, Highland Heights, KY:
The Administrator's Manual for the Mastery Test in Consumer Economics contains no information on validity or reliability. There is no evidence that either the 15 sections or the 45 individual items were ever analyzed for evidence of validity or reliability. Item difficulty data were obtained from 334 Illinois high school students. Students were from four different high schools—one urban, one rural, one suburban, and one university high school. Of these students, 292 were juniors or seniors, 173 had completed a course in consumer economics, and 161 had not completed such a course. The Administrator's Manual does not describe the students (e.g., gender, ethnicity, SES) in the report of difficulty data. The 334 scores were combined and the percentage of correct responses reported for each of the 45 items and 15 sections.

An overall objective is given for each of the 15 sections and it is then broken down into three more specific objectives for the individual test questions. These were based upon an analysis of goals objectives, competencies, and knowledge as defined by a variety of state education agencies and professional organizations. A list of these resources is included in the Administrator's Manual. A chart cross-referencing sections of the test to chapters in commonly used textbooks is also included, as are lists of supplementary instructional sources, periodicals, and newsletters. It is likely these would be useful to consumer economics teachers.

The tests may be hand scored by the teacher, and an annotated answer key with explanations for correct answers is part of the Administrator's Manual. A scoring service is also available that analyzes each item in terms of whether the item was correct, omitted, or which incorrect response was given. Mastery of each of the 15 sections is reported if the student answered all three questions correctly; nonmastery is reported for 0–1 correct responses, and partial mastery for 2 correct answers. Group scores are provided for both the percent correct and for the percent of mastery. Each student is compared to local norms. No national norms are available.

In summary, the author seems to have based his objectives upon a solid foundation of recommendations from professional organizations and state education agencies. The Administrator's Manual contains much useful information for teachers. Validity and reliability information is sorely needed. The authors may feel that content validity has been addressed through their careful item selection; however, they must do additional work to relate performance on the Mastery Test to performance on other measures. In addition, the small number of questions in each section raises concerns about reliability and adequate coverage of knowledge domains.

[39]

MD5 Mental Ability Test. Purpose: To assess mental ability quickly, easily, and over a wide range of educational and ability levels, in staff selection, placement and counselling. Supervisors to managers; no date on test materials; 1987 price data: £.45 per test booklet; £2.80 per scoring key; £5.50 per manual (17 pages); £7.85 per specimen set; (15) minutes; The Test Agency [England].*

Review of the MD5 Mental Ability Test by M. HARRY DANIELS, Associate Professor of Educational Psychology, Southern Illinois University at Carbondale, Carbondale, IL:

The MD5 Mental Ability Test was developed to provide a quick and easy-to-use test of intelligence for the purpose of selecting managerial and supervisory staff for large commercial organizations. It consists of 57 items selected from a larger item pool and administered in a standardized format. Test items assess both verbal/vocabulary and mathematical skills, including comprehension (1 item), vocabulary/semantic relationships (15 items), symbol relationships—answers as words or parts of words (16 items), alphabetical sequence relationships (6 items), symbol relationships—answers as letters (4 items), relationships between numbers and letters of words (5 items), symbol relationships—answers as numbers (1 item), mathematical relationships (9 items), and mathematical procedures (1 item). Items are arranged in order of increasing difficulty. There is a 15-minute time limit for completion. Thus, the test measures speed as well as power. The MD5 may be administered to individuals or groups as required.

Test materials include a test booklet, a scoring key, and a test manual. Directions for completing the MD5 require that responses to all test items must be made on the test booklet. Answers may be made in either pen or pencil, but erasures are not permitted (mistakes are to be crossed out). Answers require only the use of numbers, letters, or short words. The scoring key consists of a strip of posterboard on which the correct responses for each page of the test booklet are written. Answers are written in vertical columns so that they align with the appropriate answer columns in the test booklet.

Clear and concise directions for administering the MD5 are included in the manual.

Scores on the MD5 are determined by totaling the number of items answered correctly; there is no correction for either guessing or error. Raw scores are converted to percentile scores by using the MD5 percentile norms. These norms are based on the results of approximately 3,200 tests completed by middle and lower level managers, supervisors, and applicants for supervisory and managerial positions. Average scores among these groups appear to vary on the basis of education and work experience (the mean score for middle level managers was 39.0; 30.3 for lower level managers; and 26.9 for supervisors).

The manual contains very little information about the psychometric properties of the MD5. Thus, it is not possible to comment about either the internal consistency or the temporal stability of scores. Similarly, there is no empirical evidence concerning the predictive validity of the test, although the publisher asserts that it is "a useful test of mental ability for staff selection and placement at managerial and supervisory levels." On the other hand, evidence is provided demonstrating that MD5 scores correlate highly with the Watson-Glaser ($r = .52$) and the Guilford-Zimmerman II ($r = .62$).

EVALUATION. The MD5 is an example of a mental abilities test designed to serve a particular purpose: to select managerial and supervisory staff. When used with the specific population for which it was developed, it may be a very useful instrument. Due to the paucity of information about the psychometric characteristics of the test, and the lack of any independent evaluations of its content, construction, scoring procedures, and norms, it is difficult to comment on the overall quality of the instrument, or about its usefulness for other populations. The lack of evidence concerning its predictive validity represents an even greater limitation. Instruments like the MD5 are developed for the purpose of making reliable and accurate predictions concerning personnel and training. Considering the vast sums of money spent on such ventures, and the potential impact they may have on human lives, such predictors need to be as reliable and as accurate as possible. Because the MD5 does not provide adequate documentation of its predictive validity, caution should be a guide in its use.

Review of the MD5 Mental Ability Test by DAVID J. MEALOR, Associate Professor of School Psychology, University of Central Florida, Orlando, FL:

The MD5 was developed by Mackenzie Davey and Company "as a quick and easy-to-use test of intelligence," and was first used in 1972 to assist in the selection of supervisory staff for a large commercial organization in the North of England. The instrument was found to make a substantial contribution to the selection of supervisory staff and was extended to more senior levels including graduate management trainees. The author notes the primary focus of the MD5 is on the ability "to deduce relationships and to apply the rules governing them, which are generally considered to be fundamental components of intelligence." How these skills relate to supervisory functions and the weight given them in the selection of supervisory staff is not explained.

The MD5 consists of 57 items arranged in order of increasing difficulty. There is a 15-minute time limit and it is reported that the test is a measure of both speed and power. Examinees are instructed to work as "quickly and accurately as you can." The test can be administered either individually or in a group format. No specialized training on the part of the examiner is required, and the test may be administered by clerical level staff. The item content can be categorized into several areas: comprehension, vocabulary/semantic relationships, symbol relationships (answers as words or parts of words, letters, numbers), alphabetical sequence relationships, relationships between numbers and letters or words, arithmetical relationships, and arithmetical procedures. The manual provides a thorough description of administration and scoring considerations. All items require the examinee to figure out what letter(s) or figure(s) are missing, and to write them in the test booklet. The number of missing elements is determined by the number of asterisks [i.e., (black-white/short-tall/up-****), (2 4 8 16 **)]. Scoring is a simple procedure of placing a scoring key next to the answers written in the test booklet. A raw score is determined by the number of items answered correctly.

A description of the standardization sample is somewhat incomplete. While the author urges the need to construct "local norms" and make comparisons with specifically defined groups, the manual includes "some sets of norms whose data were obtained whilst the test was being developed." Unfortunately, additional demographic data regarding those in the standardization are not provided. This severely limits the use and generalizability of the MD5.

A review of the MD5 raises some serious questions. The technical documentation in the manual is woefully inadequate, and there appear to be a number of weaknesses in the development of the instrument. There is no discussion of how the items were selected or what relationship the item content has with the selection of personnel. Does a high score predict job related success? The test appears to measure a limited domain of cognitive behavior. Reliability and validity information is inadequate at best. It is noted that the instrument can be used with a wide range of educational ability levels, yet no information is presented to support this claim. The author claims there is no significant difference in performance based on sex of examinee. However, male and female performance is compared only with lower level managerial staff. It is unclear if this same pattern would hold true with other groups. A review of the raw score distributions (Appendix 1) is very disturbing. Supervisors appear to do much better than lower level managers, yet when mean scores for the groups are reported (Appendix 2), supervisors' mean scores are lower. No information is presented to determine if the MD5 does what the author intended. Comparative studies with other instruments would be most helpful.

In summary, the MD5 provides insufficient information to determine if it is a valid and reliable instrument. The item type and content limit its use with certain groups. The decision-making process warrants that instruments used be somewhat comprehensive in nature. At this time the MD5 does not appear to be that type of instrument. Significantly more work is needed with the norm groups and to establish the reliability and validity of this test.

[40]

Meadow-Kendall Social-Emotional Assessment Inventory for Deaf and Hearing Impaired Students. Purpose: "Can be used to flag students who need extra attention in particular areas . . . . useful in communicating with parents who are reluctant to admit that their child needs special attention . . . . helpful in implementing an individualized program so that social and emotional areas are emphasized in the curriculum for the child who needs them." Ages 3–6, 7–21; 1983; SEAI; behavior checklist to be completed by adult informant; 2 levels; 1987 price data: $5 per 10 forms; $15 per manual (37 pages); administration time not reported; Kathryn P. Meadow and others listed below; OUTREACH.*

a) PRE-SCHOOL. Ages 3–6; 5 scores: Sociable/Communicative Behaviors, Impulsive Dominating Behaviors, Developmental Lags, Anxious/Compulsive Behaviors, Special Items; Kathryn P. Meadow, Pamela Getson, Chi K. Lee, Linda Stamper, and the Center for Studies in Education and Human Development.

b) SCHOOL-AGE. Ages 7–21. 3 scores: Social Adjustment, Self Image, Emotional Adjustment; Kathryn P. Meadow, Michael A. Karchmer, Linda M. Petersen, and Lawrence Rudner.

TEST REFERENCES

1. Bolton, B., Turnbow, K., & Marr, J. N. (1984). Convergence of deaf children's sociometric scores and teachers' behavioral ratings. *Psychology in the Schools*, 21, 45-48.

Review of the Meadow-Kendall Social-Emotional Assessment Inventory for Deaf and Hearing Impaired Students by MARILYN E. DEMOREST, Associate Professor of Psychology, University of Maryland-Baltimore County, Catonsville, MD:

Development of the Meadow-Kendall Social-Emotional Assessment Inventory (SEAI) for Deaf and Hearing Impaired Students was motivated by the provision of Public Law 94-142, which requires a comprehensive assessment and individual educational plan for every handicapped child. The SEAI is designed for use by classroom teachers and includes observable behaviors that, at a theoretical level, are expected to reflect the social and emotional development of deaf and hearing-impaired children. One premise underlying the inventory is that development may be influenced by factors such as relative language deprivation and acceptance by significant others.

Test development procedures have ensured the content relevance of the items and the statistical integrity of the resulting scales. Content of the SEAI School-Age form was adapted from the School Behavior Check List (Miller, 1972) in consultation with more than 100 professionals knowledgeable about deaf chil-

dren. Items use a 4-point response scale ranging from *Very True* to *Very False* and describe both positive and negative behaviors in four categories: (a) sociability and interpersonal relationships, (b) individual or personal characteristics, (c) self-esteem or identity, and (d) maturity, responsibility, and independence. A 69-item Research Edition was administered to 2,365 children in 10 residential and day programs from the northeastern, north central, southern, and southwestern regions of the country. Other demographic characteristics of the sample are not reported. Ten items were eliminated for statistical reasons (low response rate, discrimination, or factor loadings) and the resulting 59-item School-Age form yields scores on three scales derived from factor analysis. Because of significant mean differences among some groups, normative data are given by gender and age group for the Social Adjustment and Self Image scales, and by age group for the Emotional Adjustment scale.

The Preschool form was developed with the same rationale and methodology as the School-Age form, which served as a starting point for item construction. A Research Edition containing 70 items was developed in consultation with teachers at the Kendall Demonstration Elementary School and 34 other professionals. Final revision and norming were based on a sample of 857 children from 54 programs in at least 10 states. Characteristics of the sample are more completely described than for the School-Age form. In addition to age and gender, information is provided on geographic distribution of programs by state, type of program, ethnic background of the child, age at onset of deafness, hearing level, and deaf relatives. Item selection procedures resulted in 46 items distributed among four scales. Three additional items related to deafness were retained as "special items" and scored separately, despite the fact that they failed to satisfy inclusion criteria. No rationale for this is given. For Scales 1, 2, and 3, norms are provided by age level and gender to reflect significant differences in mean scores among groups; for Scale 4 subgroup norms were not necessary.

Unpublished data on the reliability and validity of both forms of the SEAI are presented in the test manual but the studies are not described in detail and are quite limited in scope. For the School-Age form interrater reliability, test-retest reliability, and correlations of the scales with an index of sociometric status are reported, but the research is based on a sample of only six children from a single classroom. Some of the coefficients are quite high, but their sampling error is so large that little useful information can be derived. Further evidence of interobserver reliability and convergent validity are provided by two local studies, one conducted in Seattle as part of the evaluation of a social skills curriculum ($N = 61$) and one performed at Gallaudet College in which advisors, dormitory counselors, and parents completed the SEAI for deaf adolescents ($N = 81$) entering the Model Secondary School for the Deaf. Many of the obtained correlation coefficients are significant, and some are moderately high, but very little information is given about the samples and the conditions under which the data were collected. Consequently, the research methods and generalizability of the findings are difficult to assess. The only data reported for the School-Age form that do seem to rest on an adequate data base are the relationships between SEAI scores and the presence of other handicapping conditions in the norm sample. Given that additional handicaps were, predictably, associated with significantly lower scores on all three scales, there is some evidence of construct validity for the SEAI School-Age form.

Preliminary data are also given for the more recently developed Preschool SEAI. Test-retest reliability over a 4-week period was assessed in four preschool programs with a combined sample size of 159 children. Correlations between the SEAI ratings of teachers and teachers' aides are given for one of these programs ($N = 21$) and correlations of the SEAI scales with a global assessment of adjustment (provided by teachers in the norm sample) are also reported. As with the School-Age form, the studies are not reported in detail and are therefore difficult to evaluate.

Given that the SEAI is to be used in formulating an individual educational plan, it is essential that both interobserver and retest reliability be rigorously evaluated. Moreover, internal consistency reliability (coefficient alpha) should be reported for the norm samples since the data are already available. Because the inventories were developed to fill a particular assessment need, other comparable measures are not available for testing concurrent validity. Nevertheless, scores on the SEAI should correlate positively with other measures of social and emotional development as well as with behavioral criteria associated with that construct. Until such validity data become available, content-referenced interpretation of the scores is recommended.

In conclusion, the School-Age and Preschool forms of the SEAI fill an important assessment need for the hearing-impaired population. A judicious combination of theoretical premises, expert judgment, and data analysis has resulted in a set of scales whose potential construct validity appears great. However, there is a critical need for systematic, large-sample studies of the reliability and validity of the scales. Preliminary evidence reported in the manual is promising, but further investigation is needed if the full potential of the scales is to be realized.

REVIEWER'S REFERENCE

Miller, L. C. (1972). School Behavior Check List: An inventory of deviant behavior for elementary school children. *Journal of Consulting and Clinical Psychology*, 38, 134-144.

Review of the Meadow-Kendall Social-Emotional Assessment Inventory for Deaf and Hearing Impaired Students by KENNETH L. SHELDON, *School Psychologist, Edgecombe County Schools, Tarboro, NC:*

The Meadow-Kendall Social-Emotional Assessment Inventory for Deaf and Hearing Impaired Students (SEAI) was developed in response to the regulations of the Education for All Handicapped Children Act of 1975 (PL 94-142) and the need for an instrument to assess the social and emotional status of hearing-impaired students. Based on developmental theories and research pertaining to mental health problems of hearing-impaired individuals, the SEAI was designed for use with a wide range of hearing losses and to be used in a variety of special education settings. Two inventories were developed, one a revision of the 1980 SEAI for school age children and the other a downward extension of the SEAI for preschool and kindergarten age children. The goals that guided the development of each of these inventories included the sampling of positive and negative classroom behaviors, the creation of reliable subscales, and the generation of a final product that could be easily completed by an adult who has had contact with the student for at least 8 weeks.

SCHOOL-AGE FORM. The standardization sample was representative of both residential and day programs in states representing all but the northwestern United States. Participating sites were voluntary and not randomly selected. Through item analyses, feedback from site participants, and factor analysis, items were deleted and grouped into three subscales.

Interitem reliability (Cronbach's alpha) is in the .90s, indicating adequate item reliability. Based on ratings of six children, interrater reliability between a teacher and counselor varied for each subscale, ranging from .58 to .93. Using the same six students, test-retest reliability ranged from .79 to .86. Some evidence for concurrent validity is provided in a study ($N = 61$) in which the SEAI was correlated with the Health Resources Inventory and the Walker Problem Behavior Identification Checklist. The correlations ranged from .53 to .78. The authors believe that there is "variable but positive support for the meaningfulness of the inventory." The instrument does compare favorably with other behavior rating scales, such as the Burks Behavior Rating Scale, and seems valid. Additional data collection with larger samples is needed.

The SEAI package includes a manual and inventory booklet. The easily read manual includes a helpful scoring and interpretation sample. The inventory booklet is self-contained and includes everything needed to complete and score the inventory. The price of the inventory booklet may be prohibitive for some.

Instructions for completing the 59-item inventory require the informant to compare the child to both hearing and hearing-impaired individuals of similar age. Most items appear to be easily observed, except for item 2, "Kind and considerate," which is not as behaviorally stated as the others. A 4-point scale is used for scoring. Scoring involves some simple calculations which require attention to detail in order to avoid errors. Norms are reported as mean scores, and for two of the subscales the norms for boys and girls are separate. Also, the examiner will need to determine the chronological age since separate norms are reported for ages 7–15 and 16–21. Final scores are reported in deciles.

PRE-SCHOOL AGE FORM. This form is similar in most respects to the School-Age form in administration, scoring, and interpretation. Dif-

ferences noted are in the developmental sequence of the behaviors sampled and in the norms. Standardization procedures appear to be similar. Once again, the standardization sample was voluntary and not randomly selected. The geographical representation does appear to be more inclusive of all regions. Reliability is similar to the School-Age form and is adequate. There is, however, greater variability in scale reliability, with Scale 4 (anxious, compulsive behaviors) being the least reliable.

The test developers note the lack of validity studies and suggest instruments that can be used to conduct such studies. They do report one study that provides some evidence of validity. Results yielded low to medium correlations between teacher perceptions of the children and teacher ratings of the children using the SEAI. Like most preschool assessment instruments, reliability and validity are difficult to insure due to the changing behaviors of the developing child.

SUMMARY. This reviewer has found the SEAI to be useful in developing individualized treatment programs for hearing-impaired children. Compared to other behavior rating scales normed on hearing individuals, the SEAI is specific to the hearing-impaired population yet appears to measure the most important behaviors necessary for successful integration of any child into the educational setting. The reviewer concurs with the authors' cautions explicitly stated in the manual for using and interpreting the results. The results are only useful if completed after careful observation and should be used to identify students who need extra attention in areas of social and emotional development. Overall, the SEAI is a needed and useful addition to the small but growing list of assessment instruments for the evaluation of hearing-impaired children.

[41]

Measurement of Counselor Competencies: A Self-Assessment. Purpose: "Assesses counselor competencies necessary for the adequate performance of roles and functions." School counselors; 1973–74; ratings by self in 4 areas: Competency Level, Interest Level, Frequency, Demands; no manual (instructions and profile included on test); 1985 price data: $4.75 per manual; administration time not reported; Robert R. Percival, John W. Dahm, and Joseph D. Dameron; Dallas Educational Services.*

Review of the Measurement of Counselor Competencies: A Self-Assessment by RICHARD A. WANTZ, Associate Professor of Educational Psychology and Director of the Counseling Psychology Clinic, College of Education, University of Oklahoma, Norman, OK:

This self-assessment was designed for use by school counselors. The 18-page booklet containing this inventory provides no introduction, rationale (theoretical or otherwise), or references. The amount of time required to administer, score, and profile this inventory is not specified in the test booklet. The items appear to be chosen from some unidentified model regarding school counselors' roles and functions. Some items are broad in scope and difficult to rate. A manual is not provided; in general, the information provided in the inventory book is insufficient.

No evidence is provided regarding the psychometric properties of the instrument including external validity and reliability, nor is any normative data provided. The instrument has not been revised since the early 1970s. For example, a reference is made to the American Personnel and Guidance Association, which is known currently as the American Association for Counseling and Development. Also, since the early seventies the generic term "counselor" is less frequently used without qualifying the type of counselor: school counselor, rehabilitation counselor, marriage and family counselor, employment counselor, public offender counselor, etc. (Wantz, Scherman, & Hollis, 1982; Hollis & Wantz, 1983).

The four broad dimensions assessed—Counseling, Coordination, Consultation, and Organization and Evaluation—are logical but limited as areas to be assessed for a school counselor. No rationale is provided for choosing these or for not including other areas. Not addressed were such areas as career and life style planning, resource and information management, appraisal of students, and computer assisted career guidance systems and other utilizations of computers within an effective school counseling program.

The user would need to carefully match the counseling functions of his or her school against those assessed in this instrument. For example, users are asked to assess their ability to utilize only two specific counseling interaction skills (i.e., the Hill Interaction Matrix and the

Carkhuff Communication Scale). No provision is made for substitutions of other methods and techniques. Furthermore, no references are provided for these two approaches. It is unfortunate that a procedure is not provided to allow for adaptation of this instrument to meet local needs. Also it would appear appropriate to incorporate a "not applicable" response within the 1 (low) through 5 (high) response choices.

Profiling and assessment report worksheets are provided, but no assistance is provided in the form of suggested remedial interventions or references.

This instrument might be revised by a school counselor to incorporate specific job responsibilities in a local school setting. Without further research, development, and documentation it offers limited assistance for assessing school counselor competencies. This inventory is not recommended for use in its current state of development.

REVIEWER'S REFERENCES
Wantz, R. A., Scherman, A., & Hollis, J. W. (1982). Trends in counselor preparation: Courses, program emphases, philosophical orientation and experiential components. *Counselor Education and Supervision*, 21, 258-268.
Hollis, J. W., & Wantz, R. A. (1983). *Counselor preparation 1983–1985. Programs, personnel, trends* (5th ed.). Muncie, IN: Accelerated Development Inc.

[42]

Meeting Street School P.S.R. Test: Psychological S-R Evaluation for Severely Multiply Handicapped Children. Purpose: "Assesses the abilities of the severely multiply handicapped child," and provides alternate modes of response. Severely multiply handicapped children ages 1–5 and retarded severely multiply handicapped children ages 6–10; 1977; PSR; 2 scales: Auditory Language, Visual-Motor, plus a Tactile Differentiation section; individual; 1985 price data: $35 per complete set including 10 protocols, picture vocabulary cards and response cards, and manual (100 pages); $15 per 10 protocols; administration time not reported; Eileen M. Mullen; Meeting Street School.*

Review of the Meeting Street School P.S.R. Test: Psychological S-R Evaluation for Severely Multiply Handicapped Children by PATRICIA L. MIRENDA, Assistant Professor of Special Education and Communication Disorders, University of Nebraska-Lincoln, Lincoln, NE:

This instrument is designed to help fill the current void that exists in the area of assessment of children with severe multiple handicaps. It is composed of Auditory Language, Visual-Motor, and Tactile Differentiation subscales and is intended to provide a functional age (F.A.) score instead of a mental age (M.A.) score or intelligence quotient (IQ). The items in each subscale are arranged in chronological order from 0–1 month to 60 months for the Auditory and Visual-Motor scales, and from 0–6 months to 6 years for the Tactile Differentiation section. At least one, and up to six, references are provided as evidence for the developmental placement of each of the test items. The references are drawn primarily from assessment instruments that have been standardized for the nonhandicapped population, such as the Bayley Scales, (Bayley, 1969), Uzgiris-Hunt Scales (Uzgiris & Hunt, 1975), and the Stanford-Binet Intelligence Scale (Terman & Merrill, 1973).

The authors have changed the usual psychological assessment protocol in several ways to accommodate the needs of severely multiply handicapped children. The test (a) is not timed, (b) is to be administered by examiners who are familiar with severely handicapped children (not necessarily psychologists), and (c) provides suggestions for alternate (i.e., nonverbal) responses for most of the test items. The test manual includes information designed to help the examiner identify the stimulus modality (visual, auditory, or both) to which the child is responding. Finally, the examiner is encouraged to focus on the subscales that best suit the child's abilities, and to begin assessment at a level approximately 6 months below the child's anticipated F.A., thus allowing even more individualization and flexibility. The directions for administration of each of the test items are clearly spelled out and include reference to the materials needed, procedure to be used, and alternate responses considered acceptable.

There are also several significant problems with both the construction of the test and the protocol provided for it. First, the term "severely handicapped" is never defined, leaving the potential user in doubt as to whether the test is to be used with children who experience cognitive as well as other handicaps, or with children whose disabilities are primarily motoric and/or sensory in nature. This problem is exacerbated by the rather ambiguous statement in the test manual that "informal test data gathered over the past 2 years" indicates that the test "is particularly effective when testing very young severely multiply handicapped

children, ages 1 to 5, and older, *retarded* [italics added] severely multiply handicapped children, ages 6 to 10." The implication here is that the term "severely multiply handicapped" does *not* necessarily refer to a combination of motor/sensory problems plus retardation.

Second, aside from the normative references related to each test item, there are no reliability or validity data provided. In addition, it is unclear whether the authors primarily "borrowed" test items from the references listed, or whether the test items were created specifically for this test, using the normative information contained in the references as a guide. If the former is the case, it is unfortunate that no rationale is provided for how and why particular test items were selected from one test over others. It is also unfortunate that many of the references listed are inaccurate or incomplete, and that no bibliography is supplied for the sources cited. A related problem is that, while the authors note that the end product of the assessment is a functional age (F.A.) score as opposed to either a mental age or IQ score, the differences, if any, between F.A. and M.A. are not clear. The combined result of these ambiguities is that the potential user is left unclear as to how the test was constructed and what the results will indicate.

Third, the test provides no guidelines concerning implications of the assessment results for individual educational planning (I.E.P.) or curriculum development. This failure to discuss educational implications is problematic in that it implicitly encourages the unfortunate practice of basing I.E.P. goals on test items "failed," regardless of whether or not the skills tested by these items are relevant to the student's ability to engage in the meaningful, functional tasks necessary for maximum independence (Brown, Nietupski, & Hamre-Nietupski, 1976). Further, since the test is intended to measure only cognitive development and conceptual understanding, there are no subtest items related to skills in the areas of self-care, recreation/leisure skills, or other adaptive skills. This militates even further against the potential of using the assessment information to identify programming needs in functional curriculum areas.

Given the overall problems related to inadequate definitions of target population, absence of reliability and validity data, ambiguity about how the normative references relate to test development, and lack of direction regarding the implications of test results for educational programming, this evaluation tool appears to fall short of its intended goals. The primary advantages of the Meeting Street P.S.R. Test over already existing assessment tools seem to be the format of the test items and the provision for allowing alternate responses to be counted as "correct." However, the deficits would seem to outweigh the strengths in situations where a straightforward developmental assessment might be indicated.

REVIEWER'S REFERENCES

Bayley, N. (1969). Bayley Scales of Infant Development. New York: The Psychological Corporation.
Terman, L. M., & Merrill, M. A. (1973). Stanford-Binet Intelligence Scale, (3rd rev.). Boston: Houghton-Mifflin Co.
Užgiris, I. C., & Hunt, J. McV. (1975). *Assessment in infancy: Ordinal scales of psychological development.* Urbana, IL: University of Illinois Press.
Brown, L., Nietupski, J., & Hamre-Nietupski, S. (1976). Criterion of ultimate functioning. In M. A. Thomas (Ed.), *Hey don't forget about me!* (pp. 2-15). Reston, VA: Council for Exceptional Children.

Review of the Meeting Street School P.S.R. Test: Psychological S-R Evaluation for Severely Multiply Handicapped Children by DAVID P. WACKER, Associate Professor, Pediatrics and Special Education, University of Iowa, Iowa City, IA:

The Psychological S-R Evaluation (PSR) utilizes "stimulus and response item content [that] is designed to minimize the physical aspects of the tasks while tapping behavior which demonstrates acquisition of concepts traditionally associated with levels of intellectual development." The PSR consists of two scales: (*a*) Auditory-Language, and (*b*) Visual Motor. Both scales were "designed as a cognitive tool to assess verbal and visual-motor intelligence." Each of the scales consists of a four-step sequence beginning with basic attending behavior and ending with higher level concept formation. For children who have sensory deficits, either scale can be used for assessment. The PSR also contains a Tactile Differentiation Section which is intended to assess "tactile-kinesthetic awareness and discrimination abilities, as well as vestibular integration." The authors suggest that the PSR be used with severely handicapped children who cannot be assessed with traditional measures of intelligence.

The authors report that the PSR has been found to be especially useful in identifying learning styles in young multihandicapped children 1 to 5 years of age. The PSR provides what the authors call a "functional age" score, which is roughly equivalent to mental age scores achieved with other tests. The range in functional ages is from birth through 60 months, with increments ranging from 1 to 6 months. Directions/guidelines are provided for each item and detail the stimulus materials needed (some are included with the test), the testing procedure to be used, and the responses required.

A major strength of the PSR is the manual, which provides good information on who should administer the test, positioning of students, and the purposes of the test. In addition, relatively clear descriptions of all test items are provided.

Unfortunately, no information is provided on test construction, reliability, or validity. Given that the manual was written in 1977, perhaps reliability and validity data are available. If so, these data should be included in the manual. At present, the PSR should be considered an experimental tool of unknown reliability and validity. Additional data are needed before the PSR can be considered for use in applied settings.

[43]

Multidimensional Aptitude Battery. "Designed to provide a convenient objectively-scorable measure of general aptitude or intelligence in the form of a profile containing five verbal and five performance subtest scores." High school and adults; 1982–84; MAB; 13 scores: 6 Verbal (Information, Comprehension, Arithmetic, Similarities, Vocabulary, Total), 6 Performance (Digit Symbol, Picture Completion, Spatial, Picture Arrangement, Object Assembly, Total), Total; 1987 price data: $22 per machine-scorable examination kit including manual ('84, 94 pages), verbal battery booklet and answer sheet, performance battery booklet and answer sheet, and 1 coupon for computerized scoring; $33 per hand-scorable examination kit including same material as machine-scorable kit but with scoring templates and record form rather than coupon; $57.50 per 35 test booklets for verbal or performance battery; $16.50 per 35 answer sheets for verbal or performance battery; $6.50 per 35 record forms; $13.75 per scoring templates; $22 per cassette tape; $10.50 per manual; $3.50 per 6-page computer report; 35(50) minutes per battery; Douglas N. Jackson; Research Psychologists Press, Inc.*

TEST REFERENCES

1. Krieshok, T. S., & Harrington, R. G. (1985). A review of the Multidimensional Aptitude Battery. *Journal of Counseling and Development*, 64, 87-89.

2. Vernon, P. A., Nador, S., & Kantor, L. (1985). Reaction times and speed-of-processing: Their relationship to timed and untimed measures of intelligence. *Intelligence*, 9, 357-374.

3. Sternberg, R. J. (1986). Haste makes waste versus a stitch in time? A reply to Vernon, Nador, and Kantor. *Intelligence*, 10, 265-270.

4. Vernon, P. A. (1986). He who doesn't believe in speed should be aware of hasty judgments: A reply to Sternberg. *Intelligence*, 10, 271-275.

5. Vernon, P. A., & Kantor, L. (1986). Reaction time correlations with intelligence test scores obtained under either timed or untimed conditions. *Intelligence*, 10, 315-330.

Review of the Multidimensional Aptitude Battery by SHARON B. REYNOLDS, Assistant Professor of Education, Texas Christian University, Fort Worth, TX:

The Multidimensional Aptitude Battery (MAB) attempts to translate the basic ideas of the Wechsler intelligence measures into a format suitable for group administration. There are verbal and performance sections, each with its own test booklet, answer sheet, and scoring template. The answer sheets are standardized to correspond to the format of the test booklets. The test materials are color coded for each scale. The test booklet and answer sheet have a clear, readable format. Instructions and practice items are included in the test booklet.

MANUAL. An extensive manual is provided, including chapters describing the purpose, administration, scoring and standardization, construction, and psychometric properties of the MAB. The 12-page introduction to the manual includes a general description of the MAB, and a summary of constructs and theories of intelligence. The presentation is thorough and provides an adequate basis for understanding the place of the MAB in the context of the general notion of intelligence testing.

The description of the item selection and scale construction is preceded by a general discussion of test construction. The procedure for selecting items was clearly and thoroughly described. The items retained were selected after a series of item analyses. These analyses are described in detail in the manual. Empirical data are presented in support of the 7-minute time limit that was adopted as standard for the MAB.

Scale intercorrelations and factor analyses yielded support for the subscales being divided into Verbal and Performance scales. These data are fully described in the manual.

ADMINISTRATION AND SCORING. All necessary information for administration of the instrument is provided in an easily understandable form. Verbatim instructions are included in the manual. A cassette tape of instructions is also available. The test may be scored manually or by computer. Templates are provided for manual scoring. The templates are easy to use and are color coded to match the appropriate answer sheet to further reduce the probability of error. The MAB record form provides a simple way to record the scores and convert the raw scores to scaled scores. The layout of the record form and step-by-step directions make the recording and presentation of the scores simple and clear. The standard scores are converted to a Verbal IQ, a Performance IQ, and a Full Scale IQ by consulting an age-appropriate table provided in the manual. There are instructions for estimating a full scale score from administration of fewer than the standard five Performance scales.

STANDARDIZATION. The instrument was standardized by equating (calibrating) the MAB with the Wechsler Adult Intelligence Scale—Revised (WAIS-R). A thorough description of the method of equating was given, including the theoretical justification in terms of the application of sampling theory to test standardization. Adequate empirical evidence is presented to support the decision to use linear equating. The standardization group is adequately described as to both number and type of subject in the sample. The sample was heterogeneous with respect to age, gender, and source. The equating procedure was comprehensive and well described.

RELIABILITY AND VALIDITY. Reliabilities were computed for each age group from 15 to 20. The sample was adequate in size and was composed of males and females. These Kuder-Richardson Formula 20 reliabilities range from .94 to .97 for the Verbal Scale, .95 to .98 for the Performance Scale, and .96 to .98 for the Full Scale. Reliability data based on weighted composites, verbal/performance composite, and separately timed halves are also reported. Test-retest subtest reliabilities ranged from .83 to .97 (Verbal Scale) and from .87 to .94 (Performance Scale). Verbal Scale reliability was .95, Performance Scale was .96, and Full Scale was .97. All subscale reliabilities are reported, as are the standard errors of measurement.

Validity was assessed primarily by correlations with the WAIS-R. These correlations compare favorably with WAIS/WAIS-R correlations, which are also reported. Factor analyses of the MAB and the WAIS-R demonstrated marked congruence between the respective Verbal and Performance factors, with congruence coefficients of .97 for the Verbal factor and .96 for the Performance factor.

SUMMARY. The MAB appears to be a very good alternative to the WAIS-R in settings where group administration is appropriate. It has the advantages of standardized group administration without sacrificing reliability and validity. The empirical support for the test is impressive. The materials are easy to understand and use. The information provided in support of the instrument is thorough and provides an adequate basis for interpreting scores and evaluating the appropriateness of the test for the user's setting.

Review of the Multidimensional Aptitude Battery by ARTHUR B. SILVERSTEIN, Professor of Psychiatry, University of California, Los Angeles, CA:

For years, the instruments David Wechsler devised for the measurement and appraisal of adult intelligence have been among the most successful of all psychological tests, both scientifically and commercially. Douglas N. Jackson's intent in designing the Multidimensional Aptitude Battery (MAB) was to evaluate the degree to which it is possible to incorporate some of the positive features of Wechsler's scales into a test that does not require individual administration and scoring by a specially trained psychologist or psychometrist.

Like Wechsler's scales, the MAB consists of two groups of subtests: Five Verbal subtests are contained in one booklet, and five Performance subtests in another. Separate answer sheets that may be either hand or machine scored are provided for each booklet. Nine of the subtests have the same names as in Wechsler's scales (Digit Span is omitted and Spatial replaces Block Design), but the specific items are original and a multiple-choice format is employed throughout. Examiner's instructions are

standardized so the test can be administered by cassette, available from the publisher. Seven minutes are allowed for each subtest, and each half of the battery is said to require about 50 minutes for complete administration. For comparison, the Wechsler Adult Intelligence Scale—Revised (WAIS-R) is said to require from 60 to 90 minutes (of professional time) to administer.

Raw scores on the 10 subtests are first transformed into scaled scores with a mean of 50 and a standard deviation of 10 (on Wechsler's scales the scaled scores have a mean of 10 and a standard deviation of 3). The scaled scores for the two halves of the battery are summed separately to yield Verbal and Performance scores, and these two sums are added to yield a Full Scale score. Finally, the Verbal, Performance, and Full Scale scores are converted into IQs with a mean of 100 and a standard deviation of 15 (just as with Wechsler's scales), or alternatively, to standard scores with a mean of 500 and a standard deviation of 100 (as with the Scholastic Aptitude Test). A table is also provided so that an individual's subtest scores can be compared with those of people in the same age group, as for pattern analysis.

The procedure used to standardize the MAB is remarkable, for it was equated directly to the WAIS-R, using a rather small ($N = 160$) and extremely heterogeneous sample that took both tests: university and senior high school students, hospitalized psychiatric patients, and probationers from court-imposed prison sentences, of both sexes and ranging in age from 16 to 35 years. (Yet norms are provided for age groups up to 70–74.) In a partial check on the validity of the equating procedure, a large ($N > 5,000$) sample of Canadian high school students obtained an average Full Scale IQ of 103 on the MAB, which is very close to the expected value. Data are also given on the correlations between the MAB and the WAIS-R for a subset of the subjects in the equating sample. These range from .44 to .89 for the subtests and from .79 to .94 for the three scales, roughly comparable to the correlations between the WAIS-R and its predecessor, the 1955 WAIS. Nevertheless, much more research is required before scores on the MAB can be considered equivalent to those on the WAIS-R.

Additional information on the psychometric properties of the MAB includes internal consistency and test-retest reliability coefficients (generally > .95 for the three scales), data on the effects of speededness (they do not appear excessive), and the results of several factor analyses (yielding the same Verbal Comprehension and Perceptual Organization factors that are commonly found in Wechsler's scales).

Practitioners who stress the distinction between the psychological assessment of intelligence and the psychometric testing of intelligence (e.g., Matarazzo, 1972) will doubtless regard the MAB with skepticism (some, perhaps, with horror). Its author acknowledges that clinical observation of a subject's test-taking behavior is sometimes helpful, and that mentally retarded and some psychotic patients require individual administration, but he maintains that for most people individual administration is not only costly but unnecessary. Those who share this view are likely to find the MAB an attractive alternative.

REVIEWER'S REFERENCE

Matarazzo, J. D. (1972). *Wechsler's measurement and appraisal of adult intelligence.* Baltimore: Williams & Wilkins.

[44]

Multilevel Informal Language Inventory. Purpose: "Designed to measure a child's level of functioning in the production of critical semantic relations and syntactic constructions." Ages 4–12; 1982; MILI; no scores, semantic and syntactic developmental profiles in 8 areas: Verbs, Nominals, Modification, Interrogatives, Negation, Combining Propositions, Adverbs/Prepositions, Associative Language; individual; 1988 price data: $69 per complete set including examiner's manual (111 pages), picture manual, and 12 record forms; $15 per 12 record forms; $45 per picture manual; $25 per examiner's manual; (40–60) minutes; Candace Goldsworthy and Wayne Secord (picture manual); The Psychological Corporation.*

Review of the Multilevel Informal Language Inventory by ELIZABETH M. PRATHER, Professor of Speech and Hearing Science, Arizona State University, Tempe, AZ:

The Multilevel Informal Language Inventory (MILI) was designed to provide an efficient means of sampling 44 specific syntactic and semantic targets. Developmental profiles based on normal syntactic acquisition patterns are included. Ordering of constructions within syntactic categories is based upon a composite of findings from earlier research of Bloom and Lahey (1978), deVilliers and deVilliers (1972),

Miller (1981), and others. A check-sheet of semantic relations is provided, but sequenced order is not specified.

The MILI is designed solely for intrachild comparisons. The author uses multiple levels of tasks and probes to increase the child's opportunities to perform, to help the clinician select targets for an intervention program, and to monitor progress during the training program. No norms are provided and comparisons between children or among age-level counterparts are inappropriate.

The examiner's manual is clearly written and includes considerable detail on ways to analyze language samples. The picture manual is appropriate; it includes colored drawings with sufficient detail to provide clarity. Pictured and verbal stimuli are used to sample language at various task levels: (a) general survey level similar to traditional language sampling, as in "Tell me everything you can about this picture"; (b) specific survey stories based on story-retell from sequenced pictures; and (c) direct probes. None of the direct probes uses immediate imitation; rather three different elicitation levels are used for each potential target behavior (evoked spontaneous, elicited, and receptive understanding). For the user who wants a prepared set of stimuli to elicit language samples and a record form which provides a simple check-off system, the MILI may be very useful.

The MILI has major weaknesses. Field testing was completed with 45 children aged 4 to 12 years, but only to determine whether test stimuli produced desired responses (to allow for the revision or elimination of confusing or inappropriate stimuli). No intrasubject (test-retest) or interexaminer reliability is provided, and neither are age-level norms. Further, this test is much more effective in analyses of syntactic structures than in analyses of semantic relations, a fact recognized by the author.

The MILI is not recommended when normative comparisons are important, such as in documenting a need for speech-language services. It could, however, provide an efficient procedure for obtaining and profiling syntactic productions and identifying the child's use of various semantic relations. In recommending the MILI, I am assuming that intrasubject reliability data will be provided in a future revision.

REVIEWER'S REFERENCES

deVilliers, P. A., & deVilliers, J. G. (1972). Early judgments of semantic and syntactic acceptability by children. *Journal of Psycholinguistic Research*, 1, 299-310.

Bloom, L., & Lahey, M. (1978). *Language development and language disorders*. New York: Wiley.

Miller, J. F. (1981). *Assessing language development in children: Experimental procedures*. Baltimore: University Park Press.

Review of the Multilevel Informal Language Inventory by ROBERT RUEDA, Adjunct Assistant Professor, University of California, Santa Barbara, Santa Barbara, CA:

DESCRIPTION OF TEST. This inventory was designed to provide a developmental profile of language functioning, specifically in the areas of semantic relations and syntactic constructions. The manual suggests that this measure would be appropriately used for screening, diagnostic assessment, and ongoing assessment. Although the Multilevel Informal Language Inventory (MILI) is individually administered, it was not designed as a norm-referenced measure, but as a tool for intra-individual comparison.

The content of the MILI was based upon a review of research "on the acquisition of oral language production in children up to the approximate age at which they enter school (5 to 6 years)." The primary references used for this purpose are provided in the manual. As the introductory description points out, the items covered by this inventory are semantic relations and syntactic constructions.

The authors of the MILI have attempted to incorporate a multilevel approach to assessment, and there are three distinct ways in which this multilevel approach is embedded either in the administration procedures or the test content. First, an attempt was made to follow an approximate developmental ordering of test items within each category assessed. For example, the probe for the present progressive verb form precedes the past irregular form since this is the assumed order of developmental acquisition. Second, the inventory proceeds from less structured to more structured levels of observation. For example, the contexts for observations move from free description of a page-size cartoon-like drawing, to a somewhat more structured retelling of a story based on a series of cartoon drawings, and finally to direct probes of specific syntactic and semantic items. The third multilevel feature of the MILI is found in the administration procedures of the direct probes for specific language features. Probes may be presented to children either at the evoked spontaneous level, the elicited level, or the receptive level, thus providing an indication of the conditions under which the child was able to produce the linguistic structure being assessed.

Although the manual indicates that the MILI underwent field testing, little detailed information is provided. Forty-five children, including 15 "normal" children and 30 children "who had previously been diagnosed as language delayed and/or disordered" were administered a draft of the inventory. However, there was no information on where the field testing took place nor was any specific description of the subjects provided. The only type of validity discussed with respect to the MILI was content validity. Given the presentation in the manual on the derivation of the content of the test, the content validity of the test appears adequate.

ADMINISTRATION AND SCORING. The test authors appropriately caution that this measure should be used in conjunction with natural observation and standardized test procedures. In fact, the manual states "Use of MILI assumes that the child has already been administered one or more formal assessments of language, i.e., standardized tests or batteries, and that some estimate of his overall degree of delay/disorder has been made."

The MILI does not yield numerical scores, but rather provides separate developmental profiles for semantic relations and for syntactic features, which are taken as a summary of a child's level of language functioning. A positive feature of the syntactic profile is that it indicates the conditions under which the child produced specific target items (evoked spontaneously, specifically elicited, or responded to at the receptive level only). The MILI allows a great deal of clinical leeway in terms of specific administration procedures, order of presentation, selection of the entry level of assessment, etc. This is both a strength and a weakness. On the one hand, clinical sensitivity can be used to facilitate maximum performance levels of students without violating the structure or assumptions of the MILI. On the other hand, the clinician needs to have considerable experience, a firm grasp of language development, and well-developed clinical skills in order to effectively deal with the lack of rigid administration guidelines.

The administration time should be 15–20 minutes per session (if more than one session is needed), and results of the first session should be used to determine specific targets and levels to assess for the second administration. This procedure is meant to avoid making awkward and time-consuming test-time decisions. Overall, the manual provides adequate, clear administration instructions, and the scoring sheet appears to be well thought out. The cartoon-like drawings which are used as stimulus materials in the MILI appear to be attractive and interesting, at least to children at the lowest ages for which the inventory was designed. The stimulus drawings maintained the interest and elicited a substantial amount of language from 4-year-olds to whom it was shown by the reviewer.

The introduction in the manual provides a straightforward discussion of language assessment, which is balanced and sensitive to various aspects of testing language proficiency. In addition, the authors clearly state the assumptions guiding development of the test.

SUMMARY AND CONCLUSION. Overall, this inventory appears to fulfill what the authors promise. However, there are some factors that need consideration by clinicians using this inventory. For example, the manual states that "An underlying assumption of such measures [informal assessment instruments] is that the task will closely approximate the child's typical performance and thereby provide a representative sample of that child's current language behavior." Nevertheless, the MILI does incorporate many elements of standardized test situations, such as tape recording (where appropriate), marking of scoring forms by the clinician while recording responses, and having children interact individually with a strange adult in a test-like context around school-like tasks. It should be kept in mind that there is mounting evidence from many disciplines that both linguistic and cognitive behaviors are tremendously sensitive to contextual variations, especially in the case of young children and minority children. Given this information, the clinician needs to be aware that some of the "test-like" features of the MILI may serve to counteract the intent of the MILI to "elicit the most natural language behavior from the child." As a simple example, some children might respond very differently in a group or peer communicative context. In all fairness, the authors caution that "a child's failure to produce the intended target should first be viewed as a failure of the stimuli to elicit the target rather than as clear-cut evidence that the child is unable to produce the target under any conditions." In addition, the authors stress that the MILI should not be used as the sole indicator of language functioning. Nevertheless, clinicians will need to exercise clinical judgement in the use and interpretation of the MILI with minority and non-English-speaking students.

There are some specific features of the MILI that merit caution when used with very young children. At younger ages, for example, it is possible that the survey stories may confound short term memory capacity with language skills, especially if a child interprets the task as a strict retelling (not rephrasing) of the story provided by the clinician. Also, the survey scenes used as a stimulus for the general language sample may confound discrimination skills with linguistic features. Finally, several items appear to tap labeling (vocabulary) skills, for example, where the child's task is to "tell me about this picture."

At the more advanced levels, some of the items appear to tap cognitive rather than strictly linguistic features. For example, level AL-1 (creating words) seems, at least in part, to tap divergent thinking skills. In addition, some of the items such as AL-4 (word meanings in context) seem more like items from an intelligence test, (e.g., "How many centimeters are there in a parking meter?").

A final consideration in the use of the MILI is that the focus on specific features of syntax and semantic relations encourages a somewhat decontextualized approach to language intervention. Although the MILI has a somewhat narrow focus, it is true that the test does not promise more than it delivers, and it certainly was not meant to be used in isolation. However, the relatively recent emphasis on context as a key factor in language and development by sociolinguists, educational anthropologists, and others, should encourage consideration of the role of contextual factors and the process of natural language acquisition in a comprehensive language assessment and intervention program.

[45]
The Multiple Affect Adjective Check List, Revised. Purpose: Measures positive and negative affects as traits or states. Ages 20–79; 1960–85; MAACL-R; previous edition still available; 5 basic scores: Anxiety, Depression, Hostility, Positive Affect, Sensation Seeking, and 2 summary scores: Dysphoria, and Positive Affect and Sensation Seeking; 2 forms: State and Trait; 1987 price data: $6.50 per 25 hand-scoring or machine-scoring State or Trait forms; $10 per set of handscoring keys; $2.50 per manual ('85, 29 pages); $3.50 per bibliography ('85, 33 pages); $5.50 per specimen set including one copy of each form and manual); $1 per answer form for scoring service available from publisher; 5(10) minutes; Marvin Zuckerman and Bernard Lubin; EdITS/Educational and Industrial Testing Service.*

See 9:734 (47 references), T3:1547 (108 references), 8:628 (102 references), and T2:1293 (56 references); for reviews by E. Lowell Kelly and Edwin I. Megargee of an earlier edition, see 7:112 (60 references); see also P:176 (28 references).

TEST REFERENCES

1. Rohsenow, D. J. (1982). Control over interpersonal evaluation and alcohol consumption in male social drinkers. *Addictive Behaviors*, 7, 113-121.
2. Suedfeld, P., Ramirez, C., Deaton, J., & Baker-Brown, G. (1982). Reactions and attributes of prisoners in solitary confinement. *Criminal Justice and Behavior*, 9, 303-340.
3. Ellickson, J. L. (1983). Representational systems and eye movements in an interview. *Journal of Counseling Psychology*, 30, 339-345.
4. Fordyce, M. W. (1983). A program to increase happiness: Further studies. *Journal of Counseling Psychology*, 30, 483-498.
5. Alter, R. C. (1984). Abortion outcome as a function of sex-role identification. *Psychology of Women Quarterly*, 8, 211-233.
6. Barbaree, H. E., & Davis, R. B. (1984). Assertive behavior, self-expectations, and self-evaluations in mildly depressed university women. *Cognitive Therapy and Research*, 8, 153-172.
7. Chaplin, W. F., & Goldberg, L. R. (1984). A failure to replicate the Bem and Allen study of individual differences in cross-situational consistency. *Journal of Personality and Social Psychology*, 47, 1074-1090.
8. Cragan, M. K., & Deffenbacher, J. L. (1984). Anxiety Management Training and Relaxation as Self-Control in the treatment of generalized anxiety in medical outpatients. *Journal of Counseling Psychology*, 31, 123-131.
9. Crandall, J. E. (1984). Social interest as a moderator of life stress. *Journal of Personality and Social Psychology*, 47, 164-174.
10. Farley, R. C. (1984). Training in rational-behavior problem solving and employability enhancement of rehabilitation clients. *Rehabilitation Counseling Bulletin*, 28, 117-124.
11. Gotlib, I. H. (1984). Depression and general psychopathology in university students. *Journal of Abnormal Psychology*, 93, 19-30.
12. Greenstein, S. M. (1984). Pleasant and unpleasant slides: Their effects on pain tolerance. *Cognitive Therapy and Research*, 8, 201-210.
13. Haskett, R. F., Steiner, M., & Carroll, B. J. (1984). A psychoendocrine study of Premenstrual Tension Syndrome: A model for endogenous depression. *Journal of Affective Disorders*, 6, 191-199.
14. Hertsgaard, D., & Light, H. (1984). Anxiety, depression, and hostility in rural women. *Psychological Reports*, 55, 673-674.
15. Ingram, R. E. (1984). Information processing and feedback: Effects of mood and information favorability on the cognitive processing of personally relevant information. *Cognitive Therapy and Research*, 8, 371-386.
16. Johnson-Sabine, E. C., Wood, K. H., & Wakeling, A. (1984). Mood changes in bulimia nervosa. *British Journal of Psychiatry*, 145, 512-516.
17. King, D. A., & Heller, K. (1984). Depression and the response of others: A re-evaluation. *Journal of Abnormal Psychology*, 93, 477-480.
18. Lang, A. R., Verret, L. D., & Watt, C. (1984). Drinking and creativity: Objective and subjective effects. *Addictive Behaviors*, 9, 395-399.
19. Light, H. K. (1984). Differences in employed women's anxiety, depression, and hostility levels according to their career and family role commitment. *Psychological Reports*, 55, 290.
20. Martin, D. J., Abramson, L. Y., & Alloy, L. B. (1984). Illusion of control for self and others in depressed and nondepressed college students. *Journal of Personality and Social Psychology*, 46, 125-136.
21. Miller, L. S., & Funabiki, D. (1984). Predictive validity of the Social Performance Survey Schedule for component interpersonal behaviors. *Behavioral Assessment*, 6, 33-44.
22. Mitchell, J. E., & Madigan, R. J. (1984). The effects of induced elation and depression on interpersonal problem solving. *Cognitive Therapy and Research*, 8, 277-285.
23. Peck, D. F., Morgan, A. D., MacPherson, E. L. R., & Bramwell, L. (1984). The Multiple Affect Adjective Check List: Subscale intercorrelations from two independent studies. *Journal of Clinical Psychology*, 40, 123-125.
24. Plante, T. G., & Denney, D. R. (1984). Stress responsivity among dysmenorrheic women at different phases of their menstrual cycle: More ado about nothing. *Behaviour Research and Therapy*, 22, 249-258.
25. Powell, M., & Hemsley, D. R. (1984). Depression: A breakdown of perceptual defence. *British Journal of Psychiatry*, 145, 358-362.
26. Pretty, G. H., & Seligman, C. (1984). Affect and the overjustification effect. *Journal of Personality and Social Psychology*, 46, 1241-1253.
27. Schare, M. L., & Lisman, S. A. (1984). Self-statement induction of mood: Some variations and cautions of the Velten procedure. *Journal of Clinical Psychology*, 40, 97-99.
28. Schare, M. L., Lisman, S. A., & Spear, N. E. (1984). The effects of mood variation on state-dependent retention. *Cognitive Therapy and Research*, 8, 387-408.
29. Veleber, D. M., & Templer, D. I. (1984). Effects of caffeine on anxiety and depression. *Journal of Abnormal Psychology*, 93, 120-122.
30. Abrahamson, D. J., Barlow, D. H., Sakheim, D. K., Beck, J. G., & Athanasiou, R. (1985). Effects of distraction on sexual responding in functional and dysfunctional men. *Behavior Therapy*, 16, 503-515.
31. Brown, N. W. (1985). Assessment measures that discriminate between levels of DUI clients. *Psychological Reports*, 56, 739-742.
32. Carey, M. P., & Burish, T. G. (1985). Anxiety as a predictor of behavioral therapy outcome for cancer chemotherapy patients. *Journal of Consulting and Clinical Psychology*, 53, 860-865.
33. Dobson, K. S. (1985). Defining an interactional approach to anxiety and depression. *The Psychological Record*, 35, 471-489.
34. Dobson, K. S. (1985). An analysis of anxiety and depression scales. *Journal of Personality Assessment*, 49, 522-527.
35. Farber, S. S., Felner, R. D., & Primavera, J. (1985). Parental separation/divorce and adolescents: An examination of factors mediating adaptation. *American Journal of Community Psychology*, 13, 171-185.
36. Friedrich, W. N., Tyler, J. D., & Clark, J. A. (1985). Personality and psychophysiological variables in abusive, neglectful, and low-income control mothers. *The Journal of Nervous and Mental Disease*, 173, 449-460.

37. Gackenbach, J. I., & Auerbach, S. M. (1985). Sex-role attitudes and perceptual learning. *The Journal of Social Psychology*, 125, 233-243.

38. Gotlib, I. H., & Beatty, M. E. (1985). Negative responses to depression: The role of attributional style. *Cognitive Therapy and Research*, 9, 91-103.

39. Hasher, L., Rose, K. C., Zacks, R. T., Sanft, H., & Doren, B. (1985). Mood, recall, and selectivity effects in normal college students. *Journal of Experimental Psychology: General*, 114, 104-118.

40. Kirschenbaum, D. S., Tomarken, A. J., & Humphrey, L. L. (1985). Affect and adult self-regulation. *Journal of Personality and Social Psychology*, 48, 509-523.

41. Klein, H. A., & Rennie, S. E. (1985). Temperament as a factor in initial adjustment to college residence. *Journal of College Student Personnel*, 26, 58-62.

42. Koverola, C., Manion, I., & Wolfe, D. (1985). A microanalysis of factors associated with child-abusive families: Identifying individual treatment priorities. *Behaviour Research and Therapy*, 23, 499-506.

43. Mehlman, R. C., & Snyder, C. R. (1985). Excuse theory: A test of the self-protective role of attributions. *Journal of Personality and Social Psychology*, 49, 994-1001.

44. Ruderman, A. J. (1985). Dysphoric mood and overeating: A test of restraint theory's disinhibition hypothesis. *Journal of Abnormal Psychology*, 94, 78-85.

45. Shaw, J. B., & Weekley, J. A. (1985). The effects of objective work-load variations of psychological strain and post-work-load performance. *Journal of Management*, 11, 87-98.

46. Young, L., & Humphrey, M. (1985). Cognitive methods of preparing women for hysterectomy: Does a booklet help? *British Journal of Clinical Psychology*, 24, 303-304.

47. Adam, K., Tomeny, M., & Oswald, I. (1986). Physiological and psychological differences between good and poor sleepers. *Journal of Psychiatric Research*, 20, 301-316.

48. Anderson, C. A., & Ford, C. M. (1986). Affect of the game player: Short term effects of highly and mildly aggressive video games. *Personality and Social Psychology Bulletin*, 12, 390-402.

49. Asso, D. (1986). The relationship between menstrual cycle changes in nervous system activity and psychological, behavioural and physical variables. *Biological Psychology*, 23, 53-64.

50. Brand, A. G., & Powell, J. L. (1986). Emotions and the writing process: A description of apprentice writers. *The Journal of Educational Research*, 79, 280-285.

51. Cash, T. F., Rimm, D. C., & MacKinnon, R. (1986). Rational-irrational beliefs and the effects of the Velten Mood Induction Procedure. *Cognitive Therapy and Research*, 10, 461-467.

52. Clark, D. A. (1986). Cognitive-affective interaction: A test of the "specificity" and "generality" hypotheses. *Cognitive Therapy and Research*, 10, 607-623.

53. Daiss, S. R., Bertelson, A. D., & Benjamin, L. T., Jr. (1986). Napping versus resting: Effects on performance and mood. *Psychophysiology*, 23, 82-88.

54. Dougherty, K., Templer, D. I., & Brown, R. (1986). Psychological states in terminal cancer patients as measured over time. *Journal of Counseling Psychology*, 33, 357-359.

55. Gard, P. R., Handley, S. L., Parsons, A. D., & Waldron, G. (1986). A multivariate investigation of postpartum mood disturbance. *British Journal of Psychiatry*, 148, 567-575.

56. Glynn, S. M., & Ruderman, A. J. (1986). The development and validation of an eating self-efficacy scale. *Cognitive Therapy and Research*, 10, 403-420.

57. Gotlib, I. H., & Meyer, J. P. (1986). Factor analysis of the Multiple Affect Adjective Check List: A separation of positive and negative affect. *Journal of Personality and Social Psychology*, 50, 1161-1165.

58. Haley, W. E., & Strickland, B. R. (1986). Interpersonal betrayal and cooperation: Effects on self-evaluation in depression. *Journal of Personality and Social Psychology*, 50, 386-391.

59. Harris, R. N., Snyder, C. R., Higgins, R. L., & Schrag, J. L. (1986). Enhancing the prediction of self-handicapping. *Journal of Personality and Social Psychology*, 51, 1191-1199.

60. Herbert, J., Moore, G. F., de la Riva, C., & Watts, F. N. (1986). Endocrine responses and examination anxiety. *Biological Psychology*, 22, 215-226.

61. Higgins, E. T., Bond, R. N., Klein, R., & Strauman, T. (1986). Self-discrepancies and emotional vulnerability: How magnitude, accessibility, and type of discrepancy influence affect. *Journal of Personality and Social Psychology*, 51, 5-15.

62. Kraemer, D. L., & Hastrup, J. L. (1986). Crying in natural settings: Global estimates, self-monitored frequencies, depression and sex differences in an undergraduate population. *Behaviour Research and Therapy*, 24, 371-373.

63. Liu, T. J., & Steele, C. M. (1986). Attributional analysis of self-affirmation. *Journal of Personality and Social Psychology*, 51, 531-540.

64. Madigan, R. J., & Bollenbach, A. K. (1986). The effects of induced mood on irrational thoughts and views of the world. *Cognitive Therapy and Research*, 10, 547-562.

65. Mullins, L. L., Peterson, L., Wonderlich, S. A., & Reaven, N. M. (1986). The influence of depressive symptomatology in children on the social responses and perceptions of adults. *Journal of Clinical Child Psychology*, 15, 233-240.

66. Nickel, E. J., Lubin, B., & Rinck, C. M. (1986). The new MAACL scales with adolescents: Preliminary reliability and validity determinations. *Adolescence*, 21, 81-86.

67. Overholser, J. C., & Beck, S. (1986). Multimethod assessment of rapists, child molesters, and three control groups on behavioral and psychological measures. *Journal of Consulting and Clinical Psychology*, 54, 682-687.

68. Peterson, C., Zaccaro, S. J., & Daly, D. C. (1986). Learned helplessness and the generality of social loafing. *Cognitive Therapy and Research*, 10, 563-570.

69. Saranson, I. G., Saranson, B. R., & Shearin, E. N. (1986). Social support as an individual difference variable: Its stability, origins, and relational aspects. *Journal of Personality and Social Psychology*, 50, 845-855.

70. Schwartz, D. P., Burish, T. G., O'Rourke, D. F., & Holmes, D. S. (1986). Influence of personal and universal failure on the subsequent performance of persons with Type A and Type B behavior patterns. *Journal of Personality and Social Psychology*, 51, 459-462.

71. Snyder, C. R., Lassegard, M., & Ford, C. E. (1986). Distancing after group success and failure: Basking in reflected glory and cutting off reflected failure. *Journal of Personality and Social Psychology*, 51, 382-388.

72. Suominen-Troyer, S., Davis, K. J., Ismail, A. H., & Salvendy, G. (1986). Impact of physical fitness on strategy development in decision-making tasks. *Perceptual and Motor Skills*, 62, 71-77.

Review of The Multiple Affect Adjective Check List, Revised by JOHN A. ZARSKE, Director, Northern Arizona Psychological Services, P.C., Flagstaff, AZ:

The Multiple Affect Adjective Check List, Revised (MAACL-R) represents a revision of an earlier version first published by Zuckerman and Lubin in 1965. The previous version of the MAACL required revision due to problems affecting the test's discriminant validity. Prior to its revision, the MAACL generated considerable research activity. Included with the MAACL manual is a bibliography of over 700 of these studies, indexed according to various research and clinical topic areas. With the improved norms and psychometric properties of the MAACL-R, it is anticipated that a host of similar, new studies and clinical uses shall emerge for this popular test.

The authors have done a commendable job of addressing the several problems of the MAACL (i.e., high correlations between the subscales, acquiescence response set, and the independence of positive and negative affect scores). Additionally, the manual includes a thorough and scientific treatment of strengths and weaknesses of the revised edition. Included in the manual are several new validity and reliability studies, a comprehensive discussion of the factor analytic investigations that led to the development of the new scales, and details regarding administration, scoring, normative data, and demographic factors affecting the MAACL-R. In all, it appears the authors have made substantial improvements for a test that has already enjoyed a vast amount of research attention and use in clinical practice.

SCORING AND ADMINISTRATION. Scoring is a simple and straightforward procedure as described in the manual. Basically, all checked adjectives for the various scales are counted to compute a raw score for each of the scales or scale groupings (i.e., broader factor scales) and transformed into T scores using appendices in the back of the manual. The test publisher provides an optical scanning service for machine scoring but this reviewer was unable to establish under what conditions the user may score the test without relying upon the scoring service. The manual indicates that "local" scoring may be done "under arrangement with the test publisher." However, a one-page mailer that accompanied the manual suggests that hand-scoring keys are available (none were included in the specimen set).

Administration is simple and the test is completed in under 5 minutes in most circumstances. For the Trait form, the respondent is asked to check those adjectives which "generally apply"; for the State version, those which apply "at the present time."

VALIDITY. As mentioned above, the main problem with the MAACL was that the three subscales (Anxiety, Depression, and Hostility) were correlated with each other between .7 and .9. Research studies demonstrated that when a respondent was exposed to a stressor, concurrent changes would occur in all three scales.

Correlational studies comparing the MAACL scales with other assessment tools (observer ratings and questionnaires), typically revealed that the Anxiety and Depression scales had adequate convergent validity but not discriminant validity. To address this problem, the authors conducted a series of factor-analytic studies that resulted in a five-factor solution: Anxiety (A), Depression (D), Hostility (H), Positive Affect (PA), and Sensation Seeking (SS). The A, D, and H scales (i.e., the Negative Affect scales) now show correlations in the range of .4 to .6, revealing an improvement in the discriminant validity of these scales. However, there is still a significant intercorrelation among these scales, leading the authors to postulate a broader Dysphoria Factor, composed of these three subfactors. The PA and SS scales are significantly correlated as well, hypothetically combining to form a Positive Affect factor. Correlational studies between these two broader Positive and Negative Affect factors show evidence for convergent and discriminant validities, suggesting a new and more useful structure for the MAACL-R.

Several other validity studies are reported in the manual for various populations using peer ratings and single clinical observer ratings correlated with MAACL-R scaled scores. Peer ratings showed the highest correlation but even the observer correlations were adequate. The authors also correlated the MAACL with the Lorr Poms and the MMPI. Correlations between the Poms and MAACL were greatest for college students. The MMPI-MAACL study suggests the PA scale shows merit in predicting depression in several psychiatric diagnostic groups. Sufficient validity studies are lacking for the Sensation Seeking scale in both the Trait and State forms, indicating a need for further studies regarding this scale's construct validity.

RELIABILITY. All scales show adequate internal reliability with the exception of the Sensation Seeking scale. Of course, the Trait scales would be expected to show higher reliability coefficients and this is supported by the data. All scales, except the Positive Affect scale, show satisfactory reliabilities for periods up to 8 weeks.

NORMS. As part of the MAACL-R revision process, norms were developed for the Trait form. Analysis of information presented in the manual suggests that the Trait-form norms are based on a representative nationwide sample with proportional representation for sex, racial, regional, educational, and financial distributions in the United States. The new norms will probably result in greater research and clinical use of the MAACL-R Trait form. The norms for the State form are restricted and based only on a sample of 538 midwestern students examined in groups. As such, norms for the State version are not representative. This suggests a need for restandardization with a larger, more representative sample. The authors address this particular weakness directly in the manual and suggest that despite the lack of standardization, test-retest comparisons may still be conducted using existing State T scores as such comparisons are within subjects.

In summary, the MAACL-R is a psychometrically improved version of the popular MAACL. The Trait form is now standardized and new validity studies cited in the manual suggest direct clinical applications in assessment of affect and affective characteristics. The MAACL-R also shows promise for pre- and post-treatment measures of therapeutic effectiveness on a broad range of variables, including emotional aspects of health, stress, and stress management, as well as differential diagnosis. With its improved psychometric foundation, it is anticipated that the MAACL-R will continue to find considerable utility in psychological research and evaluation of treatment effectiveness.

[46]

National Business Competency Tests: Secretarial Procedures Test. Purpose: "To help teachers and employers determine whether prospective secretarial employees (students) are ready for entry-level jobs." Secondary and postsecondary students completing a secretarial program; 1983; 6 tasks: Filling Out a Job Application Form, Secretarial Procedures Information, Editing, Priority Assignments, Calendar Notations, Letter and Envelope; 1985 price data: $.75 per test; $.75 per manual (4 pages); (100) minutes; National Business Education Association.*

Review of the National Business Competency Tests: Secretarial Procedures Test by MICHAEL RYAN, Clinical Psychologist, West Side Family Mental Health Clinic, P. C., Kalamazoo, MI:

The National Business Competency Tests: Secretarial Procedures Test purports to measure the secretarial skills of secondary and post-secondary students completing a secretarial program. It consists of two parts which should be administered on consecutive days. A ballpoint pen is required for the first day and a typewriter for the second day. The tests take a total of 100 minutes to administer. On the first part, students are asked to fill out a job application, answer a multiple choice test on secretarial procedures, and perform a proofing and editing task. On the second part, students prioritize six tasks and then complete them. These tasks include typing minutes, a letter, an agenda, a purchase order, and a memo. In addition, each student is asked to update an employer's calendar. The directions for Part 1 are straightforward and understandable. However, the directions for Part 2 are more complex and somewhat confusing. The strength of these tests lies in the broad range of secretarial skills they measure. In addition to the clerical tasks, such as proofing, these tests ask the student to perform more cognitive tasks such as prioritizing time. A variety of typing skills are measured on Part 2. The author should be commended for the breadth of secretary abilities measured in this instrument.

However, these tests are wholly lacking in the psychometric information that is needed to make them useful to the educator, employer, or researcher. The brief (four-page) test manual includes little of the information deemed essential in the *Standards For Educational and Psychological Testing*, which was prepared by a joint committee of the American Psychological Association, the American Educational Research Association, and the National Council on Measurement in Education (APA et al., 1985). Strict scoring procedures, normative data, reliability data, and validity data are absent. Although scoring procedures for Part 1 are straightforward, scoring on Part 2 is somewhat confusing, and the manual ends by stating "follow your usual practices and standards for evaluating basic secretarial skills and job performance." Because such procedures and standards may vary greatly, this section is of questionable reliability and scores become meaningless.

The manual provides a cutoff score of 170 (85 points for each section) to indicate a good student at the secondary or post-secondary levels. However, no information was given as to how this cutoff was determined and no other normative data were provided. Furthermore, no information was provided to suggest differences in performance in regard to age, sex, or minority group membership. Although comprehensive norms would be preferable, at minimum separate means and standard deviations for secondary and post-secondary students are required to make these tests meaningful. In addition, normative data on intercorrelations on each subtest are also essential to understand the interrelationships among tests.

The authors have provided no reliability data. Therefore, it cannot be determined whether these tests will yield consistent scores over time. Furthermore, without consistent and clear scoring procedures, low reliability would be expected.

Finally, although the test purports to "help teachers and employers determine whether prospective secretarial employees (students) are ready for entry level jobs," the manual offers no validity studies whatsoever. At most, the manual states that reviewers of the tests, (unspecified) as well as the committee that developed the tests, judged these items to be significant measures of secretarial competency. This hardly suffices to prove this instrument's validity.

At first glance, the National Business Competency Test appears to possess content validity. It provides a reasonable sample of the skills needed by a typical secretary. However, the lack of consistent scoring procedures and normative data bring into question the validity of this instrument. In addition to a more rigorous psychometric foundation for this test, studies of predictive and concurrent validity are necessary. Correlations with job performed and other established tests would help substantiate the author's claims that this instrument measures secretarial skills.

Finally, the manual offers no discussion of what results mean or how to use results to remediate deficits. It is reasonable to assume that deficits on some tests are more significant than others. For example, a deficit in the knowledge of office procedures seems more detrimental than an inability to type an office memo. If this test is for use by educators, recommendations for remediating specified deficits would be extremely helpful.

In summary, the National Business Competency Tests: Secretarial Procedures Test, has some potential because of the diversity of the abilities that are measured; yet it cannot be recommended for use by educators, employers, or researchers because of a lack of consistent scoring procedures, reliability data, normative data, and validity data. Furthermore, the manual needs to include a more comprehensive discussion of the test's uses and appropriate populations. The test developers would do well to develop a clear and more consistent system of scoring, perform reliability and normative studies, and evaluate the validity of these measures against other secretarial tests and the actual success of students in secretarial positions. A similar test that provides more psychometric information, but still is somewhat flawed, is the Office Skills Test published by Science Research Associates.

REVIEWER'S REFERENCE

American Psychological Association, American Educational Research Association, & the National Council on Measurement in Education. (1985). *Standards for educational and psychological testing.* Washington, DC: American Psychological Association, Inc.

Review of the National Business Competency Tests: Secretarial Procedures Test by PAUL W. THAYER, Professor and Head of Psychology, North Carolina State University, Raleigh, NC:

The Secretarial Procedures Test presents some interesting problems for the reviewer. It has been prepared by a committee of business-procedures educators for the purpose of measuring secretarial skills. The contents look very interesting to this reviewer. I would, for example, want my secretary to know many of the things required: calling an 800 number instead of a billable number, choosing the appropriate mail service, delivering an urgent message to me during an important meeting with minimal disruption, editing rough copy, setting work priorities, etc. The test certainly has high face validity.

Unfortunately, it suffers from a host of deficiencies. I requested information concerning a number of these, but answers were not forthcoming within the time allowed for this review. The manual does not contain answers to the questions that many test users would have.

Despite my impression of face validity, there is no information as to how the contents of the test were determined. There is no indication of a series of job or curriculum analyses. Because one doesn't know the universe of possible test items, it is hard to say how representative the item sample is.

There are also some peculiarities with regard to administration instructions. The option to give the test in one or two sittings is possible, and extra points for completing part of the test early can be given. The impact of these procedures on the scoring system is not explained, nor is the rationale for them given. Further, we are informed that good students should receive 85 or more points (out of 100) on each part of the test. No other normative information is given. There are also some unusual instructions for scoring which might inadvertently penalize a student twice for an error. Students are penalized for incorrect priority assignments, and for failure to complete assignments. As different assignments get different weights, incorrect priority assignment may result in extra penalties for failing to complete a given task.

There is also a serious error in the "calendar notation" section. The student is to take two telephone memos and correct the boss's calendar. The calendar in the test booklet is already corrected and is identical to that in the scoring key booklet.

Most serious is the failure to provide any normative, reliability, or validity data. The NBEA Test Committee recommends that researchers collect such data and submit them to NBEA. The reviewer hopes that will be done. Given the mistakes and inadequate information on psychometric properties, one cannot recommend this instrument.

[47]

New England Pantomime Tests. Purpose: "Designed to investigate the nonverbal sending and receiving abilities of aphasic and other communicatively disordered adults." Communicatively disordered adolescents and adults; 1984; 4 tests: Pantomime Recognition Test (Forms A, B), Pantomime Expression Test, Pantomime Referential Abilities Test; individual; 1988 price data: $69 per complete set including manual (36 pages); administration time not reported; Robert J. Duffy and Joseph R. Duffy; PRO-ED, Inc.*

Review of the New England Pantomime Tests by RUSSELL L. ADAMS, Director, Psychology Internship Program, University of Oklahoma Health Sciences Center, Oklahoma City, OK:

The purpose of the New England Pantomime Tests is to measure quantitatively and presumably qualitatively the nonverbal sending and receiving abilities of aphasic patients and other communicationally impaired adults. All the norms are based on adult populations; however, the manual states the test can be used for children. There are actually four different tests included. These tests are the Pantomime Recognition Test, (Forms A and B), the Pantomime Expression Test, and the Pantomime Referential Abilities Test.

The manual states that nonverbal communication behaviors are important to the clinician, especially the speech therapist, because patients use nonverbal pantomimes as compensatory or augmenting mechanisms for communication. The test can be given prior to and following speech therapy in an effort to quantify improvement in sending or receiving ability of nonverbal communication. Because the test is standardized, the therapist can compare the efficacy of different therapeutic approaches.

The test, in this reviewer's opinion, is probably not appropriate for routine inclusion in most psychological or neuropsychological batteries because the amount of information gained by the test normally does not justify the time involved in gathering the data. If a specific question arises concerning the patient's ability to send or receive nonverbal communication signals, then the test could be helpful. The test may well be helpful to speech therapists or speech pathologists. The following is a brief description of each of the four tests.

PANTOMIME RECOGNITION TEST. The Pantomime Recognition Test is a nonverbal task that measures the subject's ability to recognize pantomime acts as being associated with common objects. For example, using this test, the examiner demonstrates the use of a cup for drinking, using pantomime actions. The patient's task is to point to the cup from an array of four pictures presented visually. The specific approach the examiner is to use in pantomiming drinking from a cup is clearly delineated in the manual. To pantomime drinking from a cup, the examiner is instructed to use one hand, beginning with tips of thumb and index finger almost touching and parallel to table. The side of the palm should be touching the table. The examiner is told to bring the hand close to the mouth, rounding lips slightly, and rotating the hand until the index finger is superior to the thumb. The examiner is then instructed to move the hand away from the mouth.

The written description of the pantomimes can be used in conjunction with a videotape demonstration of the pantomimes, which is available presumably from the publisher. However, specific information on how to order the videotape or the cost of the tape is not available in the manual.

Form A of the Pantomime Recognition Test contains 46 items and Form B contains 40. Specific data concerning the length of time for administration of the test are not presented in the manual. Form A differs from Form B in that Form B was developed to make the responses more difficult for aphasic patients by including distractors that are semantically related to the target object. Norms for Form B are not currently available, so this makes interpretation of the performance of a given patient on the test problematic. Norms for Form A, however, are available for three groups of patients: left hemisphere damaged, right hemisphere damaged, and normal controls. The manual provides no statistical tests to show whether the performance of aphasics is significantly different from the performance of the right hemisphere group or the control group. The mean for the aphasic patients on this test was 39.6 while the mean for the right hemisphere damaged group was 43.8. Thus the aphasia patients performed just 5 points lower on this test than did the right hemisphere group.

No test-retest reliability information on the instrument was given for the Pantomime Recognition Test. Given the fluctuation in attention seen in many brain-damaged patients, such data would be helpful in future updates of the test.

PANTOMIME EXPRESSION TEST. In this test the patient is asked to demonstrate the function of an object through pantomime. The patient's performance is videotaped and later scored according to a 16-point scoring system. The Pantomime Expression Test can be considered a measure of expressive deficit while the Pantomime Recognition Test could be considered a measure of pantomime reception deficit.

The interrater reliability of scores for the expression test was computed for only 10 aphasic patients. The correlation was .98. The intrascorer reliability for one score after a 1-year interval was .94 for 13 aphasic patients. This individual scorer looked again at the videotapes that had been made a year earlier.

The norms for 46 aphasic, 25 right hemisphere damaged, and 10 controls were presented. Again, no statistical tests were presented to determine if these groups differ significantly, although inspection of the table would certainly suggest that they do. No data are presented on important factors such as age, education, sex, length of time since onset of aphasia, etiology of aphasia, etc., of the subject population.

An important finding is that no subject in the control group or in the right-hemisphere-damaged group scored as low as the average patient (as measured by either the mean or the median) in the aphasic group. This strikingly low performance of the aphasic group was not found on the Pantomime Recognition Test.

PANTOMIME REFERENTIAL ABILITIES TEST. This test measures the ability of the patient to demonstrate the function of an object to a receiver (not the examiner) to the point that the receiver has obtained sufficient information to identify the object from an array of four pictures. This test differs from the Pantomime Expression Test in that the latter requires the patient's performance to be compared with that described on a 16-point scale. The Pantomime Referential Test uses the same 23 items as the Pantomime Expression Test; however, the distractors are different. At least one of the distractors requires the same location in space or body topography as the target. For example, for the target item "apple," a distractor of a cigarette is given. Both are associated with the mouth area. The more difficult distractor makes the test a more complicated one. No reliability or validity data are presented in the manual on this test. Because the patient demonstrates the function of an object to a receiver (not the examiner), the ability of reviewers is an important consideration. Receivers may differ greatly in the amount of information they need to recognize the pantomime. No data are presented in the manual concerning "receiver" reliability.

SUMMARY. The advantages of the Pantomime Abilities Tests are that they look at nonverbal pantomime communications skills of aphasia from both the receptive and expressive viewpoint. One recent study by the authors not described in the manual demonstrates that

Wernicke's (fluent) aphasics were also relatively fluent on the Pantomime Fluency Test, while Broca's (nonfluent aphasics) were relatively nonfluent on the Pantomime Expression Test. Thus the study demonstrated distinct differences in the pantomime fluency in these two aphasic groups which are similar to differences in their speech fluency. In another study involving the test, the test authors concluded that aphasic patients' pantomime expressive deficits are not caused by general intellectual deficits or limb apraxia; instead, these deficits are associated with a central symbolic disorder or a verbal mediation deficit.

The manual does not present concrete descriptions and case examples on how to use this test with a clinical population. The clinician is given no guidance as to why he/she should utilize this test or how it would be utilized. Perhaps the test could best be described as a research instrument in a state of development.

In summary, the tests are interesting ones, particularly because of their theoretical import (i.e., do aphasics also have an underlying impairment to communicate nonverbally through pantomime?). Some of the New England Pantomime Tests must be considered as still under construction because of the lack of adequate norms and validity and reliability studies. The tests would probably not be appropriate for regular inclusion in most neuropsychological batteries or psychological batteries because it is not clear how the results would be used clinically.

Review of the New England Pantomime Tests by JOHN A. COURTRIGHT, Professor and Chair of Communication, University of Delaware, Newark, DE:

The authors of the New England Pantomime Tests (NEPT) have used earlier versions and individual sections of these tests in their published research on aphasia (e.g., Duffy, Duffy, & Pearson, 1975; Duffy & Duffy, 1981; Duffy, Duffy, & Mercaitis, 1984). This has been excellent, trend-setting work, where the primary goal has been to investigate the causal antecedents of aphasic deficits. Unfortunately, the transition from research instrument to published test has resulted in several serious omissions. Users of the NEPT willing to take the time and energy to explore the authors' research may find these omissions less critical.

Without this exposure, however, information essential to the understanding and evaluation of the NEPT is simply not available in the test manual.

The most obvious and certainly most perplexing of these omissions is the lack of a definitive statement of purpose. What performance domain is being measured? To what evaluative or diagnostic purpose would scores from the several sections of the NEPT be put? The test manual fails to address these questions in any meaningful way. The authors suggest that nonverbal behaviors should be of interest to clinicians because of their "potential uses as compensatory or augmentative procedures for dealing with deficits in verbal/linguistic skills." This represents the beginnings of a rationale for constructing such a test, but it does not address the use or purpose of the tests per se.

There is only one statement in the manual that speaks directly to the NEPT's purpose: "The New England Pantomime Tests can serve as a standardized measure of pre- and posttraining abilities in studies of the efficacy of clinical procedures designed to enhance communicative functioning through nonverbal modes." What abilities? What procedures? What nonverbal modes? Do the authors intend, as the previous quotation implies, for the NEPT to be solely a research instrument for "studies" of therapeutic effectiveness? Certainly, the manual provides only the vaguest conception of what diagnostic or therapeutic ends the NEPT was designed to serve. As a result, the content validity of these tests is virtually impossible to evaluate.

This absence of a specific purpose also surfaces in the administration and scoring of one of the four tests: the Pantomime Referential Abilities Test (PRAT). In discussing the scoring of this test, the authors state, "Various scores may be obtained." After briefly outlining the measures obtained by Duffy et al. (1984), the authors conclude, "Other measures of accuracy, efficiency, or effectiveness of the subject's performance may also be devised."

Are users of this test really expected to devise other measures? Devise them for what purpose? With what degree of content and criterion-related validity could this be done? The authors seemingly place the burden for test construction and validation on the user, instead of accepting this essential responsibility for themselves. In the research arena, investigators frequently use instruments for a variety of unintended purposes, and thus must assume the responsibility for providing evidence of the reliability and validity of these "devised" measures.

In the clinical setting, however, clinicians have neither the time nor, in many cases, the methodological skills to explore the reliability and validity of their diagnostic instruments. Moreover, they should not be expected to investigate these issues, particularly for published instruments they have purchased! This is the responsibility of the NEPT's authors—a responsibility they have not fulfilled in these test materials.

These several concerns notwithstanding, the most salient omissions from the test manual are the complete absence of any discussion of validity, accompanied by an incomplete treatment of reliability. I will address the issue of reliability first. Although reliability is treated a bit differently for each of the four NEPT tests, it is always approached from the standpoint of scorer or rater reliability. Thus, for example, the authors claim no need to address the reliability of the two Pantomime Recognition Tests, because "there is little room for error in the examiner's recording of the response." Similarly, when presenting the reliability of the Pantomime Expression Test (PET), only interscorer reliability is considered, but the statistic used to calculate this value is not disclosed.

While it is important and necessary to know that independent scorers are highly consistent on these tests, it is, perhaps, more important to be apprised of the *internal* consistency of the tests themselves. Are the 46 items comprising the Pantomime Recognition Test measuring the same phenomenon? What about the 23 items for the PET and the Pantomime Referential Abilities Test (PRAT)? Several different indices of reliability could have provided this essential information, and the omission of internal consistency information must be considered a serious shortcoming.

Equally serious, of course, is the absence of any discussion of the validity of the four tests that comprise the NEPT. Much of this information—particularly information relevant to concurrent validity—is presented in detail in the authors' several research monographs. Moreover, those presentations make a convincing case that the four subtests of the NEPT are each related to established indices of communicative deficits in aphasics, the most notable being the Porch Index of Communicative Ability (PICA).

Despite availability elsewhere, some synthesis or summary of these findings should have been offered in the test manual. Test users have an important practical need to know what other major indices are related to the test they are using. This is especially true in the case of the NEPT, because competent clinicians dealing with aphasic clients will routinely administer the PICA. Given (*a*) the consistently high correlation (across several studies) of these two instruments, and (*b*) the authors' failure to articulate a definitive evaluative/diagnostic purpose (i.e., a performance domain) for the NEPT, one must question what nonredundant information would be obtained by administering the NEPT. The authors almost certainly have an answer to this question, but it is not made apparent in the test materials.

In conclusion, the NEPT is a set of four individual tests for which the transition from research instrument to published test has been less than successful. Information essential for a user to critically evaluate the NEPT is simply not provided. Because no domain of behavioral performance or skill is articulated, it is impossible to evaluate the content validity of the NEPT. In addition, evidence for concurrent validity, which exists in published research reports, is not presented in the test materials. Finally, reliability is incompletely treated as only the agreement among raters, rather than as additionally the internal consistency of the instruments. As a consequence, the user of the NEPT cannot be certain exactly what behavioral phenomenon is being measured, nor how accurately that measurement is being performed. Given these shortcomings and omissions, I cannot recommend the NEPT for general use by speech and language clinicians. The PICA remains a much better and more widely accepted diagnostic instrument.

REVIEWER'S REFERENCES

Duffy, R. J., Duffy, J. R., & Pearson, K. L. (1975). Pantomime recognition in aphasics. *Journal of Speech and Hearing Research*, 18, 115-132.

Duffy, R. J., & Duffy, J. R. (1981). Three studies of deficits in pantomimic expression and pantomimic recognition in aphasia. *Journal of Speech and Hearing Research*, 24, 70-84.

Duffy, R. J., Duffy, J. R., & Mercaitis, P. A. (1984). Comparison of the performances of a fluent and nonfluent aphasic on a pantomimic referential task. *Brain and Language*, 21, 260-273.

[48]

Occupational Aptitude Survey & Interest Schedule: Aptitude Survey. Purpose: Measures the career development of students. Grades 8–12; 1983; OASIS-AS; intended to be used with Occupational Interest Schedule; 6 scores: Vocabulary, Computation, Total (General Ability), Spatial Relations, Word Comparison, Making Marks; 1985 price data: $46 per complete test kit including manual (42 pages), 10 tests, 50 student profile and answer sheets, and scoring stencil; $14 per 10 tests; $18 per 50 student profile and answer sheets; $18 per manual; 35(45) minutes; Randall M. Parker; PRO-ED, Inc.

Review of the Occupational Aptitude Survey and Interest Schedule: Aptitude Survey by RODNEY L. LOWMAN, Director, Corporate Mental Health Programs, Occupational Health Service, and Faculty, Divisions of Medical Psychology and Occupational Medicine, Duke University Medical Center, Durham, NC:

The Occupational Aptitude Survey and Interest Schedule: Aptitude Survey (OASIS-AS) is intended to be like foreign automakers' answer to Detroit: a sleeker, more efficient, and in many ways, better version of the old gas-guzzling models. Analysis suggests that this instrument is an evolutionary, not revolutionary, product. By traditional standards of test validation much work remains to be done. If one word were to be used in evaluating this test it would be "promising." However, if the test is to become more than an isolated oasis in the midst of a dry and lately rather infertile desert, much more research will be required. This research should be directed especially to some troubling aspects of the validity evidence currently available.

There is little question that the five aptitudes which the OASIS-AS attempts to measure are well established as related to vocational success. Individually, these factors can be predictive of success in certain employment situations and, as a group, are generally of value in counseling high school students, the primary target population for this battery. The authors correctly note the limitations of the two major existing multi-aptitude test batteries, the Differential Aptitude Test (DAT) and the General Aptitude Test Battery (GATB). Both tests were excellent measures in their day, but they have problems, including the length of time needed to complete the instruments and, in the case of the GATB, its unavailability until recently to those outside certain government employment services. The need for an updated, reliable, valid, but shortened instrument to measure these particular aptitudes is clear.

By this standard, the OASIS has laid a good foundation on which to build. The reliability evidence for the test, though based in certain instances (especially the split-half and test-retest data) on rather small samples, is generally within professionally acceptable standards. The OASIS-AS normative data includes a national sample of about 1,400 individuals. This sample is racially imbalanced (blacks are inadequately represented and no breakdown is provided for those of Hispanic or Oriental origin). The sample is also geographically imbalanced (too many rural testees). The manner of selecting schools for inclusion in the sample is not adequately specified. Measures of central tendency for the item difficulty levels are not provided.

Except for two subtests (Making Marks and Word Comparison), the OASIS-AS is described as being primarily a power test. However, the question of the extent to which the remaining subtests are also speed tests is inadequately addressed in the manual. By its design, the OASIS-AS is a *shortened* version of longer multi-aptitude batteries. The apparent hope is that the same precision of aptitude measurement can be accomplished in less time. Indeed, the longest OASIS-AS subtest is 12 minutes; the shortest, 1 minute. While shortening does not necessarily occur at the expense of validity, the extent to which the OASIS-AS has become a speeded measure needs more research attention. This question is especially important in the case of those examinees who have the desired aptitude but who do not respond well in timed situations.

Test format and instructions are clear, except that examinees are not told that the test extracts no penalty for guessing. The booklet and test items are printed in an attractive format. However, the apparent intent to condense the Vocabulary and Computation subtests to a single page results in some very small print, especially for Computation. Students with uncorrected visual deficits may be needlessly penalized by this format.

The test falls short in the validation area. The OASIS-AS was patterned after the five factors on the GATB. However, the test manual reports only the results of a second order factor analysis (suggesting two factors), not the prior factor analyses which were said to have been conducted. It is important to know whether five factors emerged from the primary factor analyses. If not, what are the subtests really measuring, apart from the labels the author assigned to them? Moreover, the OASIS-AS does not provide evidence of adequate validation using external criteria. Although a few studies (again with small Ns) are cited that present correlations between OASIS-AS and other measures of aptitude or ability (generally suggesting that the OASIS-AS measures something akin to the GATB), it must be emphasized that the OASIS-AS is a new test and as such needs to be validated against external criteria, not just other tests.

Does the OASIS-AS meet minimally acceptable standards for commercial publication? Probably, but barely so. As an instrument for further exploration and research, it is a promising start. As a test to guide career choices and possibly for employment selection, the user should proceed with caution (especially with minorities) pending additional studies.

The authors correctly note that "the OASIS-AS should not be used as the sole predictor of job performance in a specific occupation." However, the counseling uses suggested for the OASIS-AS go beyond the validity evidence. Especially problematic is the inclusion of suggested "minimal aptitudes" needed for a variety of occupations. Although it is difficult to determine from the inadequate description in the test manual, these cutoff norms appear to be based on the GATB rather than the OASIS-AS. An example of the dangers of using this "minimal aptitudes" construct is illustrated by the case of Gloria, who is described as having "the requisite aptitudes for any of the 120 occupations listed." Any measure which suggests that the same examinee has equally sufficient aptitude for computer-applications engineer, dairy farm manager, and arc welder would appear not to be measuring aptitudes at a sufficient level of specificity to be valid or useful.

Finally, insofar as the OASIS-AS is to be used as a general aptitude battery for counsel-ing, there are areas of omission which are mildly troublesome. Here, the OASIS-AS is no oasis. It uses the same "tried (or is it 'tired'?) and true" measures of, essentially, academic aptitude. What about the student with artistic talents? The budding executive or manager? The psychotherapist? The garage mechanic? Will these individuals, who may present rather lackluster profiles on the OASIS-AS, be discouraged from pursuing their "natural talents"? Evidence has begun to emerge that artistic, social, and mechanical aptitudes are rather independent of some of the aptitudes tapped by the OASIS. (See for example, Gardner, 1983; Lowman, Williams, & Leeman, 1985.) One would like to see this battery (or some other) expand the old repertoire to include other types of "intelligence." If counseling is the goal, it is time to move beyond those aptitudes which are primarily academic and provide a measure for general counseling purposes which will tap into more of the diversity of human abilities than is captured by measures like the OASIS-AS.

SUMMARY. This could be an important new measure of basic aptitudes, primarily academic. It is a bit early in its development to advocate its use on a widespread basis, but assuming the authors and their colleagues get on with the research needed, there is great hope for this shortened multi-aptitude test battery. Although it may be criticized for omitting some important measures of aptitude (e.g., social, mechanical, artistic) the OASIS-AS hopefully will be shown to measure in only minutes what many aptitude batteries have taken many hours to do. Those with the time to administer the longer GATB or DAT will probably get more predictably reliable and valid results, but for a general screen and as a test for further validation efforts, the OASIS-AS offers much promise.

REVIEWER'S REFERENCES

Gardner, H. (1983). *Frames of mind: The theory of multiple intelligences.* New York: Basic Books.

Lowman, R. L., Williams, R. E., & Leeman, G. E. (1985). The structure and relationship of college women's primary abilities and vocational interests. *Journal of Vocational Behavior, 27,* 298-315.

Review of the Occupational Aptitude Survey and Interest Schedule: Aptitude Survey by KEVIN W. MOSSHOLDER, Associate Professor of Management, Auburn University, Auburn, AL:

The Occupational Aptitude Survey and Interest Schedule (OASIS) is a vocational exploration and career development tool for use with junior high and high school students. Only one part of OASIS, the Aptitude Survey (AS), is discussed here. The OASIS-AS is a multiple aptitude test that includes the following subtests: Vocabulary (verbal), Computation (numerical), Spatial Relations (spatial), Word Comparison (perceptual), and Making Marks (manual dexterity). The Vocabulary and Computation scores may be combined to yield a general ability score.

Published in 1983, the OASIS-AS was constructed with the idea of providing a commercially available test of multiple aptitudes encompassing the dominant factors measured by the General Aptitude Test Battery (GATB). Exploratory and Procrustes factor analyses of GATB correlation matrices were performed and interpreted as indicating that five factors underlie the GATB subtests. These factors became the constructs on which the OASIS-AS was based. Traditional item-analysis techniques were employed to construct the Vocabulary, Computation, and Spatial Relations subtests. Item-total correlations for items comprising these subtests were in the .2 to .6 range. Because Word Comparison and Making Marks were speeded subtests, standard item analysis was not used with these subtests.

Norms for the OASIS-AS were developed from a sample of 1,398 8th- through 12th-grade students residing in 11 states. The sample was predominantly white and urban, though balanced for sex. Norm tables are available in terms of percentiles, stanines, and 5-point scores. The latter are useful for comparing student scores with purported minimal aptitude requirements of various occupations.

Appropriate forms of reliability (alpha, split-half, alternate-forms, test-retest) were used to check the reliability of the five subtests. The subtests were equally reliable for males and females. Overall, the median reliability for all subtests was approximately .85, with Spatial Relations being at the low end of the range and Making Marks at the high end of the range. It should be noted that some reported reliabilities were corrected for range restriction, while others were not. Where corrected reliabilities were reported, corresponding uncorrected reliabilities should have been, but were not listed.

The validity of the OASIS-AS is reported largely in terms of concurrent criterion-related validities for subtests. Subtests of the OASIS-AS were matched and correlated with counterpart subtests from the Iowa Tests of Educational Development (ITED), SRA Achievement Series, and the GATB. Convergent validities, correlations between subtests measuring similar aptitudes, were best for OASIS-AS/GATB matches, ranging from .53 to .87. This is not surprising given that the OASIS-AS was developed with the GATB in mind. Convergent validities with ITED and SRA subtests were really only meaningful for the Vocabulary and Computation subtests of the OASIS-AS. Average correlations were approximately .70 for the Vocabulary subtest and .50 for the Computation subtest. The Spatial Relations, Work Comparison, and Making Marks subtests exhibited low to moderate correlations with verbally or numerically-loaded subtests of the ITED and SRA series.

The OASIS-AS manual is understandable, containing basic psychometric information like that described above, as well as standardized instructions for giving and scoring the subtests. The manual explains test features, and by using examples, discusses ways that the OASIS-AS might be used for counseling. Male and female norms for both grade 8–10 and grade 11–12 aggregates are reported. A table listing minimum aptitudes for 120 occupations keyed to OASIS-AS subtests is also included.

The major strength of the OASIS-AS ultimately may be its ties with the GATB, since much occupational information is keyed to the GATB. This linkage could prove beneficial when counseling students about occupational choices; however, whether the OASIS-AS can meet this objective is uncertain. There are several points concerning the OASIS-AS that may limit its utility. First, the supposition that there are five factors underlying the GATB, the five measured by the OASIS-AS, is based on an intercorrelation matrix for GATB subtests from 100 high school seniors. In order to show that these five factors could be found in data from other samples, Procrustes procedures were utilized. Such methods are notorious for yielding hypothesized factors, even in the face of many other equally plausible factor structures. Better confirmatory procedures are available and should have been used. One cannot be sure how well OASIS-AS covers the GATB construct domain until more research is completed.

Perhaps because the test was developed recently, validational evidence is not as complete as would be desired. Correlating the OASIS-AS with tests (ITED and SRA series) not designed as multiple aptitude tests does not permit completely meaningful subtest comparisons. As previously noted, convergent validities were best for OASIS-AS/GATB comparisons. However, these comparisons were based on the responses of only 72 students. Also, convergent validity may be the easiest standard for new tests to meet.

Discriminant validity, differentiation among subtests regarding what they measure, is harder to demonstrate. Data presented as supporting OASIS-AS discriminant validity was not rigorously assessed (as per a multitrait, multimethod paradigm), and is only adequate at best. It is also suggested in the manual that examining OASIS-AS subtest intercorrelations and/or factor-analyzing them is a partial means of assessing construct validity. Though not incorrect, the utility of such actions vis-a-vis construct validity is very marginal. Information about the predictive validity of the OASIS-AS with respect to any criteria of occupational success is completely omitted. Though the recency of the OASIS-AS may partly explain this shortcoming, such information is vital and must be sought.

There are other minor negative points that should be noted. The OASIS-AS has no apparent means for machine scoring. This deficiency could present extra work for counselors. Another undesirable feature is the inclusion of IQ and GATB equivalents in a conversion table, although users are cautioned about converting OASIS-AS scores in this manner. However, even printing such information creates the potential for abuse. Finally, the sampling procedures used to develop the normative sample may not have been ideal. That is, no statistically systematized sampling plan is mentioned. In fairness, demographics of the sample are fully described.

Given its current state of development, any summary judgment about the OASIS-AS must be mixed. Evidence for its reliability appears sufficient. However, more and better validational data must be gathered before one should consider this test as an alternative to some other multiple aptitude tests (e.g., Differential Aptitude Battery). The goal of providing a commercially available parallel to the GATB is laudable. Whether or not it can be attained is, at present, unknown. Use of the OASIS-AS for research and comparative purposes is encouraged. Those who wish to use it for actual counseling are advised to proceed with caution and restraint.

[49]
Occupational Aptitude Survey & Interest Schedule: Interest Schedule. Purpose: "Developed to assist students in grades 8–12 in formulating educational and vocational goals and generally in career planning." Grades 8–12; 1983; OASIS-IS; intended to be used with Occupational Aptitude Survey; 12 scores: Artistic, Scientific, Nature, Protective, Mechanical, Industrial, Business Detail, Selling, Accommodating, Humanitarian, Leading-Influencing, Physical Performing; 1985 price data: $47 per complete test kit including manual (42 pages), 25 tests, 50 profiles, and 50 answer sheets; $9 per 25 tests; $12 per 50 profiles; $12 per 50 answer sheets; $18 per manual; $49 per scoring and interpretation software package; (35) minutes; Randall M. Parker; PRO-ED, Inc.*

Review of the Occupational Aptitude Survey and Interest Schedule: Interest Schedule by CHRISTOPHER BORMAN, Professor, Department of Educational Psychology, Texas A&M University, College Station, TX:

The Occupational Aptitude Survey and Interest Schedule (OASIS) was developed "to assist junior high and high school students in vocational exploration and career development." The OASIS consists of two separate instruments—the Aptitude Survey (AS) and the Interest Schedule (IS). This review pertains only to the Interest Schedule. The IS has 240 items that are scored on a 3-point scale using the terms *like*, *neutral*, and *dislike*. This interest instrument has 12 scales with 20 items per scale. Of the 20 items for each scale, half of the items are occupational titles and the other half are job activities.

The OASIS-IS is built upon interest research conducted by the U.S. Employment Service and the early work of Cottle (1950). This research led to the identification of 12 interest factors, and the 240 items in the IS were selected to represent these 12 interest factors. Each of the 12 scales is briefly described in the test manual.

The test was standardized and normed on a sample of 1,398 students in grades 8–12 living in 11 states across the United States that seem to be representative of the country. About equal numbers of males and females were used in the sample, and the manual compares the sample to 1980 census data based on region of the country, gender, enthnicity, and urban or rural residence. Separate male and female norms are presented along with combined norms. Scores are presented in percentiles and stanines.

Alpha and test-retest reliabilities were employed in the development of the OASIS-IS. Two tables present alpha reliabilities for 260 students in grades 8, 10, and 12, and for 177 males and females, respectively. The coefficients for the 12 scales range from .85 to .95 indicating very respectable internal consistency for the OASIS-IS. Test-retest reliability was computed from data on 54 junior high and high school students over a 2-week interval, with the reliability coefficients ranging from .66 to .91 for the 12 OASIS-IS subscales. One of the most useful types of reliability evidence for an interest inventory is consistency over time, and the test-retest reliability data indicate that the IS scales are relatively stable over time.

The validation techniques used for the OASIS-IS included content and construct validity. Content validity was demonstrated by showing that the occupational titles and occupational activities listed in the OASIS-IS are representative of all the occupations listed in the *Guide for Occupational Exploration* (U.S. Department of Labor, 1979). Based on the information given in the manual, this instrument appears to have items representative of all the occupations listed in this Department of Labor publication. Factor analysis was used to provide evidence for the construct validity of the IS, and the analyses indicated that the 12 factors or components extracted could be identified as corresponding to one of the IS scales with one possible exception. This evidence seems to support the construct validity of the instrument. In this reviewer's opinion, the most serious shortcoming of the OASIS-IS is a lack of evidence of predictive validity. This absence of predictive validity data is a condition common among interest inventories, but it is a serious weakness because interest inventories are based on the assumption that predictions can be made from the scores. Although the purpose of this test may be to encourage exploration and not predict specific behaviors, information on the

predictive validity of the instrument would still be helpful.

The OASIS-IS is untimed, but most examinees should be able to complete the instrument within 30 minutes. Directions for administration of the OASIS-IS are clear and easy to follow. Scoring is facilitated by a published scoring form. Unless the computer version of the instrument is used, the test must be hand scored, and this could be quite time consuming if more than just a few answer sheets have to be scored at one time. A machine-scoring service for the OASIS-IS would be helpful. Getting the scores for the 12 scales from the back of the scoring form to the front of the form and then recording the corresponding percentiles and stanines is somewhat awkward and could lead to mistakes in recording the results.

The OASIS-IS manual gives general guidelines for interpreting an interest inventory, and then specific guidelines for interpreting the OASIS-IS results are given. These guidelines are clear and present excellent suggestions for interpreting the test results. Also, the manual refers test administrators to several very useful resource books that have particular relevance to the OASIS-IS.

A microcomputer version of the OASIS-IS is now available for use on the Apple II+, IIe, and IIc personal computers. This program administers, scores, profiles, and provides interpretative information regarding an examinee's scores on the OASIS-IS. A separate small manual describes the background of the test, gives instructions for using the computer program, and offers several guidelines or suggestions for interpreting the results. The instructions for using this software package are clear and easy to follow. If a printer is available with the microcomputer being used, the computer program will print a profile of an examinee's scores; otherwise, the scores (percentiles and stanines) can be copied on the scoring form and profile sheet used with the paper-and-pencil version. Although this computer program presents a profile of an individual's scores and some general interpretative information, the program does not analyze the test results or provide an opportunity for the examinee to interact with the computer. One real advantage of the computer program is that the computer scores the test rather quickly.

The OASIS-IS was published in 1983 and remains a relatively new entrant to the interest-inventory market. The OASIS-IS does offer the potential for being a useful and respected instrument. Reliability data indicate respectable internal consistency and stability over time. Evidence is presented supporting the content and construct validity of the OASIS-IS, but there is no data on the predictive validity of the instrument. Therefore, the OASIS-IS should be used with caution until evidence supporting the predictive validity of the instrument is available. The test manual presents convincing evidence that the OASIS-IS was normed on a sample of students in grades 8–12 that is quite representative of students in the United States in this age group. The microcomputer version of the OASIS-IS offers another means of administering and scoring the instrument, but the full potential of a computer program is not realized because the program does not interpret individual test results or interact with the individual taking the test.

REVIEWER'S REFERENCES

Cottle, W. C. (1950). A factorial study of the Multiphasic, Strong, Kuder, and Bell inventories using a population of adult males. *Psychometrika*, 15, 25-47.
U.S. Department of Labor. (1979). *Guide for occupational exploration*. Washington, DC: U. S. Government Printing Office.

Review of the Occupational Aptitude Survey and Interest Schedule: Interest Schedule by RUTH G. THOMAS, Associate Professor, College of Education, University of Minnesota, St. Paul, MN:

The basis for development of the OASIS Interest Schedule (OASIS-IS) is worker trait research. Twelve empirically-derived, occupational interest factors were identified from the factor analysis of 307 activity items covering all worker trait groups. This research, conducted by the U.S. Employment Service, defined the domains which served as the basis for the writing of the OASIS-IS items.

Recent concerns about sex bias in occupational interest inventories and their interpretation are addressed in the OASIS-IS by: (*a*) using as its basis factors that are reportedly invariant by sex, (*b*) screening scale items for sex bias, and (*c*) providing both separate and combined norms for females and males.

Items are of two types: job titles and work activities. The *Guide for Occupational Exploration* (U.S. Department of Labor, 1979) was the source document for item development. The approach to development of the OASIS-IS

beyond the identification of the original 12 interest factors is content oriented. Both items and occupations were keyed to the 12 domains on a logical basis. No evidence of empirical validation of items to occupations is provided. Item-total score correlations provided the basis for item inclusion in each scale.

While no systematically derived reading level information is provided, the OASIS-IS uses straightforward nontechnical language which should be understandable to most students in the age groups for which it is intended.

The OASIS-IS provides a profile of peer-normed percentile and stanine scores on 12 occupational interest scales that correspond to the original 12 interest factors. A computerized version of the interest schedule is available. This computer program offers immediate feedback to the student but provides less total information than does the paper-and-pencil version, omitting the stanine scores included on the original scoring sheet. However, even the paper-form version of the OASIS-IS does not provide as much information to the student as other established interest inventories. Many other inventories provide scores on other types of scales in addition to occupational interest scales.

The OASIS-IS was normed on a national sample of approximately equal numbers of male and female students in grades 8–12. Descriptive information about the norm group is provided and the manual is explicit about the norm group biases toward white, urban populations. The method by which the normative sample was drawn is not described, nor are the dates of norm data collection provided. The development of local norms is encouraged.

The manual deals with complex psychometric concepts and properties of the OASIS-IS in language aimed at a general population of users. It explains basic measurement concepts in a very readable and understandable fashion. The language used in the discussion of raw scores is of some concern since it refers to "correct" responses and to "performance," which inappropriately implies ability interpretations rather than interest interpretations.

Test-retest reliability coefficients for the 12 interest scales are slightly lower than those for the interest scales on the Strong-Campbell SVIB SC-II. While alpha internal consistency reliability coefficients are reported for three grade levels, only one standard error of measurement is reported for each subscale. The procedures and criteria used for drawing the reliability subsamples from the norm group are not explained. Means and standard deviations on each of the 12 subscales are provided for a larger norm group but not for the reliability subsamples.

Content and construct validity are identified in the OASIS-IS manual as the two types of validity most relevant to the purposes of the inventory. The purposes of the inventory are described in various sections as vocational exploration and career development, vocational goal setting, and measuring interests in a variety of occupations. It is clearly stated that the OASIS-IS is not intended for selection or prediction uses. The absence of a prediction element, particularly in relation to goal setting, is limiting in that it does not allow interpretations of scores in terms of predicted occupational satisfaction, success, entry, or tenure.

The use of judges or other types of verification of content validity is not reported, and therefore the validity of assignment of items and occupations to the 12 scales appears to be based solely on logical analysis.

Construct validity is based on data collected as part of the interest schedule development process. No research using the OASIS-IS is reported. Construct validity data is based on factor analysis and is totally internal to the inventory. It would be strengthened by empirical anchoring of scale items to occupational groups.

A means of checking for response bias with respect to social desirability and scale position is provided by two validity scales, which are designated as research scales because of their need for further empirical validation. Appropriate precautions regarding their use are given.

The length of time required to complete the interest schedule (identified as 30 minutes) is within the attention span and energy levels of the intended audience. No particular qualifications of users are indicated. Suggestions for user orientation are given. Administration and scoring instructions are detailed and could be followed by most education and counseling professionals. A hand-scoring procedure and form is provided and is reasonably simple to use. The lack of a machine-scoring option for the paper form may be a disadvantage when dealing with large numbers of students. Detailed instructions for providing interpretive feedback to students are given.

Users of the OASIS-IS should have at their disposal two publications recommended by the Interest Schedule author for use in interpreting OASIS-IS results and linking them to specific occupations: *Guide for Occupational Exploration* and *Worker Trait Group Guide*. Although the manual provides a limited summary of this type of information, it would be most helpful to have the more complete information provided in these two publications. The table in the manual appendix that is intended to link occupational titles, OASIS-IS item numbers, *Dictionary of Occupational Titles* (*DOT*) codes, and occupational interest areas to the 12 occupational interest scales is not adequately labeled for ease of interpretation. The 12 broad interest areas are not explicitly identified in the table. One can eventually infer what is missing in the table and supply it, but this is a needless task for users.

The strengths of the OASIS-IS include attention to sex bias concerns regarding occupational interest inventories, control of the scoring process by the user, and the availability of immediate computerized student feedback and scoring. Less sophisticated users might find the OASIS-IS less overwhelming and more understandable than more complex inventories with multiple dimensions. Weaknesses include the limited information the OASIS-IS provides to students and the lack of empirical, occupationally-anchored validation of scale items.

It would be difficult to recommend this interest schedule over a well established inventory like the Strong-Campbell SVIB SC-II if the goal is to provide maximum information to the student. The practical logistical advantages the OASIS-IS offers may outweigh information considerations in some instances.

[50]

Oetting's Computer Anxiety Scale. Purpose: "To provide a general measure of computer anxiety." College students; 1983; COMPAS; for research only; 8 subscale scores: Hand Calculator, Trust, General Attitude, Data Entry, Word Processing, Business Operations, Computer Science, Overall; Overall scale only for short form (10 questions from long form) and parallel forms (first or last halves of long form); norms for entering freshmen only; 1985 price data: $50 per 100 long form; $12 per manual ('83, 36 pages) including tests, scoring keys, scoring forms, and profile summary; [15] minutes; E. R. Oetting; Rocky Mountain Behavioral Science Institute, Inc.*

Review of Oetting's Computer Anxiety Scale by BENJAMIN KLEINMUNTZ, Professor of Psychology, University of Illinois at Chicago, Chicago, IL:

At the risk of questioning the purpose and rationale of 90 percent or more of the psychological tests published over the years and reviewed in these pages, I seriously challenge the importance of predicting computer anxiety. But even if one were to argue that it is meaningful to do so—an argument that would probably revolve around the issue of the computer's increasingly important role in our society and the possibility that it frightens some people some of the time—the test manual does not help us out in this regard. Nowhere does Oetting indicate the redeeming societal (i.e., clinical, industrial, practical) value of identifying, discovering, or predicting such anxiety. For example, is it a disabling disorder that warrants remediation? Does it interfere with one's performance in school, at work, or in the home? Or is it simply an inconvenience that deprives some people of their God-given privilege of participating in our high-tech society?

On the other hand, if one were to assume that it is important to measure or predict computer anxiety, then Oetting's Computer Anxiety Scale (COMPAS) is certainly the test to select. Its manual is admirably prepared in the best psychometric tradition, and the two forms of the test—Long Form (48 items) and Short Form (10 items)—are certainly to the point, and seem to have high face validity. These are advantages that should not be underestimated, given the general slovenliness and/or commercialism that one often finds in test manuals.

Oetting's manual for the COMPAS appropriately begins with a caveat that the test should be used *only* for research purposes" and "should not be used for selection if there could be negative consequences from that selection." It then formulates a general theory of computer anxiety by reviewing some of the highlights of trait and state anxiety, and concludes that computer anxiety is concept-specific, a term intended to provide "the theoretical underpinning of the COMPAS." Content-specific anxiety, Oetting believes, "may be the most useful construct for clinical practice or for many different kinds of research" and he defines it as "anxiety associated with a specified, clearly defined, and limited situation." The definition strikes me as being closer to the classical notion of phobia than to anxiety, given that the source of the emotional response is known.

Definitional considerations aside, Oetting's manual provides clear descriptions of the COMPAS and its scoring and interpretation. The internal consistency reliability data are admirably expressed in the form of Cronbach's alpha, which ranges from .88 for the Short Form to .96 for the Long Form based on 435 entering freshmen to Colorado State University. The parallel forms reliability of the test ranges from .94 to .96, and the internal consistency reliability of the subscales ranges from .71 (Business Operations) to .87 (General Attitude). The validity coefficients range from a low of .19 when the test is correlated with the criterion of Theme or Term Paper Anxiety measure, .40 with Suinn's Math Text Anxiety, .48 with the Science Test Anxiety, and a resounding .70 with a measure of computer *test* anxiety, which is a measure of "taking examinations where you would have to use a computer." No cross-validation data are presented.

Intercorrelations of COMPAS' seven subscales (Hand Calculator, Trust, General Attitude, Data Entry, Word Processing, Business Operations, and Computer Science) range from .07 to .71. These correlations, based on the normative sample of 435 entering freshman and 279 sophomores, tend to average around .50. They are all positive, and are correctly interpreted as showing that most of the subscales are related to an underlying common theme. They also help identify clusters of items that tap different dimensions of computer anxiety.

To summarize, the COMPAS is psychometrically sound, but its rationale for being is not immediately apparent. It would seem, moreover, that any subject who is afraid of computers would be as likely to say Yes or No to the following direct question as he/she would to the COMPAS' 48 or 10 item forms: "Are you afraid of, or made nervous by the idea of operating a computer?"

Review of Oetting's Computer Anxiety Scale by STEVEN L. WISE, Assistant Professor of Educa-

tional Psychology, University of Nebraska-Lincoln, Lincoln, NE:

Computers are playing an increasingly pervasive role in our society. Encounters with computers now commonly occur at home, in the workplace, and in many other aspects of our daily lives. This recent proliferation of computer use has produced an interest in the anxieties that may occur when people interact with computers. The Computer Anxiety Scale (COMPAS) was developed to measure these types of anxieties. The COMPAS is a 48-item attitude scale designed to provide a general measure of computer anxiety as well as measures of anxiety in particular situations involving computers.

The user is cautioned that the COMPAS should be used only for research purposes. The rationale behind this admonishment is unclear. Although it is true that the construct of computer anxiety is relatively new and has not been extensively studied, commercially-distributed anxiety scales are commonly used in clinical settings. A clinical interpretation of scores obtained using the COMPAS would not appear to represent a misuse of this instrument.

The items of the COMPAS were developed to measure a wide range of computer-related anxieties. I found some of the subscales to be more relevant to computer use than others. The Hand Calculator subscale, for example, appears to be, at best, marginally related to computer anxiety.

Each COMPAS item consists of a statement describing a situation involving a computer, followed by a 5-point rating scale using bipolar adjectives as scale endpoints. For a number of the items, the adjectives were not consistently used. For instance, across three of the items the adjective "anxious" is paired with "confident," "relaxed," and "comfortable," respectively. The double-barreled nature of some of the adjective pairings is particularly evident in combinations such as "anxious-confident."

The psychometric evidence for the COMPAS is fully described in the user's manual. The internal consistency reliability estimates for overall computer anxiety, across the various forms of the scale, are quite high. The reliabilities of the individual subscales are markedly lower, ranging from .71 to .87, although this is not surprising since each subscale is based on only four items. Also, while many items are reverse-keyed, the items within each subscale are all keyed in the same direction. This allows for the possibility of response sets distorting the subscale scores. Evidence for both content and construct validity of the COMPAS is well presented. It is clear that the test author paid close attention to validity issues when developing the COMPAS.

The manual contains detailed scoring information for the COMPAS. The scoring instructions, while unambiguous, are often very awkward to follow. For instance, the scoring of the subscales involves simultaneous manipulation and alignment of test form, transparent scoring key, and subscale scoring form. I generally found the scoring instructions to be unnecessarily difficult to use.

The user's manual also contains a scale profile sheet on which to plot the relative subscale and overall computer anxiety levels for a respondent. On this profile sheet there are interpretive statements beside several of the scale values. However, no evidence is provided to support the matching of the scale values with these interpretive statements. The manual implies that these statements follow from a direct interpretation of the rating scale used in the items. For example, the author claims that a score falling in the middle of the score range is indicative of a moderate level of anxiety. Without empirical evidence that people who are moderately anxious do, in fact, score in the middle of the score range, it is difficult to assess the validity of the author's claim. I recommend that the interpretive statements on the COMPAS profile sheet be used cautiously.

In summary, I feel that the overall computer anxiety scale of the COMPAS will be quite useful in measuring the levels of anxiety that people feel when interacting with computers. I am less confident in the utility of the COMPAS subscales, due primarily to modest reliabilities and susceptibility to response sets.

[51]

Oral Motor Assessment and Treatment: Improving Syllable Production. Purpose: "Designed for use with children who have subtle difficulties with rapid, accurate syllable production." Ages 4–11; 1985; 3 parts: reliability training to assess oral motor performance, Oral Motor Assessment Scale, treating oral motor discoordination; 4 scores: Accuracy, Smooth Flow, Rate, Total; individual; 1988 price data: $54 per manual (62 pages) and 2 treatment and assessment cassette tapes; administration time not reported; Glyndon D. Riley and Jeanna Riley; PRO-ED, Inc.*

Review of Oral Motor Assessment and Treatment: Improving Syllable Production by ROBERT RUEDA, Visiting Associate Professor of Curriculum, Teaching, and Learning, University of Southern California, Los Angeles, CA:

The Oral Motor Assessment and Treatment Program is a three-part system designed for "children who have subtle difficulties with rapid, accurate, syllable production," and is meant to improve "the phonological system and fluent production of syllables." The manual appropriately cautions that this program may or may not be helpful for children with overt physical disorders involving difficulty in breathing, swallowing, and other nonverbal motor systems (e.g., cerebral palsy). Additionally, the manual suggests that this program should be used only as a part of an overall management plan, since some cases may involve factors beyond the scope of this program. The test is individually administered and the equipment needed includes a high quality tape recorder with an external microphone and a stopwatch that can be read to one-tenth of a second.

The three parts of the program include: (*a*) Reliability Training needed for administration of the scale, (*b*) the Oral Motor Assessment Scale, and (*c*) the Oral Motor Discoordination Training Program. Each of these will be discussed in turn.

RELIABILITY TRAINING. The reliability training is provided on a single audiotape, and a separate worksheet is provided to allow the listener to follow each part of the training. The tape provides samples of types of errors, which are then scored by the listener and compared to a standard provided by the authors. In addition, this tape provides a section on timing the rate of production of various samples of grouped syllable sets. Normative rates based upon two empirical studies are provided for children between the ages of 3–13, with extrapolated norms for some syllable sets at the 3–5 year age level. The last part of the first tape contains samples of syllable production errors, which are then scored and compared to a standard provided by the authors.

The training appears to be well thought out and clearly presented. The training does take some time to work through, but is essential for

later use of the assessment scale. The most difficult aspects were correctly scoring the grouped syllable sequences once an error was made on the tape, and timing the rate of production. The syllable sets are timed to the tenth of a second, and it takes some effort to obtain the level of precision suggested in the manual. This is not a trivial consideration, since the norms at the lower age levels contain gradations as small as one-tenth of a second separating different age groups. In fact, analysis of variance of rate measures between the various age groups, as indicated in the normative data, did not reach significance.

ADMINISTRATION OF THE OMAS. The OMAS is based on previous versions of oral motor performance measures developed by the same authors. The specific areas of syllable production assessed in this program include accuracy (including distortion errors and voicing errors), flow (including coarticulation errors, even flow, and sequencing errors), and rate. Three syllable sets are used as the basis for scoring these categories, based upon their use in previous research in which norms were calculated. The syllable sets that the child is asked to produce are first modeled by the clinician, at age-appropriate rates, and the child's response is taped for later scoring. Scores are assigned in each of the categories, and are based on the number of errors (as indicated on the scoring sheet provided). The score for rate is based upon standard deviation units from the age-appropriate norms. Overall scores are provided for accuracy, smooth flow, and rate, and these are summed for an overall total score ranging from 0–42.

The part-to-whole correlations, based upon 103 "normal children" reported in the manual for the separate areas of the scale (not including total scores), ranged from .30 for distortions to .67 for rate. Although all correlations were significant, it seems that the scale measures distinct aspects of syllable production. Factor analysis of the scale might help clarify the relationships between the various subscales. In addition to these data, three studies of interobserver reliability conducted by the authors produced reliability coefficients ranging from .83 to .99. However, the reliability of the scale with wider use by clinicians trained only with the audiotape remains to be seen. Validity data for the OMAS was somewhat less complete.

For example, it is reported that 69% of 54 children who stuttered were 1.5 standard deviations away from normal expectations on oral motor discoordination, and a comparable figure was reported for a smaller sample of 17 students. However, this means that approximately 30% of these students scored within normal limits. Since the test is designed for children who have "subtle difficulties," it might be expected that these percentages would be higher. An additional study involving the comparison of scoring judgments of syllable sets with spectographic analysis was inconclusive.

Age-graded normative data are provided in the manuals for 206 children from ages 4 through 11. The manual does not indicate where or when the data were collected.

THE OMAS TRAINING PROGRAM. The training program is designed to impact the accuracy, smooth flow, and rate of syllable set production. Guidelines, based on OMAS scores, are provided for the selection of appropriate cases for treatment. The basic procedure is based upon the clinician's modeling the target syllable set and the child's imitation of the modeled performance. Syllable sets of increasing complexity are used as a basis for the training, and the manual as well as the audiotape provides suggestions, examples of appropriate reinforcement procedures, etc.

SUMMARY. The most positive aspect of this test is the attempt to link reliability training, assessment, and treatment into a single package. The manual is clear, well-written, and simple to follow, with an appropriate amount of detail. In spite of these positive features, however, there is a need for a wider data base on reliability and validity using practitioners in actual clinical settings. In addition, one potential problem with the scale is that the repeated production of nonsense syllables required of children may confound oral motor coordination with factors related to attention. Finally, it is not at all clear how the production of nonsense syllables generalizes to everyday language use. Given the increasing attention to function as well as form in the study of language development and assessment, this type of decontextualized approach may need to be evaluated carefully with respect to an overall language development program.

Review of Oral Motor Assessment and Treatment: Improving Syllable Production by SHELDON L. STICK, Professor, Department of Special Education and Communication Disorders, The University of Nebraska-Lincoln, Lincoln, NE:

The Oral Motor Assessment and Treatment Program was designed for use with children between 4 and 11 years of age who present subtle difficulties with rapid and accurate syllable production. The authors' stated purpose is to describe selected aspects of motor activity that commonly are associated with speech sound production. The intent is to provide a self-training package to enable a user to reliably assess selected motor aspects of speech production. A 14-level treatment program, based on the authors' model, accompanies the assessment training. Included in the purchase price are two audio cassettes that repeat information contained in the manual and also present examples of selected oral motor activity. The manual has three major sections: (1) Reliability Training To Assess Oral Motor Performance, (2) Oral Motor Assessment Scale (OMAS), and (3) Treating Oral Motor Discoordination.

CRITIQUE. As indicated earlier, this three-part Oral Motor Assessment and Treatment Program is aimed at improving syllable production. Empirically it would seem that any program that sets out to systematically increase the rate of production and length of units involved in the production would stand a reasonable chance of being successful, and that practitioners probably would welcome the addition of such an instrument. As a vehicle for improving syllable production, the Oral Motor Assessment and Treatment Program might be a reasonable approach. However, the data provided in the manual do not support its use as anything more than a procedure for assessing nonsense-syllable production and as an outline for training children to produce nonsense syllables at a more rapid rate.

The first major section of the manual addresses reliability training for an individual who would be using the program. It is in this section that the authors present their definitions of the three major categories of syllable production: Accuracy, Smooth Flow, and Rate. These three factors were identified as selected oral motor behaviors commonly observed among individuals who stuttered and/or who presented articulation disorders. It was noteworthy that the authors did not use the same terminology consistently throughout the rest of the manual. That was particularly distracting for the category of Smooth Flow. It is the authors' prerogative to define terms as they elect; however, it would have been helpful had they explained why they elected to deviate from more commonly accepted definitions. For example, the category of accuracy included distortions (lack of precision) and voicing errors (substitution of a voiced cognate for the target consonant). It is possible for a child to substitute a voiceless sound for the target sound, and other types of speech sound substitutions might appear as well as cognate substitutions. Perhaps the authors view these other forms of speech sound substitutions as within the purview of phonological processes. If so, it would have been helpful for such a clarification to be made at the outset of the manual instead of at the very end where they discuss which groups of children might benefit from the Oral Motor Assessment and Treatment Program.

Under the category of Smooth Flow the authors discussed three subareas: coarticulation, even spacing, and correct sequencing. Even spacing might be interpreted as an aspect of Rate, and it is not clear why the authors elected to put this subarea under Smooth Flow. Furthermore, the definition of correct sequencing would seem to have some elements of coarticulation, and it is not apparent why the two areas were not combined. The category of Rate is addressed mainly from the point of view of being slower than a so-called normal standard. There is some reference throughout the manual to a more rapid rate, but the norms presented address only slower than normal rates of speech production.

Training tape 1.1 is transcribed in the manual, so the individual seeking the training from this program has both auditory as well as visual input. There are some problems with this tape, as with the three other tapes, in that it contains an uncommon amount of noise, variation in apparent quality of production, unusual amounts of breathiness on the part of a speaker, apparently unusual cadence (rate), and, possibly, misarticulated speech sounds. The impression is that the tapes lack the professional quality one would expect when purchasing such a program. However, despite the apparent shortcomings of the tapes a listener can develop an understanding of the authors' intentions for Accuracy and Smooth Flow. It would be helpful if the manual contained a number of detachable copies of the various forms referenced for use during the training process instead of having to constantly flip pages or make photocopies of all forms. The manual contains what is referred to as a transcript of the tape, but it is not an exact transcription, which can become disturbing. Also, the writing style in the manual is not precise, and during the first part of the manual the authors' intention is not always apparent. Listening to the tape clarifies the ambiguity.

The second side of the first cassette tape is divided into two sections. The first section provides examples of varying rates that are referenced to an accompanying table in the manual (Table 1). In Table 1 data are presented as time in seconds required to perform selected syllable sets 10 times. Under the 50th percentile is a column heading entitled "Standard Deviation Mean." It is not clear whether that is intended to be the standard error of measurement or whether, in fact, a number of samples were averaged and that figure represents the average of all the standard deviations. Regardless, it would be helpful if information were provided on how that mean score was obtained. The samples presented on training tape 1.3 were acknowledged to be of less than good quality. However, the amount of noise present made judging the samples difficult; in some instances, it might prove detrimental for individuals attempting to become proficient in the use of the instrument.

The second major section of the manual addresses the development of the instrument and presents information on administration and scoring of the various subscales. Some reorganization of this part of the manual probably would be in order because scoring criteria are addressed before the reliability and validity information, but the last part of the section explains the administration and scoring. Perhaps the administration and scoring instruction should precede the scoring criteria and item selection sections. Training tape 2.1 accompanied this part of the manual and, as with both sides of the first training tape, there were numerous problems with this tape. For example, there was variability in terms of the carrier phrase presented to the presentation of the stimulus model in both intensity and in the actual length of time. Furthermore, the samples varied in overall intensity as a consequence of the speaker apparently attempting to get all of the syllables produced in a single breath. With the clinician holding the external microphone approximately 2 inches from a child's mouth (as recommended in the manual), this would seem to be a difficult task to accomplish without creating some distraction and/or unnaturalness in the gathering of the data. Directions for obtaining the sample state that the model presented should be at a rate that is challenging or at a faster rate than would be expected for a child at a given age. However, earlier in the manual the authors commented on the fact that presentation of a model at an uncomfortably rapid rate might cause the child's speech syllable production to deteriorate. That was substantiated by an example on the tape. Yet, during the administration and scoring section the authors recommend doing just that proce-dure. It is not clear why they suggest presenting a model in a manner that is likely to obtain less than an optimum performance from a subject. Several paragraphs later, the authors address this very issue of rate for presentation of the model and stress the importance of presenting age-appropriate rates.

The scoring criteria vary according to the major category and the subareas within the categories. It is not an easy process to follow, but with practice can be implemented. It was noted that the scoring criteria varied without an apparent explanation. For example, under the major category of Accuracy the distortion errors are scored as follows: No errors would be assigned a score of 0; 1–2 errors assigned a score of 1; and 3 or more errors would be assigned a score of 2. The second subarea in the major category of Accuracy, voicing, is scored as follows: No errors equaled 0; 1–2 errors apparently equaled 1; 3 or more errors equaled 3. It should be noted that there was an apparent typographical error in the scoring criteria be-cause the manual stated that 1–2 errors equaled a point value of 3, whereas in the sample score profile form it listed 1–2 errors as receiving a value of 1. There were also other apparent typographical errors in the manual.

Two types of reliability were reported. Part-whole reliability was determined by using 103 normal children, ages 4 through 8, and correlat-ing their scores for each of the major categories and subareas within the categories with the total Oral Motor Assessment Scale (OMAS). All of the correlation coefficients were reported as being statistically significant beyond the .001 level. The total Accuracy category had a correlation of .46, with the two subareas of distortion and voicing having correlations of .30 and .33 respectively. These were by far the lowest correlations with the total OMAS. The total Smooth Flow correlation with the OMAS was .83, with no subunit having a correlation lower than .52. Rate correlated .67 with the OMAS. It would seem that the Accuracy category probably reflects phonological aspects of speech production and, as such, is not truly an index of oral motor ability. Furthermore, since Rate had just one item considered in the correlation coefficient, and it had the single highest correlation with the total OMAS, that could be viewed as a means for obtaining an estimate on oral motor ability without doing the other subunit analyses. There were no data provided on similar correlation coefficients with children presenting articulation or stuttering problems.

The two aspects of validity reported were content and construct validity. For content validity the authors stated that since this was the third generation of an assessment instru-ment, by implication it was more valid than its predecessors. Furthermore, using the second generation instrument the authors reported that 69% of 54 children who stuttered were 1.5 standard deviations below the mean score expected on oral motor abilities. Using the OMAS the authors reported that 12 of 17 children who stuttered scored 1.5 standard deviations above the mean ("above meaning poorer performance"). This would support what was reported with the second generation instrument.

Construct validity evidence included a state-ment by the authors that the OMAS had a "close" relationship with the second generation of the instrument and that this relationship implied construct as well as content validity. Also, the authors stated that the OMAS total score had a correlation of .67 with a procedure suggested by Fletcher (1972); however, Fletch-er's reference was not included in the reference list. The remainder of the discussion on con-struct validity was fragmented and confusing and ended with the authors' statement that construct validity seemed adequate, but that further study was necessary. It is questionable whether the authors provided reasonable information in terms of content or construct validity. It seems that the data provided do little beyond indicating that the instrument has face validity.

Normative data apparently were based on 206 children between 4 and 11 years of age. There was no indication of how the children were selected nor any background information on the children in terms of demographics and/or speech sound production skills. Means and standard deviations were reported for four age groupings: age 4, age 5, ages 6–7, and ages 8–11. There were variable numbers of subjects in each group. Means and standard deviations were reported by age group for the three major categories and then for the total OMAS. When the total scores are examined they show higher means and standard deviations for each of the younger groups, and the authors comment on that difference. However, they do not indicate whether there is any statistically significant difference among any of the groups. Furthermore, the central tendency data are then arranged into levels of oral motor discoordination for each of the age groups without any explanation as to why certain levels are associated with a given number of points. In general, the information provided on the norm group was not adequate for a reader to judge whether the sample selected was representative of a normal population. Additionally, it was unclear why the authors elected to apparently extrapolate, without any explanation, cutoff levels for the oldest age group (8–11) to children of 12 and 13 years of age.

The third major section of the manual addressed a treatment program for oral motor discoordination. It focused on a systematically more complex sequence of syllables throughout a 14-level hierarchy, but there was no clear explanation as to why the various stimuli were selected as opposed to using other stimuli. It was unclear why at least a full page of the treatment section of the manual repeated, verbatim, what was on the first two pages of the manual.

A problem apparent in the training section of the manual, which occurred throughout the entire manual, was that the style of writing was not clear, and individual readers have to infer the intent of the authors. Distracting noise on training tapes was also a problem. Training tape 2.2, which presented examples of oral motor treatment, probably had the least amount of distracting noise. However, the speaker, as on the other training tapes, had apparent misarticulations. It is not known whether the misarticulations were due to the recording mechanism or the individual's manner of speaking. However, these misarticulations were apparent and distracting.

The authors' apparent intent in preparing the Oral Motor Assessment and Treatment Program was to prepare a procedure by which individuals could become reliable in terms of identifying three aspects of what were termed oral motor behaviors observable during syllable production, assessing those oral motor behaviors in a manner that would be reliable, and then providing a systematic treatment program, if necessary. In terms of assisting individuals in the identification of various aspects of speech syllable production, the OMAS does provide some direction, but practicing clinicians will need to decide whether they want to focus on the three major categories identified as reflecting oral motor behaviors (Accuracy, Smooth Flow, and Rate). The present edition of the OMAS does not provide sufficient information to determine whether the data were gathered in a reliable manner, nor is there sufficient information to indicate that the assessment protocol is valid. Furthermore, the poor quality of the accompanying audio tapes and the oftentimes confusing style of writing in the manual raise questions about the instrument's usefulness. Ultimately, each professional will need to decide whether the OMAS has sufficient merit to warrant its purchase.

[52]

Our Class and Its Work. Purpose: "To measure those teaching behaviors believed to contribute to student achievement in the classroom." Grades 3–12; 1983; OCIW; self-report instrument; 8 scales: Didactic Instruction, Enthusiasm, Feedback, Instructional Time, Opportunity to Learn, Pacing, Structuring Comments, Task Orientation, plus Total; user manual (13 pages); technical manual (47 pages); price data available from publisher; administration time not reported; Maurice J. Eash and Hersholt C. Waxman; Maurice J. Eash.*

Review of Our Class and Its Work by JAMES R. BARCLAY, Professor of Educational and

Counseling Psychology, University of Kentucky, Lexington, KY:

The Our Class and Its Work inventory is an instrument of 40 items designed to be administered in grades 3–12 to measure teaching behaviors believed to contribute to student achievement. Test materials include a brief user's manual and a technical report. Both appear to be available from the authors at the College of Education, University of Illinois at Chicago.

The inventory is described in the technical manual as the end product of a chain of research. This research included item analysis, scale formation and deletion, and the final form of the inventory that includes eight scales: Didactic Instruction, Enthusiasm, Feedback, Instructional Time, Opportunity to Learn, Pacing, Structuring Comments, and Task Orientation. The reliability studies appear to support the integrity of these scales. Validity studies include ratings of teachers by one principal and correlations with achievement tests.

The overall impression in reviewing this instrument is that it is very premature to make any judgment about it. Its use has been limited, and it appears to have been applied in various research-related studies only in the Chicago area. Item response alternatives define a 4-point system from *strongly agree* (4) to *strongly disagree* (1). Norms are not provided for interpretation but ranges of scores are divided into four statements. For example, if the total score is from 120–160, the judgment recorded is: "the teacher probably obtains increased achievement from most students." If the total score is below 80 the judgment is: "the teacher probably does *not* obtain increased achievement from most students." Scoring includes a number of items that must be scored negatively.

On the positive side, the scales appear to be related to dimensions that researchers have identified as important in teaching effectiveness. The research underlying the development of items is clear and documents the empirical reasoning used by the authors. On the negative side it is clear that this is a research effort, not a commercial one. Details of scoring may be confusing to some users. Norms are not available, and the interpretation of results is highly tentative.

In summary, much more work should be done with this inventory, relating it to the emotional and affective dimensions of teachers and students. In addition, the use of the inventory for assessment and possible remediation should be documented against other instruments and longitudinal outcomes. At present, it is a research instrument that might be used by researchers, but it does not seem ready in any way to be used for evaluating classroom-climate variables.

Review of Our Class and Its Work by F. CHARLES MACE, Associate Professor, Graduate School of Applied and Professional Psychology, Rutgers University, Piscataway, NJ:

Our Class and Its Work (OCIW) is a self-report questionnaire designed to solicit student appraisals of their teachers' instructional skills in grades 3–12. The instrument consists of 40 items selected to measure the following constructs or scales believed to be predictive of effective instruction: (*a*) Didactic Instruction, (*b*) Enthusiasm, (*c*) Feedback, (*d*) Instructional Time, (*e*) Opportunity to Learn, (*f*) Pacing, (*g*) Structuring Comments, and (*h*) Task Orientation. Each item describes an observable teacher or student activity. Students are asked to judge the extent to which each statement accurately describes their class using a *strongly agree, agree, disagree*, or *strongly disagree* format. Depending on the value of the summed raw scores, the authors suggest the following predictions: The teacher (*a*) probably (raw score = 120–160), (*b*) somewhat inconsistently (80–120), or (*c*) probably does not (below 80) obtain increased achievement from most students. The validity of these predictions and the utility of the instrument are perhaps best understood by examining the questionnaire's psychometric properties.

SAMPLES USED IN DEVELOPING THE OCIW. The OCIW is not a standardized instrument in the usual sense (i.e., norms have not been established for different grade levels against which raw scores are compared). However, during the course of the OCIW's development, various versions of the instrument were administered to approximately 1,500 students in over 100 classrooms in grades 2 through 12. The characteristics of these samples included students from public and parochial schools, urban and suburban districts, and black, Hispanic, and white racial groups. Thus, the OCIW has been extensively field tested with a wide variety of students and, as the authors note, this experience was useful in eliminating items that were vague, unreliable, or poor discriminators. In future versions of the OCIW, the authors may wish to consider establishing norms by grade and perhaps general subject matter. Student responses to many of the items could be expected to vary across grades and subject matter, thus substantially altering the interpretability of the total score. For instance, responses to item 25 ("Students are allowed to select activities on their own") are likely to be very different from a third-grade class than from tenth-grade algebra students.

RELIABILITY. Internal consistency and test-retest reliability have been established for the instrument. Intercorrelations among items were high, with total test reliability estimated at .85 and individual scale reliabilities ranging from .84 to .92. This level of internal consistency suggests a tendency for students to rate individual teachers consistently across the 40-item questionnaire. That is, teacher instructional skills generally appear to be rated by students as either "good" or "bad" (given the limited range of rating options). However, this pattern of ratings seems at odds with probable reality. It seems unlikely that teachers/classrooms are consistently favorable or unfavorable along the eight dimensions assessed by the OCIW, but rather that teachers are skilled in some areas and less so in others. Such a hypothesis is testable by assessing the correspondence between student ratings and direct observations of classroom events (see following discussion of validity).

Test-retest reliabilities assessed at a 5-month interval were rather low, ranging from .38 to .82 (6 of 8 scales were .58 or lower). As the authors note, it is not unusual to find test-retest reliabilities in this range after a long retest interval, and this may actually be expected as students and teachers adjust to one another during the course of the school year.

A measure of reliability that is perhaps more relevant to the assessment of teacher instructional skills is the extent to which students in a given class provide comparable ratings of their teacher (i.e., interrater reliability). If ratings among students in the same class are disparate, we have less confidence in the correspondence

between ratings and actual classroom events. Future versions of the OCIW could be strengthened by assessing interrater reliability which, in this reviewer's opinion, is more meaningful than measures of internal consistency and stability for the assessment of instructional skills.

VALIDITY. The authors report the results of several analyses that assessed the predictive validity of the OCIW. Findings generally showed that, when combined with previous measures of student achievement, some OCIW scales added significantly to the prediction of post achievement gains over and above the predictions based on previous achievement scores alone. It is important to note, however, that the contribution of OCIW scores to the total error variance accounted for was small and substantially less than the contribution of prior achievement despite its statistical significance. Thus, compared to other available measures (e.g., classroom achievement, standardized achievement scores, IQ), the meaningful predictive power of the OCIW appears minimal.

The stated purpose of the OCIW is to "measure those teaching behaviors believed to contribute to student achievement in the classroom." Given this objective it is important to demonstrate that the instrument is capable of providing accurate measures of teachers' instructional skills. Although the authors discuss some of the shortcomings of direct observation, repeated observational measures generally provide the most accurate representation of the subject matter available. Demonstrating the concurrence between student ratings on the OCIW and direct classroom observations is a necessary step in establishing the validity of the instrument; this should be undertaken in future versions of the OCIW.

An important limitation of the OCIW that is common to many rating scales is the instrument's insensitivity to various dimensions of behavior and the conditions under which it occurs. For instance, the *strongly agree* to *strongly disagree* format provides little or no information about the frequency, duration, celeration, latency, and interresponse time of the behaviors in question. Further, the scale does not indicate the prevailing context in which various classroom events occur. It is doubtful, for example, that a classroom is noisy or fraught with interruptions across all situations. To the extent that an assessment device can provide specific information about the dimensions of behavior and conditions under which it is likely to occur, it can be useful in planning and evaluating the effectiveness of interventions.

APPLICATIONS. Beyond its contribution to predicting future achievement, few applications of the OCIW are discussed in the manual. Although the instrument should be used with caution to assess instructional skills until it has been validated, the OCIW has potential applications in the following areas. First, the device could be very useful to assess student opinions or perspectives of their teachers' own perspectives and may set the occasion for reconciling these differences. Second, OCIW ratings may be useful in teacher-training programs to provide student teachers with feedback on how their teaching tactics are perceived by students prior to entering the profession. Third, OCIW scores may be one of several measures used by principals to evaluate teacher performance. Fourth, the OCIW may be useful in instructional research as a measure of social validity or to supplement classroom observational measures.

To summarize, the OCIW has a number of positive features that recommend its use. It has benefited from several revisions, each of which was prompted by research findings on the instrument's psychometric properties. Also contributing to the device's improvement has been its extensive field testing with heterogeneous groups of students. The history of the OCIW and its current characteristics are described in a well-written and scholarly manual. On the negative side, the instrument has not been adequately validated for assessing instructional skills, it has limited predictive validity, and it is generally insensitive to various dimensions of behavior. If the revision process continues to address these issues, the OCIW is likely to become an important instrument in the assessment of teaching skills.

[53]

Parent/Family Involvement Index. Purpose: "Measure of the extent to which parents are involved in their child's special education program." Parents with children in special education programs; 1984–85; P/FII; ratings by teachers; 13 scores: Contact With Teacher, Participation in the Special Education Process, Transportation, Observations at School, Educational Activities at Home, Attending Parent Education/Consultation Meetings, Classroom Volunteering, Involvement With Administration, Involvement in Fund Raising Activities, Involvement in Advocacy Groups, Disseminating Information, Involvement Total, Total; 1985 price data: $2.50 per index and mimeographed paper ('85, 21 pages); (12–15) minutes; John D. Cone, David D. DeLawyer, and Vicky V. Wolfe; John D. Cone.*

Review of the Parent/Family Involvement Index by MARILYN FRIEND, Assistant Professor of Learning, Development, and Special Education, Northern Illinois University, DeKalb, IL:

The Parent/Family Involvement Index (P/FII), developed by the West Virginia University Affiliated Center for Developmental Disabilities and the West Virginia Department of Health, is designed to be an easily administered and scored measure of parents' participation in the education of their handicapped children. The index consists of 63 specific statements describing parent activities in 12 education-related areas. Teachers, aides, or others familiar with the parents indicate one of four responses for each item: yes, no, don't know (DK), or not applicable (NA). A 13th area, overall involvement, is scored on a 6-point scale (1 = *not at all involved*, 6 = *extremely involved*). Separate responses for a mother and a father can be recorded on a single index. Three types of scores can be tabulated for the P/FII: (*a*) a score for each of the 12 areas; (*b*) a total score calculated by summing scores across areas; and (*c*) an overall rating, simply the score obtained for the 13th area. The first two types of scores are percentages of "yes" responses in relation to "yes" and "no" responses. DK and NA responses are excluded from all analyses.

A variation of a paper published in *Exceptional Children* (Cone, DeLawyer, & Wolfe, 1985) serves as the technical manual for the P/FII, and the manual is an appropriate starting point for a discussion of the many problems with the index. In terms of appearance, the manual is poorly arranged and badly reproduced, its single-spacing and fuzzy mimeographed print making it extremely difficult to read. In addition, three tables discussed in the text were missing from the paper.

The manual describes the instrument's development in excruciating detail. Index items were generated based on a literature search for which no parameters were included, and items were grouped on the basis of authors' judgment. Initial field testing resulted in a revision in format, the addition of 13 items, and the rewording of others. No rationale is presented for any of the changes.

The validity of the final version of the instrument is not adequately addressed. While some items clearly have face validity (e.g., "Parent has attended an IEP conference in the school setting"), others seem to have little to do with parents' participation in their handicapped children's education (e.g., "Parent has baby-sat for another handicapped child and/or has been part of a baby-sitting or respite service for parents of handicapped children"). The authors did not employ the relatively simple strategy of submitting items to an expert panel for review. The validity of the index is also suspect because of the exclusion of all DK and NA responses from scoring. A teacher answering only a few items, but positively, could rate parents as more involved than a teacher completing most items but with several negative responses. Nowhere in the manual is this anomaly addressed.

The authors determined the reliability of the P/FII using two methods. First, the instrument's internal consistency was assessed. This strategy is not particularly convincing since relatively high KR-21 values are not necessarily desirable when an instrument purports to measure distinct components of a single phenomenon. Second, interrater reliability was calculated. This was accomplished by having the aides of an unknown number of the 65 special education teachers included in the field test complete an additional P/FII for 24% ($N = 55$) of the 229 families involved in the study. Although such interrater reliability is desirable, the authors did not convincingly establish the independence of these ratings. Finally, test-retest reliability, defined here as a rater's judgments for the same cases across a short period of time (an important consideration), was simply not assessed.

Misleading norms are reported for the index. Although the information in the index booklet states the field test families came from three states and encourages users to compare parents with the included "profiles of normal scores" for mothers and fathers, the manual explains that all families were from middle Atlantic states and primarily from rural areas. Further, 79% of handicapped students in the families were in preschool or elementary school, 61% of them were either trainable mentally retarded or learning disabled, and 65% were enrolled in self-contained classes. The limitations of the reported norms are not mentioned.

From a lengthy list of additional weaknesses with the P/FII, the following three should be noted: (*a*) Several sets of items are hierarchical and thus not independent, and the effect of this factor on scores is not considered by the authors; (*b*) no type of factor analysis or cluster analysis was used to establish the 12 scales; and (*c*) numerous correlations between demographic variables and index scores are reported in a discussion of predicting parent involvement through the use of this index. In order to appropriately address this last issue, a regression analysis should have been completed.

In summary, the P/FII is too technically flawed to systematically assess parent involvement in handicapped students' education. However, because the items are for the most part objective and apparently representative of a wide range of parent involvement levels, it could be appropriately used as a reminder for educators on how to actively involve parents, or as a checklist for inviting parents to select school activities in which they would like to assist educators. Thus, it has a purpose, although not the one intended by its developers.

REVIEWER'S REFERENCE

Cone, J. D., DeLawyer, D. D., & Wolfe, V. V. (1985). Assessing parent participation: The Parent/Family Involvement Index. *Exceptional Children*, 51, 417-424.

Review of the Parent/Family Involvement Index by KORESSA KUTSICK, Assistant Professor of Psychology, James Madison University, Harrisonburg, VA:

The Parent/Family Involvement Index (P/FII) was designed to assess the level of parent participation in their handicapped child's education. The Index is completed by a classroom teacher or educational aide who is familiar with the handicapped child's family. The scale consists of 63 items reflecting parental activities which are broken into 12 categories of involvement: Contact with Teacher, Participation in Special Education Process, Transportation, Observations at School, Educational Activities at Home, Attending Parent/Education Consultation Meetings, Classroom Volunteering, Parent-Parent Contact and Support, Involvement with Administration, Involvement in Fund Raising

Activities, Involvement in Advocacy Groups, and Disseminating Information. A 13th area summarizes a rater's overall impression of the level of parent involvement with the child's educational program.

Instructions for completing the P/FII are straightforward and clear-cut. Raters are asked to check Yes, No, NA (not applicable), or DK (don't know) for each item as it describes a child's parent. Separate inventories may be completed for the mother and father. The composite list of items appears very complete and covers a wide range of parental activities.

Three types of scores may be generated from the P/FII. These include: (a) area scores summarizing each of the 12 different categories of parent involvement; (b) a total score which quantifies parental involvement across all 12 areas; and (c) an overall rating which is the rater's response to the 6-point Likert-scale items comprising area 13 of the index. Calculating the area and total scores of the P/FII are slightly confusing tasks. Raters must follow verbal descriptions of mathematical formulas in order to generate the 12 area scores and the total score. It seems that the inclusion of a printed formula where raters could plug in data and perform the necessary mathematical operations would have simplified the scoring process. Guidelines for interpreting the three scores are also vague. Procedures include transferring area, total, and overall rating scores to a rather crowded profile. A description of a "perfectly" average score is provided, but no specific information is given as to how far scores can vary from average and still be considered "normal." There are also no clear indicators of how to interpret high and low scores.

Psychometric properties of the P/FII are perhaps the weakest characteristics of this instrument. No reliability or validity data are presented in the Index materials. A supplemental paper (Cone, DeLawyer, & Wolfe, 1985) provided by the authors explains test construction procedures and the norming sample, as well as reliability and validity data. Normative data were developed from the scores of 226 mothers and 168 fathers who had handicapped children in special education programs. The majority of these parents were from rural or semi-rural areas. The sample did not reflect stratified U.S. population statistics. A truly randomized selection of families was not

achieved. Reliability data presented in the supplemental paper consisted of reported high interrater and moderate internal consistency values. No clear validity data have been established for this instrument, although it would appear to meet criteria for adequate face and content validity.

The major strengths of this test lie in its purpose and heuristic value. The authors stated that the scale could be utilized in identifying possible needs of parents in terms of their involvement with the education of their special-needs child. Results could lead to recommendations for family interventions. The tool could also be used as a program evaluation measure where documenting changes in parent involvement in a particular education process is necessary. The index should still be considered an experimental scale, however, until additional reliability and validity studies can be conducted. The authors should also be encouraged to develop a parent-completed version of this index. Such a measure would provide direct assessment of parents' perceptions of involvement in their child's educational experiences. It also seems as if it would be necessary to interpret the various scores generated by the P/FII in light of parental sociological conditions. For example, it would seem possible that a single mother who works full time to support three children would have different involvement scores than a married mother of one child who did not work outside the home. It may not be reasonable to expect the same involvement activities from both of these parents. Currently, the P/FII does not incorporate information such as marital or employment status into the interpretation of the index scores.

In summary, the Parent/Family Involvement Index holds promise of being a useful evaluation device. Due to the lack of psychometric data and need for revising the instrument, however, its current applied use should be limited. Further development of this instrument is encouraged.

REVIEWER'S REFERENCE

Cone, J. D., DeLawyer, D. D., & Wolfe, V. V. (1985). Assessing parent participation: The Parent/Family Involvement Index. *Exceptional Children, 51*, 417-424.

[54]

Performance Levels of a School Program Survey. Purpose: "For diagnosing and assessing current offerings of a school program with reported levels of performance." School teachers and administrators; 1979; PLSPS; 9 ability scores: General Intellectual Abilities, Specific Academic Abilities, Leadership Abilities, Creative Productive Thinking Abilities, Psychomotor Abilities, Visual-Performing Arts Abilities, Affective Abilities, Vocational-Career Abilities, Total, and 11 survey scores: Measurement, Enrichment, Acceleration, Individualization, Recognition, Special Activities, Special Personnel, Staff Development, Student Mentors, Out of School/Class Activities, Total; 1985 price data: $14.95 per complete kit including survey materials for 30 participants and manual ('79, 16 pages); (60) minutes; Frank Williams; D.O.K. Publishers, Inc.*

Review of the Performance Levels of a School Program Survey by TIMOTHY Z. KEITH, Associate Professor of School Psychology, Virginia Tech University, Blacksburg, VA:

The Performance Levels of a School Program Survey (PLSPS) is designed to assess whether a school measures and develops eight abilities believed to be important for all school programs. The extent to which schools foster those abilities is measured through a survey administered to teachers and administrators.

The PLSPS attempts to assess a school program's development of General Intellectual Abilities, Specific Academic Abilities, Leadership Abilities, Creative Productive Thinking Abilities, Psychomotor Abilities, Visual-Performing Arts Abilities, Affective Abilities, and Vocational-Career Abilities. Within each of these eight areas, the PLSPS includes one question designed to assess each of the following 10 dimensions: Measurement ("Are there means provided for measuring leadership abilities of students in your class or school?"), Enrichment ("Do you select students who perform well on creative thinking tasks for future experiences requiring such skills in your class or school?"), Acceleration ("Are students identified as intellectually bright accelerated in grade or subject level?"), Individualization ("Are talented students assigned to work with music and art teachers from your staff on artistic activities over and beyond that offered all students?"), Recognition and Reward ("Are academic achievers provided opportunities to pursue advanced work or interest areas as a reward for academic excellence?"), Special Activities ("Do you provide specific lessons and class activities for students which would purposely integrate their emotional along with their academic development?"), Special Personnel

("Are there provisions in your class or school for parent and community involvement in physical education and health programs for students?"), Staff Development ("Is staff development provided for training teachers what vocational-career opportunities are available for students in the local community?"), Student Mentors ("Are intellectually bright students used in and around the school to help others?"), and Out-Of-School/Class Activities ("Are identified leaders excused from classes to participate in further leadership activities in or out of school?"). For each question, respondents are directed to give their impressions of the extent to which their school program develops the activities highlighted in each question; possible ratings are: *not being done* (scored 0), *rarely being done* (1), *usually being done but need more* (2), and *adequately being done, leave as is* (3). The questionnaire is easy to use, although many of the items are difficult to rate.

The manual for the PLSPS is short, and although simple to follow, few details are provided concerning anything other than scoring. The introduction, for example, states the survey was derived from "extensive research dealing with how gifted and creative children learn." Yet none of that research is cited anywhere in the manual, and there is no evidence presented to support the notion that the areas and dimensions the survey is designed to measure are, in fact, important components of an effective school program. Furthermore, there is little attempt to justify the extension of findings from gifted students to the education of students in general. Rather, the author simply states that "by looking at what determines good education for gifted and talented students, one can then relate these findings into better education for most other students." Finally, there is no rationale provided in the manual for the suggested use of the PLSPS at all grade levels in a district, even though it seems likely the abilities and dimensions assessed should be of varying importance at different age levels.

The administration and scoring of the PLSPS is straightforward. Ideally, it is administered to an entire school or district staff, both teachers and administrators, in a group setting. Each item is weighted by its rating (0 to 3) with the ratings summed across ability areas and across dimensions. The eight ability areas and the 10 dimensions are then separately rank ordered from highest score to lowest score. The author suggests the primary interpretation be based on those ranks; areas and dimensions ranked highly should be interpreted as strengths in the school or district program and those areas ranked the lowest should be considered as weaknesses. Obviously, using this approach, even very effective schools will have weaknesses according to the survey, and even ineffective schools will have strengths according to the survey. The raw scores on the eight ability levels may also be summed to provide a total score (averaged across respondents) for the survey. The interpretation of this total score is unclear. The manual simply reports the mean score and range of scores for a sample of 450 teachers and administrators.

The manual reports this is the third version of the PLSPS; two earlier versions of the scale were field-tested and revisions made based on the results of those field tests. Yet details concerning the groups surveyed, the results of those surveys, or the modifications made to the survey are not provided. The only normative information provided in the manual is the range and mean of total scores for a sample of approximately 450 teachers and administrators. Even this group is not described. In fact, it is impossible to determine whether the total mean score reported is based on the final version of the scale or one of the earlier versions of the scale. It is similarly unclear how or where this sample was collected and how the total score should be interpreted.

Reliability and validity information are similarly scant and vague. The author reports a test-retest correlation of .61 for a sample of 51 teachers and administrators over a 6-month period. The score on which the reliability is based is not specified. Presumably the reliability coefficient is based on the total raw score, but it is unclear whether this reliability estimate is based on the current version of the scale or one of the earlier field-tested versions. Finally, no information, even grade level, is reported concerning the sample of teachers and administrators used to calculate reliability. Validity information presented in the manual is restricted to content validity; again the information is vague. The manual reports that "six specialists in evaluation and measurement of gifted and talented educational programs" evaluated the

scale and that "all reported the scale was a valid and useful instrument for assessing a broad spectrum of total human development."

SUMMARY. The PLSPS is an interesting effort to assess a school or district's efforts toward development of various skills and abilities in children. And although the intent of the scale is intriguing, in its present form the PLSPS cannot be recommended for purposes other than research. To fulfill its intended purpose, the PLSPS first needs a much stronger grounding in research, not just research about gifted children, but research concerning school attributes that produce high quality education for all children. The scale should be adequately standardized and interpretable norms presented. The reliability and validity of all recommended scores should be demonstrated, with particular attention devoted to establishing the criterion-related validity of the scale. Specifically, the author should provide evidence that the areas assessed by the scale are, in fact, important for an effective school program.

Review of the Performance Levels of a School Program Survey by LESLIE T. RASKIND, *School Psychologist, Gwinnett County Public Schools, Lawrenceville, GA:*

The Performance Levels of a School Program Survey (PLSPS) is a questionnaire and rating scale designed to survey teachers' and/or administrators' perceptions of how well their school district develops the total human potential of all students. Eight abilities are included for rating, such as General Intellectual Skill, Leadership, Affective Development, etc. (listed in the test descriptive entry above as ability scores). Additionally, ratings can be grouped according to 10 methods of developing students' abilities, such as Providing Enrichment, Special Activities, Use of Student Mentors, etc. (listed above as survey scores).

The PLSPS is designed to assess the school program's effectiveness in developing the eight abilities for most students. However, the specific questions are posed in terms of how well accelerated or talented students are served. The author's rationale is that gifted and regular students vary only in terms of degree of ability, not in kind or type of skills possessed. Because extensive research is available documenting effective ways of educating accelerated students, a survey of gifted education could serve as a blueprint for improving regular education.

The PLSPS consists of an eight-page questionnaire in which 80 items are rated on a 4-point scale ranging from *not being done* to *adequately being done*. Most items request additional qualitative, short-form responses such as who provides a service, how often it is provided, and how many students are served. The author estimates that less than an hour is needed to complete the survey, with scoring taking about 30 minutes. Scoring directions take three pages in the manual, but seem fairly simple; each check is weighted and summed, and total weighted scores are rank ordered. Scores might also be averaged across raters, but the author advises separate comparisons of teacher's perceptions with those of administrators. The only normative data given are a range of total weighted scores and a mean score from surveys completed by approximately 450 teachers and administrators. No other description of the normative group is given. The norms are based on a mixed sample, in spite of the author's admonition to compare teachers and administrators separately. Separate norms should have been provided.

The author states that interpretation of scores is best done by studying the lowest ranked abilities and then meeting with "competent professionals trained in program design to consider modifications." The author indicates that high ranks are rarely found, so that interpretation is best focused on the lowest ranks obtained. The PLSPS purports to be only an initial screening device, and so does not offer suggestions or references for further assessment and remediation of deficiencies.

The PLSPS is designed to provide an efficient and economical survey instrument. Certainly, ease of administration and scoring are strong points of this survey. The instrument is extremely economical in terms of cost. The author has attempted to meet recommended standards by providing information on test construction, reliability, and validity in the manual.

Regarding construction, there were two field tests and three revisions of the PLSPS in six western states. Only the first sample is described, consisting of 435 teachers and principals of schools serving kindergarten through twelfth grade. Only one reliability study was reported consisting of a test-retest study over 6 months. A finding of moderate reliability resulted. The sample was a small mixed group of teachers and administrators ($N = 51$). The small size and lack of descriptive information are limitations of this single study.

Content validity data were gathered by soliciting judgments from six specialists in evaluation of gifted programs. This seems to be one type of validity check for the PLSPS, but specialists in regular education evaluation should have been included because the PLSPS purports to apply to most students, gifted and regular.

This reviewer's most serious concern regarding the PLSPS is the assumption that it can be used validly to survey the offerings of a total school program. If information is desired on all students, why not directly ask teachers to assess the 8 ability areas and 10 survey areas for all students? Although research on gifted education can surely be useful in studying mainstream practices, it seems the indirect method of asking about gifted education and applying results to regular education creates an unnecessary extrapolation. Self-reports are fraught with measurement problems, and a more direct method of asking about regular education (when generalizations are to be made to regular education) would seem to improve the PLSPS. Alternatively, the author could present his instrument as a way of assessing gifted programs.

Less serious concerns include the fact that no directions are printed on the rating form. The form is somewhat self-explanatory, but questions could arise as to whether all questions must be answered and whether the rater is to score the total number of checks on each page, or leave that portion blank. Additionally, some directions should have been given for the use of the short-answer qualitative data. Otherwise, asking for such specific information seems to strain the good graces of the rater. Lastly, this reviewer felt that the test is too short (80 items) to derive the 18 scores. The grid-system used to develop the 18 scores contributed to items that seemed very repetitive. The author may be trying to investigate too many areas with too few items.

The PLSPS was found to be an economical survey in which the author attempted to adhere to accepted standards in reporting reliability, validity, and test construction information directly in the manual. However, this reviewer feels the PLSPS is better suited to be used as a survey of a gifted and talented program rather than to survey an entire curriculum. The PLSPS could be said to be an initial screening device, but to say the PLSPS diagnoses and assesses current offerings of a total school program overstates its usefulness.

[55]

Personal Outlook Inventory. Purpose: "Predicts the probability of employee theft before a person is hired." Prospective employees; 1983; POI; 5 scores: Personal Demographics, General Activity Level, Social and Moral Values, Satisfaction With Personal Circumstances, Risk-Taking Behavior; technical report (14 pages); 1985 price data: $18 or less per inventory; administration time not reported; Selection Research Publishing; Wolfe Personnel Testing and Training Systems, Inc.*

[The publisher informed us in September, 1987 that this test has been discontinued.]

Review of the Personal Outlook Inventory by ROBERT M. GUION, University Professor Emeritus of Psychology, Bowling Green State University, Bowling Green, OH:

Interest seems to be growing in using tests to tackle the problem of employee theft. This inventory is said to differ from other so-called honesty tests in that it has been developed and validated against actual theft reports.

It is not theory-based. The Technical Report, the only manual available, says that the five component parts (the subscores, for which no interpretations are offered) are related to a presumably generalized trait, "propensity to steal." This contention is based on "an extensive literature review." There is no discussion of the general propensity or of the relationship of the component traits to it, so a user can have only a vague idea of what, if anything, is being measured by this 37-item inventory. The report ignores many debatable issues. For example, on what basis is it assumed that "propensity to steal" is a general or stable trait? Are components such as high activity level and great willingness to take risks causally associated with theft, or is the relationship in the opposite direction? In many jobs, these would be considered desirable traits. How does the logic of the inventory distinguish between desirable and undesirable activity and risk taking?

The answer is not available, largely because there is no articulated logic. This inventory was developed in a strictly empirical tradition. A 378-item pool was developed and divided into two sets, set A with 178 items and set B with 200. Each set was given to recently hired employees in several stores of a retail chain (a different chain for each set). Subsequent records of those fired for theft were kept for 9 months. These cases made up one category of a dichotomous criterion with those still employed after 9 months making up the other. Voluntary terminations were excluded. For each data set, two-thirds of the data were used for item analysis, and the other third was held back for cross validation. In the primary samples, items with significantly different response rates in the two criterion categories were identified. In the holdout groups, total scores (not subscores) based on these items gave validity coefficients of .43 and .23. No reliability data are reported.

Nor are other important technical data reported. No norms (other than means and standard deviations) are provided. No item statistics are reported, even for the 37 items retained, nor were they determined within the holdout group. The level of significance required for item retention is not mentioned. The probability level required for significance is not reported. The problem of multiple significance tests, particularly severe with 378 nonindependent tests, is not mentioned. In each item set, approximately 10% of the items were keyed as significant, an unimpressive proportion when one considers that (a) the number of cases was apparently quite large, although not given, so very small differences are significant at any level; (b) the inclusion of each item in the final inventory rests on a single unreplicated significance test; and (c) the number of items in the pool was very large, making the usual problem of multiple significance tests extremely severe.

A further analysis of 549 cases "drawn from" data set B included 177 people terminated for theft and 372 others. However, only 270 of the 549 were in the holdout group. These selected cases give a higher point-biserial correlation (.39) than reported for the full data set from which they were drawn (.23). The basis for selecting cases is not clear; indeed, it is not clear why this analysis was done. One interest expressed in the Technical Report is compliance with the Uniform Guidelines, and this particular analysis does attempt to provide data for ethnic subgroups. Oddly enough, it offers ethnic group correlations not only for cases drawn from the cross-validation sample but also for those from the original item-analysis group and for the whole set of 549 cases including cases from both groups. We cannot say why these latter two sets of data were reported, but the impression of technical naivete is strong. The impression is enhanced when cross-validation subgroup analyses are reported for 22 blacks and 10 Spanish—samples clearly too small for sensible conclusions.

Other data on the use of the inventory sustain that impression. One study reports a kind of program evaluation, presented as evidence of "operational validity" of the 37-item test. Four stores using the test in preemployment screening had a 68% decrease in terminations for theft; four others without the test had a 29% increase. These data seem impressive at first, but alternative interpretations are plausible and uninvestigated. To what extent is the dramatic decrease due to the predictive validity of the test, and to what extent can it be attributed to the test as a sign that the theft problem is getting serious management attention, thereby increasing risk of getting caught? Some decrease due to the use of a valid predictor could be expected, but its storewide effect would be diluted by the presence of employees not so screened. Yet the effect reported here seems anything but diluted.

Other operational validity data show mean scores for those fired for theft, in each of 2 years, 2 points below the means for all people hired (including those later fired for theft). This very small difference raises ethical and utility problems not considered in the Technical Report. These problems are not limited to this particular inventory; they are common to efforts to screen out potential thieves. But how ethical would it be for a company to decide to reject people for having a general "propensity to steal," and tagging them so in company records, on the basis of inventory scores? The question suggests that users should be very sure they know what they are doing by having very strong validity data. For this inventory, the available validity data are sparse; although suggestive, they are far from convincing. The utility questions require attention to the relative costs of false positives and false negatives; these issues are not examined in the Technical Report.

In short, unanswered questions about logic, item analyses, predictive or follow-up validity, and utilities at different score levels are serious enough to cast doubt on the use of the inventory for anything beyond exploratory research.

Review of the Personal Outlook Inventory by KEVIN R. MURPHY, Associate Professor of Psychology, Colorado State University, Fort Collins, CO:

Employee theft is thought to account for over a billion dollars in annual losses in the retail industry alone. A variety of techniques, including polygraph examination, honesty testing, and voice analysis have been suggested as methods of reducing theft. The Personal Outlook Inventory (POI) represents a relatively new instrument designed to meet this same goal. In particular, the POI is promoted as a scientifically sound instrument that predicts the likelihood that a prospective employee will steal. The test is specifically recommended for use in personnel selection; the POI manual claims that the inventory complies with all legal regulations and that it has been shown to be highly effective in reducing theft.

The POI is an empirically keyed inventory, similar to the Minnesota Multiphasic Personality Inventory or the Strong-Campbell Interest Inventory. That is, POI items were selected on the basis of their success in discriminating employees who are caught stealing from those who are not. As with other empirically keyed inventories, the acid test of the POI rests on its ability to predict theft in some sample other than the samples used in developing the test. Little evidence exists that the POI meets this criterion.

The technical manual for the POI presents two classes of evidence that at first appear to support the validity of the POI: (*a*) cross-validation studies and (*b*) studies of operational validity. Close examination of this evidence suggests that the case for the validity of the POI is quite weak. First, the cross-validation studies employ a design that essentially guarantees a high cross-validated correlation (r) even when significant overfitting exists; this design is especially inappropriate for empirically keyed tests (Murphy, 1983, 1984). In each of three cross-validation studies described in the technical manual, a sample of employees was randomly divided into derivation and cross-validation subsamples, and that test was used to predict theft in the cross-validation subsamples. The test manual cites the high levels of cross validity as evidence of the validity of the inventory. In fact, the large cross validities are no indication of the usefulness of the test, but rather reflect the fact that the derivation and validation subsamples are (and by design must be) very similar, and that an empirically keyed test that works well in the derivation subsample *must* also work well in the cross-validation subsample (see Murphy, 1983 for an extended critique of this cross-validation design). Thus, these studies present no credible evidence that the test generalizes to samples other than those used in test development. Since empirically keyed tests can take substantial advantage of chance, this sort of evidence is crucial.

Second, the operational validity studies that describe the effects of using the POI in the field are both poorly designed and poorly reported, making their interpretation difficult. For example, the manual reports that four stores that used the test experienced a 68% decrease in negative references (persons previously terminated for theft), while four other stores that did not use the test reported a 29% increase. We do not know whether the test itself, the very fact that some stores used a test and others did not, or some other irrelevant characteristic (e.g., store location) is responsible for this difference. Later, test scores in an undetermined number of stores are reported for 1980 and 1981. These scores indicate that individuals fired for theft had lower scores than the total group hired, but it is not clear whether these differences are statistically significant, or whether differences in range restriction have been taken into account. Finally, the manual notes that in another setting (N is once again unspecified), the number of employees discharged with scores in the "reject," "questionable," and "acceptable" ranges were 6%, 2%, and .6%, respectively. The manual does not indicate whether these differences are significant.

In addition to the unimpressive validity evidence cited above, the test shows little evidence of reliability. A reliability coefficient of .58 is reported. Although the manual is unclear about the method used in estimating reliability, it appears that this coefficient describes the internal consistency of the POI. An internal consistency measure is hardly appropriate for an empirically derived test such as the POI, but even if it was appropriate, a coefficient of .58 would not indicate an acceptable level of reliability.

The technical manual is deficient in several respects. First, normative data are not reported in sufficient detail. For example, the mean and standard deviation in the theft group ($M = 28.1$, $S.D. = 6.6$) and the nontheft group ($M = 35.0$, $S.D. = 6.6$) of the test development sample are presented, but these statistics do not provide a sufficient basis for setting cutting scores or for interpreting individual scores. Second, the manual is filled with minor inconsistencies. For example, the POI is described as a 35-item test in the manual, but in fact is comprised of 37 items. Third, redundant statistics are often presented as if they conveyed new information. For example, we are told that the differences between the means of the theft and nontheft groups are significant, and that the point-biserial correlation between test scores and group membership is also significant. The significance test for the point-biserial r is in fact exactly the same as the test of the difference between group means.

The most important difficulty with the manual is the ambiguity in describing test-development procedures. We are told that two experimental forms, A and B, were used, and that 16 of 178 items (Form A) and 26 of 200 items (Form B) discriminated theft from nontheft groups. It is not clear whether the operational validity studies described earlier employed Form A, Form B, or some combination of both. The POI is described as being made up of 35 selected items, but it is not clear how these items relate to the items on Forms A and B. The manual implies that these items were somehow selected from the 42 discriminators from Forms A and B, but gives no detail. In addition, a potentially serious confounding exists, since at least some of the data involved in the development of Form B were also used in developing weights for the POI. In addition, the manual fails to discuss the relationships between the weights derived for Forms A and B and the POI weights. Assuming that items from Forms A and B were used in the POI, it is reasonable to ask whether the same weights were derived in the different item analyses.

That is, it would be useful to know whether items that discriminated theft from nontheft groups in the original analyses of Forms A and B also discriminated between groups in the item analysis conducted for the POI.

The manual does not state whether the POI has adverse impact. However, the scores of Black and Hispanic members of the test-development sample were somewhat lower than the scores of whites. In the light of these data, the claim put forth in the promotional materials that the POI complies with all legal regulations must be examined in terms of the evidence provided. Evidence concerning reliability and validity reviewed above suggests that this claim is overstated. Some features of test scoring suggest additional problems. The inventory yields scores on five separate scales; practically no detail regarding these scales is given in the manual. These five scores are sent to the publisher, who returns a single score that is described as indicating the probability of theft. Apparently, scores are reported on a 4-point scale, anchored as *low risk*, *moderate risk*, *substantial risk*, and *extreme risk*. There is no indication of the actual risk levels asociated with these labels or of the scoring procedures used to transform scale scores to a single risk measure.

In summary, the POI is advertised as a valid tool for reducing employee theft. The available evidence does not support this interpretation. Unfortunately, it is difficult to identify a superior test that can be used for this same purpose; there is little evidence that paper-and-pencil tests or physiological measures such as the polygraph provide valid predictors of theft (Lykken, 1970; Sackett & Harris, 1984). The POI claims to be superior to its competitors; those claims are yet to be validated.

REVIEWER'S REFERENCES

Lykken, D. (1979). The detection of deception. *Psychological Bulletin*, 86, 47-53.
Murphy, K. (1983). Fooling yourself with cross-validation: Single sample designs. *Personnel Psychology*, 36, 111-118.
Murphy, K. (1984). Cost-benefit considerations in choosing among cross-validation methods. *Personnel Psychology*, 37, 15-22.
Sackett, P., & Harris, M. (1984). Honesty testing for personnel selection: A review and critique. *Personnel Psychology*, 37, 221-245.

[56]

Personal Profile System. Purpose: "Helps people identify their behavioral style and pinpoints what they might do to become more effective and successful people." Employees; 1977-83; self-report instrument; 1985 price data: $7.50 per profile booklet; $10 per manual ('83, 70 pages); (60–360) minutes depending upon preferred program format; published by Performax Systems International, Inc.; distributed by Development Publications.*

Review of the Personal Profile System by ELLEN MCGINNIS, Assistant Professor of Special Education, University of Wisconsin-Eau Claire, Eau Claire, WI:

The goal of the Personal Profile System, originally published in 1979 and revised in 1983, is to help "people identify their behavioral style and pinpoints what they might do to become more effective and successful people." The Personal Profile is based on William M. Marston's theory that behavior can be viewed according to four clusters: Dominance, Inducement of Others, Steadiness, and Compliance. These behavioral clusters, according to Marston, could be described along two axes: Process Oriented and Product Oriented.

The Personal Profile is comprised of 24 descriptors, modified from Marston's 1928 work by Geier (1967). In completing this self-report scale, the user is instructed to rate each descriptor as *most* descriptive and *least* descriptive of himself/herself. These choices are then placed on three graphs yielding profiles of the person's behavior in reaction to others' expectations, in reaction to stress or pressure, and according to the interaction of the environment and the individual's response style.

The measure is designed to be self-scored and self-interpreted and is suggested for a workshop in the training/development of adults and high-school-age youth. The manual contains sections on theory, reliability and validity, administration, applications, and suggested use.

The theoretical base of the Personal Profile System and its focus on increasing individuals' understanding of their own behavioral patterns in relationship to environmental factors have value in increasing personal effectiveness. A serious concern with this instrument is its lack of reported research. While the authors state the instrument shows good reliability and validity, they provide the user with virtually no data to support these claims.

The manual refers to a study of 300 Minnesota dentists using the system, but neglects to provide the reader with statistical specifics. The manual also refers to studies involving "hundreds of thousands of people" but does not provide specific results or references, stating that these studies "are not widely available" or "cannot be included in this packet because of their confidential nature." The authors do briefly describe one study of 100 subjects who were given the Personal Profile System, the Tennessee Self-Concept Scale (TSC), and the Personal Orientation Inventory (POI). According to the authors, items on the Personal Profile System highly correlated with items on the other two measures. However, the authors fail to report complete information and conclude: "The dimensions of the Personal Profile are sufficiently represented within the POI and the TSC to assume that some of the underlying attributes of the POI and TSC are also being measured by the scales of the Personal Profile. Not having the scores on the subscales for each of the POI and TSC, it is not possible to get a direct relationship between the Personal Profile and reported scores on the POI and TSC." Clearly, such vague and incomplete information regarding the construct or convergent validities of the Personal Profile is unacceptable.

While the theory behind this instrument holds promise in increasing individuals' awareness of their behavioral styles in interactions with environmental conditions, the clear lack of data to support this instrument should preclude its use.

REVIEWER'S REFERENCES

Marston, W. M. (1928). *Emotions of normal people*. New York: Harcourt, Brace.
Geier, J. G. (1967). A trait approach to the study of personalities and their roles in task situations. *The Journal of Communication*, 17, 316-323.

[57]

Power Base Inventory. Purpose: "Designed to measure the kinds of power which a manager (or supervisor) chooses to use with subordinates." Managers and supervisors; 1985; self-administered; 6 scores: Information, Expertise, Goodwill, Authority, Reward, Discipline; manual (20 pages including inventory); 1987 price data: $5.25 per each 1–99 inventories (minimum order $20); (10) minutes; Kenneth W. Thomas; XICOM, Inc.*

Review of the Power Base Inventory by RABINDRA N. KANUNGO, Professor of Psychology and Management, McGill University, Montreal, Quebec, Canada:

The main purpose of the Power Base Inventory is to assess the reasons for subordinates' compliance with supervisors' wishes when these wishes are expressed in different ways (e.g., suggestions, directions, requests, orders, etc.). The theoretical basis of the inventory is the typology of social power and influence processes developed by French and Raven (1959). Ordinarily, operationalization of the French and Raven typology of social power deals with five bases of power: reward, coercive, legislate, expert, and referent. The Power Base Inventory is designed to measure these five power bases plus a sixth, referred to as information power. The possibility of informational influence was suggested by French and Raven (1959) but was not considered to be a primary source of power. By accepting the informational influence as a separate primary source of supervisory power and measuring it independently, the Power Base Inventory appears more inclusive in scope compared to other measures (e.g., Kanungo, 1980; Student, 1968).

In addition to the inclusiveness criterion, the Inventory is different from other measures of French and Raven social power framework in yet another way. The Inventory is designed to assess the six bases of supervisory power through supervisor's perception of subordinate's reasons for compliance. The common practice, however, following French and Raven's theoretical rationale, is to use subordinates' own perceptions of their reasons for compliance (Podsakoff & Schriesheim, 1985). Since the Inventory is meant to reveal supervisor's rather than subordinates' response, the scores cannot be interpreted as true indications of subordinates' reasons for compliance. Rather the scores indicate supervisor's perceptions of subordinates' reasons, and being one step farther removed from subordinates' reasons, such perceptions may be influenced by unknown attributional errors.

The Inventory uses a paired comparison format with 30 paired items designed to measure six power bases. The range of scores for each power base is 0 to 10. The use of multiple items forced-choice technique is a considerable improvement over other single item questionnaire formats (e.g., Kanungo, 1980) for drawing a comparative profile of six power bases. In spite of such improvements, there are serious problems with content validity. For instance, one finds no information on item construction and no justification for item content.

A careful examination of the items reveals that several items in the Inventory appear too general and vague. Such items are open to different interpretations. For example, Item 27A, "They have to agree with the facts that I use for support," can be interpreted two ways. Subordinates may agree because of the merits of the facts (informational influence) or because the facts are used by a superior (legitimate power base).

Furthermore, inclusion of several direct attributional statements such as Item 17A, "They enjoy doing what they can for me," creates problems. Inclusion of such items enhances the possibility of attributional and social desirability errors. It would be more appropriate to use only behavioral items such as Item 12B, "I show them how to properly interpret and deal with the situation, so that we agree."

A different type of problem affecting content validity stems from changing the referents across items. The Inventory uses some items that reflect the supervisor's direct perception of resources under his/her control and other items that reflect the supervisor's perception of similar resources through the eyes of subordinates. Item 25B, "I am able to get them to see why I am right" is an example of the former type, and Item 26B, "They think I could be tough with them if I had to" is an example of the latter type.

It is not clear whether an adequate sampling of the content domain was achieved. A cursory look at the five to seven items reflecting each power base reveals the item content to be very narrow. In addition, the dimensionality of a given domain remains unknown, as does the internal consistency of items measuring a given power base. Failure to provide such information makes assessment of construct validity difficult.

There is no information on how the six power bases are related to each other. Without such data, it is hard to justify informational influence as a primary power base separate from the influence exerted through supervisor's expertise.

The Inventory provides descriptions of how to score and interpret profiles of individual respondents. Percentile data based on the profiles of 317 managers from a variety of organizations are provided to serve as norms. Although the norms are useful, this information is hardly adequate considering the lack of data on reliability, dimensionality, stability, and validity of the Inventory.

A qualitative description of six bases of "managerial power," the conditions under which each power base is effective, and the interpretation of high and low scores are useful appendages from a practitioner's point of view. However, no information is available demonstrating the effectiveness of a given power under specific conditions (i.e., criterion-related validity). Furthermore, there is no information on conditions under which two or more power bases in combination may be more effective than such power bases operating in isolation.

In summary, the Power Base Inventory does not represent a reliable and valid standardized instrument for measuring bases of managerial power. Hence it cannot be useful as a diagnostic tool to identify the nature of a manager's influence over subordinates. However, it can be used during training sessions as a structured exercise or a training tool that can sensitize managers to the nature of the social influence processes within organizations.

REVIEWER'S REFERENCES
French, J. R. P., & Raven, B. (1959). The bases of social power. In D. Cartwright (Ed.), *Studies in social power*, (pp. 150-167). Ann Arbor, MI: Institute for Social Research.
Student, K. R. (1968). Supervisory influence and work group performance. *Journal of Applied Psychology*, 52, 188-194.
Kanungo, R. N. (1980). *Biculturalism and Management*. Toronto: Butterworths.
Padsakoff, P. M., & Schriesheim, C. A. (1985). Field studies of French and Raven's bases of power: Critique, reanalysis, and suggestions for future research. *Psychological Bulletin*, 97, 387-411.

Review of the Power Base Inventory by CHARLES K. PARSONS, *Professor of Management, Georgia Institute of Technology, Atlanta, GA:*

The Power Base Inventory provides a measure of a manager's perception of his/her bases of power over his/her subordinates. The instrument is based primarily on the work of French and Raven (1959). The instrument yields scores on six scales representing six bases of managerial power. These scales are (*a*) Information, (*b*) Expertise, (*c*) Goodwill, (*d*) Authority, (*e*) Reward, and (*f*) Discipline. The test booklet contains one page of introduction, three pages of forced choice items (a total of 30 item pairs), one page for self scoring the instrument, one page for graphing a power base profile, and nine pages of score interpretation. There is also a page where the respondent is asked to provide background data to be sent along with the data sheet back to the authors of the instrument.

The instructions for the forced choice items are clear. The respondent is forewarned that some item pairs may appear equally descriptive, but is instructed to choose one item from each of the 30 item pairs. The items appear to be approximately matched on social desirability, though no data concerning social desirability were provided. This might cause some uneasiness among respondents because there are likely to be times when they feel both statements are equally descriptive (or nondescriptive) of their beliefs.

For each of the 30 item pairs, the respondent simply circles the item (A or B) that is more characteristic of his/her subordinates' reasons for compliance. Some of the items are used more than once in a different pair. The basis for item construction was not included in the materials that this reviewer saw. The power base tapped by each item is apparent to one who knows the French and Raven typology.

The respondent can score the instrument by circling the letter of the item chosen for each pair on a special scoring sheet. The number of items are totaled for each of six scales. Scores can range from 0 to 10 for each scale. Because of the ipsative nature of the scales, the respondent cannot get the maximum (or minimum) number of points on all scales.

Scores on each scale can be converted to percentiles using a chart provided by the authors. The norming group is described as "317 managers in a variety of organizations." It should be noted that the authors encourage the respondent to send a copy of his/her data sheet and background information to the authors. This action leads this reviewer to believe that more specific norming data will be provided in the future.

The interpretation of scores includes a description of each of the six power bases. The descriptions are brief but clear. There are also descriptions of situations when use of each power base is desired and what is required to use this power base effectively.

Finally, there are warning signals for respondents who scored high or low on a particular scale. The signals are meant to be diagnostic and help the manager determine why he/she tends to hold certain beliefs. These warning signals are provided for high and low scorers on all six scales.

No validity or reliability data were provided to this reviewer. The construct of managerial power bases deserves further research. It is hoped that the authors will provide data in the future concerning the relationships between scores on the six scales and other managerial behaviors. Because the interpretations of the scales are situational and normative (certain power bases are more appropriately used in certain situations), research needs to be conducted to substantiate the suggestions offered as part of this instrument.

REVIEWER'S REFERENCE

French, J. R. P., & Raven, B. (1959). The bases of social power. In D. Cartwright (Ed.), *Studies in social power* (pp. 150-167). Ann Arbor, MI: Institute for Social Research, University of Michigan.

[58]

Preschool and Kindergarten Interest Descriptor. Purpose: "Identify children with attitudes and interests usually associated with preschool and kindergarten creativity." Ages 3–6; 1983; PRIDE; downward extension of the Group Inventory for Finding Creative Talent; scale for rating by parents; 4 dimension scores: Originality, Imagination-Playfulness, Independence-Perseverance, Many Interests; 1984 price data: $55 per complete set including manual (10 pages), and 30 scales; $10 per specimen set; scoring service included in the cost of the test; (20–35) minutes; Sylvia B. Rimm; Educational Assessment Service, Inc.*

Review of the Preschool and Kindergarten Interest Descriptor by GLORIA A. GALVIN, Assistant Professor and Director, School Psychology Training Program, Ohio University, Athens, OH:

The Preschool and Kindergarten Interest Descriptor (PRIDE) was developed as a screening measure for young children who may qualify for programs for the creatively gifted. The inventory contains 50 questions to which parents respond regarding their own or their child's interests and behaviors. The responses are made on a Likert-type scale. Given the question, "My child likes to do hard puzzles," parents may check "*no,*" "*to a small extent,*" "*average,*" "*more than average,*" or "*definitely.*" Group administration of the inventory to parents while visiting school is recommended.

In order to score the inventory, it must be sent to a scoring service that promises to return results within 1 month of receipt. The results are reported in percentile ranks and Normal Curve Equivalent scores for the total PRIDE inventory and in stanines for the four dimensions of the PRIDE, reportedly based on factor analysis of the inventory. Perhaps it is an understandable business decision not to allow users to score the inventory themselves; however, this requirement does introduce a significant delay in receiving the results for use in decision making. This is a problem in a screening device that should be followed by more focused assessment of creativity on those who have been screened "in." The length of time needed to receive screening results adds significantly to the amount of time in the overall assessment process.

The PRIDE inventory has several attractive features. It is brief and easy to administer; parents will not find the questions at all threatening and should, in fact, find them easy to answer. The use of parents as respondents allows for assessment of young children who would not be good candidates for self-report methods. Finally, PRIDE offers a substitute for teacher-nomination methods of identifying creative children that have been found unsatisfactory.

Unfortunately, there are also significant problems with the PRIDE inventory in regard to purpose and development. Its purpose is described in the manual as, "to screen children 'into' a program and not 'out' of a program." No cutoff scores are provided nor recommended to be developed from local norms. Although the purpose of screening should be to be overly inclusive (and to follow screening with additional assessment of those screened "in"), failure to screen anybody "out" seems to leave the PRIDE inventory without a clear purpose. Given the stated purpose, the author does not feel constrained to provide any information regarding the decision-making efficiency of PRIDE. The issue of false positives and false negatives has been avoided. Rather, users are told that students not selected by high PRIDE scores may be selected by other means such as teacher nomination, even though it is the criticisms of teacher nomination (Rimm, 1984) that has spurred the development of PRIDE.

The psychometric data gathered during the development of the PRIDE inventory appears promising. However, the data are only minimally reported. Internal consistency reliability is reported for the total inventory as .92; however, no further information is provided on the subjects upon whom this was based nor on

the details of that study. More importantly, no assessment of test stability or interrater (e.g., mother, father) reliability is presented, and these would both be useful in judging the value of this instrument.

Three studies of criterion-related validity are reported. Subjects numbered 62, 18, and 14 children, respectively. Two significant correlations (.50, .38) are reported for two of the subject groups between PRIDE and a composite criterion score based on a drawing of a picture, a "brief dictated story," and a teacher rating. This evidence is promising; however, two of the sample sizes are very small and details about the subjects and the study are not given, making judgment of the quality of the evidence impossible.

Construct validity for the PRIDE is asserted based on the evidence that test items were taken from preschool characteristics of creative children reported in papers by scholars in the area of creativity. Furthermore, the PRIDE is reported to contain four dimensions determined by factor analysis. Unfortunately, the factor analysis is not reported in the manual other than to indicate that it was performed and to name the factors (dimensions) obtained from the analysis. No report is made of how many items make up each dimension, the number of subjects on which the analysis was based, or how reliable the factors are. The norm group for the PRIDE is reported as 114 children representing urban, rural, and suburban areas. No further description as to age, sex, or any other relevant characteristics is provided. If the purported factor analysis was based on the norm group, the sample is too small to yield reliable results from a factor analysis of a 50-item inventory.

In summary, the PRIDE is a good first step towards development of a creativity screening measure for preschoolers that may eventually prove to be more useful than teacher nomination. The items have face validity and have been derived from several research sources. What is needed is an effort to administer the PRIDE to a large representative sample that could be the basis for a carefully described normative population. Then factor analytic, reliability (consistency, stability, and interrater), and validity studies need to be carried out and reported to the potential user in the manual. As currently presented, the PRIDE costs approximately $1.33 per administration and requires the examiner to wait a month for results of questionable value.

REVIEWER'S REFERENCE
Rimm, S. (1984). The characteristics approach: Identification and beyond. *Gifted Child Quarterly, 28,* 181-187.

Review of the Preschool and Kindergarten Interest Descriptor by SUE WHITE, Assistant Professor of Psychology, Case Western Reserve University, School of Medicine, Cleveland, OH:

According to the author, this assessment instrument was designed "in order to provide an easy to administer, reliable and valid instrument for use in screening preschool and kindergarten children for programs for the creatively gifted." This questionnaire consists of 50 items to which a parent responds on a 5-point scale. Scoring is to be done only by the test publisher and is included in the original cost of the test. The author indicates that this test is to be used to include a child in a creativity program, but admits that a low score should not be allowed to restrict a child's admission if the teacher feels such would be appropriate. This reviewer believes, however, that all children at this age (3–5 years) should be included in any such creativity programs.

Psychometrically this test does not meet adequate standards as its norms are based on "114 children representing urban, suburban and rural populations." The extremely small sample coupled with the lack of other demographic information makes this test unacceptable for applicability to a larger population, especially for providing for the tracking of children at a very young age. The test manual provides very scanty data relative to reliability and validity. It is felt that this test should be avoided and is inappropriate for the purpose for which it was designed.

[59]

Preschool Behavior Rating Scale. Purpose: Measures the level of children's preschool behavioral skills in the psychomotor, cognitive, and social areas. Day care, Head Start, or nursery school children ages 3–6; 1980; PBRS; ratings by teachers; 9 scores: Coordination, Expressive Language, Receptive Language, Environmental Adaptation, Social Relations, Total, Language Skills, Socialization Skills, Psychomotor Skills; individual; 1986 price data: $7 per basic packet including blank scale and manual ('80, 23 pages); $2 per blank scale; $6.50 per manual; $3.50 per technical monograph; Wil-liam F. Barker and Annick M. Doeff; Child Welfare League of America, Inc.*

Review of the Preschool Behavior Rating Scale by MARY LOU KELLEY, Assistant Professor of Psychology, Louisiana State University, Baton Rouge, LA:

The Preschool Behavior Rating Scale (PBRS) is a 20-item instrument for assessing preschoolers' psychomotor, cognitive, and social skills. The scale is completed by teachers on children aged 3–6 who are enrolled in a daycare or preschool program. As described in the scoring manual, the PBRS can be used to: (a) screen for developmental delays; (b) identify children in need of further evaluation; (c) objectively monitor children's skill acquisition over time; (d) guide teachers' selection of appropriate curriculum; and (e) evaluate program effectiveness.

The items are grouped into five domains: Coordination, Expressive Language, Receptive Language, Environmental Adaptation, and Social Relations. All items are written using a Guttman scaling format with 4–5 response choices. Item choices range from lower to higher skill levels. Raters are required to select the response choice closest to the actual behavior of the child.

In part, each item is intended to assess a child's skill level within a very broad area. In doing so, the measure can be completed in a short period of time and yields information about a variety of skills relevant to preschoolers' adaptive functioning.

The manual emphasizes evaluating children based on observed behavior rather than the child's potential. Although objectivity is emphasized, many of the items appear to lack adequate specificity for obtaining objective ratings. For example, the item used to assess fine motor skills contains response choices ranging from "1. Generally unable to use or manipulate preschool materials requiring fine motor skills, eye-hand coordination (e.g., crayons, scissors, buttoning, or unbuttoning)," to "3. Occasional awkwardness in using these materials," to "5. Easily and deftly uses preschool materials." As the above example indicates, the language of many of the items may be too complex and the discriminations too fine for some preschool teachers to accomplish easily.

The behaviors assessed by the test reportedly were chosen because they occur in a preschool setting, are observable, and are relevant to development. Although the skills covered by each item reportedly were evaluated by mental health workers and educators, they were not derived through empirical methods. In addition, given the brevity of the test it is not clear whether the items adequately represent the skill area or whether the skill areas covered by the test accurately reflect those important to preschoolers' adaptive functioning.

The PBRS has been normed on a heterogeneous sample of children ($N = 1,367$). Norms are available at 6-month intervals for both male and female children aged 3–6 years. However, the number of subjects per group is, in some cases, relatively small. Based on these normative data, children are categorized as typical, questionable, and atypical for each of the five skill areas. The authors stress that this categorization is not to be used for diagnostic purposes. However, the manual does not specify clearly how the test results are to be used to accomplish the stated purposes of the test.

The manual accompanying the test is generally well written. Like the text itself, however, the instructions for completing the test may be difficult for some preschool teachers to interpret. Furthermore, adequate information regarding the misuses of test data is not provided.

A significant amount of research has been conducted on the reliability and validity of the PBRS. Correlation coefficients were computed to assess interobserver agreement, internal consistency, and alternate-item-format reliability. The interobserver reliability coefficient for the total score was .89. However, the manual did not specify how these data were obtained (e.g., amount of training the teachers received prior to completing the instrument). Split-half and alternate-item-format reliability coefficients were acceptable. However, the authors did not adequately assess exact agreement between raters. They also did not adequately validate whether item choices were "true" Guttman scales as neither the coefficient of reproducibility nor scalability was obtained. In some instances the scale items appeared to be difficult to distinguish from one another or did not appear to represent a "true" sequence of skills.

Factor analytic studies supported the validity of the PBRS. The results of the factor analysis yielded three relatively nonoverlapping factors (Language, Social, and Psychomotor).

The predictive validity of the PBRS was evaluated by assessing the degree to which the test differentiated between children with and without a "problem." The authors did not specify criteria for subject selection. The results indicated that total test scores did not differentiate the two groups. However, when scores for all items were entered into the discriminant analyses, only 15% of the atypical children and 7% of the typical children were misclassified.

The PBRS has a number of positive features. The test is brief, relatively easy to complete and score, and apparently reliable. In spite of the positive features of the test, the test items lack specificity and in my opinion are fairly ambiguous and susceptible to rater bias. In addition, the authors failed to specify how the respondents are to use the information to accomplish the purported purposes of the test. Reliability and validity studies relevant to the stated purposes of the test have not been conducted to an adequate degree. In attempting to efficiently assess a wide variety of skills, the authors may have failed to develop a test that can be consistently administered. Unfortunately, the manual does not provide sufficient training in the interpretation and uses of test data and thus information obtained from the test could be easily misused by individuals unfamiliar with test administration and interpretation. Thus, I do not recommend use of this test for the purposes cited in the manual.

Review of the Preschool Behavior Rating Scale by F. CHARLES MACE, Associate Professor, Graduate School of Applied and Professional Psychology, Rutgers University, Piscataway, NJ:

DESCRIPTION AND PURPOSE. The Preschool Behavior Rating Scale (PBRS) is designed to assess psychomotor, cognitive, and social skills of children ages 3–6 who are enrolled in day care settings or Head Start programs. The main purposes of the PBRS are (*a*) to facilitate screening of preschoolers to identify those who show signs of developmental problems (without diagnosing or categorizing children), and (*b*) to permit monitoring of progress in preschool behavioral skill development over time.

After a minimum of 4 weeks observation, teachers are asked to rate individual children on 20 items, each of which consists of four or five

Guttman-scaled options. These options describe observable skills ordered from lower to higher skill levels according to a developmental perspective. For purposes of interpretation, PBRS items are grouped in the following ways: (a) Total Score (all 20 items); (b) 3 Factor Scores (Language, Socialization, and Psychomotor Skills); and (c) 5 Subscores (Coordination, Expressive and Receptive Language, Environmental Adaptation, and Social Relations). Within each of these groupings, summed ratings are compared to norms by sex and age group (6-month intervals) and are classified as either Typical, Questionable, or Atypical.

STANDARDIZATION. Norms for the PBRS were established on a sample of 1,367 children. Sampling procedures were not reported. The sample included male and female children of low and high socioeconomic status (SES), black and white racial groups, and ages ranging from 36 to 71 months. Statistical analyses showed that, of the four groupings (sex, SES, race, and age), PBRS scores differed significantly only by age and sex. On the basis of these findings, separate norms were developed for males and females at six different, 6-month interval age groupings. The norms for future versions of the PBRS could be strengthened by (a) describing the sampling procedures, (b) obtaining multiregional samples, and (c) including Hispanic children.

RELIABILITY. Pearson product-moment correlations were computed for interrater, split-half, and alternate forms reliability. The most important of these for an instrument measuring behavior—interrater reliability—showed that independent ratings of children by pairs of teachers correlated highly (generally > .80) for the PBRS total, three factor groupings, and five subscore groupings. One exception was the Coordination subscore, for which the median correlation was .65. This high level of correspondence between independent ratings of child behavior increases our confidence that the instrument provides reasonably accurate measures of the behaviors surveyed.

Split-half and alternate forms reliability for the PBRS total were .94 and .98, respectively. These values suggest a high degree of internal consistency among rating-scale items.

VALIDITY. Three types of validity have been assessed for the PBRS: face, factorial, and concurrent validity. With respect to face validi-ty, PBRS items were constructed, in part, on the basis of interviews with nonprofessional and professional mental health workers and educators after they examined the scale. In general, the resulting items correspond to observable child behaviors that require few inferences regarding hypothetical conditions or motives. Although generally reflecting observable behaviors, some items are ambiguous, leading to difficulties with scoring and interpretation. For example, many item options include multiple parts (e.g., item VIII: 1 "Generally avoids joining groups, disrupts or does not participate appropriately"). In such cases it is not clear how to score and interpret the item if the child exhibits some but not all of the behaviors. Guidelines for dealing with this problem are discussed in the manual, but they are complicated and seem unlikely to be followed.

Another factor contributing to the ambiguity of some items is option differentiation based on terms such as "generally," "markedly," and "occasional" (e.g., item II). Without specific criteria which differentiate such options on the basis of amount of behavior exhibited, the validity of these items is questionable.

A final concern regarding the development of the PBRS items is the lack of empirical evidence for the developmental ordering of item options. Although most item options seem to follow a logical developmental sequence, some do not. For example, it seems questionable that children normally progress from "almost never initiates any activity" to "can usually find a variety of acceptable activities" (item XV). Empirical validation of these developmental sequences would greatly strengthen the PBRS.

Factor analysis of PBRS items resulted in a solution with a clearly determined factor structure. Thus, there is empirical evidence for the existence of three factors (Language, Social, and Psychomotor Skills).

One of the most important characteristics of a screening device is its ability to discriminate those in need of additional evaluation or services. Discriminant function analyses on low SES children revealed that the PBRS, in combination with age and sex information, could differentiate between typical children and children previously diagnosed as having a problem. Only fifteen percent of atypical children and seven percent of typical children were misclassified. It is important to note that this level of differentiation was found only when all item scores were used.

Two shortcomings of the PBRS concern the scale's insensitivity to important dimensions of behavior (e.g., frequency, duration, latency, etc.) and the absence of research showing a correspondence between PBRS scores and actual child behavior. Insensitivity to dimensions of behavior places limits on the use of the scale beyond screening purposes. The authors suggest in the manual that the PBRS may be used for program development and evaluation. In this reviewer's opinion, the PBRS is not well suited for these purposes. Program development requires detailed information regarding specific skill strengths and deficits as well as the conditions that promote and inhibit their display. Such information is best obtained through curriculum-based assessment and direct observation. Similarly, program evaluation is best achieved via repeated measures of behaviors that have been targeted for improvement.

The problem of unestablished score-behavior relationships is common to behavior rating scales. In the case of the PBRS, concern is diminished somewhat by high levels of interrater reliability, which are suggestive of accurate measurement. However, the PBRS could be at the forefront of behavior rating scales if future versions addressed the problems of insensitivity to dimensions of behavior and score-behavior relationships.

In summary, the Preschool Behavior Rating Scale appears to be among the best screening devices for teachers to identify children who may have problems in the development of language, social, or psychomotor skills. Its principal strengths are the ability to facilitate agreement between independent raters and to identify those children in need of further evaluation or services. Future versions of the PBRS would be strengthened by expanding its norm groups, increasing sensitivity to various dimensions of behavior, and establishing the correspondence between PBRS scores and actual child behavior. Until these objectives are achieved, the scale should be used principally for screening purposes.

[60]

Preschool Development Inventory. Purpose: "A screening inventory designed to help identify children with developmental and other problems which may interfere with the child's ability to learn." Ages 3-0 to 5-5; 1984; parent's report of child's current functioning; 1985 price data: $6 per 25 question/answer sheets and mimeographed manual (7 pages); administration time not reported; Harold Ireton; Behavior Science Systems, Inc.*

Review of the Preschool Development Inventory by R. A. BORNSTEIN, Assistant Professor of Psychiatry, Departments of Psychiatry and Psychology, Ohio State University, Columbus, OH:

The Preschool Development Inventory (PDI) appears to be a condensation of the Minnesota Child Development Inventory (MCDI) and the Minnesota Preschool Inventory (MPI), both by the same author. Not surprisingly, the Preschool Development Inventory has the same goal, that is, the identification of children with developmental problems that could contribute to learning problems. It is unclear whether the author conceptualizes the PDI as a substitute for the previous tests, or as a "screening device" to be followed in some instances by the other inventories. Given the apparently extensive overlap of items, it may be that the PDI represents a cost- and time-effective substitute for the other measures.

The normative data base is that reported for the MCDI. That sample was sufficiently large, but (as emphasized in a previous review of the MCDI) permits generalization primarily to white, middle-class families. The PDI then suffers similar constraints. The PDI is divided into five sections. Two sections request parents to respond to questions regarding general development or specific problems. The other three sections elicit narrative descriptions aimed at obtaining parent's concerns and perceptions about the child.

The first section contains 60 items from the MCDI, and covers seven developmental areas. The items included in the PDI are described as "among the most age-discriminating items of the MCDI," although the basis for this item selection is not explicitly presented. Furthermore, the balance of item selection in the various areas is very uneven, with 33 of the items related to Language Comprehension (19) or Expressive Language (14). This very likely contributes to the differential sensitivity of the test. A child's score is compared with the mean of children who are 25% younger, and those below this cutoff are described as delayed. This operational definition has some appeal, but is not without problems. No information is provided about the variability of performance in the normal sample, which is likely to be considerable. It would be helpful to know the accuracy of the test using other types of cutoffs, such as two standard deviations from the mean of normals. No formal classification studies have been included in the manual.

The authors suggest using a cutoff score based on the combination of males and females from the normal sample. While the author is aware of the different base rates of children with delays, he suggests that a case can be made for identifying more males than females as delayed. There is some merit to this view, but there is an insufficient discussion of the issues, and no data are presented to justify the use of combined scores. If in fact males do develop more slowly than females, the intent of the test should be to identify "abnormal" delay, and thus sex-specific cutoffs should be employed. Fortunately, the author provides such sex-specific cutoff scores. The remainder of the PDI essentially serves as a broad outline for a structured interview of the parent.

In essence the PDI is an amalgamation of two previous tests. The two primary components of the test are a general developmental scale that is poorly balanced in depth of inquiry in various areas, and an outline for a structured interview. The PDI appears to be shorter and more efficient than the previous tests, and its value may be in terms of its cost and time savings. It is more likely to be useful in screening settings where potential obstacles to learning may not be readily apparent. This is consistent with the author's goals for the test, and he carefully acknowledges that the test is not intended as a substitute for more formal testing. As a screening device, the test may be a time- and cost-efficient adjunct to the early identification of children with possible developmental delays.

[61]

The Preverbal Assessment-Intervention Profile. Purpose: "Developed as an individualized assessment for severely and multihandicapped preintentional learners." Low functioning handicapped infants and children; 1984; PAIP; 7 scores for Stage One (developmental ages 0–1 month): Motor, Communication, Visual Awareness of Objects, Auditory Awareness of Sounds, Earliest Interaction Patterns, Reflex/Motor, Tactile Accep-

tance/Defensiveness; 6 scores for Stage Two (developmental ages 1–4 months): Motor, Communication, Visual Attending, Auditory Attending, Social Bond Attending, Reflex/Motor; 5 scores for Stage Three (developmental ages 4–8 months): Motor, Communication, Orienting to Objects, Orienting to Persons, Reflex/Motor; individual; 1987 price data: $14.95 per 5 assessment record booklets; $29.95 per assessment manual (46 pages); administration time not reported; Patricia Connard; ASIEP Education Co.*

Review of The Preverbal Assessment-Intervention Profile by PATRICIA MIRENDA, Assistant Professor of Special Education and Communication Disorders, University of Nebraska-Lincoln, Lincoln, NE:

The Preverbal Assessment-Intervention Profile (PAIP) was designed to evaluate sensorimotor and prelinguistic behaviors in individuals labelled severely/profoundly retarded and/or multihandicapped. The assessment manual provides protocols for determining the level at which to begin detailed assessments, as well as protocols for the in-depth assessments themselves. In addition, the manual includes a section related to developing goals and personalized objectives based on the assessment results.

The PAIP assessment is designed more as an observational protocol than as a test per se. That is, unlike many assessments used with individuals who are handicapped, there is not a series of predetermined items or skills that are either "passed" or "failed" by the person being tested. Rather, the assessment involves a series of detailed observations and analyses of learner behavior in a number of sensorimotor areas during both naturalistic and contrived interactions. The result is a profile of learner responses and initiations to caregivers under a number of conditions. This unusual mode of assessment is intuitively appealing in that it allows a great deal of flexibility to the examiner; provides for many alternative response modes by the learner; and, perhaps most importantly, potentially results in an increased appreciation by the examiner of the subtle responses (called communiques in the PAIP) of the severely handicapped individual to a variety of environmental events. Unlike most assessments that might be used with severely multihandicapped learners, this instrument provides a structure for *learning about* the person being assessed rather than simply assigning a developmental age score based on some arbitrary set of tasks.

There are several problems, however, that militate against the usefulness of the instrument. The major problem is that the protocols are extremely complex and time-consuming and would seem to be virtually impossible to utilize in a classroom situation by examiners (e.g., teachers) who have not received fairly extensive training in the assessment format. The protocols require that the examiner possess finely-tuned behavioral observation and recording skills as well as an appreciation of the subtleties of learner-caregiver interactions. Further, the directions for conducting many of the observations are so detailed that they are quite confusing and would require several careful readings by an examiner in order to understand exactly how each protocol is to be administered. In several instances, the manual contains terms that require specialized knowledge; however, these terms are left undefined. For example, the Assessment Record for Reflex/Motor Skills (Stage 3, Form C, page 32 of the manual) contains items such as "A.T.N.R. Inhibited" and "S.T.N.R. Inhibited," which require considerable knowledge of primitive reflex patterns in order to be relevant. ("A.T.N.R. Inhibited" means that the asymetric tonic neck reflex, a primitive reflex pattern normally seen in infants and elicited by turning the head to the side, does not occur. "S.T.N.R. Inhibited" means that the symetric tonic neck reflex, elicited in normal infants by extending or flexing the neck, does not occur.) In attempting to go beyond the traditional "pass-fail" assessment format (a commendable goal in itself), the author(s) seem to have gotten so entrenched in detail that the result is an extremely complex and very confusing instrument.

In addition to this major drawback, there are some rather serious flaws with the test reliability and validity studies as reported in the manual. First, the interobserver reliability measures reported (average percent agreement = 92%) are misleading in that the calculations were completed after the observers received a *total of 12 hours* of lecture, recitation, and simulation training in the assessment protocols. Thus, the calculations would seem to indicate that the *training* was effective in teaching the observers to use the instrument reliably, but not that the instrument as it stands alone (i.e., without

training) produces reliable results. In addition, the test-retest reliability report states that "all [15 individuals involved] received the same communication and reflex/motor stage placement during both testing situations." However, since there are only three stages possible for placement, this level of agreement could be easily achieved even if the specific results of the detailed profiles varied widely between the two testing sessions. Finally, the validity measure correlates the scores reported in five areas on the PAIP with analogous scores on the Early Learning Accomplishment Profile (ELAP). The latter test is not well known and is apparently quite new, as it does not appear in the most recent *Mental Measurements Yearbook* (Mitchell, 1985). Thus, it is difficult to assess the strength of the validity correlations provided for the PAIP since these depend, in turn, on the degree of validity of the ELAP for which no information is available.

Finally, the PAIP is not clear concerning the question of how the assessment results are translated in educational programs once the assessment has been completed. The test format provides a procedure to translate the observational data into a series of scores; however, these scores seem to have no bearing on the intervention goals that might be produced and serve no other discernible purpose aside from summarization of the test results. Thus, the suggestions provided for developing goals and objectives flow directly from the observational records themselves; this has the advantage of allowing maximum utilization of the results for each learner on an individualized basis. However, the suggested goals and objectives provided in the manual are problematic in that they tend to emphasize teaching tasks that are largely non-functional (and, for learners over the age of 5, chronological-age-inappropriate) in nature. That is, the goals and objectives are unlikely to result in the learner's ability to participate in meaningful domestic, recreation/leisure, vocational, and/or general community activities in integrated settings (Brown, Branston, Hamre-Nietupski, Pumpian, Certo, & Gruenewald, 1979; Brown, Falvey, Vincent, Kaye, Johnson, Ferrara-Parrish, & Gruenewald, 1980). The result may be that, after expending considerable energy in learning to conduct and in administering the assessment, the examiner is left with a large amount of very detailed information that is difficult to translate into meaningful goals, activities, and/or programs. As a tool that has the potential for teaching adults to observe and appreciate the unique and subtle behaviors exhibited by learners labelled severely/profoundly and/or multiply handicapped, the PAIP has much to offer. However, as an assessment instrument to aid in the development of functional, meaningful programs for this population, the instrument falls far short of its intended purpose.

REVIEWER'S REFERENCES

Brown, L., Branston, M. B., Hamre-Nietupski, S., Pumpian, I., Certo, N., & Gruenewald, L. (1979). A strategy for developing chronological-age-appropriate and functional curricular content for severely handicapped adolescents and young adults. *Journal of Special Education, 13,* 81-90.
Brown, L., Falvey, M., Vincent, L., Kaye, N., Johnson, F., Ferrara-Parrish, P., & Gruenewald, L. (1980). Strategies for generating comprehensive, longitudinal, and chronological-age-appropriate individualized education programs for adolescent and young-adult severely handicapped students. *Journal of Special Education, 14,* 199-215.
Mitchell, J. V., Jr. (Ed.). (1985). *The ninth mental measurements yearbook.* Lincoln, NE: The Buros Institute of Mental Measurements.

Review of The Preverbal Assessment-Intervention Profile by DAVID P. WACKER, Associate Professor of Pediatrics and Special Education, The University of Iowa, Iowa City, IA:

The Preverbal Assessment-Intervention Profile (PAIP) was "developed to assist specialists in answering the question, 'What can we do to help this child learn to communicate needs and wants?'" According to Connard, the administrative procedures of the PAIP "provide for an indepth probe that allows the examiner to obtain representative samples of an individual's abilities within the natural setting. Discrete behaviors indicative of the individual's information processing abilities (interactions with things), communication abilities (interactions with people), and motor abilities are observed and recorded." The PAIP uses a "Piagetian sensorimotor framework" to evaluate the responding of severely handicapped persons who function within the first three sensorimotor stages of development (birth to 8 months). To assist these individuals in obtaining intentional communication behavior, Connard argues that an assessment must be first conducted to "ascertain information relative to the child's ability to communicate awareness, attending, and orienting." Once these behaviors have been identified, intervention programs can then be developed which build on the child's current

skills and hopefully promote greater communication ability. The PAIP, therefore, is solidly based within the developmental orientation, and was developed specifically for use with the lowest functioning individuals within the severe/profound range of functioning.

The PAIP is comprised of four sections: (*a*) a preliminary evaluation of communication and motor abilities for deciding further assessment needs; (*b*) a diagnostic profile of variations in age-stage levels of functioning across several areas; (*c*) a narrative section arranged by developmental and functional areas providing descriptions of the child's current level of functioning, deficits, and instructional needs; and (*d*) a listing of developmentally based learning goals and objectives "to assist in appropriate program planning" (based on the results of assessment). The assessment manual provides a description of how each of these sections should be administered, how the data should be recorded in the record booklet, and also provides an example to assist the examiner in understanding how to administer the test.

To use the PAIP, the examiner begins by completing the Preliminary Placement Evaluation Profile. This can be completed either through interview, direct observation in natural situations, or through elicited responding. The preliminary placement evaluation is used as a screening procedure to determine at which stage of development the child is functioning, and consists of very few items (6 communication and 4 motor items at Stage 1). Scoring of each item (e.g., "Is the learner aroused by human voices?") is conducted by indicating "Yes," "No," or "Not applicable." The child's performance on these items is then used to determine if assessment should be conducted at a higher level (Stage 2) or if a diagnostic assessment within that stage appears appropriate. The diagnostic evaluation is then conducted to assess individual patterns of performance within a given stage of development. These patterns of performance provide the information needed to "design and implement effective intervention programs" using the goals and objectives sheets provided in the record booklet.

Connard reports that the PAIP was developed by reviewing 26 instruments used in facilities serving severely handicapped persons. An initial item pool of 785 behaviors was field-tested with 20 teachers of severely handicapped infants, children, and adults. The results of the field test led to the inclusion of the current items using the present format. No further information is provided on the construction of the test or how individual items were specifically selected.

Two reliability studies are reported in the manual. The first study evaluated interrater agreement across 25 pairs of observers each of whom assessed two severely handicapped individuals, while the second reported test/retest reliability over an average of 26 days with 15 severely handicapped persons. Interrater agreement was collapsed across all items within a stage, and ranged from 88% to 96% agreement. No data are provided for the test-retest reliability, except that the students "received the same communication and reflex/motor stage placement during both testing situations."

One validity study is also reported in the manual, where the communication and reflex/motor placement scores of the PAIP were correlated with skill areas from the Early Learning Accomplishment Profile for 35 severely handicapped persons. Five Spearman rank correlation coefficients were computed resulting in correlation coefficients ranging between .84 and .94.

In interpreting these findings, Connard states that the results of these studies "strongly suggest that the PAIP can be used reliably and validly with severely, profoundly, and multihandicapped individuals." Although these preliminary data are positive, it is premature to conclude that the test is either reliable or valid. For example, no data are provided on the intercorrelations across items or stages, and no data are provided on how successful children are in programs based on the results of assessment.

Of potential concern is the administration of the PAIP with untrained examiners. A great deal of flexibility is present in the administration procedures, which may limit the overall generalizability of the findings. For example, the directions for the Stage One Preliminary Placement Evaluation indicate that the learner should be observed "in a variety of situations." No guidelines are given regarding how many environments should be sampled, what activities should be available, how long the observation periods should be, etc. With respect to the items (e.g., "Is the learner visually aroused by

humans?"), no specific criteria are provided to evaluate this behavior, especially if inconsistent behavior occurs. For the interrater agreement investigation, Connard reported that observers received at least 4 hours of training. Given the flexibility available in the administration of the test, it would seem that at least this amount of training would be needed for examiners to achieve acceptable levels of interrater agreement.

In summary, the data presented in the manual regarding the reliability and validity of the PAIP are positive, but should be considered as preliminary data. Given the great amount of flexibility in the administration of the test, it will probably be necessary for examiners to receive at least some training (and possibly extensive training) prior to the use of the test in applied settings. Although the use of the PAIP may prove useful for programs that already emphasize a strong developmental orientation to training, it should be used with some caution given the lack of reliability and validity data reported in the manual. Especially important to note is the fact that no data are provided that establish a link between the assessment and intervention components of the PAIP.

[62]

Problem-Solving Decision-Making Style Inventory. Purpose: Provides feedback on one's perception of problem-solving and decision-making styles of self or others. High school and college and adults in organizational settings; 1982; self-administered questionnaire; ratings by self or other on 4 problem-solving and decision-making styles: Delegative, Facilitative, Consultative, Authoritative; no manual (administrative and scoring instructions included in instrument); 1984 price data: $2.95 per test booklet; administration time not reported; Paul Hersey and Walter E. Natemeyer; University Associates, Inc.*

Review of the Problem-Solving Decision-Making Style Inventory by DAVID N. DIXON, Professor and Department Chair of Counseling and Psychology Services, Ball State University, Muncie, IN:

The Problem-Solving Decision-Making Style Inventory consists of two forms, one completed by the person being rated and one completed by another person, that attempt to describe the typical style a person uses to solve problems and make decisions. The two forms consist of 12 items each that are administered in a weighted, forced-choice format. Thus, for each of four dimensions (Authoritative, Consultative, Facilitative, and Delegative) two items for each dimension are paired with the two items for each of the other three dimensions.

The inventory is more appropriately a measure of administrative style as it pertains to solving problems and making decisions. It does not consider dimensions such as impulsivity or means-ends analysis, major dimensions of problem-solving from a more internal, information-processing perspective.

There is no manual for the inventory; thus no reliability, validity, or normative data are available. For an inventory that costs $2.95 for each two-page test booklet, the user receives very little that describes the development of the inventory or information about how the inventory can validly be used.

The inventory seems to be loosely related to a Situational Leadership Model of management. This is never made explicit and whether the inventory does, in fact, measure the supportive/directive dimensions as suggested is purely speculative.

This inventory, until further developed and reported upon, is indicative of the lack of consideration of psychometrics in the management field. Until such time as this inventory and other similar administrative style inventories demonstrate they are reliable, valid instruments, consumers are strongly admonished to avoid use. Buyer beware!

Review of the Problem-Solving Decision-Making Style Inventory by PAUL MCREYNOLDS, Professor of Psychology, University of Nevada-Reno, Reno, NV:

The Problem-Solving Decision-Making Style Inventory (PDSI) is a short self-administered and self-scored form intended for use in conjunction with the theory of situational leadership developed by Paul Hersey and Kenneth Blanchard (1982). In order to describe and evaluate the PDSI it will be helpful first to briefly summarize this underlying theory.

The theory deals primarily with leadership in management situations, but is held also to be applicable in educational and family settings. Two dimensions of leadership—one concerning directive (task-oriented) behaviors and the other concerning supportive (relationship) behav-iors—are posited. By considering these two dimensions together four leadership styles are defined. Thus, Style A involves high directive behavior and low supportive behavior (Authoritative style). Style B emphasizes high directive and also high supportive behavior (Consultative style); in Style C directive behavior is low, but supportive behavior is high (Facilitative style); and in style D both directive and supportive behaviors are low (Delegative style).

The PDSI attempts to apply this model to two aspects of leadership—problem-solving and decision-making. One form of the inventory is devised to assay these two aspects in terms of the way the subject perceives his or her own behaviors, and an alternate form is designed to reveal how the subject perceives the problem-solving and decision-making behaviors of a specific other individual. The PDSI is a four-page form. Page 2 is the actual inventory. The other pages consist of instructions for self-administration, self-scoring, and interpretation. The inventory includes 12 items, each item consisting of two statements concerning how a person might behave in a problem-solving or decision-making situation, with each statement representing one of the four leadership styles (e.g., "Share ideas and attempt to reach consensus on a decision" reflects the Facilitative style). The subject is requested to answer each item by distributing a total of 3 points between the two statements. These values are then summed in such a way as to represent the relative dominance in the subject's responses of given problem-solving and decision-making styles.

The situational leadership theory of Hersey and Blanchard is plausible and worthy of respect. Further, the PDSI appears, in principle, to reflect the basic postulates of the theory. The PDSI cannot, however, be recommended as an adequate instrument for assessing individuals with respect to the different styles subsumed by the theory. The inventory is too brief (each style is represented by only two statements, which when paired with each of the other three styles yield the 12 items), and lacks the necessary psychometric bases to function as a diagnostic instrument. Moreover, it is this reviewer's understanding (personal conversation with Paul Hersey) that the PDSI authors do not conceive of the inventory as a test in the usual sense of accurately measuring individuals, but rather think of it as primarily an instructional exercise to use in classes, management workshops, lectures, and the like. Certainly, the format and clarity of the form should make it an excellent device for illustrating certain aspects of the theory of situational leadership, provided it is made clear to participants that the form cannot adequately serve to provide valid information on individuals.

Because of the possibility, however, that some workers might be tempted to employ the PDSI as a formal assessment instrument, it should be noted that internal consistency, reliability, and validity data on the instrument have not been reported, nor have the intercorrelations among the different style scores. There is no manual, and the only information on interpretation of the form is that on the form itself. No doubt an adequate test to assess situational leadership variables could be constructed, but the PDSI, at least as presently developed, does not constitute such an instrument.

In sum, the PDSI appears to be useful as an instructional aid in delineating the situational leadership theory, but it is not appropriate for use as a psychological test.

REVIEWER'S REFERENCE

Hersey, P., & Blanchard, K. H. (1982). *Management of organizational behavior: Utilizing human resources* (4th ed.). Englewood Cliffs, NJ: Prentice-Hall.

[63]

Reading Test SR-A and SR-B. Purpose: "Provide a means of estimating the reading attainment of primary school children." Ages 7-6 to 11-11; 1970-82; 2 similar tests: SR-A and SR-B; 1986 price data: £2.25 per 10 tests for either SR-A or SR-B, £1.75 per combined manual ('79, 17 pages); 20(25) minutes per test; Brian Pritchard, The National Foundation for Educational Research in England and Wales; NFER-Nelson Publishing Co., Ltd. [England].*

Review of the Reading Test SR-A and SR-B by ROBERT C. CALFEE, Professor of Education, School of Education, Stanford University, Stanford, CA:

The Reading Test SR-A/B is a 48-item group-administered sentence completion test designed to assess the reading achievement of primary school children. Each item is of the form: My dog can (talk, sing, fly, bark, draw). The student's task is to underline the word that is semantically appropriate to the context. The most difficult items deal with unfamiliar vocabulary and contexts; assuming that the student can decode the words, the primary demand is vocabulary knowledge.

The test demands are relatively slight, administration is fast and easy, and scoring would be straightforward if the test were converted to a multiple choice response format. As a screening device the instrument might have some advantages—it is fast and cheap. The reliability indices (intra-year internal consistencies) fall in the mid-.80s, somewhat low given the homogeneity of the task and the items.

I cannot recommend the instrument to most readers, however, because of several limitations. First, it will not be clear in most instances what is being assessed. Decoding skill, vocabulary knowledge, and background information are all intertwined in the task. The procedure provides no information about comprehension ability. The instrument is a thin reed whether used for student placement, diagnostic assessment, or program evaluation. The manual is quite skimpy—less than three pages of prose, and most of that on the technical aspects of norming and scoring. The instrument was developed in Great Britain, and details of the language as well as the norming population limit the utility outside of the country. Better alternatives exist.

Review of the Reading Test SR-A and SR-B by MARIAM JEAN DREHER, Associate Professor of Education, Department of Curriculum and Instruction, University of Maryland, College Park, MD:

The Reading Test SR-A and its alternate form SR-B require a child to read incomplete sentences and choose a correct last word from among either four or five choices. These sentence completion tests are intended to estimate "the reading attainment of primary school children." A prospective user of SR-A and SR-B should consider whether exclusive use of sentence completion adequately taps the reading skills being stressed in the user's reading program. For instance, because only single sentences are used, students' comprehension of connected discourse is not assessed. Thus, the tests would not match the curricular emphasis of a reading program that stresses the comprehension of passages and stories.

The author of SR-A and SR-B acknowledges the limitations of sentence completion and attempts to eliminate them by stating, "The tests do not claim to measure all aspects of reading skill but sentence completion tasks do correlate highly with other measures of reading." Unfortunately that statement is not elaborated. No information is provided on other reading measures which correlate with SR-A and SR-B or with any other sentence completion tests. Indeed, no information at all is offered regarding the validity of the tests.

SR-A and SR-B are intended for use in the first through fourth years of elementary school. Reliability coefficients ranging from .85 to .88 are reported for each school year and each test form. No correlations between the two test forms are given.

The author calculated the reliability coefficients using an index of interitem consistency (Kuder-Richardson Formula 21). But he justifies his choice of this form of reliability estimate by arguing that the procedure is acceptable because it is associated with test-retest correlation. If test-retest correlation is what the author considered ideal, it is unclear why another procedure was used. It is also unclear why the test-retest correlation would be ideal for this type of test since such a reliability procedure is aimed at establishing stability or consistency of performance over time. Yet the purpose of SR-A and SR-B is apparently to make inferences about students' ability to read at a given time; ongoing instruction should make this level of knowledge change over time. Consequently, a measure of interitem consistency such as was actually used appears to be appropriate and the justification of it in terms of an association with test-retest correlation is confusing.

The SR-A was standardized on 13,886 first through fourth year elementary school students ranging in age from 7 years 9 months to 11 years 8 months. A stratified random sampling procedure was used to make the sample representative of students in England and Wales. This sample was used to construct norm tables in which raw scores are converted to standard scores on the basis of year in school and a pupil's age. Norms for SR-B were constructed by calibrating the performance of 3,099 additional students against the original norms.

Standard scores are easily obtained from the norm tables. However, negligible information is provided to assist test users in interpreting the test scores once they are obtained. Test users are simply told that the standard scores have a mean of 100 and a standard deviation of 15. In addition, a very brief discussion of standard error of measurement is included that would be of questionable value to anyone not already very familiar with the concept.

The SR-A and SR-B can be administered quickly and easily. Students are given 20 minutes to work on the 48 items. However, a redesign of the first page of the test booklet should be considered because the first six items are in full view as children fill in identifying information and complete the practice items. Rather than allowing faster students to get a head start on this speeded test by reading ahead, the author should begin the test on the second page.

Each test form covers a wide range of difficulty because the test is to be used across first through fourth year elementary school levels; norms extend from ages 7 years 6 months to 11 years 11 months. Although such a range of difficulty may avoid the problem of ceiling and floor effects that exist when a test of more limited range is given at a particular grade level, there is a trade-off with such a wide-ranged approach. With only 48 items on each form, the difficulty of the items accelerates rapidly. Therefore, beginners may quickly find the test too difficult and perhaps become discouraged.

One must assume the author intends SR-A and SR-B to be used to track progress over the four grade levels for which the test is targeted. If so, then a discussion is needed of appropriate intervals for administering the test and appropriate use of the alternate forms. The manual for SR-A and SR-B offers no information on how the two forms are to be used. For instance, does the author recommend giving one form at the beginning of each school year and the other at the end? Or perhaps the test is to be given yearly with the two forms given in alternate years so that students encounter the same test only twice. Possible problems that may be encountered in administering the same test more than once to the same students should also be discussed in the manual.

In summary, although the Reading Tests SR-A and SR-B are easy to administer and score, the manual presents no information on the validity of the tests and next to nothing to help users interpret students' scores. In addition, the one sentence description of the purpose does not explicate such questions as why two forms are provided or how these two forms should be used in tracking students' progress over the first through fourth years in elementary school. If the SR-A and SR-B are to be useful tests, the manual needs to include a good deal more information and to clarify much of what is included. In addition, test users outside of England and Wales should develop local norms before using the tests for any important educational decision making.

[64]

Receptive One-Word Picture Vocabulary Test. Purpose: Assesses a child's ability to verbally identify pictures of objects. Ages 2-0 to 11-11; 1985; ROWPVT; individual; 1988 price data: $46 per manual (47 pages), test plates, and 25 record forms; Spanish forms available; (10–15) minutes; Morrison F. Gardner; Academic Therapy Publications.*

Review of the Receptive One-Word Picture Vocabulary Test by JANICE A. DOLE, Assistant Professor of Education, Michigan State University, East Lansing, MI:

The Receptive One-Word Picture Vocabulary Test (ROWPVT) is a norm-referenced, individually administered test designed to assess "a child's receptive single-word vocabulary." The test consists of a set of 100 plates, ordered in difficulty. Each plate has four pictures on it. The child is asked to identify the picture that matches the word presented orally by the examiner. For example, the child is shown a plate with black and white line drawings of objects such as a ball, a shoe, a doll, and a bicycle, and is asked to point to the shoe. The test can be administered to children from ages 2 through 11 years 11 months in 10 to 15 minutes.

ADMINISTRATION AND SCORING. The ROWPVT is a straightforward, easy-to-administer test. Directions for establishing basals and ceilings and for scoring the test are adequate. Appropriate cautions are provided for the examiner, and the manual points out potential difficulties in testing. However, it would be useful if the directions were scripted in bold-face. Scripted directions help ensure the standardization of testing, and directions in bold-face are especially helpful for examiners.

Directions for administering the test to Spanish-speaking children are included in the Administration and Scoring section of the manual.

These directions are wholly inadequate for the administration and interpretation of the test to Spanish-speaking children.

No standardization of the Spanish version was undertaken. Nor was the test administered to any Spanish-speaking children as part of the actual standardization process. Finally, the manual states that the test can be administered to Spanish-speaking children to assess English vocabulary, and then "a program of English development can be initiated." However, this instrument is inadequate for setting up a remedial English program because the test measures only a small portion of language acquisition.

NORMATIVE INFORMATION. Standardization was accomplished by administering the ROWPVT to 1,128 children in the San Francisco Bay area. Raw scores were converted to standard scores based on the norms from the Expressive One-Word Picture Vocabulary Test (EOWPVT), a test developed by the same author. The ROWPVT was designed and normed as a companion to the EOWPVT.

The standardization procedures described for the ROWPVT must be regarded as inadequate. The test appears to have been standardized on a relatively homogeneous sample of subjects in San Francisco, California. Socio-economic and ability levels of the subjects in the sample were not adequately reported. It is indicated that "Parents brought the very young children to the Child Development Center [at Children's Hospital in San Francisco] to be tested." It is not clear whether parents were asked to bring their children in, or whether they brought their children in for other reasons. The latter case would result in a nonrepresentative sample of subjects.

Norms for this test include standard scores comparable to those on the EOWPVT, stanines, language ages, and percentile ranks. The manual is particularly good in discussing the use and interpretation of these derived scores. Examiners with a rudimentary knowledge of descriptive statistics should be able to understand the manual's description of each of these scores, what the scores mean, and how they can be used in evaluating performance.

RELIABILITY AND VALIDITY. Reliability is determined by Cronbach's alpha. These correlation coefficients, as well as standard errors of measurement (*SEM*) for raw scores and standard scores, are reported in 6-month intervals for ages 2 through 5 and 1-year intervals for ages 6 through 12. Coefficients ranged from .81 to .93, with a median of .90. *SEM* for raw scores ranged from 2.37 to 3.79 with a median of 3.33. These figures are regarded as adequate, although test-retest reliability should be reported as well.

Content and criterion-related validity are discussed for the ROWPVT. The manual reports that "pictures and verbal descriptions that represented words and pictures that children are typically exposed to" were selected for possible inclusion in the test. These words were then reviewed and evaluated by teachers and speech and language pathologists. How representative are these words of the domain of "receptive vocabulary?" The answer to this question is important for establishing the content validity of this test. A dilemma arises if more abstract words or words that can't be easily translated into pictures are part of what we agree to be "receptive vocabulary." No data are provided to answer this concern.

However, even if we can demonstrate that the words on this test do not reflect the full scope of receptive vocabulary, it is still possible for the author to support the validity of the test by demonstrating its convergent and discriminant validity. Unfortunately, data are not provided to adequately address these issues. The manual reports an average correlation coefficient of .42 between the ROWPVT and the Vocabulary subtests of the WPPSI and the WISC-R. But this correlation is not adequate for establishing the convergent validity of the ROWPVT, or, for that matter, the manual's assertion of criterion-related validity.

Unfortunately, there are no additional criterion-related measures which would help establish the ROWPVT's validity or would explain why the ROWPVT does differ so much from the Weschler tests. Since the ROWPVT and the EOWPVT correlate so highly ($r = .89$), it is likely that these two tests measure largely the same constructs. But what are they, and how do they relate to language? This information is not provided.

These questions point out a larger problem related to the test and the manual. There is no theoretical rationale presented for the ROWPVT. The manual states that the test is designed to provide norms comparable to the EOWPVT. An examiner can use information from both tests to compare a child's performance on receptive versus expressive vocabulary. But the manual does not provide a rationale for these measures. How do expressive and receptive vocabulary relate to overall language ability? And what would be the advantage of giving one or both of these tests over other, more global measures of language?

A final problem is reflected in the stated purpose for the test. It is stated in the manual that information can be gleaned about differences in language skills caused by language impairment, language delay, bilingualism, and a host of other factors. Then the examiner is told that poor performance on the test could be due to another variety of factors, including problems in hearing, auditory discrimination, auditory memory, visual memory, etc. In fact, so many factors are included that it is difficult to evaluate what an examiner would know based on the results of this test, and what an examiner would do with what s/he finds out.

SUMMARY. The ROWPVT is an individually administered test designed to be a companion test to the EOWPVT and to measure receptive knowledge of single words. The test is easy to administer, score, and interpret. The standardization procedures reported for the test are inadequate. No theoretical rationale is given for the test. For example, the manual does not provide sufficient information for the examiner to understand how this test fits into a framework for measuring language abilities. Inadequate information is provided to the examiner for understanding the test's usefulness in assessing potential language problems. Finally, reported reliabilities for this test are adequate, but insufficient evidence is provided in the manual to establish the validity of the test. In light of the revisions and new standardization of the Peabody Picture Vocabulary Test—Revised (PPVT-R), I would recommend PPVT-R over this competitor as a measure of receptive vocabulary. Further study and additional data are needed to warrant confidence in the ROWPVT as a superior alternative to the PPVT-R.

Review of the Receptive One-Word Picture Vocabulary Test by JANICE SANTOGROSSI, Instructor of Special Education and Communica-

tion Disorders, University of Nebraska-Lincoln, Lincoln, NE:

The Receptive One-Word Picture Vocabulary Test (ROWPVT) is an untimed, individually administered measure of single-word receptive vocabulary which was designed to accompany the Expressive One-Word Picture Vocabulary Test (EOWPVT). The ROWPVT and the EOWPVT yield similar scores ($r = .89$), which makes possible direct comparisons between the two measures.

The ROWPVT contains 100 items arranged in order of increasing difficulty. The use of a basal (highest eight consecutive correct responses) and ceiling (lowest six incorrect responses out of eight consecutive items) makes administration of all the items unnecessary. The author employed evaluations by classroom teachers and speech-language pathologists and item analysis of the frequency of correct responses to each item to determine item selection and sequence.

The author states that the ROWPVT requires 10 to 15 minutes to administer and 5 minutes or less to score. Trial administration and scoring by this reviewer supported the author's claim. For the purpose of achieving consistent presentation, the author includes a pronunciation guide for stimulus words in the test manual.

The illustrations for the ROWPVT are arranged horizontally, four pictures to a $5\frac{1}{2}$ by 11 inch page in a spiral bound book. The author states that he arranged the pictures in a single, horizontal row based on a survey of 1,000 psychologists who presumably reported that left-to-right scanning is easier for young children.

The illustrations for the ROWPVT are rather crude line drawings. The poor quality of the illustrations is also a long-recognized drawback of the ROWPVT's predecessor, the EOWPVT. In addition, many of the drawings in the ROWPVT have inappropriate size relationships to each other (e.g., page 4, on which the drawings of the flower, fan, and leaf are approximately the same size as the drawing of the tree).

The examiner subtracts the number of errors from the number of the ceiling item to obtain the raw score. The raw score can be converted to a language age, standard score, and stanine score. The use of these types of scores is an improvement over the IQ score and mental age scores used for the EOWPVT. This reviewer suggests, however, that the author would have been better advised to use another term such as "receptive vocabulary age" or "age equivalent" instead of "language age," because receptive vocabulary is only one component of language. To aid in interpretation the author provides the standard error of measurement (SEM) for raw scores and standard scores at each age level.

Direct comparisons may be made between the child's performance on the ROWPVT and the EOWPVT using the standard scores. The author provides the standard error of difference for the two tests and suggests that a standard score difference of 9 or more points reflects a true difference in receptive versus expressive vocabulary while a difference of less than 9 points is indicative of error of measurement.

The author employed Cronbach's alpha, to determine the internal consistency of the ROWPVT. The reliability of coefficients for each age level range from .81 to .93 with a median of .90. The SEMs for raw scores range from 2.37 to 3.79 with a median of 3.33. For standard scores, the SEMs range from 3.97 to 6.53 with a median of 4.50. The reliability coefficients are below .90 for the 2-0 to 2-5, 2-6 to 2-11, 3-6 to 3-11, 9-0 to 9-11, and 11-0 to 11-11 age levels. The reliability data indicate adequate support for the consistency of the ROWPVT in measuring receptive vocabulary, except at those age levels indicated (i.e., where reliability coefficients are below .90). No test-retest reliability data are presented.

The author reports information about three kinds of validity: content, item, and criterion-related. The author established content validity by having classroom teachers and speech-language pathologists evaluate the pictures and verbal descriptions to determine the pictures and words to which children are typically exposed at home or at school. Pictures and verbal descriptions with possible ethnic, regional, or gender bias and words that could not be translated into Spanish were excluded from the final form of the ROWPVT. In addition, the author had classroom teachers and speech-language pathologists assign items to age levels. Item validity was established, according to the author, "by the retention of only those items that yielded a greater percent passing as chronological age increases." These are subjective methods of establishing content and item validity. In addition, the author provides no information concerning the experience or qualifications of the professionals he consulted, the criteria used to make judgements, or the extent of agreement among the professionals.

The author examined the criterion-related validity of the ROWPVT by correlating raw scores from the ROWPVT with raw scores from the vocabulary subtests of the Wechsler Preschool and Primary Scale of Intelligence (WPPSI) and the Wechsler Intelligence Scale for Children—Revised (WISC-R) for 935 children in the standardization sample. These correlation coefficients range from .23 to .70 with a median of .42. The author adds that additional criterion-related validity can be inferred from the high correlation ($r = .89$) between raw scores for the ROWPVT and the EOWPVT. The reported correlations are inadequate for establishing the criterion-related validity of the ROWPVT. This reviewer wonders why the author chose to compare the ROWPVT to the vocabulary subtests of the WPPSI and the WISC-R, since the latter, in contrast to the ROWPVT, require the child to verbally express the meanings of words. A more appropriate comparison would be to the Peabody Picture Vocabulary Test—Revised (PPVT-R), which is more like the ROWPVT. The author includes no information concerning attempts to establish the construct validity of the ROWPVT.

The similarity of the ROWPVT to the PPVT-R in purpose and design makes comparison of the two measures inevitable. In most respects, the PPVT-R is clearly superior to the ROWPVT. Most notable of the PPVT-R's advantages when compared to the ROWPVT is the size and composition of the standardization sample. The ROWPVT was normed on 1,128 children from the San Francisco Bay area, the PPVT-R on 4,200 children nationwide selected to approximate the 1970 census data. In addition, the quality and amount of reliability and validity data, the existence of two forms, and the applicability to a wider age range make the PPVT-R the clear choice for a measure of receptive vocabulary.

SUMMARY. The ROWPVT is a quick, easy method for estimating a child's single-word receptive vocabulary. Its best feature is that its norms are equivalent to those of the EOWPVT, which makes it possible to compare a child's receptive and expressive vocabulary scores. The superiority of the PPVT-R to the ROWPVT, however, is unquestionable. Further research to establish the test-retest reliability and validity of the ROWPVT, more extensive normative studies, and improvement of the illustrations are needed before this reviewer would recommend use of the ROWPVT over the PPVT-R as the better measure of receptive vocabulary.

[65]

Recognition Memory Test. Purpose: "Geared to detect minor degrees of memory deficit across a wide age range of the adult population." Adult patients referred for neuropsychological assessment; 1984; RMT; 2 scores: Words, Faces; individual; 1986 price data: £34.25 per complete kit; £25 per set of test booklets; £3.50 per 25 record forms; £5.95 per manual (16 pages); administration time not reported; Elizabeth K. Warrington; NFER-Nelson Publishing Co., Ltd. [England].*

Review of the Recognition Memory Test by RUSSELL L. ADAMS, Director, Psychology Internship Program, University of Oklahoma Health Sciences Center, Oklahoma City, OK:

This test, which is a measure of recognition memory of both words and faces, was designed to detect *minor* degrees of memory deficits in patients with known or suspected memory disorders.

The test consists of two separate instruments—Recognition Memory for Words (RMW) and Recognition Memory for Faces (RMF). In the Recognition Memory for Words Test, the patient is presented with 50 words of 4 to 6 letters in length. The words are frequently occurring words in the English vocabulary. The words are presented at the rate of one word every 3 seconds. The patient is then presented with a card containing 50 word pairs. Each pair contains a word previously presented and a distractor. The subject's task is to select the word previously presented.

The Recognition Memory for Faces is an analogous task except the test stimuli consist of 50 photographs of unfamiliar faces. After presentation of 50 faces, the patient is asked to select the previously presented face from a pair of two faces. Fifty such pairs are presented.

The test has some very strong assets. The test manual presents data on 310 volunteer subjects, ranging in age from 18 to 70. Separate norms are presented for three age groups: < 40, ages 40–54, ages > 55. Age norms are important because there is a clear decrement in the memory scores of normative subjects in the older age groups. More importantly, however, the manual also presents the results of 134 patients with right-hemisphere lesions and 145 patients with left-hemisphere lesions. These lateralized-brain-injured patients were further divided into frontal-, parietal-, temporal-, or occipital-lesion groups. The fact that this test has such a large sample of patients with lateralized damage sets it aside from most other memory measures. Getting documented cases of lateralized disorders is very difficult.

Although the manual states the pathology in these lateralized groups includes 65% neoplastic lesions and 31% vascular lesions, the reader does not know the exact type of lesions, the chronicity of the lesions, or whether testing was done prior to or after surgery. These factors can greatly affect memory disorders and, in this reviewer's opinion, should have been reported in the manual. The manual also presents performance data on a group of 112 patients with documented cerebral atrophy as measured by the CT scan. The degree of atrophy was separately assessed by both (a) width of sulci and (b) width of ventricles on a 5-point scale. Patients with obvious marked dementing processes were not included. Apparently the decision to exclude these patients was made on clinical grounds when it was felt that patients were not up to the demands of this rather complicated memory task. This procedure effectively eliminated patients with severe dementia. Unfortunately, the implication of this approach is that it would be difficult to do repeat testing of patients with progressive memory disorders who at the time of retest may be in the severe range, because no norms are available on the more significantly demented patients. The manual, however, clearly points out that this test is for patients with mild memory disorder. Of course, one test cannot be expected to do everything.

The fact that the test has both a verbal-memory measure and a nonverbal-memory measure is another real asset, because the dominant hemisphere is thought to play a major role in the verbal memory and the nondominant hemisphere in the nonverbal memory. The manual presents the very important find-

ing that there was a highly significant impairment in the right-hemisphere-lesion groups on the RMF, while there was no corresponding impairment on the RMW. Similarly, the patients with lesions in the left hemisphere were impaired on both the RMW and the RMF compared with the normal subjects. However, as expected, the left-hemisphere group was significantly worse than the right-hemisphere group on the RMW measure. In addition, the right-hemisphere group performed significantly poorer on the RMF than the left-hemisphere group. This finding would make the test useful in separating right-hemisphere-damaged from left-hemisphere-damaged patients. However, one must be careful to note this is only one of many measures that must be used in order to differentiate these two groups. The actual percent of patients with deficit scores (poorer than the performance of 95% of the normal patients) was seldom over 40%. That would mean that 60% of the brain-injury group would be misclassified as would 5% false positives in the normative sample.

No data are presented concerning an overall measure of recognition memory that would be obtained by adding together the performance scores on the RMF and RMW. Such data may be important, especially in diffuse brain-injured patients. Psychometric theory would suggest that the more items the memory measure has, the higher the reliability of the measure would be. Why this information was not included in the manual is unknown.

Also, it was noted that there was no parallel form of the test available. Again, no test can be perfect, but such parallel forms are helpful for repeat testing of a progressive disorder such as memory impairment.

Unfortunately, the reliability coefficients of these measures were not presented. Granted, test-retest reliability would be inappropriate in a memory measure because once the test is given, the patient would likely remember much of this material on the next presentation. However, some type of internal consistency reliability estimate would be in order. If parallel forms of the test were available, the reliability between these two parallel measures would also be helpful.

The manual presents data in a very scientific and appropriate manner. The test user is likely to benefit from the scholarly approach of the author. It would be helpful, however, to have a section in the manual demonstrating how performance on this test could be helpful in clinical planning. Perhaps case examples would be helpful. Also I think a section dealing with possible problems in using the instrument would be useful.

The various tables presented in the manual did not present summary information concerning false positives, false negatives, hits, and misses when the test was used with various subgroups. Such information is clearly of great importance and should be included in future revisions of the test.

In summary, the Recognition Memory Test is an excellent measurement tool. The manual presents detailed information, not only on normal test performance, but also on lateralized lesions and patients with diffuse atrophy. Moreover, the performance of patients who have lesions in particular lobes of each hemisphere is described. I would anticipate frequent use of this test in the future.

Additional studies need to be conducted and cross-validation studies undertaken. However, given the fact that this test was copyrighted only in 1984, such data may well be forthcoming in future revisions. The test has some advantages over the Wechsler Memory Scale because the Wechsler Memory Scale, as described in its manual, dilutes the various memory components of the test by averaging scores. After reviewing the test manual, this reviewer (who, parenthetically, had not used the test previously) will start to include it periodically in his test battery. This reviewer would suggest that future revisions of this test include some measure of free recall of the words rather than just recognition memory. Free recall of words could simply be obtained prior to the recognition-memory portion of the test. Similarly, perhaps the test could further be expanded by having a delayed-component recognition memory obtained 30 minutes after the initial recall. Delayed recognition may well result in additional clinical data.

[66]

Salamon-Conte Life Satisfaction in the Elderly Scale. Purpose: "Designed to reliably measure life satisfaction among the aged in a variety of settings." Older adults; 1984; LSES; 9 scores: Daily Activities, Meaning, Goals, Mood, Self-Concept, Health, Finances, Social Contacts, Total; 1987

price data: $21.95 per complete kit including 50 test booklets, 50 scoring sheets, and manual (27 pages); (15–25) minutes; Michael J. Salamon and Vincent A. Conte; Psychological Assessment Resources, Inc.*

Review of the Salamon-Conte Life Satisfaction in the Elderly Scale by DAVID N. DIXON, Professor and Department Chair of Counseling and Psychology Services, Ball State University, Muncie, IN:

The Life Satisfaction in the Elderly Scale (LSES) is one of many scales in this area. The authors establish a place for this new scale primarily on the basis of inadequate psychometric information for previous scales and expanded coverage of important domains of life satisfaction.

The LSES provides a total satisfaction score and eight subscale scores. The chosen subscales are consistent with those definitions of satisfaction found in the literature. Five of the domains of satisfaction (Daily Activities, Meaning, Goals, Mood, and Self-Concept) are also assessed by Life Satisfaction Index scales developed by Neugarten, Havighurst, and Tobin (1961). The three additional subscales are Health, Finances, and Social Contacts.

Reliability data support the internal consistency and stability of the total scale. Coefficient alpha reliabilities of .93 and .92 and test-retest reliability coefficients of .67 (6 month) and .90 (1 month) are reported. Subscale reliabilities are adequate for most subscales; however, the Goals and Self-Concept subscales are questionable (coefficient alpha reliabilities of .60, .50 and .61, .47 respectively for two different samples).

Validity data, derived by factor analysis and cluster analysis procedures, generally support the subscale structure of the LSES. These data also raise questions about the Goals and Self-Concept subscales.

No criterion-related validity is presented in the manual. Minimally, it would be useful to know how the LSES correlates with other measures of life satisfaction.

The authors report normative data from 600 individuals with total scores broken down by age groups. They encourage the development of local norms in order to consider unique characteristics of the population of interest. They state that older adults suffering from impaired physical functioning would have lower subscale scores on Health and Mood and that a clinically depressed population would be expected to score lower on Mood, Meaning, and Self-Concept. However, no norms are presented to support these assertions. For the total scale and subscales to be most useful, data for these clinical populations need to be gathered.

Instructions for administration and scoring are clear. Instructions for interpretation, unfortunately, go well beyond the current stage of development of the LSES. Four case studies are presented in the manual to illustrate how scores on the LSES are interpreted. Interpretation of scores for individuals fails to consider measurement principles such as standard error of measurement. Whether changes in subscale scores of 2 or 3 points have any clinical significance lacks validation, and the user of the LSES should be very cautious about interpreting individual scores until further research is completed.

Overall, the LSES appears to be an acceptable measure of life satisfaction. The content, as reflected by the subscales, is comprehensive. The total scale and some of the subscales are reliable. Further validity studies of the subscales are needed to provide a basis for individual interpretation.

REVIEWER'S REFERENCE
Neugarten, B. L., Havighurst, R. J., & Tobin, S. S. (1961). The measurement of life satisfaction. *Journal of Gerontology*, 16, 134-143.

Review of the Salamon-Conte Life Satisfaction in the Elderly Scale by NANCY A. BUSCH-ROSSNAGEL, Associate Professor of Psychology and Research Associate, Hispanic Research Center, Fordham University, Bronx, NY:

The authors of this scale criticize the scales frequently used to assess the well-being of the elderly population (i.e., Life-Satisfaction Indices, [LSI] devised by Neugarten, Havighurst, & Tobin, 1961) because of "the lack of information regarding the psychometric properties" and because "the domain of life satisfaction encompasses a larger number of issues than the five" constructs used by Neugarten et al. The Salamon-Conte Life Satisfaction in the Elderly Scale (LSES) has been designed to overcome these limitations. Thus, the LSES includes the five life-satisfaction constructs of the LSI—taking pleasure in daily activities, regarding life as meaningful, goodness of fit between desired and achieved goals, positive

mood, and positive self-concept—and adds three more—perceived health, financial security, and social contacts.

The LSES contains 40 items, five for each subscale, on a 5-point Likert scale. Most of the items are written in the first person. To score the subscales, the far left anchor is always given a score of 1, the next anchor is given a score of 2 and so on, so that the far right anchor is given a score of 5. This scoring procedure means that the "best" response, reflecting high satisfaction, would be a column of "Xs" down the far right anchor. No information is given about the possibility of response bias generated by this scoring procedure. The scores are written on a scoring sheet patterned to allow for easy summation to obtain the subscale score by adding down the columns; the total score is computed by summing the subscale scores.

Three different samples were used to examine reliability. The first consisted of 408 subjects, ages 55 to 90, who lived in the community. The second sample contained 241 subjects affiliated with health care providers, including in-patient and ambulatory care services and visiting nurse services provided in the subjects' own homes. The third sample consisted of 50 subjects, ages 65 to 89, residing in a housing complex for older adults. Information about both internal consistency and test-retest reliability is provided. The coefficient alphas for the total score were .93 and .92 for the first two samples respectively. The reliabilities for the subscales ranged from .60 to .79 and .47 to .78 for the first two samples respectively. The lower reliabilities were found for the subscales of Goals and Self-Concept. Six-month test-retest for 120 subjects of the first sample was .67 for the total score. One-month test-retest reliability for the third sample was .90 for the total scale and above .88 for all subscales.

Information about construct and concurrent validity is provided. The authors state the items were reviewed by a panel of four experts to establish their face validity, but no information about this process is given. More specific information about construct validity is provided by means of factor analysis and cluster analysis. A principal components analysis with the data from Sample 1 indicated that eight factors adequately summarized the data. Factor rotation, using an eight-factor solution, indicated that the subscales of Health and Finance are well determined by each of two factors. However, the loadings for the other six factors did not identify the other subscales as coherently. Using the data from Sample 2, a cluster analysis indicated that four of the five items from five of the subscales cluster together. The subscales of Self-Concept, Goals, and Daily Activities did not show such clear patterns.

A study of concurrent validity used a sample of 75 subjects who were applying to a preventative health care program. The data obtained on these subjects included the LSES, information about health background, psychosocial information, and physical assessments. Unfortunately, the authors provide no specific information about how the data other than the LSES were scored or coded, so it is impossible to interpret their table of chi-squares and correlations.

Additional concurrent validity information was obtained using the second sample. These subjects were recruited from six different types of settings. ANOVAs were used to examine group differences in the total and subscale scores. The total scores and the subscales of Daily Activities, Meaning, and Health significantly differentiated among the groups. The authors state the other subscales are "related to personal characteristics not expected to correlate with participation in health services." However, it is not clear that this was an a priori hypothesis.

The available norms are based on scores from elderly persons living primarily in the Northeastern United States, and the authors state the norms should be considered preliminary. While the sample appears to be heterogeneous in regard to age, sex, socioeconomic status, and so on, the sample is not compared to the population at large. The authors suggest establishing local norms, but do not follow their own advice of cross-tabulating norms against demographic data such as sex, service unit, or income level. The norms are separated by age group: 55–60, 61–65, etc.; the last age group is "over 80." The norms are presented as quantiles for the total scores and average quantiles for the subscales scores. The authors also suggest that the LSES may be useful for individualized assessment and present four case studies as illustrations. The preliminary nature of the norms requires that other diagnostic tools be used when developing individual treatment plans and monitoring progress.

The LSES is an adequate measure of life satisfaction among the elderly. The manual provides more psychometric information about the LSES than is easily obtainable for the widely-used LSI (Neugarten et al., 1961). While the reliability of the total score of the LSES is high, the validity evidence is mixed. The information about concurrent validity is not presented in enough detail to allow for evaluation. Construct validity information suggests that more work is needed on item development, and studies of groups that should differ on the subscales related to personal characteristics are needed to further establish validity in this area. As the authors note, further work on the norms is needed.

REVIEWER'S REFERENCE
Neugarten, B. L., Havighurst, R. J., & Tobin, S. S. (1961). The measurement of life satisfaction. *Journal of Gerontology*, 16, 134-143.

[67]

Schaie-Thurstone Adult Mental Abilities Test. Purpose: "Measuring the mental abilities of adults." Ages 22–84; 1985; STAMAT; consists of many items from the Thurstone Primary Mental Abilities Test Form 11–17; 7 scales: Recognition Vocabulary, Figure Rotation, Letter Series, Number Addition, Word Fluency, Object Rotation, Word Series; manual (86 pages); price data available from publisher; (50–60) minutes; K. Warner Schaie; Consulting Psychologists Press, Inc.*

Review of the Schaie-Thurstone Adult Mental Abilities Test by ERIC F. GARDNER, Professor of Psychology and Education Emeritus, Syracuse University, Syracuse, NY:

The Schaie-Thurstone Adult Mental Abilities Test (STAMAT) is presented as a research and assessment tool for measuring the mental abilities of adults. It consists of two forms. Form A, for adults, is "essentially the Thurstone Primary Mental Abilities Test Form 11-17 (PMA) with new adult norms." Form OA, for the "Older Adult," contains the same tests as Form A augmented by two tests paralleling two of the original tests but using stimuli less abstract and more familiar to adults.

This reviewer believes that there are very few tests that have been so thoroughly and critically reviewed in previous editions of *The Mental Measurements Yearbooks* as the Thurstone Primary Mental Ability Tests. Previous reviews, beginning with *The Second Mental Measurements Yearbook* (Buros, 1940), and continuing in each subsequent edition up to and including *The Seventh Mental Measurements Yearbook* (Buros, 1972), have pointed out the large number of deficiencies of past editions as well as what are described as partial improvements. The most recent reviews in *The Seventh Mental Measurements Yearbook* by Richard Schutz (Schutz, 1972) and M. Y. Quereshi (Quereshi, 1972) stress that many of the needed improvements have not been made and that the tests have outlived their usefulness.

Quereshi says, "The PMA tests served an important purpose as research tools in the advancement of the multiple factor notion of ability but have not fulfilled the practical promise of differential educational or vocational measurement" (Quereshi, 1972, p. 1066). Schutz is even more critical: "Neither a modern researcher nor a practitioner is likely to find it an attractive new buy, considering the other models available to him" (Schutz, 1972, p. 1067).

In view of these rather devastating criticisms, one could legitimately ask why Schaie selected the PMA tests for his extensive research. Schaie addresses this issue directly and makes a special point that the reason he selected the Thurstone tests for his work, in contrast with other possibilities, was because of their theoretical basis. Although this is a desirable objective, it should be pointed out that attempts to devise tests for intellectual abilities have been based on theories associated with three alternative hypotheses: (*a*) that the measurement of "general" intelligence is of major importance (e.g., Stanford-Binet and Otis-Lennon tests); (*b*) that different kinds of intelligence are of major importance and, therefore, each should be measured (e.g., Thurstone tests); and (*c*) that both the "general factor" of intelligence and specialized "group factors" should be measured.

The PMA, although representing only one of the various models of mental abilities stressing hypothesis *b*, has seen steady growth and has been the basis for a number of competing tests. A plausible additional explanation for its choice is that Schaie began his extensive research program in gerontology, which requires long-range longitudinal studies, years ago with data from the PMA and such studies require a constant stimulus. Of great importance is the fact that previous reviewers have indicated that the PMA tests are sound and well constructed, that the test items are well written, and the directions clear. This reviewer concurs. In any event, the use and improvement of the Primary Mental Abilities Test for the adult level is a defensible choice.

The major deficiencies have been addressed by Schaie through his gerontological research the past 20 years, and he has taken steps to rectify them. Specifically, he has: (*a*) focused on a specific portion of the age range; (*b*) defined the purpose of the Schaie-Thurstone Adult Mental Abilities Test as a research instrument; (*c*) presented data, both cross sectional and longitudinal, over an extensive period of time; (*d*) used a methodology relating both kinds of data (cross-sectional and longitudinal); (*e*) shown the interrelationships among the variables for different age groups; (*f*) shown stability over time (3 years, 7 years, 14 years, and 21 years); (*g*) presented norms separately for each sex as well as the combined group for age groups extending from 22–28-year-olds to 78–84-year-olds; (*h*) adapted a more suitable format for Form OA (Older Adult); (*i*) presented two additional tests in Form OA with stimuli more suitable for older adults; and (*j*) addressed the issue of validity directly and presented substantial amounts of data.

The manual is well written and contains the supporting data for the statements made about the tests. Data for both validity and reliability are presented and discussed in a relevant fashion. The stability indices for the 21 years of longitudinal data are amazingly high and consistent. The correlation coefficients for the three separate cohorts with a 7-year test-retest span for Form A ranged from a low of .72 to a high of .86 for the individual tests. The stability over a 21-year span for 120 of the subjects for the same tests ranged from .77 to .82. The consistency on Form OA for 256 persons, ages 55 to 85, who were followed for 3 years ranged from .80 to .86. Several of the tests are sufficiently short so as to give relatively large standard errors of measurement in spite of their respectable reliability coefficients. This matter would be serious if differential diagnosis of individuals is attempted.

An extensive discussion with considerable supporting data of content, concurrent, predictive, and construct validity is presented in the manual. Schaie makes the important point that "intelligence tests have typically been constructed to predict performance in educational or vocational entry," whereas the purposes for adult intelligence tests may stress other needs. In particular, they should be validated in terms of situations involving specific competencies, especially those related to independent living. Very little work has been done in this area and Schaie expresses hope that the STAMAT will be used for research in this field.

Voluminous tables of norms for each subtest in Form A as well as for a weighted total score are given for each sex and the total group. The individual test scores are converted to standard T-scores by sex for each age of nine age groups extending from 22–29 to 78–84. Composite intellectual ability norms expressed as deviation IQ equivalents with a mean of 100 and standard deviation of 15 are given for each sex over the nine age groups. Also, composite educational aptitude indices expressed as standard scores with a mean of 50 and standard deviation of 10 are tabled. Similar tables of norms are included for Form OA, but there are no composite intellectual ability scores or composite educational aptitude scores for this Older Adult form.

In conclusion, the Schaie-Thurstone Adult Mental Abilities Test is based upon the previous work of the Thurstones; the long range research program by Schaie has made available two instruments, measuring important cognitive variables and with excellent psychometric characteristics, for research on the mental abilities of adults.

REVIEWER'S REFERENCES

Buros, O. K. (Ed.). (1940). *The second mental measurements yearbook.* Highland Park, NJ: Gryphon Press.
Buros, O. K. (Ed.). (1972). *The seventh mental measurements yearbook.* Highland Park, NJ: Gryphon Press.
Qureshi, M. Y. (1972). [Review of SRA Primary Mental Abilities, 1962 Edition]. In O. K. Buros (Ed.). *The seventh mental measurements yearbook* (pp. 1064-1066). Highland Park, NJ: Gryphon Press.
Schutz, R. E. (1972). [Review of SRA Primary Mental Abilities, 1962 Edition]. In O. K. Buros (Ed.). *The seventh mental measurements yearbook* (pp. 1066-1068). Highland Park, NJ: Gryphon Press.

[68]
The Self-Directed Search: A Guide to Educational and Vocational Planning—1985 Revision.

Purpose: "Developed to create a scientifically sound and practical simulation of the vocational counseling experience by using a self-administered, self-scored, and self-interpreted vocational assessment booklet and compatible file of occupational possibilities." High school and college and adults; 1970–87; SDS; 6 scores (Realistic, Investigative, Artistic, Social, Enterprising, Conventional) for each of 3 scales (Activities, Competencies, Occupations) and for Self-Ratings of Abilities, Summary; 2 forms: standard, Form E ("simplified for a 4th grade reading level"); 1987 price data: $75 per 10 mail-in prepaid test booklets/answer sheets; $30 per 25 standard booklets and 25 occupations finders; $30 per 25 Form E booklets and 25 jobs finders; $19.50 per 25 alphabetized occupations finders; $27 per 20 college majors finders; $150 per computer version (50 uses); IBM or Apple computer-administered version requires 64K, 80-column card, 2 floppy disk drives (Apple); 256K and 2 disk drives (IBM); $12 per professional manual ('85, 102 pages); $9 per manual supplement ('87, 51 pages); (40–60) minutes; John L. Holland; Psychological Assessment Resources, Inc.*

Canadian Edition: 1985; edited by Lewis Miller; also available in French; Guidance Centre [Canada].

For a review by Robert H. Dolliver of an earlier edition, see 9:1098 (12 references); see also T3:2134 (55 references); for a review by John O. Crites and excerpted reviews by Fred Brown, Richard Seligman, Catherine C. Cutts, Robert H. Dolliver, and Robert N. Hansen, see 8:1022 (88 references); see also T2:2211 (1 reference).

TEST REFERENCES

1. Kerr, B. A. (1983). Raising the career aspirations of gifted girls. *The Vocational Guidance Quarterly*, 32, 37-43.
2. Winer, J. L., Wilson, D. O., & Pierce, R. A. (1983). Using the Self Directed Search—Form E with high school remedial reading students. *The Vocational Guidance Quarterly*, 32, 130-135.
3. Costa, P. T., Jr., McCrae, R. R., & Holland, J. L. (1984). Personality and vocational interests in an adult sample. *Journal of Applied Psychology*, 69, 390-400.
4. Dawis, R. V., & Sung, Y. H. (1984). The relationship of participation in school activities to abilities and interests in a high school student sample. *Journal of Vocational Behavior*, 24, 159-168.
5. Furnham, A., & Schaeffer, R. (1984). Person-environment fit, job satisfaction and mental health. *Journal of Occupational Psychology*, 57, 295-307.
6. Healy, C. C., & Mourton, D. L. (1984). The effects of an abbreviated Self-Directed Search on the career decision competencies of community college students. *Vocational Guidance Quarterly*, 33, 55-62.
7. Healy, C. C., Mourton, D. L., Anderson, E. C., & Robinson, E. (1984). Career maturity and the achievement of community college students and disadvantaged university students. *Journal of College Student Personnel*, 25, 347-352.
8. Hollinger, C. L. (1984). The impact of gender schematic processing on the Self Directed Search responses of gifted and talented female adolescents. *Journal of Vocational Behavior*, 24, 15-27.
9. Iachan, R. (1984). Measures of agreement for incompletely ranked data. *Educational and Psychological Measurement*, 44, 823-830.
10. Pichl, H. A., & Clark, A. K. (1984). Congruency, achievement, and the Self Directed Search. *Canadian Counsellor*, 18, 79-86.

11. Aronowitz, A., Bridge, R. G., & Jones, P. (1985). Sex bias in the Self-Directed Search Investigative subscale. *Journal of Vocational Behavior*, 26, 146-154.

12. Elliott, T. R., & Byrd, E. K. (1985). Scoring accuracy of the Self-Directed Search with ninth-grade students. *Vocational Guidance Quarterly*, 34, 85-90.

13. Galassi, M. D., Jones, L. K., & Britt, M. N. (1985). Nontraditional career options for women: An evaluation of career guidance instruments. *Vocational Guidance Quarterly*, 34, 124-130.

14. Healy, C. C., & Mourton, D. L. (1985). Congruence and vocational identity: Outcomes of career counseling with persuasive power. *Journal of Counseling Psychology*, 32, 441-444.

15. Lowman, R. L., Williams, R. E., & Leeman, G. E. (1985). The structure and relationship of college women's primary abilities and vocational interests. *Journal of Vocational Behavior*, 27, 298-315.

16. Neimeyer, G. J., & Ebben, R. (1985). The effects of vocational interventions on the complexity and positivity of occupational judgments. *Journal of Vocational Behavior*, 27, 87-97.

17. Kerr, B. A. (1986). Career counseling for the gifted: Assessments and interventions. *Journal of Counseling and Development*, 64, 602-604.

18. Schwartz, R. H., Andiappan, P., & Nelson, M. (1986). Reconsidering the support for Holland's congruence-achievement hypothesis. *Journal of Counseling Psychology*, 33, 425-428.

Review of The Self-Directed Search: A Guide to Educational and Vocational Planning—1985 Revision by M. HARRY DANIELS, Associate Professor of Educational Psychology, Southern Illinois University at Carbondale, Carbondale, IL:

Since its initial publication in 1971, John Holland proposed that the Self-Directed Search (SDS) would provide vocational counselors with a "self-administered, self-scored, and self-interpreted vocational counseling tool" that could be used to serve a large portion of the adolescent and adult population. Additionally, he intended that the SDS would provide a framework for users to organize occupational and personal information and would be a means for researchers to investigate both the theoretical and practical utility of its underlying typology. Holland has achieved his purposes.

The SDS is based on Holland's theory of vocational choice, which postulates the existence of six types of work environments: Realistic (R), Investigative (I), Artistic (A), Social (S), Enterprising (E), and Conventional (C). The theory also states that most people can be categorized into one of six matching personality types, and that individuals will seek out environments in which they will have the greatest opportunity to act out those values, interests, and competencies consistent with their personality. The SDS represents a popular means for conducting a search for the proper person-environment match. It is widely used as the vocational instrument of choice with adolescent, young adult, and adult populations throughout the United States and in several other countries. Related research has stimulated a reexamination of the vocational counseling process as well as improvements in the instrument itself.

Its apparent usefulness notwithstanding, the SDS and its underlying typology have been the focus of frequent evaluation and criticism. Issues related to the presence of cultural, gender, or age biases represent the most persistent and frequent criticisms. Other concerns have focused on the simplicity of Holland's personality typology, the problems associated with self-scoring and self-interpretation, the unavailability of appropriate and adequate statistical procedures to utilize essential psychological constructs (e.g., differentiation and consistency) when interpreting or comparing results, and the lack of adequate support materials to guide users' career information-seeking behavior.

Although it appears to be virtually unchanged from the 1977 version, the 1985 version of the SDS both addresses and answers most of the criticisms previously leveled against it. The goals in developing the 1985 revision were (*a*) to make the new SDS more practical and easier to use, (*b*) to increase the benefits of the SDS, (*c*) to make assessment more scientific, (*d*) to consider the evaluations of test reviewers and users, and (*e*) to weigh the implications of Title IX, the *Standards for Educational and Psychological Testing*, and the NIE guidelines. It is my judgment that Holland achieved the majority of his goals.

As with previous versions, the SDS consists of an assessment booklet and an Occupations Finder (OF). The assessment booklet consists of six scales: Occupational Daydreams (up to eight self-identified occupations can be listed), Activities (11 items for each of the six personality types), Competencies (11 items for each of the six personality types), Occupations (14 items for each of the six personality types), and two Self-Estimates (two 7-point scales for each of the six personality types). Except for Occupational Daydreams, all of the scales are used to calculate the total score for each of the six personality types (each total score equals the sum of the five raw scores). The ordinal relationship of the magnitude of the three highest total scores determines the three-letter Holland occupational code. (It is recommended that the Occupational Daydreams section be used as a cross-validation of the obtained occupational code.) Once obtained, the summary code represents a simple way of organizing information about occupations. Users are directed to search the OF for every possible ordering of their three-letter code. Form E (Easy) of the SDS, which contains the same sections but with fewer items per section and different labels for each section, is available for use with individuals with limited reading skills. There is also a separate OF for Form E.

Revising approximately one-fourth of the items (59 of 228) with the intent of increasing the validity of the scales and of eliminating gender and age biases represents one of the major changes in the new SDS. This change should not be interpreted to mean that Holland has set aside his position that gender does influence career choices. According to Holland, gender bias is a complex social-emotional issue that involves more than reducing mean differences between sexes. It is his contention that "anyone can write items that make men and women look alike. It is another matter to write items that will withstand the variety of standard psychometric and content validity tests" (Holland, 1985, p. 375). There is a growing body of literature supporting the validity of Holland's view that gender does influence career. Assuming that such a conclusion is indeed valid, it would not be unreasonable to argue that the accurate assessment of those influences by instruments like the SDS would promote rather than prohibit satisfactory career choices.

Other important differences between the old and the new SDS include enlarging the OF to include "all of the most common occupations in the United States," rewriting the directions to improve clarity of understanding, and providing a more useful list of resources in the assessment booklet. This revision of the OF represents a marked improvement over previous ones. The actual number of occupations increased from 500 to 1,156, which accounts for "approximately 99% of all workers." As before, individual occupations included in the OF are arranged according to personality types and subtypes. Occupational subtypes are also arranged according to the general educational development (GED) that an occupation requires according to the *Dictionary of Occupational Titles*, (*DOT*). Most occupations are also designated by their current *DOT* number. The availability of the revised OF greatly enhances the potential of the SDS to stimulate career information-seeking behavior.

The 1985 SDS Professional Manual is as impressive as its predecessor. It contains a total of 69 tables (37 in the text and 32 in the appendices), four figures, and 35 SDS profiles. (The chapter on the interpretation and use of the SDS is most informative. Questions concerning score consistency and score differentiation as well as other problems related to scoring and interpreting the SDS are addressed through the interpretation of 35 profiles.) The lack of tables of contents for these information sources greatly reduces their utilization. One entire appendix is devoted to normative data (i.e., percentile ranks, mean scores, frequency of code combinations, and distribution of people and jobs). Another appendix contains an eight-page alphabetical listing of occupational classifications and codes. Two appendices emphasize scoring accuracy, and one contains technical information for the 1985 revision. The reference section has been updated, but otherwise is almost identical to the one in the 1977 Revision.

Estimates of the internal consistency of the 1985 SDS are slightly higher overall than those reported for the 1977 version. For the Summary Scales, 69% had higher alphas, 17% showed no change, and 14% had lower alphas. The range of summary-scale alphas varied by age and gender. For ages 14–18, estimates for females ranged from .81 (Realistic) to .91 (Investigative), while males ranged from .81 (Social) to .92 (Realistic). For ages 19–25, alphas ranged from .87 (Social) to .92 (Artistic and Enterprising) for females, and from .83 (Social) to .92 (Artistic) for males. Estimates for females in the 26–74 age range varied between .85 (Artistic and Social) to .91 (Realistic, Enterprising, and Conventional), and between .87 (Artistic) to .93 (Investigative and Realistic) for males. No estimates of the temporal stability of the 1985 SDS were reported in the Professional Manual. The concurrent validity of the 1985 SDS, which is determined by assessing the "percentage of hits" (i.e., the percentage of a sample whose high-point code and occupational code agree), is comparable to that reported for the 1977 version.

Although many of the limitations of previous versions of the SDS have been satisfactorily addressed, others persist. Two problems are of special concern. The first is the use of raw score data to determine total scores and, subsequently, the summary codes. Holland has provided a detailed rationale for his use of raw scores, and many of his arguments are good ones. However, his arguments fail to provide a satisfactory explanation of the practice, especially in light of the construction of the instrument. Holland describes the SDS as having four sections (totaling 228 items) that are used to determine the summary codes. Because the scales do not contain the identical number of items, they contribute unequally to the total scores. Activities and Competencies have 11 items for each of six scales, while Occupations has 14 items per scale. Self-Estimates contains 12 items (two sets of six ratings, each rating corresponding to a type). Because raw scores rather than standard scores are used to calculate the total score for each type, Occupations contributes more to the total than either Self-Estimates, Activities, or Competencies, and Self-Estimates contributes more than either Activities or Competencies. Such a scoring protocol places undue emphasis on fantasy as opposed to experience, which may result in unrealistic and unsatisfactory career choices. (This explanation becomes more plausible if occupations are considered as an "objectively determined" set of occupational daydreams.)

The second concern is Holland's inconsistent use of his typology in the different sections. In three of the sections (Activities, Competencies, and Occupations), the typology serves as a framework for listing items (each item of each scale in each section has an assigned value of 1). In the Self-Estimates section, however, the types become items, and the items may have an assigned value ranging from 1–7. Such a practice maximizes the weighted value of the very thing (occupational type) that is being determined. (It is conceivable, for example, that the sum of the Self-Estimates could total 14, which is more than 25% of even the largest possible score, and which may represent up to 100% of an obtained score.) It also raises questions about the necessity of including all the items from each of the other sections. Finally, it may represent a potential source of

the reported confusion about the scoring procedures.

In sum, the 1985 version of the SDS reflects Holland's continuing commitment to provide vocational clients, counselors, and researchers with an accurate, inexpensive, and simple means for addressing questions that are related to occupational choice. Its popularity among practitioners and researchers alike is testimony to its perceived utility and effectiveness. The expanded OF will enhance its use as a stimulus for vocational exploration. Despite its many positive features, however, it is important to remember that it may not be the instrument of choice for all clients, and that some clients will need to see a counselor even after completing the SDS. (According to the manual the SDS will only satisfy the vocational assistance needs of approximately 50% of the people.) Similarly, users need to remember that the SDS, like other vocational choice instruments, has limited predictive validity. This limitation notwithstanding, the SDS remains an excellent vocational counseling tool that can be used with most adolescents and adults.

REVIEWER'S REFERENCE
Holland, J. L. (1985). Author biases, errors, and omissions in an evaluation of the SDS Investigative Scale: A response to Aronowitz, Bridge and Jones (1985). *Journal of Vocational Behavior*, 27 (3), 374-376.

Review of The Self-Directed Search: A Guide to Educational and Vocational Planning—1985 Revision by *CAROLINE MANUELE-ADKINS, Associate Professor, Counseling, Department of Educational Foundations, Hunter College of the City University of New York, New York, NY:*

The Self-Directed Search (SDS) is a self-administered, self-scored, and self-interpreted inventory of a person's occupationally related characteristics. The purpose of the SDS is to provide people with "a vocational counseling experience by simulating what a person and counselor might do together in several interviews." The SDS was developed from Holland's Vocational Preference Inventory and is based on his theory of vocational choice.

The Holland theory proposes that "most people can be categorized as one of six personality types labeled realistic, investigative, artistic, social, enterprising, or conventional." The theory also predicts that work environments can be classified in the same way because specific work environments are dominated by people who share the same "interests, competencies, and outlook on the world," (e.g., a social work environment is dominated by many social personality types). Good vocational choices then consist of helping people find a work environment congruent with their personality orientation. The SDS operationalizes this theory by providing people with information about their personality types and by helping them identify occupations congruent with their types.

The 1985 version of the SDS consists of an assessment booklet divided into six sections. These include Occupational Daydreams, Activities (liked and disliked), Competencies (activities performed well or poorly), Occupations (interesting or uninteresting), and Self-Estimates (high to low ratings of various abilities). The last section is a scoring section in which a three-letter summary code is obtained for the person's personality types. Accompanying the booklet is the Occupations Finder in which occupations are classified according to personality type and subtypes, and a *Dictionary of Occupational Titles (DOT)* with required educational level. The 1985 version of the SDS is similar to the 1977 version except that 59 of the 228 items were revised and the Occupations Finder has been increased from 500 to 1,156 occupations. According to the manual, the scoring directions were also changed to "stimulate completing of the SDS and to increase understanding of the results." These appear, however, to be minor changes. Form E of the SDS is for people with limited reading skills. It is similar to the standard form except that it is shorter (203 items) and a two-letter rather than three-letter code is obtained. No mention is made in the manual as to whether this form was revised for the 1985 edition.

The SDS is easy to read and understand. Each scale includes items that are clearly worded and obviously related to the area being assessed. In this revision efforts were made to make the items more contemporary and in some instances more occupationally related (e.g., social activities such as going to a party or dance have been replaced by items such as teaching in a college or taking a human relations course). A possible item-related problem appears in the content of the Conventional Competencies subscale. Items in that scale are so consistently directed at secretarial and office competencies that many females who have these competen-

cies may receive an inflated Conventional score. Including more diverse Conventional Competency items may alleviate this problem.

Directions for taking and scoring the SDS appear to be clear but questions have been raised about the accuracy of client self-scoring of the SDS. Studies on the 1977 version of the SDS indicate that about 40% of a sample of high school students made errors in scoring. Some of these were minor and did not affect the accuracy of the 3-point code. The manual does caution that "the scoring of the SDS should be supervised and checked." One area of scoring and interpretation that may need more attention is the Occupational Daydreams section. The instructions for this section include obtaining a three-letter code (in the Occupations Finder) for each of the career choices or aspirations listed, and then later comparing these codes to the person's summary code. The problem is that scoring directions for this part tend to minimize the importance and significance of the information obtained. First, the scoring is not part of the primary scoring directions but is buried under "some next steps" which may be easily ignored or skimmed over by some test takers. Second, the directions do not fully explain to the self-scorer what similarities or disagreements may mean. They are advised only that the codes should have some resemblance to each other and that if there is no relation they should talk to a counselor or friend. Because the manual points out that these comparisons provide extremely important information about the nature of a person's choices and agreement between codes is valuable for predicting actual career choices, more specific instructions seem warranted. Disagreements imply the person is making noncongruent choices. Evidence of self-concept clarity and confusion can also be obtained by looking at these comparisons. Thus it would seem important to include this area in the primary scoring directions and to point out to the self-scorer more extensively what agreements and disagreements might mean.

Extensive information is presented in the manual regarding the validity, reliability, and norming of the SDS. These areas of the manual could be improved in their clarity of presentation. The item content and format demonstrate good content validity. One of the purposes of this revision was to increase validity by reducing item overlap across scales, by writing better items, by omitting items with extreme endorsement rates for males and females, and by making items more applicable to a broader age range. This revision's summary scale intercorrelations indicate they are similar to the correlational hexagon pattern obtained on studies done with the earlier versions. Predictive validity studies done over time are not presented for this version but studies on the earlier versions indicate that the SDS has moderate validity for predicting actual occupational choice. The Occupations Finder is an integral part of the SDS. Many studies described in the manual seem to indirectly address the question of the accuracy of the codes assigned to various occupations. More direct studies, (e.g., testing many different occupational groups to determine their actual Holland code), would provide more evidence for the validity of the occupational codes.

Extensive normative data are also supplied in the manual. Different age groups (including high school, college, and adult) are consistently described with respect to their percentile ranks, mean scores, and frequency of code occurrences for both scale scores and summary code scores. What is missing are normative data regarding the performance of different samples on Form E. Populations with literacy problems for whom norms would be useful include people who are high school dropouts, disadvantaged, learning disabled, and people for whom English is a second language. As in previous editions, women receive different Holland codes than men. For the 1985 revision female average scores, ranked from highest to lowest, were Social (33.56), Enterprising (26.14), Artistic (23.50), Conventional (21.27), Investigative (20.47), and Realistic (14.36). Male average scores, ranked from highest to lowest, were Enterprising (27.57), Social (26.68), Realistic (24.39), Investigative (23.43), Artistic (20.45), and Conventional (19.35). These findings indicate that results on the SDS are still gender-related and reflect the cultural differences of males and females in this society.

The SDS is promoted as an inventory requiring little assistance from a counselor. In fact, the manual indicates the SDS alone is sufficient for about 50% of the test takers. For a measure that is supposed to "stand on its own" it is paradoxical to find such extensive information

available in the manual to assist the counselor with SDS interpretation and almost no information available to the test taker who is attempting to understand it without guidance. This problem is somewhat alleviated with the 1985 edition because this revision includes a new booklet by Holland entitled "You and Your Career." The booklet provides users with some basic theoretical concepts, (e.g., descriptions of the different personality types). The usefulness of the booklet should be highlighted for users. All test takers should have access to it as a means of helping them understand their SDS results more completely.

The SDS has been well received and extensively used. Its strengths are that it meets the objectives the author set out for it—to produce a simple self-report, self-scoring measure that could be used by a wide variety of people. It is well grounded in theory and has an extensive cadre of research studies providing evidence for its validity and reliability. The SDS is, however, a measure requiring more assistance from a counselor than is acknowledged in the manual. The SDS compares quite favorably to other self-administered and handscored measures (e.g., the Career Decision Making System).

REVIEWER'S REFERENCE
Harrington, T. F., & O'Shea, A. J. (1982). The Harrington-O'Shea Career Decision-Making System. Circle Pines, MN: American Guidance Service.

[69]

Signals Listening Tests. Purpose: "Assist in identifying students who are not meeting minimum standards in listening." Grades 3, 5; 1982; 3 objectives: Listening for the Main Idea, Following Geographical Directions, Following Instructions; test administered by cassette tape; 1 form for each of 2 levels: grade 3, 5; 1985 price data: $75 per 2-level sets including 30 tests for each level, directions for administering (19 pages) for each level, and technical manual (27-32 pages) for each level; $40 per 1-level set; $.95 per test; $8 per technical manual; $10 per specimen set; (35) minutes; Project Signals; Project SPOKE.*

Review of the Signals Listening Test by MARTIN FUJIKI, Associate Professor of Speech Pathology and Audiology, University of Nevada School of Medicine, Reno, NV:

The Signals Listening Test is designed to provide the test user with an effective means of quickly screening a classroom of third or fifth grade children for listening problems. To do this, performance is evaluated in three tasks:

Listening for the Main Idea, Following Geographical Directions, and Following Instructions.

Because the test is designed to be administered to an entire classroom, it may be a highly efficient means of screening large numbers of children. Additionally, the tape-recorded instructions insure consistency from administration to administration. However, just as these procedures have certain advantages, they also bring certain disadvantages to the testing situation. For example, any test simultaneously administered to large numbers of individuals is subject to certain problems. Some children may perform poorly because they did not understand the directions. Other children may do well because they are helped, although inadvertently, by other students. The fact that the test directions are tape recorded, and that the examiner is instructed not to stop the tape, may add to these difficulties. Test users should consider their specific needs in relation to these advantages and disadvantages in using this test.

A discussion of content validity is presented in the statistical manual; however, criterion validity and construct validity are not addressed. Some discussion of construct validity would have been especially helpful in that the term "listening" is a particularly nebulous one. It is difficult to determine if the test is designed to identify children with specific clinical deficits, or children who are generally within normal developmental limits but whose listening skills are not as refined as those of their peer group.

On a related note, it is likely that a variety of disorders might cause a child to fail the test. For example, children with attending problems, language comprehension disorders, memory difficulties, and auditory acuity problems might be expected to have difficulty. Although this is not necessarily a weakness in a screening measure (depending upon what behaviors one considers to fall within the domain of listening), it is a consideration that the potential test user should keep in mind.

The administration instructions are generally well written, and the test itself is easy to administer. The testing materials are acceptable. The cassette-tape recordings used in testing are professionally done, both with respect to recording quality and content.

There is one point of possible confusion between the statistical manual and the test administration manual having to do with the cutoff point between passing and failing the test. The administration manuals for both forms of the test state, "Most students will score between 13 and 15 correct out of 15 items." This statement can be interpreted to indicate that a score of 12 or lower is failing. However, in the statistical manual for both forms, it is stated that, "A school system which wishes to maintain a criteria [sic] of seventy-five percent correct will consider a raw score of 12 or above as passing the Listening Basic Skills test and a raw score of 11 or below as indicating non-competency." The first statement could be misinterpreted by test users.

It is clearly stated in the administration directions and the statistical manual for both grade levels that the test is a screening instrument. As such, it can be used to identify only those children who are candidates for further evaluation, and cannot differentiate levels of acceptable performance (e.g., fair, good, excellent). This caution might be logically extended by also stating that the test cannot be used to identify treatment goals. Although the child is presented with three specific tasks, performance on any one of these tasks is not sampled in great enough detail to allow in-depth interpretation of performance.

The test manuals for both levels emphasize the need for further evaluation once a child fails the test. This is of particular importance in that, as noted previously, failure may stem from a variety of sources. Further assessment will be critical in providing such children with proper services. Discussion of this point is not intended as criticism, but is provided to emphasize the importance of close adherence to guidelines presented by the test designers.

In summary, the Signals Listening Test, Grades 3 and 5, can be a useful assessment tool if used within the guidelines specified in the test manual. Test users should be aware of the behaviors that constitute listening as identified and probed by this test measure. Unfortunately, determining what specific behaviors are actually measured by the Signals Listening Test is a task largely left to the test user. Although the test lacks sensitivity to specific types of problems, it may provide the clinician or teacher with an efficient screening tool if the user's concept of listening is similar to that represented by the test.

Silver Drawing Test of Cognitive and Creative Skills. Purpose: Designed to assess levels of ability in three areas of cognition: sequential concepts, spatial concepts, and association and formation of concepts. Ages 6 and over; 1983; SDT; 4 scores: Predictive Drawing, Drawing From Observation, Drawing From Imagination, Total; 1984 price data: $35 per complete kit including manual (95 pages), 10 test booklets, and 1 individual/classroom record sheet; $18 per specimen set; (30) minutes; Rawley A. Silver; Special Child Publications.*

[The publisher informed us in November, 1987 that this test would be discontinued. Remaining copies are available from author, Rawley A. Silver, 5 Woodland Dr., Rye, NY 10580.]

Review of the Silver Drawing Test of Cognitive and Creative Skills by CLINTON I. CHASE, Director, Bureau of Evaluative Studies and Testing, Indiana University, Bloomington, IN:

The Silver Drawing Test of Cognitive and Creative Skills (SDT) is based on the idea that cognitive skills are evident in visual as well as in verbal conventions, and that drawing can be an avenue of cognitive expression paralleling verbal expression. From this perspective, drawing takes the place of language as the primary channel of receiving and expressing ideas.

The test is divided into three parts. In the Predictive Drawing section, which purports to assess sequencing of concepts, outline drawings are provided and the test taker draws a line or lines to elaborate the outline. For example, an outline of a full soda glass is provided and the client is told to show how the picture would look if a few sips were taken from the glass. Spatial concepts are assessed in the Drawing From Observation section. Here an arrangement of objects (a can, a rock, a cylinder) is given to the client and the task is to draw a picture of the arrangement. In the Drawing From Imagination section, the ability to associate form and concept is tested. In this part of the test, the examinee is given two pages with six pictures on each page. The instructions are to take one picture from each page and combine them into a single picture. Scoring is based not only on selection and combination, but also on originality.

Tests of psychological constructs must rely on the adequacy of their nomological net for validity. Although some research is cited by Silver in the manual (the tests involve Piagetian concepts and, in part, rest on research in the deficiencies found among reading disabled youngsters), there is no theory of cognition or cognitive development spelled out as a base for the construct validity of the tests. This is a serious deficiency in that no guide is provided to determine which classes of behaviors are tied to the construct and which are not. Silver has assumed that increasing age should be correlated with increasing test scores, and that the test should correlate with other intelligence and achievement tests. The empirical data related to the convergent validity of the Silver test are, however, a bit bewildering. For example, the three Silver test scores are correlated .32, .03, and .31 with the Metropolitan Achievement Test Reading score and .36, -.15, and .37 with the SRA Achievement Series Mathematics score. No rationale is provided on why these tests were chosen to establish "validity" or how these tests should relate to the Silver test. If the Silver test is a measure of general cognitive ability, the correlations should have been much more substantial. Indeed, these figures would be better evidence for discriminant validity, but the presentation of the data suggests they are intended to be evidence of convergent validity.

The Silver tests were also correlated with the Wechsler Intelligence Scale for Children Performance IQ (why not the Verbal, too?) and with IQs from the Otis Lennon School Ability Test. Here correlations at best were .39 (Imagination with the Otis Lennon) and at worst .05 (Observation with the Otis Lennon). Normally one would expect that correlations between tests intended to measure cognitive functioning would be higher than this. The lack of a clearly defined construct for the Silver test means there is little or no basis for deciding how the test should relate to anything.

Reliability is assessed by two methods: correlation among scorers and the test-retest method. The evidence for acceptable interrater reliability is tenuous because of the small number of cases involved. For example, in one study seven judges scored tests of six children; in another, 10 judges' data were correlated with the scores of the instructor who was teaching the judges to score; in a third case, an art therapist's scores for nine mentally retarded children were correlated with the scores for these children reported by the test author. The correlations are typically moderate to high, but one must wonder about their usefulness because of the small group sizes. Data on the means and standard deviations generated in these studies are not given and would be useful for prospective test users.

The test-retest data do not fare much better. The time lapse between the two testings is not provided, but the coefficients ranged from .56 for Imagination to .84 for Observation. Unfortunately, the data were based on only 12 learning-disabled children, where the range of scores is likely to be constricted. Although the correlations are cited as significantly larger than zero, they are unimpressive as reliability coefficients given that the time between the testings is not provided and that the coefficients are based on only one small sample.

Silver reviews some studies in which the Silver tests have been used. These studies suffer from the same problem as those used to establish reliability data—the number of cases is typically very small (less than 20). For this reason the conclusions must be regarded as, at best, tentative.

The manual provides only a page and a half of instructions for administration and 5 pages of scoring instructions, with several pages of sample drawings and their scores. Judgment plays such a large role in scoring that these few pages devoted to test administration and scoring seem inadequate. In actually trying out the tests, however, I found that I could at least find my way through the procedures based on these parsimonious leads. The greatest difficulties come in the scoring, especially in deciding what was "creative." Much more detail (and theory) would have been an aid to the scorer.

In sum, the Silver tests represent a novel idea, but are lacking in a solid theoretical foundation. No information is provided to relate Silver's conceptualization of cognitive and creative skills to other behaviors or test scores thought to represent cognitive and creative abilities. The data on reliability and on application of the test are based on too few cases to allow a reasonable conclusion about the utility of the tests. Until the psychometric qualities of the Silver tests are more clearly established, these tests should be used only as experimental tools. Their design and departure from typical paper-and-pencil cognitive measures are intriguing but not convincing.

Review of the Silver Drawing Test of Cognitive and Creative Skills by DAVID J. MEALOR, Associate Professor of School Psychology, University of Central Florida, Orlando, FL:

The Silver Drawing Test of Cognitive and Creative Skills (SDT) is a carefully thought out instrument that allows drawing to take "the place of language as the primary channel for receiving and expressing ideas." The premise of the SDT is that art and art activities can be a language of cognition paralleling language skills and may yield more meaningful information for some groups of children and adults than traditional measures of intelligence and achievement. The objective of the test is to assess the effectiveness of educational and therapeutic programs as well as monitor individual progress with pretest and posttest measures. The SDT is appropriate for age ranges from 6 years to adult and can be administered either individually or in a group format by teachers, therapists, or psychologists. The SDT is comprised of three subtests: Predictive Drawing (responses are scored for sequencing, horizontality, and verticality), Drawing from Observation (responses scored for left-right, above-below, and front-back), and Drawing from Imagination (responses scored for selecting, combining, and representing). Each subtest reportedly measures specific areas of cognition. Predictive Drawing assesses sequential concepts, Drawing from Observation assesses spatial concepts, and Drawing from Imagination assesses the ability to associate and form concepts. Although there is no time limit, administration should take less than 20–30 minutes. Examinees are given a test booklet in which to complete their drawings. Scoring principles are based on the works of Piaget and Inhelder as well as Bruner and his associates. Performance in each area is rated from 0–5 points for a maximum subtest score of 15. The maximum total score is 45. Raw scores can be converted to percentile ranks and *T*-scores.

While it is apparent that a great deal of effort has gone into the development of the SDT, several perplexing issues surface. The most noticeable involves the technical documentation found in the test manual. It is insufficient at best. As the author notes, "to compare the scores of particular children with typical scores," the standardization group was comprised of 513 children, ages 7 to 16, in heterogeneous classes from nine schools. Sample sizes for grades ranged from 16 (tenth) to 106 (fourth). Five of the classes were located in New York, one each in New Jersey, Pennsylvania, California, and Canada. Twenty subjects comprised the adult group. Unfortunately, no demographic data are presented regarding the individuals selected. How "typical" this group is remains unclear.

The reliability and validity information is inadequate in scope. Reliability investigations are reported by interscorer and test-retest methods. All are comprised of limited sample sizes and did not appear to include those in the standardization group. Of particular concern to this reviewer is the manner in which the reliability information is presented. While the correlation coefficients are high, in two of the studies raters participated "in a series of training sessions." The third and fourth studies "were undertaken to determine the adequacy of the scoring guidelines for scorers who did not participate in training sessions." The two raters selected for "non-training" were a university director of art therapy and a registered art therapist. The generalizability of their performance to regular classroom teachers and psychologists without special training is suspect. Yet, no mention of the need for training in scoring techniques appears in the administration section of the manual. The manual does contain a number of drawings with examples of scoring. It would be beneficial for potential users if explanations for assigned scores were included with the examples.

As the author notes, the purpose of the statistical development was to determine if test items in the SDT "were related primarily to age and cognitive maturity, with scores increasing as children grow older" and "to test the hypothesis that scores on the test can be used to assess intellectual functioning." Statements made are intended to lead the reader to believe that skills measured by the SDT "are closely related to the skills measured by commonly used tests of intellectual excellence." Based on information presented in the manual, it is most difficult to find any empirical support for these claims. More care is needed in the construction of the statistical tables.

In summary, the author provides theoretical support for the SDT. However, it is uncertain that this instrument does what it purports to do.

If scores increase with age, is a high score indicative of creativity? In its present form reliability of scoring is questionable. The author has put a great deal of effort into the development of an instrument that is surely needed. An instrument such as the SDT can assist in the measurement of nonverbal concept formation, visual-motor coordination, spatial relations, and visual perception. However, substantially more work is needed in the development of norms and support for the reliability and validity of this instrument.

[71]

Situation Diagnosis Questionnaire. Purpose: To understand the concept of situational management, recognize situations in which various management styles are most appropriate, identify the management style(s) most appropriate for the individual's situation, and develop a plan to use a more appropriate management style on the job. Managers and employees; 1974–83; 1987 price data: $6 per set including 1 participant form, 2 companion forms, and scoring and interpretation booklet ('83, 10 pages); $15 per leader's guide ('83, 15 pages); 115(135) minutes; Don Michalak; Michalak Training Associates, Inc.*

Review of the Situation Diagnosis Questionnaire by RABINDRA N. KANUNGO, Professor of Management and Psychology, Faculty of Management, McGill University, Montreal, Quebec, Canada:

The Situation Diagnosis Questionnaire (SDQ) is designed primarily for use in training sessions for managers. With the help of SDQ, the training program is supposed to achieve the following four objectives for the participant managers: (a) The managers would be able to understand the concept of "situational management"; (b) they would develop an appreciation of the appropriateness of different "management styles" for different situations; (c) they would identify the management style(s) appropriate for their own job situations; and finally, (d) they would be able to articulate the specific manner in which they can use the appropriate management style in their job.

In order to achieve these objectives, the trainer is provided with a Leader's Guide that spells out the specific step-by-step details of the training session including the time needed for each step. Overall, the design of the training session and the packaging of the SDQ materials (e.g., questionnaire forms, scoring and interpretation booklet, and the Leader's Guide) are done quite well, with trainers' needs in mind.

The four objectives listed above and specified in the Leader's Guide appear quite sound and attractive from the practitioner's point of view. However, the "situation management" and "management styles" constructs that form the basis of SDQ are conceptually ambiguous and hence provoke serious questions about the content validity of SDQ as a measuring or diagnostic instrument of work situation characteristics requiring specific management styles.

The theoretical rationale for SDQ is derived from the earlier works on the managerial grid (Blake & Mouton, 1964) and contingency or situational theory of leadership (Hersey & Blanchard, 1977). Several management styles are identified on the basis of two dimensions of "concern for task" and "concern for people." For instance, managers showing low levels of both people and task concerns are characterized as showing an "administrator" style of management, whereas managers showing high levels of both task and people concerns are labelled as showing a "team" approach to management. Such labelling of management styles on the basis of two very broad and vaguely defined dimensions of managerial behavior is simplistic and confusing. Broadly defined categorization of managers' behavior overlooks many important distinctions between different aspects of each category of behavior. The simplistic dichotomy between people and task concerns expresses the behavioral dimensions of looking after the "needs-of-the-task" versus the "needs-of-the-subordinates." This dimension, however, is confused with "direction and control" versus "participation" of subordinates. Such confusion is reflected in the SDQ scoring and interpretation booklet by equating "autocratic control" of managers as "task" concern, and "permissiveness" of managers as "people" concern. In actual practice, a manager can use either autocratic or participative styles of management while trying to meet the needs of either task or people under his/her supervision. For such reasons, current theories of organizational leadership (Yukl, 1981) have argued in favour of making a clear distinction between participation behavior (decision-centralization dimension) and behavior showing "task" or "people" concern.

The type of conceptual ambiguity mentioned above is reflected in the item contents of SDQ. Hence, the content validity of SDQ is suspect. The SDQ items represent various work situation characteristics but are scored in terms of the styles of management most appropriate for such situational characteristics. However, the criterion-related validity of the items is difficult to judge in the absence of any empirical data. One simply does not know how the items were chosen and whether in fact a given situational characteristic requires a specific management style. Furthermore, some items are scored to represent a fit for both "task" and "people" concern and some others represent a fit for "administrative concern" (defined as being low on both task and people concern) along with task or people concern. Items representing such combinations, particularly of the latter type, are not very meaningful without proper content validity checks.

The use of SDQ in a training session requires a participant manager to previously obtain two subordinates' perception of the work situation using the "Companion" forms. The subordinates' characterization of the work situation is compared with the participant's own perception in order to arrive at a more realistic recognition of the work situation. The participant is then encouraged to think of specific behaviors (management style) most appropriate to his/her situation. Such procedure achieves the objectives of getting feedback from subordinates and developing an awareness of how to behave in the future for managerial effectiveness. Although the procedure is commendable, the questionable content validity of the questionnaire casts a shadow of doubt on the effectiveness of such training to achieve stated objectives.

In summary, the SDQ provides a convenient training package with explicit instructions to the trainers. It can be used as a training tool in both organizational and academic settings. However, considerable caution needs to be exercised in interpreting the item contents and the management styles profiles based on SDQ, primarily because of the weak conceptual basis of the "task-people concern" dichotomy of managerial behavior and the lack of data on the criterion-related validity of the measure.

REVIEWER'S REFERENCES

Blake, R., & Mouton, J. S. (1964). *The managerial grid.* Houston: Gulf Publishing Co.

Hersey, P., & Blanchard, K. H. (1977). *Management of organizational behavior: Utilizing human resources* (3rd ed.). Englewood Cliffs, NJ: Prentice-Hall.

Yukl, G. A. (1981). *Leadership in organizations.* Englewood Cliffs, NJ: Prentice-Hall.

Review of the Situation Diagnosis Questionnaire by CHARLES K. PARSONS, Professor of Management, Georgia Institute of Technology, Atlanta, GA:

The Situation Diagnosis Questionnaire provides a measure of a manager's work situation. This information is then used to suggest an appropriate style of management to fit the situation. The instrument and suggestions are based on the work of Blake and Mouton (1964), Reddin (1967), and Hersey and Blanchard (1969). The explicit purpose of the authors of the Situation Diagnosis Questionnaire is to assess the manager's situation at work rather than the manager's current style. The instrument yields scores on three situational scales: (*a*) the required task-orientation, (*b*) the required people-orientation, and (*c*) the required pure administrative orientation. There is a test booklet for the participating manager, test booklets for two employees or coworkers, and a scoring and interpretation booklet.

The Participant form is designed to be self-administered and completed before attending a workshop on situational management. The instructions on this form are minimal. The workshop leader is supposed to prepare a cover letter to accompany the form and hopefully give further explanation as to the purpose of the instrument. There are 21 items that purportedly assess important aspects of the work situation such as presence of quantifiable output, intellectual versus physical task demands, existence of clear procedures for work performance, and so forth. The items are answered on a 5-point verbally anchored scale (from 0 to 4). The verbal anchors are 4 = *almost always*, 3 = *regularly*, 2 = *often*, 1 = *sometimes*, 0 = *almost never.* This reviewer was a bit confused by the implied frequency scale and how the scale points were determined. Do most respondents believe "regularly" is more frequent than "often"? The participants are instructed (in the cover letter) to bring the completed instrument to the workshop.

Companion forms are sent to two coworkers or employees of the participant. The Companion forms are to be completed and returned to the personnel department (or whoever is coordinating the program). The instructions on this form are also minimal. The cover letter can provide some more information. The same 21 items from the Participant form are included on the Companion form. The response scale is the same. The two completed Companion forms are taken to the workshop on situational management.

The author of the instrument gives a step-by-step Leader's Guide for sending out instruments. There are also sample cover letters that would accompany the Participant Form and Companion Form. The sample cover letters are clearly written. I would suggest to potential users that some further explanation be given to the participants and coworkers concerning the nature of the information to be disclosed. Suggestions for respondents would be to be honest, to realize that the instruments are not for evaluating anyone's job performance, to understand that the results will not affect jobs or assignments, and so forth. One final point of interest is the fact that the author shows no preferences concerning the use of coworkers or employees as "companions," though he later notes that the responses could be quite different depending on the perspective.

Scoring of both the Participant Form and Companion Form occurs at the workshop. The Scoring and Interpretation Booklet gives directions on deriving and interpreting scores on three scales: the required task orientation (T-scores), the required people orientation (P-scores), and the required administrative orientation (A-scores). The T-scores and P-scores are plotted on a grid similar to that used by Blake and Mouton. In addition, the A-score is interpreted as meaning the degree to which the manager should act as a pure administrator.

The Scoring and Interpretation Booklet describes the meaning of various combinations of T-scores and P-scores, but is deficient in explaining what is meant by the Administrative style of management. This is additionally troublesome because users who are familiar with Blake and Mouton's Managerial Grid will have little trouble understanding the T-score/P-score combinations and labels, but will probably struggle (as did this reviewer) to understand the meaning and rationale for the A-scores.

The Leader's Guide gives suggestions on helping participants interpret differences between their responses and those on the Companion form. The meaning of these differences (or similarities) could potentially be quite beneficial to the manager, especially if the Companion forms were those of employees rather than coworkers.

In the materials seen by this reviewer, there was no evidence of normative, reliability, or validity data. Many of the 21 items included in the instrument are used in two of the three scales. Without any evidence of scale homogeneity or discriminant or convergent validity, this approach to scoring is questionnable. Some psychometric evidence should be made available so that users can better judge the merits of the scales.

One strength of the instruments is that they are part of a package of workshop exercises and discussion. The user can benefit from the author's experience in using the scales. Discussion questions and exercises are included as part of the Leader's Guide.

Another strength of the package is that independent observations of the work situation are obtained from employees or coworkers. Therefore, differences between perceptions of different people must be confronted and become part of the training exercise. This reduces the likelihood of purely socially desirable responding.

Finally, because the diagnosis of work situations leads to a discussion of "appropriate management styles," this reviewer would recommend further research on the effectiveness of the situational management approach.

An alternative training package that is based on situational management is that of Fiedler (1967). In Fiedler's contingency theory of leadership, people have a more or less stable disposition to be People-oriented or Task-oriented. Upon assessing their work situation, Fiedler suggests that leaders try to change the situation to be compatible with their style. The advantage of the Fiedler approach is that a great deal of research has been done on the leadership model, the measure of leader disposition (the Least Preferred Coworker Scale), and a specific training program called Leader Match. The user has a much better idea of the characteristics of the instrumentation and effectiveness of the training program in various settings.

REVIEWER'S REFERENCES

Blake, R. R., & Mouton, J. S. (1964). *The managerial grid.* Houston: Gulf Publishing Co.
Fiedler, F. E. (1967). *A theory of leadership effectiveness.* New York: McGraw-Hill.
Reddin, W. J. (1967). The 3-D management style theory. *Training and Development Journal*, 21, 8-17.
Hersey, P., & Blanchard, K. H. (1969). Life cycle theory of leadership. *Training and Development Journal*, 23, 26-34.

[72]

Sklar Aphasia Scale, Revised 1983. Purpose: "Developed as a clinical procedure to provide systematic information about the severity and nature of language disorders following brain damage in adults." Brain damaged adults; 1966–83; SAS; 5 scores: Auditory Decoding, Visual Decoding, Oral Encoding, Graphic Encoding, Total Impairment; individual; 1986 price data: $45 per complete kit including 25 test booklets, stimulus cards, and manual ('83, 25 pages); $11.85 per 25 test booklets; $22.50 per set of stimulus cards; $12.50 per manual; administration time not reported; Maurice Sklar; Western Psychological Services.*

See T3:2213 (1 reference); for a review by Manfred J. Meier, see 8:976 (1 reference); for reviews by Arthur L. Benton and Daniel R. Boone of the original edition, see 7:970; see also P:247 (2 references).

TEST REFERENCES

1. Thompson, C. K., & McReynolds, L. V. (1986). Wh interrogative production in agrammatic aphasia: An experimental analysis of auditory-visual stimulation and direct-production treatment. *Journal of Speech and Hearing Research*, 29, 193-206.

Review of the Sklar Aphasia Scale, Revised 1983, by LINDA CROCKER, Professor of Foundations of Education, University of Florida, Gainesville, FL:

The 1983 edition of the Sklar Aphasia Scale (SAS) is the second revision since the original publication of the SAS in 1966. The current edition features pictorial stimuli (rather than actual objects used in earlier editions) and some updated normative data. The test author suggests that this scale is intended for use by examiners with a general background knowledge of common speech and language disorders, but the manual does provide fairly clear functional definitions for a variety of clinical terms often used in classification and discussion of speech disorders.

The SAS is administered in two parts. The first part is an informal but structured interview requiring approximately 15 minutes for completion. The interview is designed to allow the examiner to form an initial impression of the client's functional level, estimating the overall degree of impairment on a 3-point scale. The primary usefulness of this interview would appear to be establishing rapport with the client and/or screening clients who may be too severely disabled to participate in the formal testing procedure that follows the interview. Because one of the tasks in the formal interview requires reading a passage, the examiner should check to insure that the client has minimal literacy skills and normal intelligence before administration of this test.

The second part of the SAS is composed of five 25-item subtests in which each item is rated by the examiner on a 0–4-point scale (with high scores indicating greater degree of impairment). Some subjective judgement on the part of the examiner is required for scoring the items, but the scoring criteria are straightforward and the instructions for numeric scoring are easy to follow. A particularly helpful feature of the manual is the inclusion of an illustrative case study to demonstrate subtest and total score interpretation.

The normative data for interpretation of the subtest and total scores are based on a relatively small sample ($N = 69$). Subscale and total score ranges are divided into three broad categories ranging from minimal-mild to severe. Placement of the cutting scores that discriminate between these diagnostic categories was determined empirically from the frequency distribution data of the norming sample. This process raises serious questions about use of these diagnostic categories in score interpretation, particularly for clients who score near the cutting scores.

Another question that might be raised about the new edition of the SAS is whether substitution of pictorial stimuli for actual objects in the naming tasks has an effect on examinee performance. Results of a study comparing examinee performance on 10 items using pictured stimuli and the same items using objects are reported. Although significant differences occurred for performance on only 3 of the 10 items, this investigation was based on an extremely small sample (11 subjects), which greatly reduced the chance of observing statistically significant differences. Thus evidence of similar performance on the two types of items is not convincing.

A decided shortcoming of the SAS is apparent in the psychometric data reported. Reliability evidence consists of only one investigation, and the data reported are for interrater reliability for a German translation of the scale. No internal consistency estimates for the subscales or total test are reported although these could have been readily determined from the responses of the standardization sample. Even more serious is the lack of any evidence of test-retest reliability.

Validity evidence is presented in the form of a variety of studies dating back to 1963. Results of factor analytic studies give some general support to organization of the scale into subscales, and correlational studies of the SAS and other measures of aphasia and verbal aptitude offer some evidence of construct validity. Users must be willing to assume that these results have applicability for the present edition since no validation studies with the current edition of the scale are reported.

In summary, the strengths of the SAS include its breadth of coverage, subscales of reasonable length, factor analytic evidence to support the subscale structure, clear instructions for scoring, and an illustrative case study to aid users in interpretation of test results. The author's suggestions for future research needed with this scale deserve attention. The weaknesses of this test include the small standardization sample, diagnostic categories of questionable stability, lack of essential reliability data, and lack of recent research on the scale's validity. Considering the lengthy history of this instrument, it is disappointing that these weaknesses were not addressed in the recent revision.

Review of the Sklar Aphasia Scale, Revised 1983, by LAWRENCE J. TURTON, Professor of Speech-Language Pathology, Indiana University of Pennsylvania, Indiana, PA:

The 1983 version of the Sklar Aphasia Scale (SAS) is the third version of this instrument. No significant changes were made in test design. The SAS continues to assess four areas: Auditory Decoding, Visual Decoding, Oral Encoding, and Graphic Encoding. The only change in the test stimuli was a substitution of pictures for objects in the Auditory Decoding subtest. New norms were obtained on 69 aphasic patients and cutoff points were identified from these data to create three impairment categories: mild, moderate, and severe. The last change, integration of the Preliminary Interview into the protocol booklet, was not central to the test and will not be addressed in this review.

The significance of the revision of the SAS is what was omitted rather than what was changed. This is the third review of this test in the *Mental Measurements Yearbooks* (Benton and Boone, 1972; Meier, 1978). In the first set of reviews, Benton expressed serious reservations about the SAS due to the poor quality of test design and standardization procedures. Meier's review stressed the same problems and this reviewer is in complete concurrence with their concerns. Unfortunately, these concerns were ignored by the author and publisher in the current revision of the SAS.

The only reliability indices reported for the SAS were taken from a study done in Germany in 1977 and consist of percentage of agreement measures for interrater reliability. There are no reliability indices to indicate that scores and severity ratings are stable. Given the fact that this test was designed to be administered in the hospital setting shortly after onset of problems, this failure is a most serious deficiency. Yet the author has failed to address the problem after 20 years of marketing and numerous complaints by reviewers.

The scoring for the SAS consists of a 5-point scale (0 = correct, 4 = incorrect or no response). Although broad descriptions for each category are included in the manual, there are no indices for reliability of the ratings as they are used by certified clinicians or by subtests. The author fails to point out that for many of the items the 5-point scale may not be applicable. For example, virtually the entire Auditory Decoding subtest requires yes/no responses (either oral or manual). Without specific scoring protocols, clinicians must decide on their own whether a response is delayed (1), assisted (2), or distorted (3). A clinician can create his/her own standards and score a response differently than a colleague, resulting in a different final score and severity rating. If a yes/no standard is used, only options 0 and 4 are possible for an item.

There is very little to be said about the validity measures in the manual. They were derived from mini-studies using the first version of the SAS, which did not use the 5-point scale.

Furthermore, the tests used for comparison no longer constitute state-of-the-art aphasia diagnosis. The change in the scoring system was a major change; indeed, it resulted in a new test with new standards. However, users are expected to rely upon reliability and validity measures computed from a totally different set of scoring standards. This is one more critical testing concept ignored in the preparation of this revision.

The author reports new standardization data on 69 patients selected on the basis of availability from five states and an unspecified number of treatment sites. The data from these patients constitute the new norms in the form of profiles for the severity categories. These norms, however, are only as good as the reliability of the data collection procedures. Once again, the author fails to provide the user with this important information. The fact that these norms were collected from geographically disparate sites with small samples at each site suggests that different examiners may have done the testing. If this is true, the lack of reliability indices takes on greater prominence. Very simply, the norms cannot be accepted as having any degree of validity as presented in the manual.

Despite the negative reviews, this test has managed to survive over 20 years and the publisher was willing to invest in a new edition. From a clinical perspective, this test is a good *screening* device. It provides a clinician with a fast method of obtaining global information to use to advise family and medical staff on appropriate steps to follow in establishing a rehabilitation program. However, it should not be used for a true diagnostic evaluation from which a comprehensive program will be designed. The problems of reliability and validity raise the possibility of serious errors in classification and identification of the total pattern of aphasia.

[73]

The Southern California Ordinal Scales of Development. Purpose: Provide a clear guide to what is profitable to teach a given child at a given time. Multihandicapped, developmentally delayed, and learning disabled children, and normal children; 1977-85; SCOSD; a Piagetian-based assessment system; 6 scales: Cognition, Communication, Social-Affective Behavior, Practical Abilities, Fine Motor Abilities, Gross Motor Abilities; individual;

1988 price data: $18–$25 per scale including manual ('85, 61–182 pages) and 10 record booklets; $7–$10 per 25 record booklets; (60–120) minutes per scale; Donald I. Ashurst, Elaine Bamberg, Julika Barrett, Ann Bisno, Artice Burke, David C. Chambers, Jean Fentiman, Ronald Kadish, Mary Lou Mitchell, Lambert Neeley, Todd Thorne, and Doris Wents; Foreworks.*

Review of The Southern California Ordinal Scales of Development by CAMERON J. CAMP, Associate Professor of Psychology, University of New Orleans, New Orleans, LA:

The 1985 edition of The Southern California Ordinal Scales of Development (SCOSD) consists of six scales—Cognition, Communication, Social-Affective Behavior, Practical Abilities, Fine Motor Abilities, Gross Motor Abilities—that were "designed to be used especially with developmentally and learning disabled children," though "they are equally effective with all other children." The SCOSD is said to differ from most other intelligence and ability tests in three ways: "(1) It is criterion-referenced rather than norm-referenced; (2) assessment procedures are flexible rather than fixed; (3) the scoring system takes into account the quality as well as the quantity of responses."

Criterion-referencing is achieved by basing the scales on Piagetian theory and methodology. "Each scale is divided according to the levels and stages that Piaget describes in his writings on human development." Therefore, test items are arranged according to the four major periods or stages of Piaget's theory: Sensorimotor (appearing at approximately 0–24 months of age), Preoperational (2–7 years), Concrete Operational (7–11 years), and Formal Operations (11+ years). Sensorimotor is further divided into six (sub)stages, while Preoperational is subdivided into two (sub)stages. Within stages, items are grouped according to specific concepts or abilities. For example, in the Cognition scale at the Sensorimotor stage, (sub)stage 4, the ability to know that an object exists even though it cannot be directly perceived is tested using the set of items grouped under the heading "Awareness of Object Constancy." Items here include Finds Hidden Object Under a Cloth, Retrieves Object Hidden Under a Cup or Box, Recognizes Reversal of Objects, and Looks for Contents of Box.

The administration of these scales is flexible in that the materials used are chosen by individual test administrators. "You are encouraged to vary materials to suit your needs, the children's handicaps, or a particular child's observed interests or cultural background." For example, in the Social-Affective Behavior scale at Preoperational stage, (sub)stage 2, one of the items under the heading "Self-Awareness" is Shows Interest in Projects. Materials can be clay, blocks, drawing materials, or any others the examiner wishes to use. Through observation, the examiner determines if the child "shows interest in planning small projects with definite goals in mind, carries her plans to completion, and shows regard for meeting some standard." Uses Language To Express Feeling, another item under the "Self-Awareness" heading, can be measured through spoken language, gesture, signing, or (with nonverbal children) through body gestures and/or facial expression. Examiners are encouraged to "observe the subject in his/her natural environment, using materials that are readily available and familiar." If a child doesn't perform a task that the examiner believes to be within his or her ability, a parent or teacher may administer the item in the presence of the examiner. Limits testing and repeated presentations of some of the same items are also encouraged.

Scoring reflects quality of responses. Test items are "passed" when the child exhibits a minimum level of performance. If passed, an item is scored according to the following criteria: Sometimes Observed (SO)—ability or concept only seen in highly structured environments; Frequently Observed (FO)—ability or concept seen with moderate structuring, but is in transition and is not automatic; or Regularly Observed (RO)—ability or concept is typical mode of functioning and is generalizable. Scores on items are used to create a developmental profile for each scale. Three levels of development are derived for each child. These are: Functional level—highest stage of development (Sensorimotor, Preoperational, etc.) in which the child obtains RO scores for at least 66 percent of items; Basal Level—highest stage in which the child obtains RO scores on all items; and Ceiling Level—highest stage at which a child passes one or more items with a score of SO or above. Items which a child cannot "pass" because a sensory or physical deficit prevents the demonstration of a concept or ability are labelled "Not Applicable" and are omitted in computing Functional, Basal, and Ceiling levels.

All six scales have separate manuals, though general instructions, references, and validation data are identical in all manuals. Responses are made in answer booklets that accompany each scale. Scales vary in length and in the number of items used at each stage. For example, the Cognition scale has many more items at the Formal Operations stage than the Gross Motor Skills scale, as would be expected.

Test items were selected from existing tests and research literature "on the basis of empirical evidence of validity." The field study sample used to "standardize" the scales was composed of 508 children, 505 of whom were classified as having some type of disability based on "diagnostic impression." Data were gathered from 1977 to 1980. Males comprised approximately 65 percent of the sample. Anglos comprised 68 percent of the sample, Hispanics 20 percent, and Blacks 6 percent. The geographic region from which the sample was selected is not mentioned (presumably it is Southern California). Disability categories included severely emotionally disturbed (20 percent), TMR (13 percent), aphasia (13 percent), deafness (13 percent), multihandicapped (23 percent), among others. Mean chronological ages for each disability category ranged from 102 months for aphasics to 131 months for TMRs. The manual contains the statement that "Criterion-group validity is easily established by a visual comparison of scores between groups," but this point is never elaborated nor are the figures being referenced totally clear as to how this validation is established.

Mean scores for each disability group for each scale are shown in the manuals in a series of tables and figures. However, these mean scores are given in terms of "months." It is unclear how these scores were derived. Presumably, a child with a Basal level of Concrete Operations (7–11 years) was given a score of 11 years (132 months), though this is unspecified in the manuals. This "mental age," however it was computed, was then somehow compared to IQ. Thus, the manual contains the statement that ceiling levels are "roughly equivalent to expected IQ measures for various categories of handicaps," but no correlational data are cited to support this statement. The manual also contains the claim that for disability groups where program admission required an IQ within 1 standard deviation of national norms, "the Ceiling scores very closely approximate the chronological ages." Basal and Functional levels were consistently below Ceiling levels. The manual therefore includes the claim that "these findings indicate that instruction based upon age and measured IQ is not appropriate for children in these categories. Rather, the levels at which they are routinely proficient (Basal and Functional) provide a more realistic foundation for instructional planning." No other attempts to relate Scale scores to other measures of intelligence are to be found.

No data on test-retest reliability are reported, nor are there data on reliability between different examiners. Internal consistency of the six scales was studied using Cronbach's alpha after assigning unweighted numeric values to the criterion-referenced designations used in the scales. "Almost all items show correlations above .75."

The strength of the SCOSD is its solid connection with Piaget's work. The test uses many of his tasks in an ordering that is consistent with his theory, and is a truly "developmental" scale. Central concepts such as object permanence are tested with multiple items, materials, and operations. Other strengths include the flexibility/adaptability of procedures and the attempt to give qualitative scores to responses. The item instructions are stated clearly, and the manuals are well designed for ease of use while testing. The focus of the SCOSD is to allow the development of educational programs based on abilities and concepts that a child has mastered, which is a worthwhile goal.

The weaknesses of the SCOSD, paradoxically, derive from the same sources as its strengths. A "thorough grounding in Piagetian developmental theory" is required if valid assessments are to be made using such flexible procedures and qualitative scoring. Thus, reliability is probably at risk with this instrument. Given that Piaget's ideas about intelligence are far removed from the individual differences approach of standardized intelligence testing, concurrent validity is difficult to achieve. No real effort to assess concurrent validity is found in these materials. The use of Functional, Basal, and Ceiling levels also seems inappropriate. Labelling a child as a "Concrete Operational" child is simply of little use. Piaget's concepts of decalage (both horizontal and vertical) would seem to militate against the use of such labels. It would seem to be best to look at profiles across tasks rather than to assign a child to a stage. Even adults will not always generalize formal operational thought to all tasks, as Piaget himself noted.

Finally, by adhering so closely to Piaget's theory, the SCOSD also is open to the general criticisms of Piaget's theory. Though space does not allow an elaboration of these criticisms, it should be sufficient to note that educators and psychologists who are not enamored with Piaget's work will not wish to develop the expertise necessary to administer these scales, nor will they likely accept the validity of the SCOSD as a means of assessing the abilities and concepts it purportedly measures.

SUMMARY. The Southern California Ordinal Scales of Development represent an attempt to use Piagetian theory to create a standardized assessment battery for use with disabled children. Its chief strength is that it is based on a widely-known and respected theory which describes cognitive development in a cohesive, developmental framework from birth to adolescence. It is also flexible and adaptable for use with a wide variety of populations, and allows qualitative measurement of performance. Its weaknesses are the high level of familiarity with Piagetian theory needed to administer the Scales, the lack of data on reliability and concurrent validity, and the attempt to attach stage labels to children based on performance with these tasks. The Scales may best be used as a means of creating a developmental profile of abilities which seem to be automatic, partially obtained, or lacking. These data might be useful in constructing educational or training programs, if there is sufficient understanding of how such abilities relate to specific academic behaviors. The SCOSD is not a "standardized" test in the classic use of the term, and should not be viewed as a substitute for more traditional intelligence tests.

Review of The Southern California Ordinal Scales of Development by ARLENE C. ROSENTHAL, Department of Educational and Counseling Psychology, College of Education, University of Kentucky, Lexington, KY:

The Southern California Ordinal Scales of Development are comprised of six developmental scales. The scales are comprised of approximately 500 items. The instrument was developed to provide a guide for what is profitable to teach a given child at a given time. Although the scales were developed for use with developmentally and learning disabled children the authors report that "they are equally effective with all other children." The scales draw on the developmental theories of Jean Piaget. They are (*a*) criterion as opposed to norm referenced, (*b*) comprised of flexible as opposed to fixed administration procedures, (*c*) scored qualitatively as well as quantitatively, and (*d*) used to obtain a Basal, Functional, and Ceiling Level.

There is no single comprehensive manual; each scale has its own manual and scoring form. Each manual is divided into 14 sections: General Instructions, Scale Instructions, Sensorimotor Stages 1–6, Preoperational Stages 1–2, Concrete Operations, Formal Operations, Technical, and Appendix.

The authors emphasize that these scales are criterion-referenced measures rather than norm-referenced measures. The issue of norm- versus criterion-referenced tests in the overall pupil evaluation and instructional process is controversial. In most assessment processes both types are generally used and each has its advantages and disadvantages. Perhaps most important is that the selected test match the purpose of the assessment. Each item on this test is criterion referenced and is scored as pass or fail. Each passed item is then scored qualitatively (i.e., how often it is observed). Generally, all items of a scale need not be administered to obtain a Basal, Functional, or Ceiling Level.

Performance on the scales is used to provide information about a child's overall range of functioning (e.g., areas of strength). Analysis of a child's profile can be used to "produce comprehensive individualized education plans." Essentially, the scales serve a diagnostic prescriptive function and are, purportedly, particularly suitable in teaching the handicapped. Careful analysis of performance on many traditional, standardized tests will also reveal areas of deficits and strengths. The ordinal scales are not remarkable in this sense.

The general instructions section of each manual describes procedures to ensure reliable administration, scoring, and interpretation.

Each of the manuals contains additional admin-istration and scoring directions unique to the abilities assessed. In the general instructions section, directions for administering each scale cover: procedure, method of communication, item repetition, time, materials, structure of the environment, and alternative methods of ad-ministration. In the technical section the au-thors indicate that instruction based on the Basal and Functional Levels "provide a more realistic foundation for instructional planning," whereas the Ceiling Level is the "least stable foundation for planning instruction."

A brief description of each scale will be provided below. The scale of Fine Motor Abilities assesses dexterity, perceptual motor, and graphomotor abilities at each of Piaget's developmental levels. The Cognition Scale assesses the development of: (a) methods of problem solving, (b) classification processes, and (c) linguistic and intellectual processes that require reasoning, logical thought, and the understanding of causality. The scale of Gross Motor Abilities assesses strength, balance, mo-bility, and coordination which, when combined, form the basis of many large muscle motor tasks. Items on this scale assess abilities ranging from simple reflexes to complicated motor actions. The scale of Practical Abilities assesses personal independence and the capacity to care for basic needs. The Communication Scale assesses oral and gestural expression, which together comprise total communication. Recep-tive and expressive behavior are assessed inde-pendently in each of four areas: (a) Awareness of Self and Environment, (b) Imitation, (c) Communicative Mediation, and (d) Symboliza-tion. The scale of Social-Affective Behavior assesses: (a) self awareness, that is, emotional responses, self-initiated activities, and self im-age; and (b) relationships with others: aware-ness of others, responses to others, initiation of interaction with others, acquisition of social norms, development of sensitivity to others, and acquisition of social values.

The flexibility of the scales permits the examiner to adapt the assessment procedures to the needs of the child. In exchange for this flexibility, the examiner must be well grounded in Piagetian theory, assessment techniques, and clinical acumen. This is stated explicitly by the authors although a paragraph later they state "given some understanding of Piagetian epis-temology, anyone can administer them." The examiner must react quickly to the examinee's performance and must not waiver deciding in which direction to proceed. The scales offer tips on how to conduct such interviews in order to solicit the most useful information and ancillary behaviors to observe (e.g., delayed responses).

Prior to utilizing the scales it is highly recommended that the examiner be familiar with each item in the six scales in order to establish Functional, Basal, and Ceiling Levels in a timely manner. Inadequate preparation for this task on the part of the examiner would seem to militate against the valid use of the results.

Technical data are provided in each scale manual and the data reported are identical in all six manuals. Why the general instructions, technical data, and bibliography are repeated verbatim in each of the six manuals is unclear, although presumably for convenience. The scales were administered to several hundred children collected over a 3-year period. Samples from this population were selected to provide data for item analysis and reliability studies. Each technical data section contains three tables reporting, respectively: (a) demographic charac-teristics, (b) type and frequency of various handicaps, and (c) mean Functional, Basal, and Ceiling Level scores in all scales for each handicap, and (d) analysis of variance across all handicaps all of which were statistically signifi-cant at the .001 level. Of 508 children, the socioeconomic status of approximately 35% are professional with the remainder including the unemployed, semi-skilled, and skilled crafts-men. The majority are of White or Hispanic background with 12.2% of Black, Asian Indian, or other ethnicity. Children ranged in age from, approximately, 8 years to 11 years. Of 508 children only .6% were in the regular class-room, 20.1% were severely emotionally dis-turbed/autistic, 30.8% were mentally retarded, and 23.5% multiply handicapped.

Approximately half a page each is given to the issues of validity and reliability. The validity of the scales is asserted by having selected items from existing developmental scales based on *normally developing* children at each level of development. This seems ques-tionable given that items were empirically selected based on normal children but are to be used with handicapped youngsters. The authors suggest that criterion group validity is easily established by statistically significant differences between diagnostic groups on Basal, Functional, and Ceiling Levels. A single *F*-test across the standardization samples is given such that while an overall statistically significant result is achieved, the reader does not know what groups are responsible for this overall result. That is, there are no post-hoc analyses. With respect to reliability, a 250-page printout of reliability tables for each scale is available upon special request. The manual reports that almost all items show correlations above .75 "indicating excellent internal consistency."

It is distressing and erroneous that the authors claim the test assesses intelligence as well as ability. Intelligence is a controversial construct and current research suggests there may be a number of "intelligences" (e.g., social, artistic, etc.). There is not one piece of evidence given that relates performance on the scales to the more widely used measures of intelligence. Users of the scales should be aware of this, and this test in no way should be used to assess intellectual capacity. It is further stated that "The Ceiling levels are roughly equivalent to expected IQ measures for the various categories of handicap." There are several problems with this. First, expected IQ is not defined. Second, the manner in which the authors make the conceptual leap from Ceiling Level to IQ is unclear and therefore not interpretable. What this statement suggests is that an examiner can determine a child's Ceiling Level and extrapolate an IQ score based on the figures in the manual for the appropriate group. Third, Ceiling Levels are provided for each of the six scales. The unstated suggestion is that an "expected IQ" score can be obtained for each scale giving a "communication IQ," "gross motor IQ," etc. Clearly this paradigm is questionable given the oft debated construct of "intelligence."

In summary, the scales seem to be useful if used in a clinical versus an "absolute" (i.e., numerical) sense. The scales were developed to identify, developmentally, a child's placement in a variety of areas. The scales seem to do this and are appropriate for this purpose. While the scales are criterion referenced for the purpose of providing a total picture of a child's abilities, the manuals do not suggest a single intervention nor how to interpret/summarize the ple-

thora of results. Given that intervention is the purported aim of this test, the lack of suggestions is a shortcoming. It would be useful to provide some continuity from the test results to the practical world (i.e., classroom). Psychometrically the test is touted as criterion versus norm referenced. That's fine. But more complete validity and reliability data are required before a practitioner can use the instrument with confidence.

Currently, numerous texts and periodicals address assessment of special or exceptional children in the same areas as do these scales. I would recommend that currently available commercial tests be used instead of, or in addition to, these scales. Tests in each area can be found in many special education assessment texts, in various test catalogues, and in the *Mental Measurements Yearbooks*. It is also of note that of approximately 30 references, only 2 are more recent than 1975 and approximately 16 appeared prior to 1970. The area of special education, in general, has undergone great change since 1975. The references given by the authors are outdated and do not integrate recent research.

The behaviors assessed in the early stages of this instrument have limited application to exceptional child assessment. Additionally, given that the scales are for prescriptive programming for the school-aged child, recommendations for interface with the school are absent. Generally, to receive special education in the school system the student must go through several stages in the assessment program. How the results of the scales fit into this process is not explained.

The scales attempt to do too much and cover too many areas, so that their utility in any one area is diminished. Again, the user should be cautious in making the conceptual leap from performance on the scales to intellectual capacity. The quantitative measurement of intellectual capacity has a long and rich heritage. Evidence that the scales measure intellectual capacity is lacking and should not supplant/uproot the more traditional measures. The scales represent a first step towards building an assessment model of intelligence.

[74]

Sports Emotion Test. Purpose: "Designed to show how an athlete responds affectively to a competition." High school through adult athletes;

1980–83; SET; 24 scores: 4 scores (Intensity, Concentration, Anxiety, Physical Readiness) for 6 different points in time (24 Hours Before, At Breakfast, Just Before, After Start, At Peak, Something Wrong); 1982 price data: $50 per 100 scales and profiles; $15 per manual ('83, 75 pages); (10–20) minutes; E. R. Oetting and C. W. Cole (profile); Rocky Mountain Behavioral Science Institute, Inc.*

Review of the Sports Emotion Test by ROBERT D. BROWN, Professor of Educational Psychology, University of Nebraska-Lincoln, Lincoln, NE:

The Sports Emotion Test (SET) is a self-report scale asking athletes to indicate how they feel when they are performing in athletic competition. The SET is made up of four scales: Anxiety, Intensity, Concentration, and Physical Readiness. The Anxiety Scale is intended to capture feelings of anxiety, the Intensity Scale indicates whether or not the athlete is "psyched up," the Concentration Scale suggests how well the athlete is able to focus on the event, and Physical Readiness indicates the athlete's perceptions of how well his or her body is working. The author stresses that these are measures of the athlete's perceptions of his or her emotional state and these may or may not reflect physiological anxiety or readiness.

Each scale is a semantic differential consisting of six bipolar adjectives with specific concepts as the stimulus for each item within the differential. The concepts are: "How I feel" for the Anxiety and Intensity scales, "What my thoughts are like" for the Concentration scale, and "What my body is like" for the Physical Readiness scale. Each scale is administered six times at different periods prior to and during competition. There is no testing period for after the competition per se, but rather athletes are asked to indicate how they feel after "something goes wrong."

A scoring template is provided and normative data are available based on slightly over 100 athletes. Most of these were male and female college athletes from Colorado State University, but the group included a few high school and professional athletes as well. The author emphasizes the norms may not be as helpful as noting how the individual athlete responds to different periods of time surrounding the competition and how the responses may vary by scale. A validity-check process (to determine whether or not the respondent answered honestly) is described and several individual SET profiles are presented with helpful case illustrations of a particular athletes' performances and unique problems.

The manual provides an interesting discussion of anxiety and other emotions believed to be related to athletic performance. Rather fine, but important, distinctions are made between perceptions and physiological effects and between anxiety and intensity.

The manual includes a more than adequate discussion of overall validity and the validity of each scale. Three psychologists served as judges of the content validity. All items in the current version of the SET were correctly sorted into the scale categories. Cluster analysis was used to assess discrimant validity. A separate cluster analysis was done for each scale using 118 athletes.

The author is to be commended for the excellent presentation of the cluster-analysis results. A spherical graph of the results provides a clear portrayal of the summary of the analyses suggesting that the items do cluster within the scale categories and that the scales are relatively independent of each other.

Evidence for construct validity is also presented for each scale. The empirical evidence (e.g., patterns of concentration before and during a race) are consistent with expectations, though based on limited sample sizes. Internal consistency measures of reliability resulted in Cronbach alphas ranging from .83 to .94 across time periods and scales. Test-retest reliability was .85 for Anxiety, .79 for Intensity, .75 for Concentration, and .70 for Physical Readiness. These latter indices of reliability were based on a sample of 18 athletes.

The work that this manual traces and the manual itself could easily serve as a model for independent test developers. The author considers and confronts most of the major steps and concerns in test and scale construction. Theory development is briefly but adequately explored, reliability and validity issues are addressed, and case illustrations make it possible for potential users to see how the instrument might be used.

Not everyone is likely to agree with the theoretical premises of the SET. Psychologists are still debating the causes and effects of stress and even coaches disagree on when athletes should be "psyched up" or how important it is for them to be "fired up." Further research with this instrument may help our understanding.

Users need to remember that this is a self-report instrument and in most instances depends on recall. It undoubtedly suffers from limitations as do all self-report instruments. Further research with athletes completing appropriate scales at the moments related to competition rather than depending upon recall may be fruitful, though the reactive effects of being tested need to be considered.

The evidence is too limited at this point to use the SET for predictive purposes. As the author cautions, the SET is primarily a research tool. It has the potential, however, for being useful for individual counseling with athletes without paying attention to normative information. Group or individual conversations with a trained psychologist around issues raised by the SET could not only improve the athletes' performances but could also result in a clearer and enhanced self-concept. This in itself could be a major accomplishment within a society in which adolescent and post-adolescent athletes often find themselves under severe stress.

Review of the Sports Emotion Test by ROBERT P. MARKLEY, Professor of Psychology, Fort Hays State University, Hays, KS:

The Sports Emotion Test is a set of scales attempting to measure a performer's emotional responses to a situation involving athletic competition. The scales ask the performer to provide self ratings of their feelings and reactions to the stress of competition on four theoretically derived dimensions (Anxiety, Intensity, Concentration, and Physical Readiness). The athlete is asked to retrospect about emotional feelings experienced at six times: 24 hours before competition, breakfast on the day of a meet, just before competition, just after the start of competition, at the peak of a competition, and "just after something goes wrong." Twenty-two check-mark responses are required at each time period. When the competitor completes the entire test, there are 24 scores that can be profiled in a variety of ways. Available from the publisher are a test booklet, a profile sheet, and a technical handbook.

This test attempts to capture some good ideas: that emotional responses (Anxiety) are situationally specific, are different at various times within a situation, are multidimensional, and that one's evaluative construction of stress and arousal is perhaps as important as the actual presence of physiological stress and arousal responses. The test's Anxiety dimension assesses the athlete's perception of the amount of emotional or physiological arousal that is interpreted by the athlete as anxiety. The authors postulate a phenomenal distinction between Anxiety feelings and the emotional Intensity the performer experiences. They suggest that the profile (over time) of Intensity is different than the profile for Anxiety. For example, in successful athletes anxiety often drops after the start of a meet while intensity stays constant or increases.

The Concentration dimension asks whether the athlete can stay attentionally focussed upon the performance or is distracted and experiences anxiety-related thought interference. The authors report some construct validity data for this scale from prior test-anxiety research. The Physical Readiness scale measures perceptions of bodily strength and coordination, for example, how weak (or powerful) the legs feel at a particular time before or during a meet.

Cronbach alpha reliabilities are reported ranging from .83 to .94 for a sample of $N = 118$ university, high school, and professional athletes. Test-retest reliability is a problematic concept when dealing with these sorts of idiographic measures of affective responses. These measures are specific to a particular point in the time course of a specific event; however, the authors report small sample estimates that range from .85 (Anxiety scale) to .70 (Physical Readiness scale).

Content, discriminant, and some construct validity data are provided in the test manual. Three qualified judges agreed about the scale placement of each item. A cluster analysis of data from the 118 athletes located items from each scale in separate clusters. The Anxiety scale is essentially identical to a previous scale published by the same authors in the 1960s. Validity data for the previous scale are reported in the manual. The other three dimensions represent new scales for which very limited validity data are presented.

The manual contains some discussion of scale profiles. These may be useful to a clinician working with a client on a sports-related performance-anxiety problem. Such a clinician will have to acquire some experience using the test with several clients and, because there is no single simple score, the user must also be one who enjoys the intellectual challenge of interpreting the spaghetti strands of multiple profiles.

The idea embodied in this instrument, of assessment at various times prior to and during an athletic event, is a good one. It is not clear, however, that this set of scales, with a wealth of measures, would be more useful than something simpler, for example, Martens' (1977) shortened form of the State Anxiety Inventory, as a situational measure of competition anxiety. Also, I am unconvinced that the Intensity or Concentration subscales are valid assessments of physiological arousal. In particular, the issue of the personal meaning one gives to various physical states—"I am excited and therefore am going to perform well (or poorly),"—is not clearly addressed. The opportunity for more experimental research is clear. For example, it may be possible to construct modifications of the scales to deal with other performance-anxiety situations (e.g., music, theater, speech, and so on).

This test may be a useful tool to examine the dynamics of performance and anxiety in the sports setting. What is missing is evidence of refereed published research using this instrument. It is my opinion that an author's responsibility extends beyond simply publishing the test and manual. Test users will benefit from carefully researched demonstrations of the substantive usefulness of the test.

REVIEWER'S REFERENCE

Martens, R. (1977). Sport Competition Anxiety Test. Champaign, IL: Human Kinetics Publishers.

[75]

Stanford-Binet Intelligence Scale, Fourth Edition. Purpose: "An instrument for measuring cognitive abilities that provides an analysis of the pattern as well as the overall level of an individual's cognitive development." Ages 2–adult; 1916–86; S-B; Third Revision is still available; 20 scores: Verbal Reasoning (Vocabulary, Comprehension, Absurdities, Verbal Relations, Total), Abstract/Visual Reasoning (Pattern Analysis, Copying, Matrices, Paper Folding and Cutting, Total), Quantitative Reasoning (Quantitive, Number Series, Equation Building, Total), Short-Term Memory (Bead Memory, Memory for Sentences, Memory for Digits, Memory for Objects, Total), Total; individual; 1987 price data: $297 per complete examiner's kit;

$24.30 per 35 record booklets ('86, 40 pages); $24 per Guide for Administering and Scoring the Fourth Edition ('86, 196 pages); $15 per Examiner's Handbook; $8.55 per Technical Manual ('86, 142 pages); administration time not reported; Robert L. Thorndike, Elizabeth P. Hagen, and Jerome M. Sattler; The Riverside Publishing Co.*

See 9:1176 (41 references), T3:2289 (203 references), 8:229 (176 references), and T2:525 (428 references); for a review by David Freides, see 7:425 (258 references); for a review by Elizabeth D. Fraser and excerpted reviews by Benjamin Balinski, L. B. Birch, James Maxwell, Marie D. Neale, and Julian C. Stanley, see 6:536 (110 references); for reviews by Mary R. Haworth and Norman D. Sundberg of the second revision, see 5:413 (121 references); for a review by Boyd R. McCandless, see 4:358 (142 references); see also 3:292 (217 references); for excerpted reviews by Cyril Burt, Grace H. Kent, and M. Krugman, see 2:1420 (132 references); for reviews by Francis N. Maxfield, J. W. M. Rothney, and F. L. Wells, see 1:1062.

TEST REFERENCES

1. Bouchard, T. J., Jr. (1983). Do environmental similarities explain the similarity in intelligence of identical twins reared apart? *Intelligence, 7,* 175-184.
2. Hartsough, C. S., Elias, P., & Wheeler, P. (1983). Evaluation of a nonintellectual assessment procedure for the early screening of exceptionality. *Journal of School Psychology, 21,* 133-142.
3. Morrison, G. M., & Borthwick, S. (1983). Patterns of behavior, cognitive competence, and social status for educable mentally retarded children. *The Journal of Special Education, 17,* 441-452.
4. Teglasi, H., & Freeman, R. W. (1983). Rapport pitfalls of beginning testers. *Journal of School Psychology, 21,* 229-240.
5. Tsai, L. Y., & Beisler, J. M. (1983). The development of sex differences in infantile autism. *British Journal of Psychiatry, 142,* 373-378.
6. Wilson, R. S., & Matheny, A. P., Jr. (1983). Mental development: Family environment and genetic influences. *Intelligence, 7,* 195-215.
7. Adams, J. L., Campbell, F. A., & Ramey, C. T. (1984). Infants' home environments: A study of screening efficiency. *American Journal of Mental Deficiency, 89,* 133-139.
8. Bickett, L., Reuter, J., & Stancin, T. (1984). The use of the McCarthy Scales of Children's Abilities to assess moderately mentally retarded children. *Psychology in the Schools, 21,* 305-312.
9. Bradley, R. H., & Caldwell, B. M. (1984). The relation of infants' home environments to achievement test performance in first grade: A follow-up study. *Child Development, 55,* 803-809.
10. Deckner, C. W., Soraci, S. A., Jr., Blanton, R. L., & Deckner, P. O. (1984). The relationships among two experimental and four psychometric assessments of abnormal children. *Journal of Clinical and Child Psychology, 13,* 157-164.
11. Flynn, J. R. (1984). The mean IQ of Americans: Massive gains 1932 to 1978. *Psychological Bulletin, 95,* 29-51.
12. Furrow, D. (1984). Social and private speech at two years. *Child Development, 55,* 355-362.
13. Guidubaldi, J., & Perry, J. D. (1984). Concurrent and predictive validity of the Battelle Development Inventory at the first grade level. *Educational and Psychological Measurement, 44,* 977-985.
14. Hoffman-Plotkin, D., & Twentyman, C. T. (1984). A multimodal assessment of behavioral and cognitive deficits in

abused and neglected preschoolers. *Child Development*, 55, 794-802.

15. Honig, A. S. (1984). Risk factors in infants and young children. *Young Children*, 39 (4), 60-73.

16. Kaufman, A. S. (1984). K-ABC and controversy. *The Journal of Special Education*, 18, 409-444.

17. Kohlberg, L., Ricks, D., & Snarey, J. (1984). Childhood development as a predictor of adaptation in adulthood. *Genetic Psychology Monographs*, 110, 91-172.

18. Maheady, L., Maitland, G., & Sainato, D. (1984). The interpretation of social interactions by mildly handicapped and nondisabled children. *The Journal of Special Education*, 18, 151-159.

19. Martin, N. D. T., Snodgrass, G. J. A. I., & Cohen, R. D. (1984). Idiopathic infantile hypercalcaemia—A continuing enigma. *Archives of Disease in Childhood*, 59, 605-613.

20. McCall, R. B. (1984). Developmental changes in mental performance: The effect of the birth of a sibling. *Child Development*, 55, 1317-1321.

21. McGowan, R. J., & Johnson, D. J. (1984). The mother-child relationship and other antecedents of academic performance: A causal analysis. *Hispanic Journal of Behavioral Sciences*, 6, 205-224.

22. McGowan, R. J., & Johnson, D. L. (1984). The mother-child relationship and other antecedents of childhood intelligence: A causal analysis. *Child Development*, 55, 810-820.

23. Mehrens, W. A. (1984). A critical analysis of the psychometric properties of the K-ABC. *The Journal of Special Education*, 18, 297-310.

24. Miller, L. B., & Bizzell, R. P. (1984). Long-term effects of four preschool programs: Ninth- and tenth-grade results. *Child Development*, 55, 1570-1587.

25. Obrzut, A., Nelson, R. B., & Obrzut, J. E. (1984). Early school entrance for intellectually superior children: An analysis. *Psychology in the Schools*, 21, 71-77.

26. Odom, S. L., Deklyen, M., & Jenkins, J. R. (1984). Integrating handicapped and nonhandicapped preschoolers: Developmental impact on nonhandicapped children. *Exceptional Children*, 51, 41-48.

27. Ramey, C. T., & Campbell, F. A. (1984). Preventive education for high-risk children: Cognitive consequences of the Carolina Abecedarian Project. *American Journal of Mental Deficiency*, 88, 515-523.

28. Ramey, C. T., Yeates, K. O., & Short, E. J. (1984). The plasticity of intellectual development: Insights from preventive intervention. *Child Development*, 55, 1913-1925.

29. Ritvo, E. R., Freeman, B. J., Yuwiler, A., Geller, E., Yokota, A., Schroth, P., & Novak, P. (1984). Study of fenfluramine in outpatients with the syndrome of autism. *The Journal of Pediatrics*, 105, 823-828.

30. Runco, M. A. (1984). Teachers' judgements of creativity and social validation of divergent thinking tests. *Perceptual and Motor Skills*, 59, 711-717.

31. Sternberg, R. J. (1984). The Kaufman Assessment Battery for Children: An information-processing analysis and critique. *The Journal of Special Education*, 18, 269-279.

32. Tobey, E. A., & Cullen, J. K., Jr. (1984). Temporal integration of tone glides by children with auditory-memory and reading problems. *Journal of Speech and Hearing Research*, 27, 527-533.

33. Zins, J. E., & Barnett, D. W. (1984). A validity study of the K-ABC, the WISC-R, and the Stanford-Binet with nonreferred children. *Journal of School Psychology*, 22, 369-371.

34. Berbaum, M. L., & Moreland, R. L. (1985). Intellectual development within transracial adoptive families: Retesting the confluence model. *Child Development*, 56, 207-216.

35. Blackwell, S. C., Dial, J. G., Chan, F., & McCollum, P. S. (1985). Discriminating functional levels of independent living: A neuropsychological evaluation of mentally retarded adults. *Rehabilitation Counseling Bulletin*, 29, 42-52.

36. Cardoso-Martins, C., Mervis, C. B., & Mervis, C. A. (1985). Early vocabulary acquisition by children with Down syndrome. *American Journal of Mental Deficiency*, 90, 177-184.

37. Coleman, M., Sobel, S., Bhagavan, H. N., Coursin, D., Marquardt, A., Guay, M., & Hunt, C. (1985). A double blind study of vitamin B6 in Down's syndrome infants. Part 1-Clinical and biochemical results. *Journal of Mental Deficiency Research*, 29, 233-240.

38. Covin, T. M., & Sattler, J. M. (1985). A longitudinal study of the Stanford-Binet and WISC-R with special education students. *Psychology in the Schools*, 22, 274-276.

39. Cunningham, C. C., Glenn, S. M., Wilkinson, P., & Sloper, P. (1985). Mental ability, symbolic play and receptive and expressive language of young children with Down's syndrome. *Journal of Child Psychology and Psychiatry and Allied Disciplines*, 26, 255-265.

40. Durham, T. W. (1985). Extrapolated Stanford-Binet IQs for severely and profoundly retarded adults. *Psychological Reports*, 56, 189-190.

41. Gunn, P., & Berry, P. (1985). The temperament of Down's syndrome toddlers and their siblings. *Journal of Child Psychology and Psychiatry and Allied Disciplines*, 26, 973-979.

42. Hewitt, K. E., Carter, G., & Jancar, J. (1985). Ageing in Down's syndrome. *British Journal of Psychiatry*, 147, 58-62.

43. Kashani, J. H., Carlson, G. A., Horwitz, E., & Reid, J. C. (1985). Dysphoric mood in young children referred to a child development unit. *Child Psychiatry and Human Development*, 15, 234-242.

44. Kavale, K. A., & Nye, C. (1985). Parameters of learning disabilities in achievement, linguistic, neuropsychological, and social/behavioral domains. *Journal of Special Education*, 19, 443-458.

45. Klanderman, J., Devine, J., & Mollner, C. (1985). The K-ABC: A construct validity study with the WISC-R and Stanford-Binet. *Journal of Clinical Psychology*, 41, 273-281.

46. Latorre, R. A. (1985). Kindergarten screening: A cross-validation of the Florida Kindergarten Screening Battery. *The Alberta Journal of Educational Research*, 31, 174-190.

47. Marcell, M. M., & Jett, D. A. (1985). Identification of vocally expressed emotions by mentally retarded and nonretarded individuals. *American Journal of Mental Deficiency*, 89, 537-545.

48. Plomin, R., & DeFries, J. C. (1985). A parent-offspring adoption study of cognitive abilities in early childhood. *Intelligence*, 9, 341-356.

49. Richardson, S. A., Koller, H., & Katz, M. (1985). Appearance and mental retardation: Some first steps in the development and application of a measure. *American Journal of Mental Deficiency*, 89, 475-484.

50. Rose, S. A., & Wallace, I. F. (1985). Cross-modal and intramodal transfer as predictors of mental development in full-term and preterm infants. *Developmental Psychology*, 21, 949-962.

51. Rose, S. A., & Wallace, I. F. (1985). Visual recognition memory: A predictor of later cognitive functioning in preterms. *Child Development*, 56, 843-852.

52. Sinclair, E., Forness, S. R., & Alexson, J. (1985). Psychiatric diagnosis: A study of its relationship to school needs. *Journal of Special Education*, 19, 333-344.

53. Templer, D. I., Schmitz, S. P., & Corgiat, M. D. (1985). Comparison of the Stanford-Binet with the Wechsler Adult Intelligence Scale—Revised: Preliminary report. *Psychological Reports*, 57, 335-336.

54. Wasserman, G. A., Allen, R., & Solomon, C. R. (1985). At-risk toddlers and their mothers: The special case of the physical handicap. *Child Development*, 56, 73-83.

55. Wilson, R. S. (1985). Risk and resilience in early mental development. *Developmental Psychology*, 21, 795-805.

56. Breitmayer, B. J., & Ramey, C. T. (1986). Biological nonoptimality and quality of postnatal environment as codeterminants of intellectual development. *Child Development*, 57, 1151-1165.

57. Carvajal, H., & Weyand, K. (1986). Relationships between scores on Stanford-Binet IV and Wechsler Intelligence Scale for Children—Revised. *Psychological Reports*, 59, 963-966.

58. Chomsky, C. (1986). Analytic study of the tacloma method: Language abilities of three deaf-blind subjects. *Journal of Speech and Hearing Research*, 29, 332-347.

59. Goldstein, D. J., Smith, K. B., & Waldrep, E. E. (1986). Factor analytic study of the Kaufman Assessment Battery for Children. *Journal of Clinical Psychology*, 42, 890-894.

60. Hewitt, K. E., Fenner, M. E., & Torpy, D. (1986). Cognitive and behavioural profiles of the elderly mentally handicapped. *Journal of Mental Deficiency Research*, 30, 217-225.

61. Karnes, F. A., Whorton, J. E., Currie, B. B., & Cantrall, S. W. (1986). Correlations of scores on the WISC-R, Stanford-Binet, the Slosson Intelligence Test, and the Developing Cognitive Abilities Test for intellectually gifted youth. *Psychological Reports*, 58, 887-889.

62. Kashani, J. H., Horwitz, E., Ray, J. S., & Reid, J. C. (1986). DSM-III diagnostic classification of 100 preschoolers in a child development unit. *Child Psychiatry and Human Development*, 16, 137-147.

63. Lewis, M., Jaskir, J., & Enright, M. K. (1986). The development of mental abilities in infancy. *Intelligence*, 10, 331-354.

64. Lidz, C. S., & Ballester, L. E. (1986). Diagnostic implications of McCarthy Scale General Cognitive Index/Binet IQ discrepancies for low-socioeconomic-status preschool children. *Journal of School Psychology*, 24, 381-385.

65. Maisto, A. A., & German, M. L. (1986). Reliability, predictive validity, and interrelationships of early assessment indices used with developmentally delayed infants and children. *Journal of Clinical Child Psychology*, 15, 327-332.

66. Mannarino, A. P., & Cohen, J. A. (1986). A clinical-demographic study of sexually abused children. *Child Abuse and Neglect*, 10, 17-23.

67. Mundy, P., Sigman, M., Ungerer, J., & Sherman, T. (1986). Defining the social deficits of autism: The contribution of non-verbal communication measures. *Journal of Child Psychology and Psychiatry and Allied Disciplines*, 27, 657-669.

68. Palisin, H. (1986). Preschool temperament and performance on achievement tests. *Developmental Psychology*, 22, 766-770.

69. Rantakallio, P., & von Wendt, L. (1986). Mental retardation and subnormality in a birth cohort of 12,000 children in Northern Finland. *American Journal of Mental Deficiency*, 90, 380-387.

70. Rice, T., Corley, R., Fulker, D. W., & Plomin, R. (1986). The development and validation of a test battery measuring specific cognitive abilities in four-year-old children. *Educational and Psychological Measurement*, 46, 699-708.

71. Roth, F. P., & Spekman, N. J. (1986). Narrative discourse: Spontaneously generated stories of learning-disabled and normally achieving students. *The Journal of Speech and Hearing Disorders*, 51, 8-23.

72. Silva, P. A., Chalmers, D., & Stewart, I. (1986). Some audiological, psychological, educational and behavioral characteristics of children with bilateral otitis media with effusion: A longitudinal study. *Journal of Learning Disabilities*, 19, 165-169.

73. Simmons, C. H., & Zumpf, C. (1986). The gifted child: Perceived competence, prosocial moral reasoning, and charitable donations. *The Journal of Genetic Psychology*, 147, 97-105.

74. Singer, L. (1986). Long-term hospitalization of failure-to-thrive infants: Developmental outcome at three years. *Child Abuse and Neglect*, 10, 479-486.

75. Spitz, H. H. (1986). Disparities in mentally retarded persons' IQs derived from different intelligence tests. *American Journal of Mental Deficiency*, 90, 588-591.

76. Wasserman, G. A., Shilansky, M., & Hahn, H. (1986). A matter of degree: Maternal interaction with infants of varying levels of retardation. *Child Study Journal*, 16, 241-253.

77. Gollob, H. F., & Reichardt, C. S. (1987). Taking account of time lags in causal models. *Child Development*, 58, 80-92.

78. Loveland, K. A. (1987). Behavior of young children with down syndrome before the mirror: Exploration. *Child Development*, 58, 768-778.

79. Lukose, S. (1987). Knowledge and behavior relationships in the memory ability of retarded and nonretarded students. *Journal of Experimental Child Psychology*, 43, 13-24.

Review of the Stanford-Binet Intelligence Scale, Fourth Edition by ANNE ANASTASI, Professor Emeritus of Psychology, Fordham University, Bronx, NY:

This revision of the Stanford-Binet is the most extensive ever undertaken, including basic changes in content coverage, administration, scoring, and interpretation, as well as a complete restandardization on a representative national sample. Continuity with the earlier editions was maintained in part by retaining many of the item types from the earlier forms. Even more important is the retention of the adaptive testing procedure, whereby each individual takes only those items whose difficulty is appropriate for his or her performance level.

ADMINISTRATION AND SCORING. In this edition, adaptive testing is achieved by a two-stage process. In the first stage, the examiner gives the Vocabulary Test, which serves as a routing test to select the *entry level* for all remaining tests. Where to begin on the Vocabulary test depends solely on chronological age. For all other tests, the entry level is found from a chart reproduced on the record booklet, which combines Vocabulary score and chronological age. In the second stage, the examiner follows specified rules to establish a *basal level* and a *ceiling level* for each test on the basis of the individual's actual performance.

Unlike the age grouping followed in earlier editions, items of each type are now placed in separate tests in increasing order of difficulty. Item difficulty is incorporated in the scoring by recording the item number of the highest item administered, from which is subtracted the total number of attempted items that were failed. There are 15 tests, chosen to represent four major cognitive areas: Verbal Reasoning, Quantitative Reasoning, Abstract/Visual Reasoning, and Short-Term Memory. No one individual, however, takes all 15 tests, because some are suitable only within limited age ranges. In general, the complete battery may include from 8 to 13 tests, depending on the test taker's age and performance on the routing test. For some testing purposes, moreover, special abbreviated batteries of 4 to 8 tests are suggested in the Guide.

Testing procedures are facilitated in several ways. Four item books, conveniently designed for flip-over presentation, display stimulus material on the test taker's side and condensed directions on the examiner's side. For most tests, each item has only one correct answer, available to the examiner on the record booklet and in the item books. All items are passed or failed according to specified standards. Five tests call for free responses, thus requiring the use of expanded scoring guidelines included in the Guide.

STANDARDIZATION AND NORMS. The standardization sample comprised slightly over 5,000 cases between the ages of 2 and 23 years, tested in 47 states (including Alaska and Hawaii) and the District of Columbia. The sample was stratified to match the proportions in the 1980 U.S. Census in geographic region, community size, ethnicity, and sex. Socioeconomic status, assessed by parental educational and occupational levels, revealed some overrepresentation at the upper and underrepresentation at the lower levels. This imbalance was adjusted through differential weighting of frequencies in the computation of normative values.

Raw scores on each of the 15 tests are converted to Standard Age Scores (SAS); these are normalized standard scores with mean of 50 and standard deviation of 8, within each of 30 age levels (ranging from 4-month intervals for ages 2 to 5 to a single interval for ages 17-11 to 23-11). The record booklet provides a chart for plotting a profile of the SASs on each test administered. It would have been desirable to give the test user some further guidance in the interpretation of this profile, beyond the simple statement in the Guide that the profile "shows at a glance the strengths and weaknesses of the examinee's cognitive abilities." At the very least, there should have been a reference to the table of minimum significant differences in the Appendix of the Technical Manual. Not all users will read the Technical Manual, much less its Appendices. It might also have been helpful to give the user some overall guidelines to follow, such as plotting score bands ($\pm$ SEM) and observing overlap, as is done in some published group tests. To be sure, the present procedure is a marked improvement over the traditional clinical practice of comparing performance on subjectively grouped items of unknown reliability. Nevertheless, the technical improvements introduced in this regard could have been carried a bit farther through integration of available data in the Guide.

The normative tables also provide SASs for the four cognitive areas and for a composite score on the entire scale. These SASs have a mean of 100 and a standard deviation of 16, thus using the same units as the deviation IQs of the earlier editions. In addition, the normative tables permit the examiner to find SASs for any desired combination of two or more area scores ("partial composites"). For example, a combination of verbal and quantitative reasoning corresponds closely to scholastic aptitude and may be of particular interest in academic settings. In the introductory discussions in both Guide and Technical Manual, this composite is designated a measure of "crystallized abilities," in contrast to the "fluid-analytic abilities" identified with the single area score in abstract/visual reasoning. This distinction is of questionable value and is not well supported by the Stanford-Binet data themselves. The "fluid-analytic score" seems to be more a measure of spatial ability than of abstract-visual reasoning. Of the four tests in this area, only Pattern Analysis has a substantial loading on the abstract-visual factor; the other three tests have their major nongeneral loading in specificity factors (Technical Manual). Although introduced in discussing the theoretical rationale for the Fourth Edition, the crystallized-fluid distinction does not play a significant part in the actual processing of scores. The available procedures permit considerable flexibility in combining and interpreting area scores. For the well-qualified and sophisticated user, this is an advantage.

RELIABILITY AND VALIDITY. K-R 20 reliabilities were found for each 1-year age group in the standardization sample for ages 2 to 17, and for the 18–23-year group. Reliabilities of the composite score ranged from .95 to .99. Reliabilities were also high for the four cognitive area scores; although varying with the number of tests included, they ranged from .80 to .97. For the separate tests, most reliabilities fell in the .80s and low .90s, except for Memory for Objects, a short, 15-item test whose reliabilities ranged from .66 to .78. In general, all reliabilities tended to be slightly higher at the upper age levels. SEMs are also reported for each test, each area score, total composite, and all partial composites. Some retest reliabilities (2–8 month intervals) showed coefficients in the .90s for composite score, but the other results are difficult to interpret because of small samples, restricted ranges on some tests, and an appreciable practice effect.

Beginning with a hierarchical model of cognitive abilities, the test construction process (spanning some 8 years) pursued the dual goal of retaining as many item types as possible from the earlier editions while incorporating current ability constructs. Of the final tests, nine evolved from earlier item types, six used new types. Field trials on different age groups provided data for both quantitative and qualitative item analyses, including item-fairness reviews, as well as intercorrelations and factor analyses of preliminary tests. For the final scale, intercorrelations of all scores within the 17 age groups of the standardization sample were used in confirmatory factor analyses. By far the largest loadings were on a general factor. There was also some support for the area scores, although the identification of the abstract/visual factor appears questionable, and the evidence for a memory factor is weak, especially in the Bead Memory test. Special studies were conducted on "non-exceptional samples" and on exceptional samples (gifted, mentally retarded, and learning disabled) to find (a) correlations with Stanford-Binet (Form L-M), Wechsler scales, and the Kaufman Assessment Battery for Children (K-ABC), and (b) performance level on composite and area scores. In general, all the results conformed to expectations.

OVERVIEW. This basic restructuring of a well-established clinical instrument shows a high level of technical quality in its test construction procedures. At this stage, its principal limitation centers on communications with test users, especially in clinical settings. This limitation has been met in part by the subsequently published Examiner's Handbook (Delaney & Hopkins, 1987). This volume includes cautions regarding possible misuse of scores, together with examples of clinical interpretations and some illustrative case reports. Moreover, it provides thorough and sophisticated procedures for profile analysis of subtest scores, which are lacking in the Guide and the Technical Manual.

REVIEWER'S REFERENCE

Delaney, E., & Hopkins, T. (1987). *Stanford-Binet Intelligence Scale examiner's handbook: An expanded guide for fourth edition users.* Chicago: The Riverside Publishing Company.

Review of the Stanford-Binet Intelligence Scale, Fourth Edition by LEE J. CRONBACH, Fellow, Center for the Study of Families, Children, and Youth, Stanford University, Stanford, CA:

This essentially new instrument (hereafter, SB4) is not much like the Stanford-Binet of former years. Traces of the thinking of Terman and Merrill survive in SB4 and its manuals—notably, some wise counsel on how to conduct individual tests. Many of the 15 subtests are ingenious modifications and extensions of tasks devised by Binet or Terman; others are adapted from the Cognitive Abilities Test (CogAT), the group test of Thorndike and Hagen; one, Matrices, descends from Spearman. The structure resembles that of CogAT, setting out to measure four correlated dimensions: Short-Term Memory, plus Verbal, Quantitative, and Abstract/Visual Reasoning. These combine into a Composite SAS ("standard age score"). I shall refer to the scores as M, V, Q, A, and CSAS. For possible supplementary use, the tester also records subtest scores.

Six subtests have a low floor and a high ceiling: Vocabulary, Comprehension, Quantitative, Pattern Analysis, Bead Memory, and Memory for Sentences. Two further subtests top out in early adolescence; three more have floors near the 12-year level, and four serve from age 7 upward. Above age 7, the older Stanford-Binet was predominantly a verbal test, whereas SB4 has a balance of the four dimensions at age 7 and above. Although Q and M are measured by few subtests at earlier ages, the sections are weighted equally in obtaining the CSAS.

Easy and hard items within a subtest often differ in character. In Pattern Analysis, for example, easy items use a three-piece form-board; intermediate items require matching a model made of cubes by arranging one to four cubes that have patterned faces; and in advanced items intricate printed designs are to be reproduced with many cubes. (This is the only subtest with strict time limits.) The brief verbal directions for A subtests are supplemented by sufficient pantomime to reduce the influence of listening comprehension.

My impression is that SB4 is less game-like than some other individual tests and will be less attractive to children. Some items call for choice response. Less can be inferred from styles and strategies when interaction with materials and with the examiner is reduced; and perhaps SB4 will elicit fewer idiosyncratic, clinically suggestive responses than the Wechsler Intelligence Scale for Children (WISC) or the traditional SB. A countervailing virtue is that the austerity of SB4 encourages conservative interpretation.

ADMINISTRATION AND SCORING. SB4 is efficient to administer. Items within a subtest are ordered by difficulty, which ascends rapidly; each pair of items is labeled with a letter. Vocabulary is given first as a "routing" test. Subsequently, M, V, Q, and A subtests are interspersed. Entering a chart with the subject's age and the performance on Vocabulary pinpoints a letter that identifies the level at which every further subtest is to begin. When the examinee has trouble on a subtest at this entry level, the tester backs down to where the person consistently passes. Otherwise, the examiner works upward until items are consistently failed. The examinee finds few items very easy or very hard, and encounters together all items of the same kind (an improvement over Binet's format). The examiner must judge rapidly whether to credit a response, deny credit, or probe further; scoring guides are succinct and handy.

Test development sought to enhance objectivity, subtest homogeneity, and comparability over ages. The publisher reports only a fraction of the findings made during test development. Thus, when a clinician tells me that items in a certain subtest are ordered incorrectly, according to her trials with children, I cannot review the authors' evidence for their ordering.

Some judgments can be questioned. I regret that the authors catered to tradition with an archaic 100 ± 16 scale for CSAS and for section SAS scores, then introduced for subtests an unprecedented 50 ± 8 scale. I favor the 50 ± 10 scale for all standard scores, to facilitate communication. If a child scores zero on a subtest (not rare at ages 2 and 3), the subtest is treated as spoiled and not counted. This would bias upward the section score, and could be critical in evaluating the severity of mental handicaps. Many Vocabulary and Comprehension items have more than one defensible answer, and usually any of them is credited. For "Why do people read newspapers?" answers listed in the scoring guide include "To find out what the news is," "Because it's fun," "To see what's on TV," and "Because the TV is broken." Full credit is given to any of the first three, none to the fourth. I doubt that there is empirical evidence to justify such scoring; from my armchair, I prefer Wechsler's principle of giving greater credit for a more basic answer.

The norming plan specified selection of communities, schools, and classrooms. Children were tested after their parents mailed to the publisher an agreement to participate. Parents from high occupational and educational strata responded more often and are overrepresented. Weighting adjusted the score distributions, but undersampling of lower strata reduces the accuracy of the norms. A side effect: the manual's statistical tables vary between unweighted and weighted calculations. This makes it hard to pursue some technical questions.

For a subtest too easy or too hard to be given to all members of an age sample, the reliabilities and correlations with other subtests are hard to interpret; some calculations are restricted to abler examinees, others to less able ones. Toward the end of the age range for such a subtest, norms were created by extrapolation. The procedures seem appropriate, but the extrapolation makes it more important than usual not to take seriously the numerical value of a low score.

RELIABILITY OF SCORES AND CONTRASTS. Users are given poor information on accuracy. The manual relies almost wholly on KR20 coefficients for subtests, compositing them into reliability coefficients for sections and CSAS. Because of the termination rule, items within subtests are not independent and all coefficients are inflated. The presentation, especially in Appendix F on differences between scores required for "significance," is misleading.

Far too little was invested in retest studies; retests, with a time lapse of 4 months or so, were made on fewer than 60 cases at age 5 and at age 8. The retest coefficients imply a standard error for CSAS nearly twice as great as those based on KR20. It seems likely that CSAS retest reliability is around .90. In small samples, the correlations of CSAS with IQ from Wechsler Preschool and Primary Scale of Intelligence (WPPSI) and Wechsler Intelligence Scale for Children—Revised (WISC-R) were .80 and .83, respectively. Retests with a change of examiners should be made on 100 cases at each early age and at spaced later ages;

reliabilities for all contrasts in the profile should be reported; and, to minimize memory effects, the coefficients for subtests and broader scores should be derived from the stepped-up correlation of odd items on the first trial with even items on the second (and vice versa).

Until near-term stability is verified, it is especially important to be wary of measurement error at the lowest ages and in a section score based on one or two subtests. The full SB4 requires somewhat more testing time than its competitors, and shortened scales must be considered dubious until their reliability is established.

How useful is the profile? As the test is planned primarily to measure four categories of ability, subtest-specific factors constitute noise rather than signal. Therefore, I treat subtests as random representatives of their domains in evaluating how well each section score measures its postulated latent trait. For age 9, my coefficients are: CSAS, .91; V, .84; M, .73; A, .71; Q, .64. Coefficients tend to be larger in adolescence, lower in early childhood. These "domain validity" coefficients count subtest-specific variance as error, but not instability from session to session. (See Tryon, 1957; for a similar analysis of WPPSI, see Cronbach, Gleser, Rajaratnam, & Nanda, 1972, pp. 234-256, under "Universe 3.") Surprisingly, domain true scores for Q and A correlate perfectly at age 9.

Are differences between CSAS and a section SAS meaningful? It would be exceedingly liberal to take seriously a part-whole contrast having a domain validity of .40; V and M generally satisfy this standard at ages 8 and above, whereas Q and A almost never do. This conclusion appears consistent with the authors' factor analyses.

To speak in practical terms, assume that someone wants to identify persons whose true scores on a dimension are $1/2$ standard deviation above or below their true Composite scores, and not persons with smaller differences. At the ages where V is most reliable an examiner with 100 cases, flagging V-minus-CSAS differences "significant at the .05 level," would have about 5 hits (worthwhile true difference, flagged), 5 misses, and 10 false positives. These proportions would not become more encouraging with other cut scores or a section other than V. So SB4

profile shape provides nothing beyond suggestions to be checked with additional evidence.

The SB4 selection of content is plausible especially for school-related testing, and the general factor is strong. At age 9, 88 per cent of the within-occasion variance comes from the child's *attention and adaptation to intellectual demands from an authority figure*. It appears entirely safe to impute importance to CSAS, on the basis of the vast body of research on ability to reason and to learn. Although CSAS appears to measure most English-speaking persons well, it of course does not indicate how well a person with limited command of English can function in his or her own community.

COMPARISON WITH OTHER TESTS. Further research on stability, especially at ages 2 through 6, may show SB4 to be as accurate as its competitors; I shall compare tests on the assumption that this uncertainty is resolved favorably. SB4 is shaped much less by clinical aims and experience than the competing batteries (or Binet's own scale). It concentrates on quantifying the attribute that a century of psychometrics has proved central to educational and vocational success. The unique feature of SB4 is continuity of subtests over a wide age range. This enables one to compare scores over a span of 20 years; but not many testers need to do that.

Testers familiar with a Wechsler scale can take advantage of years of personal experience and published suggestions for interpretation. They may find Wechsler performance subtests more informative for diagnosing educational difficulties and for cases with language handicaps than subtests of SB4. SB4 provides more information on memory than Wechsler scales do, and its well-engineered subtests may take on subtle interpretations as experience accumulates. Those who take norms most seriously may be uneasy with WISC-R and WPPSI norms compiled in the early 1970s, but when these tests and SB4 were given to the same children the Wechsler means ran only 3–5 IQ points higher. (I understand that new norms for WPPSI will soon be available, with a renormed WISC-R in a few years.)

The Kaufman Assessment Battery for Children (K-ABC) evidently assembled a better standardization sample than SB4. I surmise that it outdoes SB4 with respect to children's responsiveness to the tasks, and the richness of clinical clues in the performance. The sections of K-ABC are more distinct than those of SB4, and clinicians who like its structure of scores and norms are unlikely to find SB4 appealing. (SB4 V correlates .87 with K-ABC "Achievement," so the two instruments give similar weight to verbal abilities.) SB4 does not present separate norms for the disadvantaged; some users of K-ABC or the Wechsler-related System of Multicultural Pluralistic Assessment (SOMPA) will regret this, but I do not.

The McCarthy scales, despite out-of-date norms, appear to be the instrument of choice at early ages. For individualized educational planning in the primary grades, the British Ability Scales and Feuerstein's LPAD (Learning Potential Assessment Device) have special virtues. If SB4 has advantages over WISC-R and K-ABC for measurement at later ages, the case has not been made.

REVIEWER'S REFERENCES

Tryon, R. C. (1957). Reliability and behavior domain validity: Reformulation and historical critique. *Psychological Bulletin*, 54, 229-249.

Cronbach, L. J., Gleser, G. C., Nanda, H., & Rajaratnam, N. (1972). *The dependability of behavioral measurements: Theory of generalizability for scores and profiles.* New York: John Wiley & Sons, Inc.

[76]

Stress Analysis System. Purpose: Helps to identify possible sources of negative stress in ones life and recognize the symptoms of stress and provides techniques for modifying ones reactions to stress. Adults; 1983–85; self-administered, self-scored; 6 scores: Type A, Anger In, Situational, Health, Accountability, Interpersonal; 1985 price data: $6.50 per booklet ('85, 13 pages) including test and profile; administration time not reported; P. B. Nelson, K. M. Schmidt, and Noel Nelson; Interdatum, Inc.*

Review of the Stress Analysis System by MARY LOU KELLEY, Assistant Professor of Psychology, Louisiana State University, Baton Rouge, LA:

The Stress Analysis System is a 114-item instrument designed to evaluate the amount of stress experienced by an individual across six different domains. The test is apparently completed, scored, and interpreted by the test taker. The stated purpose of the test is to help the respondent identify sources of negative stress and recognize symptoms of stress. Test materials include a number of techniques for modifying reactions to stress. The test is packaged in a professional and appealing manner. The test booklet is divided into several sections including directions for completing and interpreting the results of the test, discussion of the nature and types of stress, and a description of various interventions for alleviating specific types of stress.

The instructions for completing and scoring the test are simple and straightforward. The respondent determines whether each statement is true or false. Next, the test taker sums the items endorsed in each of six areas. Scores obtained in each area are plotted on a profile that indicates the degree to which a given score reflects low or high stress levels.

The six areas of stress purportedly measured by the test are described as:
1. The Type "A" Controller Personality. This personality type is characteristic of individuals who are high achieving, driven to succeed, never happy with their performance, and have a strong desire to control themselves and their environment.

2. The Anger-In Personality. This type is characteristic of individuals who are unassertive and/or find it difficult to express feelings.

3. Situational Stress and Life Readjustments. These items reflect stress due to life changes such as a divorce.

4. Corollary Health Habits. Health habits are measured by items on substance abuse, diet, and exercise.

5. Low Accountability/Victim Syndrome. This pattern is characteristic of individuals who do not assume responsibility for their circumstances, believe they have little influence over their environment, or blame others for their shortcomings or problems.

6. Interpersonal Stress. These stressors are related to a lack of adequate social support.

The items making up each of the six areas appear to correspond with the author's descriptions of types of stress, thus demonstrating face validity, at least. The items themselves are brief and clear. The stress domains targeted on the test correspond to commonly held notions about stress and are, in fact, constructs with some research support in terms of their relationship to stress reactions. However, the authors did not provide any data on or description of test construction. Apparently, the items were intuitively selected and grouped rather than empirically derived.

With regard to other aspects of reliability and validity, absolutely no data were provided on the psychometric characteristics of the test. Thus, it is not known whether the test measures what it is intended to measure or in any way is a useful instrument. Although the profile sheet indicates whether a score represents a low or high amount of stress in a specific domain, the authors did not substantiate empirically the validity of their stress "barometers." The references cited as support for the stress domains and treatment suggestions incorporated in the test are, primarily, self-help books. No mention was made of any data available in support of the instrument.

A serious concern related to the use of the Stress Analysis System is that the test manual offers an array of interventions for reducing stress yet fails to mention the importance of professional help in assisting individuals in stress management. Discussions on alleviating stress present fairly sound advice, yet do not mention the difficulty that may be experienced by many individuals who attempt to carry out the suggestions. Nor did the authors mention any of the negative consequences that may be encountered when a suggestion is used incompetently, ineffectively, or just used at all. For example, the authors discuss the importance of communicating assertively yet fail to mention that changes in one's assertiveness may not always be well received by important people in the subject's life.

In summary, the Stress Analysis System is a slickly-packaged instrument designed to assist individuals in evaluating the degree to which they experience stress. Test materials provide information on methods of alleviating stress. The instrument is apparently completed, scored, and interpreted by the test taker. As the authors did not report any data on the reliability, validity, or standardization of the test, the utility of the test is unknown. Therefore, I recommend that the test not be used for any purpose other than research aimed at establishing its psychometric characteristics. Results from the test have unknown validity and reliability and, in my opinion, could be easily misinterpreted by individuals unfamiliar with psychological evaluation.

Review of the Stress Analysis System by JAYNE E. STAKE, Professor of Psychology, University of Missouri-St. Louis, St. Louis, MO:

P. B. Nelson developed the first version of the Stress Analysis System (SAS) in 1978. The SAS was originally designed for use in training physicians to be better aware of psychological factors in stress-related disease. The items were rationally derived, based upon stress theory. The current form of the SAS was first published in 1981.

The SAS comprises six scales purported to measure six factors that can lead to stress: Type A tendencies, involving preoccupation with time and results; Anger In tendencies, the inability to express anger appropriately; Situational, the number of major adjustments and changes experienced within the past 12 months; Health, hazardous health habits, including poor eating patterns, smoking, and excessive alcoholic consumption; Accountability, the tendency to see oneself as a victim, rather than in control of one's life situation; and Interpersonal, problems in interpersonal relationships.

Also included in the SAS booklet are directions for obtaining a score for each scale, a Stress Profile for charting the six scores, information for interpreting the meaning of each scale, and suggestions for possible changes in behavior and attitudes for participants scoring high on the scales.

There are virtually no data available regarding the psychometric properties of the SAS. Information regarding the reliability and validity of the scales has not been obtained. Of prime importance is the lack of evidence demonstrating that scores on any of the scales are associated with stress-related disease. This is a key assumption made by the authors, and it has not been tested.

A related psychometric problem is that no information is available to justify the scaling of items on any of the six measures. Participants are instructed that if they have scored above a certain level on each scale they have a high potential for stress symptoms. There is no evidence provided to substantiate a relationship between the stated cutoff scores and stress symptoms.

An additional limitation of the SAS is that the internal consistency of the scales has not been established. The authors have assumed that each scale measures one factor in stress-related disease, but the scales may not be factorially pure. This possibility is most evident in the Accountability scale, which includes a number of items that may not be closely related to one another. That is, items on the scale may measure more than one factor or dimension, leading to a summary score of unknown properties. A factor-analysis study is clearly needed.

On the positive side, the SAS provides a clear and helpful explanation to the layperson about the relationship between stress factors and health problems. Participants who are high scorers are given a rationale for changes in their attitudes and life styles, and specific suggestions for changes are provided for each of the six scales. The suggestions could provide a beginning for those seeking better ways of coping with and avoiding stress.

In summary, the SAS has some potential as a self-help tool for diagnosing potential sources of stress and for finding new strategies for reducing stress. Scores should be interpreted with caution, however, as the validity of the scales has not been established.

[77]

Student Rights Scales. Purpose: Determines student and teacher perceptions of student rights in junior and senior high school. Grades 7–12; 1982; SRS; for research use only; 5 subscales: General Rights, Due Process, Academic Self Determination, Freedom of Expression, Personal Conduct; price data available from publisher for manual ('82, 9 pages including test); administration time not reported; T. R. F. Oaster; the Author.*

Review of the Student Rights Scales by STEVEN W. LEE, Assistant Professor of Educational and School Psychology, Indiana State University, Terre Haute, IN:

The Student Rights Scales—Revised (SRSR) was designed to measure and "compare student and teacher perceptions" of rights that students have in junior high and high school. The manual states that the SRSR was designed for use with students and teachers, but parents are also listed as possible respondents. The SRSR materials include a manual and a copy of the Student Rights Scale. According to the manual, the "best use of the current form of the SRSR is as a research tool." The manual presents little research on the topic of student rights. Some of the relevant literature on student rights provid-

ed in the accompanying studies should be incorporated in the manual.

The SRSR is an untimed test that apparently can be administered individually or in groups. However, little information about the appropriate administrative conditions is reported in the manual. The directions for self administration are reported on the first page of the test form with two examples. The directions for administration are clear, but the method of scoring the protocol is not discernable due to discrepancies in the procedure for item weighting. No information on interpretation of the scale is provided either in the manual or on the test form. The SRSR purports to measure five categories of students' rights, identified by the following subscales: General Rights, Due Process, Personal Conduct, Academic Self Determination, and Freedom of Self-Expression.

Apparently the items on the SRSR were generated in a study by Oaster (1983), who reports that "several school teachers were involved in the generation of original item stems." The items in the current form of the SRSR were divided into five "rights categories" on the basis of item intercorrelations and a literature review by Price, Babcock, and Oaster (1982). However, these item intercorrelations could not be found in the above mentioned study. Not only is the development of items for the SRSR not clear in the manual; the development of the "subscales" is equally mysterious.

The norms for the SRSR are provided for 113 students, grades 7 through 12 in two rural school districts. These students volunteered to complete the instrument in their social studies classes. No stratification of the sample was attempted. While the scale is not recommended for clinical or educational uses, the fact that the SRSR has not been sufficiently normed or standardized deserves more emphasis in the manual.

While norms may not be important when the SRSR is used as a research tool, the reliability and validity of the scales are essential. A coefficient alpha of .74 was reported for Form 1. Identical forms with Likert-scale choice points ranging from 3 to 9 yielded coefficient alpha reliabilities ranging from .65 (Form 3) to .78 (Form 7). No estimates of temporal stability or interrater reliabilities were reported in the manual.

Some evidence of content validity exists simply by virtue of a rational examination of the test items. However, no empirical evidence is reported in the manual for the validity of the SRSR as a measure of students' or teachers' perceptions of rights in school. No factor analytic or concurrent validity studies are reported that may help to confirm the SRSR as a measure of students' rights. Furthermore, other than the item intercorrelations, which the manual states are reported in a manuscript by Oaster (1983), no empirical evidence exists for the identified subscales of the SRSR. The item intercorrelations reported to be in Oaster (1983) were not found. These concerns suggest the SRSR cannot demonstrate empirically that it measures what it purports to measure. With these fundamental problems of reliability and validity in mind, the SRSR manual should provide cautions regarding the use of the scale and the limits of generalizability. Unfortunately, the manual does not provide the necessary cautions.

In summary, the SRSR was designed as a research instrument to measure students' and teachers' perceptions of students' rights in school. The procedure used to develop items for the SRSR was not clearly stated in the manual and appears to lack scientific rigor. Because little information was provided in the manual regarding research in the area of students' rights and the development of the SRSR, definite conclusions regarding the theory and development of the SRSR are difficult to draw. A research scale should demonstrate adequate reliability and validity even though completely developed norms are not essential. The norms for the SRSR are quite insufficient. While this is not a major problem in a research scale, more cautions against the use of the SRSR clinically or educationally should be provided in the manual. The internal consistency of the SRSR appeared adequate (coefficient alpha = .74) but no estimates of temporal stability or interrater reliabilities are provided. With the exception of content validity, the SRSR manual offers no empirical support for the scale as a measure of students' rights nor of its subscales. More fundamental research in the area of temporal stability, interrater reliability, and concurrent and construct validity are needed before the SRSR can be considered a viable tool measuring perceptions of students' rights.

REVIEWER'S REFERENCES

Price, L. B., Babcock, S. K., & Oaster, T. R. (1982, February). *Teacher and student perceptions of student rights*. Paper presented at the meeting of the American Association of Colleges for Teacher Education. Houston, TX.

Oaster, T. R. F. (1983). *Reservation and off-reservation parent, teacher and student perceptions of student rights*. Kansas City: University of Missouri-Kansas City. (ERIC Document Reproduction Service No. ED 220 740)

Review of the Student Rights Scales by DAVID MOSHMAN, Associate Professor of Educational Psychology, University of Nebraska-Lincoln, Lincoln, NE:

Public school controversies have made student rights a matter of national attention. Do students have a right to encounter a variety of books, ideas, and points of view? To express their own views? To make curriculum decisions? To wear what they please? To pray in school? Do they have a right to freedom from religious indoctrination? From searches of their desks, lockers, clothes, and bodies? From corporal punishment? Do they have a right to due process if accused of wrongdoing? To equal protection and opportunity regardless of race? Regardless of sex?

Although all of the above questions are raised frequently and have been the subject of substantial legal controversy, relatively little is known about the attitudes of parents, teachers, administrators, and students themselves on these issues. The purpose of the Student Rights Scales is to assess attitudes toward a wide range of student rights. It is a worthy aim.

Unfortunately, the psychometric properties of the scale are, at present, not well established. The items themselves cover a range of rights that are divided into five subscales: General Rights, Due Process, Personal Conduct, Academic Self-Determination, and Freedom of Self-Expression. The subscales do cover a variety of important rights and the distinctions among them are reasonable. On the other hand, there is little attempt to show that these scales adequately encompass the relevant domain or that the differentiation of the student rights domain into these five categories is legally, theoretically, or empirically justified. Why not, for example, a category labeled something like Equal Protection and Opportunity?

In several studies using the scale, the coefficient alpha estimate of reliability has ranged from .52 to .79. The meaning of these figures is unclear in that the populations tested were quite diverse, the samples were usually small, the test itself varied from study to study as items were added or dropped, and even *within* several of the studies items judged inappropriate were dropped prior to calculating reliability. Given these limitations, it cannot be said that the test has been convincingly normed for any definable population.

In its present state of development, the Student Rights Scales cannot be considered a definitive assessment device. Nevertheless, its existence does focus attention on an area worthy of serious research. Do students, teachers, administrators, and parents differ in their overall level of support for student rights? Does this support vary as a function of category of rights (e.g., free speech vs. due process)? Does it vary as a function of individual personality, social class, or school climate? How does *attitude* toward student rights (which is what these scales assess) relate to *knowledge* about relevant legal, moral, or educational considerations? In the absence of other measures, the Student Rights Scales may be useful as a beginning strategy to address questions of this sort. In the course of such research, however, the scale itself must be scrutinized and improved.

[78]

Survey of Personal Values. Purpose: "Measure certain critical values that help determine the manner in which individuals cope with the problems of everyday living." High school and college and adults; 1964–84; SPV; self-administered; test identical to 1965 edition, some additional material provided in manual; 6 scores: Practical Mindedness, Achievement, Variety, Decisiveness, Orderliness, Goal Orientation; 1987 price data: $33 per 25 tests; $5.50 per scoring stencil; $10 per examiner's manual ('84, 49 pages); (15) minutes; Leonard V. Gordon; Science Research Associates, Inc.*

See T3:2370 (5 references) and T2:1409 (5 references); for a review by Gene V Glass, see 7:148 (6 references); see also P:263 (3 references).

Review of the Survey of Personal Values by WILLIAM P. ERCHUL, *Assistant Professor of Psychology, North Carolina State University, Raleigh, NC:*

The Survey of Personal Values (SPV) is a brief, self-administered instrument that reportedly measures temperaments and values that influence a person's behavior. Such information may be useful for the purposes of personnel selection, vocational guidance, and individual counseling. Before proceeding further, two

observations regarding the SPV are warranted. First, the word "personal" in its title refers to the author's claim that the SPV assesses the individual's values in coping with life's problems; Gordon's Survey of Interpersonal Values (a companion test) purports to measure a different set of values concerned with one's interpersonal relationships. Second, the SPV's use of the word "values" is somewhat misleading; as has been noted previously, the test more accurately measures "broad areas of interest" rather than "values" (Glass, 1972). Thus, potential users should be aware that the SPV is not concerned with "values" in the sense of standards by which good/evil and moral/immoral behavior is evaluated.

The SPV employs a forced-choice format and consists of 30 sets of three statements. Within each triad, the respondent is instructed to choose the statement considered "most important" and the statement judged "least important." Each triad presents statements matched for social desirability drawn from three different value dimensions. In all, six dimensions (i.e., scales) are represented: Practical Mindedness (being materialistically-oriented); Achievement (accepting and successfully completing challenging tasks); Variety (engaging in diverse and novel activities); Decisiveness (stating and defending one's opinions); Orderliness (approaching matters in an organized, systematic way); and Goal Orientation (having task-oriented, problem-solving tendencies). Decisiveness and Goal Orientation derive from Guilford's Convergent Thinking and Dislike of Ambiguity factors, respectively; the remaining four scales were developed from "a review of the relevant literature."

Interestingly, scale intercorrelations are such that an ordering of the scales resembling a circumplex model (e.g., Leary, 1957; Olson, Sprenkle, & Russell, 1979) is possible. Two major axes, Organization-Fluidity and Challenge-Security define this model, and individual scales cluster around each of the four poles. Gordon appropriately acknowledges the model's preliminary nature and its oversimplification of human behavior. It is, however, conceptually intriguing and merits further attention.

NORMS. Percentile ranks based on raw scores for each of the six scales are presented for eight nonoccupational and two occupational groups: vocational ninth grade male ($N = 1,096$), vocational ninth grade female (N = 1,571), high school male (N = 1,644), high school female (N = 1,392), vocational junior college male (N = 2,311), vocational junior college female (N = 587), college male (N = 984), college female (N = 1,080), "workers in routinized jobs" (N = 1,461), and managerial (N = 1,089). These numbers appear adequate and can be expected to grow through further test development. The composition of the entire sample seems to be representative of the U.S. in general, although minority group representation data are unavailable for the college and occupational groups. Finally, no standard errors or standard scores are offered, but percentile ranges based on equal standard score intervals are given to aid in interpretation.

RELIABILITY. Using coefficient alpha, internal consistency for the six scales ranges from .77 (Achievement) to .87 (Variety). The test-retest reliability over a 7–10 day period extends from .74 (Decisiveness) to .92 (Variety) as calculated on scores of 97 college students. Reliability coefficients for a 1-year interval collapsed across four educational levels range from .38 (vocational ninth graders' scores on Practical Mindedness) to .74 (eleventh graders' scores on Orderliness), with a mean 1-year test-retest reliability of .58 (N = 207). Taken together, these figures indicate the SPV to be a reliable instrument.

VALIDITY. The manual cites over 20 studies concerned with establishing the validity of the test. In terms of concurrent validity, the SPV scales (with the exception of Variety) correlate significantly with logically related scales of Cattell's Sixteen Personality Factor Questionnaire, and five of six SPV scales correlate significantly with either the Economic or Aesthetic scale of the Allport-Vernon-Lindzey Study of Values. In addition, SPV scores appear to be unrelated to cognitive ability and Caucasian/Black racial class membership (when socioeconomic status is held constant). Other correlational findings raise questions such as: Why are measures of authoritarianism, dogmatism, and self-esteem all significantly related to most SPV scales? And why are the disparate constructs of Acquiescence (Couch & Keniston, 1960) and Authoritarianism (Adorno, Frenkel-Brunswik, Levinson, & Sanford, 1950) both positively related to Practical Mindedness? One begins to wonder what the SPV scales actually measure.

The author relies largely on the contrasting-group approach to establish construct validity; however, in most cases, there are no generally agreed-upon, a priori hypotheses regarding group performance that data can support or fail to support. For example, are faculty members expected to have lower scores on Goal Orientation and Orderliness than their students? Gordon apparently believes so, and presents these results to support the test's construct validity. The strongest argument for using a contrasting-group approach can be made for the Achievement scale, for which meaningful comparisons between groups (e.g., enrolled students and drop-outs) can be and are made. As a final note, Gordon's inclusion of cross-cultural research is inherently interesting, but does little to convince one of the SPV's validity.

SUMMARY. Numerous refinements of the SPV have occurred since the time of Glass' (1972) review. Specifically, the test presents better norms developed on more diverse populations and acceptable long-term reliability data. However, basic questions surrounding the test's validity still remain (e.g., What do the individual scales actually measure?). In the final analysis, the SPV appears to have risen above the status of a research instrument but continues to walk in the shadow of the more well-established Study of Values.

REVIEWER'S REFERENCES

Adorno, T. W., Frenkel-Brunswik, E., Levinson, D. J., & Stanford, R. N. (1950). *The authoritarian personality.* New York: Harper & Row.

Leary, T. (1957). *Interpersonal diagnosis of personality.* New York: Ronald Press Co.

Couch, A., & Keniston, K. (1960). Yeasayers and naysayers: Agreeing response set as a personality variable. *Journal of Abnormal and Social Psychology,* 60, 151-174.

Glass, G. V. (1972). [Review of Survey of Personal Values]. In O. K. Buros (Ed.), *The seventh mental measurements yearbook* (Vol. 1, pp. 359-360). Highland Park, NJ: The Gryphon Press.

Olson, D. H., Sprenkle, D. H., & Russell, C. S. (1979). Circumplex model of marital and family systems: I. Cohesion and adaptability dimensions, family types, and clinical applications. *Family Process,* 18, 3-28.

Review of the Survey of Personal Values by RODNEY L. LOWMAN, *Director, Corporate Division, Personal Assistance Service, Occupational Health Service, and Faculty, Divisions of Medical Psychology and Occupational Medicine, Duke University Medical Center, Durham, NC:*

In reviewing the Survey of Personal Values (SPV), one is reminded of Peter Drucker's old differentiation between organizational efficiency and effectiveness. Efficiency, said Drucker, is doing the job right, while effectiveness is doing the right job. The SPV is more problematic concerning *what* it measures than for *how* it goes about the process of measuring it. It is the test's conceptualization of values that raises the most concern.

What are values? How do they relate to decisions and behaviors that are of interest to psychologists who would use such a test, presumably, to advise and counsel persons about real-life choices and decisions? Does this test really measure values or some related construct such as vocational interests? These are important, and largely unanswered, questions raised by this measure. The answers matter a great deal because they help to determine whether this test is of use outside of a very narrow research context and they guide the question of whether this is the most efficient test of its genre.

Conceptually, this measure is rather confused. It comes narrowly close to being a set of items (or scales) in search of constructs to measure. The closest definition of "values" provided is "the relative importance individuals ascribe to various activities." The "various activities" measured here include six scales of what are presumed to be stable (typological) characteristics of persons: Practical Mindedness, Achievement, Variety, Decisiveness, Orderliness, and Goal Orientation. In post-hoc analyses, these scales are said to reduce to two underlying dimensions: Organization-Fluidity and Challenge-Security. Yet, the loadings on each scale do not add up to a conceptually satisfactory (much less elegant) solution. The Challenge-Security dimension seems especially muddled.

Although the SPV's test manual has been revised and updated, the instrument was last revised over 20 years ago (1965). The format requires the respondent to select the items in each of 30 triads that are most and least liked. No formal validity or fakability scales are incorporated. Although norms are provided for high school students, the measure remains one requiring a fairly high degree of reading comprehension and test sophistication. It is difficult to imagine the test being used with students or others of below average intelligence and reading level.

Normative data are included for several groups. Unfortunately, the data are not ade-

quately elaborated as to geographic, racial, and socioeconomic distributions. Although minorities were included in the normative samples, no breakdown for each race is provided. (Buried in the manual's validity section are normative data for Japanese college students and Indian high school students.) Norms are provided for two industrial samples (managers and "workers in routinized jobs"), but only combined sample data are presented (without age, sex, or experience level breakdowns). Given the profound societal changes of the last 20 years, a need for new normative data and more sophisticated elaboration of norms is suggested.

An abundance of types of validity evidence is presented on behalf of the SPV: factorial, correlations with other tests, and descriptive data for groups of known characteristics. The test is differentiated from abilities, but in considering its relationship with other personality-like variables, the author follows an unfortunate practice of correlating the SPV with other tests produced by him, (viz., the Survey of Interpersonal Values, the Gordon Personal Profile, the Gordon Personal Inventory, and the Work Environment Preference Schedule). Both with his own instrumentation and when comparing the SPV with other measures, the samples are small and the results rather mixed. For example, in correlating scores of 58 Peace Corps volunteers on the SPV and the more widely known Allport-Vernon-Lindzey Study of Values, four of the latter's values (Theoretical, Social, Political, and Religious) have no statistically significant correlations with any of the SPV scales. Although some of the correlations with the Economic and Aesthetic values are in an interpretable direction, there is a statistically significant negative correlation of "Economic Man" with scores on the SPV's achievement scale, and its modest correlation with Goal Orientation is not statistically significant. Whatever the SPV is measuring, it would appear to be something rather different from what is measured by the Study of Values. Similarly, some of the correlations between the SPV and scores on the 16PF for a sample of 172 men make good sense (e.g., Goal Orientation with the 16PF's self-discipline measure), but many do not (e.g., Variety with scales described as "tense, suspicious, and apprehensive"; no correlation between "Practical-Imaginative" scale on the 16PF and the Practical Mindedness scale on the SPV, etc.).

Validity concerns are also raised by the data provided for various occupational groups. This is particularly troubling since the SPV is suggested by its author to be appropriate for use in personnel selection as well as student-counseling contexts. At first, one is impressed with the finding, in three samples of managers from diverse cultural settings, that Achievement and Goal Orientation are the first and second highest scoring patterns for each group. However, in reviewing the normative data provided for 44 occupational samples cited in the Appendix to the test manual, it is noted that in 29 of these diverse occupations, Goal Orientation was the highest endorsed scale (in two additional cases, it ties for first place). In all but three of the remaining cases, Achievement Orientation was the highest score. If there is a theory to explain why record clerks, high school teachers, chemical sales representatives, and retail chain managers all share the same pattern of highest-held values, it is certainly not elaborated. The test author also includes, without discussion, data indicating that a sample of prisoners scored higher on the SPV's achievement scale than did a sample of college students, community college students, and a variety of high school students.

The careful reader is left with the conclusion that there is considerable confusion about exactly what is being measured by this test and a need for clarification before it can usefully be applied in clinical practice. Differential validity for the various scales is insufficiently demonstrated. Whether the test indeed measures "values" as the author contends is open to question. Moreover, variables such as "variety" and "goal orientation" may be more appropriate for describing characteristics of jobs or of the *interaction* between individuals and jobs rather than regarded as typological characteristics of persons. Longitudinal research to assess changes in persons over time as they interact with jobs or other life circumstances of known dimensions is recommended in order to better understand this issue.

Finally, the author's suggestions concerning possible uses for personnel selection are troublesome, especially the author's contention of the need for situational validation. In the context of the manual's 1984 copyright date, this recommendation suggests a curious unfamiliarity with the personnel selection literature of the last decade moving the field toward validity generalization and away from the situational specificity approach advocated by the author.

SUMMARY. The SPV itself was last revised in 1965 and there are only two references in the current (1984) manual as recent as the 1980s. This measure has had many reliability and validity studies, but remains problematic for contemporary use. Although it appears to measure its constructs reliably, there is a much more ambiguous pattern to the validity data presented. There is evidence that the test is measuring something different from abilities. There is less evidence that it is measuring something different from vocational interests.

When this test (and the more widely utilized Survey of Values) were first promulgated, there was a scarcity of tests on the commercial market and the absence of conceptual clarity was perhaps more understandable. Today, there are thousands of tests readily available for a wide variety of personality and vocational constructs and conceptual specificity is appropriately demanded. Considerable updating of this instrument and its research literature are called for if the SPV is to be of more than passing historical interest.

[79]

Teacher Assessment of Grammatical Structures. Purpose: "Developed to evaluate a child's understanding and use of the grammatical structures of English and to suggest a sequence for teaching these structures." Ages 2–4, 5–9, 9 and over; 1983; TAGS; 3 ratings per level on Imitated, Prompted, or Spontaneous Production; ratings are based on informal administration in classroom or therapy setting; individual; 3 levels; 1985 price data: $6 per 25 rating forms per level; $15 per manual (203 pages); administration time not reported; Jean S. Moog and Victoria J. Kozak; Central Institute for the Deaf.*

a) TAGS-P, PRE-SENTENCE LEVEL. Ages up to 6 years for hearing impaired, ages 2–4 for language impaired children; receptive and expressive skills.

b) TAGS-S, SIMPLE SENTENCE LEVEL. Ages 5–9 years for hearing impaired, ages 3 and over for language impaired children; expressive skills.

c) TAGS-C, COMPLEX SENTENCE LEVEL. Ages 8 and over for hearing impaired, 3.5 and over for language impaired.

Review of the Teacher Assessment of Grammatical Structures by ELIZABETH M. PRATHER,

Professor of Speech and Hearing Science, Arizona State University, Tempe, AZ:

Teacher Assessment of Grammatical Structures (TAGS) is a series of rating forms designed primarily for use by teachers of hearing-impaired children. It is reportedly also appropriate for rating normal-hearing children with serious delays in English syntax. The authors suggest that the forms are useful for (*a*) specifying the child's use of syntactic structures, (*b*) planning language instruction, (*c*) measuring and recording progress, and (*d*) reporting to parents.

No normative data have been provided to interpret a child's level of performance; the grammatical structures on each of the three forms, however, are listed in an "expected order of development." The sequenced orders were determined by the authors from experiences in teaching the hearing impaired, experiences with standardized language tests, knowledge of normal language development, and understanding how teaching the hearing-impaired parallels normal language development.

The TAGS closely resembles in content and format the Grammatical Analysis of Elicited Language (GAEL) (Moog, Kozak, & Geers, 1983). There are, however, important differences. The GAEL was standardized on hearing-impaired (aged 3 to 12 years) and normal-hearing children (aged 2½ to 5½ years) for use in a formal test setting. The TAGS provides no standardization data and no reliability or validity data. Teachers are asked to rate each structure as *Acquired* or *Emerging* from observations made during classroom activities. The teacher notes whether the child comprehends, imitates, shows prompted production, or shows spontaneous production by checking the appropriate box. The acquired-emerging distinction is made on the basis of ease of facility with which the child comprehends or uses the structure. Criteria for ratings are specified and teachers are encouraged to observe the child in enough situations to make accurate judgments.

The TAGS was developed to chart a child's understanding and use of structures in everyday environments. This information could be used to plan instructional targets and to assign children to appropriate instructional groups. Because the structures are ordered developmentally, the forms might serve as a guide to the selection of the next targets.

It would be inappropriate to categorize the TAGS as a test. It is a series of check sheets designed to help teachers observe a child's comprehension, imitation, and production of various grammatic forms. With our current emphasis on functional communication and pragmatics, these forms limited to grammar seem almost outdated.

It is unfortunate that no evidence of validity is provided. One wonders whether teachers' ratings would closely resemble those completed by trained observers within the classroom. It would also be of interest to know how a child's GAEL performance (in a structured testing session) compares to the TAGS ratings completed by the teacher. These data are not provided.

The usefulness of the TAGS would depend upon (*a*) the degree of emphasis a given teaching program places on grammatic development, and (*b*) the ability of the classroom teacher to observe and record accurately the various aspects of grammatical language.

REVIEWER'S REFERENCE

Moog, J. S., Kozak, V. J., & Geers, A. E. (1983). *Grammatical analysis of elicited language.* St. Louis, MO: Central Institute for the Deaf.

Review of the Teacher Assessment of Grammatical Structures by KENNETH G. SHIPLEY, Professor and Chairman, Department of Communicative Disorders, Laboratory School-MS 80, California State University-Fresno, Fresno, CA:

The Teacher Assessment of Grammatical Structures (TAGS) consists of an instructional manual and different rating forms for evaluating aspects of hearing-impaired children's abilities with a variety of syntactic constructions. The three scales generally correspond to children's language development and language age.

TAGS-P focuses on six types of language constructions. These include single words, two-word combinations, three-word combinations, pronouns, wh-questions, and tense markers. TAGS-S attempts to evaluate children's use of six more advanced constructions which range from noun modifiers (e.g., adjectives to demonstratives) to questions (e.g., *where* to modals like *can* and *may*). Each of these more advanced constructions is subdivided into four to six levels of specific language substructures.

The third form, TAGS-C, views six even more complex sentence-level constructions. Categories range from certain types of nouns to various question types. Again, each of these six categories contains four to six levels of substructures available for evaluation. Thus, the three rating forms include more than 220 language features and structures available for evaluation.

Each of the three TAG rating forms is administered by teacher observation. Essentially, the teacher is looking for the presence or absence of the specific words or structures under study in various classroom situations. Productions are rated as follows: imitated productions, prompted productions, and spontaneous productions. Based on multiple observations, each structure is subsequently rated as being acquired, emerging, or a possible teaching objective.

There are several very positive aspects of the TAGS. Among the most positive are the range and large number of language features that can be evaluated. Other positive features include the readability of the manual and some of the teaching examples and appropriate cautions that are outlined in the manual. For example, the authors caution that:

> Since not all possible structures are included on the TAGS rating forms, the teacher should not let the forms limit what is taught, but . . . as a guide to organize instruction. Rather than dictating what to teach, the TAGS rating forms should serve as a reminder of the wide variety of structures possible and should stimulate the teacher to think of others.

Although there are several strengths of TAGS, there are also several major weaknesses that must be noted. The most noticeable problems are the failure to address issues of validity or reliability. Validity seems to be assumed, but neither data nor an ample review of appropriate literature are presented to the reader. This is particularly apparent in the 203-page instructional manual, which contains only two fully cited references and four nonreferenced bibliographic works by TAGS' senior author.

There are vague references to validity issues as when the authors state the belief that teachers know the child best and indicate that teacher ratings are based on multiple observations. However, this does not speak to the instrument's basic validity. This surfaces as a problem because the authors recommend using a developmental teaching sequence and present verti-

cal teaching levels for "the sequence for teaching [language] structures within each grammatical category." Unfortunately, a number of these sequences fail to correspond to the current literature on children's language development. The authors offer little evidence to substantiate the developmental sequences, and no direct data are offered to the reader.

There is also a very sparse discussion of reliability issues. Reliability is affected by a variety of factors: observer's backgrounds, their training and experience, the time they have to study a child, and their knowledge of language and its development. In the absence of more precise information on how these factors affect the administration and scoring of the TAGS, users must remain cautious about the test's reliability.

In summary, TAGS presents a novel and structured method for viewing language and its development with hearing-impaired youngsters. It has been used in a number of settings and has an appearance of relatively good face validity. However, educators and clinicians need to read the manual very carefully, understand the appropriate applications of such a model, and be judicious in their consideration of the validity and reliability issues posed within this review.

[80]

A Teacher Attitude Inventory: Identifying Teacher Positions in Relation to Educational Issues and Decisions. Purpose: "Indicator of teacher attitudes regarding philosophical issues and contrasting educational practices." Teachers; 1986; TAI; for evaluation and research purposes; 5 scores: Controlling, Rigidity, Individualism, Professionalism, Total; 1986 price date: $19.95 per complete kit including 25 Inventories, 25 scoring sheets, and manual ('86, 16 pages); $6 per 25 Inventories; $6 per 25 scoring sheets; $10 per manual; (10–15) minutes; Joanne Rand Whitmore; United Educational Services, Inc.*

Review of A Teacher Attitude Inventory: Identifying Teacher Positions in Relation to Educational Issues and Decisions by MARY HENNING-STOUT, Assistant Professor, Austin College, Sherman, TX:

The Teacher Attitude Inventory (TAI) is a descriptive instrument designed to measure teacher attitudes relative to two divergent philosophical positions regarding education. This scale was originally developed to serve as a measure of the effectiveness of an inservice program designed to "encourage teachers to break away from traditional methods and to experiment with new alternatives; to attend more to individual students and their emotional needs; and to individualize instruction more often in order to increase pupil success and opportunities for self-correction." Thus, the original intent of the scale was to gauge movement toward more flexible, child-centered attitudes toward teaching.

In the 16-page manual accompanying the scale, the author suggests that application of the TAI in other educational settings could occur for purposes of evaluation and research. A number of potential uses for the inventory are presented in the manual and discussed below. Among these uses is the evaluation of prevailing attitudes to illustrate intraorganizational matches, for example, among teachers and between teachers and administrators or teachers and students.

ADMINISTRATION. The TAI takes the form of a questionnaire with 24 items. These items are presented in a 5-point Likert-type format with two contrasting educational positions at the opposite poles (e.g., "Schools are too structured these days" vs. "A major problem in today's schools is a lack of well defined structure"). Teachers indicate their position relative to these statements by marking an "X" in one of the five blanks between them. The TAI is reported to require 10–15 minutes for completion.

The author suggests that the inventory be administered in an atmosphere that encourages "unreserved self-disclosure" of educational philosophy by establishing "an open, trusting, nonjudgmental climate for 'testing.'" Although this suggestion would seem to lead to the most candid responses to the TAI, contriving such an environment would seem to be an organizational intervention that could contaminate the data gathered. This would especially be the case if the TAI were being administered in any sort of descriptive manner (i.e., for describing current attitudes in a particular educational setting). The author does briefly suggest that, for use in more rigid organizations, the TAI should be administered in such a way that the responses are anonymous. Her other suggestions for informing the respondents of the nature and use of the inventory include ethical considerations that are impressively complete.

Along with the 25 questionnaire copies included in the standard inventory packet, there are 25 scoring sheets for tabulating individual responses. This useful sheet allows for tabulation of a total score and four subscale scores. The subscales identified are intuitive and, according to the author, have not been verified with factor analysis. These subscales include items reflecting the following dimensions: "Controlling vs. Releasing, Rigidity vs. Flexibility, Individualism vs. Group-Orientation, and Interest vs. Disinterest in Professionalism." The author suggests that these subscale scores should be used with caution and that the total score seems of greater value.

PSYCHOMETRIC PROPERTIES. One distracting feature of the TAI is the significant number of typographical errors in both the manual and questionnaire. This weakness is mentioned in this section of the review because additional evidence of careless construction of the manual detracts significantly from the claims regarding the inventory's psychometric properties. The report of the project for which this scale was developed is referred to quite frequently as a source for additional statistical information. There is also frequent reference in the manual to a section of that text that would explain and present such data. No such section exists. Therefore, in spite of the author's convincing prose regarding the inventory's content validity (factor analysis reportedly supported the dichotomous nature of the polar stems) and predictive validity (evidence that attitudes indicated match with behavioral practices), the lack of supporting data presentation requires the consumer to take a great deal "on faith."

The description of the scale's construction also leaves several questions. The author reports that the items making up the scale were selected by "the research staff" as fitting with one of the dichotomous styles. There is no indication of the criteria used to select these questions. Again, the author reports successful item analysis, test-retest results, and within- and between-scale correlations but provides no data to support her statements.

A review of the project report to which the author frequently refers (Whitmore, 1974) did provide the statistical results of efforts to establish the psychometric viability of this instrument. Reliability was described as moderate and seemed low for one of the two school districts tested in the original application of this instrument. Construct validity was established with factor analysis, which verified the dichotomy represented by the items but failed to support the existence of the postulated subscales. Predictive validity was weakly supported by the data in the project report.

Whitmore (1974) called for additional research to establish the psychometric strength of the instrument. The original project employing the TAI was completed in the early 1970s. Apparently no research in response to the report author's call has occurred. The 1985 manual cites no other research beyond the 1974 project report.

PRACTICAL AND RESEARCH UTILITY. The author of the TAI presents an impressive number of practical uses for this scale. The TAI could be used by school building administrators to determine the most effective match between teachers and children with specific learning needs (e.g., more "rigid" teachers with children requiring more structure). Findings could also be used to group teachers in teams according to their educational views or to match an administrator's characteristics with those of the teachers with whom s/he will work. Measurement of faculty attitudes regarding education could guide program planners in deciding which approaches would be most effective in a given school or classroom. TAI results could also provide information useful for determining faculty development needs.

This inventory also seems to have a variety of potential uses for research. Results could be used to determine the correlation between faculty positions on the scale and the relative success of specific programs. The original use of the TAI was to measure attitude change in a pre-post test design. This use is potentially generalizable. Finally, the TAI could be used as a covariate in studies considering the success of district- or state-wide programs. The utility of this inventory is restricted only by its incomplete development as described in the preceding section.

In summary, the TAI has significant potential as a practical and research tool for individuals involved in the planning and evaluation of educational programs and organizations. The incompleteness of the inventory in its current presentation restricts its utility. Without verification of the psychometric strength of the TAI,

the consumer would be remiss in choosing this inventory for any but descriptive uses, and then without reliance on the reportedly dichotomous items as accurately representative of disparate behavioral tendencies.

REVIEWER'S REFERENCE

Whitmore, J. R. (1974). *A teacher attitude inventory: Identifying teacher positions in relation to educational issues and decisions.* (Research and Development Memorandum No. 118). Stanford, CA: Stanford University, Stanford Center for Research and Development in Teaching.

Review of A Teacher Attitude Inventory: Identifying Teacher Positions in Relation to Educational Issues and Decisions by SYLVIA ROSENFIELD, Professor of School Psychology, Temple University, Philadelphia, PA:

A Teacher Attitude Inventory (TAI), a self-report questionnaire for elementary school teachers, was developed as an indicator of teacher attitudes about philosophical issues related to contrasting educational practices. Specifically, the instrument attempted to divide teachers along a continuum between two contrasting styles: (*a*) Style One was assigned to "traditional, teacher-centered" methodology; (*b*) Style Two represented progressive, pupil-centered approaches and experimentation. Characteristics of the contrasting basic styles are described in the manual. In addition, the scale itself was divided by the author into four theoretical subscales: Rigidity, Controlling, Professionalism, and Individualism.

The instrument contains 24 items, divided into the four theoretical subscales (Rigidity, Controlling, Professionalism, and Individualism), each consisting of six items. Items were constructed by preparing statements to reflect basic attitudes along these dimensions; each statement was paired with its opposite to formulate an item. Teachers place a mark on a 5-point Likert scale between the paired dichotomous statements, expressing their tendency to agree or disagree with one of the statements in each pair.

Administration time is considered by the authors to be 10 to 15 minutes. Suggestions are given to facilitate teacher responding, including sensitivity to issues of confidentiality and explanation of the purpose of the questionnaire. Two sample items are included in the manual. Scoring is done by hand using an individual scoring sheet that enables the scorer to group the items on the subscales and indicates which 13 items are reverse scored.

The TAI was developed for a field-based project of the Stanford Center for Research and Development in Teaching (SCRDT). This project was designed as an intervention in an elementary school with a predominantly black, low SES population. The objective of the inservice program, which formed the basis of the project, was to enable the teachers to "break away from traditional methods and to experiment with new alternatives." The inventory was developed to measure the change in teacher attitudes as a result of the inservice training.

The manual indicates that SCRDT Research and Development Memorandum No. 118 (Whitmore, 1974) contains the bulk of the technical data on the TAI. No data on reliability and validity are presented in the manual itself, although there are some general statements about the research presented in the Memorandum. The Memorandum, which can be obtained for cost of xeroxing and mailing from the Center for Educational Research, cautions with the following statement: "At this stage, there is not enough evidence of the reliability and validity of the instrument for its use to be extended beyond that of qualified researchers desiring to obtain more data." No additional data are provided in the TAI Manual since the publication of the 1974 Memorandum, however.

The data presented in the Memorandum are essential to the potential user of the TAI. It is important, for example, to know that there is little evidence in the Memorandum to support the use of subscores, although the test scoring sheet continues to divide the items into the four hypothesized subscales. Factor analysis of the TAI did not support either a 2-factor or a 4-factor construct, but rather suggested a general factor. In addition, the samples used in the initial construction and validation of the questionnaire are limited to two California school districts. One was the predominantly low-SES black community with a tradition of emphasizing the 3-Rs and with firm discipline and control of pupils as the principal concern of the teachers (the district in which the inservice was provided). The contrasting district was a predominantly white, middle class community, with teachers who were frequently engaged in some form of innovative experiment in grouping or instruction. The descriptions of the schools were based on the direct experience of the test author.

Statistical analysis of the original questionnaire, which consisted of 40 items, is not reported in the Memorandum. On the revised 24-item TAI, interitem correlations were low to moderate, with low correlations between similar items. Whitmore (1974) suggested that errors may have occurred in the original pairing of statements assumed to be dichotomous and/or in assigning items to subscales. Coefficients of internal consistency for the total test varied between .76 and .84 for the samples at different times, indicating some degree of internal consistency. Test-retest reliability is hard to evaluate on the data provided, given the long period of time between testings (October and May). In the middle class school, without an intervention project, the questionnaire was moderately stable over the year (.66 for total score on an N of 29). Primary teachers appeared to be more stable than intermediate teachers, but the sample was small.

Validation studies included a factor analysis, with both a 4-factor and a 2-factor rotation examined. The findings, as noted above, indicated that one general attitude factor is the best fit for the inventory. Low reliabilities on individual items suggest caution in the use of the factor analysis results, however.

Criterion-related validity was also attempted, to predict whether teachers observed as exhibiting behavior described as Style One (traditional "3-R" teacher behavior) would receive significantly lower scores on the TAI than teachers behaving as described by Style Two (innovative, experimental teaching behavior). There were, however, large within-group variances and lack of consistent differences between groups, although Whitmore notes that differences between group means were usually in the predicted direction. There were significant differences between teachers in the two districts (which Whitmore had described as reflecting the two different styles) on TAI Total, Rigidity, and Controlling scale means; these findings were due to differences between the intermediate teachers in the two districts. Based on the informal descriptions of the two districts by Whitmore, the instrument did seem to validate her perception of the attitudes displayed. Although Whitmore provides cutoff scores for differentiating teachers as Style One or Style

Two in the manual, there does not seem to be a sound empirical foundation for their use, and she concludes the Memorandum with a call for norms to be obtained on large heterogeneous samples.

Whitmore concludes the test manual with a caution: "Until there is more extensive testing of the reliability and validity of the instrument . . . users should be cautious and tentative in using test scores in practical decision making." The instrument as developed thus far has, in fact, very limited reliability and validity data, with no compelling case for the subscales. No additional research on the TAI is reported by Whitmore between the 1974 Memorandum and the publication of the manual in 1985. However, given the increasing interest in adaptive instruction and the continuing interest in evaluating the effectiveness of inservice training, the inventory may be useful to researchers in education who are interested in teacher style and its underlying philosophical base.

REVIEWER'S REFERENCE

Whitmore, J. R. (1974). *A teacher attitude inventory: Identifying teacher positions in relation to educational issues and decisions.* (Research and Development Memorandum No. 118). Stanford, CA: Stanford University, Stanford Center for Research and Development in Teaching.

[81]

Test for Auditory Comprehension of Language, Revised Edition. Purpose: Provides a means of assessing a child's auditory-comprehension, helps to identify individuals having receptive language disorders, helps to guide the clinician toward specific areas that need additional testing, and provides a means of measuring change in auditory comprehension. Ages 3–10; 1973–85; TACL-R; guidelines for use with adults are provided; 4 scores: Word Classes and Relations, Grammatical Morphemes, Elaborated Sentences, Total; individual; 1988 price data: $105 per examiner's manual ('85, 195 pages), test book, and 25 individual record forms; $20 per 25 individual record forms; $23 per examiner's manual; $109 per microcomputer scoring program; (10–20) minutes; Elizabeth Carrow-Woolfolk; DLM Teaching Resources.*

See T3:2472 (25 references); for reviews by John T. Hatten and Huberto Molina, see 8:454 (6 references); see also T2:997A (2 references).

TEST REFERENCES

1. Fey, M. E., & Leonard, L. B. (1984). Partner age as a variable in the conversational performance of specifically language-impaired and normal-language children. *Journal of Speech and Hearing Research, 27,* 413-423.
2. Terrell, B. Y., Schwartz, R. G., Prelock, P. A., & Messick, C. K. (1984). Symbolic play in normal and language-impaired children. *Journal of Speech and Hearing Research, 27,* 424-429.
3. Tallal, P., Stark, R. E., & Mellits, D. (1985). The relationship between auditory temporal analysis and receptive language development: Evidence from studies of developmental language disorder. *Neuropsychologia, 23,* 527-534.
4. Beitchman, J. H., Nair, R., Clegg, M., & Patel, P. G. (1986). Prevalence of speech and language disorders in 5-year-old kindergarten children in the Ottawa-Carleton region. *Journal of Speech and Hearing Disorders, 51,* 98-110.
5. Brinton, B., Fujiki, M., Winkler, E., & Loeb, D. F. (1986). Responses to requests for clarification in linguistically normal and language-impaired children. *Journal of Speech and Hearing Disorders, 51,* 370-378.
6. Dollaghan, C., & Kaston, N. (1986). A comprehension monitoring program for language impaired children. *Journal of Speech and Hearing Disorders, 51,* 264-271.

Review of the Test for Auditory Comprehension of Language, Revised Edition by NICHOLAS W. BANKSON, Professor and Chair, Department of Communication Disorders, Boston University, Boston, MA:

The Test for Auditory Comprehension of Language, Revised Edition (TACL-R) is an improved version of the original TACL. The need for a revision was based on studies and critiques of the original test. While the test organization, format, and construction of the TACL-R are similar to the original, there is substantial increase in the depth of performance assessed with the revised version.

The TACL-R is an individually administered test for measuring auditory comprehension of language. Specifically, test items are organized into three, 40-item sections, with each section assessing several linguistic categories. Section I assesses word classes and relations, and is comprised of 33 single word stimuli (e.g., girl, box, round, giving), and seven items that involve "word relations" (e.g., a bird and a cat; riding a little bicycle). Included among the single word stimuli are several items from each of the following categories: nouns, verbs, modifiers/qualifiers, quantity, and direction.

Section II is called Grammatical Morphemes, and is comprised of short sentence verbal stimuli (e.g., The circle is around the car) that are designed to reflect semantic modulations of other structures, such as specificity, number, aspect, tense, and mood. Items reflecting each of the following categories are included in this section: prepositions, pronouns (the manual provides the rationale for placement of pronouns in this section, rather than Section I), noun number, noun case, verb tense, verb number, noun-verb agreement, and derivational suffixes. Section III, Elaborated Sentences, assesses comprehension of more complex sentences of various types including interrogatives, negatives, active and passive voice, direct and indirect object, embedded and partially and completely conjoined sentences.

Each stimulus item is comprised of a word or sentence presented by the examiner, and a corresponding pictorial plate that has three black and white line drawings. One of the three pictures for each item illustrates the meaning of the word, morpheme, or syntactic structure being tested. The other two pictures illustrate either two semantic or grammatical contrasts of the stimulus, or one contrast and one decoy. The subject is required to point to the picture that he or she believes best represents the meaning of that which is spoken by the examiner. Test items within each section are ordered according to difficulty. Basal and ceiling rules for scoring are provided. Although the test manual indicates that the average testing time is 10 minutes, children with language difficulties are likely to require more time.

The TACL-R Examiner's Manual is a more thorough manual than is often available for speech and language tests. Items such as the theoretical base of the test, the revision process, item selection, test standardization, reliability and validity, and interpretation and use of the test, represent individual chapters in this manual. The test user can obtain a great deal of information about assessment of language comprehension, test construction, and the nature of TACL-R with this manual.

Several measures of test reliability are reported. Standard errors of measurement are reported for each section by age groupings, and are relatively low. Internal consistency is demonstrated with a split-half reliability of .96 for the total score. Test-retest reliabilities range from .89 to .91 across the various age levels. Because test scoring is a straightforward, objective procedure, intertester reliability was not reported.

Three types of validity assessments are reported for the TACL-R. Content validity is supported by descriptions of the rationale and procedures involved in item selection, including examination of the instrument by numerous reviewers and test users. One emergent issue is the relationship between language comprehension and sentence length. In other words, an examiner may wonder whether a child's failure on an item is a function of item complexity or the length of the stimulus itself. This question was addressed by correlating the percentage of subjects in the norming and in the clinical samples that passed each item in Section III, Elaborated Sentences, with the number of syllables in each item. On the basis of these figures the author reported "this amount of variance represents such a negligible effect when compared to the remaining variance (92.2% to 98.8%), that one can confidently conclude that item length has little effect on a subject's performance on the TACL-R."

Construct validity is demonstrated through data indicating that subject performance is better on simpler as opposed to complex items, that performance improves with age, and that subjects identified as having language disorders performed more poorly than normals. Concurrent validity is reflected in high correlation between scores on the TACL-R and each of the following: the original TACL; Auditory Association, Auditory Reception, and Grammatic Closure subtests of the Illinois Test of Psycholinguistic Abilities; the Peabody Picture Vocabulary Test; the Sequences Inventory of Communication Development; and the Stanford-Binet Intelligence Scale.

Normative data on the TACL-R are provided for children ages 36–119 months and for grades kindergarten through four. Raw scores can be transformed to percentile ranks, z-scores, and T scores. Non-normalized standard scores are also provided for use with extremely low or high scores. The norming sample represented four geographical regions of the United States, and included 1,003 children, including a total of 161 from ethnic/minority groups. In addition, three levels of family occupation groups were included in the sample.

Although the current trend in language assessment is away from the administration of formal tests that focus on one aspect of language behavior (in this instance auditory comprehension), the test can be highly useful if norm referenced data on a language skill is needed. This would be the case if one needs to know where a particular child stands with regard to his or her peer group, or one wishes to measure changes in behavior over time. The careful work undertaken on this instrument will allow one to use the instrument with confidence for such purposes.

Assuming the clinicians who use the TACL-R may be as interested in guidelines for remediation as in normative data, we must also consider the instrument from this perspective. Although knowing the section level(s) (I, II, III) in which a client has difficulties has clinical utility, of more interest may be the specific categories within each section that may have posed problems. While the score form for the original TACL provided for this type of analysis, the revised scoring form does not. Rather, the clinician must consult page 92 of the Examiner's Manual and do his/her own item analysis. Since this process is cumbersome, the test would be improved, in my opinion, by more readily accommodating this type of analysis through the scoring form. I would see this type of analysis being primarily of benefit to clinicians in the early years of their career, since it provides a way of structuring observations that often come more readily to experienced diagnosticians.

In summary, this test is as thorough a formal measure of auditory comprehension of language as is on the market. The revised form represents careful and systematic efforts by the author to develop a standardized test that measures particular facets of auditory comprehension in a controlled situation. It can be particularly useful as part of a comprehensive language evaluation of children referred for language disorders.

Review of the Test for Auditory Comprehension of Language, Revised Edition by WILLIAM O. HAYNES, Associate Professor, Department of Communication Disorders, Auburn University, Auburn, AL:

The Test for Auditory Comprehension of Language, Revised Edition (TACL-R) has been changed significantly from the previous editions of the TACL. Carrow-Woolfolk and her associates have done a competent job of researching, piloting, and presenting the TACL-R. All aspects of the revision are explained in detail in a 185-page examiner's manual. The documentation is extensive and a significant improvement over the 30 pages of explanation and data that preceded the 1973 version of the test. The plan for the revision of the TACL was well thought out and systemati-

cally completed. The revisions began with a thorough literature review including surveys of working clinicians, published reviews of the TACL, and studies published between 1971–85. The literature review also included new information on language development and the processes involved in comprehension. Pilot administrations of the TACL-R were used to evaluate needed changes in test items and scoring conventions. The revision plan resulted in alterations in the general format of the test, standardization methods, and the documentation provided in the manual.

THEORETICAL FRAMEWORK AND PURPOSE. A criticism of the TACL had been that it was not broad enough to really assess comprehension and that it focused on literal meanings of linguistic forms (Rees and Shulman, 1978). In short, the TACL did not measure comprehension as it occurs in the natural environment with discourse situations, idiomatic usage, metaphoric language, and inferencing. The TACL-R is quite clear in its stated purpose: It was not designed to test all aspects of comprehension, just literal meanings in a very specific examination context. Thus, the TACL-R does not purport to be an all-inclusive comprehension measure, which would be all but impossible to design. Many authorities have recommended nonstandardized assessment of comprehension, but still there remains a need for standardized instruments to help determine if behavior falls within the range of normal variation. The TACL-R certainly does not claim to do anything it does not accomplish. The examiners' manual has many disclaimers and cautions regarding test theory, interpretation, and use. These are appropriate and useful for both novice and experienced test users. An informative review of comprehension theory, ways to measure comprehension, test content, standardized versus nonstandardized approaches, comprehension in language disordered populations, and comparisons of the content and format of various comprehension tests is included.

GENERAL FORMAT. Several changes have been made in the organization of the test. First, the Spanish version of the instrument has been eliminated. Second, the TACL-R is divided into three sections which analyze the comprehension of word classes and relations, grammatical morphemes, and elaborated sentences (coordination, negatives, imperatives, passives, subordination, and embedding). The section on elaborated sentences has been greatly expanded in the TACL-R. A third change is the expansion of the age range, from a ceiling age of 6-11 to 9-11. Fourth, the picture stimuli have been redrawn and include more minorities. Fifth, the sections are organized in developmental order according to Brown (1973). A final format change is that basal and ceiling scores have been established so that the time of test administration can be more efficiently related to both lower and higher achieving children.

STANDARDIZATION. The norms for the TACL-R were based on 1,003 normal language children between 3-0 and 9-11 years. In addition, 60 normal adults, 234 speech/language disordered children, 16 hearing impaired children, 11 mentally retarded children, and 7 adult aphasic patients were tested. The normal subjects were selected using stratified random sampling. There were a variety of geographical, occupational, and minority populations represented. Several reliability coefficients were calculated on the TACL-R. Standard errors of measurement are available for each grade and age level on all three sections and appear acceptable. Both split-half and test-retest reliabilities were well within acceptable limits. The manual includes a discussion of content validity, construct validity, and criterion-related validity. The normal age groups differed significantly from one another and the norm sample also differed significantly from a sample of language impaired children in a series of comparisons. The TACL-R was correlated with the Illinois Test of Psycholinguistic Abilities (ITPA), Peabody Picture Vocabulary Test (PPVT), Sequenced Inventory of Communicative Development (SICD), and the Stanford-Binet Intelligence Scale; the majority of correlations were significant. Finally, the normative sample showed no significant performance difference among groups based on sex, socioeconomic status, or ethnic origin. Thus, the author suggests that only a single set of norms is necessary for scoring.

The inclusion of normalized standard scores in addition to percentile ranks is an improvement over earlier editions. The TACL-R provides z-scores, T scores, deviation quotients, and normal curve equivalents in addition to percentile ranks for age and grade level. A table of age equivalent scores is also included. The inclusion of standard scores allows more precise interpretation and comparison of TACL-R scores with other tests.

ADMINISTRATION AND SCORING. The TACL-R takes between 5–20 minutes to administer depending on the child. Strict guidelines are provided regarding instruction, establishing basal and ceiling levels, marking responses, and use of the tables to convert raw scores to any of the measures mentioned in the previous section. It is recommended that the scores be graphically displayed on the record form as standard scores with the confidence intervals calculated using the *SEM* data provided in tabular form. The final two chapters in the manual are devoted to test interpretation and case examples.

In sum, this reviewer feels that the TACL-R is a well-designed and psychometrically sound instrument for evaluating limited aspects of comprehension. Carrow-Woolfolk realistically views the TACL-R as a general guide that may suggest problem areas in need of further exploration with specific informal measures.

[82]

Test for Examining Expressive Morphology. Purpose: "Developed to help clinicians evaluate expressive morpheme development with children whose language skills range from three to eight years of age." Ages 3-0 to 8-12; 1983; TEEM; individual; 1987 price data: $24.95 per complete set including 25 scoring forms, test, and manual (43 pages); $10 per 25 scoring forms; (5–7) minutes; Kenneth G. Shipley, Terry A. Stone, and Marlene B. Sue; Communication Skill Builders.*

Review of the Test for Examining Expressive Morphology by DORIS V. ALLEN, Professor of Audiology, Wayne State University, Detroit, MI:

The Test for Examining Expressive Morphology (TEEM) is a well-constructed instrument that provides information about a child's development of bound morphemes. The test contains 54 items distributed as follows: present progressive (4), plurals (14), possessives (7), third person singular (7), past tense (12), and derived adjectives (10). A picture-presentation format is used, accompanied by sentence-completion statements by the examiner, such as "Here is a boat. Here are two _____." The pictures are standard black-and-white line drawings similar to those used in many other instruments for young children. The test booklet is approximately 5 x 8 inches and spiral bound—a convenient size and format for presentation. Average test time is 6.5 minutes.

The instrument was thoroughly researched in its preliminary as well as its final stages. Prestandardization testing was conducted with 40 normally developing children ranging in age from 3 years through 6 years 12 months. Construct validity and concurrent validity were estimated for this sample; estimates of validity were above .8 and the choice of criterion for each was logical. High inter- and intratester reliability were also obtained (.95 and .94).

Standardization on 500 children, ages 3 through 7 years 12 months, followed. Descriptions of various characteristics of the sample and where/how the children were obtained are reported, important information for users. The results of data analyses for age and sex differences are described. At the youngest age levels (3-year-olds), significant differences at 6-month age intervals were reported, while differences at 12-month intervals were significant at 4 years and older. Sex differences were not found at any age level. The data for the standardization sample and the prestandardization sample were comparable even though the samples differed in terms of size, location, and researcher. Thus, the test deserves to be characterized as well researched and well documented.

The instructions for administration and scoring are clear and detailed. Directions for interpretation of scores are given with suggestions for intervention/therapy programs. The authors point out the limitations of their instrument and make suggestions for alternate procedures (e.g., language samples or presentation of additional items testing the target concept) to confirm morphemes for which the child may need clinical intervention.

Overall, this is a well-designed instrument that should be useful to speech-language pathologists who wish to evaluate expressive morpheme development in children. It is a test designed for clinical use—examiners should be knowledgeable about child language development and experienced in phonetics, both for recording responses and for hearing subtle differences between endings. The authors are to be especially commended for the manual—it is a model of clarity and completeness while remaining brief and direct.

Review of the Test for Examining Expressive Morphology by JANICE A. DOLE, Assistant Professor of Education, Michigan State University, East Lansing, MI:

The Test for Examining Expressive Morphology (TEEM) was developed "to help clinicians evaluate expressive morpheme development" in young children. The individually administered test consists of 54 items designed to measure children's correct use of six major morphemes (present progressive, plurals, possessives, third person singulars, past tense, and derived adjectives). Children are presented with a stimulus picture and asked to complete a target sentence, (e.g., "Here is a boat. Here are two _____."). The test is designed to be used with children ranging from 3 to 8 years of age.

ADMINISTRATION AND SCORING. The test is simple and straightforward to administer. Directions in the manual are clear. Examiners are presented with helpful information about what to do if children do not respond appropriately to the practice items. The information also details how much prompting can be given legitimately.

Explicit information about scoring the responses also is found in the manual. Care is taken to caution the examiner not to count subtle speech idiosyncracies as errors. In addition, sample test protocols are provided to demonstrate the entire scoring procedure. The scoring procedures are easy to follow, and should present no problems for examiners.

NORMATIVE INFORMATION. The TEEM was standardized by comparing the results of tests administered to a group of 40 subjects in Reno, Nevada (prestandardization) to a group of 500 subjects in Fresno, California (standardization). Preschools and schools used during standardization were selected to represent "middle class" populations and achievement test scores near the "national median." Students in both samples were said to exhibit "normal speech, language, and hearing abilities."

Statistical results from the prestandardization and standardization samples are quite similar. Reliability coefficients and age differences were comparable, and no significant differences in scores emerged between the two groups. Despite these similarities, the standardization of the TEEM must be regarded as inadequate. Larger sample sizes and a more heterogeneous population are needed to justify placing confidence in this test.

RELIABILITY. Test-retest reliability was determined by having a clinician administer the test to 12 randomly selected children on two occasions. An r of .94 was reported, a correlation sufficiently high to establish more than adequate reliability. But, considerably larger numbers of students are needed to have any confidence in the reported reliability. Intertester reliability was determined by having different clinicians administer the test to 12 different, randomly selected children. The obtained scores were then used to calculate an intertester reliability of .95. Again, this correlation is high and would, with larger samples of students, buttress confidence in the reliability of the test.

VALIDITY. The manual reports data on three types of validity: content, construct, and concurrent. The reporting of content validity is confusing. I had to reread different parts of the manual to see how content validity was established. The allomorph variations used in the test were determined through research on children's language development at different ages. The stimulus word items, the morphemes, were selected from lists of words children first learn and lists of words for primary readers. These words were then tested for familiarity with normal preschoolers. These procedures appear to be adequate for establishing content validity.

Construct and concurrent validity present more serious problems for interpretation. First, the manual states that research indicates that morpheme development is "related to children's overall language development and, to a lesser degree, their age." Construct validity therefore was determined by correlating the TEEM scores with children's ages. A Pearson r of .87 was reported. This correlation, in and of itself, is not adequate to establish the construct validity of the TEEM. After all, we know that many cognitive as well as linguistic abilities improve with age—children's abilities to infer, to recall, and to remember, etc. A better indicator of the test's validity would be to correlate the test with an established test of children's overall early language development. The Test of Early Language Development (TELD) is one such measure, and this reviewer would have far more confidence if the TEEM correlated highly with a language measure such

as the TELD. Or, better still, the TEEM should be correlated with a battery of language measures which clearly reflect the language abilities of children. Thus the manual is inadequate in providing sufficient evidence for the construct validity of the TEEM.

The manual does report the correlation between the TEEM and the Peabody Picture Vocabulary Test (PPVT), and this correlation of .8 is used as evidence for the concurrent validity of the TEEM. But the TEEM manual states that the PPVT is a language measure, when, in fact, it is not. The PPVT is a vocabulary test, and therefore inadequate for demonstrating either the construct or concurrent validity of the TEEM. The correlation of .84 between the PPVT and the TEEM is problematic, because it suggests that the TEEM measures something very similar to what the PPVT measures—perhaps natural language development, intelligence, or both.

There are additional problems with the validity of the TEEM. The manual states that the test could be administered by a "clinician or an educator," but why would either want to give this test? Research clearly demonstrates, and this test corroborates the fact that morphologic development advances with age and is part of natural language development. Why, then, would someone give this test as opposed to a test that measures more globally expressive and/or receptive language? One answer might be to screen children who are having language problems in this particular area. This use of the test is hinted at in the manual, which indicates that "the TEEM may be useful for. . . . language-delayed or language-disordered children," but absolutely no information or guidance is provided for clinicians or educators about how to use the test for this purpose. Furthermore, the test was not administered to any language-delayed or disordered children as part of the standardization process. Is there any relationship between children who are language-delayed and low scores on this test? The answer to this question is important for determining the usefulness of the TEEM with this particular population.

Another reason to give the TEEM might be to diagnose certain morphological problems exhibited by second language learners or dialect differences exhibited by nonstandard speakers of English. These purposes are also suggested in the manual, but no assistance is provided as to what differences might be found, or what those differences might suggest for remediation. The manual does caution the clinician about interpreting and reporting results obtained from nonstandard speakers of English, but this caution is inadequate.

SUMMARY. The TEEM is an individually administered measure of young children's morphological development. It is a quick, easy-to-administer test, but its usefulness to clinicians and educators is questionable. First, the standardization sample must be regarded as inadequate. Second, reliability coefficients, though high, were established with very small samples. Third, the test has not been adequately correlated with more global language measures.

Perhaps the biggest problem with this test is that clinicians and educators who might want to use the test are not provided with enough information in the manual to guide them beyond the administration and scoring of the test. How should clinicians interpret the test results? What do they mean? And what should clinicians do with the information? Should they teach morphemes and allomorphs directly? What are the consequences of direct teaching for different language abilities of children? And how does morphological development relate to overall language development? Until some of these practical, philosophical, and research questions are answered, consumers might be well advised to seek more global measures of language development.

[83]

Test of Articulation Performance—Diagnostic. Purpose: "Designed to provide information that is useful in planning and implementing remedial programs." Ages 3–8; 1983; TAP-D; 6 areas: Isolated Words, Distinctive Features, Selective Deep Test, Continuous Speech, Stimulability, Verbal Communication Scales; Verbal Communication Scales available as separate; individual; 1985 price data: $68 per test kit including manual (53 pages), diagnostic picture cards, 25 test forms, and complete verbal communication scales; $12 per 25 test forms; $25 per diagnostic picture cards; $18 per verbal communication scales; $17 per manual; no time limit; Brian R. Bryant and Deborah L. Bryant; PRO-ED, Inc.*

Review of the Test of Articulation Performance—Diagnostic by NICHOLAS W. BANKSON, Professor and Chair, Department of Com- munication Disorders, Boston University, Boston, MA:

Bryant and Bryant have made a commendable attempt to develop in a single articulation assessment instrument the breadth of phonological sampling that is called for in a diagnostic battery. Although there are some notable shortcomings, there are also some very positive attributes to this multi-step assessment tool.

First, by assessing two consonants in each of 81 stimulus words, an acceptable sample is obtained of consonant productions in single words. The scoring sheet is designed to reflect the fact that most phonemes are sampled more than three times and is organized so that the examiner can record the percentage of time a sound is produced correctly in the isolated words sample. The scoring sheet also facilitates a place, manner, and voicing pattern analysis (erroneously referred to in the test as a "distinctive feature" analysis).

The Test of Articulation Performance—Diagnostic (TAP-D) calls for stimulability testing of error productions at syllable, word, and sentence levels. Continuous speech is also assessed using the same words sampled in the isolated words portion of the instrument. Continuous speech can be assessed either through sentences that are imitated, or a list of sentences that are read. A truly unique aspect of the instrument consists of guidelines for the clinician to use stimulus words to assess "adjacent phonemes," or in other words to perform a "deep test" on selected error productions.

Test reliability is well documented as far as internal consistency and test-retest performance are concerned. Although interjudge reliability for scoring the instrument is reported as 95% among eight judges, the exact procedure for determining reliability is not reported. Whether this figure reflects point-to-point agreement or some overall averaging of correct/incorrect judgements is not clear. Intrajudge reliability on the instrument is not reported. Concurrent and construct validity of the test are acceptable.

A major shortcoming of an instrument such as this, which seeks to be broad based enough to be considered "diagnostic" and also includes phonological pattern analysis among its aims, is the manner in which patterns among errors are analyzed. The place-manner-voicing analysis mentioned earlier is fine, but is a very basic type of pattern analysis. Current emphasis on phonological process occurrence and analysis suggests that some type of process analysis could strengthen the instrument. By transcribing all segments in the 81 stimulus words and then looking for processes among these transcriptions, response data could be more efficaciously analyzed. Clinically, phonological process analysis has been shown to be more relevant than distinctive feature-type pattern analysis; however, as indicated earlier, this instrument does not really facilitate the distinctive feature-type pattern analysis that clinicians look for when they see this term.

Although the instrument provides for a deep test analysis of error productions, the procedures for doing this are cumbersome. The examiner must determine the contexts he/she wishes to test by reviewing the contextual possibilities among the stimulus words and then employ selected stimulus pictures. It would save considerable examiner time if the manual prescribed the items that could be used for contextual testing of each target sound.

Clinicians should be aware that the instrument does not assess all consonant sounds, but only those "that occurred most frequently" on two measures of sound productions. In addition, vowel sounds are not formally assessed. Consonant blends are tested. The instrument does not include a sample of "spontaneous" continuous speech (not imitated, not read), which is something that should be a part of any articulation assessment that is considered "diagnostic" in nature.

An interesting procedure that is related to the phonological assessment, and yet is a separate instrument, is the Verbal Communication Scale. There are three separate scales: student, teacher, and parent scales. These scales, which include separate sets of 20–25 questions each, are designed to assess attitudes toward the clients' speech and language. This information may ultimately be of value in case selection and/or treatment. Limited reliability and validity data are presented. However, the ultimate value of the instrument will be determined by the extent to which a clinician may make practical use of the information. The student scale appears to have value for older children, and the other scales may have value with particular parents and teachers.

The test manual is clear and concise in its presentation; however, the background information regarding phonology/articulation is often superficial and dated. For example, the term "articulation" is used throughout, even though the term "phonology" is increasingly being used in the literature. The inappropriate use of the term "distinctive features" has already been cited. Although the manual indicates that articulation and intelligence are related, this statement is true only for those with below normal intelligence. Information contained in the manual could easily be corrected and made more substantial and does not constitute a flaw of the instrument itself.

In summary, this test pulls together procedures that traditionally have been a part of separate tests that have been used together as a phonological/articulation test battery. Physical properties of this test (black and white pictures, small print for scoring sheet) may make it hard to compete with some of the existing, more attractively produced instruments. In addition, the lack of normative data may decrease its viability compared to other instruments. In spite of these limitations, however, the TAP-D can provide clinicians with a reasonably comprehensive sample of a client's phonological/articulatory productions.

Review of the Test of Articulation Performance—Diagnostic by LAWRENCE J. TURTON, Professor of Speech-Language Pathology, Indiana University of Pennsylvania, Indiana, PA:

The Test of Articulation Performance—Diagnostic (TAP-D) is an ambitious attempt to provide a comprehensive test for articulation disorders. Bryant and Bryant have taken the major step of trying to include multiple testing modes and analytical procedures in one testing battery. The TAP-D consists of single word stimuli, deep-testing, and sentence testing through imitation or reading. Not all tests are administered to each child; the tests administered depend upon the age level of the child. The manual provides for analysis by percent correct, coarticulation effects, error pattern, distinctive features, phonetic inventory, continuous speech, and stimulability. Only phonological analyses are omitted as a possible source of interpretive data for a clinician.

The core stimulus for virtually all of these analyses is a set of 81 words depicted with line drawings to test 23 consonants in the word-initial or word-final positions, 12 blends, and 13 vowels. The words were selected from standard word lists to control for familiarity and age. All of the analyses except continuous speech and stimulability are computed on the responses to words. The deep-testing is performed on those phonemes judged by the clinician to be misarticulated and is accomplished by combining pictures from the single word stimuli. Clinicians will find this very awkward because the picture cards are relatively large and are not bound, making attempts to combine them into spondaic word patterns most difficult.

Only the responses to single words testing word-initial or word-final are incorporated into the distinctive feature analysis. For some reason, the authors decided to disregard responses for blends or sentence stimuli from this analysis. Indeed, clinicians need to be aware of the fact that the "distinctive feature" analysis is actually a phonetic feature analysis and not truly a distinctive feature analysis. This decision is most remarkable in light of the fact that the authors indicate in the manual that they reviewed all the primary sources on distinctive features but still elected to adopt an analysis that stresses phonetic features.

The decision to use a phonetic feature model preempts the need to do the phonetic inventory described separately from the "distinctive feature" analysis, if the clinician includes all instances of the production of a sound disregarding correctness (Turton, 1973). Furthermore, inclusion of the data from the sentences would strengthen this analysis because the words are embedded in the sentences in such a way that all responses are utterance-medial and will yield more information on coarticulation effects.

Clinicians will also get a more accurate percentage of correctness in the single word test if they ignore the vowel productions and divide the total correct for consonants by 146 rather than 164 (74 for initial position; 72 for final). There are so few instances of vowels in the test that there is a high probability that the children will produce them correctly and the percentage derived from the computation will be inflated.

Bryant and Bryant are to be congratulated for actually attempting to obtain data on the reliability and validity of their instrument. It was most refreshing to open a manual on an articulation test and find a comprehensive section on these critical measures. Unfortunate-

ly, except for two measures, they apparently used only normal children in the standardization studies. Their data base would have been strengthened considerably if they had repeated the reliability and validity studies with samples of children who misarticulate. Reliability can be demonstrated easily with normal children who make few errors, yielding virtually exact patterns of variance on all measures. Clinicians need to know how stable scores are with children who have problems.

Validity studies provide some evidence of the appropriateness of this test with handicapped children. One construct-validity study involved a comparison between normal and misarticulating children. The differences between the groups were statistically significant at the .001 level, suggesting that the test could distinguish between two different populations. The most striking observation based upon the validity studies is that the TAP-D correlates so highly with other instruments that one has to question why it should be chosen over older tests. Bryant and Bryant fail to point out that using their test would be more efficient because a clinician has all the various testing modes available in one packet. This fact would preclude the need for a school clinician to carry multiple tests as she/he travels from school to school, a strong argument in its favor.

Included in the test packet is a set of attitudinal scales called the Verbal Communication Scales. These scales are designed to be administered to the child using a yes/no response or to parents or teachers using a Likert-type scale. Standardization data and percentiles are included in a separate manual. However, the authors do not provide an analytical system to allow a clinician to use the data in the decision-making process. The scales are an interesting attempt to highlight the social impact of an articulation disorder but they are not central to the decision to place a child in therapy. More importantly, the authors do not provide specific treatment procedures to help the clinician and child cope with the social impact other than articulation treatment.

The TAP-D fails at the same clinical step as most of its predecessors. Decision making is left totally to the discretion of the individual clinician. There are no norms or standards available to suggest who is placed in treatment or the course of treatment. Indeed, a clinician can ignore the elaborate analyses described in the manual and make the diagnostic decisions on the basis of any standard she/he selects. Once again, the profession has an elaborate set of stimuli to purchase but no standards for determining whether a child is normal or handicapped. Consequently, clinicians would be wise to save money and create their own set of testing stimuli and make decisions from the responses to those stimuli.

REVIEWER'S REFERENCE

Turton, L. J. (1973). Diagnostic implications of articulation testing. In W. D. Wolfe & D. J. Goulding (Eds.), *Articulation and learning* (pp. 195-218). Springfield, IL: Charles C. Thomas.

[84]

Test of Pragmatic Skills, Revised Edition.
Purpose: Designed to provide information on children's use of language to signify conversational intent. Ages 3-0 to 8-11; 1985–86; optional language sampling supplement is provided in test materials; 5 scores: Playing With Puppets, Playing With Pencil and Sheet of Paper, Playing With Telephones, Playing With Blocks, Total; individual; 1987 price data: $59 per manipulatives, manual (23 pages), and 25 scoring forms; $24.95 per 25 scoring forms; administration time not reported; Brian B. Shulman; Communication Skill Builders.*

Review of the Test of Pragmatic Skills, Revised Edition by MARTIN FUJIKI, Associate Professor of Speech Pathology and Audiology, University of Nevada School of Medicine, Reno, NV:

In recent years pragmatics has attracted increased attention from individuals interested in language disorders in children. With this increased interest has come the need for clinical tools to assess this area. The Test of Pragmatic Skills is an attempt to address this need.

The Test of Pragmatic Skills is designed to assess "children's use of language to signify conversational intent." As such, the test examines the child's ability to produce 10 different "conversational intentions." This is done in four assessment tasks (playing with puppets, playing with pencil and sheets of paper, playing with telephones, and playing with blocks). In each of these tasks, the examiner provides the child with various probes (questions and statements) designed to elicit various speech acts. The child receives a score representing his/her performance on each of the four tasks, as well as a mean composite score. These scores are used to compare the child's performance to that of the normative population.

The value of calculating scores for each of the individual assessment tasks is questionable. Although the normative data suggest that certain tasks are more difficult than others for various age groups, there does not appear to be any diagnostic significance in these differences. If there is specific information to be gained from these scores, it is not indicated in the manual. The test user should be aware that scores for specific intentions (e.g., requesting) are not provided.

High interexaminer and test-retest reliability figures are reported in the test manual; however, internal consistency is not addressed. Test validity is only briefly discussed. For example, the entire discussion of the test's construct and content validity is as follows: "To ensure that the Test of Pragmatic Skills sampled pragmatic behavior, a variety of speech acts and assessment contexts was included in the test construction. The test elicits conversational intentions from the child in a variety of guided play contexts. The test's theoretical bases substantiate and describe its construct and content validity." Although more extensive, the discussion of criterion-related validity is also limited. Such a brief treatment of validity is unacceptable in a standardized measure. Without further data, the validity of this measure is questionable. Further, the situations in which the conversational intentions are elicited are relatively limited compared to the number of situations a child deals with each day.

The manual implies that information from the test may be used to identify treatment targets (see discussion on page 10 of the manual). In this regard, the author states that specific deficit areas may be identified by examining the summary sheet and score sheet, and that specific attention should be focused on items receiving a score of 1 or 0 (the two lowest scores possible on a 0 through 5 scale). It is the opinion of this reviewer that specific treatment decisions cannot be made on the basis of these test results alone. Any attempt to do so would be at best problematic for the following reasons. First, the test evaluates specific conversational intentions on a limited number of trials in a limited conversational setting. As such it does not test a broad spectrum of behaviors. Further, the test items are not analyzed in enough detail to make a sound clinical decision possible. Before it would be possible to confidently make treatment decisions regarding the child's ability to produce a specific conversational intention, the behavior would have to be observed in a variety of situations on numerous occasions.

Secondly, there are a number of other linguistic deficits outside the realm of pragmatics that might be the basis for a low score on this instrument. For example, a child with severe verbal apraxia might produce limited responses, and thus earn a poor score, even though the child might not demonstrate specific pragmatic difficulties. To the author's credit, it is noted in the test manual that this instrument should be used in conjunction with other language assessment tools.

The Language Sampling Supplement is an optional section of the test evaluating four aspects of discourse: verbal turntaking, speaker dominance, topic maintenance, and topic change. A major weakness of this supplement is the simplified manner in which these parameters are examined. For example, consider topic maintenance and topic change. As viewed by the Language Sampling Supplement, topic maintenance and change are examined only in terms of how long the child talks on topic. However, such a procedure fails to deal with a number of significant variables. For example, topic maintenance may be heavily influenced by the speaker's interest and knowledge of the topic, the speaker's social relationship with the listener, and the conversational situation.

No normative data are provided for the Language Sampling Supplement. To be fair, this measure is an informal procedure, and as such might not be expected to provide norms. However, the question of separating normal from disordered behavior is one of central importance, and the test user is left to his/her own devices to make this decision. Because current research has not definitively specified normative information on these conversational parameters, this is an extremely difficult task. Further, the casual manner in which these behaviors are approached in the manual may suggest to some test users that these judgments can be made confidently on the basis of linguistic intuition. This is a questionable assumption. Those users who are searching for clinical guidelines will be disappointed.

In summary, although the Test of Pragmatic Skills provides the clinician with a certain amount of structure with which to view prag- matic behavior, it also has a number of limitations. When the advantages of using the test are considered in conjunction with these limitations, the Test of Pragmatic Skills, Revised Edition has little to offer the clinician that could not be obtained in a traditional language sample.

Review of the Test of Pragmatic Skills, Revised Edition by BARBARA LAPP GUTKIN, Speech-Language Clinician, Lincoln Public Schools, Lincoln, NE:

The Test of Pragmatic Skills by Brian B. Schulman is a unique language test designed to measure the ability of children ages 3 years to 8 years 11 months to use language appropriately in different natural contexts. Given the growing body of literature on the importance of pragmatic language abilities, a standardized measure designed to evaluate these abilities in young children is essential. The Test of Pragmatic Skills purports to address this need. Responses are quantified through a norm-referenced standardized test that is more conversational and naturalistic than most standardized language measures currently available. Children's abilities to express specific conversational intentions through speech acts are measured. A list of 10 conversational intentions probed by the test (e.g., requesting information, rejection, responding, informing) is provided by the author along with a description of behaviors the child could exhibit to demonstrate these intentions. To understand the intention or purpose of the child's speech acts, the discourse must be viewed in the context of the conversation, observing both the verbal and nonverbal cues used by the speaker to express meaning to the listener.

The author operationalizes his purpose through the use of four tasks likely to be of high interest to young children: puppet play, a pencil and paper task, toy telephones, and wooden blocks. A clinician, while taking on the role of a child's playmate, is able to systematically observe a child's performance in using language for varying speech acts in the listener and speaker roles. During administration, video taping or audio taperecording with written notes on nonverbal behaviors is crucial for the accurate recording and scoring of results. Responses are rated for their appropriateness in the conversational context and for response length on a 5-point scale.

When scoring responses, this test provides greater flexibility than found in the majority of commercially available language tests because responses can receive full credit even if the response does not contain the specific words shown on the sample response form. Because specific words are not required, children who may feel uncooperative during the test administration or who do not know certain information can receive credit for context-appropriate expressions of negative intentions such as statements like "I don't know" or "I don't want to tell you."

For children who approximate or exceed the mean performance value on the Test of Pragmatic Skills or for whom the clinician thinks the problem lies in discourse rather than specific conversational intention, the author provides the Language Sampling Supplement. The use of this supplement is optional. Specific discourse behaviors that can be evaluated in the Language Sampling Supplement include verbal turntaking, speaker dominance, topic maintenance, and topic change. The author describes various formulas for analyzing the discourse behaviors but supplies no theoretical or statistical basis for his analysis.

Unfortunately, the Test of Pragmatic Skills is quite weak from a psychometric perspective. For example, the manual does not provide enough information regarding the reliability of the test. While impressive interexaminer and test-retest (3-week interval) reliability coefficients are reported (.92 and .96, respectively), these data are the result of only two studies. Above and beyond this, the manual devotes a total of only five sentences to these topics, leaving the reader with no clear understanding of the quality of these studies. There is no examination of internal consistency reliability, a crucial oversight in light of the fact that task scores are combined to yield a total score. Most importantly, even though clinicians are encouraged to determine deficit areas based on subjects' performance on small groups of items (e.g., items pertaining to informing), there is absolutely no information regarding the reliability of these item clusters.

The validity section of the manual is also inadequate. Content and construct validity are dismissed by noting that "a variety of speech acts and assessment contexts was included in the test construction" and that "the test elicits conversational intentions from the child in a variety of guided play contexts." No data or meaningful theoretical discussions are provided. Criterion-related validity is based entirely on the analysis of two subjects from the standardization sample by two clinicians, and a very brief analysis of how predictive validity could be investigated in the future.

The Test of Pragmatic Skills suffers from a number of other technical shortcomings. First, the standardization sample includes only middle-class Anglo children and thus, as acknowledged in the manual, may not be appropriate for children from diverse racial and socioeconomic backgrounds. While the authors state that the standardization sample geographically reflects the 1980 U.S. Census, no data are presented to support this claim. Second, the norm tables provided in the manual transform raw scores into percentiles rather than standard score units; this makes the interpretation of test scores unnecessarily cumbersome. Finally, the manual fails to present the intercorrelations among childrens' scores on the four tasks. As a result, it is not possible to assess the adequacy of the prescribed method of combining these four scores into a Mean Composite Score.

In summary, the Test of Pragmatic Skills is an exploratory attempt to provide clinicians and researchers with a standardized instrument for assessing children's language in a natural context. As such, it is one of the few tests that provide information that is appropriate for use within the increasingly important pragmatic perspective of language development and language disorders. The Test of Pragmatic Skills is thus an important addition to our body of existing tools for assessing language. Unfortunately, the test is seriously flawed from a technical perspective. Substantial additional research is needed to assess its reliability and validity. Clinicians would be well advised to exercise considerable caution when using this test in their daily practice.

[85]

Test of Written Spelling [Revised Edition]. Purpose: "Assesses the student's ability to spell words whose spellings are (a) readily predictable in sound-letter patterns, (b) words whose spellings are less predictable (i.e., the demons), and (c) both types of words considered together." Grades 1–12;

1976–86; TWS-2; 3 scores: Predictable Words, Unpredictable Words, Total; 1986 price data: $32 per complete kit including manual ('86, 42 pages), and 50 answer sheets; $13 per 50 answer sheets; $21 per manual; (15–25) minutes; Stephen C. Larsen and Donald D. Hammill; PRO-ED, Inc.*

For reviews by John M. Bradley and Deborah B. Erickson of an earlier edition, see 9:1279 (1 reference).

Review of the Test of Written Spelling [Revised Edition] by DEBORAH B. ERICKSON, Assistant Professor of Psychology, Rochester Institute of Technology, and Monroe Community College, Rochester, NY:

The Test of Written Spelling [Revised Edition] (TWS-2) is designed to assess written spelling from ages 5 to 18. Larsen and Hammill describe an unmet need for adequate spelling assessment and instruction. They define spelling skills as the ability to properly arrange letters in words. They cite research supporting the contention that analysis of the student's knowledge of English orthographic rules and memorization of specific nonconforming exceptions provides an adequate basis for the assessment of spelling ability. Their suggested testing approach thus divides spelling of English words into two categories: those that follow orthographic rules ("predictable words") and those that do not ("unpredictable words"). The authors suggest that this division will assist teachers in planning an appropriate instructional program. In adherence to the new emphasis on creating tests to directly assist in the educational process, these authors sought to develop a test of written spelling that could be linked to an educational program of spelling. However, caution should be exercised before planning a total educational program in spelling from a test of 100 words covering 12 grades.

The manual developed for the TWS-2 is clear and concise. It follows the guidelines of reporting test construction data recommended by the joint committee of the American Educational Research Association, the American Psychological Association, and the National Council on Measurement in Education (1974). The thoroughness with which the authors have described the purpose of the test, the directions to administer and interpret the test, and the technical development of the test are commendable.

Specifically, the administration and scoring section of the manual details the basal, ceiling, and scoring procedures. The interpretation section gives examples of how to use the profile of scores. Scores are reported in percentiles and standard scores. Grade equivalents are not given due to the recent controversy and dissatisfaction over the abuse of grade equivalent scores. In the development section of the TWS-2, differences from the TWS are outlined. Item selection was redone to allow for the extension into upper grades. Five basal series and an upper level vocabulary series were used in the selection of the words. Item analyses consisted of item difficulty data and item discrimination indices (point biserial correlations). Normative data include a thorough description of demographic characteristics of the sample population.

Test-retest reliability and internal-consistency data are reported in the TWS-2 manual. The test-retest reliability coefficients for the total scores on the test range from .91 to .99 with a median of .96. Coefficient alpha reliabilities range from .92 to .98 with a median of .98. Reliability estimates indicate that the test can be accepted as a consistent measure of written spelling ability. However, sample sizes of the studies were limited to 20 students per grade in each of grades 1–8 for the interval from 6 to 18 years for the coefficient alpha data. Future revisions should consider larger sample sizes representative of all age and grade levels.

Content validity is inferred through a thorough discussion of the item-selection process. Concurrent validity for the TWS-2 is based upon studies of its predecessor, the TWS. Concurrent validity of the TWS was established through correlations with other measures of spelling in studies of 63 students in 3 different fourth grade classrooms in Austin, Texas. Demonstrating equivalence of the TWS and the TWS-2 was attempted by comparing 300 cases of similar items from the TWS and the TWS-2. From this comparison the authors concluded that the studies reported in the 1976 manual support the validity of the present TWS-2. While all other aspects of the test manual used rigorous methods of test development, it is disappointing that concurrent test validity was approached in this manner. Again, future revisions should expand upon this study. Construct validity is inferred through a focus upon the developmental nature of spelling ability. The authors compared the spelling ability of younger and older children and of normal and learning-disabled students. Studies comparing different populations indicated that the TWS-2 does discriminate between groups of students with different spelling abilities. This evidence for the discriminatory power of the test is a significant factor in establishing validity of the TWS-2.

SUMMARY. The revisions of the test manual and the additional information regarding the discriminatory power of the TWS-2 make this test an excellent screening instrument for assessing written spelling ability. Spelling is a complex function and the TWS-2 does not assess all aspects of the spelling process. However, it is useful in analyzing a student's strengths and weaknesses in spelling predictable and unpredictable words. This analysis can assist a teacher to develop appropriate teaching strategies for spelling. Further diagnostic assessment is recommended before developing a total educational program in the area of spelling.

REVIEWER'S REFERENCE

American Psychological Association, American Educational Research Association, & National Council on Measurement in Education. (1974). *Standards for educational and psychological tests.* Washington, DC: American Psychological Association.

Review of the Test of Written Spelling [Revised Edition] by RUTH M. NOYCE, Professor of Curriculum and Instruction, The University of Kansas, Lawrence, KS:

Using a dictated word format, the Test of Written Spelling (TWS-2) measures the ability of students in grades 1 through 12 to spell both "predictable" and "unpredictable" words. It is composed of two subtests, one comprised of words conforming to the rules of English orthography and the other made up of irregular words. The test has two unique features that separate it from other commercial spelling tests. One is the capacity to provide diagnostic information relative to specific teaching strategies; the other is the requirement that the examinee actually write the word. Both features contribute to the appeal of the instrument when it is compared to existing tests. Most commercial spelling tests report general progress without discriminating between rule-governed words and "spelling demons"; therefore, they are not useful for the purpose of identifying the specific problems of individuals. In addition, the majority of current tests require the examin-

ee to select a correctly-spelled word from among four or five choices, a practice which has been criticized by some authorities for possibly reinforcing incorrect spellings. While most current formats measure editing ability, they do not determine the student's capability to correctly spell words in written form without a visual stimulus.

The theoretical base for TWS-2 is derived from the research of Hanna, Hanna, Hodges, and Rudorf (1966), who reported that knowledge of the linguistic nature of English orthography is useful to spellers due to the fact that a considerable number of spellings are rule-governed. The authors of TWS-2 have taken this into account, maintaining that teachers need a valid tool for identifying specific error patterns in order to accurately diagnose a pupil's spelling difficulties.

An excellent test manual provides a clear explanation of procedures for administering the TWS-2. Examiners are instructed to allow 15 to 25 minutes for administration and advised that young or immature pupils may require two or more sessions to complete the test, because they are required to write dictated words. The use of entry levels, basals, and ceilings is thoroughly explained in the manual. Five consecutive items must be answered correctly in the establishment of a basal. Otherwise, the examiner returns to the entry point (determined by grade level) and tests downward until five consecutive items are answered correctly. The examiner says the word in isolation, reads a sentence from the manual containing the word, and then repeats the word, while the examinee writes the word on a response form. The words written by the subject are scored "correct," earning one point, or "incorrect," receiving no credit, and the raw score is the sum of the correct answers. Each subtest yields raw scores, percentiles, and standard scores that are recorded on a summary form on the reverse side of the word-list page written by the student. This information is recorded graphically in the form of a profile on the Summary/Response Form.

Illustrative features of the test manual that are particularly helpful to the examiner are a completed sample Summary/Response Form and a chart showing the relationship of TWS-2 words to the word lists of five current (1982–84) spelling programs. A glossary of pronunciation symbols is also included. Adequate information for interpreting the three types of scores is provided. However, no grade equivalents are given, due to dissatisfaction expressed over their use since the 1976 edition of the test. The authors acknowledge a recommendation from the International Reading Association requesting test publishers not to provide this information. The problem becomes obvious when the reader of the test manual observes the inconsistency with which words are placed at grade levels in the five spelling series. Grade level placement is not a stated purpose of the developers of this instrument, who purport to have created a valid device for measuring individual progress in spelling and for determining the kinds of instruction needed to remedy spelling problems.

The validation data reported are satisfactory. Content validity was addressed through controlled item-selection and item-analysis procedures. Words for grades 9 through 12 were selected from the EDL Reading Core Vocabulary; words for the elementary grades were derived from the EDL list and current spelling programs for grades 1 through 8. The criteria for word selection were that the word could be easily categorized as rule-governed or irregular and that the word appear in the five current basal spelling program word lists compared by the authors. Concurrent validity data indicate substantial correlation with the spelling subtests of four well-established tests: California Achievement Tests (CAT), Durrell Analysis of Reading Difficulty (DARD), SRA Achievement Series (SRA), and Wide Range Achievement Test (WRAT).

Adequate normative data were collected from a nationally representative sample of 3,805 children and reported as standard scores and percentile ranks. The developers report acceptable results from both test-retest and internal consistency reliability estimates. In this revised version of the test, the reliability at younger age levels has been strengthened.

The TWS-2 appears to measure what it was designed to measure efficiently and consistently. It is a well-constructed, easily-administered test to be used in diagnosing and prescribing for spelling instruction. Its unique purpose is to distinguish between the ability to spell rule-governed words and the ability to spell irregular words. However, the extent of its utility is difficult to predict. An underlying assumption

is that children who don't "spell by the rules" can be taught to do so by learning certain rules that have "broad application." Spelling authorities are not in agreement about this issue. The value of the TWS-2 as a diagnostic tool for educators will be directly proportionate to the willingness of teachers to follow up the testing by modifying instructional practices.

REVIEWER'S REFERENCE

Hanna, P. R., Hanna, J. S., Hodges, R. G., & Rudorf, E. H. (1966). *Phoneme-grapheme correspondences to spelling improvement.* Washington, DC: Office of Education, United States Department of Health, Education, and Welfare.

[86]

The Vane Kindergarten Test (1984 Revision). Purpose: "Evaluate the intellectual and academic potential and behavior adjustment of young children." Ages 4–6; 1968–84; VKT; 4 scores: Perceptual Motor, Vocabulary, Drawing a Man, Total; 1987 price data: $8 per 50 record sheets; $7.50 per manual ('84, 61 pages); (30) minutes; Julia R. Vane; Clinical Psychology Publishing Co., Inc.*

See T3:2548 (4 references) and T2:528 (7 references); for reviews by Dorothy H. Eichorn and Marcel L. Goldschmid, see 7:428 (3 references).

TEST REFERENCES

1. Kaplan, H. B. (1985). A comparison of the Vane Kindergarten Test with the WPPSI and a measure of self-control. *Psychology in the Schools, 22,* 277-282.
2. Schmidt, S., & Perino, J. (1985). Kindergarten screening results as predictors of academic achievement, potential, and placement in second grade. *Psychology in the Schools, 22,* 146-151.

Review of The Vane Kindergarten Test (1984 Revision) by DAVID W. BARNETT, Associate Professor, School Psychology, University of Cincinnati, Cincinnati, OH:

The Vane Kindergarten Test (VKT) is a screening measure developed to assist with the identification of cognitive and social behaviors related to early school success or failure. However, the reader is also given the unwarranted impression that the VKT yields an adequate estimate of intelligence and enables the *determination* (emphasis added) of the effects of motivation, attention, perceptual skills, and behavior on performance. The scale is intended for use by school psychologists.

The VKT is comprised of three subtests: Perceptual Motor, Vocabulary, and Intelligence ("a Man subtest"). In addition, a number of unstructured observations are suggested.

PERCEPTUAL MOTOR SUBTEST. This subtest is similar to many other drawing tasks such as the Bender-Gestalt and the Geometric Design subtest of the Wechsler Preschool and Primary Scale of Intelligence (WPPSI). The author states that performance on this subtest is related to early reading and writing skills, and difficulties are possibly indicative of a "developmental lag." If the performance is extremely "poor," central nervous system dysfunction (or brain injury) is implicated. Only three forms are included in the scale: a square, a cross formed by double lines, and a hexagon. Each is drawn three times.

VOCABULARY. Verbal expressive skills are required. The child is asked to define 11 words similar to the words on the WPPSI Vocabulary subtest and other language tests. General information is an important determinant of success on this subtest.

MAN SUBTEST. The child is asked to draw a person, a technique similar to that used in other tests (e.g., Harris, 1963; Koppitz, 1968). Details and features of the drawing contribute to the developmental scoring, yielding a "man IQ." In addition, various psychopathological signs found in the literature on children's drawings are used to evaluate adjustment (e.g., absence of mouth, grotesque drawing).

ADDITIONAL OBSERVATIONS. Although the author refers to a section describing additional measures, no objective guidelines are offered for the subsequent observations. One "measure" is the child's skill in writing his or her name. The author states that a child's skill in this task "contains a number of clues that are helpful in reaching an evaluation regarding the child's motivation, learning ability, and perceptual motor development." A second category includes test observations of such factors as hand dominance, attention, following directions, self-control, cooperation and turn taking, interference, motivation, spontaneity, and related behaviors.

RESTANDARDIZATION. The original VKT was published in 1968. The present norms are based on the performance of 800 children, ages 4 to 6-5, from three states (New Jersey, New York, and Vermont). Equal numbers of boys and girls were included at each age level and the 1980 census was used as a guide for selection based on occupation, rural versus urban residence, and racial group (described as white and nonwhite). Non-English-speaking children were not represented. Sample selection procedures are not adequately described.

VALIDITY. Each subtest is substantially correlated with the full score (Perceptual Motor = .78; Vocabulary = .74; Man = .82; N = 800). The intercorrelations between the subtests are at a high, but reasonable level (e.g., the highest, between Man and Perceptual Motor, is .58).

Four studies reported correlations between the VKT and the Stanford-Binet. The median correlation was .73. Two studies reported correlations between the VKT and the WPPSI (.70, N = 33; .75, N = 18).

Various achievement measures also have been used to study the validity of the VKT. The range of correlations was from .52 (N = 213), based on a comparison between the VKT given in kindergarten and the Stanford Achievement test given one year later, to .60 (N = 304), the correlation between the VKT administered in kindergarten and the Stanford Achievement test given in third grade.

Other studies reported the use of the VKT with test batteries and other types of tests. In general, the VKT was substantially correlated with other academic, language, and perceptual motor measures.

RELIABILITY. Test-retest reliability information was examined in six different samples with various intervals between tests. The results ranged from a high of .97 (N = 14, 1-week interval) to .70 (N = 29, 5-to-6-week interval).

ADMINISTRATION AND SCORING. The Perceptual Motor and Man subtests can be group administered to 10–12 children. The Vocabulary subtest is individually administered. Scoring instructions for the Man and Vocabulary subtests are clearly presented with sufficient examples of successful and unsuccessful performances.

An IQ is derived for each subtest. Tables enable the determination of IQ relative to the child's age and performance. One month increments are used. The three subtests are simply averaged to obtain a "Full IQ."

Mental age equivalents of subtest scores are available from ages 3-9 to 7-6 for the Perceptual Motor subtest, ages 4-0 to 8-0 on the Vocabulary subtest, and 3-0 to 10-3 for the Man subtests. However, it should be noted that many of these ages were *not* included in the standardization and information is not present-ed on the derivation of the mental ages.

CONCLUSIONS. The evidence for both validi-ty, and, to a lesser extent, reliability of the VKT seems to be comparable to individually adminis-tered IQ tests for preschool children. However, numerous preschool measures correlate in a similar manner and the concerns identified below preclude the recommendation of the VKT as a screening measure.

The psychometric development of the scale does not use contemporary techniques or sug-gested guidelines for scale development. Infor-mation is not included concerning the construc-tion of the IQ tables. Standard scores are not used.

Concerns can be raised with respect to the labeling of subscales (e.g., *Man* IQ), mislead-ing floor and inadequate ceiling (e.g., a child of 6-11 with a perfect score receives an IQ of 105), derivation of composite scores, derivation of mental ages for children not included in standardization, the standardization itself, and other factors. The standard deviations of sub-tests range from 15.1 (Perceptual Motor) to 20.3 (Vocabulary) at various ages. Reliabilities of subtests and standard errors for all scales are not included in the manual. No guidelines are suggested for interpretations of subtests or for screening decisions. The case studies included serve as testimonials and are potentially mis-leading.

The most important criticism of the VKT is conceptual in nature. Many contemporary re-views of preschool screening suggest that this process should be curricular based, ongoing, include adult or caregiver behaviors in addition to child behaviors as targets of assessment, and be systematic. Assessment tasks should have direct links to interventions. The use of the VKT as a screening instrument is inconsistent with these guidelines.

REVIEWER'S REFERENCES

Harris, D. B. (1963). *Children's drawings as measures of intellectual maturity.* New York: Harcourt, Brace & World.
Koppitz, E. M. (1968). *Psychological evaluation of children's human figure drawings.* New York: Grune & Stratton.

Review of The Vane Kindergarten Test (1984 Revision) by WILLIAM B. MICHAEL, Profes-sor of Education and Psychology, University of Southern California, Los Angeles, CA:

The 1984 edition of The Vane Kindergarten Test (VKT) represents a revision of the earlier 1968 form, which has been designed to evalu-ate not only the intellectual and academic potential of young children, but also their behavioral adjustment. The first two of the three parts of the VKT, which can be adminis-tered to groups of 10 to 12 children at one sitting, include the following: (*a*) the Perceptu-al Motor Subtest, in which the examinee is directed to make copies of three boxes, three crosses, and three hexagons, and (*b*) the Man Subtest, in which the child draws a picture of an entire man. The third part of the VKT, which is individually administered, is named Vocabu-lary Subtest. It requires the examinee to tell the examiner what each of 11 different words means. The instructions for administration and scoring of the three parts of the VKT are clear, detailed, and quite specific. Examiners would be expected to be qualified school psychologists. Specific criteria (signs) have been given to the examiner so that he or she can use them during the process of test taking as indicators of behavioral characteristics associated with diffi-culties or problems in perceptual-motor devel-opment and emotional-social adjustment. In addition, the examiner is also urged to observe test behaviors that might suggest possible defi-ciencies in motivation or cognitive functioning.

In the restandardization of the VKT, sub-stantial effort has been expended to obtain a representative population of children under 6-6 years of age relative to socio-economic level, urban or rural background, ethnicity, and sex. Selected from an initial population of more than 2,000 children, the final standardization sample of 800 consisted of (*a*) subgroups of 100 boys and 100 girls within each of three age levels of 4-6 to 4-11 years, 5-0 to 5-5 years, and 5-6 to 5-11 years, and (*b*) subgroups of 50 boys and 50 girls at ages 4-0 to 4-5 years and 6-0 to 6-5 years. Although efforts were made to allocate percentages of children in the various strata according to the population distribution throughout the United States, all those tested came only from the states of New York, New Jersey, and Vermont. In this restandardization, one of the main objectives was to correct for inflation in test scores that had occurred subsequent to 1968. A second goal was to simplify the scoring system for the Man Subtest. To minimize scoring errors, certain test items requiring difficult judgmental decisions concerning the appropriateness of responses were eliminated. A comparatively simple scoring system of 31 points was devised. The test author has recommended that this new system should be used only with young children, as it may underestimate the intellectual level of very bright children of 6-6 to 7-0 years. She also has suggested that for older children the well-known Goodenough scoring method be applied to the Man Subtest.

The restandardization effort has led to the generation of a considerable amount of new normative, reliability, and validity data. In the case of normative data, three kinds of evidence are represented by (a) mean IQs and standard deviations of the normative population relative to each of the three subtests and the full scale for each age subgroup as well as for the total population, (b) mean IQs and standard deviations on the same measures according to sex of child and occupation of parent, and (c) IQs converted from raw scores on each of the subtests by each month of chronological age over an age span from 3-6 to 6-11 years.

Virtually all reliability data were cited in the form of test-retest coefficients involving the use of comparatively small samples. Seven reported coefficients varied between .70 to .97 with an approximate median value of .81. Evidence that might be considered indicative of the internal consistency of the VKT was apparent in coefficients among the subtests for the total sample of 800 children. Coefficients of .43, .58, and .45 were found between the Perceptual Motor and Vocabulary, Perceptual Motor and Man, and Vocabulary and Man subtests, respectively.

Concurrent validity data have been presented in terms of the correlation of the VKT with other widely used standardized measures of intelligence. The range of correlation coefficients found in five different samples fell between .62 and .76 with a median value of approximately .74. Predictive validity information has been reported in the form of coefficients between the VKT and three different, widely employed standardized tests of achievement. The five validity coefficients varied between .52 and .60 with a median entry of .59. Additional evidence for validity was cited in the form of correlations between the VKT and other types of tests indicative of perceptual-motor and cognitive development. The result-

ing validity coefficients were comparable to those already mentioned.

Additional noteworthy features occur in the manual. Studies pertaining to the performance of minority populations on the VKT have been cited, although the information presented is not sufficient to permit any reliable degree of generalization. Of potential assistance in the interpretation of subtest and full-scale IQ scores is Chapter 5 of the manual. This chapter includes six case studies that are anchored to detailed information presented in the form of reproductions of drawings representing the two nonverbal parts of the test. These case studies also provide information on vocabulary responses, age of child, school attended, handedness, and IQs earned on the three subtests as well as on the full scale.

In summary, the VKT is a relatively easy test to administer and to score in the hands of a well-trained school psychologist. The 1984 revision furnishes what may be considered quite adequate normative and interpretive score information on each subtest as well as on the full scale. Although additional data on reliability and validity would be welcome, the initial evidence has been quite promising. In comparison with other widely used measures of early childhood perceptual-motor and cognitive development, the VKT would appear to be comparable, if not possibly superior, in its psychometric adequacy and clinical usefulness.

[87]

Waksman Social Skills Rating Scale. Purpose: "Developed to assist psychologists, educators, and other clinicians to identify specific and clinically important social skill deficits in children and adolescents." Grades K–12; 1983–84; WSSRS; 3 scores: Aggressive, Passive, Total; individual; separate forms for males and females; 1987 price data: $5.45 per 25 male or female rating forms; $21.95 per manual ('84, 15 pages); administration time not reported; Steven A. Waksman; ASIEP Education Co.*

Review of the Waksman Social Skills Rating Scale by HAROLD R. KELLER, Associate Professor of Psychology and Education, Syracuse University, Syracuse, NY:

The Waksman Social Skills Rating Scale (WSSRS) was designed to aid in the assessment of social competence or specific social skills. After carefully defining social competence as those abilities required to perform competently at a social task, the author indicates that the WSSRS was developed "to identify specific and clinically important social skill deficits in children and adolescents." It is apparent from examination of the items and the two factors on the scale (Aggressive and Passive domains) that the focus of the scale is upon problematic behaviors. The behavior descriptors for the items were selected as representative of behaviors taught by a number of social skills training programs. While the programs cited train specific social competencies, the WSSRS items address problematic behaviors.

The 21 items on the scale were selected on the basis of ratings of 29 original items by 50 mental health professionals and/or educators and 50 graduate students in counseling psychology. The raters were asked to judge whether the behaviors were "important for a child's development" on a scale of 0–5 (with 5 indicating extreme importance). To be retained in the final pool, an item had to have a mean rating over 2.5 and at least 50% of the ratings for that item had to be 3, 4, and 5.

Administration and scoring of the WSSRS is very simple, with each behavior rated on a scale of 0 (never) to 3 (usually). Domain subtotal and total scores are easily obtained, as are corresponding percentile scores from the profile table on the front of the respective rating forms for males and females. The rating forms and manual indicate the WSSRS should be completed by classroom teachers, counselors, or childcare workers who have "daily contact with the child or adolescent." There is no indication of a minimum period of familiarity or daily contact with the child before ratings are done. Classroom teachers who had had the students enrolled in their classes for a minimum of 2 months did the ratings for the normative sample. In order to make valid normative comparisons, the manual should state explicitly that ratings be made only after a minimum of 2 months contact with the student. Further, it should be noted that behavior ratings by teachers do not correlate consistently highly with those of mental health professionals (Achenbach & Edelbrock, 1978), so the source of the ratings must be considered.

The normative sample consists of 331 students in kindergarten through high school, randomly selected from 10 schools in the metropolitan area of Portland, Oregon. Given the limited nature of the sample, much more descriptive information is needed in order for users to judge the comparability of their settings and children with those of the normative sample. What was the basis for selecting the 10 schools? Are the schools public or private? The sample must be described more specifically in terms of numbers of children by grade, gender, race, socioeconomic status, or census tract data. The explicit basis for the grade grouping in the norm tables is not provided, though the groupings fit elementary school, middle school, and high school breakdowns.

The factor analysis appears to be appropriate. Consistent with the apparent focus of the WSSRS on problematic behaviors rather than on social skills and competence, the factors identified appear to match closely the primary factors that emerge from factor analyses of most behavior problem rating scales. That is, the Aggressive and Passive domains appear to be versions of externalizing (undercontrolled) and internalizing (overcontrolled) factors obtained in previous research (Achenbach & Edelbrock, 1978). Research is needed on the WSSRS within the context of multitrait (or multibehavior), multimethod designs to determine whether this scale and its factors are any different from already existing, high-quality, general behavior problem rating scales (e.g., the Child Behavior Checklist, Achenbach & Edelbrock, 1983). The author did correlate the WSSRS with the Portland Problem Behavior Checklist (Waksman, 1980; Waksman & Loveland, 1980) and found a substantial relationship between the measures. This result raises the question of whether the WSSRS is a measure of social skills, or an alternative behavior problem checklist.

The internal consistency reported was very high (.92). Test-retest reliabilities were moderately high (.63 to .74). Interrater reliabilities showed mixed results, being particularly low for the Passive domain with a randomly selected sample of high school students and a small sample of emotionally disturbed children. Such interrater reliabilities are, of course, subject to rater differences, setting differences, and/or setting specificity of behaviors.

The author attempted to demonstrate validity by a comparison group approach. Rating scale scores differentiated significantly among the normative sample and two small samples of emotionally disturbed children in the public schools and a residential setting, with the residential children having the highest scores. The samples were very small (7 and 32, respectively) and genders and ages are not specified. A comparison group approach involving emotionally disturbed children appears to be based upon the assumption that emotionally disturbed children are children with social skills deficits. A more appropriate comparison would be to identify groups with and without social skills, as determined by independent assessment of social skills. Then, in addition to mean score differences, information on hit/miss ratios would be very helpful. However, more importantly, a critical validity test would involve determining the relationship among WSSRS ratings and independent measures of social skills. As indicated earlier, a multitrait (or multibehavior), multimethod design is needed to determine the relationship of the WSSRS with other social skills measures and its independence from general behavior problem rating scales.

The author suggests a number of uses for the WSSRS, including identification of students and behaviors for social skills training programs, behavioral interventions, and for individual education programs. In addition, the author suggests the scale can be used to evaluate social skills training programs or other counseling programs. However, no studies of treatment validity are presented, and there is no indication of the measure's sensitivity to interventions.

In summary, the WSSRS is an easily administered and scored rating scale, though a minimum time frame for the rater to gain familiarity with the child or adolescent is not specified. The normative sample is quite limited and largely unspecified, a limitation making it difficult for users to determine comparability to their own children and settings. Reliabilities are mixed, particularly for the Passive domain. Validity data are extremely limited, particularly as they relate to suggested uses for the scale. Perhaps most importantly, the author has failed to present data to demonstrate the scale is assessing the stated skills (i.e., social skills), independent of behavior problems.

REVIEWER'S REFERENCES

Achenbach, T. M., & Edelbrock, C. S. (1978). The classification of child psychopathology: A review and analysis of empirical efforts. *Psychological Bulletin, 85*, 1275-1301.

Waksman, S. A. (1980). *The Portland Problem Behavior Checklist test and manual.* Portland, OR: Enrichment Press.
Waksman, S. A., & Loveland, R. J. (1980). The Portland Problem Behavior Checklist. *Psychology in the Schools,* 17, 25-29.
Achenbach, T. M., & Edelbrock, C. S. (1983). *Manual for the Child Behavior Checklist and the Revised Child Behavior Profile.* Burlington, VT: Author.

Review of the Waksman Social Skills Rating Scale by ELLEN McGINNIS, Assistant Professor of Special Education, University of Wisconsin-Eau Claire, Eau Claire, WI:

The Waksman Social Skills Rating Scale (WSSRS) is a brief normative checklist (21 items) designed to screen children and adolescents with social skill deficits. Possible uses suggested by the author include identifying students with social skills deficits and evaluating success of special counseling or social skills training programs.

The scale consists of 9 behavioral descriptors which factor into the "Aggressive domain" and 12 factoring into the "Passive domain." The rating scale is designed for use by classroom teachers, counselors, or child care workers who rate the descriptors on a 4-point scale of 0 (never) exhibited by this child to 3 (usually) exhibited.

The author, recognizing the limitations of using only rating scales to assess social skills, suggests this scale be used as only one piece of information to identify social skills deficits in children and also encourages completion of the scale by more than one educator due to the variability of student behavior.

Research suggests that many handicapped children are deficient in social skills. With the current interest in and development of social skills training programs, methods to assess these deficits are in high demand. The WSSRS, while having a strength in its prescriptive nature, falls short in many critical areas.

First, the brevity of the scale, while allowing for quick administration, measures a very narrow range of behaviors. Additionally, the majority of the behavioral descriptors are related to teacher acceptability. This scale does not attend adequately to behaviors related to positive relationships with peers.

Other serious drawbacks relate to psychometric issues. The descriptors comprising each of the subscales are grouped together under the headings "Passive" or "Aggressive," which may create a serious biasing effect. If the author believed that this grouping of the rating scale descriptors was desirable, statistical procedures should have been done to rule out possible biasing effects of this format.

The sample size of 331 was randomly selected from one metropolitan area, resulting in a small normative sample size when broken down into subsamples (male, female, grades K–5, grades 6–8, and grades 9–12) for units of comparison. For example, the norms for females in grades 6–8 were based on a sample of only 43 pupils. In addition, by grouping several grade levels together for normative purposes, the author has failed to attend to critical age differences found with other rating scale measures (i.e., Matson, Rotatari, & Helsel, 1985).

While the author has suggested that the WSSRS does discriminate between a normal group ($N = 32$) and a group of emotionally disturbed students ($N = 32$), the latter group was comprised of youngsters in residential treatment facilities. The user should be cautioned that this scale may discriminate only between normal and severely emotionally disturbed groups of youngsters, as adequate information was not provided on a sample of less severely handicapped youth.

Although the author stated that WSSRS scores were highly correlated with scores on the Portland Problem Behavior Checklist, this was not the case across all subgroups. Additionally, test-retest correlations were not high, especially for scores in the Passive domain. Test-retest item correlation coefficients were also below .55 on one-third of the items of this rating scale.

With the increase in awareness of the need to assess children's social behaviors for identification and documentation of the effectiveness of interventions, social skills rating scales will be in demand. While the Waksman Social Skills Rating Scale allows for quick administration, is prescriptive in nature, and does provide the user with a normative base, it seeks to measure only a narrow range of social behaviors, and the scale itself and the norms provided are of highly questionable utility. Those interested in using a social skills rating scale would be wise to look for alternatives, such as the Matson Evaluation of Social Skills with Youngsters (Matson, Rotatori, & Helsel, 1985). The Matson scale, while still in need of additional research, has more items and is more realistically evaluated by its authors.

REVIEWER'S REFERENCE

Matson, J. L., Rotatori, A. F., & Helsel, W. J. (1985). Development of a rating scale to measure social skills in children: The Matson Evaluation of Social Skills with Youngsters (MESSY). *Psychopharmacology Bulletin*, 21 (4), 855-868.

[88]

Wide Range Achievement Test—Revised. Purpose: "To measure the codes which are needed to learn the basic skills of reading, spelling, and arithmetic." Ages 5-0 to 11-11, 12-0 to 75; 1940–84; WRAT-R; 3 scores: Reading, Spelling, Arithmetic; individual in part; 2 forms; 2 levels; reading and spelling lists available on cassette tape for examiner training or group administration of spelling test; 1987 price data: $10 per 25 test forms (level 1 or level 2); $15 per 10 large print edition test forms (level 1 or level 2); $10 per set of 2 plastic word list cards; $25 per tape cassette; $20 per manual ('84, 82 pages); $45 per starter set including test forms for both Level 1 and Level 2, set of plastic cards, and manual; large print edition available; (15–30) minutes; Sarah Jastak, Gary S. Wilkinson, and Joseph Jastak (earlier editions); Jastak Associates, Inc.*

For reviews by Paula Matuszek and Philip A. Saigh of an earlier edition, see 9:1364 (103 references); see also T3:2621 (249 references), 8:37 (117 references), and T2:50 (35 references); for reviews by Jack C. Merwin and Robert L. Thorndike of an earlier edition, see 7:36 (49 references); see also 6:27 (15 references); for reviews by Paul Douglas Courtney, Verner M. Sims, and Louis P. Thorpe of the 1946 edition, see 3:21.

TEST REFERENCES

1. Epperson, D. L., Hannum, T. E., & Datwyler, M. L. (1982). Women incarcerated in 1960, 1970, and 1980: Implications of demographic, educational, and personality characteristics for earlier research. *Criminal Justice and Behavior*, 9, 352-363.
2. August, G. J., Stewart, M. A., & Holmes, C. S. (1983). A four-year follow-up of hyperactive boys with and without conduct disorder. *British Journal of Psychiatry*, 143, 192-198.
3. Berg, R. A., Ch'ien, L. T., Bownan, W. P., Ochs, J., Lancaster, W., Goff, J. R., & Anderson, H. R., Jr. (1983). The neuropsychological effects of acute lymphocytic leukemia and its treatment—a three year report: Intellectual functioning and academic achievement. *Clinical Neuropsychology*, 5, 9-13.
4. Elliott, S. N., Piersel, W. C., & Galvin, G. A. (1983). Psychological re-evaluations: A survey of practices and perceptions of school psychologists. *Journal of School Psychology*, 21, 99-105.
5. Epstein, M. H., & Cullinan, D. (1983). Academic performance of behaviorally disordered and learning-disabled pupils. *The Journal of Special Education*, 17, 303-307.
6. Feitel, B., & Sano, M. (1983). Intellectual assessment of young adult chronic patients. *Hospital and Community Psychiatry*, 34, 1153-1155.
7. Fogel, L. S., & Nelson, R. O. (1983). The effects of special education labels on teachers' behavioral observations, checklist scores, and grading of academic work. *Journal of School Psychology*, 21, 241-251.
8. Gettinger, M., & Lyon, M. A. (1983). Predictors of the discrepancy between time needed and time spent in learning among boys exhibiting behavior problems. *Journal of Educational Psychology*, 75, 491-499.

9. Lomax, R. G. (1983). Applying structural modeling to some component processes of reading comprehension development. *Journal of Experimental Education*, 52, 33-40.

10. McDermott, P. A., & Watkins, M. W. (1983). Computerized vs. conventional remedial instruction for learning-disabled pupils. *The Journal of Special Education*, 17, 81-88.

11. Morrison, G. M., Forness, S. R., & MacMillan, D. L. (1983). Influences on the sociometric ratings of mildly handicapped children: A path analysis. *Journal of Educational Psychology*, 75, 63-74.

12. Silverstein, A. B., Brownlee, L., Legutki, G., & MacMillan, D. L. (1983). Convergent and discriminant validation of two methods of assessing three academic traits. *The Journal of Special Education*, 17, 63-68.

13. Thurber, S., & Walker, C. E. (1983). Medication and hyperactivity: A meta-analysis. *Journal of General Psychology*, 108, 79-86.

14. White, M., & Miller, S. R. (1983). Dyslexia: A term in search of a definition. *The Journal of Special Education*, 17, 5-10.

15. Ysseldyke, J., Algozzine, B., & Epps, S. (1983). A logical and empirical analysis of current practice in classifying students as handicapped. *Exceptional Children*, 50, 160-166.

16. Aram, D. M., Ekelman, B. L., & Nation, J. E. (1984). Preschoolers with language disorders: 10 years later. *Journal of Speech and Hearing Research*, 27, 232-244.

17. Barth, J. T., Macciocchi, S. N., Ranseen, J., Boyd, T., & Mills, G. (1984). The effects of prefontal leucotomy: Neuropsychological findings in long term chronic psychiatric patients. *Clinical Neuropsychology*, 6, 120-123.

18. Bissell, J. C., & Clark, F. (1984). Dichotic listening performance in normal children and adults. *The American Journal of Occupational Therapy*, 38, 176-183.

19. Blachman, B. A. (1984). Relationship of rapid naming ability and language analysis skills to kindergarten and first-grade reading achievement. *Journal of Educational Psychology*, 76, 610-622.

20. Black, J. L., Collins, D. W. K., Deroach, J. N., & Zubrick, S. (1984). A detailed study of sequential saccadic eye movements for normal- and poor-reading children. *Perceptual and Motor Skills*, 59, 423-434.

21. Black, J. L., Collins, D. W. K., DeRoach, J. N., & Zubrick, S. R. (1984). Smooth pursuit eye movements in normal and dyslexic children. *Perceptual and Motor Skills*, 59, 91-100.

22. Bookman, M. O. (1984). Spelling as a cognitive-developmental linguistic process. *Academic Therapy*, 20, 21-32.

23. Cermak, S. A., & Ayres, A. J. (1984). Crossing the body midline in learning-disabled and normal children. *The American Journal of Occupational Therapy*, 38, 35-39.

24. Champion, L., Doughtie, E. B., Johnson, P. J., & McCreary, J. H. (1984). Preliminary investigation into the Rorschach response patterns of children with documented learning disabilities. *Journal of Clinical Psychology*, 40, 329-333.

25. Chandler, H. N. (1984). The American public school: Yes, we have no standards. *Journal of Learning Disabilities*, 17, 186-187.

26. Christie, D., DeWitt, R. A., Kaltenbach, P., & Reed, D. (1984). Hyperactivity in children: Evidence for differences between parents' and teachers' perceptions of predominant features. *Psychological Reports*, 54, 771-774.

27. Cohen, R. L., Netley, C., & Clarke, M. A. (1984). On the generality of the short-term memory/reading ability relationship. *Journal of Learning Disabilities*, 17, 218-221.

28. Colligan, R. C., & Bajuniemi, L. E. (1984). Multiple definitions of reading disability: Implications for preschool screening. *Perceptual and Motor Skills*, 59, 467-475.

29. Copeland, A. P., & Reiner, E. M. (1984). The selective attention of learning-disabled children: Three studies. *Journal of Abnormal Child Psychology*, 12, 455-470.

30. DeWolfe, A. S., & Ryan, J. J. (1984). Wechsler Performance IQ > Verbal IQ index in a forensic sample: A reconsideration. *Journal of Clinical Psychology*, 40, 291-294.

31. Dishion, T. J., Loeber, R., Stouthamer-Loeber, M., & Patterson, G. R. (1984). Skill deficits and male adolescent delinquency. *Journal of Abnormal Child Psychology*, 12, 37-54.

32. Dorman, C., Hurley, A. D., & Laatsch, L. (1984). Prediction of spelling and reading performance in cerebral palsied adolescents using neuropsychological tests. *Clinical Neuropsychology*, 6, 142-144.

33. Doyle, B. A., & Higginson, D. C. (1984). Relationships among self-concept and school achievement, maternal self-esteem and sensory integration abilities for learning disabled children, ages 7 to 12 years. *Perceptual and Motor Skills*, 58, 177-178.

34. Elbert, J. C. (1984). Short-term memory encoding and memory search in the word recognition of learning-disabled children. *Journal of Learning Disabilities*, 17, 342-345.

35. Eno, L., & Woehlke, P. (1984). Relationship between grammatical errors on Rotter's Scale and performance on educational tests for students suspected of having learning problems. *Perceptual and Motor Skills*, 58, 75-78.

36. Frane, R. E., Clarizio, H. F., & Porter, A. (1984). Diagnostic and prescriptive bias in school psychologists' reports of a learning disabled child. *Journal of Learning Disabilities*, 17, 12-15.

37. Friedrich, D., Fuller, G. B., & Davis, D. (1984). Learning disability: Fact and fiction. *Journal of Learning Disabilities*, 17, 205-209.

38. Garrison, W., Earls, F., & Kindlor, D. (1984). Temperament characteristics in the third year of life and behavioral adjustment at school entry. *Journal of Clinical Child Psychology*, 13, 298-303.

39. Grossman, F. M., & Clark, J. H. (1984). Concurrent validity of WISC-R factor scores for educable mentally handicapped children. *Perceptual and Motor Skills*, 58, 227-230.

40. Guidubaldi, J., & Perry, J. D. (1984). Concurrent and predictive validity of the Battelle Development Inventory at the first grade level. *Educational and Psychological Measurement*, 44, 977-985.

41. Hale, R. L., & McDermott, P. A. (1984). Pattern analysis of an actuarial strategy for computerized diagnosis of childhood exceptionality. *Journal of Learning Disabilities*, 17, 30-37.

42. Hall, R. J., Reeve, R. E., & Zakreski, R. (1984). Validity of the Woodcock-Johnson Tests of Achievement for Learning-Disabled Students. *Journal of School Psychology*, 22, 193-200.

43. Halperin, J. M., Gittelman, R., Klein, D. F., & Rudel, R. B. (1984). Reading disabled hyperactive children: A distinct subgroup of Attention Deficit Disorder with hyperactivity? *Journal of Abnormal Child Psychology*, 12, 1-14.

44. Harvey, S., & Seeley, K. R. (1984). An investigation of the relationships among intellectual and creative abilities, extracurricular activities, achievement, and giftedness in a delinquent population. *Gifted Child Quarterly*, 28, 73-79.

45. Huesmann, L. R., Eron, L. D., Lefkowitz, M. M., & Walder, L. O. (1984). Stability of aggression over time and generations. *Developmental Psychology*, 20, 1120-1134.

46. Karnes, F. A., Whorton, J. E., & Currie, B. B. (1984). Correlations between the Wide Range Achievement Test and the California Achievement Test with intellectually gifted students. *Psychological Reports*, 54, 189-190.

47. Karnes, F. A., Whorton, J. E., & Currie, B. B. (1984). Correlations between WISC-R IQs and Wide Range Achievement Test grade equivalents for intellectually gifted students. *Psychological Reports*, 54, 69-70.

48. Kaufman, A. S. (1984). K-ABC and controversy. *The Journal of Special Education*, 18, 409-444.

49. Lindgren, S. D., & Richman, L. C. (1984). Immediate memory functions of verbally deficient reading-disabled children. *Journal of Learning Disabilities*, 17, 222-225.

50. Lindsey, J. D., & Armstrong, S. W. (1984). Performance of EMR and learning-disabled students on the Brigance, Peabody, and Wide Range Achievement Tests. *American Journal of Mental Deficiency*, 89, 197-201.

51. Lomax, R. G. (1984). A component processes model of reading comprehension development: A comparison of normal

and learning disabled children. *National Reading Conference Yearbook*, 33, 308-316.

52. Mattes, J. A., Boswell, L., & Oliver, H. (1984). Methylphenidate effects on symptoms of attention deficit disorder in adults. *Archives of General Psychiatry*, 41, 1059-1063.

53. Meltzer, L. J., Levine, M. D., Karniski, W., Palfrey, J. S., & Clarke, S. (1984). An analysis of the learning styles of adolescent delinquents. *Journal of Learning Disabilities*, 17, 600-608.

54. Newman, R. S. (1984). Children's achievement and self-evaluations in mathematics: A longitudinal study. *Journal of Educational Psychology*, 76, 857-873.

55. Niklason, L. B. (1984). Nonpromotion: A pseudoscientific solution. *Psychology in the Schools*, 21, 485-499.

56. Nolen, P., & McCartin, R. (1984). Spelling strategies on the Wide Range Achievement Test. *The Reading Teacher*, 38, 148-158.

57. Obrzut, A., Nelson, R. B., & Obrzut, J. E. (1984). Early school entrance for intellectually superior children: An analysis. *Psychology in the Schools*, 21, 71-77.

58. Olson, J., & Midgett, J. (1984). Alternative placements: Does a difference exist in the LD populations? *Journal of Learning Disabilities*, 17, 101-103.

59. Perlmutter, B. F., & Bryan, J. H. (1984). First impressions, ingratiation, and the learning disabled child. *Journal of Learning Disabilities*, 17, 157-161.

60. Phelps, L., Rosso, M., & Falasco, S. L. (1984). Correlations between the Woodcock-Johnson and the WISC-R for a behavior disordered population. *Psychology in the Schools*, 21, 442-446.

61. Punnett, A. F., & Steinhauer, G. D. (1984). Relationship between reinforcement and eye movements during ocular motor training with learning disabled children. *Journal of Learning Disabilities*, 17, 16-19.

62. Ryan, M. C., Miller, C. D., & Witt, J. C. (1984). A comparison of the use of orthographic structure in word discrimination by learning disabled and normal children. *Journal of Learning Disabilities*, 17, 38-40.

63. Scarborough, H. S. (1984). Continuity between childhood dyslexia and adult reading. *British Journal of Psychology*, 75, 329-348.

64. Schiller, J. J. (1984). Neuropsychological foundations of spelling and reading difficulty. *Clinical Neuropsychology*, 6, 255-261.

65. Schneider, B. H., & Byrne, B. M. (1984). Predictors of successful transition from self-contained special education to regular class settings. *Psychology in the Schools*, 21, 375-380.

66. Schulte, A., & Borich, G. D. (1984). Considerations in the use of difference scores to identify learning-disabled children. *Journal of School Psychology*, 22, 381-390.

67. Siegel, L. S., & Linder, B. A. (1984). Short-term memory processes in children with reading and arithmetic learning disabilities. *Developmental Psychology*, 20, 200-207.

68. Sinatra, R. C., Stahl-Gemake, J., & Berg, D. N. (1984). Improving reading comprehension of disabled readers through semantic mapping. *The Reading Teacher*, 38, 22-29.

69. Spellacy, F. J., & Brown, W. G. (1984). Prediction of recidivism in young offenders after brief institutionalization. *Journal of Clinical Psychology*, 40, 1070-1074.

70. Wilson, L. R., & Cone, T. (1984). The regression equation method of determining academic discrepancy. *Journal of School Psychology*, 22, 95-110.

71. Wolff, D. E., Desberg, P., & Marsh, G. (1985). Analogy strategies for improving word recognition in competent and learning disabled readers. *The Reading Teacher*, 38, 412-416.

72. Worland, J., Weeks, D. G., Janes, C. L., & Strock, B. D. (1984). Intelligence, classroom behavior, and academic achievement in children at high and low risk for psychopathology: A structural equation analysis. *Journal of Abnormal Child Psychology*, 12, 437-454.

73. Wright, L. (1984). Modifying the Bond and Tinker formula for use with low IQ adolescents. *Journal of Reading*, 28, 224-227.

74. Altepeter, T., & Handal, P. J. (1985). A factor analytic investigation of the use of the PPVT-R as a measure of general achievement. *Journal of Clinical Psychology*, 41, 540-543.

75. Baker, E. L., White, R. F., & Murawski, B. J. (1985). Clinical evaluation of neurobehavioral effects of occupational exposure to organic solvents and lead. *International Journal of Mental Health*, 14 (3), 135-158.

76. Brown, R. T., & Alford, N. (1984). Ameliorating attentional deficits and concomitant academic deficiencies in learning disabled children through cognitive training. *Journal of Learning Disabilities*, 17, 20-26.

77. Carnine, D., Gersten, R., Darch, C., & Eaves, R. (1985). Attention and cognitive deficits in learning-disabled students. *Journal of Special Education*, 19, 319-331.

78. Cohen, N. J., Gotlieb, H., Kershner, J., & Wehrspann, W. (1985). Concurrent validity of the internalizing and externalizing profile patterns of the Achenbach Child Behavior Checklist. *Journal of Consulting and Clinical Psychology*, 53, 724-728.

79. Connelly, J. B. (1985). Published tests—which ones do special education teachers perceive as useful? *Journal of Special Education*, 19, 149-155.

80. Dalby, J. T. (1985). Taxonomic separation of attention deficit disorders and developmental reading disorders. *Contemporary Educational Psychology*, 10, 228-234.

81. Derr, A. M. (1985). Conservation and mathematics achievement in the learning disabled child. *Journal of Learning Disabilities*, 18, 333-336.

82. Estes, R. E., Hallock, J. E., & Bray, N. M. (1985). Comparison of arithmetic measures with learning disabled students. *Perceptual and Motor Skills*, 61, 711-716.

83. Feldman, M. J. (1985). Evaluating pre-primer basal readers using story grammar. *American Educational Research Journal*, 22, 527-547.

84. Fischer, F. W., Shankweiler, D., & Liberman, I. Y. (1985). Spelling proficiency and sensitivity to word structure. *Journal of Memory and Language*, 24, 423-441.

85. Fletcher, J. M. (1985). Memory for verbal and nonverbal stimuli in learning disability subgroups: Analysis by selective reminding. *Journal of Experimental Child Psychology*, 40, 244-259.

86. Guy, E., Platt, J. J., Zwerling, I., & Bullock, S. (1985). Mental health status of prisoners in an urban jail. *Criminal Justice and Behavior*, 12, 29-53.

87. Heilbrun, A. B., Jr., & Heilbrun, M. R. (1985). Psychopathy and dangerousness: Comparison, integration and extension of two psychopathic typologies. *British Journal of Clinical Psychology*, 24, 181-195.

88. Hilgert, L. D., & Treloar, J. H. (1985). The relationship of the Hooper Visual Organization Test to sex, age, and intelligence of elementary school children. *Measurement and Evaluation in Counseling and Development*, 17, 203-206.

89. Humphreys, L. G., Rich, S. A., & Davey, T. C. (1985). A Piagetian test of general intelligence. *Developmental Psychology*, 21, 872-877.

90. Kraft, R. H. (1985). Laterality and school achievement: Interactions between familial handedness and assessed laterality. *Perceptual and Motor Skills*, 61, 1147-1156.

91. Kupke, T., & Lewis, R. (1985). WAIS and neuropsychological tests: Common and unique variance within an epileptic population. *Journal of Clinical and Experimental Neuropsychology*, 7, 353-366.

92. Lowman, R. L., Williams, R. E., & Leeman, G. E. (1985). The structure and relationship of college women's primary abilities and vocational interests. *Journal of Vocational Behavior*, 27, 298-315.

93. Lueger, R. J., Albott, W. L., Hilgendorf, W. A., & Gill, K. J. (1985). Neuropsychological and academic achievement correlates of abnormal WISC-R Verbal-Performance discrepancies. *Journal of Clinical Psychology*, 41, 801-805.

94. Margolis, R. B., Greenlief, C. L., & Taylor, J. M. (1985). Relationship between the WAIS-R and the WRAT in a geriatric sample with suspected dementia. *Psychological Reports*, 56, 287-292.

95. Mayberry, W., & Gilligan, M. B. (1985). Ocular pursuit in mentally retarded, cerebral-palsied, and learning-disabled children. *The American Journal of Occupational Therapy*, 39, 589-595.

96. Moon, C., Marlowe, M., Stellern, J., & Errera, J. (1985). Main and interaction effects of metallic pollutants on cognitive functioning. *Journal of Learning Disabilities*, 18, 217-221.

97. Newville, L., & Hamm, N. H. (1985). Content validity of the WRAT and grade level achievement of primary grade students. *Journal of School Psychology*, 23, 91-93.

98. Ormrod, J. E. (1985). Proofreading *The Cat in the Hat*: Evidence for different reading styles of good and poor spellers. *Psychological Reports*, 57, 863-867.

99. Ormrod, J. E. (1985). Visual memory in a spelling matching task: Comparison of good and poor spellers. *Perceptual and Motor Skills*, 61, 183-188.

100. Reilly, T. P., Drudge, O. W., Rosen, J. C., Loew, D. E., & Fischer, M. (1985). Concurrent and predictive validity of the WISC-R, McCarthy Scales, Woodcock-Johnson, and academic achievement. *Psychology in the Schools*, 22, 380-382.

101. Reitsma-Street, M., Offord, D. R., & Finch, T. (1985). Pairs of same-sexed siblings discordant for antisocial behaviour. *British Journal of Psychiatry*, 146, 415-423.

102. Saldate, M., IV, Mishra, S. P., & Medina, M., Jr. (1985). Bilingual instruction and academic achievement: A longitudinal study. *Journal of Instructional Psychology*, 12, 24-30.

103. Shelton, T. L., Anastopoulos, A. D., & Linden, J. D. (1985). An attribution training program with learning disabled children. *Journal of Learning Disabilities*, 18, 261-265.

104. Sherman, R. G., Berling, B. S., & Oppenheimer, S. (1985). Increasing community independence for adolescents with spina bifida. *Adolescence*, 20, 1-13.

105. Sinclair, E., Forness, S. R., & Alexson, J. (1985). Psychiatric diagnosis: A study of its relationship to school needs. *Journal of Special Education*, 19, 333-344.

106. Smith, E. R. (1985). Community college reading tests: A statewide survey. *Journal of Reading*, 28, 52-55.

107. Treiman, R. (1985). Phonemic awareness and spelling: Children's judgments do not always agree with adults'. *Journal of Experimental Child Psychology*, 39, 182-201.

108. Vance, B., Kitson, D., & Singer, M. G. (1985). Relationship between the standard scores of Peabody Picture Vocabulary Test—Revised and Wide Range Achievement Test. *Journal of Clinical Psychology*, 41, 691-697.

109. Wagner, S. R. (1985). Handedness and higher mental functions. *Claremont Reading Conference Yearbook*, 49, 258-266.

110. Webster, R. E. (1985). The criterion-related validity of psychoeducational tests for actual reading ability of learning disabled students. *Psychology in the Schools*, 22, 152-159.

111. Wright, P. G., & Friesen, W. J. (1985). The Carlson Psychological Survey with adolescents: Norms and scales reliabilities. *Canadian Journal of Behavioural Science*, 17, 389-399.

112. Wurtz, R. G., Sewell, T., & Manni, J. L. (1985). The relationship of estimated learning potential to performance on a learning task and achievement. *Psychology in the Schools*, 22, 293-302.

113. Ackerman, P. T., Anhalt, J. M., & Dykman, R. A. (1986). Arithmetic automatization failure in children with attention and reading disorders: Associations and sequela. *Journal of Learning Disabilities*, 19, 222-232.

114. Bellemare, F. G., Inglis, J., & Lawson, J. S. (1986). Learning disability indices derived from a principal components analysis of the WISC-R: A study of learning disabled and normal boys. *Canadian Journal of Behavioural Science*, 18, 86-91.

115. Berninger, V. W. (1986). Normal variation in reading acquisition. *Perceptual and Motor Skills*, 62, 691-716.

116. Burton, L., & Elliott, R. N., Jr. (1986). Evaluation of a mathematics peer-tutoring program. *Journal of College Student Personnel*, 27, 80-81.

117. Catts, H. W. (1986). Speech production/phonological deficits in reading-disordered children. *Journal of Learning Disabilities*, 19, 504-508.

118. Davenport, L., Yingling, C. D., Fein, G., Galin, D., & Johnstone, J. (1986). Narrative speech deficits in dyslexics. *Journal of Clinical and Experimental Neuropsychology*, 8, 347-361.

119. Fowler, P. C. (1986). Cognitive differentiation of learning-disabled children on the WISC-R: A canonical model of achievement correlates. *Child Study Journal*, 16, 25-38.

120. Gersten, R., Carnine, D., Zoref, L., & Cronin, D. (1986). A multifaceted study of change in seven inner-city schools. *Elementary School Journal*, 86, 257-276.

121. Goldstein, H. S. (1986). Conduct problems, parental supervision, and cognitive development of 12- to 17-year-olds. *Psychological Reports*, 59, 651-658.

122. Guidubaldi, J., Cleminshaw, H. K., Perry, J. D., Nastasi, B. K., & Lightel, J. (1986). The role of selected family environment factors in children's post-divorce adjustment. *Family Relations*, 35, 141-151.

123. Hinshaw, S. P., Carte, E. T., & Morrison, D. C. (1986). Concurrent prediction of academic achievement in reading disabled children: The role of neuropsychological and intellectual measures at different ages. *Clinical Neuropsychology*, 8, 3-8.

124. Holmes, C. S. (1986). Neuropsychological profiles in men with insulin-dependent diabetes. *Journal of Consulting and Clinical Psychology*, 54, 386-389.

125. Jason, L. A., Pillen, B., & Olson, T. (1986). Comp-tutor: A computer-based prevention program. *The School Counselor*, 34, 116-122.

126. Juel, C., Griffith, P. L., & Gough, P. B. (1986). Acquisition of literacy: A longitudinal study of children in first and second grade. *Journal of Educational Psychology*, 78, 243-255.

127. Livesay, J. R. (1986). Clinical utility of Wechsler's deterioration index in screening for behavioral impairment. *Perceptual and Motor Skills*, 63, 619-626.

128. McCue, P. M., Shelly, C., & Goldstein, G. (1986). Intellectual, academic and neuropsychological performance levels in learning disabled adults. *Journal of Learning Disabilities*, 19, 233-236.

129. Miezejeski, C. M., Jenkins, E. C., Hill, A. L., Wisniewski, K., French, J. H., & Brown, W. T. (1986). A profile of cognitive deficit in females from fragile X families. *Neuropsychologia*, 24, 405-409.

130. Newsome, G. L., III. (1986). The effects of reader perspective and cognitive style on remembering important information from texts. *Journal of Reading Behavior*, 18, 117-133.

131. Nici, J., & Reitan, R. M. (1986). Patterns of neuropsychological ability in brain-disordered versus normal children. *Journal of Consulting and Clinical Psychology*, 54, 542-545.

132. Nussbaum, N. L., & Bigler, E. D. (1986). Neuropsychological and behavioral profiles of empirically derived subgroups of learning disabled children. *Clinical Neuropsychology*, 8, 82-89.

133. Nussbaum, N. L., Bigler, E. D., & Koch, W. (1986). Neuropsychologically derived subgroups of learning disabled children: Personality/behavioral dimensions. *Journal of Learning Disabilities*, 19, 57-67.

134. Pennington, B. F., McCabe, L. L., Smith, S. D., Lefly, D. L., Bookman, M. O., Kimberling, W. J., & Lubs, H. A. (1986). Spelling errors in adults with a form of familial dyslexia. *Child Development*, 57, 1001-1013.

135. Perlick, D., Stastny, P., Katz, I., Mayer, M., & Mattis, S. (1986). Memory deficits and anticholinergic levels in chronic schizophrenia. *American Journal of Psychiatry*, 143, 230-232.

136. Reid, N. (1986). Wide Range Achievement Test: 1984 revised edition. *Journal of Counseling and Development*, 64, 538-539.

137. Reynolds, C. R. (1986). Wide Range Achievement Test (WRAT-R), 1984 edition. *Journal of Counseling and Development*, 64, 540-541.

138. Sarazin, F. A., & Spreen, O. (1986). Fifteen year stability of some neuropsychological tests in learning disabled subjects with and without neurological impairment. *Journal of Clinical and Experimental Neuropsychology*, 8, 190-200.

139. Sears, N. C., & Johnson, D. M. (1986). The effects of visual imagery on spelling performance and retention among

elementary students. *The Journal of Educational Research*, 79, 230-233.

140. Shapiro, A. H. (1986). Projection of body image and printing the alphabet. *Journal of Learning Disabilities*, 19, 107-111.

141. Sinclair, E., & Alexson, J. (1986). Factor analysis and discriminant analysis of psychoeducational report contents. *Journal of School Psychology*, 24, 363-371.

142. Spruill, J., & Beck, B. (1986). Relationship between the WAIS-R and Wide Range Achievement Test—Revised. *Educational and Psychological Measurement*, 46, 1037-1040.

143. Stevenson, H. W., & Newman, R. S. (1986). Long-term prediction of achievement and attitudes in mathematics and reading. *Child Development*, 57, 646-659.

144. Stiffman, A. R., Jung, K. G., & Feldman, R. A. (1986). A multivariate risk model for childhood behavior problems. *American Journal of Orthopsychiatry*, 56, 204-211.

145. Vance, B., Fuller, G. B., & Lester, M. L. (1986). A comparison of the Minnesota Perceptual Diagnostic Test Revised and the Bender Gestalt. *Journal of Learning Disabilities*, 19, 211-214.

146. Vance, H. R., Hankins, N., & Brown, W. (1986). Predictive validity of the McCarthy Screening Test based on Wide Range Achievement Test. *Psychological Reports*, 59, 1060-1062.

147. Voeller, K. K. S. (1986). Right-hemisphere deficit syndrome in children. *American Journal of Psychiatry*, 143, 1004-1009.

148. Wharry, R. E., & Kirkpatrick, S. W. (1986). Vision and academic performance of learning disabled children. *Perceptual and Motor Skills*, 62, 323-336.

149. Lovett, M. W. (1987). A developmental approach to reading disability: Accuracy and speed criteria of normal and deficient reading skill. *Child Development*, 58, 234-260.

Review of the Wide Range Achievement Test—Revised by ELAINE CLARK, Assistant Professor of Educational Psychology, University of Utah, Salt Lake City, UT:

The Wide Range Achievement Test—Revised (WRAT-R) is the most recent of five revisions of the original 1936 test. As with most revised editions, this test was intended as a refinement and restandardization of the earlier version. Although the test looks different than its predecessors (e.g., spiral-bound test manual and separate and different colored test forms for the two levels), the content and format are virtually unchanged. The items are identical to the 1965 test edition except for the addition of two counting problems and one subtraction problem to Level 1 of the Arithmetic subtest, and the addition of 10 simple arithmetic items to Level 2. The correlation coefficients between the two editions range from .91 to .99. Nonetheless, the authors report that substantive, though not necessarily perceptible, changes have been made that contribute to the psychometric soundness of the measure.

The Rasch model for item analysis and scaling was used. It is unclear, however, in what way the results of these analyses were used. For example, although the rank order of item difficulty was different for White and non-White samples on the two versions of the Arithmetic subtest, the WRAT-R items and order of presentation are virtually the same as on the WRAT.

Standard scores and grade equivalents were revised based on the newly developed and extended norms. The normative data have been extended to include individuals between the ages of 65 and 75. Norms are now available for individuals ranging in age from 5 years, 0 months, to 74 years, 11 months. Like the earlier version, the WRAT-R has two levels: Level 1 for children ages 5 years, 0 months, to 11 years, 11 months; and Level 2 for persons over 12 years of age.

STANDARDIZATION. The standardization sample of 5,600 was stratified by age (28 age groups, each with 200 persons), sex, race (White/non-White), geographic region, and community residence (metropolitan/non-metropolitan). Unfortunately, with the exception of age, no demographic characteristics of the sample are described in the manual. The rationale underlying the decision to collapse all non-White individuals into one group is absent. For example, there is no information about the individuals who comprise the non-White group. Without such information, it is impossible to evaluate the representativeness of the sample; however, the limited information presented suggests that it was not representative. For instance, Illinois was the only state to represent the entire north central region, a region which is comprised of 26% of the U.S. population (according to the 1982 Rand McNally *Commercial Atlas and Marketing Guide*, which is used as the source of the population figures cited in the WRAT-R manual). Sampling from 1 of 12 north central states, of course, is no more disturbing than sampling 5 of 13 states in the west region, a region where 19% of the U.S. population reside. Without a breakdown of subjects according to states, and other variables on which the sample was stratified, there is no way of evaluating the representativeness of the sample.

The description of procedures used during the standardization are similarly inadequate. The authors do not describe specifically how the subjects were recruited or selected; in fact, randomization procedures were reportedly abandoned with the "difficult-to-find" adult subjects.

RELIABILITY. Consequent to selecting test items using the Rasch model, indices of person and item separation were used, in part, to assess reliability. With the exception of a coefficient of .82 for Level 1 Arithmetic, all median coefficients across subtests for person separation (test reliability) and item separation (sample reliability) are above .91. Test users who are unfamiliar with the Rasch scaling techniques may find it difficult to understand what these coefficients mean. Test-retest reliabilities were calculated for 81 individuals in Level 1 and 67 individuals in Level 2. Given the relatively small sample size, it would have been beneficial to have demographic information about this group. Without a sample description and information regarding the testing procedure (e.g., length of time between the two administrations), all the test user knows is that the coefficients for Level 1 subtests range from .94 to .97, and for Level 2 the range is .79 to .90. Further elaboration and clarification would have been helpful.

VALIDITY. The authors state that "the content validity of the WRAT-R is apparent." What is apparent to this reviewer is that the test has "face validity." Considering the fact that the parameters of the WRAT-R domains (e.g., Reading, Spelling, and Arithmetic) are not adequately defined, content validity cannot be judged. Furthermore, given the stated purpose of the test, "to measure the codes which are needed to learn the basic skills of reading, spelling, and arithmetic," it is not at all clear what the test is measuring. Nonetheless, the authors use the Rasch analysis of item difficulty as a source of evidence. The inclusion of both easy and difficult items does not constitute content validity. The evidence provided by the author for construct validity comes from two sources, item separation coefficients and increasing raw scores with age. However, it is unclear how item separation coefficients pertain to construct validity. Similarly, there is little support for concurrent validity. Not only is minimal information provided, but the studies referred to in the manual pertain to the 1978 version of the WRAT instead of the WRAT-R. Despite the similarity in content of the WRAT and WRAT-R, studies using the new version would be more meaningful.

ADMINISTRATION AND SCORING. The instructions for administering and scoring the individual subtests are clearly presented, as are the procedures for converting raw scores to standard scores and grade equivalents. What is not clear is the procedure used to "smooth" the raw data, nor the reason behind the procedure. In any case, the resultant standard scores have a mean of 100 and standard deviation of 15. The presentation of the grade equivalents has been changed, and now reflects more accurately the ordinal nature of the data. For example, instead of reporting an equivalent of 4.8 (eighth month of the fourth grade), a 4E (end of fourth grade) is reported. Since it is unclear whether the assignment of grade equivalents is arbitrary or based on objective indices, standard scores should be used for score comparisons.

Interpretation of test scores seems further confounded by the fact that test users may administer the test individually or in a group (the training cassette tape can be used for group administrations). Furthermore, the examiner may administer the subtests in a "convenient" order, a provision that was also made for examiners during standardization. Not only are there no data to suggest that the scores derived under the various conditions are comparable, there are no separate norms.

SUMMARY. Perhaps the worst thing that can be said about the WRAT-R is that the more it changes, the more it stays the same. At the present time there is no evidence to suggest that the WRAT-R is an improvement over previous editions. Although the publishing company has indicated to the reviewer that it no longer plans to publish the Diagnostic and Technical Manual as once intended, they will be publishing six monographs pertaining to (a) studies of the WRAT/WRAT-R and other instruments; (b) comparisons between the WRAT and WRAT-R; (c) reliability; (d) case studies; (e) test development; and (f) validity. These monographs should fill in some of the information missing in the Administration Manual. This test seems to have potential as a research and clinical tool; however, until documentation is available, test users should be cautious when using the test to assist in the diagnosis of learning disabilities, help determine personality structure, or check school achievement for vocational assessment, job placement, and training. The fact that this test can be administered and scored quickly will continue to contribute to its popularity. And like its predecessors, the WRAT-R will undoubtedly continue to be one of the most widely used instruments to estimate academic achievement.

Review of the Wide Range Achievement Test— Revised by PATTI L. HARRISON, Assistant Professor of Behavioral Studies, College of Education, The University of Alabama, Tuscaloosa, AL:

The Wide Range Achievement Test—Revised (WRAT-R) is the sixth edition of the popular test that was first published in 1936. Like the earlier versions, the WRAT-R contains three subtests: Reading (recognizing and naming letters and words), Spelling (writing symbols, name, and words), and Arithmetic (solving oral problems and written computations). The authors of the WRAT-R stress that the test is designed to measure basic school codes rather than comprehension, reasoning, and judgement processes. General uses for the test described in the manual include comparing achievement of one person to another, determining learning ability or learning disability, comparing codes with comprehension in order to prescribe remedial programs, and informally assessing error patterns to plan instructional programs.

The items of the WRAT-R are virtually unchanged from earlier versions. The Reading and Spelling subtests contain no changes, while the Arithmetic subtest contains a few additional problems. The administration and scoring procedures also remain unchanged, with a few exceptions that are mostly cosmetic in nature.

The major change intended by the authors of the WRAT-R, and their primary goal in restandardization, was improvement of the psychometric qualities of the test. Critics of previous editions pointed out inadequate standardization and questionable reliability and validity as major problems. The authors of the WRAT-R undoubtedly attempted to answer the criticisms. This review addresses the extent to which they were successful.

DEVELOPMENT AND STANDARDIZATION. One of the new features incorporated into the WRAT-R is the use of the Rasch item-response-theory model. The manual contains a description of the basic premises of the Rasch model, but gives little information about how the model was actually applied to test development.

The manual and a later publication (Jastak Associates, in press) describe the use of Rasch item difficulty estimates to determine that the items ranged from easy to hard. However, the estimates were not used to determine the order of item administration, a logical use of the item statistics because the cutoff rule of 10 consecutive errors on the Reading and Spelling subtests assumes the items are administered in order of difficulty. The manual also indicates that the Rasch model was used to investigate item bias, but this approach to item bias is recognized as inappropriate (Shepard, Camilli, & Williams, 1984). More details about the use of the Rasch model have been promised in forthcoming publications; however, no information was available at the time of this review (three years after the WRAT-R was published).

In contrast to earlier editions, a stratified national sampling plan was used for the standardization of the WRAT-R. A total of 5,600 subjects, or 200 subjects in each of 28 age groups from 5 to 74 years, composed the sample. Stratification variables included age, sex, race, geographical region, and metropolitan versus nonmetropolitan residence. The efforts to obtain a representative national sample are laudable, but concerns about the standardization procedures result in questions about the adequacy of the sample.

Socioeconomic status was not used as a stratification variable, although research clearly shows that socioeconomic status has a stronger relationship with achievement than does race or many other variables. In addition, race was designated as white versus nonwhite, a questionable practice. Perhaps the greatest concern is the failure to describe the actual composition of the sample. Population percentages for each stratification variable, taken from a Rand McNally guide instead of U.S. census reports, are reported in the manual, but there is no indication that the WRAT-R sample matched these percentages. One piece of evidence to support that the percentages were not matched is the states included in the norming program. For example, a total of 17 states were used during standardization, but only one state was located in the north central region of the country.

The characteristics of the adult sample are so vague and confusing that the use of the WRAT-R with individuals above age 18 is probably not advisable. The authors state, "Because of the difficulty in selecting an adult sample, randomization was not as carefully followed." A need to carefully consider amount of higher education is described, but there is no indication of the number of college graduates in the sample. College students (but not college graduates) were excluded from the sample for some reason, resulting in a biased sample. The authors indicate that correction of the norms was necessary to make the results more sensible, but test users should wonder what the WRAT-R norms indicate for adult subjects.

The manual contains adequate guidelines for interpreting the standard scores, percentile ranks, and grade equivalents obtained from the WRAT-R. The authors recommend wisely that only standard scores be used for making subtest comparisons, but do not provide standard errors of difference. The norm tables were constructed to provide standard scores for half-year age intervals at younger ages and wider intervals at older ages. Quarter-year age intervals at younger ages would be more appropriate, given the rapid development of achievement skills at younger ages.

RELIABILITY AND VALIDITY. The Rasch analysis provided person-separation and item-separation values and these are given as evidence of internal consistency. Traditional internal-consistency data, such as split-half or alpha coefficients, are not provided and are needed. Test-retest reliability coefficients range from .79 (Level 2 Arithmetic) to .97 (Level 1 Spelling), but are virtually useless. No indication of the time interval between test and retest is given and the coefficients are based on small samples for only a few age groups in the school-age range. The authors recommend the practice of using standard errors of measurement when interpreting scores, but the values are questionable since they are based on the test-retest reliability coefficients.

One of the major sources of criticism about previous editions was lack of evidence for content validity. Although the current manual provides little information about content validity, a report by Jastak Associates (in press) addresses the issue in greater detail. The following evidence is given for content validity: The first edition sampled dictionaries to obtain reading and spelling items, Rasch statistics support the wide range of item coverage, the

test exhibits evidence of internal consistency, there is a developmental progression of raw scores, WRAT-R subtests have moderately high correlations with Woodcock-Johnson achievement subtests, and the format of administration is similar to classroom activities. None of this evidence supports content validity and test users cannot be assured that the WRAT-R systematically and adequately samples the content taught in today's schools.

The manual supplies two sources of evidence for construct validity: person and item-separation values and increasing raw scores with age. As indicated by Anastasi (1982), internal consistency and developmental progression of scores are necessary but insufficient conditions for construct validity. The raw score means obtained by the standardization sample also do not indicate a clear developmental progression. Some adjacent age groups have small differences in raw score means. The means for 18-to-19-year-olds are always lower than the means for 16-to-17-year-olds, presumably because of the exclusion of college students.

The evidence for concurrent validity consists primarily of a summary of studies comparing the WRAT with other achievement tests. The manual reports very high correlations (i.e., .91 to .99) between the WRAT and WRAT-R, but the correlations were calculated using the WRAT-R norm sample and an "arbitrary" sample of previously administered WRATs. It appears that the correlations are not based on a sample of subjects who took both tests. A few recent studies not presented in the manual investigated concurrent validity. Spruill and Beck (1986a) found WRAT/WRAT-R correlations of .98, .97, and .71 for the Reading, Spelling, and Arithmetic subtests, respectively. Merrill (1985) reports correlations of .70 to .85 for the WRAT-R and Woodcock-Johnson achievement tests. Jastak Associates (1985) found correlations ranging from .37 to .72 for the WRAT-R subtests and WISC-R Verbal, Performance, and Full scales. Smith and Smith (1986) report correlations ranging from .21 to .64 for the WRAT-R subtests and WISC-R Verbal and Performance scales. Spruill and Beck (1986b) found correlations of .47 to .71 for the WRAT-R subtests and WAIS-R Verbal, Performance, and Full scales.

CONCLUSIONS. Does the WRAT-R meet psychometric standards for an achievement test?

This reviewer must answer "No" given available information. Although there seem to be some improvements over earlier editions, the development of the WRAT-R either did not include many recommended practices or the authors did not report them. There are many questions about the applications of the Rasch model, and the standardization sample is not described in enough detail to determine adequacy. Traditional internal consistency coefficients are not available and test-retest reliability coefficients are questionable. Content validity is not supported and information about construct and concurrent validity is limited.

The general uses of the WRAT-R given in the manual are not supported by the test's psychometric qualities. There is no supporting evidence that the WRAT-R can be used for placement of children into special education and remedial programs or for prescribing instruction. Some practitioners justify their use of the WRAT-R by saying, "I use it for screening purposes only." There is no support for this use, either. Using the WRAT-R for screening may result in a great disservice to students. The WRAT-R yields a limited sample of behavior. Although the WRAT-R measures codes, an important aspect of achievement, it does not measure comprehension. A child with comprehension problems could obtain high scores and, thus, not be identified as a child with special academic needs.

REVIEWER'S REFERENCES

Anastasi, A. (1982). *Psychological testing* (5th ed.). New York: MacMillan.
Shepard, L., Camilli, G., & Williams, D. M. (1984). Accounting for statistical artifacts in item bias research. *Journal of Educational Statistics*, 9, 93-128.
Jastak Associates. (1985). *WRAT-R/WISC-R correlations*. Wilmington, DE: Author.
Merrill, K. H. (1985). *Analysis: The new WRAT-R compared with Woodcock-Johnson achievement and WISC-R*. Unpublished manuscript, Mesa Public Schools, Mesa, AZ.
Smith, T. C., & Smith, B. L. (1986). The relationship between the WISC-R and WRAT-R for a sample of rural referred children. *Psychology in the Schools*, 23, 252-254.
Spruill, J., & Beck, B. (1986a). Relationship between the WRAT and WRAT-R. *Psychology in the Schools*, 23, 357-360.
Spruill, J., & Beck, B. (1986b). Relationship between the WAIS-R and Wide Range Achievement Test—Revised. *Educational and Psychological Measurement*, 46, 1037-1040.
Jastak Associates. (in press). *WRAT-R monograph #1: Content validity*. Wilmington, DE: Author.

[89]

Wide-Span Reading Test. Purpose: Assesses a "child's skills in decoding printed symbols into meaningful sounds of language, in fitting meanings to groups of sounds, and in construing the structural relationship of meanings in their total semantic and syntactical context." Ages 7-10 to 14-11; 1972–84; 2 parallel forms, Form A and Form B; 1986 price data: £20.95 per introductory set containing 25 reusable pupils' booklets Forms A and B, 50 answer sheets, and teachers' manual ('83, 36 pages); £6.35 per 25 pupils' booklets, Form A or B; £2.35 per 25 answer sheets; £3.80 per teachers' manual; £4.25 per specimen set containing one each pupils' booklets Forms A and B, answer sheet, and teachers' manual; 30(40) minutes; Alan Brimer; NFER-Nelson Publishing Co., Ltd. [England].*

See T3:2625 (1 reference); for additional information and reviews by David J. Carroll and William Yule, see 8:747.

Review of the Wide-Span Reading Test by MARIAM JEAN DREHER, Associate Professor of Education, Department of Curriculum and Instruction, University of Maryland, College Park, MD:

The Wide-Span Reading Test is intended to assess the reading comprehension level of students aged 7 through 14 years who are in the first through fourth years of junior school and the first through fourth years of secondary school. Students' raw scores on this test are converted to standard scores based on year in school and chronological age in years and months. In addition to standard scores, a nominal scale score can be derived, which is said to represent a student's highest level of functioning. This level is determined by locating the last place in the test where a student has three out of four consecutive items correct; the nominal score is then the item number of the middle of the three correct answers. Although these nominal scores are said to be meaningful on their own, their value is not completely clear; however, there is a table to convert them to reading ages.

The test was standardized on a sample of 7,503 students who are said to represent the different types of schools and locations in England and Wales. However, no information is given to indicate how the sample was selected. There is also no indication of when the test was standardized. Although the test manual was revised in 1984, the test itself was copyrighted in 1972. If the standardization was conducted for the 1972 test, then the sample may be 15 or more years old and therefore may no longer be an appropriate reference group.

The Wide-Span Reading Test presents students with unrelated pairs of sentences. One sentence in each pair has a missing word that must be filled in by selecting an appropriate word from the other sentence. For example, students are asked to fill the blank in "Turn _____ the light" with one of the words from the sentence, "One of them went out the door and into the street."

By having students engage in a series of such tasks, the author of the test claims that "level of reading comprehension" will be measured. However, the author acknowledges that the test does not assess "the sustaining of comprehension throughout continuous passages." This limitation seems a critical one because a major goal of reading-comprehension instruction, and therefore of comprehension assessment, is most certainly to produce students capable of comprehending continuous passages.

Because the task requirement of the test is limited to the comprehension of single sentences, with some degree of reference to a second sentence, it appears that the type of comprehension measured is rather narrow. In fact, the test seems to have more in common with vocabulary rather than comprehension measures. Moreover, the task requirement does not appear to reflect typical modes of responding during common reading activities. Nevertheless, it is possible that performance on these paired sentence completion exercises might be correlated with aspects of reading comprehension that are important for teachers to know. However, no data are presented to support such a claim. Indeed, no information on the validity of the test is offered.

Reliability data are provided by reporting the intercorrelation of the two forms of the Wide-Span Reading Test, Forms A and B. Since the correlation between the two forms at each grade level ranges from .89 to .95, the two forms appear to be measuring much the same thing.

The instructions for administering the test are straightforward. However, since the manual stresses the need to time the 30-minute work period accurately to the second, it is odd that the first four items are in view on the first page while instructions and examples are being discussed. Since accuracy in timing is so important, the test items should begin on the next page to avoid having students read ahead.

The scoring procedures are clear except for an instruction to enter the total number correct in a cell marked "I" at the bottom of the answer sheet. Since there are several cells at the bottom of the page, but none marked "I," users may be confused. Apparently the intended cell is the one marked l on the answer sheet.

Besides measuring level of reading comprehension, another purpose of the Wide-Span Reading Test is "to indicate the areas of reading skill within which low-scoring children may have difficulty." To achieve this purpose, teachers are directed to have students take the test in the usual manner (i.e., students are given 30 minutes to work on the test beginning at the designated starting point for their grade level). Then, immediately afterward, students are instructed to go back to a specific earlier point and work those problems as well. Because first and second year junior school students begin the test at item 1, they of course do not have to go back; but all other students do.

There are some problems with the instructions for using the test for diagnosis. First, the section opens with a sentence that seems to say that the diagnostic use is only for third year juniors and up: "The method of working the test for the purposes of diagnosis (third year juniors and above only) is . . ." Actually, the sentence is misleading because the test is claimed to be useful diagnostically even for the younger grades. Second, teachers are given contradictory instructions regarding how long students should be allowed to work once they are sent back to earlier test sections. Teachers are told to "Allow as much time as is necessary for each child to reach the point at which he first began." But then the very next sentence says "Allow no more than thirty minutes."

After scoring the students' responses, teachers are to identify which students have at least 10 errors within a specified set of items for their grade level. The author notes that only those students' papers can be marked diagnostically. The teacher is then to examine each incorrect item within the designated set and classify the error as a decoding, linguistic (syntax), or vocabulary error. The error is to be marked "decoding" if the student has inverted letter order, or omitted, substituted, or added letters "which detract from the phonetic representation of the word." The question arises as to whether an error in writing can be equated with ability to decode, but the point is not discussed.

A key is provided to guide teachers in categorizing linguistic and vocabulary errors.

For instance, for the sentence "When logs _____, smoke rises," students are to select the missing word from "Brush up the leaves and burn them." The correct answer is "burn." The diagnostic answer key indicates that if the incorrect response is "brush," it is a vocabulary error. However, it is not always clear why a given response is classified in a certain way. Why, for instance, could not "brush" be a decoding error? Errors can also be coded as being from two "error" categories. But the marking key gives no examples to assist teachers in making such a judgement.

If half or more of the total errors occur in any of the three areas, then the claim is made that a "positive diagnostic indication is given" that indicates "prima facie evidence of the general nature of the handicap that contributes to the child's reading comprehension difficulty." However, because no evidence is offered regarding the validity or reliability of the results, it does not seem worthwhile to expend the effort required to obtain this diagnostic information. Indeed, even if teachers make the effort, they are told that the lack of "diagnostic indication" does not rule out a reading difficulty. Moreover, even when a "diagnostic indication" is found, more specific diagnosis is recommended. Consequently, it would seem more productive simply to omit the diagnostic use of this test. Instead, teachers could give an in-depth diagnostic measure to students who do not do well in reading.

In summary, although the Wide-Span Reading Test is reliable and easy to administer, there is no information on its validity for the stated purpose of assessing students' reading comprehension level. Moreover, neither reliability nor validity data are provided for the diagnostic use of the test. The manual's acknowledgement that the test does not measure the comprehension of continuous passages, along with the lack of data on how the test correlates with different aspects of typical reading, should signal prospective users to consider carefully whether this test meets their needs.

Review of the Wide-Span Reading Test by PRISCILLA A. DRUM, Associate Professor of Education, Graduate School of Education, University of California at Santa Barbara, Santa Barbara, CA:

The purpose of the Wide-Span Reading Test is to measure the level of reading comprehension "within the range defined by the beginning of competent silent reading and the full development of reading comprehension effectiveness." The test was developed and normed in Great Britain in 1972. The 1984 revision is limited to changes in the test manual, for both the actual tests and the standardization sample appear to be those obtained in 1972.

DESCRIPTION. This is a group test with exactly 30 minutes allotted for answering the questions after the preliminary instructions are provided. There are two forms of the test, Form A and Form B, so pre- and post-tests can be given to measure increases in level of comprehension. The intercorrelations between the two forms are quite high, ranging from .89 to .95 for the eight grades tested, with relatively small estimates of the standard error of measurement. However, parallel-forms reliability is the only type of reliability information provided; no test-retest, internal consistency, or item data are given.

The standardization sample appears adequate, though again, only the number and sex at each grade are noted. The manual attests to the representativeness of the sample for types of schools and geographical regions throughout England and Wales. No breakdown is provided.

FORMAT. This test differs from the typical question-stem and multiple-choice-recognition formats of most reading achievement tests. The format of the test is a modified Cloze, with each item consisting of two sentences placed side by side on the page. The stem sentence on the right side has one word deleted. The deleted item can occur at any position within the sentence from the first to the last word. The task is to select the most appropriate word from the sentence on the left side to complete the meaning of the stem sentence on the right side. The number of choices depends on the length of the left sentence, from 6 to 22 words. The guessing factor of selecting one out of four or five choices is avoided. Also, the answer cannot be selected without examining both sentences.

STUDENT LEVEL. The age range given for the test is 7-0 to 14-11 years, or the four junior years and the first four secondary years in English schools (equivalent to second grade through ninth grade in the United States). The item suggested for beginning the test increases from item 1 for the first and second junior years up to item 57 for the fourth secondary year. However, the average performance of 7-year-olds is 1 to 6 items correct and for 8-year-olds 3 to 12 items correct. Since the intent is to measure competent silent reading comprehension, this test should probably not be used until the third year of school. Also, the number of items available for the fourth secondary year, 24 items, is too few to establish adequate discrimination between students of differing abilities. Based on data from the "second occasion" (or second testing) tables, a raw score of one item correct is equivalent to a -1.33 standard deviation for a 14-year-old on the fourth year test, while the same score for a 14-year-old on the 35-item third year test is equivalent to a -2.40 standard deviation. The age for testing and the raw scores have not changed, only the entry level and the number of items available have. Thus, the effective range for this test is somewhat more limited than that recommended by the author.

The sentence items do increase in difficulty, but not just in the manner described in the manual (i.e., "complexity of the incomplete sentence, the embeddedness of the missing word in the second sentence, and the counter-suggestions of inappropriate alternatives"). Both the target and the cue sentences do increase in length, resulting in more elaborated phrases and dependent clauses. However, the target sentence for item 1, Form B, ends with a subordinate clause. Passive constructions and the use of verbals are more prevalent in the later items. But the two major sources of difficulty are the decreasing frequency of the vocabulary used and the changing content of the sentences from familiar, concrete events to abstractions and/or more technical information. The lack of any systematic description for the content of this test beyond the phrases quoted above is the major weakness of this test.

VALIDITY. The test looks like a reading comprehension test; it has face validity. But there is no reference in the manual to any theory of reading comprehension; no model is provided for levels of comprehension. In fact, there is no attempt to provide any type of validity information. How the test was developed and evaluated cannot be determined. The conversion tables for reading age, percentile rankings, and standard scores indicate that older students have more correct answers, but do these scores correlate with school performance measures or with subsequent educational attainments? These questions are not answered. More than this, if a class or a school performs poorly as compared with similar grades in the normative sample, what instruction should be provided? Without attention to construct and content validity, a score on this test can only provide comparative standings. Items are not categorized into types, nor is any item data provided except for a few brief notes on the recommended diagnostic procedures.

The diagnostic portion of the test would be difficult to implement and the results not particularly informative if done. The test administrator would have to decide in advance to proceed with the diagnostic phase because it follows immediately after the regular 30-minute test. The students in the third year and beyond now begin at a designated item prior to the item where they initially began. Each student is given an additional 30 minutes to answer the earlier items and to "look over the work you have already done." The error responses are then individually scored as indicating decoding problems (any type of misspelling), linguistic problems (selection of any word from the cue sentence other than the correct choice or an incorrect choice that is identified as a vocabulary error), and vocabulary problems (selection of a designated vocabulary word error from the cue sentence). Ten or more errors in any of the three error categories indicate the general nature of the child's reading difficulties. It is noted that an error can indicate conjoint problems, for instance, both linguistic and vocabulary. Again, no rationale is provided for the diagnostic procedures, nor any substantiation that 10 or more errors do identify a general problem area. There appears to be little point, even if feasible, to follow the diagnostic steps.

RECOMMENDATION. In summary, the Wide-Span Reading Test is an imaginative test of reading comprehension that could be useful in numerous research studies in both timed and untimed sessions to see if those students who do not have knowledge of the vocabulary used could figure out the answers by using the information in both the cue and the target sentence. As described, this test provides a measure of a student's ability to evaluate vocabulary in context. Also, major test publishers in the United States should examine this test as a basis for constructing reading comprehension tests. The format offers many ideas for better testing procedures.

However, this test cannot be recommended for classroom testing; too much of the information required by the American Psychological Association's *Standards for Educational and Psychological Testing* (AERA, APA, NCME, 1985) is simply not provided, particularly answers concerning the validity of the test.

REVIEWER'S REFERENCE

American Educational Research Association, American Psychological Association, & National Council on Measurement in Education. (1985). *Standards for educational and psychological testing*. Washington, DC: American Psychological Association, Inc.

CONTRIBUTING TEST REVIEWERS

IRA E. AARON, Professor Emeritus, University of Georgia, Athens, GA

RUSSELL L. ADAMS, Director, Psychology Internship Program, University of Oklahoma Health Sciences Center, Oklahoma City, OK

DORIS V. ALLEN, Professor of Audiology, Wayne State University, Detroit, MI

ANNE ANASTASI, Professor Emeritus of Psychology, Fordham University, Bronx, NY

NICHOLAS W. BANKSON, Professor and Chair, Department of Communication Disorders, Boston University, Boston, MA

JAMES R. BARCLAY, Professor of Educational and Counseling Psychology, University of Kentucky, Lexington, KY

DAVID W. BARNETT, Associate Professor, School Psychology, University of Cincinnati, Cincinnati, OH

CHRISTOPHER BORMAN, Professor of Educational Psychology, Texas A&M University, College Station, TX

R. A. BORNSTEIN, Assistant Professor of Psychiatry, Departments of Psychiatry and Psychology, Ohio State University, Columbus, OH

BRUCE A. BRACKEN, Associate Professor, Department of Psychology, Memphis State University, Memphis, TN

LINDA E. BRODY, Assistant Director, Study of Mathematically Precocious Youth (SMPY), The Johns Hopkins University, Baltimore, MD

ROBERT D. BROWN, Professor of Educational Psychology, University of Nebraska-Lincoln, Lincoln, NE

ROGER H. BRUNING, Professor of Educational Psychology, University of Nebraska-Lincoln, Lincoln, NE

NANCY A. BUSCH-ROSSNAGEL, Associate Professor of Psychology and Research Associate, Hispanic Research Center, Fordham University, Bronx, NY

ROBERT C. CALFEE, Professor of Education, School of Education, Stanford University, Stanford, CA

CAMERON J. CAMP, Associate Professor of Psychology, University of New Orleans, New Orleans, LA

SYLVIA M. CARTER, Associate Professor of Reading Education, University of Georgia, Athens, GA

J. MANUEL CASAS, Associate Professor of Counseling Psychology, Department of Education, University of California, Santa Barbara, CA

CLINTON I. CHASE, Director, Bureau of Evaluative Studies and Testing, Indiana University, Bloomington, IN

ELAINE CLARK, Assistant Professor of Educational Psychology, University of Utah, Salt Lake City, UT

NICHOLAS COLANGELO, Professor and Chair of Counselor Education, University of Iowa, Iowa City, IA

RICHARD COLWELL, Professor of Music and Secondary Education, University of Illinois at Urbana-Champaign, Urbana, IL

JOHN A. COURTRIGHT, Professor and Chair of Communication, University of Delaware, Newark, DE

LINDA CROCKER, Professor of Foundations of Education, University of Florida, Gainesville, FL

LEE J. CRONBACH, Fellow, Center for the Study of Families, Children, and Youth, Stanford University, Stanford, CA

BERT P. CUNDICK, Professor of Psychology, Brigham Young University, Provo, UT

M. HARRY DANIELS, Associate Professor of

Educational Psychology, Southern Illinois University at Carbondale, Carbondale, IL

MARILYN E. DEMOREST, Associate Professor of Psychology, University of Maryland-Baltimore County, Catonsville, MD

DAVID N. DIXON, Professor and Department Chair, Counseling and Psychology Services, Ball State University, Muncie, IN

JANICE A. DOLE, Assistant Professor of Education, Michigan State University, East Lansing, MI

GEORGE DOMINO, Professor of Psychology, University of Arizona, Tucson, AZ

MARIAM JEAN DREHER, Associate Professor of Education, Department of Curriculum and Instruction, University of Maryland, College Park, MD

PRISCILLA A. DRUM, Associate Professor of Education, Graduate School of Education, University of California at Santa Barbara, Santa Barbara, CA

CARL J. DUNST, Director, Family, Infant and Preschool Program, Western Carolina Center, Morganton, NC

BRUCE J. EBERHARDT, Associate Professor of Management, University of North Dakota, Grand Forks, ND

WILLIAM P. ERCHUL, Assistant Professor of Psychology, North Carolina State University, Raleigh, NC

DEBORAH B. ERICKSON, Assistant Professor of Psychology, Rochester Institute of Technology, and Monroe Community College, Rochester, NY

CANDICE FEIRING, Associate Professor of Pediatrics, Robert Wood Johnson Medical School, University of Medicine and Dentistry of New Jersey, New Brunswick, NJ

AMY FINCH-WILLIAMS, Assistant Professor of Speech/Language Pathology, University of Wyoming, Laramie, WY

MARILYN FRIEND, Assistant Professor of Learning, Development, and Special Education, Northern Illinois University, DeKalb, IL

LYNN S. FUCHS, Assistant Professor of Special Education, George Peabody College, Vanderbilt University, Nashville, TN

MARTIN FUJIKI, Associate Professor of Speech Pathology and Audiology, University of Nevada School of Medicine, Reno, NV

GLORIA A. GALVIN, Assistant Professor and Director, School Psychology Training Program, Ohio University, Athens, OH

EUGENE E. GARCIA, Professor/Director, Center for Bilingual/Bicultural Education, Arizona State University, Tempe, AZ

ERIC F. GARDNER, Professor of Psychology and Education Emeritus, Syracuse University, Syracuse, NY

FRED M. GROSSMAN, Assistant Professor of Special Education and Communication Disorders, University of Nebraska-Lincoln, Lincoln, NE

ROBERT M. GUION, University Professor Emeritus of Psychology, Bowling Green State University, Bowling Green, OH

BARBARA LAPP GUTKIN, Speech-Language Clinician, Lincoln Public Schools, Lincoln, NE

PATTI L. HARRISON, Assistant Professor of Behavioral Studies, College of Education, The University of Alabama, Tuscaloosa, AL

WILLIAM O. HAYNES, Associate Professor, Department of Communication Disorders, Auburn University, Auburn, AL

E. CHARLES HEALEY, Associate Professor of Speech-Language Pathology, University of Nebraska-Lincoln, Lincoln, NE

MARY HENNING-STOUT, Assistant Professor, Austin College, Sherman, TX

DAVID O. HERMAN, Measurement Research Services, Inc., New York, NY

JULIA A. HICKMAN, Assistant Professor of School Psychology, The University of Texas at Austin, Austin, TX

RICHARD W. JOHNSON, Associate Director and Adjunct Professor, University Counseling Service, University of Wisconsin-Madison, Madison, WI

RABINDRA N. KANUNGO, Professor of Management and Psychology, McGill University, Montreal, Quebec, Canada

ALAN S. KAUFMAN, Research Professor of School Psychology, The University of Alabama, Tuscaloosa, AL

TIMOTHY Z. KEITH, Associate Professor of School Psychology, Virginia Tech University, Blacksburg, VA

HAROLD R. KELLER, Associate Professor of Psychology and Education, Syracuse University, Syracuse, NY

MARY LOU KELLEY, Assistant Professor of Psychology, Louisiana State University, Baton Rouge, LA

BARBARA A. KERR, Assistant Professor of

Counselor Education, The University of Iowa, Iowa City, IA

BENJAMIN KLEINMUNTZ, Professor of Psychology, University of Illinois at Chicago, Chicago, IL

HOWARD M. KNOFF, Associate Professor of School Psychology, Department of Psychological Foundations, University of South Florida, Tampa, FL

DEBORAH KING KUNDERT, Educational Psychology and Statistics, University at Albany, State University of New York, Albany, NY

KORESSA KUTSICK, Assistant Professor of Psychology, James Madison University, Harrisonburg, VA

STEVEN W. LEE, Assistant Professor, Department of Educational and School Psychology, Indiana State University, Terre Haute, IN

PAUL R. LEHMAN, Professor and Associate Dean, School of Music, The University of Michigan, Ann Arbor, MI

IRVIN J. LEHMANN, Professor of Measurement, Michigan State University, East Lansing, MI

RODNEY L. LOWMAN, Director, Corporate Mental Health Programs, Occupational Health Service, and Faculty, Divisions of Medical Psychology and Occupational Medicine, Duke University Medical Center, Durham, NC

F. CHARLES MACE, Associate Professor, Graduate School of Applied and Professional Psychology, Rutgers University, Piscataway, NJ

CAROLINE MANUELE-ADKINS, Associate Professor of Counseling, Department of Educational Foundations, Hunter College of the City University of New York, New York, NY

ROBERT P. MARKLEY, Professor of Psychology, Fort Hays State University, Hays, KS

ELLEN MCGINNIS, Assistant Professor of Special Education, University of Wisconsin-Eau Claire, Eau Claire, WI

PAUL MCREYNOLDS, Professor of Psychology, University of Nevada-Reno, Reno, NV

DAVID J. MEALOR, Associate Professor of School Psychology, University of Central Florida, Orlando, FL

WILLIAM B. MICHAEL, Professor of Education and Psychology, University of Southern California, Los Angeles, CA

GLORIA E. MILLER, Associate Professor of Psychology, University of South Carolina, Columbia, SC

PATRICIA L. MIRENDA, Assistant Professor of Special Education and Communication Disorders, University of Nebraska-Lincoln, Lincoln, NE

DAVID MOSHMAN, Associate Professor of Educational Psychology, University of Nebraska-Lincoln, Lincoln, NE

KEVIN W. MOSSHOLDER, Associate Professor of Management, Auburn University, Auburn, AL

CAROLYN COLVIN MURPHY, Assistant Professor of Teacher Education, San Diego State University, San Diego, CA

KEVIN R. MURPHY, Associate Professor of Psychology, Colorado State University, Fort Collins, CO

JANET A. NORRIS, Assistant Professor of Communication Disorders, Louisiana State University, Baton Rouge, LA

RUTH M. NOYCE, Professor of Curriculum and Instruction, The University of Kansas, Lawrence, KS

CHARLES K. PARSONS, Professor of Management, Georgia Institute of Technology, Atlanta, GA

CHARLES A. PETERSON, Staff Clinical Psychologist, VA Minneapolis Medical Center, Minneapolis, MN

JAMES A. POTEET, Professor of Special Education, Ball State University, Muncie, IN

ELIZABETH M. PRATHER, Professor of Speech and Hearing Science, Arizona State University, Tempe, AZ

LESLIE T. RASKIND, School Psychologist, Gwinnett County Public Schools, Lawrenceville, GA

SHARON B. REYNOLDS, Assistant Professor of Education, Texas Christian University, Fort Worth, TX

SYLVIA ROSENFIELD, Professor of School Psychology, Temple University, Philadelphia, PA

ARLENE C. ROSENTHAL, Department of Educational and Counseling Psychology, College of Education, University of Kentucky, Lexington, KY

ROBERT RUEDA, Visiting Associate Professor of Curriculum, Teaching, and Learning, University of Southern California, Los Angeles, CA

MICHAEL RYAN, Clinical Psychologist, West Side Family Mental Health Clinic, P.C., Kalamazoo, MI

JANICE SANTOGROSSI, Instructor of Special Education and Communication Disorders, University of Nebraska-Lincoln, Lincoln, NE

RICHARD J. SCHISSEL, Associate Professor and Chair, Department of Speech Pathology and Audiology, Ithaca College, Ithaca, NY

MARCIA B. SHAFFER, School Psychologist, Steuben/Allegany BOCES, Bath, NY

EDWARD S. SHAPIRO, Associate Professor and Director, School Psychology Program, Lehigh University, Bethlehem, PA

LINDA JENSEN SHEFFIELD, Professor of Education and Mathematics, Northern Kentucky University, Highland Heights, KY

KENNETH L. SHELDON, School Psychologist, Edgecombe County Schools, Tarboro, NC

KENNETH G. SHIPLEY, Professor and Chairman, Department of Communicative Disorders, Laboratory School-MS 80, California State University-Fresno, Fresno, CA

ARTHUR B. SILVERSTEIN, Professor of Psychiatry, University of California, Los Angeles, CA

JOAN SILVERSTEIN, Assistant Professor of Psychology and Director, School Psychology Program, Montclair State College, Upper Montclair, NJ

JAYNE E. STAKE, Professor of Psychology, University of Missouri-St. Louis, St. Louis, MO

CHARLES W. STANSFIELD, Director, Division of Foreign Language Education and Testing, Center for Applied Linguistics, Washington, DC

KRISTA J. STEWART, Associate Professor of Psychology and Director of the School Psychology Training Program, Tulane University, New Orleans, LA

SHELDON L. STICK, Professor, Department of Special Education and Communication Disorders, University of Nebraska-Lincoln, Lincoln, NE

DAVID STRAND, Ph.D. Candidate in Counseling Psychology, Department of Education, University of California, Santa Barbara, CA

CATHY F. TELZROW, Psychologist and Director, Educational Assessment Project, Cuyahoga Special Education Service Center, Maple Heights, OH

PAUL W. THAYER, Professor and Head of Psychology, North Carolina State University, Raleigh, NC

RUTH G. THOMAS, Associate Professor, College of Education, University of Minnesota, St. Paul, MN

GAIL E. TOMPKINS, Associate Professor of Language Arts Education, University of Oklahoma, Norman, OK

LAWRENCE J. TURTON, Professor of Speech-Language Pathology, Indiana University of Pennsylvania, Indiana, PA

NICHOLAS A. VACC, Professor and Coordinator of Counselor Education, University of North Carolina, Greensboro, NC

STANLEY F. VASA, Professor of Special Education and Communication Disorders, University of Nebraska-Lincoln, Lincoln, NE

DAVID P. WACKER, Associate Professor of Pediatrics and Special Education, The University of Iowa, Iowa City, IA

RICHARD A. WANTZ, Associate Professor of Educational Psychology and Director of Counseling Psychology Clinic, College of Education, University of Oklahoma, Norman, OK

RICHARD A. WEINBERG, Professor, Educational Psychology and Co-Director, Center for Early Education and Development, University of Minnesota, Minneapolis, MN

SUE WHITE, Assistant Professor of Psychology, Case Western Reserve University, School of Medicine, Cleveland, OH

ROBERT T. WILLIAMS, Associate Professor of Occupational and Educational Studies, Colorado State University, Fort Collins, CO

STEVEN L. WISE, Assistant Professor of Educational Psychology, University of Nebraska-Lincoln, Lincoln, NE

DAN WRIGHT, School Psychologist, Ralston Public Schools, Ralston, NE

JOHN A. ZARSKE, Director, Northern Arizona Psychological Services, P.C., Flagstaff, AZ

INDEX OF TITLES

This title index lists all the tests included in The Supplement to the Ninth Mental Measurements Yearbook. Citations are to test entry numbers, not to pages—e.g., 54 refers to test 54 and not page 54. (Test numbers along with test titles are indicated in the running heads at the top of each page, while page numbers, used only in the Table of Contents but not in the indexes, appear at the bottom of each page.) Superseded titles are listed with cross references to current titles, and alternative titles are also cross referenced.

An (N) appearing immediately after a test number indicates that the test is a new, recently published test, and/or that it has not appeared before in a Buros Institute publication. An (R) indicates that the test has been revised or supplemented since last reviewed in a Mental Measurements Yearbook.

INDEX OF ACRONYMS

This Index of Acronyms refers the reader to the appropriate test in The Supplement to the Ninth Mental Measurements Yearbook. *In some cases tests are better known by their acronyms than by their full titles, and this index can be of substantial help to the person who knows the former but not the latter. Acronyms are only listed if the author or publisher has made substantial use of the acronym in referring to the test, or if the test is widely known by the acronym. A few acronyms are also registered trademarks (e.g., SAT); where this is known to us, only the test with the registered trademark is referenced. There is some danger in the overuse of acronyms, but this index, like all other indexes in this work, is provided to make the task of identifying a test as easy as possible. All numbers refer to test numbers, not page numbers.*

CLASSIFIED SUBJECT INDEX

The Classified Subject Index classifies all tests included in The Supplement to the Ninth Mental Measurements Yearbook *into 12 major categories: Achievement, Developmental, English, Fine Arts, Intelligence and Scholastic Aptitude, Mathematics, Miscellaneous, Neuropsychological, Personality, Reading, Speech and Hearing, and Vocations. Each category appears in alphabetical order and tests are ordered alphabetically within each category. Each test entry includes test title (first letters capitalized), population for which the test is intended (lower case), and the test entry number in* The Supplement to the Ninth Mental Measurements Yearbook. *All numbers refer to test entry numbers, not to page numbers. Brief suggestions for the use of this index are presented in the Introduction.*

ACHIEVEMENT

Maculaitis Assessment Program, Commercial Edition, ESL students in grades K–12, see 37

Wide Range Achievement Test—Revised, ages 5-0 to 11-11, 12-0 to 75, see 88

DEVELOPMENTAL

Howell Prekindergarten Screening Test, prekindergarten students, see 29

Infant Screening, ages 5–6, see 30

Meeting Street School P.S.R. Test: Psychological S-R Evaluation for Severely Multiply Handicapped Children, severely multiply handicapped children ages 1–5 and retarded severely multiply handicapped children ages 6–10, see 42

Preschool Behavior Rating Scale, day care, Head Start, or nursery school children ages 3–6, see 50

Preschool Development Inventory, ages 3-0 to 5-5, see 60

The Preverbal Assessment-Intervention Profile, low functioning handicapped infants and children, see 61

The Southern California Ordinal Scales of Development, multihandicapped, developmentally delayed, and learning disabled children, and normal children, see 73

The Vane Kindergarten Test (1984 Revision), ages 4–6, see 86

EDUCATION

Evaluating Educational Programs for Intellectually Gifted Students, learning environments for grades K–12, see 25

Our Class and Its Work, grades 3–12, see 52

ENGLISH

FINE ARTS

INTELLIGENCE AND SCHOLASTIC APTITUDE

MATHEMATICS

MISCELLANEOUS

NEUROPSYCHOLOGICAL

PERSONALITY

READING

SPEECH AND HEARING

VOCATIONS

PUBLISHERS DIRECTORY AND INDEX

Heinemann Publishers Australia Pty Ltd., 85 Abinger Street, Box 133, Richmond 3121, Victoria, Australia: 26

Houghton Mifflin, One Beacon Street, Boston, MA 02108: 11

Interdatum, 600 Montgomery Street, 37th Floor, San Francisco, CA 94111: 76

INTERSTATE Printers & Publishers, Inc. (The), 19 North Jackson Street, Danville, IL 61832-0594: 7

Jastak Associates, Inc., 1526 Gilpin Avenue, Wilmington, DE 19806: 88

Macmillan Education Ltd., Registered Office, 4 Little Essex Street, London, WC2R 3LF, England: 30, 35, 36

Macmillan Publishing Co., Inc., 866 Third Avenue, New York, NY 10022: 8

Maculaitis, Jean D'Arcy, Ph.D., P.O. Box 56, Sea Bright, NJ 07760: 34

Marathon Consulting & Press, P.O. Box 09189, 575 Enfield Road, Columbus, OH 43209-0189: 20

Meeting Street School, 667 Waterman Avenue, East Providence, RI 02914: 42

Michalak Training Associates, Inc., 875 Pinto Place, South, Tucson, AZ 85748-7921: 71

Midwest Publications, Inc., P.O. Box 448, Pacific, CA 93950: 24

National Business Education Association, 1914 Association Drive, Reston, VA 22091: 46

NFER-Nelson Publishing Co., Ltd., Darville House, 2 Oxford Road East, Windsor, Berkshire SL4 1DF, England: 63, 65, 89

Oaster, T. R. F., School of Education, Educational Research and Psychology, University of Missouri, 5100 Rockhill Road, Kansas City, MO 64110: 77

OUTREACH, Pre-College Programs, KDES PAS6, Gallaudet University, Washington, DC 20002: 40

PRO-ED, Inc., 5341 Industrial Oaks Blvd., Austin, TX 78735: 5, 14, 16, 21, 47, 48, 49, 51, 83, 85

Project SPOKE, Vincent IGO Administration Center, South Street, Foxboro, MA 02035: 69

Psychological Assessment Resources, Inc., P.O. Box 998, Odessa, FL 33556-0998: 4, 66, 68

Psychological Corporation (The), 555 Academic Court, San Antonio, TX 78204-0952: 44

Research Psychologists Press, Inc., P.O. Box 984, 1110 Military Street, Port Huron, MI 48060: 43

Riverside Publishing Co. (The), 8420 Bryn Mawr Avenue, Chicago, IL 60631: 75

Rocky Mountain Behavioral Science Institute, Inc., P.O. Box 1066, Fort Collins, CO 80522: 50, 74

Scholastic Testing Service, Inc., 480 Meyer Road, P.O. Box 1056, Bensenville, IL 60106-0856: 38

Science Research Associates, Inc., 155 North Wacker Drive, Chicago, IL 60606-1780: 78

Slosson Educational Publications, Inc., P.O. Box 280, East Aurora, NY 14052: 13

Special Child Publications, P.O. Box 33548, Seattle, WA 98133: 70

Test Agency (The), Cournswood House, North Dean, High Wycombe, Bucks, HP14 4NW, England: 39

United Educational Services, Inc., P.O. Box 605, East Aurora, NY 14052: 18, 80

University Associates, Inc., 8517 Production Avenue, San Diego, CA 92121: 62

Western Psychological Services, 12031 Wilshire Blvd., Los Angeles, CA 90025: 6, 32, 72

Wolfe Personnel Testing & Training Systems, Inc., Box 319, Oradell, NJ 07649: 19, 55

XICOM, Inc., Sterling Forest, Tuxedo, NY 10987: 57

INDEX OF NAMES

This analytical index indicates whether a citation refers to authorship of a test, a test review, an excerpted review, or a reference for a specific test. Numbers refer to test entries, not to pages. The abbreviations and numbers following the names may be interpreted as follows: "test, 73" indicates authorship of test 73; "rev, 86" indicates authorship of a review of test 86; "exc, 68" indicates authorship of an excerpted review of test 68; "ref, 45(30)" indicates authorship of reference number 30 in the "Test References" section for test 45; "ref, 13r" indicates a reference (unnumbered) in one of the "Reviewer's References" sections for test 13. Names mentioned in cross references are also indexed.

Clark, F.: ref, 88(18)
Clark, J. A.: ref, 45(36)
Clark, J. H.: ref, 88(39)
Clarke, M. A.: ref, 88(27)
Clarke, S.: ref, 88(53)
Clarkson, C.: ref, 10(4)
Clegg, M.: ref, 81(4)
Cleland, D. L.: exc, 15
Cleminshaw, H. K.: ref, 88(122)
Close, J. S.: test, 22
Cochran, C. D.: ref, 10(1), 10r
Cohen, J. A.: ref, 75(66)
Cohen, N. J.: ref, 88(78)
Cohen, R. D.: ref, 75(19)
Cohen, R. L.: ref, 88(27)
Colangelo, N.: rev, 25, 27
Cole, C. W.: test, 74
Coleman, M.: ref, 75(37)
Colligan, R. C.: ref, 88(28)
Collins, D. W. K.: ref, 88(20,21)
Colwell, R.: rev, 31
Cone, J. D.: test, 53; ref, 53r
Cone, T.: ref, 88(70)
Connard, P.: test, 61
Connelly, J. B.: ref, 15(2), 88(79)
Conte, V. A.: test, 66
Cooley, W. W.: ref, 11r
Copeland, A. P.: ref, 88(29)
Corey, S. M.: exc, 21
Corgiat, M. D.: ref, 75(53)
Corley, R.: ref, 75(70)
Coscarelli, W. C.: test, 20; ref, 6(8), 20(1,3)
Costa, P. T., Jr.: ref, 68(3)
Cottle, W. C.: ref, 49r
Couch, A.: ref, 78r
Coursin, D.: ref, 75(37)
Courtney, P. D.: rev, 88
Courtright, J. A.: rev, 16, 47
Covin, T. M.: ref, 75(38)
Cragan, M. K.: ref, 45(8)
Crandall, J. E.: ref, 45(9)
Crites, J. O.: rev, 68
Crocker, L.: rev, 5, 72
Cronbach, L. J.: rev, 75; ref, 75r
Cronin, D.: ref, 88(120)
Crowe, R. R.: ref, 10(4)
Cullen, J. K., Jr.: ref, 21(5), 75(32)
Cullinan, D.: ref, 88(5)
Cundick, B. P.: rev, 10, 32
Cunningham, C. C.: ref, 75(39)
Currie, B. B.: ref, 75(61), 88(46,47)
Cutts, C. C.: exc, 68

Dahm, J. W.: test, 41
Daiss, S. R.: ref, 45(53)
Dalby, J. T.: ref, 88(80)
Dallas Educational Services: test, 27
Daly, D. C.: ref, 45(68)
Dameron, J. D.: test, 41
Daniels, M. H.: test, 6; rev, 39, 68
Darch, C.: ref, 88(77)
Datwyler, M. L.: ref, 88(1)
Davenport, L.: ref, 88(118)
Davey, T. C.: ref, 88(89)
Davis, D.: ref, 88(37)

Davis, K. J.: ref, 45(72)
Davis, R. B.: ref, 45(6)
Dawis, R. V.: ref, 68(4)
Deaton, J.: ref, 45(2)
Deckner, C. W.: ref, 75(10)
Deckner, P.: ref, 75(10)
Deffenbacher, J. L.: ref, 45(8)
DeFries, J. C.: ref, 75(48)
Deklyen, M.: ref, 75(26)
Delaney, E.: ref, 75r
de la Riva, C.: ref, 45(60)
DeLawyer, D. D.: test, 53; ref, 53r
Demorest, M. E.: rev, 18, 40
Denney, D. R.: ref, 45(24)
Deroach, J. N.: ref, 88(20)
DeRoach, J. N.: ref, 88(21)
Derogatis, L. R.: test, 10
Derr, A. M.: ref, 88(81)
Desberg, P.: ref, 88(71)
DeSoto, C. B.: ref, 21(1)
DeSoto, J. L.: ref, 21(1)
deVilliers, J. G.: ref, 44r
deVilliers, P. A.: ref, 44r
Devine, J.: ref, 75(45)
DeWitt, R. A.: ref, 88(26)
DeWolfe, A. S.: ref, 88(30)
Dial, J. G.: ref, 75(35)
Dishion, T. J.: ref, 88(31)
Dixon, D. N.: rev, 62, 66
Dlabay, L.: test, 38
Dobson, K. S.: ref, 45(33,34)
Doeff, A. M.: test, 59
Dole, J. A.: rev, 64, 82
Dollaghan, C.: ref, 81(6)
Dolliver, R. H.: rev, 68; exc, 68
Domino, G.: rev, 12, 20
Doren, B.: ref, 45(39)
Dorman, C.: ref, 88(32)
Dougherty, K.: ref, 45(54)
Doughtie, E. B.: ref, 32(1), 88(24)
Doyle, B. A.: ref, 88(33)
Dreher, M. J.: rev, 63, 89
Drudge, O. W.: ref, 88(100)
Drum, P. A.: rev, 89
Duffy, J. R.: test, 47; ref, 47r
Duffy, R. J.: test, 47; ref, 47r
Dunst, C. J.: rev, 29
Durham, T. W.: ref, 75(40)
Dykman, R. A.: ref, 88(113)

Earls, F.: ref, 88(38)
Eash, M. J.: test, 52
Eaves, R.: ref, 88(77)
Ebben, R.: ref, 68(16)
Eberhardt, B. J.: rev, 6
Edelbrock, C. S.: ref, 87r
Edwards, A. L.: ref, 33r
Eichorn, D. H.: rev, 86
Ekelman, B. L.: ref, 88(16)
Elbert, J. C.: ref, 88(34)
Elias, P.: ref, 75(2)
Ellickson, J. L.: ref, 45(3)
Elliott, R. N., Jr.: ref, 88(116)
Elliott, S. N.: ref, 88(4)
Elliott, T. R.: ref, 68(12)

Engelmann, S.: ref, 5r
Ennis, R. H.: test, 24
Eno, L.: ref, 88(35)
Enright, M. K.: ref, 75(63)
Epperson, D. L.: ref, 88(1)
Epps, S.: ref, 88(15)
Epstein, M. H.: ref, 88(5)
Erchul, W. P.: rev, 78
Erickson, D. B.: rev, 35, 85
Eron, L. D.: ref, 88(45)
Errera, J.: ref, 88(96)
Estes, R. E.: ref, 88(82)

Falasco, S. L.: ref, 88(60)
Falvey, M.: ref, 61r
Farber, S. S.: ref, 45(35)
Farley, R. C.: ref, 45(10)
Fein, G.: ref, 88(118)
Feinburg, H.: rev, 21
Feiring, C.: rev, 29
Feitel, B.: ref, 88(6)
Feldman, M. J.: ref, 88(83)
Feldman, R. A.: ref, 88(144)
Felner, R. D.: ref, 45(35)
Fenner, M. E.: ref, 75(60)
Fentiman, J.: test, 73
Ferrara-Parrish, P.: ref, 61r
Ferrell, B. G.: ref, 20(2)
Ferrin, H. H.: ref, 6(3)
Fey, M. E.: ref, 81(1)
Fiedler, F. E.: ref, 71r
Finch, T.: ref, 88(101)
Finch-Williams, A.: rev, 5
Fischer, F. W.: ref, 88(84)
Fischer, M.: ref, 88(100)
Fitzgerald, P. W.: ref, 6(2)
Fletcher, J.: ref, 30r
Fletcher, J. M.: ref, 88(85)
Flynn, J. R.: ref, 75(11)
Fogel, L. S.: ref, 88(7)
Ford, C. E.: ref, 45(71)
Ford, C. M.: ref, 45(48)
Fordyce, M. W.: ref, 45(4)
Forness, S. R.: ref, 75(52), 88(11,105)
Fowler, P. C.: ref, 88(119)
Frane, R. E.: ref, 88(36)
Fraser, E. D.: rev, 75
Freeman, B. J.: ref, 75(29)
Freeman, R. W.: ref, 75(4)
Freides, D.: rev, 75
French, J. H.: ref, 88(129)
French, J. R. P.: ref, 57r
Frenkel-Brunswik, E.: ref, 78r
Friedlander, M. L.: ref, 6(7)
Friedman, P.: ref, 15(4)
Friedrich, D.: ref, 88(37)
Friedrich, W. N.: ref, 45(36)
Friend, M.: rev, 1, 53
Friesen, W. J.: ref, 88(111)
Fuchs, L. S.: rev, 7, 16
Fujiki, M.: rev, 69, 84; ref, 81(5)
Fulker, D. W.: ref, 75(70)
Fuller, G. B.: ref, 88(37,145)
Funabiki, D.: ref, 45(21)
Furnham, A.: ref, 68(5)

Furrow, D.: ref, 75(12)

Gackenbach, J. I.: ref, 45(37)
Galassi, M. D.: ref, 28(1), 68(13)
Galin, D.: ref, 88(118)
Galvin, G. A: rev, 58; ref, 88(4)
Garcia, E. E.: rev, 34, 37
Gard, P. R.: ref, 45(55)
Gardner, E. F.: rev, 67
Gardner, H.: ref, 48r
Gardner, M. F.: test, 64
Garrison, W.: ref, 88(38)
Geers, A. E.: ref, 79r
Geier, J. G.: ref, 56r
Geller, E.: ref, 75(29)
German, M. L.: ref, 75(65)
Gersten, J. C.: ref, 32r
Gersten, R.: ref, 88(77,120)
Getson, P.: test, 40
Gettinger, M.: ref, 88(8)
Gildemeister, J.: ref, 15(4)
Gill, K. J.: ref, 88(93)
Gilligan, M. B.: ref, 88(95)
Gittelman, R.: ref, 88(43)
Glass, G. V: rev, 78; ref, 78r
Glenn, S. M.: ref, 75(39)
Gleser, G. C.: ref, 75r
Glynn, S. M.: ref, 45(56)
Goff, J. R.: ref, 88(3)
Gohs, D. E.: ref, 6(5)
Goldberg, L. R.: ref, 45(7)
Goldschmid, M. L.: rev, 86
Goldstein, D. J.: ref, 75(59)
Goldstein, G.: ref, 88(128)
Goldstein, H. S.: ref, 88(121)
Goldsworthy, C.: test, 44
Gollob, H. F.: ref, 75(77)
Gordon, E. E.: test, 31
Gordon, L. V.: test, 78
Gordon, V. N.: ref, 6(8), 20(3)
Gotlib, I. H.: ref, 45(11,38,57)
Gotlieb, H.: ref, 88(78)
Gough, P. B.: ref, 88(126)
Greenlief, C. L.: ref, 88(94)
Greenstein, S. M.: ref, 45(12)
Gregory, H.: ref, 7r
Griffith, P. L.: ref, 88(126)
Grossman, F. M.: rev, 4, 23; ref, 88(39)
Gruenewald, L.: ref, 61r
Guay, M.: ref, 75(37)
Guidubaldi, J.: ref, 75(13), 88(40,122)
Guilford, A. M.: test, 5
Guion, R. M.: rev, 55
Gunn, P.: ref, 75(41)
Gutkin, B. L.: rev, 84
Guy, E.: ref, 88(86)

Hagen, E.: ref, 75r
Hagen, E. P.: test, 75
Hahn, H.: ref, 75(76)
Hale, R. L.: ref, 88(41)
Hale, W. D.: ref, 10(1), 10r
Haley, W. E.: ref, 45(58)
Hall, R. J.: ref, 88(42)
Hallock, J. E.: ref, 88(82)

Suedfeld, P.: ref, 45(2)
Sundberg, N. D.: rev, 75
Sung, Y. H.: ref, 68(4)
Suominen-Troyer, S.: ref, 45(72)
Swanson, L. B.: ref, 21(10)

Tallal, P.: ref, 81(3)
Tanner, D. C.: test, 14
Taylor, J. M.: ref, 88(94)
Teglasi, H.: ref, 75(4)
Telzrow, C. F.: rev, 30
Templer, D. I.: ref, 45(29,54), 75(53)
Terman, L. M.: ref, 42r
Terrell, B. Y.: ref, 81(2)
Test Agency (The): test, 39
Thayer, P. W.: rev, 46
Thomas, K. W.: test, 57
Thomas, R. G.: rev, 49; ref, 6(6)
Thompson, C. K.: ref, 72(1)
Thompson, J.: test, 7
Thorndike, R. L.: test, 75; rev, 88
Thorne, T.: test, 73
Thorpe, L. P.: rev, 88
Thurber, S.: ref, 88(13)
Tobey, E. A.: ref, 21(5), 75(32)
Tobin, S. S.: ref, 66r
Tomarken, A. J.: ref, 45(40)
Tomeny, M.: ref, 45(47)
Tompkins, G. E.: rev, 24, 36
Torpy, D.: ref, 75(60)
Treiman, R.: ref, 88(107)
Treloar, J. H.: ref, 88(88)
Tross, S.: ref, 10(2)
Tryon, R. C.: ref, 75r
Tsai, L. Y.: ref, 75(5)
Turnbow, K.: ref, 40(1)
Turton, L. J.: rev, 72, 83; ref, 83r
Twentyman, C. T.: ref, 75(14)
Tyler, J. D.: ref, 45(36)

Ungerer, J.: ref, 75(67)
University of the State of New York Faculty: test, 3
U.S. Department of Labor: ref, 49r
Užgiris, I. C.: ref, 42r

Vacc, N. A.: rev, 6
Valett, R. E.: test, 23; ref, 23r
Vance, B.: ref, 88(108,145)
Vance, H. R.: ref, 88(146)
Vanderporten, A.: ref, 10(3)
Vane, J. R.: test, 86
Vasa, S. F.: rev, 30
Veleber, D. M.: ref, 45(29)
Verinis, J. S.: ref, 10(3)
Vernon, P. A.: ref, 43(2,4,5)
Verret, L. D.: ref, 45(18)
Vincent, L.: ref, 61r
Voeller, K. K. S.: ref, 88(147)
von Wendt, L.: ref, 75(69)

Wacker, D. P.: rev, 42, 61
Wagner, S. R.: ref, 88(109)
Wakeling, A.: ref, 45(16)
Waksman, S. A.: test, 87; ref, 87r
Walder, L. O.: ref, 88(45)

Waldrep, E. E.: ref, 75(59)
Waldron, G.: ref, 45(55)
Walker, C. E.: ref, 88(13)
Wallace, I. F.: ref, 75(50,51)
Walsh, D. J.: ref, 6(4)
Wantz, R. A.: rev, 41; ref, 41r
Ward, G.: test, 1
Warrington, E. K.: test, 65
Wasserman, G. A.: ref, 75(54,76)
Watkins, M. W.: ref, 88(10)
Watt, C.: ref, 45(18)
Watts, F. N.: ref, 45(60)
Waxman, H. C.: test, 52
Webster, R. E.: ref, 21(9), 88(110)
Weekley, J. A.: ref, 45(45)
Weeks, D. G.: ref, 88(72)
Wehrspann, W.: ref, 88(78)
Weinberg, R. A.: rev, 32
Weir, E.: test, 24
Weithorn, C. J.: ref, 21(6,7)
Wells, F. L.: rev, 21, 75
Wents, D.: test, 73
Wetzel, L.: ref, 10(3)
Weyand, K.: ref, 75(57)
Wharry, R. E.: ref, 88(148)
Wheeler, P.: ref, 75(2)
White, M.: ref, 88(14)
White, R. F.: ref, 88(75)
White, S.: rev, 58
Whitmore, J. R.: test, 25, 80; ref, 80r
Whorton, J. E.: ref, 75(61), 88(46,47)
Wiig, E. H.: ref, 17r
Wilkinson, G. S.: test, 88
Wilkinson, P.: ref, 75(39)
Williams, D. M.: ref, 88r
Williams, F.: test, 54
Williams, R. E.: ref, 48r, 68(15), 88(92)
Williams, R. T.: rev, 5
Willis, C. G.: rev, 28
Wilson, D. O.: ref, 68(2)
Wilson, L. R.: ref, 88(70)
Wilson, R. S.: ref, 75(6,55)
Winer, J. L.: ref, 68(2)
Winkler, E.: ref, 81(5)
Wise, S. L.: rev, 3, 50
Wisniewski, K.: ref, 88(129)
Witt, J. C.: ref, 88(62)
Woehlke, P.: ref, 88(35)
Wolfe, D.: ref, 45(42)
Wolfe Personnel Testing & Training Systems, Inc.: test, 19
Wolfe, V. V.: test, 53; ref, 53r
Wolff, D. E.: ref, 88(71)
Wonderlich, S. A.: ref, 45(65)
Wood, B.: ref, 32(4)
Wood, K. H.: ref, 45(16)
Worcester, D. A.: exc, 21
Worland, J.: ref, 88(72)
Wright, D.: rev, 8
Wright, L.: ref, 88(73)
Wright, P. G.: ref, 88(111)
Wurtz, R. G.: ref, 88(112)

Yalow, E. S.: ref, 16r
Yates, W. R.: ref, 10(4)

SCORE INDEX

This Score Index lists all the scores, in alphabetical order, for all the tests included in The Supplement to the Ninth Mental Measurements Yearbook. Because test scores can be regarded as operational definitions of the variables measured, sometimes the scores provide better leads to what a test actually measures than the test title or whatever else is available. The Score Index is very detailed, and the reader should keep in mind that a given variable (or concept) of interest may be defined in several different ways. Thus the reader should look up these several possible alternative definitions before drawing final conclusions about whether tests measuring a particular variable of interest can be located in the 9MMY-S. If the kind of score sought is located in a particular test or tests, the reader should then read the test descriptive information carefully to determine whether the test(s) in which the score is found is (are) consistent with reader purpose. Used wisely, the Score Index can be another useful resource in locating the right score in the right test. As usual, all numbers in the index are test numbers, not page numbers.

The Supplement to the Ninth Mental Measurements Yearbook

Edited by Jane Close Conoley, Jack J. Kramer, and
James V. Mitchell, Jr.
Published by the Buros Institute of Mental Measurements
of The University of Nebraska-Lincoln
Distributed by The University of Nebraska Press
Typeset by Port City Press, Inc.
in Caslon Old Style and Antique
by the Videocomp/570 system
Printed and bound by Port City Press, Inc.
on 50 lb. Glatfelter B-31 machine-finished paper